The
Hallmark
Features

A COMPLETE LEARNING PACKAGE

Essentials of Sociology, Third Edition
explains traditional sociological concepts and
theories as well as some of the most compelling
contemporary social phenomena, including
globalization, consumer culture, the internet,
and the "McDonaldization" of society.

- **TRENDING** boxes highlight influential sociology
  books that have become a part of public
  conversation about important issues, such
  as Michelle Alexander's *The New Jim Crow*
  and Arlie Hochschild's *Strangers in Their
  Own Land.*

- **DIGITAL LIVING** boxes help students recognize
  how their everyday lives are influenced by
  mass media, the internet, and social media.

DIGITAL LIVING: DIGITAL CURRENCY

One relatively recent addition to the global financescape is Bitcoin, a digital currency, which is popularly referred to as "digital gold." It is a universal currency that can be used in all countries, so a Bitcoin user does not need to exchange it for local currencies when he or she crosses national borders (Popper 2015). Bitcoin was created in 2008, since then, more than 41 million Bitcoin accounts have been opened around the world. Unlike national currencies that are created by central banks and controlled by national governments, Bitcoin is decentralized and overseen by volunteers, who authenticate encrypted electronic signatures on transactions (Kharif 2014; Popper 2015). Bitcoins can be accrued through extensive data mining or purchased on Bitcoin currency exchanges. These online exchanges require consumers to open an account and create a digital wallet. They can then transfer money into the digital wallet, buy and sell bitcoins, and purchase products and services from individuals and companies that accept bitcoins e-into the

Bitcoin ATMs, like this one, allow users to exchange their currency for the digital money.

use (Kharif 2014). Because of the digital nature of bitcoins, they are easy to transfer and difficult to trace, especially their sources and destinations, which remain anonymous. Thus, they are favored by those involved in criminal activities, as well as by those active in the dark web, where cyberpunks challenge the dominance of large global financial in (Popper 20

While still tainted by its association with criminality, Bitcoin has begun to move into the mainstream. Parents are using the digital currency to pay babysitters or distribute allowances to their children (Kharif 2014). It is a quick and convenient way to electroni fer money to

TRENDING

Gang Leader for a Day: A Rogue Sociologist Takes to the Streets (Penguin Books, 2008)

Sudhir Venkatesh (William B. Ransford Professor of Sociology at Columbia University; PhD, University of Chicago, 1997)

One of many provocative findings discussed in Sudhir Venkatesh's *Gang Leader for a Day* is that the organization of street gangs is similar to bureaucracies, such as corporations and the military. The original intent of Venkatesh's research was to study how African Americans experience urban poverty. But after Venkatesh is unexpectedly befriended by J. T., the charismatic leader of a Chicago gang, he learns that in order to carry out his study, he needs J. T.'s guidance and protection. Venkatesh discovers that J. T.'s gang, the Black Kings, controls the territory that includes one of Chicago's largest public housing projects, the Robert Taylor Homes. The absence of official authority, particularly law enforcement, and steady, full-time employment creates a vacuum of power and jobs that the Black Kings fill through its illegal drug trade. Like any other trade, the illegal drug trade requires a hierarchical organization to ensure that it operate efficiently. Careful bookkeeping and calculation are crucial to keeping a record of supply, wages, profits, and losses. Customer demand for a predictable product necessitates quality control measures. A clear division of labor and chain of command exists in the Black Kings. Numerous low-wage street dealers, or foot

soldiers, sell the drugs, while only a few high-ranking officials, such as J. T., manage the trade within their respective territory. J. T. must report his affiliated gang's activities to a regional board of directors, who occupy the positions at the very top of the Black Kings hierarchy. While being the leader of a gang might appear to be a glamorous job, Venkatesh comments that J. T.'s daily routines are quite mundane, albeit with the potential risk of encountering violence from a rival gang.

Through J. T.'s friendship Venkatesh is able to gain access to the residents of the Robert Taylor Homes, who are mostly impoverished African American women and their children. In order for the Black Kings to conduct its illegal drug trade smoothly, the gang performs certain services for these residents, such as buying school supplies for the children or cleaning up dirty hallways. J. T. even refers to himself as a philanthropist, using drug profits to help the community survive. The gang, however, holds a monopoly of power over the residents and of "taxes" activities that generate any revenue, including prostitution, child care, and selling food. Money from the drug trade and these taxes fuels the informal economy coordinated by the Black Kings in

the Robert Taylor Homes. It also accounts for why street gangs such as the Black Kings are prosecuted by the federal government as organized criminal enterprises under the Racketeer Influenced and Corrupt Organizations Act (RICO).

Supplementary Resources
- Venkatesh briefly describes *Gang Leader for a Day* in this video trailer: www.youtube.com/watch?v=yRq1AhFAN-4.
- Steven Levitt uses Venkatesh's research to explain the economics of gangs in his TED talk "The Freakonomics of Crack Dealing": www.ted.com/talks/steven_levitt_analyzes_crack_economics?language=en
- *Dislocation* (2005) is a documentary directed by Venkatesh that portrays the demolition of the Robert Taylor Homes.

Chapter 5. Organizations, Societies, and Global Relationships   119

Sara Miller McCune founded SAGE Publishing in 1965 to support the dissemination of usable knowledge and educate a global community. SAGE publishes more than 1000 journals and over 800 new books each year, spanning a wide range of subject areas. Our growing selection of library products includes archives, data, case studies and video. SAGE remains majority owned by our founder and after her lifetime will become owned by a charitable trust that secures the company's continued independence.

Los Angeles | London | New Delhi | Singapore | Washington DC | Melbourne

Essentials of Sociology
Third Edition

To Sue, from George: With much love for enduring, mostly with her usual good humor intact, all the years I was often unavailable while writing this book

Essentials of Sociology

Third Edition

George Ritzer

University of Maryland

Wendy Wiedenhoft Murphy

John Carroll University

Los Angeles | London | New Delhi
Singapore | Washington DC | Melbourne

FOR INFORMATION:

SAGE Publications, Inc.
2455 Teller Road
Thousand Oaks, California 91320
E-mail: order@sagepub.com

SAGE Publications Ltd.
1 Oliver's Yard
55 City Road
London EC1Y 1SP
United Kingdom

SAGE Publications India Pvt. Ltd.
B 1/I 1 Mohan Cooperative Industrial Area
Mathura Road, New Delhi 110 044
India

SAGE Publications Asia-Pacific Pte. Ltd.
3 Church Street
#10-04 Samsung Hub
Singapore 049483

Acquisitions Editor: Jeff Lasser
Content Development Editor: Nancy Matuszak
Editorial Assistant: Adeline Wilson
Marketing Manager: Kara Kindstrom
Production Editor: Veronica Stapleton Hooper
Copy Editor: Laureen Gleason
Typesetter: C&M Digitals (P) Ltd.
Proofreader: Dennis W. Webb
Indexer: Jeanne R. Busemeyer
Cover Designer: Scott Van Atta

Printed in Canada

Library of Congress Cataloging-in-Publication Data

Names: Ritzer, George, author. | Wiedenhoft Murphy, Wendy A., author.

Title: Essentials of sociology / George Ritzer, University of Maryland, Wendy Wiedenhoft Murphy, John Carroll University.

Description: Third edition. | Thousand Oaks : Sage, [2019] | Includes bibliographical references and index.

Identifiers: LCCN 2017041110 | ISBN 9781506388953 (pbk. : alk. paper)

Subjects: LCSH: Sociology.

Classification: LCC HM585 .R567 2019 | DDC 301—dc23
LC record available at https://lccn.loc.gov/2017041110

This book is printed on acid-free paper.

18 19 20 21 22 10 9 8 7 6 5 4 3 2 1

BRIEF CONTENTS

DETAILED CONTENTS

9   GENDER AND SEXUALITY   229

10   FAMILIES   259

11 EDUCATION AND RELIGION 285

12 POLITICS AND THE ECONOMY 317

13 THE BODY, MEDICINE, HEALTH, AND HEALTH CARE   345

14 POPULATION, URBANIZATION, AND THE ENVIRONMENT   375

LETTER FROM THE AUTHORS

To us, the social world, as well as the field of sociology that studies that world, is always interesting, exciting, and ever-changing. Our goal for this newly revised third edition of *Essentials of Sociology* is not only to introduce you to sociology, but also to discuss what has inspired—and what continues to inspire—our dedication to the field. Our hope is that you will learn a good deal about the social world from the perspective of sociology, as well as how our interests have shaped our personal sociological journeys.

George: My initial interests in the field were the sociology of work and the sociology of organizations, but I was quickly drawn to sociological theory and how even the most classical theories were relevant to my everyday life. My interest came to fruition in the publication of *The McDonaldization of Society* in 1993 (now being released in its ninth edition). In that book, I apply and expand on Max Weber's famous classical theoretical ideas on rationality. I saw those ideas at work in my local fast-food restaurant, as well as in many other contemporary settings. After the publication of *The McDonaldization of Society,* I grew interested in consumption, including credit card debt and the places of consumption, and I authored two texts on these topics, *Expressing America: A Critique of the Global Credit Card Society* and *Enchanting a Disenchanted World: Continuity and Change in the Cathedrals of Consumption.* I developed a curiosity about globalization after recognizing that McDonaldization and consumer culture had spread rapidly throughout much of the world. This inspired me to write *The Globalization of Nothing* and *Globalization: A Basic Text.* Most recently, my sociological journey has led me to the Internet, especially social networking sites, which are highly rationalized, are often places to consume, and are all globalized.

Wendy: I developed my primary interests in consumer culture and sociological theory when I was assigned to read Thorstein Veblen's *The Theory of the Leisure Class* as an undergraduate. Veblen's work inspired me to write my master's thesis on fashion and semiotics. I continued my study of consumption in the doctoral program at the University of Maryland, where I was one of George's students. Much of my work has explored the political dimensions of consumption, particularly how consumers use their purchasing power to effect social change. Recently, I published an introductory text on consumption called *Consumer Culture and Society.* My sociological journey has led me to the intersection of poverty and consumption as well as studying debt from a social justice perspective.

You will discover how our interests have shaped this book in a variety of ways. Consumption figures prominently in most chapters; this reflects our belief that this topic should be a central concern for sociologists. This book also includes a strong emphasis on globalization to encourage you to better understand and appreciate how your daily lives are shaped by global processes. Each chapter contains a primary section on globalization that explains why and how globalization has influenced an array of sociological issues, including the discipline itself. Throughout this book—in boxes headed "Digital Living"—the sociological implications of the internet and technology are explored. Pedagogical exercises featured in these boxes will require you to actively engage the digital world and contemplate its advantages and shortcomings. To demonstrate the relevance of sociology not just within academia but to the broader public, we have included an additional pedagogical feature, "Trending" boxes. These features highlight recently published books written by sociologists and scholars in related fields that have gained mainstream popularity. Most of these books are based on extensive ethnographic research about current sociological problems, and their narratives are readable and relatable, not to mention fascinating to us—we hope the same will be true for you. The Trending boxes also include links to webpages where you can watch videos of authors discussing their books and read reviews of their books from popular newspapers and magazines.

Here we have described a bit about our personal sociological journeys. We hope that this book will provide you with a starting point to begin your own journey, to examine your social world critically, and to develop your own sociological ideas and opinions. Our aim in writing this book is to equip you to see the social world in a different way and, more important, to use the ideas discussed here to help to create a better world.

—George Ritzer, University of Maryland
—Wendy Wiedenhoft Murphy,
John Carroll University

ACKNOWLEDGMENTS

From George: I need to begin with my friends for decades, and coauthors of a previous introductory textbook, Kenneth C. W. Kammeyer and Norman R. Yetman. That book went through seven editions, the last of which was published in 1997. It was most useful to me in this text in helping define various sociological concepts that have changed little over the years. I have also been able to build on discussions of many issues covered in that text. However, because of the passage of almost two decades in sociology and in the social world (an eternity in both), as well as the innumerable changes in them, this text has comparatively little in common with the earlier one. Nonetheless, my perspective on sociology was strongly shaped by that book and the many insights and ideas provided by my friends and coauthors before, during, and in the many years after the writing of that book.

Professor Rebecca Plante played a key role in the second edition of this book. She offered useful comments and suggestions throughout, and she was especially central in the revision of Chapter 9, on gender and sexuality. These are her areas of expertise, and the chapter is much improved because of her contributions to it. I would also like to thank Professor Paul Dean, coauthor of the second edition of my book *Globalization: A Basic Text,* for his numerous and important contributions to Chapter 7, on social stratification.

Thanks also to P. J. Rey, William Yagatich, Jillet Sam, Zeynep Tufekci, and Margaret Austin Smith for their contributions. Also to be thanked for writing first drafts of parts of earlier versions of chapters are Professors William Carbonaro (Chapter 11, on education), Deric Shannon (Chapter 12, on politics), and Lester Kurtz (Chapter 11, on religion). Professor Peter Kivisto made particularly important and numerous contributions to the second edition of this book. I'm especially thankful for his work on the religion and education chapters.

At SAGE Publications, I am especially grateful for Senior Vice President Michele Sordi's confidence in, and support for, the project. She agreed from the beginning to do and spend whatever was necessary to make this a first-class introductory sociology text. As you can see from the finished project, she was true to her word. Michele also worked closely with me in an editorial capacity on the first edition to help get the project through some of its most difficult periods. Michele was a positive force and upbeat presence throughout the writing of this book, and I am deeply grateful for who she is and what she has done. Late in the process Brenda Carter took over Michele's role and performed it with the same level of expertise, good humor, and good sense (plus she got me prime seats to a game in New York involving my beloved Yankees). Jeff Lasser came on board at SAGE as sociology publisher during production of the first edition, in which he played a key role, and he has played a much more important role in the second and third editions. Jeff has proven to be not only easy to work with but a sage (pun intended) adviser on many aspects of the book and its publication. Unfortunately, he is a Boston Red Sox fan, but nobody is perfect.

I also need to thank Nathan Davidson at SAGE. The production of the first edition of this book really took off when he took over its day-to-day management. We worked together closely for about a year on virtually every aspect of the final project. Before Nathan came on board, I was in danger of being overwhelmed by the demands of finishing this book, but he provided the hard work, great organizational abilities, and good sense that helped me complete it—and on time. Nathan continued to manage the second edition of this book and, if possible, he did an even better job with it. While his imprint is found throughout this book, it is especially notable in the selection of an excellent set of photographs.

From George and Wendy: Nancy Matuszak took over from Nathan as the developmental editor for the third edition of this book. She has been amazing, demonstrating great competence, good sense, and a great sense of humor. She has managed the myriad details associated with a revision of a book of this magnitude with great aplomb. We would like to see her named "Developmental Editor for Life," but we suspect she has bigger plans and wider horizons.

To be thanked for her work on the second edition is Elisa Adams, who, first as a consultant and later as developmental editor, was instrumental in editing the entire book as well as helping create various features of the book. Sheri Gilbert is to be thanked for her work on the many permissions needed for material included in this edition, as well as the last. Scott Van Atta did great work on the cover of the book, for both this edition and the previous one. Thanks to Gabrielle Piccininni, digital content editor, for her work on the ancillary materials and e-book resources. Many thanks also to Adeline Wilson, editorial assistant, who held steady oversight over all of the small details needed to get this book into production. Thanks also to Veronica Stapleton Hooper, who amiably and capably managed the production of this book, as well as to Laureen Gleason, who capably handled the copyediting. Laureen also proved to be quite an expert on popular culture and contributed insights on that topic throughout the book.

PUBLISHER'S ACKNOWLEDGMENTS

SAGE wishes to acknowledge the valuable contributions of the following reviewers:

Miguel Centellas, University of Mississippi

James A. Curiel, Norfolk State University

Barry D. Kass, SUNY Orange

Gary Maynard, University of Michigan at Flint

Lori Park-Smith, Ridgewater College

ABOUT THE AUTHORS

George Ritzer is Distinguished University Professor at the University of Maryland. Among his awards are Honorary Doctorate from La Trobe University, Melbourne, Australia; Honorary Patron, University Philosophical Society, Trinity College, Dublin; American Sociological Association's Distinguished Contribution to Teaching Award; and being named the 2013 Eastern Sociological Society's Robin Williams Lecturer. He has chaired four sections of the American Sociological Association: Theoretical Sociology, Organizations and Occupations, Global and Transnational Sociology, and the History of Sociology. In the application of social theory to the social world, his books include *The McDonaldization of Society* (8th ed., 2015; 9th ed., forthcoming), *Enchanting a Disenchanted World* (3rd ed., 2010), and *The Globalization of Nothing* (2nd ed., 2007). He is the author of *Globalization: A Basic Text* (Blackwell, 2010; 2nd ed., 2015, with Paul Dean). He edited the *Wiley-Blackwell Companion to Sociology* (2012) and *The Blackwell Companion to Globalization* (2008) and co-edited (with Jeff Stepnisky) the *Wiley-Blackwell Companions to Classical and Contemporary Major Social Theorists* (2012) and the *Handbook of Social Theory* (2001). He was founding editor of the *Journal of Consumer Culture*. He also edited the eleven-volume *Encyclopedia of Sociology* (2007; 2nd ed., forthcoming, with Chris Rojek), the two-volume *Encyclopedia of Social Theory* (2005), and the five-volume *Encyclopedia of Globalization* (2012). He co-edited a special double issue (2012) of the *American Behavioral Scientist* on prosumption and edited a symposium on prosumer capitalism in *Sociological Quarterly* (2015). His books have been translated into more than twenty languages, with more than a dozen translations of *The McDonaldization of Society* alone.

Wendy Wiedenhoft Murphy is Associate Professor of Sociology at John Carroll University. She joined the department in 2003 after completing her doctorate at the University of Maryland. Her specialty areas are sociological theory, consumer culture and society, and environmental justice. She has published work on consumer activism in the *Journal of Consumer Culture and Social Movement Studies,* work on tourism in *Peace and Conflict Studies,* and work on the Ulster-Scots diaspora in an edited collection. She is the past director of the Environmental Studies concentration at John Carroll University and has been involved with its summer program on conflict transformation in Northern Ireland. Currently, she is researching the limited but significant and active role of poor consumers in American society, and she has been working with George Ritzer on editing the second edition of *The Wiley-Blackwell Companion to Sociology.*

AN INTRODUCTION TO SOCIOLOGY IN THE GLOBAL AGE

A Sociology of Revolutions and Counterrevolutions

In December 2010, street demonstrations, labor strikes, and other acts of civil resistance swept through the small North African nation of Tunisia. The demonstrators met strong resistance from the Tunisian government. Nevertheless, their protests eventually resulted in the overthrow of autocratic President Ben Ali after 23 years in power.

The trigger for the Tunisian protests was the self-immolation of Mohamed Bouazizi, a 26-year-old street vendor who claimed he had been harassed and humiliated by authorities. Bouazizi died in a burn and trauma center 18 days after setting himself on fire. The Tunisian revolution was at the root of the "Arab Spring"—the wave of social unrest and social revolution that Tunisia's uprising inspired throughout the Middle East. Such events are not only important in themselves; so too are the counterreactions to them by other individuals as well as by larger organizations. Those responses have since undermined the revolutions that occurred during the Arab Spring (Worth 2016). In some cases, such as in Egypt, counterreaction by the military led to a return to the kind of autocratic government that was a cause of the protests in the first place.

LEARNING OBJECTIVES

1.1 Identify major social changes since the 1880s studied by sociologists.

1.2 Explain why sociologists today focus on globalization, consumption, and the digital world.

1.3 Describe how sociologists understand continuity and change, particularly in the context of the sociological imagination and the social construction of reality.

1.4 Differentiate between sociology's two possible purposes, science and social reform.

1.5 Evaluate how sociology relates to other social sciences and how sociological knowledge differs from common sense.

edge.sagepub.com/ritzeressentials3e

- Take the chapter quiz
- Review key terms with eFlashcards
- Explore multimedia links and SAGE readings

⑤SAGE edge™

In the Persian Gulf states (Saudi Arabia, the United Arab Emirates, Kuwait, and Bahrain), monarchs have suppressed dissidents and thwarted efforts aimed at greater democratization (Fahim 2016). In the aftermath of the 2011 overthrow of dictator Muammar Qaddafi, Libya (and Yemen) have descended into civil wars, vicious fights for power, and, at least at the moment, large-scale anarchy.

In Libya, but, more important, in Syria and Iraq, a radical Islamic group—the Islamic State (IS, also known as the Islamic State of Iraq and the Levant [ISIL], the Islamic State of Iraq and Syria [ISIS], or Da'ish, from an acronym for a name of the group in Arabic)—has swept through large portions of those countries and succeeded in dismembering them in its effort to form an independent state that spans much of the Middle East. That new state is envisioned to be a caliphate, dominated by a leader—a caliph—devoted to a strict interpretation of Islam. The success of IS led, in turn, to other counterreactions, both locally (especially by the Kurds and Iranians) and globally (with the United States helping the Iraqi government and Russia aiding the Syrian government), designed to limit the IS's gains, if not to defeat it. By mid-2017, IS had been pushed back on a variety of fronts, but it still controlled large parts of Syria, as well as a shrinking territory in Iraq, and it remained a force in Libya (and elsewhere).

By drawing on modern sociology's 200-year history while looking to the future, sociologists today can find the tools and resources to gain a better understanding of where we have been, where we are, and, perhaps most important, where we are going. Sociology has traditionally tried to understand the place of the individual—even a Tunisian street vendor—within society and society's effect on the individual. In today's global age, however, we need to look beyond given individuals and societies to global realities and processes. For example, IS has grown in strength through the influx of individual supporters and fighters from other parts of the world, including the United States and Great Britain. To take a more general example of globalization—one that is more directly relevant to most readers of this book—online networks that transcend national boundaries, such as Facebook and Twitter, have forever altered the ways in which we interact with each other as well as the societies that we shape and that shape us. As the world has become increasingly globalized, sociology has developed an increasingly global perspective. ●

One of the most important lessons that you will learn in your study of sociology is that what you think and do as an individual is affected by what is happening in groups, organizations, cultures, societies, and the world. This is especially true of social changes, even those that are global in scope and seem at first glance to be remote from you, such as Mohamed Bouazizi's public suicide and the revolution throughout much of the Middle East that it helped set in motion. The roots of that dramatic act of protest lay in poverty, high unemployment, an authoritarian government, and political corruption that affected Bouazizi personally. Before his actions, most Tunisians would never have risked their lives to protest against their country's repressive regime. Yet he and tens of thousands of others in countries across the region did just that. While you may or may not be motivated to engage in revolutionary activities, you are continually affected by the social changes taking place around you.

A second important lesson in sociology is that you are not only affected by larger events, but also capable to some degree of having an impact on large-scale structures and processes. This is an example of the **butterfly effect** (Lorenz 1995). While this concept is generally applied to physical phenomena, it also applies to social phenomena (Daipha 2012). The idea is that a relatively small change in a specific location can have far-ranging, even global, effects over both time and distance. For example, Bouazizi's actions helped lead to the Tunisian revolution and, more generally, to street demonstrations and civil war, as well as counterreactions elsewhere in the Arab world that continue to reverberate throughout the region and many other parts of the world. Perhaps the arc of your life and career will be affected by the upheavals that began with the Arab Spring. More important, it is very possible that actions you take in your lifetime will have wide-ranging, perhaps global, effects.

These examples of the relationships between people and larger social realities and changes set the stage for the definition of **sociology** as the systematic study of the ways in which people are affected by and affect the social structures and social processes associated with the groups, organizations, cultures, societies, and world in which they exist.

Will our highways be safer and injury rates lower because of the sensors in self-driving cars, like this one developed by Google's car project (which is now operating as Waymo)? Or will we have more air pollution and therefore more illness because there will be so many self-driving cars on the road? Sociologists assess the so-called butterfly effects of changes such as driverless cars.

THE CHANGING NATURE OF THE SOCIAL WORLD— AND SOCIOLOGY

Sociology deals with contemporary phenomena, as you have seen, but its deep historical roots have led to many longer-term interests. In the fourteenth century, for instance, the Muslim scholar Abdel Rahman Ibn Khaldun studied various social relationships, including those between politics and economics. Of special importance to the founding of sociology was the eighteenth- and nineteenth-century Industrial Revolution. During this "industrial age," many early sociologists concentrated on factories, the production that took place in those settings, and those who worked there, especially blue-collar, manual workers. Sociologists also came to focus on the relationship between industry and the rest of society, including, for example, the state and the family.

By the middle of the twentieth century, manufacturing in the United States was in the early stages of a long decline that continues to this day. (However, manufacturing in other parts of the world, most notably China, is booming.) The United States had moved from the industrial age to the "postindustrial age" (Bell 1973; Leicht and Fitzgerald 2006). In the United States, as well as in the Western world more generally, the center of the economy and the attention of many sociologists shifted from the factory to the office. That is, the focus moved from blue-collar manual work to white-collar office work (Mills 1951) as well as to the bureaucracies in which many people worked (Clegg and Lounsbury 2009; Weber [1921] 1968). Another change in the postindustrial age was the growth of the service sector of the economy, involving everyone from high-status service providers such as physicians and lawyers to lower-status workers behind the counters of fast-food restaurants and now those who drive for Uber.

The more recent rise of the "information age" (Castells 2010; David and Millwood 2012) can be seen as a part, or an extension, of the postindustrial age. Knowledge and information are critical in today's world. So, too, are the technologies—computers, smartphones, the world wide web—that have greatly increased the productivity of individual workers and altered the nature of their work. Rather than designers drawing designs by hand, computer-assisted technologies are now used to create designs for everything from electric power grids to patterned fabrics. The widespread use of smartphones has enabled, among many other things, the rise of companies such as Uber and Lyft, whose success is threatening the rental car industry and especially the taxicab industry and the livelihoods of many taxi drivers (who are also threatened by driverless cars). A passenger uses an app to indicate that he or she needs a ride, and one is provided by an independent car owner for a set fee, which is automatically charged to the passenger's credit card (no tipping is allowed). Some of the drivers work a few hours per day for these services in search of a little extra money, while others work full-time for the services. Their willingness to do this work has had the result of reducing the need for taxicabs and full-time taxi drivers.

However, it is not just work that has been affected by new technologies; virtually everyone and everything is being affected by them. Uber is part of the growing "sharing economy" (Sundarajan 2016), in which people share (for a fee) many things; most notably, some share their homes through websites such as Airbnb.com (Pogue 2014). One key component of this new technological world, Google (see the previous mention of Google's driverless car project, Waymo), is so powerful that a 2011 book is entitled *The Googlization of Everything* (Vaidhyanathan 2011). Thus, much sociological attention has shifted to computers and the internet, as well as those who work with them (Lynch 2016; Scholz 2013).

The transition from the industrial to the postindustrial and now to the information age has important personal implications. Had you been a man who lived in the industrial age, you would have worked (if you could find a job) for money (pay). You would have done so to be able to buy what you needed and wanted. Women working in the private sphere were largely uncompensated or compensated at a lower rate, as is often still the case. However, in the postindustrial age, it is increasingly likely that men and women will be willing, or forced, to work for free (Anderson 2009; Ritzer 2015b; Ritzer and Jurgenson 2010; Terranova 2013), as in the case of interns, bloggers, and contributors to YouTube and Wikipedia.

Many hope that the labor they currently perform for free will eventually have an economic payoff. One person (known as PewDiePie) played video games on YouTube, garnered about 24 million subscribers, and reputedly earned millions of dollars per year (Jacobs 2014). Playing video games has become big business—one tournament drew 11,000 fans to a stadium and offered $11 million in prize money. Many hope that their work as bloggers or on YouTube will lead to full-time jobs.

These are but a few of the many social changes to be discussed in this book. The essential point is that the social world (people, groups, organizations, and so on)—*your* social world—is continually changing. Sociology is a field that is, and must be, constantly attuned to and involved in studying those changes.

CENTRAL CONCERNS FOR A TWENTY-FIRST-CENTURY SOCIOLOGY

While the social world has been changing dramatically over the last two centuries or so and sociology has adapted to those changes, sociology has continued to focus on many of its traditional concerns. We have already mentioned industry, production, and work as long-term sociological interests; others include deviance and crime (see Chapter 6), the family (see Chapter 10), and the city (see Chapter 14). Of particular concern to many sociologists has been, and continues to be, the issue of inequality as it affects the poor, particular racial and ethnic groups, women, and LGBTQ individuals (see Chapters 8 and 9). The bulk of this book will be devoted to these basic sociological topics and concerns, but the discussion will also encompass the nontraditional and very contemporary issues of consumption, the digital world, and especially globalization.

GLOBALIZATION

No social change is as important today as globalization, because it is continually affecting all aspects of the social world everywhere on the globe. A date marking the beginning of globalization cannot be given with any precision, and in fact is in great dispute (Ritzer 2012b; Ritzer and Dean 2015). However, the concept of globalization first began to appear in the popular and academic literature around 1990. Today, globalization is a central issue in the social world as a whole as well as in sociology; globalization and talk about it are all around

Blogging and Tweeting about Sociology

Blogging and tweeting are two popular ways to transmit and acquire information today. Current events are often posted in real time, sometimes by individuals who are witnessing them. For example, the Arab Spring was referred to as the Twitter Revolution because people around the world were able to follow these political uprisings through tweets posted by protestors. Sports fans can follow their favorite teams and on game day receive instantaneous alerts when their team scores a touchdown or scores a run. Individuals who want to find alternative perspectives on social issues from the mainstream press can follow a variety of alternate online sites (e.g., the far right-wing Breitbart News) and blogs (e.g., the left-leaning Mother Jones). Blogging and tweeting encourage individual agency. They offer the opportunity for all of us to participate in the social construction of reality and can be used as platforms to promote social reforms, such as #BlackLivesMatter. But there are a few structural constraints attached to these methods of communication. Twitter limits tweets to only 140 characters. Many popular blogs and Twitter accounts are written and maintained by celebrities, professional experts, and representatives of formal organizations (some of which are highly politicized), who have more power to shape reality than the average person does. Indeed, President Trump has made tweeting a commonplace communication method for the highest government office in the country.

Sociologists and organizations devoted to sociological theory and research use blogs and tweets to expose others to the sociological imagination, helping individuals at the micro level realize that their private troubles are connected to larger public issues. Popular sociologists who blog include George Ritzer (https://georgeritzer.word press.com), who discusses themes addressed in this book, such as McDonaldization, globalization, and consumption, and Philip Cohen, who writes about family inequality (https://familyinequality .wordpress.com). The Society Pages blog ring (http://thesocietypages .org) provides a set of sociology blogs such as The Color Line (https://thesocietypages.org/col orline) and Sociology Lens (https:// thesocietypages.org/sociologylens) that keep readers current on issues pertaining to inequality, race, gender, crime, and health. The American Sociology Association's blog (http://speak4sociology.org) offers a forum for its followers to debate sociological issues. A variety of Twitter accounts regularly post comments about and links to relevant sociological topics, including @Soc_Imagination, @SociologyLens, @DiscoverSoc, @SocWomen, and @SocImages. In addition, professional sociologists such as Michael Burawoy (@bura woy), Matthew Desmond (@just_shelter), Zeynep Tufekci (@zeynep), and Sudhir Venkatesh (@avsudhir) tweet to promote awareness about social problems and publicize their research and social activism.

Engaging the Digital World

Select one of the sociology blogs or Twitter accounts listed previously. Check this digital source periodically throughout the semester, keeping track of issues that you find most interesting or problematic. You can create your own blog to do this, or if you have a Twitter account, you can tweet about them. At the end of the semester, write a summary of what you have learned, which you can include on your blog or as a link posted to your Twitter account.

us. In fact, we can be said to be living in the "global age" (Albrow 1996). However, this fact as well as the advantages of globalization for the United States were questioned by Donald Trump in the 2016 presidential campaign. In 2017, in the early days of his presidency, Trump adopted a slightly more balanced position by, for example, coming to see the merit in the North Atlantic Treaty Organization (NATO). Such questioning has led to talk of "deglobalization" (however, see George Ritzer's blog post "Deglobalization? Not a Chance" [2016]). Deglobalization was also behind the decision of the United Kingdom to exit the European Union (called Brexit), as well as actions by other European nations to create border restrictions. However, none of these actions are going to impact globalization as a whole or in such areas as the internet, the media, and culture.

Society is a complex pattern of social relationships that is bounded in space and persists over time. The society has traditionally been the largest unit of analysis in sociology. However, in the global age, societies are seen as of declining importance (Holton 2011; Meyer, Boli, and Ramirez 1997). This is the case, in part, because larger transnational and global social structures are growing in importance. These include the United Nations (UN), the European Union (EU), the Organization of the Petroleum Exporting Countries (OPEC), multinational corporations (MNCs) such as Google and ExxonMobil, and multinational nongovernmental organizations (NGOs) such as Amnesty International. In at least some cases, these transnational structures are becoming more important than individual societies. OPEC, for example, is more important to the rest of the world's well-being than are the organization's key member societies, such as Abu Dhabi or even Saudi Arabia.

Social processes, like social structures, exist not only at the societal level but also at the global level, and these global processes are increasing in importance. Consider migration (see Chapter 14). People move about, or migrate, within and between societies. For example, many people have moved from the northeastern United States to the West and the South. However, in the global age, people are increasingly moving between societies, some halfway around the world. The United States now has a higher percentage of immigrants than it has had in almost a

century (see Figure 1.1). Many have migrated from and through Mexico to the United States (Massey 2003; Ortmeyer and Quinn 2012). More generally, large numbers of people are migrating from a number of predominantly Islamic societies in the Middle East and Africa to the West (Caldwell 2009; Voas and Fleischmann 2012). In many cases, they are fleeing from war-torn countries such as Syria, Iraq, and Libya (Yeginsu and Hartocollis 2015). In addition, the movement of thousands of people from the West to join radical Islamist organizations (such as the Islamic State), especially in Syria and Iraq, has been of major concern to Western governments. Some fear that at least some of those involved in radical Islamist activities there will migrate back to the West and engage in terrorist acts.

There have always been large-scale population movements. However, in the global age, and even with recent restrictions, people generally move around the world far more freely and travel much greater distances than ever before. Another way of saying this is that people—and much else—are more "fluid." That is, they move farther, more easily, and more quickly than ever before. Younger people, especially millennials (or Generation Y, those born from the early 1980s through the late 1990s), are likely to be especially mobile, including globally. Their greater fluidity is reflected in, among many other things, the fact that they are more likely to book airline tickets and to check in online, and to use boarding passes sent directly to their smartphones (Lee 2013).

The movement of products of all types is also more fluid as a result of the existence of massive container ships, jet cargo planes, and package delivery services such as FedEx and UPS. Even more fluid is the digital "stuff" you buy on the internet when you download music, videos, movies, and so on. And in the realm of the family, tasks once confined to the home, such as caregiving and housework, have become increasingly fluid, as those who can afford to do so often outsource domestic labor (van der Lippe, Frey, and Tsvetkova 2012; Yeates 2009). More generally, that greater fluidity is manifested in the information that flows throughout the world in the blink of an eye as a result of the internet, texting, e-mail, and social networking sites such as Facebook, Instagram, Snapchat, and Twitter.

FIGURE 1.1 • Number of Immigrants and Their Share of the Total U.S. Population, 1850–2015

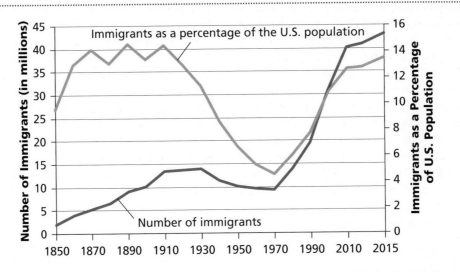

SOURCES: Migration Policy Institute tabulation of data from the U.S. Census Bureau's 2012, 2011, and 2010 American Community Surveys and 1970, 1990, and 2000 decennial Census data. All other data are from Campbell J. Gibson and Emily Lennon, *Historical Census Statistics on the Foreign-Born Population of the United States: 1850 to 1990*, Working Paper 29, U.S. Census Bureau (Washington, DC: Government Printing Office, 1999).

ASK YOURSELF

Have you ever thought of your posts on Facebook, Instagram, Snapchat, or Twitter as part of a global flow of information? In what ways do they actually fit this description? What does your position in this global flow of information reveal about you?

These flows can be expedited by structures of various types. For instance, air cargo delivery will increasingly be facilitated by the development of the "aerotropolis" (Kasarda and Lindsay 2011), a pre-planned "city of the future" that is developed because of proximity and access to a large, modern airport (Kasarda 2016). For example, New Songdo, South Korea, is being built (it is more than 50 percent completed) because such an airport (Incheon) is nearby and easily reached via a 12-mile-long bridge. The European Union, founded in 1993, is an example of a social structure that serves to ease the flow of citizens among member nations (but not of people living outside the EU). Although they have been increasing in recent years because of the flow of undocumented immigrants, border restrictions were reduced or eliminated completely among the 27 EU member nations.

Similarly, the creation in 1975 of the euro greatly simplified economic transactions among the 18 EU countries that accept it as their currency.

There are also structures that impede various kinds of global flows. National borders, passports and passport controls (Robertson 2010; Torpey 2000, 2012), security checks, and customs controls limit the movement of people throughout the world. Such restrictions were greatly increased in many parts of the world after the terrorist attacks on New York City and Washington, D.C., on September 11, 2001. This made global travel and border crossing more difficult and time-consuming. Then there are the even more obvious structures designed to limit the movement of people across borders. Examples include the fences between Israel and the West Bank, as well as one between Israel and Egypt, which was completed in 2013. Even more recent are border fences under construction or completed in several European countries (e.g., Hungary, Slovenia), which are designed to limit, direct, or stop the flow of migrants from Syria and elsewhere (Surk 2015). Donald Trump promised to turn the fence between the United States and Mexico into a wall, at least for part of the length of the distance required. In the early days of his presidency, Trump encountered opposition to the expanded wall because of its high cost and environmental concerns. It remains to be seen how much of the extended wall will actually be built. The existing fences across the Mexican border, and increased border police and patrols, have led unauthorized migrants to take longer and riskier routes into the United States. There are more than 200 immigration detention centers in the United States (see Figure 1.2), and Human Rights Watch found that 18 immigrants died in them between 2012 and 2015 due to negligent medical care (Jula and Preston 2016). There are, of course, many other structural barriers in the world, most notably trade barriers and tariffs, which limit the free movement of goods and services of many kinds.

In sum, **globalization** is defined by increasingly fluid global flows and the structures that expedite and impede those flows. Globalization is certainly increasing, and it brings with it a variety of both positive and negative developments (Ritzer and Dean 2015). On one side, most people throughout the world now have far greater access to goods, services, and information from around the globe than did people during the industrial age. On the other side, a variety of highly undesirable things also flow more easily around the world, including diseases such as Zika, HIV/AIDS, and Ebola and pollution released by industrialized countries that worsens the adverse effects of climate change (including global warming). Also on the negative side are the flows of such forms of "deviant globalization" as terrorism, sex trafficking, and the black markets for human organs and drugs (Gilman, Goldhammer, and Weber 2011).

CONSUMPTION

While consumption has been a central feature of societies for centuries, it is only in recent years that we can think in terms of a "world of consumers" (Trentmann 2016). Beginning in the 1950s, the center of many capitalist economies began to shift from production and work to **consumption**, or the process by which people obtain and utilize goods and services. During that period, the center of the U.S. economy shifted from the factory and the office to the shopping mall (Baudrillard [1970] 1998; Lipovetsky 2005). For many, work and production became less important than consumption.

FIGURE 1.2 • U.S. Immigration Detention Facilities

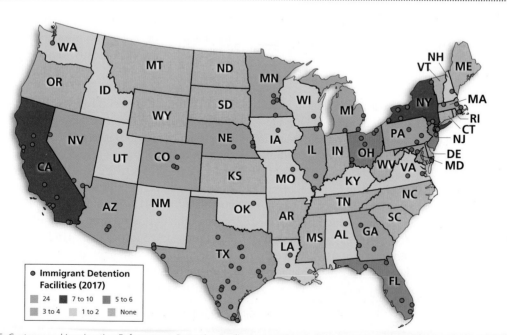

SOURCE: Customs and Immigration Enforcement, Detention Facility Locator, March 2017 (https://www.ice.gov/detention-facilities).

Essentials of Sociology

The dramatic rise in consumption was made possible by, among other things, the growing affluence of the population. A more specific factor was the introduction (in the 1950s and 1960s) and increasing availability of credit cards. The use of credit cards has now become widespread at shopping malls, on the internet, and in many other settings. One indicator of the increase in consumption in the United States is the increase in credit card debt. As you can see in Figure 1.3, credit card debt per household grew astronomically in the early years of credit card use (the figure begins with $37 in 1969). Credit card debt reached its high point, $8,729, in 2008 and has been steadily declining since the Great Recession to an average of $5,946 per household. However, households that are classified as indebted, or that carry a balance, have an average credit card debt of $16,060.

ASK YOURSELF

Have your consumption habits or credit card use changed over the last six months? The last three years? Do you anticipate that your habits will change in the next three years? If so, how and why? Will you consume more or less?

Consumption is certainly significant economically, but it is significant in other ways as well. For example, culture is very much shaped by consumption, and various aspects of consumption become cultural phenomena. A good example is the iPhone, which is used in many ways to consume, but more generally has revolutionized culture in innumerable ways. Millions of people have bought iPhones and similar smartphones, as well as the ever-increasing number of apps associated with them. These phones have altered how and where people meet to socialize and the ways in which they socialize. In addition, the media and people in general spend so much time discussing the implications of the latest iPhone and similar products that these devices have become central to the larger culture in which we live. Rumors about the characteristics and release date of the next version of the iPhone continually add to the excitement.

Consumption and globalization are also deeply intertwined. Much of what we consume in the developed world comes from other countries. In 2015 alone, the United States imported more than $480 billion worth of goods from China; the comparable figure in 1985 was only $4 million in goods (https://www.census.gov/foreign-trade/balance/c5700.html; U.S. Census Bureau 2013). Furthermore, the speed and convenience of internet commerce tend to make

FIGURE 1.3 • U.S. Credit Card Debt, 1969–2015

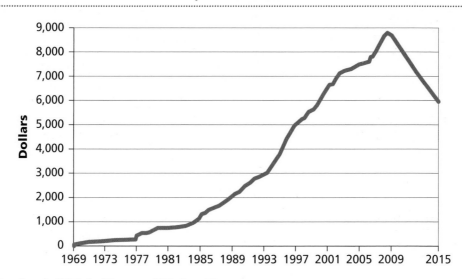

SOURCE: Data from the U.S. Federal Reserve and U.S. Census Bureau.

New consumption sites and products are often a hot cultural phenomenon. Many people will line up for hours, even camp out overnight, just to be among the first to be at such an event or to get such a product. This is clear in the crowd at the opening of a Kanye West pop-up store.

global realities and distances irrelevant to consumers. Finally, travel to other parts of the world—a form of consumption itself—is increasingly affordable and common. A major objective of tourists is often the sampling of the foods of foreign lands, as well as the purchase of souvenirs (Chambers 2010; Gmelch 2010; Mak, Lumbers, and Eves 2012). Sociologists are understandably interested in these developments in the realm of consumption. Early sociologists completed many studies of work, production, factories, and factory workers. Today's sociologists continue to study work-related issues, but they are devoting increasing attention to consumption in general (Sassatelli 2007) and more specifically to such phenomena as online shopping, done increasingly through the use of smartphones (Horrigan 2008; Morris 2013), the behavior of shoppers in more material locales such as department stores (Miller 1998; Zukin 2004), and the development of more recent consumption sites, such as fast-food restaurants (Ritzer, forthcoming) and shopping malls (Ritzer 2010b).

McDonaldization

Ritzer's study of fast-food restaurants led to the development of the concept of **McDonaldization**, or the process by which the rational principles of the fast-food restaurant are coming to dominate more

and more sectors of society and more societies throughout the world (Ritzer, forthcoming; for a number of critical essays on this perspective, see Ritzer 2010c, 275–357). This process leads to the creation of rational systems—like fast-food restaurants—that have four defining characteristics:

- *Efficiency.* The emphasis is on the use of the quickest and least costly means to whatever end is desired. Perhaps the best example of efficiency is the drive-through window, a highly organized means for employees to dole out meals in a matter of seconds.

- *Calculability.* You hear a lot at McDonald's about quantities: how large the food portions are— the Big Mac—and how low the prices are—the dollar breakfast. You don't hear as much, however, about the quality of the restaurant's ingredients or its products.

- *Predictability.* McDonaldization ensures that the entire experience of patronizing a fast-food chain is nearly identical from one geographic setting to another—even globally—and from one time to another. For example, when customers enter a McDonald's restaurant, employees ask what they wish to order, following scripts created by the corporation.

- *Control.* In McDonaldized systems, technology exerts a good deal of control over people, processes, and products. French fry machines buzz when the fries are done and even automatically lift them out of the hot oil when they've reached just the right amount of crispiness. Workers must load fry baskets with uncooked fries and unload them when the baskets emerge from the oil.

Paradoxically, rationality often seems to lead to its exact opposite—irrationality. Just consider the problems of meaningless work, roadside litter due to drive-through services at fast-food restaurants, or the societal problems associated with childhood obesity, which has been blamed, in part, on the ubiquity of fast food. Another of the irrationalities of rationality is dehumanization. Fast-food employees are forced to work in dehumanizing jobs, which can lead to job dissatisfaction and high turnover rates. Fast-food customers are forced to eat in dehumanizing settings, such as in the cold and impersonal atmosphere of the fast-food restaurant or in their car. As more of the world succumbs to McDonaldization, dehumanization becomes increasingly pervasive.

Critiquing Consumption

The sociological study of consumption sites involves, among many other things, a critical look at the ways in which they are structured. These sites may be set up to lead people to consume certain things and not others, to consume more than they might have intended, and to go into debt (Brubaker, Lawless, and Tabb 2012; Manning 2001; Marron 2009; Ritzer 1995). Take, for example, the website Shoedazzle (www.shoedazzle.com), a site that uses commercials and "style quizzes" to recruit new members. Shoedazzle highlights an "exclusive" VIP membership status on its webpage, which anyone can join. Making its members feel special through seemingly personalized style quizzes and VIP memberships lures consumers into buying more shoes than they really need.

Sociologists are also interested in how consumers use shopping malls and e-tailers in ways that were not anticipated by their designers. For example, people often wander through shopping malls and their many shops, which have been designed to spur consumption, without buying anything. Travelers are using internet sites such as Expedia and KAYAK to compare prices but then buying airplane tickets on the airlines' own websites.

Social change continues. The Great Recession and its ongoing aftermath have altered many things, including the degree to which society is dominated by consumption. Even today, long after the onset of the recession in 2007 and its supposed end, many U.S. consumers remain reluctant to spend money, or at least as much as they did in the past, on consumption (Kurtz 2014). As a result, consumption sites have experienced great difficulties. Many outdoor strip malls and some indoor malls have emptied; they have become "dead malls" (as documented on the site http://deadmalls.com). Las Vegas, which has long been a capital for the consumption of entertainment and high-end goods and services, has been hurting (Nagourney 2013). It seems possible, although highly unlikely, that even though we entered the consumption age only about half a century ago, we now may be on the verge of what could be called the "postconsumption age." While excessive consumption and the related high level of debt were key factors in causing the Great Recession, a postconsumption age would bring with it problems of its own, such as fewer jobs and a declining standard of living for many.

ASK YOURSELF

What would your life be like in a postconsumption age? In what ways might it be better? Worse? Why?

THE DIGITAL WORLD

Sociology has always concerned itself with the social aspects and implications of **technology**, or the interplay of machines, tools, skills, and procedures for the accomplishment of tasks. One example is the assembly line, a defining feature of early twentieth-century factories. Later, sociologists became interested in the automated technologies that came to define factories. However, technologies have continued to evolve considerably since then. Sociologists are now devoting an increasing amount of attention to the digital world that has emerged as a result of new technologies already mentioned in this chapter, such as computers, smartphones, the internet, and social networking sites such as Facebook and Twitter (Clough 2013).

The networking sites on the internet that involve social interaction are the most obviously sociological in character (Aleman and Wartman 2008; Patchin and Hinduja 2010). For example, Hodkinson (2015) has recently pointed out the similarities between teenagers' bedrooms and their social networking sites in terms of privacy issues. Both are intimate personal spaces where teenagers socialize and individualize in ways that express their identities. Social networking sites are especially important in North America, where the percentage of those with access

The McDonaldization of Society (SAGE, 2015)

George Ritzer (Distinguished University Professor at the University of Maryland; PhD, Cornell University, 1968)

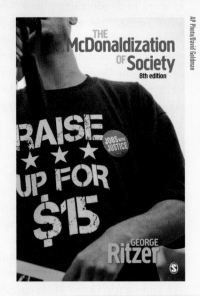

Currently in its eighth edition, *The McDonaldization of Society* continues to be relevant in its analysis of not just American society, but also the global domain. The four defining characteristics of McDonaldization—efficiency, calculability, predictability, and control—have been exported to and adopted by other countries in addition to McDonald's restaurants themselves. Like globalization, McDonaldization is a process that involves multidirectional "global flows of people, objects, places, and information" (Ritzer and Dean 2015:187). Indeed, Ritzer argues that McDonaldization is a type of globalization, what he calls the "globalization of nothing" (2015a:185). McDonaldization is a type of "nothing" because it and its offerings are centrally conceived, controlled, and lacking in distinctive content. In contrast, "something" (say, a home-cooked meal) is locally conceived, controlled, and rich in content (2015a:188–189). McDonald's, like other chain fast-food restaurants, is created and controlled by a central office. Most of its franchised restaurants look identical, offer similar food options, and treat their workers and customers in the same way. Ritzer explains that the global ambitions of the McDonald's corporation to impose its norms and values on other geographic regions is an example of *gro*balization. He argues that we are witnessing the grobalization of nothing because nothing is usually less expensive than something, appeals to a wider range of consumer tastes, and seamlessly fits into other cultures.

However, no social form or process is completely devoid of something—even one that is McDonaldized. While chain fast-food restaurants are less distinctive than indigenous restaurants, some do adapt their food options and practices to local cultures. This is an example of *glocalization,* or the "interpenetration of the global and the local," which results "in unique outcomes in different geographic areas" (Ritzer 2015a:190). For example, McDonald's offers the McAloo Tikki burger in India, which is made with a potato patty instead of beef to accommodate Hindus who do not eat beef. Offering different food options to satisfy the cultural and religious preferences of consumers in different counties is a weak form of glocalization because it does not necessarily challenge McDonaldization—the McAloo Tikki burger in India is just as efficiently mass-produced, calculable, and predictable as the Big Mac in the United States is. Efforts of *DeMcDonaldization* face a similar dilemma. Starbucks might appear to be the antithesis of McDonald's, with its supposedly caring corporate image and its inviting cafes that encourage customers to linger for hours. However, the vast majority of Starbucks' customers do not even enter the stores; they use the drive-through windows. Like McDonald's, Starbucks cafes and products are standardized and predictable, and workers are controlled by technologies, such as automated espresso machines (2015a:198–199).

Supplementary Resources

- Watch an interview with George Ritzer about his book *The McDonaldization of Society* at https://georgeritzer .wordpress.com/interviews.
- Examine photographs and learn more about what *Smithsonian* magazine has identified as the most unique McDonald's restaurants in the world at www .smithsonianmag.com/travel/ most-unique-mcdonalds-around-world-180955090. You can also look at menu items from different McDonald's restaurants on BuzzFeed, at https://www .buzzfeed.com/gavon/45-mcdonalds-items-not-available-in-the-us-that?utm_term= .ljPKeMDK9W#.tbpJqb3JlV.

to the internet is highest (see Figure 1.4). However, their importance is increasing elsewhere, especially in the Middle East and North Africa, as reflected in the role they played there in recent social revolutions. Protesters used cell phones and the internet to inform each other, and the world, about the evolving scene. To take another example, Facebook.com/yalaYL has become a key site where Israelis, Palestinians, and other Arabs communicate with each other about both everyday concerns and big issues such as the prospect for peace in the Middle East. This social networking takes place online, while peaceful face-to-face interaction between such people, and between their leaders, is difficult or nonexistent, especially in light of the 2014 war in and around Gaza, as well as the continuing violence there and elsewhere in and around Israel (Bronner 2011).

While social networking sites can bring about greater interaction, they also come between people and affect the nature of interaction. For example, Twitter limits each message to 140 characters, but face-to-face communication has no such limits. On the other hand, face-to-face communication is limited to a shared physical space, whereas communication via Twitter travels anywhere there is a device connected to the internet. Sociologists are interested in getting a better handle on the nature of the differences, as well as the similarities, between mediated and nonmediated (e.g., face-to-face) interaction. In technologically **mediated interaction**, technology such as the internet and the smartphone comes between the people who are communicating, while there is no such interference in nonmediated interaction. People who are shy and insecure when it comes to dating or sex, for example, may be much more comfortable relating to others on mediated websites such as Match.com or OkCupid.

Another sociological issue related to the internet is the impact on our lives of spending so much time interacting on social networking sites. For example, are you more likely to write term papers for your college classes using shorter sentences and more abbreviations because of your experience on Twitter or with texting? Consider also the impact of the nine hours per day that young people between the ages of 13 and 18 spend on entertainment or screen media (Common Sense Media 2015). In some cases, little time remains for other activities (schoolwork, face-to-face interaction). Increasing the ability of children to spend time on screen media is the growing availability of mobile devices such as smartphones and tablets. In 2013, about 75 percent of children in the United States under eight years of age lived in homes with mobile devices, compared to 52 percent just two years earlier. They were also more than twice as likely to use such devices in 2013 than they were in 2011 (Common Sense Media 2013).

Internet technology also affects the nature of consumption. More of it is taking place on such sites as eBay and Amazon.com, and that trend is expected to continue to grow. In 2010, a Pew study found that, during an average day, 21 percent of

FIGURE 1.4 • Internet Access by Geographic Region, 2016

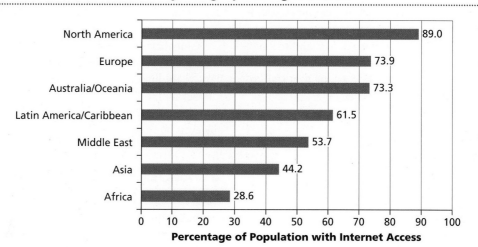

SOURCE: Data from Internet World Stats, "Internet Users in the World By Regions," http://www.internetworldstats.com/stats.htm.

Social changes brought about by the thorough integration of the internet in most areas of our lives have been enormously influential—and the changes are far from over. Teenagers and even very young children take our constant connectivity for granted, suggesting that most of the changes we are witnessing will become ever more pervasive.

As a college student, you live a truly global existence in a college or university. A significant number of your classmates may come from elsewhere in the world. Your classes are increasingly being taught by teaching assistants and professors from other parts of the globe. The ideas you are learning are the most global of all, flowing freely from virtually everywhere in the world to become part of lectures and textbooks.

As consumers, you and your classmates are likely well acquainted with Amazon.com and the nearby shopping mall. In addition, on the internet you are able to find a nearly infinite variety of goods (including this textbook) and services, the majority of which are likely to come from the far reaches of the world.

internet users in the United States look for information about a service or product they are thinking about buying (Jansen 2010). It is also easier for people to spend money on consumption on internet sites than it is in the material world. It is worth noting that these sites, as well as the internet in general, are global in their scope. The ease with which global interactions and transactions occur on the internet is a powerful indicator of, and spur to, the process of globalization.

Smartphones are also having a variety of effects on consumption. For example, on one hand, they are making it easier for people to find particular kinds of restaurants and to get to them quickly and efficiently. On the other hand, when people are eating in those restaurants, smartphones tend to slow down service because diners take time photographing the meal, taking selfies, and asking wait staff to take photos of them (Griswold 2014).

GLOBALIZATION, CONSUMPTION, THE DIGITAL WORLD, AND YOU

The three main issues discussed previously, taken singly and collectively, are of great concern not only to society in general and to sociologists but also to you as a college student. You live a good part of your life in these three interrelated domains.

Finally, an increasing portion of your education is obtained through the inherently global internet—for example, through e-learning on web-based courses and online degree programs. In 2013 the number of students taking at least one online course nearly doubled, to 45 percent, from 23 percent five years before (Bolkan 2013). With the emergence of massive open online courses (MOOCs), you, and perhaps hundreds of thousands of students from around the globe, are increasingly likely to participate in global classes (including courses in sociology; Behbehanian and Burawoy 2014) and other programs available on the internet (see Chapter 11 for more on MOOCs; see also Heller 2013; Lewin 2012).

Globalization, consumption, and the internet are of great importance on their own. However, perhaps more important are the ways in which they interact with one another and interpenetrate with your life as a college student—and the lives of virtually everyone else.

SOCIOLOGY: CONTINUITY AND CHANGE

This chapter has emphasized recent social changes and their impact on society and on sociology, but there is also much continuity in society, as well as in the field of sociology. This section deals with a number of traditional approaches and concerns in sociology that are of continuing relevance to even the most recent sociological issues.

THE SOCIOLOGICAL IMAGINATION

The systematic study of the social world has always required imagination on the part of sociologists. There are various ways to look at the social world. For example, instead of looking at the world from the point of view of an insider, one can, at least psychologically, place oneself outside that world. The U.S. "War on Terror" might look defensible from the perspective of an American, especially one who lived through 9/11, but it would look quite different if you imagined yourself in the place of an innocent Muslim caught in the middle of that war (Philips 2016).

The phenomenon of being able to look at the social world from different, imaginative perspectives attracted the attention of the famous sociologist C. Wright Mills (1916–1962), who in 1959 wrote a very important book titled *The Sociological Imagination*. He argued that sociologists have a unique perspective— the **sociological imagination**—that gives them a distinctive way of looking at data or reflecting on the world around them (Scott and Nilsen 2013). The sociological imagination challenges us to situate our personal biographies in a historical context. For example, the fact that many of us no longer use cash is not simply an individual preference, but the consequence of technological changes. Cash is not a viable option for online shopping. Most retailers make it easy and convenient to use credit cards instead of cash at drive-through windows and gasoline stations. Recently, Amazon opened physical grocery stores that require consumers to use a mobile app on their smartphones to purchase items. Consumers scan their smartphones when they enter the store, and digital technology detects what they place in their carts. There is no need to stand in line to pay for any items because they are charged to a customer's Amazon account when the person leaves the store (Rao 2016).

Private Troubles and Public Issues

The sociological imagination may be most useful in helping sociologists see the linkage between private

C. Wright Mills (1916–1962) was a prominent post–World War II sociologist who urged the use of the "sociological imagination" to study such issues as the power elite and the military-industrial complex.

troubles and public issues. For example, ADHD— attention-deficit/hyperactivity disorder—can easily be seen as a private trouble. For years there was little public awareness of ADHD, and those who had it were likely to suffer alone. But since the 1980s, it has become clear that ADHD is also a public issue, and it is becoming an increasingly important one not only in the United States but also globally (Ellison 2015). The number of children in the United States ages 3 to 17 diagnosed with ADHD increased from 6 percent in 1997 to 1999 to 9 percent in 2014 (Bloom, Jones, and Freeman 2013; Centers for Disease Control and Prevention 2014; Goodwin 2011). It is clear that many people suffer from ADHD, which creates a number of larger problems for schools, employers, and society as a whole. The fact that it has become a public issue may make ADHD less of a private trouble for some, as there is now greater public understanding of the problem, and many more support groups are available.

In another example, a 2011 White House report details the fact that women are more likely than men to be concentrated in lower-paying jobs (see Figure 1.5; U.S. Department of Commerce 2011). For example, women are much more likely to be comparatively poorly paid dental hygienists than dentists, or legal assistants rather than lawyers. Being limited occupationally creates personal troubles for many women, such as inadequate income and job dissatisfaction. This is also a public issue, not only because the discrepancy between the sexes is unfair to women as a whole but also because society is not benefiting from the many contributions women could be making.

The decision to pursue one college major or career path over another could become a private trouble if a student makes a poor choice or has one forced upon him or her. Sociologists have also shown that such choices are very much related to larger public issues. If many people make poor choices, or are forced into them—as women and other minorities often are—this will lead to public issues such as wide-scale job dissatisfaction and poor performance on the job. Culturally based ideas about gender often shape personal preferences in choosing a college major (Charles and Bradley 2009), and gendered beliefs about career competence steer women and men toward different types of jobs and away from others (Correll 2001, 2004; Ridgeway and Correll 2004). Being in a poorly paid and unsatisfying job is a personal trouble for an individual woman, but it is a public issue when large numbers of women find themselves in this situation.

ASK YOURSELF

Do you agree that private choices sometimes lead to, or are part of, public issues? Can you think of an example from your own life or the life of a family member?

The Micro–Macro Relationship

The interest in personal troubles and public issues is a specific example of a larger and more basic sociological concern with the relationship between microscopic (**micro**, or small-scale) social phenomena, such as individuals and their thoughts and actions, and macroscopic (**macro**, or large-scale) social phenomena, such as groups, organizations, cultures, society, and the world, as well as the relationships among them (Turner 2005). For example, Karl Marx, often considered one of the earliest and most important sociologists, was interested in the relationship between what workers do and think (micro issues) and the capitalist economic system in which the workers exist (a macro issue). To take

FIGURE 1.5 • Percentages of Women in Selected Occupations, 2014

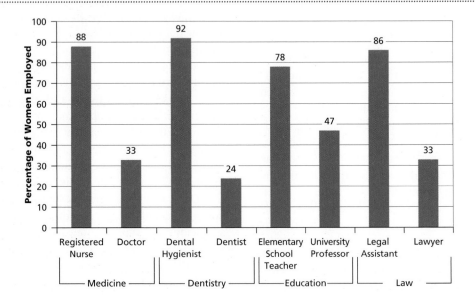

SOURCE: U.S. Census Bureau, Full-Time, Year-Round Workers and Median Earnings in the Past 12 Months by Sex and Detailed Occupation: 2014.

As they watch in real time the locating—and killing—of Osama bin Laden in 2011, the tension shows on the faces and the body language of the highest officials of the United States—including President Barack Obama.

a more contemporary example, Randall Collins (2009) has sought to develop a theory of violence that deals with everything from individuals skilled in violent interactions, such as attacking those who are weak, to the material resources needed by violent organizations to cause the destruction of other violent organizations. An example of the former type of violent organization is the well-equipped U.S. Navy SEALs team that killed Osama bin Laden in 2011 and through that act helped hasten the decline of al-Qaeda. However, the decline of al-Qaeda helped lead to the rise of a new, even more violent, organization, the Islamic State.

In fact, there is a continuum that runs from the most microscopic to the most macroscopic of social realities, with phenomena at roughly the midpoint of this continuum best thought of as meso (middle or intermediate) realities. The definition of sociology presented at the beginning of this chapter fits this continuum quite well. Individual actions and thoughts lie on the micro end of the continuum;

groups, organizations, cultures, and societies fall more toward the macro end; and worldwide structures and processes are at the end point on the macro side of the continuum. Although in their own work the vast majority of individual sociologists focus on only very limited segments of this continuum, the field as a whole is concerned with the continuum in its entirety, as well as with the interrelationships among its various components.

The Agency–Structure Relationship

American sociologists tend to think in terms of the micro–macro relationship. In other parts of the world, especially in Europe, sociologists are more oriented to the agency–structure relationship. The agency–structure continuum is complex, but for our purposes we can think of agency as resembling the micro level and structure as resembling the macro level.

The utility of the agency–structure terminology is that it highlights several important social realities and aspects of the field of sociology. Of greatest

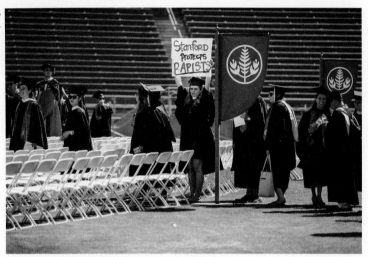

Students at many universities, including the elite Stanford University, have organized to protest rape on campus and the failure of school administrators to deal with the problem and to punish the rapists sufficiently, if at all.

significance is the fact that the term **agency** gives great importance to the individual—the "agent"—as having power and a capacity for creativity (Giddens 1984). In sociological work on agency, great emphasis is placed on the individual's mental abilities and the ways in which these abilities are used to create important, if not decisive, actions.

However, these agents are seen as enmeshed in macro-level social and cultural structures that they create and by which they are constrained (King 2004). For example, as a student, you help create the universities you attend, but you are also constrained by them and the power they have over you. Your university can require you to do certain things (such as take specific courses in order to earn your degree) and prevent you from doing other things (such as taking courses that might be of greater interest, or even taking no courses at all). On the other hand, you as a student can act to change or overthrow those structures. You might organize student-run groups on topics of interest, such as religious rights or manga cartoons, attract many participants to the groups, and eventually prompt the university to add courses on those topics. Or perhaps you might organize students to stop enrolling in an elective course that seems irrelevant to their lives, causing that elective to be dropped from the course catalog.

Agents (you as a student, in this case) have great power. In the words of another important sociologist, Erving Goffman (1961b, 81), individuals are **dangerous giants**. That is, they have the potential to disrupt and destroy the structures in which they find themselves. Yet agents often do not realize the power they possess. As a result, social structures such as the university and the class you are currently taking function for long periods of time with little or no disruption by individual agents.

However, there are times, such as during the anti–Vietnam War protests of the late 1960s and early 1970s, when students come to realize that they are dangerous giants and act to change not only the university but also the larger society (Gitlin 1993). For example, students at some universities are protesting against the possible deportation of undocumented immigrants by pressuring school administrators to create "sanctuary campuses" that protect faculty, students, and staff from federal immigration authorities.

There are far more minor, everyday actions that reflect the fact that people can be dangerous giants. Examples involving students include questioning a professor's argument or going to the dean to protest the excessive absences of an instructor. However, most people most of the time do not realize that they are dangerous giants—that they have the capacity to greatly alter the social structures that surround them and in which they are enmeshed.

THE SOCIAL CONSTRUCTION OF REALITY

The discussion of agency and structure leads to another basic concept in sociology: the **social construction of reality** (Berger and Luckmann 1967; Knoblauch and Wilke 2016). People at the agency end of the continuum are seen as creating social reality, basically macro-level phenomena, through their thoughts and actions. That reality then comes to have a life of its own. That is, it becomes a structure that is partly or wholly separate from the people who created it and exist in it. Once macro phenomena have lives of their own, they constrain and even control what people do. Of course, people can refuse to accept these constraints and controls and create new social realities. This process of individual creation of structural realities, constraint, and coercion then begins anew, in a continuing loop. It is this continuous loop that is the heart of agency–structure and micro–macro relationships, the social world, and the field of sociology.

For example, in the realm of consumption, it is people—as designers, manufacturers, consumers, and bloggers—who create the world of fashion (Entwhistle 2015). However, once the fashion world comes into existence, that world has a great deal of influence over the social constructions, especially the tastes, of individuals who purchase the fashions it produces. Famous fashion houses such as Dior and Givenchy dominate the industry and perpetuate their existence through continual fashion changes. These companies—and, more important, the "fast-fashion" companies that copy and mass-produce their products, such as H&M, Forever 21, and Zara—control people's tastes in fashion and thereby the nature of the clothing they buy and wear. Changing fashions are highly profitable for the companies involved. Consumers are led to be eager to buy the latest fashions, although most often in the form of relatively inexpensive fast-fashion knockoffs.

Of course, many people do not accept such social constructions; they do not go along with the constraints of the fashion industry. They do not wear what the industry wants them to wear, and they do not change the way they dress because of changes in fashion induced by the fashion industry. Many people have their own sense of fashion and create their own way of dressing. Others ignore fashion altogether. Of greatest importance from this perspective is the fact that the idea of what is in fashion often comes not from the fashion industry but rather from the ways of dressing that people put together themselves. These people, in a real sense, construct their own social reality. In fact, in a process known as "cool hunting" (Gloor and Cooper 2007), scouts for the fashion industry seek out new and interesting ways of dressing, often focusing on what young people in the suburbs and the inner cities are wearing. They bring those innovative ideas back to the fashion industry, and some of them are turned into next year's fashions.

SOCIAL STRUCTURES AND PROCESSES

A nineteenth-century sociologist, Auguste Comte (1798–1857), was important not only for inventing the term *sociology* in 1839 but also for being the originator of sociology as a field. Crucial for our purposes here is his early distinction between what he called "social statics" and "social dynamics." In his social statics, Comte looked at the various "parts" (structures) of society, such as the manufacturers and retailers of clothing fashions, and the ways in which they relate to one another as well as to the whole of society. In examining such relationships, Comte investigated social processes among and between parts of society as well as in society as a whole. However, under the heading of social dynamics, his main focus was on a specific social process—social change—and how the various parts of society change.

It is important to emphasize here that **social structures** are enduring and regular social arrangements, such as the family and the state. While social structures do change, they are generally not very dynamic; they change very slowly. **Social processes** are the dynamic and ever-changing aspects of the social world.

Auguste Comte (1798–1857) invented the term "sociology," argued that the discipline should be a science, and created a general theory of the social world.

The elements of globalization can be divided between structures (e.g., the United Nations) and a variety of more specific social processes (e.g., the migration of people across national borders). In terms of consumption, we can think of the shopping mall (or Amazon.com) as a structure and the shopping (or consumption) that takes place in it as a process. Finally, the internet as a whole and social networking sites in particular are structures, while the communication and the social interaction that take place in them can be viewed as processes.

Needless to say, neither the shopping mall nor the internet existed in Comte's day. Once again, we see that the social world is constantly changing and that sociologists, as well as students of sociology, must be sensitive to those changes. However, some of sociology's earliest concepts continue to be applicable, and usefully applied, to the social world.

SOCIOLOGY'S PURPOSE: SCIENCE OR SOCIAL REFORM?

Comte was famous not only for examining the relationship between structure and process but also for arguing that such study ought to be scientific. He believed that the social world was dominated by laws and that sociology's task was to uncover those laws. As those laws were uncovered, the science of sociology would develop. But Comte was also concerned about the problems of his day and interested in solving them through social reform. In fact, to Comte, science and reform should not be separated from one another. A number of classical sociologists—Karl Marx, Émile Durkheim, Jane Addams, and others—shared this view. Marx and Engels's *Communist Manifesto* (1848) was not only a commentary on the social ills of the capitalist economy but also a rallying cry to workers to organize and abolish capitalism.

Many of today's sociologists study social problems of all sorts, such as poverty and crime. They use a variety of scientific methods to collect large amounts of data on such problems (see Chapter 2). They also seek to use what they learn about those problems to suggest ways of reforming society. They believe that these two activities—scientific research

and social reform—are not necessarily distinct; they can and should be mutually enriching. While many contemporary sociologists accept this position, a division has developed over time, with some sociologists focusing more on scientific research and others more engaged in activities designed to reform society and address social problems. The sociologists who engage in "pure science" operate with the conviction that we need to have a better understanding of how the social world operates before we can change it, if that's what we want to do. The knowledge gained through social research may ultimately be used by those who want to change society, or to keep it as it is, but that is not the immediate concern of these researchers.

Other sociologists take the opposite position. C. Wright Mills, for example, was little interested in doing scientific research. He was mostly interested in such social reforms as limiting or eliminating the unwholesome and worrisome ties between the military and industry in the United States. He was also critical of many of the most prominent sociologists of his day for their orientation toward being pure scientists, their lack of concern for the pressing problems of the day, and their unwillingness to do anything about those problems. Feminist sociologists have extended the argument, pointing out that the topics and methods of objective, scientific sociology themselves sometimes reflect, and ultimately reinforce, social inequality along the lines of race, gender, and class because they are based on the assumptions of society's elite.

ASK YOURSELF

What do you believe is the best purpose of sociology: pure science or social reform? Why? Make a note to ask yourself this question again at the end of your course. Did you answer it differently?

SOCIOLOGY, THE OTHER SOCIAL SCIENCES, AND COMMON SENSE

Sociology is one of the social sciences—that is, it is one of the fields that studies various aspects of the social world. Among the others are anthropology, communication studies, economics, geography, political science, and psychology. Generally speaking, sociology is the broadest of these fields; social scientists in other fields are more likely than sociologists to delve into specific aspects of the social world in much greater depth. Sociological study touches on the culture of concern to anthropologists, the nation-state of interest to political scientists, and the mental processes that are the focus of psychologists. However, that does not mean that sociology is in any sense "better" than—or, conversely, not as good as— the other social sciences.

Rather than comparing and contrasting these fields in general terms, this concluding section will focus on the different ways in which these fields approach one of this book's signature concerns— globalization.

- *Anthropology:* Focuses on cultural aspects of societies around the world, such as the foods people eat and how they eat them, as well as the differences among cultures around the globe (Inda and Rosaldo 2008).

- *Communication studies:* Examines communications across the globe, with the internet obviously of focal concern in the contemporary world.

- *Economics:* Investigates the production, distribution, and consumption of resources through markets and other structures that span much of the globe, especially those based on and involving money.

- *Geography:* Studies spatial relationships on a global scale and maps those spaces (Herod 2009).

- *Political science:* Studies nation-states, especially the ways in which they relate to one another around the world as well as how they have grown increasingly unable to control global flows of migrants, viruses, recreational drugs, internet scams, and the like.

- *Psychology:* Examines the ways in which individual identities are shaped by increased awareness of the rest of the world and tensions associated with globalization (e.g., job loss), which may lead to individual psychological problems such as depression (Lemert and Elliott 2006).

Sociology encompasses all these concerns, and many others, in its approach to globalization. It studies globe-straddling cultures (such as consumer or fast-food culture), relationships between political systems (the European Union and its member nations, for example), communication networks (such as CNN and Al Jazeera or Twitter and Facebook), and markets (for labor or stocks and bonds, for example) that cover vast expanses of the globe. Sociology maps all of these, and even their impacts (both good and bad) on individuals. You might want to study the other fields to get a sense of the depth of what they have to offer on specific aspects of globalization. However, if you are looking for the field that gives you the broadest possible view of all of these things as well as the ways in which they interrelate, that field is sociology.

While sociology and the other social sciences differ from one another in important ways, they are all quite different from commonsense understandings of the social world. Everyone participates in globalization in one way or another. However, few if any people research these phenomena in the same rigorous way and to the same degree that social scientists examine them. That research leads, among other things, to a greater understanding of the nature of globalization. For example, you probably have a sense that globalization has changed society—perhaps even an impression that it is changing your life. What you are unlikely to know are globalization's causes, effects, and linkages to other social phenomena, or its largely invisible effects on society and the world. Research on the topic is also likely to yield much more insight into the pros and cons of globalization on the personal, societal, and global levels. Such detailed knowledge and insight will help you, and others, more successfully navigate the accompanying changes in social processes and structures.

One example of the gap between common sense and social scientific knowledge relates to perceptions of the causes of global warming. There is strong consensus in the global scientific community that global warming is occurring and that it is caused primarily by human activities, especially the burning of fossil fuels. However, data from a recent survey, illustrated in Figure 1.6, show that only 70 percent of Americans believe that global warming is happening and just 53 percent believe that it is caused by human activity. Furthermore, 28 percent

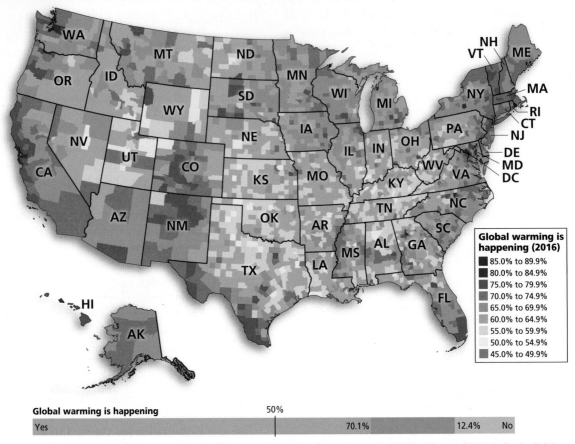

Global warming is happening (2016)

- 85.0% to 89.9%
- 80.0% to 84.9%
- 75.0% to 79.9%
- 70.0% to 74.9%
- 65.0% to 69.9%
- 60.0% to 64.9%
- 55.0% to 59.9%
- 50.0% to 54.9%
- 45.0% to 49.9%

Global warming is happening

| Yes | 50% | | 70.1% | 12.4% | No |

SOURCE: Howe, Peter D., Matto Mildenberger, Jennifer R. Marlon, and Anthony Leiserowitz (2015). "Geographic Variation in Opinions on Climate Change at State and Local Scales in the USA." Nature Climate Change, doi: 10.1038/nclimate2583, via Yale Climate Opinion Maps–U.S. 2016, (http://climatecommunication.yale.edu/visualizations-data/ycom-us-2016/).

think that there is a lot of disagreement among scientists about the causes of global warming (Howe et al. 2016). While common sense is important, even to sociologists, there is no substitute for the systematic study of the social world in both its minutest detail and its broadest manifestations.

SUMMARY

Sociology is the systematic examination of the ways in which people are affected by and affect the social structures and social processes associated with the groups, organizations, cultures, societies, and world in which they exist. Social changes in the last few centuries, including the Industrial Revolution, the growth of the service sector, and the arrival of the information age, have strongly influenced the field of sociology. This book deals with innumerable social issues, but it focuses especially on three powerful structural forces in the social world that have drawn the attention of contemporary sociologists: globalization, consumption, and digital technology.

As the world has become more globalized, it has become more fluid as people, products, and information flow more quickly and easily across national borders. The role of consumption in our daily lives over the past few decades has resulted in the increasing use of credit cards and the growing popularity of online shopping. Digital technology is changing how and when we interact with others, including the near ubiquitous use of smartphones and social media. The process of McDonaldization, or an emphasis on efficiency, calculability, predictability, and technological control, characterizes many aspects of globalization, consumption, and digital technology.

Social changes such as globalization, consumption, and digital technology can be understood using C. Wright Mills's "sociological imagination," which calls on us to look at social phenomena not just from a personal perspective but also from the outside, from a distinctively sociological perspective. In addition, recognizing that much of our reality is socially constructed can help us comprehend how the agency of individuals can bring about social change; at the same time, these changes become structures that both enable and constrain social action. These social structures become enduring and slow to change, while social processes represent the more dynamic aspects of society.

Sociologists study many issues, sometimes to understand them through scientific research and sometimes to help generate change and reform. The goal of sociology as a pure science is to collect large quantities of data about the social world to build knowledge, while the goal of sociology as a means of social reform aims to use this knowledge for social change.

Sociology, like other social sciences, distinguishes itself from commonsense opinions about the social world by developing rigorous theories and engaging in systematic research to study social phenomena. Sociology, the least specialized of the social sciences, encompasses aspects of anthropology, political science, psychology, economics, and communication.

KEY TERMS

agency, 18
butterfly effect, 2
consumption, 8
dangerous giants, 18
globalization, 8

macro, 16
McDonaldization, 10
mediated interaction, 13
micro, 16

social construction of
 reality, 18
social processes, 19
social structures, 19
society, 6

sociological
 imagination, 15
sociology, 3
technology, 11

REVIEW QUESTIONS

1. How is the projected impact of Google's driverless car project, Waymo, an example of the butterfly effect? Use your sociological imagination to think of ways in which your individual choices and actions will be influenced by this development.

2. Your social world is continually changing. What are some examples of new technologies that have been developed during your lifetime? How have they changed the way you interact with and relate to others?

3. How do shopping malls reflect increasing globalization? Do you think shopping malls lead to a sameness of culture around the world, or do they allow local areas to retain their differences?

4. What items are you most likely to buy using the internet? How do social networking sites (e.g., Facebook, Twitter, Instagram) influence what you consume?

5. WikiLeaks has released thousands of confidential documents obtained from government, military, and corporate sources. Is this an example of an information war? Why or why not? What social structures have impeded the flow of this kind of information in the past? How have the internet and social networking sites made it easier to get around these structural barriers?

6. According to C. Wright Mills, how are private troubles different from public issues? How can we use the micro/macro distinction to show how private troubles are related to public issues?

7. What is the difference between structure and agency? Within your classroom, could you be a "dangerous giant"? In what ways does your school prevent you from becoming a dangerous giant?

8. What do sociologists mean by the social construction of reality? How can you apply this perspective to better understand trends in the fashion industry?

9. Can you think of ways in which we can use "pure science" to better understand the process of McDonaldization? What do you believe should be the goal of research?

10. How is sociology's approach to globalization different from that of other social sciences? What are the advantages of using a sociological approach to understand globalization?

$SAGE edge™ **Want a better grade?**

Get the tools you need to sharpen your study skills. Access practice quizzes, eFlashcards, video, and multimedia at **edge.sagepub.com/ritzeressentials3e.**

PRACTICE AND APPLY WHAT YOU'VE LEARNED

▶ **edge.sagepub.com/ ritzeressentials3e**

CHECK YOUR COMPREHENSION ON THE STUDY SITE WITH:

- **Diagnostic pre-tests** to identify opportunities for improvement.

- **eFlashcards** that strengthen your understanding of key terms and concepts.

- **Post-tests** to check your progress and ensure mastery of key learning objectives.

THINKING ABOUT AND RESEARCHING THE SOCIAL WORLD

Sociologists Theorize about and Research Climate Change

Humankind has made amazing advances during its short existence on Earth. From the development of agriculture to the Industrial Revolution to the advent of the digital and the global ages, each generation has pushed further into an unknown future. Many, especially in the developed world, enjoy longer lives, improved standards of living, a plethora of inexpensive manufactured goods, affordable and readily available food, quick and effortless communication, and the ability to travel, even around the world. But this advancement, especially of those in the developed world, has come at a significant ecological price.

Climate change, marked by long-term fluctuations in Earth's intricate and interwoven weather patterns, has occurred since the formation of the planet. Some fluctuations affect only specific regions, while others affect the entire world. Some span decades; others occur over millions of years. Although gradual climate change is a natural process, a growing body of careful research suggests that significant recent changes, including fossil fuel combustion

LEARNING OBJECTIVES

2.1 Relate notable contributions from influential classical sociological theorists.

2.2 Explain the three major categories of contemporary theories.

2.3 Describe the scientific method and various methods of sociological research.

2.4 Summarize five key issues in social research.

edge.sagepub.com/
ritzeressentials3e

- Take the chapter quiz
- Review key terms with eFlashcards
- Explore multimedia links and SAGE readings

and deforestation, are directly attributable to human activities, especially in the developed world.

Despite this scientific consensus, our impact on climate change remains a hotly debated issue. If the available geological, atmospheric, and oceanographic evidence is solid enough to convince the scientific community, why do so many people remain fiercely unconvinced? Who is opposed to the notion that human actions are a major cause of climate change, and how have institutional forces influenced their personal beliefs over time?

Physical science can help us understand and explain climate change, but to understand the motivations, beliefs, and actions that affect our response to it, we need sociologists and their theories and research methods. A sociologist's perspective is framed by the theories to which he or she subscribes. For example, a conflict theorist would frame the debate over climate change as a struggle between the strong and the weak. Powerful oil companies might deny that climate change is a result of the burning of fossil fuels and therefore claim it is not their responsibility. Weaker groups suffering from the effects of climate change, such as the Tuvaluans, whose island is threatened by rising sea levels, might blame the oil companies for this catastrophe.

Sociologists not only have a number of theories to choose from; they also have many different research methods at their disposal to study the debate about climate change. For example, they could use surveys to gather quantitative data on how many Tuvaluans believe human activities are causing climate change or conduct open-ended interviews with Tuvaluans to collect descriptive data on how they experience this debate in their everyday lives. With its many theories and methods, sociology is a science, like—and also unlike—any other. ●

THEORIZING THE SOCIAL WORLD

Theories are sets of interrelated ideas that have a wide range of applications, deal with centrally important issues, and have stood the test of time (Ritzer and Stepnisky 2017). Theories have stood the test of time when they continue to be applicable to the changing social world and have withstood challenges from those who accept other theories. Sociological theories are necessary to make sense of both the innumerable social phenomena and the many highly detailed findings of sociological research. Without such theories, we would have little more than knowledge of isolated bits of the social world. Once those theories have been created, however, they can be applied broadly to such areas as the economy, organizations, religion, society as a whole, and even the globe. The theories to be discussed in this chapter deal with very important social issues that have affected the social world for centuries and will likely continue to affect it.

CLASSICAL SOCIOLOGICAL THEORY

The emergence of sociological theory was closely related to intellectual and social developments throughout the nineteenth century in Europe. It is important to recognize that sociological theory did not develop in isolation or come of age in a social vacuum. In Chapter 1, we briefly mentioned the impact of the Industrial Revolution. Other changes that profoundly affected sociological theorizing were the political revolutions that wracked European society (especially the French Revolution, 1789–1799), the rise of socialism, the women's rights movement, the urbanization occurring throughout Europe, ferment in the religious realm, and the growth of science.

Among the most important early sociological theorists are Auguste Comte, Harriet Martineau, and Herbert Spencer:

- *Auguste Comte* (1798–1857) is noted, as pointed out in Chapter 1, for the invention of the term

sociology, the development of a general theory of the social world, and an interest in developing a science of sociology (Pickering 2011).

- *Harriet Martineau* (1802–1876), like Comte, developed a scientific and general theory, although she is best known today for her feminist, women-centered sociology (Hoecker-Drysdale 2011).

- *Herbert Spencer* (1820–1903) also developed a general, scientific theory of society, but his overriding theoretical interest was in social change, specifically evolution in not only the physical domain but also the intellectual and social domains (Francis 2011).

Although Comte, Martineau, and Spencer were important predecessors, the three theorists to be discussed in this section—Karl Marx, Max Weber, and Émile Durkheim—are the most significant of the classical era's social theorists and of the greatest continuing contemporary relevance to sociology (and other fields).

Karl Marx

Marx (1818–1883) focused most of his attention on the structure of capitalist society, a relatively new phenomenon in his day. Marx defined **capitalism** as an economic system based on the fact that one group of people—the **capitalists**—owns what is needed for production, including factories, machines, and tools. A second group—the **proletariat**, or workers—owns little or nothing except their capacity for work and labor. In order to work and survive, the workers must sell their labor time, primarily their working hours, to the capitalists in exchange for wages. In Marx's view, the capitalist system is marked by **exploitation**. The proletariat produces virtually everything but gets only a small portion of the income derived from the sale of the products. The capitalists, who do little productive work, reap the vast majority of the rewards. In other words, the capitalists *exploit* the workers. Furthermore, driven by the need to compete in the marketplace, the capitalists are forced to keep costs, including wages, as low as possible.

Then, as competition with other capitalists intensifies, the pressure is on to reduce wages further. As a result, the proletariat barely subsists, living a miserable, animal-like existence.

In addition, the workers experience **alienation** on the job and in the workplace (Mészáros 2006). They are alienated because

- The work they do—for example, repetitively and mechanically inserting wicks into candles or attaching hubcaps to cars—is not a natural expression of human skills, abilities, and creativity.

- They have little or no connection to the finished product.

- Instead of working harmoniously with their fellow workers, they may have little or no contact with them. In fact, they are likely to be in competition or outright conflict with them over, for example, who keeps and who loses their jobs.

Thus, what defines people as human beings—their ability to think, to act on the basis of that thought, to be creative, to interact with other human beings—is denied to the workers in capitalism. As capitalists adopt new technologies to make their companies more competitive, alienation among the workers increases. For example, faster, more mechanized assembly lines make it even more difficult for coworkers to relate to one another.

Over time, Marx believed, the workers' situation would grow much worse as the capitalists increased the level of exploitation and restructured the work so that the proletariat became even more alienated. The gap between these two social classes would grow wider and increasingly visible in terms of both the two groups' economic position and the nature of their work. Once workers understood how capitalism "really" worked, especially the ways in which it worked to their detriment, they would rise up and overthrow that system in what Marx called a proletarian revolution.

Marx believed that his work was needed because the capitalist class tried hard to make sure

that the proletariat did not truly understand the nature of capitalism. One of the ways in which the capitalists did this was to produce a set of ideas, an ideology, that distorted the reality of capitalism and concealed the ways in which it really operated. As a result, the proletariat suffered from **false consciousness**—the workers did not truly understand capitalism and may have even believed, erroneously, that the system operated fairly and perhaps even to their benefit. Marx's work was devoted to providing the members of the proletariat with the knowledge they needed to see through these false ideas and achieve a truer understanding of the workings of capitalism.

Marx hypothesized that the workers could develop **class consciousness** and that such a collective consciousness would lead them to truly understand capitalism, their role in it, and their relationship to one another as well as to the capitalists. Class consciousness was a prerequisite of the revolutionary actions to be undertaken by the proletariat. In contrast, the capitalists could never achieve class consciousness because, in Marx's view, they were too deeply involved in capitalism ever to be able to see how it truly operated.

ASK YOURSELF

Do you agree with Marx's characterizations of false consciousness and class consciousness? Why or why not? Give some examples from your own experience to support your answer.

Marx's theories about capitalism are relevant to contemporary society. For example, in the United States, a capitalist country, the income gap Marx predicted between those at the top of the economic system and the rest of the population is huge and growing. In 2014, the top 20 percent of the population in terms of household income had a greater average income than the rest of the population combined. Furthermore, as you can see in Figure 2.1, those at the top have greatly increased their average income since 1967; this is especially true of the top 5 percent of the population. In contrast, the lowest fifth has a lower average income than it had in 1967 (DeNavas-Walt, Proctor, and Smith 2012).

Marx also theorized that capitalism would force the capitalists to find the cheapest sources of labor

and resources wherever they existed in the world (Panitch 2009). As Marx predicted, corporations continue to scour the globe for workers willing to work for lower wages, driving down pay closer to home and reaping as much profit as possible from lower labor costs.

However, history has failed to bear out much of Marx's thinking about the demise of capitalism. For example, there has been no proletarian revolution, and one seems less likely than ever. This is the case, if for no other reason, because the members of the proletariat of greatest interest to Marx—manufacturing workers—are rapidly declining in number and importance, at least in developed countries like the United States (Rifkin 1995; Schwartz 2016). Despite the threats to the proletariat, capitalism continues to exist, and Marx's ways of thinking about it, and the concepts he developed for that analysis, continue to be useful.

Max Weber

Although Karl Marx was a very important social theorist, he developed his ideas outside the academic world. It took time for those radical ideas to gain recognition from scholars. In contrast, Max Weber (1864–1920; pronounced VAY-ber) was a leading academician of his day (Kalberg 2011, 2017). Weber, like Marx, devoted great attention to the economy.

Weber's best-known work—*The Protestant Ethic and the Spirit of Capitalism* ([1904–1905] 1958)—is part of his historical-comparative study of religion in various societies throughout the world (see the discussion later in the chapter). One of his main objectives was to analyze the relationship between the economy and religion. Weber focused on the central role religion had played in the Western world's economic development.

Beginning in the seventeenth century, it was Protestantism in general, and especially Calvinism, that led to the rise of capitalism in the West and not in other areas of the world. Calvinists believed that people were predestined to go to heaven or hell; that is, they would end up in heaven or hell no matter what they did or did not do. While they could not affect their destiny, they could uncover "signs" that indicated whether or not they were "saved" and going to heaven. Economic success was a particularly important sign that one was saved. However, isolated successful economic successes were not sufficient.

FIGURE 2.1 • Mean Household Income Received by Each Fifth and Top 5 Percent, All Races: 1967 to 2014

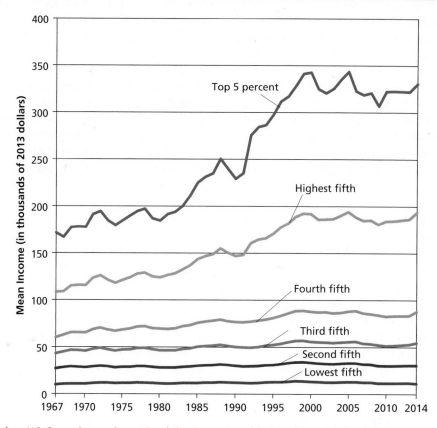

SOURCE: Data from U.S. Census Bureau, Current Population Survey, Annual Social and Economic Supplements.

Calvinists had to devote their lives to hard work and economic success, as well as to other "good works." At the same time, the Calvinists were quite frugal. All of this was central to the distinctive ethical system of the Calvinists, and more generally Protestants, that Weber referred to as the **Protestant ethic**.

Weber was interested not only in the Protestant ethic but also in the "spirit of capitalism" that it helped spawn. The Protestant ethic was a system of ideas closely associated with religion, while the spirit of capitalism involved a transformation of those ideas into a perspective linked directly to the economy. As the economy came to be infused with the spirit of capitalism, it was transformed into a capitalist economic system. Eventually, however, the spirit of capitalism, and later capitalism itself, grew apart from its roots in Calvinism and the Protestant ethic. Capitalist thinking eventually could not accommodate such irrational forms of thought as ethics and religion.

Despite his attention to it, Weber was *not* interested in capitalism per se. He was more interested in the broader phenomenon of **rationalization**, or the process by which social structures are increasingly characterized by the most direct and efficient means to their ends. In Weber's view, this process was becoming more and more common in many sectors of society, including the economy, especially in bureaucracies and in the most rational economic system—capitalism. Capitalism is rational because of, for example, its continual efforts to find ways to produce more profitable products efficiently, with fewer inputs and simpler processes. A specific and early example of rationalization in capitalism is the assembly line, in which raw materials enter the line and finished products emerge at the end. Fewer workers performed very simple tasks in order to allow the assembly line to function efficiently. More recently, manufacturers have added more rational, "lean" production methods, such as the just-in-time inventory system (Janoski 2015). Instead of storing extra components in case they are needed, the just-in-time system relies on the delivery of materials when they are needed in the production process. This makes for highly efficient use of storage space and of the funds needed to purchase materials.

Weber saw rationalization as leading to an "iron cage" of rationalized systems. Such a cage makes it increasingly difficult for people to escape the process. This gives a clear sense of his negative opinion of rationalization.

Such a negative view of rationalization and its constraints and socially harmful effects has persisted. It is frequently portrayed in popular entertainment, including George Orwell's novel, and later movie, *Nineteen Eighty-Four* (1949), as well as movies such as *Brazil* (1985), *V for Vendetta* (2005), and the *Hunger Games* series (2012–2015).

In sum, while for Marx the key problems in the modern world were the exploitation and alienation that are part of the capitalist economy, for Weber the central problem was the control that rationalized structures such as capitalism exercise over us in virtually all aspects of our lives. Furthermore, while Marx was optimistic and had great hope for socialism and communism, Weber was a pessimist about most things. Socialism and communism, he felt, would not eliminate or prevent the iron cage from enveloping us.

ASK YOURSELF

Efforts to exploit, alienate, and control us continue to this day. Is only capitalism to blame for this? Are there causes to be found in even larger systems in the modern world? Or are more microscopic sources, such as the nature of human beings, responsible for these efforts?

Émile Durkheim

Émile Durkheim (1858–1917) developed a theoretical orientation that was very different from those of his peers (Fournier 2013; Milibrandt and Pearce 2011). For Durkheim, the major concern of the science of sociology was **social facts**. These are macro-level phenomena, such as social structures and cultural norms and values, that stand apart from people and, more important, impose themselves on people. Examples of social facts that impose themselves on you include the structures of your university and the U.S. government. Durkheim felt that such structures and their constraints were not only necessary but also highly desirable.

Karl Marx, Émile Durkheim, and Max Weber were three of the most significant social theorists of their era. Though their theories were very different in many ways, all three were interested in the effect of social control on people.

Both Marx and Weber had a generally positive sense of people as thoughtful, creative, and naturally social. They criticized social structures for stifling people's innate characteristics. In contrast, Durkheim saw people as being slaves to their passions. Left to their own devices, he believed, people would relentlessly seek to satisfy those passions. However, the satisfaction of one passion would simply lead to the need to satisfy others. In Durkheim's view, passions should be limited, but people are unable to exercise this control themselves. They need social facts that are capable of limiting and controlling their passions.

The most important of these social facts is the **collective conscience**, or the set of beliefs shared by people throughout society (Bowring 2016). In Durkheim's view, the collective conscience is highly desirable not only for society but also for individuals. The collective conscience is highly beneficial to society because it provides social integration and regulation.

Durkheim's understanding of the collective conscience informed his book *Suicide* ([1897] 1951), one of the most famous research studies in the history of sociology. Because he was a sociologist, Durkheim did not focus on why any given individual committed suicide. Rather, he dealt with the more collective issue of suicide rates and why one group of people had a higher rate of suicide than another. The study was in many ways an ideal example of the power of sociological research. Using publicly available data, Durkheim found, for example, that suicide rates were not related to psychological or biological factors such as alcoholism or race and heredity. The causes of differences in suicide rates were *not* to be found within individuals. Rather, suicide rates were related to social factors that exert negative pressure on the individual.

ASK YOURSELF

Does the publicity associated with the suicide of a famous person, such as that of comedian Robin Williams in 2014, lead other people to commit suicide? Why? How do you think Durkheim would answer this question?

Durkheim differentiated among four different types of suicide. The most important one for our purposes is *anomic suicide*. **Anomie** is defined as people's feeling that they do not know what is expected of them in society—the feeling of being adrift in society without any clear or secure moorings. According to Durkheim, the risk of anomic suicide increases when people do not know what is expected of them, when society's regulation over them is low, and when their passions are allowed to run wild.

More generally, Durkheim believed that anomie is the defining problem of the modern world. This belief is central to another of his famous works, *The Division of Labor in Society* ([1893] 1964). He began by describing an early form of society with little division of labor. People there were held together by a type of solidarity—**mechanical solidarity**—stemming from the fact that they all did pretty much the same kinds of work, including hunting, gathering, and cooking. More important, people in this type of society had a strong collective conscience.

However, as Durkheim demonstrated, an increasing division of labor took place over time. Instead of continuing to do the same sorts of things, people began to specialize. What held them together was not their similarities but their differences. That is, they had become more dependent on one another; people needed what others did and produced in order to survive. Durkheim called this later form of social organization **organic solidarity**. This can be a powerful form of solidarity, but it is accompanied by a decline in the power of the collective conscience.

Although Marx, Weber, and Durkheim are the classical sociologists whose theories have most shaped contemporary sociology, several others made important contributions as well. Georg Simmel, W. E. B. Du Bois, and Thorstein Veblen all had grand theories of society, and you will see references to their ideas throughout this book.

Georg Simmel

Georg Simmel's (1858–1918) major importance in contemporary sociology lies in his contributions to micro theory. Simmel believed that sociologists should focus on the way in which conscious individuals interact and associate with one another (Scaff 2011).

Simmel was interested in the *forms* taken by social interaction. One such form involves the interaction between superiors and subordinates. He was also interested in the *types* of people who engage in interaction. In one of his most popular essays, Simmel describes the stranger as a social type, who is physically close to others, but psychologically and socially distant from them. For Simmel, it was the nature of the interaction between types of people and not the nature of the people themselves that was of greatest importance.

W. E. B. Du Bois

W. E. B. Du Bois (1868–1963) is best known in sociology for his theoretical ideas, in particular concerning the "color line" existing between whites and blacks in the United States (Taylor 2011).

This barrier was physical in the sense that African Americans could be distinguished visually, through their darker skin color, from white Americans. And the barrier was psychological because, among other things, African Americans found it difficult to see themselves in ways other than the ways in which white society saw them.

One of Du Bois's goals, especially in *The Souls of Black Folk* ([1903] 1966), was to lift the veil of race and give whites a glimpse of "Negroes" in America. He also wanted to show blacks that they could see themselves in a different way, especially outside the view that white society had prescribed for them. Another of Du Bois's important ideas is **double consciousness**. By this he meant that black Americans have a sense of "two-ness," of being American and of being African American. Black Americans want to tear down the barriers that confront them but do not want to give up their identity, traditions, knowledge, and experience. That is, black Americans, including former president Barack Obama (Terrill 2015), are both inside and outside dominant, white American society.

ASK YOURSELF

How many "consciousnesses" do you have? What are they? In what ways are they sources of satisfaction for you? In what ways do they stress you?

W. E. B. Du Bois, left, and Harriet Martineau, right, were essential to efforts to bring a focus on race and gender, respectively, to the field of sociology.

Thorstein Veblen

Thorstein Veblen (1857–1929) was concerned with the ways in which the upper classes demonstrate their wealth, which he described in his book *The Theory of the Leisure Class* ([1899] 1994). One way to show off wealth is through *conspicuous leisure,* or doing things that demonstrate quite publicly that one does not need to do what most people consider to be work. However, the problem with conspicuous leisure is that it is often difficult for very many others to witness these displays.

Thus, over time, the focus for the wealthy shifts from publicly demonstrating a waste of time to publicly demonstrating a waste of money. The waste of money is central to Veblen's most famous idea, **conspicuous consumption**. It is much easier for others to see conspicuous consumption than it is for them to see conspicuous leisure.

Veblen is important because he focused on consumption at a time when it was largely ignored by other social theorists. Furthermore, his specific ideas, especially conspicuous consumption, continue to be applied to the social world.

ASK YOURSELF

Picture in your mind some of the many examples of conspicuous consumption. Consider the brand names on your clothing, cell phone, and laptop. Are they expensive brands with visible logos and high status, or less expensive, no-name brands with little or no status? Are you less likely these days to buy clothing (and other products) with visible brand names because you are more interested in creating your own style?

CONTEMPORARY SOCIOLOGICAL THEORY

As sociology has grown as a discipline, the theories of earlier sociologists have evolved and branched out into at least a dozen newer theories. The work of the classical theorists has influenced each of these theories. As Table 2.1 shows, these contemporary theories can be categorized under three broad headings: structural/functional, conflict/critical, and inter/actionist theories.

TABLE 2.1 • Major Sociological Theories

STRUCTURAL/ FUNCTIONAL THEORIES	CONFLICT/ CRITICAL THEORIES	INTER/ ACTIONIST THEORIES
Structural-functionalism	Conflict theory	Symbolic interactionism
Structuralism	Critical theory	Ethnomethodology
	Feminist theory	Exchange theory
	Queer theory	Rational choice theory
	Critical theories of race and racism	
	Postmodern theory	

STRUCTURAL/FUNCTIONAL THEORIES

Structural/functional theories focus on large-scale social phenomena, including the state and culture (see Chapter 3 for more on culture). The two major theories under the broad heading of structural/functional theories are *structural-functionalism,* which looks at both social structures and their functions, and *structuralism,* which concerns itself solely with social structures, without concern for their functions. Note that while the names sound similar, structural-functionalism is one theory under the broader heading of structural/functional theories.

Structural-Functionalism

Structural-functionalism focuses on social structures as well as the functions that such structures perform. Structural-functionalists are influenced by the work of, among others, Émile Durkheim, who discussed, for example, the functions of and structural limits placed on deviance. Like Durkheim, structural-functionalists have a positive view of social structures, such as the police and military, seeing them as desirable, necessary, and even impossible to do without. Structural-functionalism tends to be a "conservative" theory. The dominant view is that if given structures exist and are functional, they ought to be retained and conserved.

A series of well-known and useful concepts have been developed by structural-functionalists, especially Robert Merton ([1949] 1968; see also Crothers 2011). One central concept in Merton's version of structural-functionalism is the idea of **functions**. These are the observable, positive consequences of a structure that help it survive, adapt, and adjust. For example, national borders are functional in various ways. The passport controls at borders allow a country to monitor who is entering the country and to refuse entry to those it considers undesirable or dangerous (Torpey 2012). Merton further elaborated on his basic theory by differentiating between two types of functions. The first is **manifest functions**, or positive consequences that are brought about consciously and purposely. For example, taxes (tariffs) are imposed on goods imported into the United States from elsewhere in the world in order to make the prices of those goods higher compared with American-made goods and thus protect U.S.-based producers. That is a manifest function of tariffs. However, such actions often have **latent functions**, or unintended positive consequences. For example, when foreign products become more expensive and therefore less desirable, U.S. manufacturers may produce more and perhaps better goods in the United States. In addition, more jobs for Americans may be created. In addition, functions can have either positive or negative **unanticipated consequences**. A negative unanticipated consequence of tariffs is a trade war with China. China might respond to an increase in U.S. tariffs by raisings its own tariffs on U.S. imports.

Structural-functionalism is greatly enriched when we add the concept of **dysfunctions**, which are observable consequences that negatively affect the ability of a given system to survive, adapt, or adjust. While border and passport controls clearly have functions, they also have dysfunctions. For example, President Donald Trump has attempted to restrict immigration to the United States from several Muslim-majority countries in an effort to prevent terrorists from entering the country. However, this is making it more difficult for everyone from these countries to enter the United States, including legitimate workers, businesspeople, and students. U.S. universities could lose up to $700 million per year if international students and faculty from these countries are banned (Reilly 2017).

Structuralism

Structuralism focuses on structures but is not concerned with their functions. While structural-functionalism focuses on quite visible structures, such as border fences, structuralism is more interested in the social impacts of hidden or underlying structures, such as the global economic order or gender relations. It adopts the view that these hidden structures determine what transpires on the surface of the social world. This perspective comes from the field of linguistics, which has largely adopted the view that the surface—the way we speak and express ourselves—is determined by an underlying grammatical system (Saussure [1916] 1966). A sociological example would be that behind-the-scenes actions of capitalists and the capitalist system determine the public positions taken by political leaders.

Marx's frequent collaborator Friedrich Engels ([1884] 1970) looked at relationships between women and men and theorized that the structures of capitalism and patriarchy kept women subordinated to men. Engels believed that female oppression was rooted in the hidden and underlying structure of private property rights in capitalism. When men gained control of agricultural production and wealth began to accumulate, men claimed more power over women. To guarantee the fidelity of wives and therefore the paternity of their children, men sought to claim women as their property. As a result, Engels thought that the key to ending that oppression was to abolish private property. The connections he drew between gender inequality and the underlying structure of society have proved to be enduring, and many contemporary feminist theorists have built more sophisticated analyses upon them (Chae 2014).

A structuralist approach is useful because it leads sociologists to look beyond the surface for underlying structures and realities, which determine what transpires on the surface. Thus, for example, military threats made by North Korea, and its test firing of missiles, may not really be about military matters at all but instead about that country's failing economic system. North Korea may hope that the symbolic expression of military power will distract its citizens, strengthen its global prestige, frighten others, and perhaps coerce other countries, especially the United States, into providing economic aid.

CONFLICT/CRITICAL THEORIES

Several different theories are discussed under this heading: conflict theory, critical theory, feminist theory, queer theory, critical theories of race and racism, and postmodern theory. They all tend to emphasize stresses, strains, and conflicts in society. They are critical of society in a variety of different ways, especially of the power that is exercised over less powerful members of society.

Conflict Theory

The best known of these theories is **conflict theory** (R. Collins 2012). It has roots in Marx's theory, and much of it can be seen as an inversion of structural-functionalism. While structural-functionalism emphasizes what is positive about society, conflict theory focuses on its negative aspects. To the structural-functionalist, society is held together by consensus; virtually everyone accepts the social structure, its

legitimacy, and its benefits. To the conflict theorist, in contrast, society is held together by coercion. Those who are adversely affected by society, especially economically, would rebel were it not for coercive forces such as the police, the courts, and the military.

Ralf Dahrendorf (1959) was influenced by Marx, but he was more strongly motivated by a desire to develop a viable alternative to structural-functionalism. For example, while structural-functionalists tend to see society as static, conflict theorists like Dahrendorf emphasize the ever-present possibility of change. Where structural-functionalists see the orderliness of society, conflict theorists see dissension and conflict everywhere. Finally, structural-functionalists focus on the sources of cohesion internal to society, while conflict theorists stress the coercion and power that holds together an otherwise fractious society.

Dahrendorf offered a very sociological view of authority, arguing that it resides not in individuals

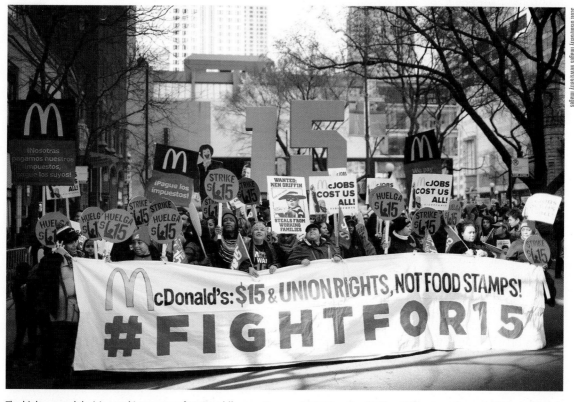

The high pay and decision-making power of McDonald's executives contrasts sharply with the relative powerlessness of the company's low-paid employees. Some of those employees and their supporters are shown here demonstrating for higher pay. Structural conflicts like this one are the focus of conflict theory.

(e.g., Donald Trump) but in positions (e.g., the presidency of the United States) and in various associations of people. In his view, those associations are controlled by a hierarchy of authority positions and the people who occupy them. However, there are many such associations in any society. Thus, a person may be in authority in one type of association but be subordinate in many others.

Dahrendorf was especially interested in the potential for conflict between those in positions of authority and those who are subordinate because they usually hold different interests. For example, the top management of a retail or fast-food corporation such as Walmart or McDonald's is interested in making the corporation more profitable by keeping wages low. In contrast, those who hold such low-level jobs as cashier or stock clerk are interested in increasing their wages to meet basic needs.

Critical Theory

While Marx's work was critical of the capitalist economy, **critical theory** shifts the focus to culture. Marx believed that culture is shaped by the economic system. In contrast, the critical school has argued that by the early twentieth century, and at an ever-accelerating rate to this day, culture has become important in its own right. Furthermore, in many ways it has come to be more important than the economic system. Instead of being controlled by the capitalist economy, more of us are controlled, and controlled more often, by culture in general, specifically by the culture industry.

The **culture industry** consists of the rationalized and bureaucratized structures that control modern culture. In their early years, the 1920s and 1930s, critical theorists focused on radio, magazines, and movies. Today, the movies remain important, but the focus has shifted to television and various aspects of the internet. These are critiqued for producing, or serving as an outlet for, **mass culture**, or cultural elements that are administered by organizations, lack spontaneity, and are phony. Two features of mass culture and its dissemination by the culture industry are of particular concern to critical theorists:

- *Falseness.* True culture should emanate from the people, but mass culture involves prepackaged sets of ideas that falsify reality. The so-called reality shows (e.g., *Survivor*) that dominate television today are a contemporary example of mass culture. These programs are also highly formulaic. They are presented as if they are authentic, but in fact they are scripted, highly controlled, and selectively edited—although in a different way than fictional dramas, comedies, and soap operas are. They are also false in the sense that they give consumers of mass culture the sense that there is a quick and easy route to fame and fortune.

- *Repressiveness.* Like Marx, critical theorists feel that the masses need to be informed about things such as the falseness of culture so that they can develop a clear sense of society's failings and the need to rebel against them.

ASK YOURSELF

Do you see evidence of critical theory's ideas of falseness and repressiveness in the elements of mass culture to which you are exposed? If so, what form do they take?

Critical theory can be applied to some of the newest media forms, such as YouTube, Facebook, Twitter, Snapchat, and Instagram (Denegri-Knott and Zwick 2012). Despite there being plenty of false and stupefying content on these sites along with all the edifying material, the sites are not controlled by large rationalized bureaucracies—at least not yet. Almost all the content that appears on sites such as YouTube, Facebook, and eBay is provided by those who also consume material on the sites. The sites exercise little control over original content; they are arguably spontaneous and authentic. It's tempting to conclude that these new aspects of the culture industry are not assailable from a traditional critical theory perspective.

Feminist Theory

A central aspect of **feminist theory** is the critique of patriarchy (male dominance) and the problems it poses not only for women but also for men. Feminist theory also offers ideas on how everyone's (women's *and* men's) situation can be bettered, if not revolutionized (Lengermann and Niebrugge-Brantly 2014; Tong 2009).

Despite the many global and individual changes in women's lives over the almost two centuries since sociology came into existence, there is also a broad consensus among feminist theorists that women continue to face extraordinary problems related directly to gender inequality. As you will learn about more in Chapter 9, these problems include, among innumerable others, a persistent wage gap between men and women in the United States and systematic and widespread rape by invading forces in wartime. These extraordinary problems require extraordinary solutions. However, feminist theories vary in the degree to which they support dramatic, even revolutionary, changes in women's situation. Some feminist theories suggest that the solution to gender inequality is to change social structures and institutions so that they are more inclusive of women and allow more gender diversity. Other feminist theories argue that because those very structures and institutions create gender difference and inequality, we must first deconstruct and then rebuild them in a wholly different way.

Women of color have sometimes been dissatisfied with feminist theory for not representing their interests very well. Several scholars argue that feminist theory generally reflects the perspective of white women while ignoring the unique experiences and viewpoints of women of color (Collins 2000; hooks 2000; Moraga and Anzaldua 2015; Zinn 2012). Similarly, studies related to race tend to focus largely (or wholly) on the position of men. Thus, many contemporary feminists have advocated for scholarship that takes into account not just gender but also how it intersects with race and ethnicity, social class, and sexuality. The upcoming discussion of critical theories of race and racism provides more detail on this view.

Queer Theory

The term *queer* was originally used as a negative term for gay men. Contemporary gay men, lesbians, bisexuals, and transgender and intersexed people have reclaimed the label *queer,* but now with a positive connotation. **Queer theory** is based on the argument that there are no fixed and stable identities that determine who we are (McCann 2016). The theory also unsettles identities that have long been thought to be fixed, stable, or natural. Among others, it unsettles *queers* as a noun, as well as gender

identities in general (Butler 1990). Some queer theorists use the term **genderqueer** to refer to gender identities that are not exclusively male or female. Others believe that it is possible to be **pangender**, or to identify as all genders. New pronouns such as *xe* and *ze* have been created to replace *he* and *she* (Scelfo 2015). While queer theory does not focus exclusively on homosexuality, it does examine the dynamics of the relationship between heterosexuals and gay males and lesbians. It is especially concerned with the historic, systematic exercise of power by heterosexuals over gay males and lesbians. For example, gay males and lesbians have often, at least in the past, governed their own behavior in public to avoid making heterosexuals uncomfortable, such as by forgoing mild displays of affection.

Critical Theories of Race and Racism

Critical theories of race and racism argue that race continues to matter globally and that racism continues to have adverse effects on people of color (Ray et al. 2017; Slatton and Feagin 2012). Critical theorists of race argue that "color blindness," or the notion that race no longer matters in determining an individual's life chances and experiences, ignores the past and present realities facing racial minorities. Some suggest that color blindness is little more than a "new racism," a smoke screen that allows whites to practice and perpetuate racial discrimination (Bonilla-Silva 2009, 2015). See the differing perceptions about employment opportunities illustrated in Figure 2.2, for example. The vast majority of white Americans believe that there is equal employment opportunity, but only a minority of black Americans subscribe to that view. The white belief in the smoke screen of equal opportunity serves to rationalize continued discrimination against blacks. Of particular importance is the idea of **intersectionality**, the concept that people are affected, often adversely, not only by their race but also by their gender, sexual orientation, class, age, and global location (Collins 1990; Collins and Bilge 2016). The confluence, or intersection, of these various statuses and the inequality and oppression associated with the intersections are what matter most. For example, a poor black female lesbian faces a complex of issues different from, and perhaps more difficult than, the issues faced by a poor white heterosexual female.

The Voluntariat

A new term that builds on Karl Marx's concept of the proletariat (see p. **29**) has recently been coined—*voluntariat*. While the proletariat works for low pay, the voluntariat works for *no pay*. Like the proletariat, the voluntariat does work that requires little skill, such as posting a peer review on Amazon.com or tweeting a comment on Twitter. However, some members of the voluntariat engage in free labor that otherwise would likely be carried out by highly paid skilled workers. For example, individuals who possess advanced university degrees perform free labor for massive open online courses, or MOOCs (Shullenberger 2014; see Chapter 1 and especially Chapter 11). Other highly skilled voluntarians translate courses taught in English into other languages at no charge, doing the work for its intrinsic reward. They are seen as "voluntarian scabs" because they threaten the livelihood of professional translators who do such work for a living. Regardless of work skills, the free labor of the voluntariat contributes to a corporation's profitability just as the poorly paid labor of the proletariat does.

In the broader context of free, value-creating activity on social media, we are all voluntarians now, because we are increasingly engaged, usually unknowingly, in advancing the interests of profit-making organizations. When we post on Facebook or buy products on Amazon.com, we are voluntarily

The free labor of the "voluntariat" has replaced the paid labor of innumerable workers in, for example, self-checkouts in supermarkets and gas stations. What are corporations giving you as a member of the voluntariat in return for your free labor?

providing lots of invaluable and free information, or "big data," about ourselves that these organizations could not otherwise obtain, and that is the major source of their market value. Amazon's chairman and CEO Jeff Bezos believes that Amazon.com can earn far more money by exploiting the data provided by voluntarians than it can by selling products. It is arguable whether or not many popular internet sites, such as Facebook, YouTube, or Flickr, could even exist without the free labor of thousands of people around the world.

We are also increasingly voluntarians when we act as "working consumers" (Dujarier 2014) in using ATMs, scanning and bagging our own groceries in the supermarket, and putting our own IKEA furniture together. These are all jobs that required wage workers not long ago. The fact that many consumers do this work without protest, and often happily, saves corporations millions of dollars because they can reduce the number of workers they hire. The point is that "voluntarianism" is a widespread phenomenon that increasingly pervades our lives on- and offline.

Engaging the Digital World

Keep a record of how much unpaid labor you engage in for one week. You should list the type of activity you performed and how much time you spent doing it. If you were to be paid the minimum wage for this labor, how much would you receive? Do you feel like you are being exploited by corporations that are taking advantage of your free labor? Why or why not?

FIGURE 2.2 • Do Black Americans Have the Same Chances as White Americans to Obtain the Same Level of Employment? (1963–2012, responses divided by race)

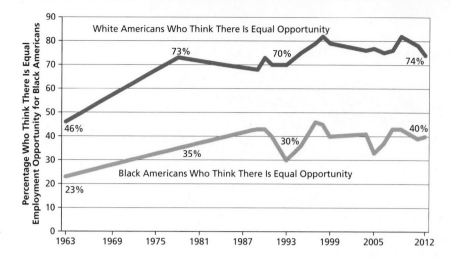

Actual question: In general, do you think that blacks have as good a chance as white people in your community to get any kind of job for which they are qualified, or don't you think they have as good a chance?

SOURCE: Gallup (2014). Gallup Review: Black and White Differences in Views on Race (2014), http://www.gallup.com/poll/180107/gallup-review-black-white-differences-views-race.aspx.

ASK YOURSELF

Is your life affected by intersectionality? How many different statuses do you hold, and to which social and cultural groups do you belong?

Postmodern Theory

The term *postmodern* refers to a world that has moved beyond the modern era. **Postmodern theory** deals with this new epoch and is also a reaction against modern theory. Postmodern theorists are opposed to broad depictions of history and society offered by modern theorists. An example of such a narrative is Weber's theory of the increasing rationalization of the world and the rise of an "iron cage" constraining our thoughts and activities. Instead, postmodernists often deconstruct, or take apart, such modern grand narratives. Postmodernists are also opposed to the scientific pretensions of much modern social theory. They often look at familiar social phenomena in different ways or adopt very different focuses for their work. For example, in

his study of the history of prisons, Michel Foucault ([1975] 1979) was critical of the modernist view that criminal justice had grown progressively liberal. He contended that prisons had, in fact, grown increasingly oppressive through the use of techniques such as constant, enhanced surveillance of prisoners.

Jean Baudrillard described the postmodern world as characterized by **hyperconsumption**, which involves consuming more than we need, more than we really want, and more than we can afford. Baudrillard also saw the postmodern world as increasingly dominated by **simulations**—that is, inauthentic or fake versions of real things. For example, when we eat at McDonald's, we consume Chicken McNuggets, or simulated chicken. It is fake in the sense that it is often not meat from one chicken, but bits of meat that come from many different chickens and that contain many other ingredients. The idea that we increasingly consume simulations and live a simulated life is a powerful critique of consumer society and, more generally, of the contemporary world.

This is not New York City but the hotel-casino called New York–New York in Las Vegas, Nevada. One hypothesis of postmodern theory is that we live in a world characterized by an increasing number of simulations of reality. How many others can you think of?

ASK YOURSELF

Does a life devoted to hyperconsumption, especially online, cause you to become disconnected from others? Are new kinds of human connections created by a common investment in a life devoted to excessive consumption?

INTER/ACTIONIST THEORIES

The slash between *inter* and *action(ist)* in the heading to this section is meant to communicate the fact that we will deal with two closely related sets of theories here. The first consists of those theories that deal mainly with the interaction of two or more people (symbolic interactionism, ethnomethodology, and exchange theory). The second comprises those that focus more on the actions of individuals (rational choice theory). A common factor among these theories is that they focus on the micro level of individuals and groups. This is in contrast to the theories discussed previously that focus on the macro structures of society.

Symbolic Interactionism

Symbolic interactionism is concerned with the interaction of two or more people through the use of symbols (Kotarba, Salvini, and Merrill 2012). We all engage in interaction on a daily basis, whether it be face-to-face or more indirectly via cell phone, e-mail, or social media. But interaction could not take place without symbols: words, gestures, and even objects that stand for things. Symbols allow the communication of meaning among a group of people. Although we can interact with one another without words, such as through physical gestures like the shrug of a shoulder, in the vast majority of cases we need and use words to interact. Symbolic interactionism has several basic principles:

- Human beings have a great capacity for thought, which differentiates them from lower animals. That innate capacity for thought is greatly shaped by social interaction. It is during social interaction that people acquire the symbolic meanings that allow them to exercise their distinctive ability to think. Symbolic meanings are not set in stone. People are able to modify them based on a given situation and their interpretation of it. The Christian cross, for example, is a symbol whose meaning can vary. Christians throughout the world define it in positive religious ways, but many in the Islamic world view it as a negative symbol. Muslims associate the cross with the medieval Crusades waged against their world by the Christian West.

- People are able to modify symbolic meanings because of their unique ability to think. Symbolic interactionists frame thinking as people's ability to interact with themselves. Through interaction people are able to examine various courses of action open to them in given situations, to assess the relative advantages and disadvantages of each, and then to choose among them.

- It is the pattern of those choices, of individual action and interaction, that is the basis of groups, larger structures such as bureaucracies, and society as a whole.

While symbolic interactionism deals primarily with people's interactions, it is also concerned with the mental processes, such as mind and self, that are deeply implicated in these interactions.

Ethnomethodology

Ethnomethodology is another inter/actionist theory, but it focuses on what people *do* rather than on what they think (Liu 2012). Ethnomethodologists study the ways in which people organize everyday life.

Their view of large-scale social structures differs from that of structural-functionalists, who tend to see those structures as highly constraining. Ethnomethodologists argue that this view tells us very little about what really goes on within structures such as courtrooms, hospitals, and police departments. Rather than being constrained, people act within these structures and go about much of their business using common sense rather than official procedures. The best-known example of an ethnomethodological approach relates to gender (O'Brien 2016; Stokoe 2006). Ethnomethodologists point out that people often erroneously think of gender as being biologically based. It is generally assumed that we do not have to do or say anything in order to be considered masculine or feminine; we are born that way. But, in fact, there are things we all do (e.g., the way we walk) and say (e.g., the tone of our voice) that allow us to accomplish being masculine or feminine. That is, being masculine or feminine is based on what people do on a regular basis. This is clearest in the case of those who are defined as being male or female at birth (based on biological characteristics) but then later do and say things that lead others to see them as belonging to the other gender (based on social characteristics).

Exchange Theory

Like ethnomethodologists, exchange theorists are not concerned with what goes on in people's minds and how that affects behavior. Instead, they are interested in the behavior itself and the rewards and costs associated with it (Molm, Whithama, and Melameda 2012). The key figure in **exchange theory**, George Homans (1910–1989), argued that instead of studying large-scale structures, sociologists should study the "elementary forms of social life" (Homans 1961, 13).

Exchange theorists are particularly interested in social behavior that usually involves two or more people and a variety of tangible and intangible exchanges. For example, you can reward someone who does you a favor with a tangible gift or with more intangible words of praise. Those exchanges are not always rewarding; they also can be punitive. You could, for example, punish someone who wrongs you by slapping him or complaining about him to mutual acquaintances.

While exchange theory retains an interest in the elementary forms of social behavior, over the years it has grown more concerned with how those forms lead to more complex social situations. That is, individual exchanges can become stable over time and develop into persistent **exchange relationships**. One particular type of exchange relationship is "hooking up," or forming sexual relationships that are also sometimes called "friends with benefits." For example, because you and another person find your initial sexual interactions rewarding, you may develop a pattern of repeat interactions (also known as "hookups" or "booty calls"). Exchange relationships, including hookups, rarely develop in isolation from other exchange relationships. Sociologists study how hooking up is not an isolated occurrence—it happens within the context of college campuses, for example, where it has been normalized (Kuperberg and Padgett 2015).

Rational Choice Theory

In **rational choice theory**, people are regarded as rational, but the focus is not exchange, rewards, and costs. Rather, the focus is on people having goals and intending to do certain things. To achieve their goals, people have a variety of means available to them; on a rational basis, they choose the means that are likely to best satisfy their needs and wants—in other words, they choose on the basis of "utility" (Kroneberg and Kalter 2012). Important variables that constrain the ability to act rationally are access to scarce resources and the rules within social structures that restrict particular actions (Friedman and Hechter 1988). For example, if you do not have access to sufficient money, you cannot purchase a new car. If you are confined within a prison, you do not have the opportunity to drive a car, much less purchase one.

Rational choice theorists understand that people do not always act rationally. They argue, however, that their predictions will generally hold despite these occasional deviations (Coleman 1990; Zafirovski 2013).

RESEARCHING THE SOCIAL WORLD

Sociology is a science of the social world, and research is absolutely central to such a science. All sociologists study others' research, and most do research of their own. Sociologists may theorize, speculate, and even rely on their imaginations for answers to questions about society. However, they almost always do so on the basis of data or information derived from research. Put another way, sociologists practice **empiricism**, which means that they gather information and evidence using their senses, especially their eyes and ears. Because we all do that in order to experience the world, what make sociology different? In addition to using their senses, sociologists adopt the scientific method, or a similarly *systematic* approach, in search of a thorough understanding of the social world. They have a variety of methods at their disposal in researching and analyzing society.

THE SCIENTIFIC METHOD

The **scientific method** is a structured way of finding answers to questions about the world (Carey 2011). The scientific method employed by sociologists is much the same as that used in other sciences. Although in practice creative sociological research often does not slavishly adhere to the following steps, they constitute the basic scientific method:

1. A sociologist uncovers *questions in need of answers*. These questions can be inspired by key issues in the larger society, personal experiences, or topics of concern specifically in sociology. The best and most durable research and findings often stem from issues that the researcher connects with personally. Karl Marx, for example, detested the exploitation of workers that characterized capitalism; Max Weber feared the depersonalizing impact of bureaucracies.

2. Sociologists review the *relevant literature* on the questions of interest to them. This is because others have likely done similar or related research in the past. After more than a century of doing scientific research, sociologists have learned a great deal about many things. It would make no sense to start over from the beginning. For example, Ritzer's work on McDonaldization (2015a) is based on the study of the work on rationalization by Max Weber ([1921] 1968), his successors (such as Kalberg [1980]), and contemporary researchers (such as Ram [2007]). Other scholars have since reviewed Ritzer's work and that of other scholars of McDonaldization (for a collection of this work, see Ritzer 2010c) and have extended it to religion (Drane 2008, 2012), higher education (Hayes and Wynyard 2002), social work (Dustin 2007), psychotherapy (Goodman 2016), and Disney World (Bryman 2004; Huddleston, Garlen, and Sandlin 2016).

3. Researchers often develop *hypotheses,* or educated guesses, about how social phenomena can be expected to relate to one another. For example, Uri Ram (2007) hypothesized that Israeli society would grow increasingly McDonaldized, and he found evidence to support that idea. As another example, Marx hypothesized that the conflict between capitalists and workers would ultimately lead to the collapse of capitalism; however, capitalism has not yet collapsed. This makes it clear that hypotheses may not be confirmed by research or borne out by social developments, but such speculation is important to the scientific method.

4. Researchers must choose *research methods* that will help them answer their research questions. Sociology offers diverse methodological tools; some are better than others for answering certain kinds of questions. For example, some sociologists are interested in how a person's social class shapes his or her opinions about social issues. Surveys and other quantitative tools may be most useful to evaluate the relationship between class and attitudes. Other sociologists may want to know how social class influences how people interpret and make sense of their social world, and how this shapes

social action. Qualitative methods, such as observations and interviews, may be helpful for studying these issues.

5. Researchers use their chosen methods to *collect data* that can confirm—or fail to confirm—their hypotheses. Most sociologists venture into the field to collect original data through observations, interviews, questionnaires, and other means.

6. Researchers *analyze the data* collected, assessing their meaning in light of the hypotheses that guided the research. For example, Émile Durkheim hypothesized that those who were involved with other people would be less likely to commit suicide than those who lived more isolated existences and were experiencing what he called *anomie*. Analyzing data from several nineteenth-century European countries, Durkheim ([1897] 1951) found that the suicide rates were, in fact, higher for widowed or divorced people than for those who were married and therefore presumably better integrated socially.

SOCIOLOGICAL RESEARCH

Sociological knowledge is derived from research that may use a variety of different methods. Typically, the method chosen is and should be driven by the nature of the research question. Imagine that you are a sociologist interested in studying differences in the behavior of people who visit Las Vegas. You might start by observing, perhaps by watching people gamble. You might look for variations: Are men and women equally represented at the slot machines? Are they equally likely to play craps or blackjack? Are there age differences in who plays which games? You could do much the same thing in looking for differences among those who attend the shows and musical events at the casinos. Are there gender differences between the audience of, say, Cirque du Soleil's *Mystère* or *KÀ* and the audience of a Penn & Teller magic show? In order to better understand such differences, you might be inspired to participate, or to become a *participant-observer,* by gambling or being entertained alongside those whom you are studying. Or you may realize that your research question is better answered through

interviewing those who have come to Las Vegas to gamble, asking about their expectations for winning a lot of money. Or you might administer an anonymous questionnaire or survey to find out how much money people who gamble have lost.

You could also create an experiment. Using a social science lab at your university, you could set up a Las Vegas–style poker table and recruit students as participants. You could tell them that the typical player loses 90 percent of the time and that previous research has shown that *most* players lose *most of the time*. You could then ask whether, in spite of that information, they still want to gamble at your poker table. Of greatest interest would be those who say yes. You could interview them before they start "gambling" at your table, observe them as they gamble, and interview them again after they finish gambling. Did they start out believing, despite all the evidence to the contrary, that they would win? How likely are they to gamble again? Are there important differences between women and men in terms of their answers to these questions?

Observation, interviews, surveys, experiments, and other research methods are all useful and important to sociologists. All have strengths but also limitations. Before we examine these methods and their strengths and limitations in more detail, there is an important distinction between two broad types of research methods—qualitative and quantitative—that should be clarified.

Qualitative and Quantitative Research

Qualitative research involves studies done in natural settings that produce in-depth, descriptive information about the social world (Denzin and Lincoln 2011; Silverman 2016). Such research does not necessarily require statistical methods for collecting and reporting data (Marshall and Rossman 2010). Observation—watching, listening, and taking detailed notes—and open-ended interviews are just two of the qualitative methods used by sociologists. Because qualitative methods usually rely on small sample sizes, the findings cannot be generalized to the broader population; for this, we use quantitative methods.

Quantitative research involves the analysis of numerical data, usually derived from surveys and experiments, to better understand important

Observation is a primary method in sociological research. Do you think people behave differently when they know they are being observed?

empirical social realities (Creswell 2008). The mathematical method used to analyze numerical data is **statistics**, which can aid researchers in two ways. When researchers want to see trends over time or compare differences between groups, they use **descriptive statistics**. The purpose of such statistics is to *describe* some particular body of data that is based on a phenomenon in the real world (Salkind 2004, 8–10). To test hypotheses, researchers use **inferential statistics**. Such statistics allow researchers to use data from a relatively small group to speculate with some level of certainty about a larger group. While such data allow researchers to make broad generalizations, they do not provide insight into people's lived experiences and interpretation of particular issues and events. Each method has its own set of strengths and limitations in terms of what it can do to help a researcher answer a specific question. Sociologists often debate the relative merits of quantitative versus qualitative methods, but they generally recognize that each method has

value. There is a broad consensus that quantitative and qualitative research methods can complement one another (Ragin 2014; Riis 2012; Rueschemeyer, Stephens, and Stephens 1992). In practice, sociologists (and other social scientists) may combine both quantitative and qualitative research methods in a single study (*mixed-method research;* Guetterman, Fetters, and Creswell 2015).

Observational Research

Observation is one of the qualitative methods. It consists of systematically watching, listening to, and recording what takes place in a natural social setting over some, usually extended, period of time (Hammersley 2007). There are several key dimensions to any type of observation in sociology:

- *The degree to which those being observed are aware that they are being observed.* This can vary from everyone being fully informed about the research to participants being observed from afar or through hidden cameras, one-way mirrors, and the like.

- *The degree to which the presence of the observer affects the actions of those being observed.* When people are aware that they are being observed, they often present themselves in the way they think the observer expects or will accept. For instance, gang members might not engage in illegal activities in the presence of a researcher.

- *The degree to which the process is structured.* Highly structured observational research might use preset categories, codes, or a checklist to guide observations, while less structured observation studies attempt to take note of as much as possible in the field setting with a totally open method.

Some of the most famous pieces of sociological research have used the observational method. Examples include studies of the social and economic contexts of people's lives, such as *The Philadelphia Negro* (Du Bois [1899] 1996), *Street Corner Society* (Whyte 1943), *Tally's Corner: A Study of Negro Streetcorner Men* (Liebow 1967), *Floating City: A Rogue Sociologist Lost and Found in New York's Underground Economy* (Venkatesh 2014), and *On the Run: Fugitive Life in an American City* (Goffman 2014; see the Trending box in this chapter, page 58). Most of the studies discussed in the Trending boxes throughout this book use observational methods.

Participant and Nonparticipant Observation. There are two major types of observational methods. One is **participant observation**, in which the researcher actually plays a role in the group or setting being observed. A participant observer might become a hostess or bartender to study the sex industry in Ho Chi Minh City, Vietnam (Hoang 2015), sell books on the sidewalk to watch what happens on a busy city street (Duneier 1999), or live in a trailer park to witness how individuals cope with poverty (Desmond 2016; see the Trending box in Chapter 7, page 187). CNN's *Somebody's Gotta Do It* is essentially an informal exercise in the participant observation of work. The host, Mike Rowe, is *not* a trained sociologist and he is *not* trying to uncover the sociological aspects of the jobs he is participating in, but he *is* a participant observer. In each episode, he actually does the job being examined—he is a participant—and he observes the workers doing their jobs. Anthony Bourdain does much the same in the places he visits on his CNN show, *Parts Unknown*.

In the second observational method, **nonparticipant observation**, the sociologist plays little or no role in what is being observed. Gary Fine has done nonparticipant observation research on Little League baseball (1987), restaurant kitchens (2008), meteorologists (2010), and chess players involved in a chess tournament (2015). Digital media provides a new way to engage in nonparticipant observation. **Netnography**, or an account of what transpires online, allows researchers to observe thousands of phenomena online in virtual anonymity—and without actively participating (Kozinets 2015). One recent study used netnography to examine the blogs of female Chinese tourists in Macao, discovering how crossing the border influenced perceptions of their self-identity and enhanced their personal relationships (Zhang and Hitchcock 2014).

There are no firm dividing lines between participant and nonparticipant observation, and at times the two blend imperceptibly into one another. The participant often becomes simply an observer. An example is the sociologist who begins with participant observation of a gang, hanging out with members in casual settings, but becomes a nonparticipant when illegal activities such as drug deals take place. And the nonparticipant observer sometimes becomes a participant. An example is the sociologist who is unable to avoid being asked to take sides or share opinions in squabbles among members of a Little League team or, more likely, among their parents.

ASK YOURSELF

Do you think participant observers risk losing their objectivity when they grow too close to the subjects under study? Why or why not? What about nonparticipant observers? How can sociologists conducting observational research avoid becoming too involved with subjects?

Ethnography. **Ethnography** is the creation of a detailed account of what a group of people do and the way they live (Adler and Adler 2012; Hammersley 2007), usually entailing much more intensive, immersive, and lengthy periods of qualitative research. Researchers may live for years with the groups, tribes, or subcultures (such as gamblers) being studied. Ethnographic research can reveal much about the experiences of traditionally understudied and marginalized groups of women—for example, Latina girls (Garcia 2012), lap dancers (Colosi 2010), and ex-convicts (Opsal 2011). Some suggest that the personal relationships that develop between researchers and subjects in ethnographic studies make it less likely that the power researchers exert over subjects will distort the results (Bourdieu 1992). Normally ethnographies are small in scale, micro, and local. Researchers observe people, talk to them, hang out with them, sometimes live with them, and conduct formal and informal interviews with them over an extended period of time.

The ethnographic method has now been extended to the global level. Michael Burawoy (2000; see also Tsuda, Tapias, and Escandell 2014) argues that a **global ethnography** is the best way to understand globalization. This is a type of ethnography that is grounded in various parts of the world and seeks to understand globalization as it exists in people's social lives. For example, Hung Cam Thai (2014) spent time with more than 100 members of Vietnamese transnational families, in both the United States and Vietnam, to study global remittances. He found that low-wage Vietnamese immigrants in the United States sent a significant portion of their income to relatives in Vietnam because of a sense of social obligation and to feel more confident in their social status.

Interviews

While observers often interview those they are studying, they usually do so very informally and on the spur of the moment. Other sociologists rely mainly, or exclusively, on **interviews**, in which they seek information from participants (respondents) by asking a series of questions that have been spelled out, at least to some degree, before the research is conducted (Gubrium et al. 2012). Interviews are usually conducted face-to-face, although they can be done by phone and are increasingly being done via the internet (Farrell and Peterson 2010; Fontana

2007; James 2016). In addition, large-scale national surveys are increasingly including interviews. The use of interviews has a long history in sociology. One very early example is W. E. B. Du Bois's ([1899] 1996) study of the "Philadelphia Negro." A watershed in the history of interviewing in sociology was reached during World War II when large-scale interview studies of members of the American military were conducted. Some of the data from those studies were reported in a landmark study, *The American Soldier* (Stouffer et al. 1949). More recently, Jennifer Silva (2015) interviewed working-class young adults to understand how they were transitioning into adulthood. She learned that their economic struggles were preventing many of them from developing long-term romantic relationships.

Types of Interviews. The questions asked in an interview may be preselected and prestructured so that respondents must choose from sets of preselected answers, such as *agree* and *disagree*. Or an interview may be more unstructured with no preset questions or answers; respondents are free to say anything they want to say.

Prestructured interviews are attractive when the researcher wants to avoid any unanticipated reactions or responses from those being studied.

The interviewer attempts to

- Behave in the same way in each interview

- Ask the same questions, using the same exact words, and in the same sequence

- Ask closed-ended questions that the participant must answer by choosing from a set of preselected responses

- Offer the same explanations when they are requested by respondents

- Not show any kind of reaction to the answers, no matter what they might be

Interviews conducted in this way often yield information that, like data obtained from questionnaires, can be coded numerically and then analyzed statistically.

There are problems associated with prestructured interviews. First, interviewers often find it difficult to live up to the guidelines for such interviews because they are frequently unable to avoid reacting to answers. Furthermore, they may use different intonation from one interview to another or change the wording, and even the order, of the questions asked, which can affect respondents' answers.

Another problem is that respondents may not respond accurately or truthfully. For example, they may want to conceal things or give answers that they believe the interviewer wants to hear. Third, and most important, closed-ended questions limit the responses, possibly cutting off useful unanticipated information.

The last problem is solved by the use of open-ended or *unstructured interviews*. The interviewer begins with only a general idea of the topics to be covered and the direction to be taken in the interview. The answers in unstructured interviews offer a good understanding of the respondents and what the issues under study mean to them. Such understandings and meanings are generally not obtained through structured interviews. However, unstructured interviews create problems of their own, such as yielding so much information that it is hard to offer a coherent summary and interpretation of the results.

The Interview Process. Conducting interviews, especially those that are prestructured, usually involves several steps:

1. The interviewer must *gain access* to the setting being studied. This is relatively easy in some cases, such as when interviewing one's friends in the student union or at a local bar. However, access would likely be much more difficult if one wanted to interview one's friends in a sorority house or on the job. They might be less eager to talk to a researcher—to any outsider—in such settings.

2. The interviewer must often seek to *locate a key informant* (Brown, Bankston, and Forsyth 2013; Rieger 2007). This is a person who has intimate knowledge of the group being studied and is willing to talk openly to the researcher about the group. A key informant can help the researcher gain access to the larger group of respondents and verify the information being provided by them.

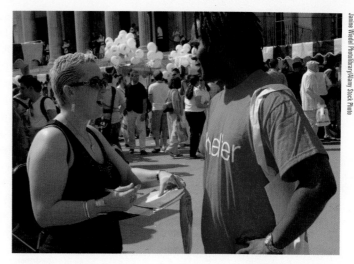

Interviews can take many forms and can be more or less structured depending on the researcher's needs. Here an interviewer stops passersby.

3. The interviewer must seek to *understand the language and culture* of the people being interviewed. In some cases, this is very easy. For example, it is not a great problem for an academic interviewer to understand the language and culture of college students. However, it is more difficult if the academician interviews members of motorcycle gangs or prostitutes. In these kinds of cases, it is all too easy for the researcher to misunderstand or to impose incorrect meanings on the words of respondents.

4. The researcher must *gain the trust of the respondents and develop a rapport* with them. Establishing trust and rapport can be easy or difficult, depending on the characteristics of the researcher. Well-educated and relatively powerful male researchers may intimidate less privileged female respondents. Older researchers may have trouble interviewing traditional-age college students. Depending on the field site, a researcher's point of view and (perceived) similarities with the respondents may ease rapport.

ASK YOURSELF

Have you ever conducted or participated in an interview, perhaps for a job or as part of a study? How closely did it adhere to the guidelines mentioned here?

Survey Research

Survey research involves the collection of information from a population, or more usually a representative portion of a population, through the use of interviews and, most important, questionnaires. While some sociologists do their own surveys, most rely on data derived from surveys done by others, such as the U.S. government (the U.S. census, for example) and the National Opinion Research Center, which conducts various opinion polls.

Most survey research relies on **questionnaires**, which are self-administered, written sets of questions. While the questions can be presented to respondents on a face-to-face basis, they are more often delivered to them by mail; they are also increasingly being filled out on personal computers or over the phone (Snyder 2007).

Types of Surveys. There are two broad types of surveys. A **descriptive survey** is designed to gather accurate information about, for example, members of a certain group, people in a given geographic area, or people in a particular organization. The best-known descriptive surveys are those conducted by organizations such as Gallup to gather information on the preferences, beliefs, and attitudes of given samples of people.

For many years, the Institute for Social Research at the University of Michigan has conducted a descriptive survey of high school seniors in the United States. One of the subjects has been marijuana use. As you can see in Figure 2.3, the prevalence of marijuana use among high school seniors has risen and fallen, as if in waves. Marijuana use in this group peaked in 1979 (with more than half of students admitting use of the drug), reached a low of 22 percent in 1992, and has generally been rising since then, although it has never again approached the 1979 level. In 2015, slightly less than 35 percent of twelfth graders reported having used marijuana in the previous 12 months.

ASK YOURSELF

Has the increasing legalization of marijuana throughout the United States altered the data on marijuana use among high school seniors? Why or why not? How might any change affect data on the use of other drugs?

The data in Figure 2.3 are derived from descriptive surveys, but what if we wanted to explain, and not just statistically describe, changes in marijuana

FIGURE 2.3 • Marijuana Use among U.S. High School Seniors, 1976–2015

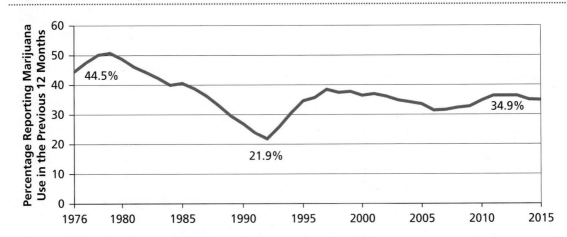

SOURCE: Data from Lloyd D. Johnston, Patrick O'Malley, Richard A. Miech, Jerald G. Bachman, and John E. Schulenberg. *Monitoring the Future: National Survey Results on Drug Use, 1975–2015: Overview, Key Findings on Adolescent Drug Use,* Table 6 (Ann Arbor: Institute for Social Research, University of Michigan, 2015).

use among high school seniors? To get at this, we would need to do an **explanatory survey**, which seeks to uncover potential causes of, in this case, changes in marijuana use (e.g., the legalization of marijuana in states such as Colorado, California, and Maine [Monte, Zane, and Heard 2015]). For example, having discovered variations in marijuana use by high school students over the years, we might hypothesize that the variation is linked to students' (and perhaps the general public's) changing perceptions about the riskiness of marijuana use. In this case, we would use the survey to learn more about respondents' attitudes toward and beliefs about the riskiness of marijuana use and not simply measure student use of marijuana.

Sampling. It is almost never possible to survey an entire population, such as all Americans or even all students at your college or university. Thus, survey researchers usually need to construct a **sample**, or a representative portion of the overall population. The more careful the researcher is in avoiding biases in

selecting the sample, the more likely the findings are to be representative of the whole group.

The most common way to avoid bias is to create a **random sample**, a sample in which every member of the group has an equal chance of being included. One way of obtaining a random sample is by using a list—for example, a list of the names of all the professors at your university. A coin is tossed for each name on the list, and those professors for whom the toss results in heads are included in the sample. More typical and efficient is the use of random number tables, found in most statistics textbooks, to select those in the sample (Kirk 2007). In our example, each professor is assigned a number, and those whose numbers come up in the random number table are included in the sample. More recently, use is being made of computer-generated random numbers. Other sampling techniques are used in survey research as well. For example, the researcher might create a **stratified sample**, in which a larger group is divided into a series of subgroups (e.g., assistant, associate, and full professors) and then random

FIGURE 2.4 • Random Samples and Stratified Samples

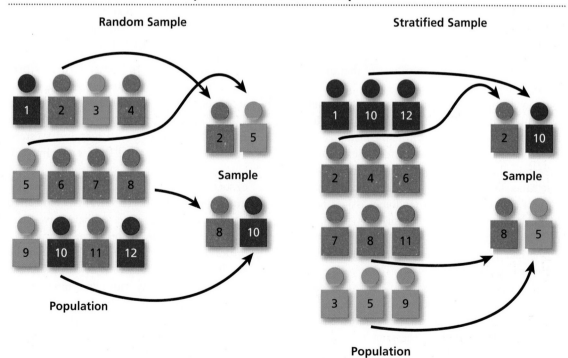

SOURCE: Random Samples and Stratified Samples is reprinted with permission of Dan Kernler, Associate Professor of Mathematics, Elgin Community College, Elgin, IL.

samples are taken within each of these groups. This ensures representation from each group in the final sample, something that might not occur if one simply does a random sample of the larger group.

Random and stratified sampling are the safest ways of drawing accurate conclusions about a population as a whole. However, there is an element of chance in all sampling, especially random sampling, with the result that findings can vary from one sample to another. Even though sampling is the safest way to reach conclusions about a population, errors are possible. Random and stratified sampling are depicted in Figure 2.4.

Sometimes researchers use **convenience samples**, which avoid systematic sampling and simply include those who are conveniently available to participate in a research project. An example of a convenience sample might involve researchers passing out surveys to the students in their classes (Lunneborg 2007). These nonrandom samples are rarely ever representative of the larger population whose opinions the researcher is interested in knowing. Nonrandom samples therefore may create a substantial bias in researchers' results (Popham and Sirotnik 1973, 44).

Experiments

Some sociologists conduct **experiments**, which involve the manipulation of one or more characteristics in order to examine the effect of that manipulation (Jackson and Cox 2013; Kirk 2007). The condition being manipulated is referred to as an **independent variable**, while the **dependent variable** is the measurement that results from the manipulation.

Devah Pager (2009) conducted an experiment to examine how the background of a job applicant affects the likelihood of that individual's being called back for an interview. Pager randomly assigned fake criminal records to pairs of similar young men, one in each pair black and one white. In each pair, one person had a criminal record and one did not, and one was white and one was not. These young men then sent résumés to companies in Milwaukee, seeking entry-level jobs. One major finding of this experiment was that black men without criminal records received callbacks at about the same rate as white men with criminal records. In this experiment, we can clearly see the relationship between the independent variable, the job applicants' combination of race

and criminal record, and the dependent variable, whether or not the applicant was called for an interview. There are several different types of experiments (Walker and Willer 2007):

- *Laboratory experiments.* **Laboratory experiments** take place in controlled settings. The "laboratory" may be, for example, a classroom or a simulated environment. The setting offers the researcher great control over the selection of the participants as well as the independent variables—the conditions to which the participants are exposed (Lucas, Graif, and Lovaglia 2008).

- *Natural experiments.* **Natural experiments** are those in which researchers take advantage of a naturally occurring event to study its effect on one or more dependent variables. Such experiments offer the experimenter little or no control over independent variables (De Silva et al. 2010). For example, a recent natural experiment at Harvard University assigned first-year students from different races as roommates. Among the findings was that breakups among the roommates were more likely when an East Asian student lived with two white students (Chakravarti, Menon, and Winship 2014).

- *Field experiments.* In some natural situations, researchers are able to exert at least some control over who participates and what happens during experiments (Bertrand and Mullainathan 2004; Pager and Western 2012). These are called **field experiments**. One of the most famous studies in the history of sociology is the "Robbers Cave" field experiment (Sherif et al. [1954] 1961), so called because it took place in Robbers Cave State Park in Oklahoma. The researchers controlled important aspects of what took place at the site. For example, they were able to assign the 22 boys in the study into two groups, called the Rattlers and the Eagles. The researchers were also able to create various situations that led to rivalry, bickering, and hostility between the groups. At the end of the experiment, they had each group rate the other: 53 percent of ratings of the Eagles were unfavorable, while

FIGURE 2.5 • World Happiness: Rankings of 158 Countries

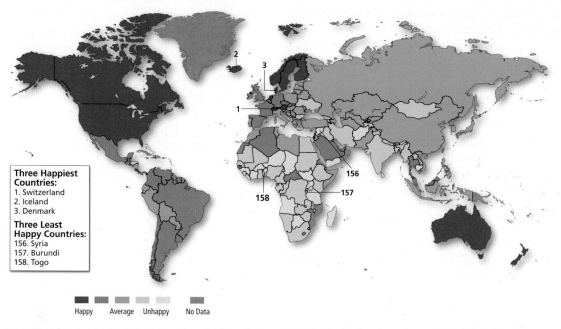

Three Happiest Countries:
1. Switzerland
2. Iceland
3. Denmark

Three Least Happy Countries:
156. Syria
157. Burundi
158. Togo

Happy   Average   Unhappy   No Data

SOURCE: Helliwell, John F., Richard Layard, and Jeffrey Sachs, eds. 2015. *World Happiness Report 2015*. New York: Sustainable Development Solutions Network.

NOTE: The World Happiness map is a global projection of subjective well-being based on a battery of statistical data, plus the subjective responses of 80,000 people worldwide, to map out well-being across 158 countries.

nearly 77 percent of ratings of the Rattlers were unfavorable. Later, the researchers introduced conditions that they hoped would reduce bad feelings and friction between the groups. In fact, greater harmony between the groups was created by having them work together on tasks such as securing needed water and paying collectively and equitably for a movie that everyone wanted to see. By the end of the latter part of the experiment, just 5 percent of the ratings of the Eagles were unfavorable, and unfavorable ratings of the Rattlers had dropped to 23 percent.

SECONDARY DATA ANALYSIS

All of the methods discussed thus far involve the collection of new and original data, but many sociologists engage in **secondary data analysis**, in which they reanalyze data collected by others. Secondary analysis can involve a wide variety of different types of data, from censuses and other surveys to historical records and old transcripts of interviews and focus groups. Until recently, obtaining and using some of these secondary data sets was laborious and time-consuming. Today, however, thousands of data sets are available online, and they can be accessed with a few keystrokes (Schutt 2007).

Secondary data analysis very often involves statistical analysis of government surveys and census data. For example, researchers studying multi-racial identity used data from the 2000 and 2010 censuses and found that individuals who identified as two or more races increased from 7 million in 2000 to 9 million in 2010 (Jones and Bullock 2013). It is not unusual for one body of data to lead to hundreds of secondary analyses. For example, the World Values Survey (WVS) is conducted in nearly 100 countries containing almost 90 percent of the world's population. Its six waves—a seventh wave is planned for 2017–2018—have been used to produce more than 1,000 research publications in more than 20 different languages. Some of this research has used the WVS to examine what social, cultural, and economic factors contribute to an individual's happiness. Figure 2.5 shows a "happiness map" depicting levels of happiness among the citizens of various countries included in the surveys from 2010 to 2014.

Historical-Comparative Method

The goal of **historical-comparative research** is to contrast how different historical events and conditions in various societies have led to different societal outcomes. The historical component involves the study of the history of societies as well as of the major components of society such as the state, religious system, and economy. The addition of the comparative element, comparing the histories of two or more societies, or of components of societies, makes this method more distinctively sociological.

Historians go into much more detail, and collect far more original historical data, than do sociologists. In contrast, sociologists are much more interested in generalizing about society than are historians. Weber is the preeminent historical-comparative sociologist (Mahoney and Rueschemeyer 2003; Mahoney and Thelen 2015; Ragin 2014; Varcoe 2007). He did comparative analyses of the histories of Protestantism in the West, Confucianism in China, and Hinduism in India. He sought to determine which religions fostered the development of capitalism and which served to impede its development. Of course, Weber knew that capitalism had developed in the West and not in China and India. The issue, then, was what about these religions did or did not foster the emergence of capitalism. A key factor was that in contrast to Protestantism, Confucianism and Hinduism did not foster rationality and efficiency and a striving for material success.

More recent instances of historical-comparative research have covered a wide range of issues. One researcher used historical-comparative research to examine whether internal wars could lead to state formation. Using the ability to collect taxes as a key factor, internal wars were found to strengthen states if solidarity existed among the elite (Rodriguez-Franco 2016; for a review of work on the relationship between the state and war, see Kestnbaum 2012).

Content Analysis

Another type of secondary analysis, called **content analysis**, relies on the systematic and objective analysis of the content of cultural artifacts in print, visual, audio, and digital media, including photographs, movies, advertisements, speeches, and newspaper articles (Wolff 2007). The goal is to use qualitative and especially quantitative methods to understand the content of messages. In one well-known study, Herbert Gans (1979) did a quantitative and qualitative content analysis of news on television and in newsmagazines to identify patterns in the reporting of news. For example, he found that well-known people were dealt with much more frequently than unknowns. More recently, Marleen Klaasen and Jochen Peter (2015) did a content analysis of 400 popular pornographic videos derived from the most frequently visited pornographic websites. They were focally interested in the issue of gender inequality in pornography. One of their findings was that women were more frequently depicted as being submissive and men were more often shown as dominant during sexual activities. Another finding was that there was more gender inequality in amateur pornography as far as women are concerned than in professional pornography.

ISSUES IN SOCIAL RESEARCH

The research conducted by sociologists raises a number of issues of great importance. These include the reliability and validity of findings and the ethics involved in the research process.

RELIABILITY AND VALIDITY

A key issue with sociological data relates to one's ability to trust the findings. **Reliability** involves the degree to which a given question, or another kind of measure, produces the same results time after time. In other words, would the same question asked one day get the same response from the participants or the same measurement on the scale the following day, or week, or month?

The other dimension of trustworthiness is **validity**, or the degree to which a question, or another kind of measure, gets an accurate response. In other words, does the question measure what it is supposed to measure?

RESEARCH ETHICS

Ethics is concerned with issues of right and wrong, the choices that people make, and how they justify them (Hedgecoe 2016). World War II and the behavior of the Nazis helped make ethics a central issue in research. The Nazis engaged in horrendous medical experiments on inmates in concentration camps. Unethical research was also conducted between 1932 and 1972 at Tuskegee Institute in Alabama on hundreds of poor black American men suffering from syphilis. The researchers, who were interested in studying the natural progression of the disease over time, never told the participants that they had syphilis. Despite regular visits to collect data from and about the participants, the researchers did not treat them for the disease and allowed them to suffer over long periods of time before they died painfully (Reverby 2009).

No research undertaken by sociologists has caused the kind of suffering and death experienced by the people studied in Nazi Germany or at Tuskegee Institute. Nonetheless, such research is the context and background for ethical concerns about the harmful or negative effects of research on participants in sociological research (the code of ethics of the American Sociological Association can be found online at www.asanet.org/about/ethics.cfm). There are three main areas of concern: physical and psychological harm to participants, illegal acts by researchers, and deception and violation of participants' trust.

Physical and Psychological Harm

The first issue is concern over whether the research can actually cause participants physical harm. Most sociological research is not likely to cause such

This photo shows participants in the infamous Tuskegee Institute research on syphilis. Several hundred poor black men who suffered from the disease and eventually died from it were never informed that they had the disease and never treated for it. How did this change the way in which such a disease would be studied today?

harm. However, physical harm may be an unintended consequence. In the Robbers Cave research, the hostility reached such a peak that the boys engaged in apple-throwing fights and in raids on one another's compounds.

A much greater issue in sociological research is the possibility of psychological harm to those being studied. Even questionnaire or interview studies can cause psychological harm, merely by asking people about sensitive issues such as sexual orientation, drug use, and experience with abortion. This risk is greatly increased when, unbeknownst to the researcher, a participant is hypersensitive to these issues because of a difficult or traumatic personal experience.

Some of the more extreme risks of psychological harm have occurred in experiments. The most famous example is Stanley Milgram's (1974) laboratory study of how far people will go when they are given orders by those in authority (the 2015 movie *Experimenter* deals in a fictionalized way with Milgram and his research). In the Milgram experiment, one group, the "learners," were secretly paid to pretend that painful shocks were being applied to them by the other group of participants, the "teachers," who were led to believe that the shocks they thought they were applying were very real (see Figure 2.6). The researcher, dressed officially in a white coat and projecting an aura of scientific respectability, ordered the teachers to apply shocks that appeared to be potentially lethal. The teachers did so even though the learners, who were in another room and not visible, were screaming with increasing intensity. The research clearly showed that if people were ordered to do so by authority figures, they would violate the social norms against inflicting pain on, and even possibly endangering the lives of, others.

The results of the Milgram experiment are important in many senses, especially regarding what the study did to the psyches of the people involved. The "teachers" came to know that they were very responsive to the dictates of authority figures, even if they were ordered to commit immoral acts. Some of them certainly realized that their behavior indicated that they were perfectly capable in such circumstances of harming, if not killing, other human beings. Such realizations had the possibility of adversely affecting the way participants viewed, and felt about, themselves. But the research has had several benefits as well, for both participants and others who have read about the Milgram studies. For example, those in powerful positions can better understand, and therefore limit, the potential impact of their orders to

subordinates, and subordinates can more successfully limit how far they are willing to go in carrying out the orders of their superiors.

Another famous study that raises similar ethical issues was conducted by Philip Zimbardo (1973). (The 2010 movie *The Experiment* is a fictionalized depiction of this experiment.) Zimbardo set up a prisonlike structure called "Stanford County Prison" as a setting in which to conduct his experiment. Participants were recruited to serve as either prisoners or guards. The "prison" was very realistic, with windowless cells, minimal toilet facilities, and strict regulations imposed on the inmates. The guards had uniforms, badges, keys, and clubs. They were also trained in the methods of managing prisoners.

The experiment was supposed to last six weeks, but it was ended after only six days, when the researchers grew fearful about the health and sanity of the prisoners, whom some of the guards insulted, degraded, and dehumanized. Only a few guards were helpful and supportive. However, even the helpful guards refused to intervene when prisoners were being abused. The prisoners could have left, but they tended to go along with the situation, accepting both the authority of the guards and their own lowly and abused position. Some of the guards experienced psychological distress, but it was worse for the prisoners when they realized how much they had contributed to their own difficulties. Social researchers learned that a real or perceived imbalance of power between researcher and participant may lead the participant to comply with a researcher's demands, even though they cause distress.

FIGURE 2.6 • The Teacher (T), Learner (L), and Experimenter (E) in the Milgram Experiment

Illegal Acts

In the course of ethnographic fieldwork, a researcher might witness or even become entangled in illegal acts. This problem confronted Randol Contreras in his research on a group of Dominican men who robbed upper-level drug dealers in the South Bronx (Contreras 2017). These "stickup kids" engaged in brutal acts of violence and possessed illegal drugs and cash. Contreras, himself a former—though admittedly unsuccessful—drug dealer, had to be careful to avoid participating in illegal activities that the stickup kids were describing to him, particularly because some of them were childhood friends. Alice Goffman faced similar issues while doing the research published in her book *On the Run* (2014; see the Trending box on page 58).

Philip Zimbardo's experimental re-creation of prison conditions was so realistic, and the participants were so severely affected by their involvement in it, that the experiment had to be cut short by several weeks. Could this early cutoff have invalidated the research?

Stanford Historical Photograph Collection (SC1071). Used with permission.

Researchers must weigh sticky legal and ethical ramifications for participants and themselves. Publishing an account of such dramatic illegal acts might help the researcher's career, but it might also send the perpetrator of those acts to jail. It is also possible that not informing the police of illegal acts, or refusing to turn over field notes, could lead to imprisonment for the researchers.

Violation of Trust

Researchers can betray participants' trust in several ways. For instance, the researcher might inadvertently divulge the identity of respondents, even though they were promised anonymity. There is also the possibility of exploitative relationships, especially with key informants. Exploitation is of special concern in cases where there is a real or perceived imbalance of power—often related to race, class, or gender—between researcher and participant. In the Tuskegee case, for example, African American men suffered the adverse effects of the research, even though syphilis is distributed throughout the larger population. Although this research should not have occurred under any circumstances, a more equitable research design would have meant that most of the participants were white males.

It is also a betrayal of trust for the researcher to develop inappropriate relationships with participants. One noteworthy example of this is a study conducted by Erich Goode (2002) to better understand the stigma of obesity. Goode has publicly acknowledged that he had sexual relations with some of his female informants. He argues that because of this, he was able to obtain information that may not have been obtainable by any other means. However, one must ask about the cost to his participants of his obtaining the knowledge in this way. Because Goode's participants did not have full knowledge of his motives, they were unable to make informed choices about engaging in sexual relations with him. In this case, the power imbalance between researcher and participant led to exploitation.

The best-known example of sociological research involving deception and intrusion into people's lives is Laud Humphreys's (1970) study of the activities of gay men in public restrooms ("tearooms"). Humphreys (1930–1988) acted as a lookout outside tearooms and signaled men engaged in anonymous acts of fellatio when members of the public or the police were approaching. He interviewed some of the men with full disclosure. However, he also noted the license plate numbers of some of those he observed and tracked down their

On the Run: Fugitive Life in an American City

(Picador, 2014)

Alice Goffman (Assistant Professor of Sociology at University of Wisconsin; PhD, Princeton University, 2010)

Mark Makela/Getty Images News/Getty Images

Maintaining a certain level of objectivity and distance from the individuals one is researching can prove challenging, especially when one is immersed in their daily lives for an extended period of time. Ethical dilemmas can arise when researchers empathize too much with the people being studied. Alice Goffman found herself facing just such a dilemma when conducting fieldwork on how young black men and their families negotiate the criminal justice system in one Philadelphia neighborhood she calls 6th Street. Most of these men were on parole or probation or had outstanding warrants. They spent much of their time trying to avoid the police and incarceration. Law enforcement does not make this easy for them. Goffman observed the police harassing these men in a variety of ways, from stopping and frisking them on the streets to searching their homes, often without probable cause. The courts offer little recourse. Missed court dates and failure to pay court fees make it difficult for these men—and by extension their families

and friends—to avoid the legal system.

During the six years that Goffman was in the field, she developed close relationships with two men in particular, Mike and Chuck. For a time, she even became their roommate. While establishing strong connections is important to build trust and gain access to research sites and subjects, Goffman found herself spending more time—and feeling more comfortable—with her friends on 6th Street than at the university at which she was studying. She also found herself engaging in legally questionable activities. One night she spent "on the run" with Chuck and his brother Reggie, hiding with them in a neighbor's house from the police. After Chuck was shot and killed, Goffman drove Mike around to try to find his killer. During one of these drives, Goffman waited in the car when Mike, who was carrying a loaded gun, got out and followed a man who he thought shot Chuck. Luckily, Mike determined that this was the wrong man and returned to the car. If Mike had shot and killed this man, Goffman could have

been an accomplice in a conspiracy to commit murder. On the Run reveals that the decision of when to observe and when to participate is complicated both ethically and legally when conducting ethnographic research.

Supplementary Resources

- Goffman discusses her research findings from On the Run in her TED Talk, "How We're Priming Some Kids for College—and Others for Prison": https://www.ted.com/talks/alice_goffman_college_or_prison_two_destinies_one_blatant_injustice?language=en.
- Criticisms about the reliability of Goffman's ethnographic methodology are examined in an article by Gideon Lewis-Kraus (2016), "The Trials of Alice Goffman": http://www.nytimes.com/2016/01/17/magazine/the-trials-of-alice-goffman.html?_r=0.

addresses. Humphreys appeared at their homes a year or so later, in disguise, to interview them under false pretenses. In this way he uncovered one of the most important findings of his study: More than half the men were married, with wives and families. They were active in the tearoom trade not because they were gay but because sexual relations in their marriages were problematic.

Humphreys deceived these men by not telling them from the outset that he was doing research on them and, with those he interviewed under false pretenses, by not revealing the true nature of the research. His research had at least the potential of revealing something that most of the participants wanted to conceal. But the research itself is not without merit. It helped distinguish between same-sex acts and gay identity. Humphreys's research, while ethically flawed and harmful to the unwitting participants, did have some benefit: It provided much-needed insight into the social construction of sexuality and the difficulties involved in understanding how people develop their sexual selves.

OBJECTIVITY, OR "VALUE-FREE" SOCIOLOGY

Another issue relating to sociological research is whether or not researchers are, or can be, objective. That is, do they allow personal preferences and judgments to bias their research? Many argue that value-laden research jeopardizes the entire field of sociology. The publication of such research—and public revelations about researcher biases—erodes and could destroy the credibility of the field as a whole. In the history of sociology, this discussion is traceable, once again, to the work of Max Weber (Black 2013). Taken to its extreme, *value-free sociology* means preventing all personal values from affecting any phase of the research process. However, this is not what Weber intended in his work on values, and it is instructive to take a brief look at what he actually meant.

In fact, Weber saw at least two roles for values in social research. The first is in the selection of a question to be researched. In that case, it is perfectly appropriate for researchers to be guided by their personal values, or the values that predominate in the society of the day. The second is in the analysis of the results of a research study. In that analysis, sociologists can, and should, use personal and social values to help them make sense of their findings. These values are an aid in interpretation and understanding. However, they are not to be used purposely to distort the findings or mislead the reader of a report on the study. This is a particularly important issue today given the proliferation of "fake news" based on unscientific opinions and political ideology. As an example of an effort to combat this phenomenon, the March for Science in April 2017 was organized to support objective research and fight for its continued funding by the federal government.

SUMMARY

The main theorists of classical sociology are Karl Marx, Max Weber, and Émile Durkheim. Marx focused the majority of his attention on macro issues, particularly the structure of capitalist society. Unlike Marx, Weber did not focus exclusively on the economy but considered the importance of other social structures, particularly religion. Durkheim believed that social structures and cultural norms and values exert control over individuals that is not only necessary but also desirable. Among other early sociological theorists, Georg Simmel focused on micro-level issues, specifically interactions among individuals. W. E. B. Du Bois was a pioneering researcher of race in America at the beginning of the twentieth century. Thorstein Veblen studied consumption, particularly the ways in which the rich show off their wealth through conspicuous consumption.

Structural/functional, conflict/critical, and inter/actionist theories are the three main types of contemporary sociological theories. Two influential structural/functional theories are structural-functionalism, which is concerned with both social structures and the functions and dysfunctions they perform, and structuralism, which uncovers the social impact of hidden or underlying structures. There are several conflict/critical theories. Conflict theory stresses the ways in which society is held together by power and coercion. Critical theory analyzes culture, feminist theory critiques patriarchy, and queer theory suggests that there are no stable or fixed identities that determine who we are. Critical theories of race and racism argue that race continues to matter and intersects with other social statuses. Postmodern theory is concerned that society is coming to be dominated by simulations. Inter/actionist theories deal mostly with micro-level interaction among people. Symbolic interactionism studies the effect of symbols on social interactions, and ethnomethodology focuses on what people do rather than on what they think. Exchange theory analyzes people's behavior based on rewards and costs, while rational choice theory considers how the rational evaluation of goals and the means to achieve them influence behavior.

Sociologists use different research methods depending on the research questions they are studying. Quantitative research yields data in the form of numbers, usually derived from surveys and experiments. Qualitative research is conducted in natural settings and yields descriptive information. Researchers may choose to participate and play a role in what they are observing or engage in nonparticipant observation. Ethnographic research is more likely to be based on participant observation over an extended length of time. In interviews, respondents are asked a series of questions, usually on a face-to-face basis. Survey research collects data through interviews and questionnaires. Experimentation manipulates one or more independent variables to examine their effect on one or more dependent variables. Sociologists also often engage in secondary data analysis, in which they reanalyze data collected by others. Secondary data may consist of statistical information, historical documents and analyses, or the content of cultural artifacts and messages.

Sociologists encounter several key issues when conducting research, including reliability, validity, and ethical concerns. Reliability is the degree to which a given measure produces the same results time after time. Validity is the degree to which a measure is accurate. Ethical issues that sociologists need to be mindful of during the research process include preventing physical and psychological harm to their subjects, dealing with illegal acts that they may witness, and avoiding violating the trust of the people whom they are studying.

KEY TERMS

alienation, 29
anomie, 33
capitalism, 29
capitalists, 29
class consciousness, 30
collective conscience, 33
conflict theory, 37
conspicuous
    consumption, 35
content analysis, 54
convenience samples, 52
critical theories of race
    and racism, 39
critical theory, 38
culture industry, 38
dependent variable, 52
descriptive statistics, 46
descriptive survey, 50

double
    consciousness, 34
dysfunctions, 36
empiricism, 44
ethics, 55
ethnography, 47
ethnomethodology, 43
exchange
    relationships, 43
exchange theory, 43
experiments, 52
explanatory survey, 51
exploitation, 29
false consciousness, 30
feminist theory, 38
field experiments, 52
functions, 36
genderqueer, 39

global ethnography, 48
historical-comparative
    research, 54
hyperconsumption, 41
independent variable, 52
inferential statistics, 46
intersectionality, 39
interviews, 48
laboratory
    experiments, 52
latent functions, 36
manifest functions, 36
mass culture, 38
mechanical solidarity, 33
natural experiments, 52
netnography, 47
nonparticipant
    observation, 47

observation, 46
organic solidarity, 33
pangender, 39
participant
    observation, 47
postmodern theory, 41
proletariat, 29
Protestant ethic, 31
qualitative research, 45
quantitative research, 45
queer theory, 39
questionnaires, 50
random sample, 51
rational choice
    theory, 43
rationalization, 31
reliability, 54
sample, 51

REVIEW QUESTIONS

1. What are theories, and how do sociologists use theories to make sense of the social world? In what ways are theories developed by sociologists better than your own theorizing?

2. Max Weber said the world is becoming increasingly rationalized. What are the benefits and disadvantages of rationality?

3. Do your consumption habits reflect Veblen's theory of conspicuous consumption? Consider the brand names on your clothing, cell phone, and laptop.

4. What are the functions and dysfunctions of using the internet to consume goods and services? On balance, do you think that consumption through the internet is positive or negative?

5. How is your life affected by intersectionality? Do you think these intersections affect you positively or negatively?

6. What are the differences between participant and nonparticipant observational methods? How do sociologists ensure that their observations are systematic using both approaches?

7. Researchers use interviews to gather data by asking individuals a series of questions. How do researchers choose between prestructured and unstructured interviews? What are the advantages and disadvantages of each type of interview?

8. Some experiments allow researchers to take advantage of a naturally occurring event to study its effect on one or more dependent variables. Can you think of any recent events that might have been conducive to natural experiments? What would be the dependent variable or variables in your example?

9. A researcher uses the World Values Survey (WVS) to examine the relationship between people's religious beliefs and their level of happiness. In this study, what is the independent variable, and what is the dependent variable? What reliability and validity issues could arise in conducting this survey across countries?

10. What role do values play in the research process? According to Weber, when is objectivity most important?

$SAGE edge™ **Want a better grade?**

Get the tools you need to sharpen your study skills. Access practice quizzes, eFlashcards, video, and multimedia at **edge.sagepub.com/ritzeressentials3e.**

CULTURE

A Reflection of U.S. Culture

A jazz musician, Miles Davis, gave new life to the term *cool* in his 1957 album *Birth of the Cool*. Being cool—calm and steady as cool water—remains part of American culture, though that culture has many other characteristics. One influential cultural force today is HBO's *Girls* and its decidedly "uncool," even geeky, characters, especially its 30ish star, executive producer, writer, and director Lena Dunham.

Girls and Lena Dunham have become cultural phenomena by portraying, and helping define, the culture of urban millennials (those born between the early 1980s and the early 2000s). The show, which is somewhat autobiographical (like Dunham's book, *Not That Kind of Girl*), deals fearlessly with a wide range of topics, particularly the many varieties of human relationships, including between female friends and the sexual politics of male-female and homosexual and lesbian relationships. The characters are young, flawed, unstable, vulnerable, self-involved, somewhat immature people whose relationships are fraught with difficulties. Their jobs and careers, such as they are, exist mainly at the bottom of the occupational hierarchy and are, if anything, more problematic than their social relationships.

Dunham's character, Hannah, is a paradigm of a millennial woman. A writer, she is a narcissistic, striving careerist who fails more often than not. She is irrepressible but anxious, self-loathing, often depressed, frequently

LEARNING OBJECTIVES

 3.1 Define culture.

 3.2 Identify the basic elements of culture.

3.3 Discuss cultural differences.

3.4 Explain characteristics of global culture.

3.5 Outline the characteristics of consumer culture.

badly treated by friends and lovers, and in need of drugs—prescription and nonprescription—and therapy. She hates her overweight body and alternates between dieting and binge eating. When not clothed in some bizarre, unflattering outfit, she often unselfconsciously displays her nude, decidedly un-model-like body. Sex for Hannah often seems unsatisfying, and many of the problems that she and her friends have appear to stem from the fact that they are women. *Girls* seems to get at the essence of millennial culture, at least for women, in the early twenty-first century.

Because you were likely born in the 1990s, you are considered part of the millennial generation. However, you also belong to many different cultures and subcultures. For example, you are likely to be engaged to some degree or another in consumer and digital culture, as well as the culture of college life. You are continually learning the dimensions and the rules of these and other cultures. Much of that learning happens almost effortlessly, as you live your daily life. But cultures that are new to you, such as university culture, or that are evolving rapidly, such as digital culture, are likely to require much, and continuing, effort, alertness, and flexibility on your part for you to learn how to behave in them. ●

A DEFINITION OF CULTURE

Culture encompasses the ideas, values, practices, and material objects that allow a group of people, even an entire society, to carry out their collective lives in relative order and harmony. There are innumerable ideas, values, practices, and material objects associated with most cultures. As a result, no one individual can possibly know them all or what they all mean. But people must know at least the most basic and important elements of their culture. Knowledge of a shared culture leads people to behave in similar ways and to adopt a similar way of looking at the world. However, it is important to remember that there are differences within, as well as between, cultures. This point was reflected in the December 2016 terrorist attack in Berlin by an Islamic radical at a Christmas market—an obvious cultural symbol of Christianity. There are profound differences in Germany today among German, Muslim, and Jewish cultures.

Closer to home, consider the cultures of the Bloods and the Crips, two street gangs with origins in Los Angeles in the early 1970s but now existing nationwide (Covey 2015; Deutsch 2014). Members of the two gangs distinguish themselves from each other in a variety of ways, but most notably by their defining colors—red for Bloods and blue for Crips. These colors and other symbols are very meaningful to gang members, helping them mark territories, easily identify friends and foes, and signify their values. The symbols—and their meanings—have been created by the group itself and passed down from one gang member to another. In contrast, for those who are not members of the group, an idea, a value, a practice, or an object may have little meaning, may mean something completely different, or may even have no meaning at all. For example, to members of the general public, a person wearing a red shirt is simply wearing a red shirt.

The existence of a culture and common knowledge of it are so important that newcomers to any group, especially children, are taught its basic elements early. They then expand on that knowledge as they mature and become more integral members of the group.

At the same time, culture is constantly being affected by changes both internal and external to the group. Among the *internal changes* are the average age of the population within that group. Depending on whether the average age increases or decreases, a culture will need to reflect the needs and interests of either younger or older people. For example, in the United States, television programs and the advertisements associated with them often target specific age groups, such as Baby Boomers, Gen Xers, or Millennials (Elliot 2014). A good example of this is the great popularity, especially among older viewers, of CBS's *NCIS*. On the other hand, television certainly cannot and does not ignore its younger audience. The great popularity and cultural influence of Fox's *Empire* is indicative of that.

Similarly, cultures need to adapt to other changes, such as a group's gender composition. For example, today there are more female gang members in general, and this is also true of the membership of the Bloods and the Crips (Goldman, Giles, and Hogg 2014). As a result of this shift, a gang's culture needs to change to deal with things such as the tasks to be allotted to female members (e.g., carrying concealed weapons) and, more specifically, to those who are pregnant or have young children.

Technological innovations are among the *external changes* likely to alter a group's culture significantly.

There are few rules on what should and should not be discussed on a cell phone in places where others, especially strangers, are close enough to overhear what is being said.

For example, with the growth of smartphone use, texting has become wildly popular as a communication method (including among street gang members), and cell phone conversations have become proportionally less common. Thus, not only newcomers to the group but also those who have participated for years must constantly learn new aspects of culture (e.g., gang members using prepaid "burner" cell phones that are difficult or impossible to trace) and perhaps unlearn others (using traditional cell phones) that are no longer considered desirable.

The increasing ubiquity of the smartphone has created a whole new set of realities for which clear and firm cultural rules are not yet in place. There are few rules about texting, and those few that do exist are notoriously difficult to monitor and police, especially in settings such as classrooms (Pettijohn et al. 2015).There are also few rules on what should and should not be discussed on a cell phone in places where others, especially strangers, are close enough to overhear what is being said. Long, loud, and frequent phone conversations are not a problem in the privacy of one's home, but they are a problem in public areas where there is an expectation of quietude, for example, at a nice restaurant.

A more formal set of rules regarding talking and texting on cell phones is being developed to control these activities on the part of drivers. It has become apparent—both from insurance company statistics and from experimental research—that using a handheld cell phone while driving increases the risk of accidents (Richtel 2016). In 2015, more than a quarter of automobile crashes in the United States involved the use of cell phones while driving (Smith 2015). A very active media campaign has developed to discourage people from using handheld cell phones while driving. As shown in Figure 3.1, many states have enacted laws against the practice, and some safety advocates are pressing for a similar federal law. If both campaigns succeed, using a handheld cell phone while driving will no longer be culturally acceptable and will in fact become illegal across the nation.

Although we generally accept and learn the various components of culture, sometimes we refuse to comply with, or even accept, them. For example, many continue to talk and text on cell phones while driving even though they know that it is illegal and that the larger culture and legal system are increasingly characterized by negative views on such behaviors. To take a different example, premarital and extramarital sexual relationships continue to be disapproved of by traditional American culture, but many people have come to reject these ideas and to engage increasingly in these behaviors (on premarital sex, see Elias, Fullerton, and Simpson 2015). Indeed, it could be argued that both these forms of sexual behavior have come to be widely tolerated; premarital sex in particular has become an accepted part of the culture.

FIGURE 3.1 • Cell Phone Use and Texting-while-Driving Laws, 2016

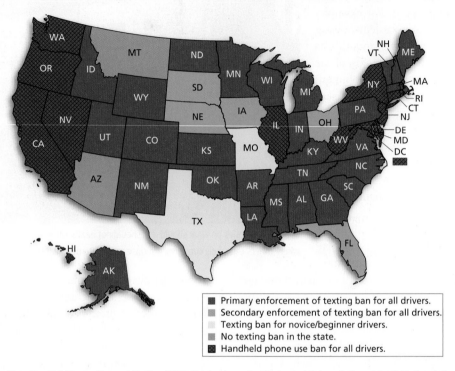

■ Primary enforcement of texting ban for all drivers.
■ Secondary enforcement of texting ban for all drivers.
□ Texting ban for novice/beginner drivers.
■ No texting ban in the state.
▨ Handheld phone use ban for all drivers.

SOURCE: Map Showing Cell Phone Use and Texting While Driving Laws in "Distracted Drivers." Copyright © National Conference of State Legislatures. Reprinted with permission.

NOTE: Under "secondary" laws, an officer must have some other reason to stop a vehicle before citing the driver for using a cell phone. Laws without this restriction are called "primary." Many states that have passed hand-held phone bans and texting bans provide for various exemptions for emergencies, law enforcement personnel, emergency medical technicians, firefighters, state DOT employees, etc.

THE BASIC ELEMENTS OF CULTURE

As pointed out earlier, every group and society has a culture. Culture surrounds such diverse social phenomena as athletics, cooking, funeral ceremonies, courtship, medicine, marriage, sexual restrictions and taboos, bodily adornment, calendars, dancing, games, greetings, hairstyles, personal names, religion, and myths. However, the specific content of each of these domains, and many more, varies from culture to culture. Cultures differ from one another mainly because each represents a unique mix of values, norms, objects, and language inherited from the past, derived from other groups, and created anew by each group.

VALUES

The broadest element of culture is **values**, the general and abstract standards defining what a group or society as a whole considers good, desirable, right, or important. Values express the ideals of society, as well as of groups of every size.

In his classic work *Democracy in America* ([1835–1840] 1969), the French scholar Alexis de Tocqueville detailed what he perceived to be America's values. Among the things Americans valued in the early nineteenth century were democracy, equality, individualism, a "taste for physical comfort," spirituality, and economic prosperity. Although Tocqueville wrote about his impressions of the United States almost 200 years ago, the vast majority of Americans today would accept most, if not all, of the values he described.

Indeed, Americans find these values so natural that they expect them to be accepted in other cultures around the world. However, this expectation has had some disappointing, even disastrous, consequences for the United States. For example, when the United States undertook invasions of Iraq and Afghanistan, one of the objectives was the creation of democratic regimes in those societies. The assumption was that Iraqis and Afghanis wanted the same kind of democracy as the one that exists in the United States. But creating democracies in those countries has proven to be extremely difficult for a variety of reasons, including the fact that their cultures lack a tradition of democratic government. It is extremely difficult, if not impossible, to impose a value, such as the value of democracy, on a society where it does not already exist, or where it exists in a very different form. Researchers using data collected through the World Values Survey (WVS) have found support for the idea that democracy is a hard, if not impossible, sell in many parts of the world (Welzel and Inglehart 2009). As you may recall from Chapter 2, the WVS has gathered data from a variety of countries around the world on individual views on topics such as gender equality; tolerance for abortion, homosexuality, and divorce; desire for autonomy over authority (for example, obedience and faith); and democratic participation over security. Respondents in countries where personal freedom is not valued highly—such as Pakistan, Jordan, and Nigeria—tend to think of antidemocratic authoritarian regimes as being democratic. The data also show that citizens within these countries have little knowledge of the meaning of liberal democracy.

Of course, there are many other reasons why democracy has a difficult time succeeding in some countries. Among other things, before democracy can be established, people need to have enough to eat, to feel safe, to be able to get an education, and to trust the government. Unfortunately, many, if not all, of these needs are not being met in many parts of the world.

Have you ever deliberately broken a social norm? Some of the passengers on this New York City subway are participating in an annual "No-Pants Subway Ride" event.

NORMS

Based on values, **norms** are the informal rules that guide what people do and how they live. Norms tell us what we should and should not do in a given situation. Many norms are informal. That is, they are not formally codified, not written down in any one place. **Laws** are norms that *have* been codified. They are written down and formally enforced through institutions such as the state. Rules prohibiting speaking and texting on handheld cell phones while driving are examples of how informal norms can come to be codified into laws.

You are expected to follow norms and obey laws, but the consequences of failing to do so are usually very different in the two cases. If you violate the law against homicide, you can expect to be arrested, incarcerated, and perhaps even executed. But if you fail to follow the norm of using utensils to eat your dinner and use your fingers instead, you can expect merely a few raised eyebrows and a "tsk tsk" or two from your dinner companions. However, reactions to violating norms are not always so gentle. For example, a gang member's violation of a norm against fleeing a fight with another gang may lead to physical violence or death.

Norms are reinforced through **sanctions**, which can take the form of punishments (negative sanctions) or rewards (positive sanctions). In general, when norms have been violated, punishments are used, while rewards are employed when norms have been followed. For example, dinner companions might frown when you eat with your hands and grin approvingly when you use the right utensil. Gang members would be likely to disapprove of those who flee and approve of those who stay and fight. In other words, sanctions may be applied when norms are observed as well as when they are violated. Sometimes either positive or negative sanctions are enough to enforce norms. However, enforcement is generally more effective when positive and negative sanctions are used in tandem—when *both* the "carrot" (reward) and the "stick" (punishment) are applied. Most people follow norms primarily because sanctions are associated with them.

ASK YOURSELF

What norms are operating in your classroom, dorm, or apartment? What negative sanctions have you observed when these norms have been violated?

Not all norms are the same, are equally important, or carry with them the same penalties if they are violated. On the one hand, there are **folkways**, or relatively unimportant norms. Whether they are observed or violated, they carry with them few if any sanctions (Sumner [1906] 1940). Not intruding on the space of the passenger sitting next to you on a plane is an example of a folkway. In contrast, **mores** (pronounced MOR-ays) are more important norms whose violation is likely to be met with severe negative sanctions. Airplane passengers who are belligerent toward other passengers or crew members are violating mores and may be forcibly ejected from the plane. While a clear distinction is often made between folkways and mores, in fact, they exist along a continuum; it is often hard to distinguish where folkways end and mores begin.

MATERIAL CULTURE

Values and norms exist within the realm of ideas (see the following section for a related definition and discussion of symbolic, or nonmaterial, culture). However, culture also takes material—that is, tangible—forms. **Material culture** encompasses all the artifacts, the "stuff" in which culture is reflected or manifested. A wide range of things can be included under the heading of material culture, including this book, the clothes we wear, the homes in which we live, our computers and iPhones, the toys children play with, and even the weapons used by our military.

Sharing an armrest on a train can be a fraught experience. How do you react if someone violates what you see as an established social norm? For a good example of the differences between laws and the various types of norms, consider the situations you may encounter at Walmart. There are laws against shoplifting, there are mores against damaging store displays, and folkways exist about lining up and waiting your turn to check out.

Culture shapes such objects. For instance, the value Americans place on economic prosperity is reflected in material objects such as the game Monopoly. This game was first patented in the mid-1930s, and its icon is a well-dressed, economically successful tycoon. The goal of the game is to accumulate the most property and money. There are now also nonmaterial games, such as Minecraft and Pokémon Go, which are not only enjoyed by millions of people online but also played by thousands in quite material sports arenas, for millions of dollars in very real and material prize money (Wingfield 2014a, 2014b).

Material culture also shapes the larger culture in various ways. For example, when playing Monopoly, children are learning about, helping support, and furthering a culture that values wealth and material success. To take a different example, the centuries-old American value of individual freedom and individualism has been greatly enhanced by the widespread adoption of such material objects as the automobile, the single-family home, and the smartphone. The last of these, for example, gives us highly individualized and mobile access to the vast world available on the phone and the internet.

SYMBOLIC CULTURE AND LANGUAGE

Symbolic culture includes the nonmaterial, intangible aspects of culture. In fact, we have already discussed two key forms of symbolic culture—values and norms. However, there is no clear line between material and nonmaterial culture. Most, if not all, material phenomena have symbolic aspects, and various aspects of symbolic culture are manifest in material objects. Our symbolic culture is manifest when we buy American-made rather than Japanese or Korean automobiles in a show of patriotism, purchase the latest iPhone as soon as it is released to denote our technological sophistication, or choose cloth diapers over disposables as a symbol of our commitment to "green" parenting.

One important aspect of symbolic culture is **language**, a set of meaningful symbols that enables communication. Language, especially in its written form, allows for the storage and development of culture. Cultures with largely oral traditions do manage to accumulate culture and transmit it from one generation or group to another, but written language is a far more effective way of retaining and expanding upon a culture.

Perhaps more important, language facilitates communication within a culture. Our words reflect the way in which we think about and see the world. They also shape and influence culture. Suppose a time traveler from the 1950s arrived at a modern-day supermarket to buy something to eat for breakfast. Our time traveler would be bewildered by cereals with brand names like Froot Loops, Fruity Pebbles, and Lucky Charms. The exotic and varied cereals we have now would be considered a marvel by someone from the 1950s. The point, however, is that having names for many different kinds of cereals allows consumers to make much finer distinctions about breakfast and to communicate more precisely what it is they wish to eat.

The contemporary world has given us a wealth of new words. For example, in the digital era, e-mail and advertisers have given us the word *spam* for the avalanche of unwanted messages. In the world of social networking, Twitter has given us the word *hashtag* to describe a label that helps us in searching *tweets*. The term *trolls* refers to those who seek to instigate arguments on social media forums. The consumption-oriented nature of our society has also led to the creation of many new words, a large number of them brand names. For example, the now nearly extinct *iPod* was the leading portable music device; it led to the development of *iTunes*. The *iPhone* is the leading *smartphone* (another new word), and it has replaced the iPod as well as leading to a booming industry in *apps* (applications) of all sorts. Similarly, globalization has led to new words, including *globalization* itself, which was virtually unused prior to 1990 (Ritzer and Dean 2015). Words like these are shared by people all over the world and allow them to communicate with one another. Communication among people of different cultures is also easier if they share a mother tongue. As you can see in the simplified map of world languages in Figure 3.2, African cultures use a variety of official and national languages. People in countries where French is the official language, such as Burkina Faso and Niger, can transact their business more easily with one another than they can with nations where Arabic or Portuguese is the primary language, such as Mauritania and Cape Verde.

In a world dominated by consumption, communication between cultures also takes place through the viewing of common brands. However, brand names well known in some cultures may not translate well in other cultures. As a result, brands are often renamed to better reflect the cultures in which they are being sold. The following list shows the names of some well-known brands in the United States and elsewhere and the way they are translated into Chinese:

BRAND	CHINESE TRANSLATION
Nike	Enduring and Persevering
BMW	Precious Horse
Heineken	Happiness Power
Coca-Cola	Tasty Fun
Marriott	10,000 Wealthy Elites

While such name changes are common, some Chinese brand names are simply phonetic translations

FIGURE 3.2 • Distribution of Major Languages

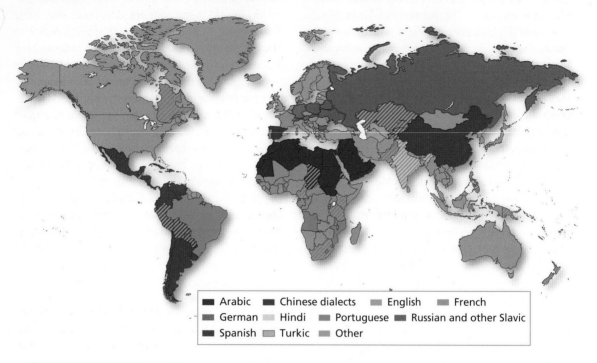

Legend:
- Arabic
- Chinese dialects
- English
- French
- German
- Hindi
- Portuguese
- Russian and other Slavic
- Spanish
- Turkic
- Other

- Official language for every country.
- Other languages spoken and percentage of English speakers.

SOURCES: Data from Languages of the World, One World, Nations Online Project.

of the brands' names into Chinese. For example, Cadillac is translated "Ka di la ke." Although this name means nothing to the Chinese, the fact that it is foreign gives it an aura of status and respectability. However, if Microsoft had used a phonetic Chinese translation of the name of its search engine Bing, it would have been in big trouble. In Chinese, the word *bing* translates into "disease" or "virus." To avoid being seen as disease-ridden or a carrier of a virus, Microsoft changed the search engine's Chinese name to Bi ying. This has the far more appealing meaning of "responding without fail" (Wines 2011).

ASK YOURSELF

Have you ever been in a situation, such as a trip abroad, in which understanding and communicating were difficult for you because you were unfamiliar with the language and symbols around you? How did you cope? Have you ever helped someone else who was in a similar situation? What did you do?

CULTURAL DIFFERENCES

As you have seen so far, we can think in terms of the culture of a society as a whole (for example, American culture), and later in this chapter we will even conceive of the possibility of a global culture. But you have also seen that there is great diversity within cultures, from gang culture to internet culture and too many other variants of culture for us to enumerate. Studying and understanding culture becomes easier, however, with the aid of a few key ideas: ideal and real culture, ideology, subculture and counterculture, culture war, and multiculturalism.

IDEAL AND REAL CULTURE

There is often a large gap, if not a chasm, between **ideal culture**, or what the norms and values of society lead us to think people should believe and do, and **real culture**, or what people actually think and do in their everyday lives. For example, as we have seen, a major American value is democracy. However, barely a majority of Americans bother to vote in presidential elections—only 60 percent of eligible voters voted in the 2016 election, about 1 percent above the figure four years earlier (United States Elections Project 2016; see Chapter 12). A far smaller percentage of those who are eligible vote in state and local elections. Worse, very few Americans are active in politics in other ways, such as canvassing on behalf of a political party or working to get people out to vote.

In another example, the cultural ideal that mothers should be completely devoted to their children often comes into conflict with the lived reality for many women who work outside the home and must balance their time between job and family (Blair-Loy 2003; Hays 1998). This contradiction is apparent in the incidence of breastfeeding, which at least for some women is once again a norm of motherhood (Avishai 2007; Stearns 2009). Breastfeeding is difficult or impossible for many mothers because it is labor- and time-intensive, and given work and all the other constraints they face in their lives, it is difficult for them to find the time and energy to do it. Despite its health benefits for baby and mother, under such circumstances, breastfeeding can have adverse social and economic consequences for women. One study demonstrated that women who breastfed for more than six months suffered greater economic losses than those who did so for less time or not at all (Rippeyoug and Noonan 2012). Women who do not breastfeed, however, can feel they have failed to live up to cultural standards of being a "good mom."

IDEOLOGY

An **ideology** is a set of shared beliefs that explains the social world and guides people's actions. There are many ideologies in any society, and some of them become dominant. For example, in the United States, *meritocracy* is a dominant ideology involving the widely shared belief that all people have an equal chance of succeeding economically based on their hard work and skills. Many people act on the basis of that belief and, among other things, seek the education and training they think they need to succeed.

However, even with dedication and adequate education and training, not everyone succeeds. Among many other things, some people are luckier than others (Frank 2016). Even though they don't deserve it, some people succeed because of a lucky break; others who deserve to succeed don't because they are unlucky. This reflects the key fact that not all ideologies are true. For one thing, they may come from, and be true for, some groups of people (such as those in the upper classes) and not for others (those in the lower classes; Mannheim [1931] 1936). For another, they may be outright distortions used by one group to hide reality from another group (Marx [1857–1858] 1964). In this sense, it could be argued that meritocracy is an ideology created by the upper classes to hide the fact that those in the lower classes have little or no chance of succeeding. This fact is hidden from them to prevent them from becoming dissatisfied and rebellious. If the lower classes accept the ideology of meritocracy, they may be more likely to blame themselves for failing rather than the upper classes or the American economic system as a whole.

SUBCULTURES

Within any culture there are **subcultures**, or groups of people who accept much of the dominant culture but are set apart from it by one or more culturally significant characteristics. In the United States, major subcultures include the LGBTQ community (lesbian, gay, bisexual, transgender, and queer people), Hispanics, the Tea Party, Hasidic Jews, hip-hop fans, and youth. Muslims are becoming an increasingly important subculture in the United States (especially in cities such as Detroit). They already constitute a major subculture in many European countries, most notably France and Great Britain.

Subcultures arise in the realm of consumption as well. For example, "brand communities" develop around particular brand-name products (Meister 2012; Stratton and Northcote 2014). Harley-Davidson motorcycle riders are one such subculture (called HOGS, for Harley Owners Group), with distinctive clothing, events, and norms. Brand communities have formed around a number of Apple products, such as the Macintosh computer (the "Mac") and the iPad. The members of these communities share a number of cultural elements, including norms. In the case of the Mac, for example, some community members positively sanction "jailbreaking," a method for hacking into Apple's software in order to get around its restrictions and limitations.

Any society includes many subcultures, such as hackers or those devoted to fishing, that develop around particular styles of life and share special

MOHAMMED ABED/AFP/Getty Images

Parkour has developed a subculture with its own norms, values, language, and environments. Do you belong to any similar subcultures?

vocabularies. A great deal of attention has been devoted to "deviant" subcultures, such as those of punks, goths, and the like (Barmaki 2016). In Great Britain, "football hooligans," those who often engage in violence at or in regard to soccer matches, constitute a deviant subculture largely specific to that society (Ayres and Treadwell 2012; Dunning, Murphy, and Williams 1988). However, there are also many "straight" youth subcultures, such as those who play online games (e.g., Pokémon Go) or "straight" fans of clean eating (e.g., the Whole30 program or the Paleo diet).

Another example of a subculture is the world of parkour. The majority of those who practice parkour accept most of the larger society's culture, norms, values, and language, but they also differ in some ways. For instance, many are more willing than most members of society to take physical risks, such as using their bodies to overcome urban obstacles such as walls and ledges (Kidder 2012; Thorpe and Ahmad 2015). They see such obstacles as enhancing the thrill of their activity. Those who practice parkour also have their own vocabulary, using such terms as "tricking" and "freerunning" to describe their activities.

COUNTERCULTURES

Countercultures are groups that not only differ from the dominant culture but also adhere to norms and values that may be incompatible with those of the dominant culture (Zellner 1995). They may, in fact, consciously and overtly act in opposition to the dominant culture. The term *counterculture* was introduced by Theodore Roszak ([1968] 1995) in the late 1960s in reference to hippies, antiwar activists, and radical students.

Computer hackers are a contemporary example of a counterculture (Corbett 2014; Levy 2010). Many hackers simply seek to show their technical mastery of computers through relatively benign actions, such as writing free computer software, but a minority are devoted to subverting authority and disrupting the internet, and some are involved in stealing personal identification data ("identity theft") and money. They may write malicious code in order to interrupt or even shut down the normal operations of computers. Many attempted and successful break-ins have threatened government and corporate computer systems; the hackers' goal has been to steal secret or personal information. In mid-2015, hackers exposed the names of 30 million people who had accounts with Ashley Madison. This was particularly troublesome to the account holders because those who participated on Ashley Madison were interested in having adulterous affairs. (The site's slogan was "Life is short; have an affair" [McPhate 2016].) Personal accounts have also been hacked and locked until the account holders paid ransom demanded by the hackers (Simone 2015). Hacking became a huge public issue in late 2016 when the Russians were caught hacking the accounts of Hillary Clinton and her supporters during the U.S. presidential campaign. Many believe that the Russians' goal was to help Donald Trump win the election (Lipton, Sanger, and Shane 2016). This continues to be an important issue in late 2017, and we can expect more revelations about it in the future.

In the realm of consumption, an important contemporary counterculture is formed by those who are associated with or sympathetic to the "voluntary simplicity" movement (Elgin 2010; Zammuel, Sasson-Levy, and Ben-Porat 2014). Sociologist

Juliet Schor (1993, 1998) has critiqued the dominant American culture's emphasis on what she calls "work and spend." That is, we are willing to work long hours so that we can spend a great deal on consumption and live an ever-more elaborate lifestyle. In addition, Schor (2005) points out the ways in which our consumer culture has led to the commercialization of childhood, with advertising pervading all aspects of children's lives. As a countercultural alternative, she suggests that we both work less and spend less and instead devote ourselves to more meaningful activities. Living a simpler life means avoiding overconsumption, minimizing the work needed to pay for consumption, and doing less harm to the environment.

Globalization, especially economic globalization, has also spawned a number of very active countercultural groups. They are not necessarily antiglobalization, but they favor alternative forms of globalization (Obara-Minnitt 2014; Pleyers 2010). In fact, many of them are part of the process of globalization. The World Social Forum (WSF) was created in 2001 following a series of antiglobalization protests, particularly one in Seattle in 1999. Its members come from all over the world. The WSF's slogan is "Another world is possible." That other world would be less capitalistic. It would also allow for more democratic decision making on matters that affect large portions of the world's population. Those who accept this kind of perspective are clearly part of a counterculture. They oppose the global spread of the dominant capitalist culture that prioritizes maximizing profits over democratic decision making.

CULTURE WARS

In the 1960s, the hippies, student radicals, and anti–Vietnam War activists vocally, visibly, and sometimes violently rejected traditional American norms and values. Among other things, they rejected unthinking patriotism and taboos against recreational drugs and sexual freedom. The term *culture war* was used to describe the social upheaval that ensued. More generally, a **culture war** is a conflict pitting a subculture or counterculture against the dominant culture, or a conflict between dominant groups within a society. Culture wars sometimes lead to the disruption of the social, economic, and political status quo (Hunter 1992; Luker 1984).

In the United States today, the major culture war is being fought between those who place themselves on the conservative end of the sociopolitical spectrum and those who place themselves on the liberal end. It is largely viewed as a political battle over such things as government spending, taxes, social services, national defense, and environmental measures. Conservatives generally favor less government spending, lower taxes for the wealthy, fewer entitlements for the poor, aggressive national defense, and minimal environmental regulations. Liberals usually support higher government spending on education, health care, and services for the poor; less spending on national defense; and stricter environmental regulations (see the Trending box in Chapter 15). Today, this battle is epitomized by struggles between Donald Trump and his conservative allies in the Republican Party and liberal Democrats in Congress.

ASK YOURSELF

Do you think a culture war between political conservatives and liberals is inevitable? Must it be ongoing? Why or why not?

There are important differences in fundamental values between these groups. Consider, for example, the long-running battle over abortion. The political battle is over legal limits to abortion and contraception. However, the underlying values have to do with varying definitions of life and attitudes toward women's role in society. Similarly, much heat is generated over "family values," with conservatives worrying about the decline in the traditional nuclear family, the increasing prevalence of cohabitation and single parenthood, homosexual marriage, and the adoption of children by same-sex couples (Murray 2013). They place more emphasis on strict moral codes and self-discipline, whereas liberals, in contrast, place more significance on empathy, openness, and fairness (McAdams et al. 2008). Liberals tend to see the developments in the family as signs of greater acceptance of people's differences and circumstances (Gerson 2011). Within the field of sociology, in fact, there is intense debate between family scholars who argue that the family is in decline and those who feel the concept of the family needs to be broadened to embrace the many ways in which people experience kin connections (see Chapter 10).

The conservative–liberal culture war is debated endlessly in the popular media. The media themselves tend to be increasingly divided along conservative (Fox News) and liberal (MSNBC) lines. Examples of culture wars are also to be found in the digital world. For example, open-source advocates believe that the internet, or at least large portions of it, should be protected from control by governments or corporations. They support free open-source software (e.g., Linux, Firefox, OpenOffice, GNU Image Manipulation Program) as well as free access to information. One of their models is Wikipedia, where anyone can create entries and modify them. They oppose the dominant players on the internet, including Microsoft, Google, Apple, and internet service providers. These large corporations are seen as carving up the digital world and controlling access in order to generate huge profits. There is a constant low-level conflict going on between members of these two cultures and the groups that support them. More recently, a culture war broke out between those who want to give some corporations (such as Comcast and Verizon) control over the internet and those who favor "net neutrality," in which the internet is free and open to all. The issue seemed settled when in mid-2016 a federal court ruled in favor of net neutrality, but it is far from dead. In mid-2017, the Trump administration sought to unwind some net neutrality rules. Large corporations that want to control the internet have vowed to take the case to the Supreme Court (Kang 2016).

MULTICULTURALISM AND ASSIMILATION

A great deal of attention has been paid in recent years to another aspect of cultural diversity—**multiculturalism**, or an environment in which cultural differences are accepted and appreciated both by the state and by the majority group (Pakulski 2014). The cultural groups may be based on race, ethnicity, nationality, or language. They may also be based on age and other dimensions of difference. People in the United States, for example, generally accept that young and old people have their own cultural preferences. Americans for the most part tolerate—sometimes even celebrate—the coexistence of different cultural groups within the larger culture.

FIGURE 3.3 • Legal Migration to the United States by Region of Origin, 1820–2014

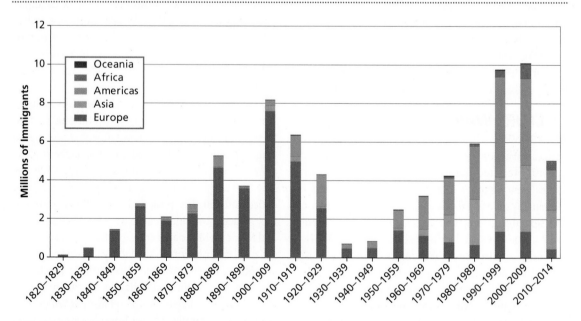

SOURCE: Data from Table 2, "Persons Obtaining Legal Permanent Resident Status by Region and Selected Country of Last Residence: Fiscal Years 1820 to 2014," Washington, DC: U.S. Department of Homeland Security, 2014.

TRENDING

The Spirit Catches You and You Fall Down: A Hmong Child, Her American Doctors, and the Collision of Two Cultures (Farrar, Straus and Giroux, 2012)

Anne Fadiman (Adjunct Professor of English, Francis Writer-in-Residence at Yale University; Essayist and Reporter; BA, Harvard University, 1975)

Foua Yang weeps as she describes her daughter Lia Lee, whose 30-year struggle with epilepsy, cerebral palsy, pneumonia, and sepsis is chronicled in *The Spirit Catches You and You Fall Down*.

Ignorance and confusion about cultural differences often result in awkward social interactions that can be momentarily embarrassing. Cultural misunderstandings, however, can have life-or-death consequences. Take, for example, situations in which doctors and patients believe in different values and practice different norms. Anne Fadiman spent eight years studying encounters between immigrant Hmong parents and the American doctors who treated their epileptic daughter, Lia. Lia's condition was not diagnosed initially because she was not having seizures when she arrived at the emergency room. Further, her parents did not speak English, so they could not communicate her symptoms to the doctors on duty. After Lia's doctors made the correct diagnosis, her condition did not improve, because her parents did not dispense her medicines properly. Lia's parents did not trust Western doctors, the medicine they prescribed, or even the idea that biology was the basis of their daughter's epilepsy. They adhered to the Hmong belief that Lia's epilepsy was caused by her soul

escaping her body. Her symptoms were seen as the result of a soul-stealing spirit that made Lia fall down, or have seizures. According to the Hmong, being epileptic is a sign of distinction and indicates that an individual has special powers (Fadiman 2012, 20–21). Even if Lia's parents did believe that Western medicine could help her, they could not read the instructions on giving her the right dosages. Their lack of compliance—whether intentional or accidental—resulted in Lia's being removed from their custody and placed in foster care.

Lia's parents eventually regained custody of their child by agreeing to dispense her prescriptions according to her doctor's orders. However, six months later, Lia unexpectedly suffered a massive seizure that resulted in septic shock and rendered her brain dead. The doctors removed her from life support so that her parents could take her home and presumably die. But, to their surprise, she survived, even though her parents refused to give her more Western medicine or use a feeding tube. Using traditional Hmong rituals and medicines, Lia's

mother constantly cared for her body and her soul. Though Ladiman admits she does not know whether Lia would become a fully functioning adult, she argues that cross-cultural misunderstandings between Lia's parents and her doctors played a key role in how epilepsy affected her life (Fadiman 2012, 263). Many Hmong in the United States, like Lia's parents, want "to be left alone to be Hmong" and refuse to assimilate (2012, 183). They value self-sufficiency and believe that surgery and drawing blood from the body are taboo. When sick, they prefer to be treated by a shaman, who will come to their homes and spend hours with them (2012, 33). In contrast, American medical professionals value science and rationality. They have their patients

Chapter 3: Culture   75

visit them in impersonal office buildings or hospitals and often spend only a few minutes with them. Undoubtedly, the ethnocentrism expressed by both the Hmong and American doctors can be tempered with a dose of cultural relativism.

Supplementary Resources

- You can read more about Fadiman's book, including the fate of Lia and her family and how it has influenced the medical field, at www .nytimes.com/2012/09/15/ us/life-went-on-around-her- redefining-care-by-bridging- a-divide.html?_r=0.
- Learn more about why cultural competency in the healthcare professions is important by watching this training video: www.youtube .com/watch?v=dNLtAj0wy6l.

When it comes to ethnicity and national origin, however, multiculturalism has not always been celebrated in this country. The dominant culture has been interested primarily in **assimilation**, or integrating the minority group into the mainstream. As a so-called nation of immigrants, the United States has always had to resolve issues of cultural diversity. Until late in the twentieth century, most immigrants to the United States were from Europe, especially Eastern and Southern Europe (see Figure 3.3). Many of these groups did assimilate to a large degree, even if their assimilation occurred over a couple of generations. Today we do not think twice about whether or not Polish Americans or Italian Americans, for instance, are "regular" Americans.

But immigrants from the next large wave, in the 1990s and 2000s, have not assimilated so well. If you refer again to Figure 3.3, you can see that the largest flow of immigrants is now from the Americas, with another large—and growing—group from Asia. These immigrants, especially those from Mexico and China, often live in largely separate enclaves and speak their native languages (see Figure 3.4 for a map depicting the percentage of the population speaking a language other than English at home). They also often retain their basic cultures, such as their tastes in food. It remains to be seen whether, and to what degree, these groups will be assimilated into mainstream culture or their culture will be accepted as a valued element of American culture.

In the past, Muslims have generally assimilated well in the United States (Freedman 2016). The future of their assimilation, however, is in doubt (Bulut 2016). This is a result of the current widespread hostility toward Muslims (especially toward radical Islamic extremists) because of their perceived association with 9/11 and terrorism in the United States and many other parts of the world. This hostility increased greatly during the 2016 presidential campaign, when then-candidate Donald Trump suggested at least a temporary ban on Muslim immigration to the United States. As president, Trump has tried to implement such a ban, at least for a few primarily Islamic countries, but his efforts have thus far been stymied by the courts. It remains to be seen how this will be resolved, but Muslims, as well as members and supporters of the rights of all minority groups, have every reason to be alarmed.

Multiculturalism is a relatively recent issue for many European societies, particularly the Scandinavian countries and the Netherlands. They have traditionally been almost monocultures, and even now, during a period of widespread global migration, they have a smaller proportion of foreign-born residents than the United States. However, beginning in the 1950s, many European countries began to experience labor shortages (Fassmann and Munz 1992; Fielding 1989). Large numbers of people from poorer Southern European countries such as Spain and Italy migrated to Northern European countries. Later, migration flowed from less developed countries outside Europe, such as Turkestan, other largely Islamic countries, and many African countries. The fall of the Soviet Union in 1991 brought additional Eastern Europeans from places such as Albania. Most recently, the conflict in Syria has led to an influx of refugees into many European countries. Though some immigrants were meant to stay only a short time to help with labor shortages, many immigrants built lives for themselves, brought their families, and chose to remain. The result is that European countries today are far more multicultural than they were several decades ago.

FIGURE 3.4 • Percentage of U.S. Population Speaking a Language Other Than English at Home, by County, 2007–2011

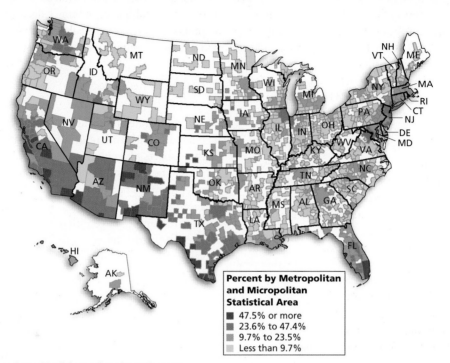

Percent by Metropolitan and Micropolitan Statistical Area
- 47.5% or more
- 23.6% to 47.4%
- 9.7% to 23.5%
- Less than 9.7%

- Percentage of non-English speakers in each county.
- Major languages spoken other than English.

SOURCE: Camille Ryan, "Language Use in the United States: 2011," American Community Survey Reports ACS-22, U.S. Census Bureau, August 2013, p. 12.

ASK YOURSELF

If you were born in the United States, imagine yourself as an immigrant to another country, one to which you have no cultural or genealogical ties and where you know no one. What would you do on your arrival in order to survive? Would you seek out other Americans? Why or why not? Would you try to assimilate? How?

More recent immigrants to largely Christian Europe bring with them very different cultures and very different religions (Islam, for example). They are also likely to be relatively poor. A relatively small, monocultural country like the Netherlands has had trouble integrating its roughly 850,000 Muslim immigrants, and relations with non-Muslims have grown increasingly polarized (Maliepaard and Alba 2016). The same is true in Belgium, which has sought to accommodate the burgeoning Muslim population by de-Christianizing its own holidays (for example, All Saints Day was renamed Autumn Holiday; Kern 2014). In spite of such efforts, concerns about the Muslim population in Belgium continue, epitomized by the coordinated attacks in Brussels in March 2016, which killed 35 people and injured hundreds of others.

Southern and Eastern European countries, such as Italy and Hungary, are increasingly having difficulty dealing with waves of refugees from the Middle East and North Africa. The Hungarian government built a fence to prevent the entry of migrants moving through its borders and interested in going on to wealthier countries in Western Europe, especially Germany. While many Germans see this as a cultural threat, Germany is more welcoming to migrants—and willing to put up with the cultural challenges posed by them—than most other European countries for a variety of reasons, including the fact that its aging population needs an influx of young people.

In short, European countries today have more cultural diversity than ever. However, the situation is fraught with tension, conflict, and danger as people from very different cultures, religions, and languages struggle to find a way to live side by side. Given these recent developments in Europe, the United States, and elsewhere in the world, some are declaring multiculturalism a failure. States, and especially majority groups, are growing less appreciative of, and less willing to accept, groups that represent different cultures (Gozdecka, Ercan, and Kmak 2014).

Identity Politics

While some majority groups have come to oppose multiculturalism, various minority groups have grown impatient with the dominant culture's limited view of multiculturalism and its unwillingness to accept them for who they are. Such minorities have asserted their right to retain their distinctive cultures and even their right *not* to assimilate, at least totally. These groups have engaged in **identity politics** in using their power to strengthen the position of the cultural groups with which they identify (Nicholson 2008; Wasson 2007). Identity politics has a long history in recent decades, including the black power, feminist, and gay pride movements in many parts of the world. The goal of such movements has been the creation of a true multicultural society, one that accepts minorities for who they are.

Identity politics has played out not only on streets in public protests and demonstrations but also in schools and especially in universities. In the latter, the central issue has been whether all students should be required to learn the "canon"—a common set of texts, sometimes referred to as the "great books"—a body of knowledge long regarded as of central importance. For example, the works of Marx, Weber, and Durkheim are often thought to be the canonical texts in sociology. Minority cultures claim that the canon in sociology and many other fields reflects the interests and experiences of white middle- and upper-class males. They argue that alternative bodies of knowledge, such as those created by women, people of color, and the LGBTQ community, are at least as

important. The result has been a proliferation of programs such as those devoted to black, Chicano, and feminist studies, where the focus is on those alternative texts and bodies of knowledge. However, such programs have been the subject of much controversy and political scrutiny (Lacey 2011).

Cultural Relativism and Ethnocentrism

Multiculturalism and identity politics are closely related to **cultural relativism**, which is the idea that aspects of a culture such as norms and values need to be understood within the context of that culture; there are no cultural universals, or universally accepted norms and values. In this view, different cultures simply have different norms and values. There is no basis for saying that one set of norms and values is better than another (Weiler 2007). Thus, for example, those in Western countries should not judge Islamic women's use of headscarves. Conversely, those in the Islamic world should not judge Western women who bare their midriffs.

Cultural relativism runs counter to the tendency in many cultures toward **ethnocentrism**, or the belief that the norms, values, traditions, and material and symbolic aspects of one's own culture are better than those of other cultures (S. E. Brown 2007; Machida 2012). The tendency toward ethnocentrism both among subcultures within the United States and in cultures throughout the world represents a huge barrier to greater cultural understanding. However, to be fair, a belief in one's own culture can be of great value to a culture. It gives the people of that culture a sense of pride and identity. Problems arise when ethnocentrism serves as a barrier to understanding other cultures, a source of conflict among cultures, or an excuse for one culture to deny rights or privileges to another.

GLOBAL CULTURE

There are certainly major differences within American culture, such as those that exist among subcultures. Yet few would dispute the idea that it is possible to talk about American culture in general. However, discussing a global culture, a culture common to the world as a whole, is not as easy. Some elements of material culture, including hamburgers, sushi, cars, and communication technology, have spread widely around the world. However, the global diffusion of nonmaterial culture—values, norms, and symbolic culture—is somewhat more difficult.

THE GLOBALIZATION OF VALUES

We have already discussed how values differ, sometimes greatly, from one society to another. How, then, can we discuss global values—values that are shared throughout the world? Some scholars argue that global values exist because all people share a biological structure that produces universal tendencies, including common values. Others contend that while particular values vary from country to country, the underlying structure of values is much the same across societies. However, the most persuasive argument for the existence of global values is traceable to the process of globalization. The global flow of all sorts of things—information, ideas, products, and people—produces realities in most parts of the world that are more similar than ever before in history (Lechner and Boli 2005). If these realities are increasingly similar, it seems likely that what people value will come to be increasingly similar throughout the world as well.

CULTURAL IMPERIALISM

- Many have the strong view that what affects global culture most of all is **cultural imperialism**, or the imposition of one dominant culture on other cultures (Tomlinson 2012). Cultural imperialism tends to destroy local cultures. For example, there is a long tradition in India of professional letter writers, men who place themselves in prominent locations (e.g., near train stations) and offer their services writing letters for poor, illiterate migrants. Many of these letter writers are able to survive on the pittance they are paid for each letter. However, the adoption of elements of Western culture—the cell phone, texting, and so on—is rendering the professional letter writers, and the cultural traditions associated with them, obsolete.

There is certainly a great deal of cultural imperialism in the world today, much of it associated with the United States (Crothers 2010). The process of **Americanization** includes the importation by other countries of a variety of cultural elements—products, images, technologies, practices, norms, values, and behaviors—that are closely associated with the United States. One example is the American movie industry: The popularity of American movies around the world has decimated the film industries of many countries, including Great Britain and France. (India is one exception, with its thriving Bollywood productions, including the 2009 Academy Award winner for Best Picture, *Slumdog Millionaire*.) Another successful U.S. cultural export is Americans' taste for food, especially fast food and the way in which it is eaten (quickly, with one's hands, standing up or in the car). McDonald's is a prime example, but another of note is Starbucks (Simon 2009), which has been surprisingly successful in exporting its model of large, slowly consumed cups of coffee. In contrast, in France and Italy and other countries, the historic preference has been for tiny cups of espresso quickly consumed. There are now more than 24,000 Starbucks stores located around the world, in more than 70 countries.

Cultural imperialism certainly exists, but it would be wrong to overestimate its power. Local cultures can be quite resilient. Not all cultures suffer the fate of French movie producers and Indian letter writers. For example:

- The powerful process of Americanization is often countered by **anti-Americanism**, which is an aversion to the United States in general, as well as to the influence of its culture abroad (Huntington 1996; O'Connor and Griffiths 2005).

- Many cultures—Chinese and Islamic cultures, for example—have long, even ancient, histories. These cultures have resisted at least some impositions from other cultures for centuries. They are likely to continue to resist changes that threaten their basic values and beliefs.

- Local cultures modify inputs and impositions from other cultures by integrating them with local realities and in the process produce cultural hybrids that combine elements of both original cultures (Nederveen Pieterse 2015). Hybridization occurs when, for instance, the Dutch watch Moroccan women engage in Thai boxing. McDonald's sells such hybrid foods as

McChicken Korma Naan, which caters to those in Great Britain who have developed a taste for Indian food (including the many Indians who live there); McLaks, a grilled salmon sandwich served in Norway; and McHuevos, a hamburger with a poached egg served in Uruguay.

- Additionally, it would be remiss to assume that the United States has been immune to the influence of cultures from other countries. Some of our most popular food, like pizza and tacos, originated in Italy and Mexico. Unbeknownst to many U.S. viewers, television shows such as *Big Brother, American Ninja Warrior,* and *Homeland* are reproductions based on foreign programs from Denmark, Japan, and Israel, respectively.

Thus, cultural imperialism needs to be examined in the context of the counterreactions to it, counterflows from elsewhere in the world, and the combination of global and local influences to produce unique cultural elements.

EMERGING ISSUES IN CULTURE

CONSUMER CULTURE

Consumption is clearly highly valued in the United States (and elsewhere; see Nwachukwu and Dant 2014). That makes American culture a **consumer culture**, one in which the core ideas and material objects relate to consumption and in which consumption is a primary source of meaning in life (Berger 2015; Slater 2015; Wiedenhoft Murphy 2017b). In a consumer culture, meaning may be found in the goods and services that you buy, in the process of buying them (in shopping malls, cybermalls, and so on), in the social aspects of consumption (shopping with your friends or family), and even in the settings in which consumption takes place (e.g., the Venetian or some other Las Vegas hotel-casino, or eBay; Ritzer, Goodman, and Wiedenhoft 2001). There are norms for the consumption process as well. For example, customers should wait patiently in the queue for the cashier, gamblers at a Las Vegas casino should not flaunt their winnings in front of other gamblers and should tip dealers, and so on.

Consumer culture is unique in the history of the world. In the past, culture has generally focused on some other aspect of social life such as religion, warfare, citizenship, or work. In fact, in the not-too-distant past in the United States and other developed countries, the core ideas and material objects of culture related to work and production. People were thought to derive their greatest meaning from their work. This was true from the Industrial Revolution until approximately 1970, when observers began to realize that developed societies, especially the United States, were beginning to derive more meaning from consumption (Baudrillard [1970] 1998). Of course, work continues to be important, as do religion, warfare, and citizenship, but many people in the world now live in a culture dominated by consumption.

While the roots of today's consumer culture can be traced further back in history (Trentman 2016), the rise of consumer culture was linked to the rise of the modern world in the West (Campbell 1987). Today, of course, consumer culture has arguably become *the* culture of the modern West and indeed of modernity in general. But consumer culture has also globalized to a great degree. It has become firmly entrenched in such non-Western places as Singapore, Hong Kong, and Dubai. For example, Japan has been called the premier consumer culture. Consumers in Japan prefer rationalized or McDonaldized ways of eating, and Japan has many fast-food restaurants to fulfill their desires. Kura is a Japanese restaurant chain of 262 sushi restaurants with conveyor belts instead of waiters carrying food to the diners (Tabuchi 2010). In these restaurants, the highly skilled and valued traditional sushi chef has been largely replaced by robots. Diners order from touch screens and put finished plates in a table-side bay so that their bills can be calculated automatically. Video cameras let supervisors in three control centers watch over each restaurant. All this allows Kura to operate with relatively few workers, with a high degree of efficiency and much lower costs, and therefore greater predictability, than traditional sushi restaurants.

CHILDREN IN A CONSUMER CULTURE

The most controversial aspect of consumer culture may be the involvement of children (Sparman

DIGITAL LIVING: NETIQUETTE

Social media websites are developing faster than the norms that can help guide and regulate the behavior of their users (McLaughlin and Vitak 2011, 300). Online etiquette, or netiquette, tends to be implicit—there are few if any formal rules on how to use Snapchat or Instagram. Norms for these sites often emerge when users directly sanction the behavior of each other and content that they feel is inappropriate. They may flag a sexually explicit photograph or hide a person from their Facebook feed who posts too many status updates. Our understanding and practice of online norms typically reflect the habits of our close friends, whom we are more likely to confront with norm violations than acquaintances. For example, if our friends are discrete about the photos they post of us, we will likely reproduce this norm of being considerate when we post photos that include them (McLaughlin and Vitak 2011). Reciprocity, or sharing, is one of the most important norms currently guiding online behavior. Adherence to these norms allow us to build trust and gain access to information (Palfrey and Gasser 2008, 25).

Netiquette can be complicated considering the diversity of our online audience—what might be appropriate for our close friends to read or see might not be acceptable to our teachers or bosses. Furthermore, some sites might encourage people to behave in ways online that might not be acceptable in the real world. Snapchat can automatically delete photos, which might encourage users to post inappropriate or unflattering pictures of themselves or their friends. The legality of such practices has become an issue with teenagers when they send sexual images of themselves to each other. In some states, this is considered to be the distribution of child pornography. Likewise, the anonymity of Yik Yak can prompt users to post racist or sexist comments without fear of being held accountable. These same users might never make such derogatory statements when they interact in face-to-face conversations. In addition, cyberbullying occurs on a variety of social media sites, such as Tumblr, Twitter, and Facebook, prompting some people to question whether these digital means of communication are making cruelty more normative (boyd 2014).

Engaging the Digital World
Select one social media site and list five norms that are regulating, or you think should be used to regulate, the behavior of its users. Explain what you think should happen if a user violates each of these norms. Are there any behaviors that are so extreme that they should result in the user's being denied access to the site? Have you ever tried to directly sanction the behavior of someone on a social media site? If yes, what norm did this person violate, and how did he or she respond to your sanction?

2015). In a consumer culture, it is important that children be socialized into, and become actively involved in, consuming (Cook 2004; Pilcher 2013). Consumption by children has not always been valued, however. In fact, there were once strong norms against it. Children were not considered able to make informed choices about consumption and were therefore seen as even more susceptible than adults to exploitation by advertisers and marketers.

An important change began to take place in the mid-nineteenth century with the advent of department stores. Some stores offered supervised play areas so that parents could shop more easily. A key development by the mid-twentieth century was children's sections in department stores; they were eventually subdivided into shops for babies, children, and teens. Also during this period, radio programs, movies, and TV shows were

Some parents see buying and collecting certain toys, such as the American Girl dolls these girls are holding, as valuable activities. What cultural values are being promoted when young children are encouraged to participate actively in consumer culture?

NONTRADITIONAL SETTINGS FOR CONSUMPTION

An interesting aspect of consumer culture is the way in which it has spread beyond the economy to other aspects of society. For example, higher education is increasingly characterized by consumer culture. Students and their parents shop around for the best colleges and the most conspicuous degrees or for the best values in a college education. College rankings, such as those published by *Kiplinger* and *U.S. News & World Report,* are a big business. For-profit colleges have become a booming industry, with enterprises like the University of Phoenix and Kaplan University enrolling hundreds of thousands of students who pay for the opportunity to earn their degrees on a flexible schedule. Not long ago, students were largely passive recipients of what educational systems had to offer, but now they are more active consumers of education. For example, college students shop for the best classes, or the best class times, and regularly rate their professors (see Chapter 11).

A key site of consumption is now the internet (Miller and Slater 2000; Zuev 2015). A good portion of the time people spend online is related to consumption, either directly (e.g., purchasing items on sites such as Etsy or Amazon) or indirectly (e.g., buying World of Warcraft tokens with real dollars). Among the changes wrought by the internet is a great increase in consumer-to-consumer sales on sites such as eBay. In 2000, only 22 percent of Americans had used the internet to buy products online, including books, music, toys, and clothing. By 2013, that number had increased to 80 percent (Weinstein 2013). In 2014, 69 percent of American adults shopped online at least once per month (Mintel 2015). The growing importance of online consumption is reflected in the increasing amount spent each year on "Cyber Monday" (the Monday after Thanksgiving). Cyber Monday 2016 set a new record for online shopping, generating $3.45 billion in sales. In addition, in a process known as "contextual advertising," advertisements are often woven seamlessly into the content of internet sites—even into games designed for children.

increasingly directed at children. More recently, children have come to be targeted directly by advertisers on Saturday-morning TV shows and cable channels such as Nickelodeon that specialize in children's programming.

In fact, marketing aimed at children is now pervasive. For example, the Walt Disney Company directly markets baby products, and thus the Disney brand, to new mothers in maternity wards. In schools, branded products are sold at book fairs, and corporate sponsorships adorn everything from sports stadiums to classroom supplies. Brands and logos are woven into textbook problems and examples. Market researchers observe the way in which children use and respond to products and advertising messages, not just in focus groups and in the lab, but also in natural settings such as school and the home. Marketers have also discovered the importance of the "pester power" of children. This is the ability of children to nag their parents into buying things. It is effective not only for selling children's products but also for getting children to influence their parents' purchases.

Overall, children are much more immersed in consumer culture today than ever before. They learn at an early age to value it as well as the norms involved in participating in it. As adults, then, they will fit well into a culture with consumption at its core.

Beyond that, many websites carry pop-up ads for goods and services targeted to the interests of the individuals who are viewing the sites. More specifically, if you use Google to shop for shoes or Amazon for books, ads for shoes and books will pop up for days, or even months, later on many of the sites you visit.

YouTube offers several innovations in consumption, including "shopping haul" and "unboxing" videos. In shopping haul videos, consumers, often women, show viewers the results of their recent shopping trips. Haulers describe and display clothing, accessories, and cosmetics from popular chain stores (such as Superdry, Bebe, and Victoria's Secret) in malls and shopping strips around the world. Prices and bargains are mentioned frequently. Unboxing videos are a curious hybrid of unofficial marketing and product demonstration. Technology unboxers might demonstrate the features of new iPhones or computer games, while toy unboxers film children playing with various toys. Unboxers might assemble Lego kits or open up McDonald's Happy Meals and then have children play with the toys.

It could be argued that people in general, especially children and teens, are becoming more immersed in consumer culture as they become more deeply enmeshed with the internet. This is even more the case now because we increasingly carry the internet—and the ability to shop there—with us all the time on our smartphones. As a result, consumer culture has become an even more inescapable part of our daily lives. Furthermore, consumption on the internet is increasingly wedded to the material world. You can pay for parking and rental cars using smartphone apps. An iPhone app allows a driver to open the doors of her rented Zipcar with her phone and honk the car's horn to locate it. The Hunt is an app that brings into play a community of fashion-minded people to help hunt down desired fashion items.

ASK YOURSELF

How much of the time you spend online is devoted to shopping or purchasing? Try keeping a log of your internet use for a few days. Note how many times you went online and on how many of those occasions you bought something or browsed sites devoted to consumption. Are you a typical internet consumer? Why or why not?

A POSTCONSUMER CULTURE?

Many people are also doing something that would have been unthinkable only a few years ago—saving money. The personal savings rate in the United States has changed over the past few years. In late 2007, it dipped to close to 3 percent of disposable income. At the height of the Great Recession in 2008 and 2009, it spiked to more than 8 percent. By mid-2015, even though the economy had improved considerably, the personal savings rate still exceeded 5 percent. People who are saving more of their money are obviously using less of it to consume.

These changes in the behavior of consumers and their attitudes speak to a change in the larger value system. Consuming less is a sure indication of at least a temporary decline of consumer culture. It may even be the beginning of a postconsumer culture. Among the characteristics of such a culture, beyond buying less and saving more, are sharing more things in the "sharing economy" (Belk 2014; Sundarajan 2016), renting consumer items (such as dresses on sites like Rent the Runway), taking pride in buying less expensive or even recycled items, buying less showy brands (a Kia rather than a BMW), purchasing preowned clothing and shoes at vintage shops or on thredUP, dining at home more often than eating at restaurants, and showing a greater concern for the environment in terms of what we buy and, more important, do not buy. It is not clear that we are in a postconsumer culture, and if we are, it is uncertain how long it will last. However, just as we entered what is best described as a consumer culture in the last half of the twentieth century, it is at least possible that we are entering a postconsumer culture in the first half of the twenty-first century.

CULTURE JAMMING

Another chink in consumer culture has been created by organized groups actively seeking to subvert aspects of both consumer culture and the larger culture. The success of Burning Man is one indication of such subversion. Begun in 1986, this annual weeklong event in Nevada's Black Rock Desert today attracts 50,000 participants, who commit themselves during their stay to self-expression, decommodification (for example, cash transactions between participants are banned), and community building (Chen 2009; Jones 2011).

"Absolut Impotence" is an example of culture jamming intended to counter the alcohol industry's influence by suggesting that alcohol will negatively impact drinkers' sex lives. Is this an effective way to change consumption?

This is an example of **culture jamming**, which radically transforms mass media messages, often turning them on their heads completely (Kuehn 2015; Lasn 2000). It is a form of social protest aimed at revealing underlying realities of which consumers may be unaware. The hope is that once people are made aware of these realities by culture jamming, they will change their behaviors or perhaps even band together to change those underlying realities.

The best examples of culture jamming are to be found in the magazine *Adbusters* and the media campaigns it sponsors. The magazine's main targets are in the realm of consumption, especially web and magazine advertisements and billboards. The idea is to transform a corporation's ads into anticorporate, anticonsumption advertisements (Handelman and Kozinets 2007).

The following are some additional examples of the ways in which culture jamming turns commercial messages inside out:

- "Tommy Sheep" is a spoof of a Tommy Hilfiger ad, with sheep (presumably representing the conformists who buy such clothing) pictured in front of a huge American flag.

- "Absolute on Ice," spoofing an Absolut vodka ad, depicts the foot of a corpse (presumably someone killed by excessive alcohol consumption) with a toe tag.

- People for the Ethical Treatment of Animals (PETA) uses the Burger King logo with the phrase "Murder King" to raise awareness of animal brutality in the beef industry.

All these examples show the hidden realities (sickness, death, and other miseries) and goals (conformist consumers, obscene profits) of corporations. A broader objective is to show viewers the folly of consumer culture, which encourages the consumption of numerous harmful and wasteful goods and services. In addition to advertisements, culture jammers create memes to spread ideas and information that challenge the status quo (Lasn 2012). For example, one meme designed by culture jammers depicts a photo of Walmart with the following words: "One of the biggest companies in the world owned by one of the richest families in America . . . holds food drive for needy employees instead of paying them a living wage" (CursedByTheDiceGods 2017).

CYBERCULTURE

The internet is, as mentioned before, one site for the proliferation of consumer culture and perhaps postconsumer culture. It is also the site of an entirely new culture—**cyberculture** (F. Turner 2008). That is, the internet as a whole (as well as the individual websites that it comprises) has the characteristics of all culture, including distinctive values and norms.

Some of the distinctive values within cyberculture are openness, knowledge sharing, and access. These values have their roots in the open-source software that emerged before computing became an attractive commercial opportunity. They are also rooted in the knowledge sharing and continuous improvement that were the practice when early computer professionals survived through reciprocity (Bergquist 2003). These roots have been maintained through the open-source movement, through actions against censorship, and through organizations such as the Free Software Foundation and the "copyleft" movement. In line with the values of a postconsumer society, these "cyber-libertarians" favor user control of information and applications and free products (Dahlberg 2010; Himanen 2001). They are in conflict with the more dominant values of profit maximization and control of the internet by large corporations. This conflict of values, a culture war by the definition offered earlier in this chapter, goes a long way toward defining the internet today.

Various norms have also come to be a part of cyberculture. Internet users are not supposed to hack into websites, create and disseminate spam, unleash destructive worms and viruses, maliciously and erroneously edit user-generated sites such as Wikipedia, and so on. Many norms relate to desirable behavior on the internet. For example, creating and editing entries on Wikipedia is supposed to be taken seriously and done to the best of one's ability. Once an entry exists, the many people who offer additions and deletions are expected to do so in a similar spirit. Those who purposely add erroneous information on Wikipedia will suffer the stern disapproval of other contributors to, and users of, the site. They may even be banned from the site by those who manage it.

There is, of course, much more to the culture of the internet. For example, in addition to a general cyberculture, there are a number of cybercultures that vary from nation to nation. But the point is that cyberculture, like all culture, is emerging and evolving as other changes take place within and around it. The biggest difference between cyberculture and other cultures is that because the internet is so new and the changes in it are so rapid, cyberculture is far more fluid than culture in general.

People need to be socialized in order to learn how to use the internet, and they increasingly interact online rather than on a face-to-face basis. In Chapter 4 we turn to a broad discussion of the sociological perspective on socialization and interaction.

SUMMARY

Culture encompasses the ideas, values, norms, practices, and objects that allow a group of people, or even an entire society, to carry out their collective lives with a minimum of friction. Values are the general, abstract standards defining what a group or society as a whole considers good, right, or important. Norms are the rules that guide what people do and how they live. Culture has material and symbolic elements. Material culture encompasses all the objects and technologies that are manifestations of a culture. Symbolic culture, the nonmaterial side of culture, is best represented by language.

We are surrounded by cultural differences. Subcultures include people who may accept much of the dominant culture but are set apart from it by one or more culturally significant characteristics. Countercultures are groups of people who differ in certain ways from the dominant culture and whose norms and values may be incompatible with it. Culture wars pit one subculture or counterculture against another or against the dominant culture.

Many societies tend to be ethnocentric—those living in them believe that their own culture's norms, values, and traditions are better than those of other cultures. Many times newcomers are expected to assimilate, or to replace elements of their own culture with elements of the dominant culture. Groups that do not want to assimilate entirely may engage in identity politics, or try to use their power to strengthen the position of the cultural groups with which they identify. A society that values multiculturalism accepts and even embraces the cultures of many different groups and encourages cultural diversity. Multicultural societies often embrace cultural relativism, or the belief that there are no cultural universals.

Some scholars argue that globalization has increasingly led to a global culture of shared norms and values. Others attribute the growing cultural similarity around the world to cultural imperialism, or the imposition of one dominant culture on other cultures. American culture, in particular, has been exported around the world. But some countries have challenged this process of Americanization with anti-American sentiment and emphasis on their own culture.

Emerging cultural issues today include the growth and significance of consumer culture and cyberculture in our daily lives. Consumer goods provide many of us with a sense of meaning and identity. The internet is a new setting where consumers are increasingly purchasing goods. This is contributing to the norms and values that constitute cyberculture, which also involves online activities such as sharing information on Wikipedia and interacting with others on social media.

KEY TERMS

Americanization, 79
anti-Americanism, 79
assimilation, 76
consumer culture, 80
counterculture, 72
cultural imperialism, 79
cultural relativism, 78

culture, 64
culture jamming, 84
culture war, 73
cyberculture, 84
ethnocentrism, 78
folkways, 68
ideal culture, 70

identity politics, 78
ideology, 71
language, 69
laws, 67
material culture, 68
mores, 68
multiculturalism, 74

norms, 67
real culture, 70
sanctions, 67
subculture, 71
symbolic culture, 69
values, 66

REVIEW QUESTIONS

1. What do you and your peers think of the millennial culture depicted in HBO's *Girls*? Are you as "uncool" as the characters on that show? You are likely the right age to be considered a millennial, but do you feel that you are part of that culture?

2. How and why might the American value of democracy have created tensions in Iraq and Afghanistan?

3. As part of our material culture, what values do smartphones reflect? In what ways have "brand communities" or other subcultures formed around smartphones and their use?

4. Consider the terminology that has developed around the internet. How does this language reflect changes in the world around us? In what ways does it shape the world around us?

5. Skateboarders constitute a subculture because they have certain cultural differences (in language, dress, and values) that set them apart from other groups in society. What is another example of a subculture in the United States, and what elements of this culture (both material and symbolic) make it unique?

6. How does a counterculture differ from a subculture? Is it reasonable to say that computer hackers are part of a counterculture? Can you think of other examples of countercultures?

7. What is the difference between assimilation and multiculturalism? Would you say that the United States is an assimilationist or a multiculturalist society? Would you say that multiculturalism is more a part of the ideal culture or the real culture of the United States? Why?

8. What are some of today's important culture wars? In what ways and to what degree are you engaged in them? Even if you are not active in them, how is your life affected by them?

9. What do we mean by the term *global culture*? Do you think the evolution of popular social networking sites such as Facebook and Twitter is related more to the evolution of a global culture or to Americanization? In what ways are these sites reflective of cultural hybridization?

10. To what extent are you and your friends embedded in a consumer culture? How has the development of technology (the internet, smartphones, and so forth) helped create this consumer culture?

$SAGE edge™ Want a better grade?

Get the tools you need to sharpen your study skills. Access practice quizzes, eFlashcards, video, and multimedia at **edge.sagepub.com/ritzeressentials3e.**

PRACTICE AND APPLY WHAT YOU'VE LEARNED

▶ edge.sagepub.com/ ritzeressentials3e

SOCIALIZATION AND INTERACTION

Socialization and Variance

Mack Beggs won his weight class in the Texas state wrestling championships in February 2017—in the girls' league. Mack is a 17-year-old transgender boy, but state rules bar him from competing in the boys' league. The rules say that boys cannot compete against girls, and that students are required to compete as the gender noted on their birth certificate. After Beggs's final competition in an undefeated season, the crowd erupted in both cheers and boos.

Beggs, who began transitioning a year and a half prior to the championship, has been taking testosterone as part of that process. Some felt he shouldn't have been competing against girls, that testosterone gave him an unfair advantage. A few parents even attempted legal injunctions to prevent Beggs from competing. Ignoring the controversy, Beggs credited his success to his teammates, noting that they all worked hard together. While the public, schools, and politicians debate the fluidity of gender, transgender students like Beggs face pressure to fit in with the social expectations of their peers, families, and the wider world—and the repercussions when they don't.

The majority of transgender students from kindergarten through twelfth grade who were out or perceived as transgender while in school experience some form of

LEARNING OBJECTIVES

4.1 Describe the development of the self.

4.2 Discuss the concept of the individual as performer.

4.3 Explain the significance of socialization in childhood and adulthood.

4.4 Describe the key aspects of interaction with others.

4.5 Identify micro-level social structures.

edge.sagepub.com/
ritzeressentials3e

- Take the chapter quiz
- Review key terms with eFlashcards
- Explore multimedia links and SAGE readings

$SAGE edge™

mistreatment. In 2015, 54 percent acknowledged being verbally harassed; 24 percent said they had been physically attacked; and 13 percent were sexually assaulted because they were transgender. Some, 17 percent, experienced such severe treatment that they left school (James et al. 2016). Such mistreatment due to gender identity or expression is not restricted to peers and schools, but may also pervade family and work life. Transgender people have an attempted suicide rate *nine times* that of the general U.S. population.

Yet despite sometimes violent disapproval from the dominant society, many transgender people continue to express their gender identity. Research suggests a biological basis for transgender identity. At the same time, behavior and experiences are as influential as biology. You are who you are because of the people, institutions, and social structures that have surrounded you since birth (and even before). You have been socialized to look, think, act, and interact in ways that allow you to live harmoniously, at least most of the time, with those around you. However, at times you may come into contact with those who socialize you into ways that are at variance with the dominant culture. In extreme cases, such socialization can lead to actions like those taken by abusers of transgender people. Discovering how socialization and social interaction shape who we are and how we act, as we will do in this chapter, is the most basic level of sociological analysis. But, in fact, sociologists are concerned with everything along the micro-macro continuum, which was introduced in Chapter 1. That includes the individual's mind and self, interactions among individuals, and interactions within and between groups, formally structured organizations, entire societies, and the world as a whole, as well as all the new global relationships of the "global age."

Sociology's micro-macro continuum means that rather than being clearly distinct, social phenomena tend to blend into one another, often without

our noticing. For example, the interaction that takes place in a group is difficult to distinguish from the group itself. The relationships between countries are difficult to distinguish from their regional and even global connections. Everything in the social world, and on the micro-macro continuum, interpenetrates. ●

This chapter and the next will introduce you, at least briefly, to the full range of sociological concerns along the **micro–macro continuum**. We will start with the smallest-scale social phenomena and work our way to ever larger ones as these two chapters progress.

THE INDIVIDUAL AND THE SELF

Sociologists rarely, if ever, concern themselves with any particular individual. Rather, their concern is with individuals in general. A primary sociological question is what, if anything, distinguishes humans as individuals from other animals. Some would argue it stems from characteristics such as a larger brain or an opposable thumb. However, most sociologists believe the essential difference between humans and other animals is the distinctive interaction humans are capable of having with other humans.

An important source of this view is data about individuals who grew up in social isolation and did not experience normal human interaction during their development. For instance, we have information on cases in which children have been locked in closets or in single rooms for much or all of their childhoods (Curtiss 1977; Davis 1940, 1947). In a more recent example, five children, ages 2 through 13, were discovered by authorities in York, Pennsylvania. They had lived their entire lives with their parents in a single room in a private home without any functioning utilities; their water source was rain dripping through the roof. The children had no birth certificates and had received no formal schooling, and there was no evidence that they had ever received any medical care, including vaccinations. They suffered from physical and mental health problems and were not where they should have been in terms of educational level ("Police Discover Five Children" 2010).

Of related interest is the existence of feral, or wild, children—that is, children who have been raised by animals in the wilderness (Benzaquen 2006; Dombrowski, Gischlar, and Mrazik 2011; Friedmann and Rusou 2015; Newton 2002). Oxana Malaya is from a small village in Ukraine (Grice 2006). In 1986, after being abandoned by her parents at age three, she crawled into a hovel housing dogs. The "Dog Girl" lived there for five years before a neighbor reported her existence. When she emerged, she could hardly speak. Like the dogs she lived with, she barked, ate with her tongue, and ran about on all fours. Years later, when she was living in a home for the mentally disabled, Oxana was found to have the mental capacity of a six-year-old. Among other things, she could not spell her name or read. She was able to communicate like other humans and talk because she had acquired some speech before she began living with dogs. She had also learned to eat with her hands and to walk upright (Lane 1975; Shattuck 1980).

The concept of feral children relates to the fundamental question of the relationship between "nature" and "nurture." The nature argument is that we are born to be the kinds of human beings that we ultimately become; it is built into our "human nature" (Settle et al. 2010). The nurture argument is that we are human beings because of the way we are nurtured—that is, the way we are raised by other human beings, who teach us what it is to be human. Of course, both nature and nurture are important (Meloni 2014). However, the cases of feral children indicate that nurture is in many ways more important than nature in determining the human beings we become.

SYMBOLIC INTERACTION AND DEVELOPMENT OF THE SELF

As the example of feral and isolated children suggests, development as a human presupposes the existence of other humans and interaction with and among them. This is the domain of symbolic interactionism, which developed many ideas of great relevance to this view of humans. In general, the interaction that takes place between parents and children is loaded with symbols and symbolic meaning.

One early symbolic interactionist, Charles Horton Cooley (1864–1929), explained how parents help children develop the ability to interact with others with his famous concept of the **looking-glass self**. This is the idea that as humans we develop a self-image that reflects how others see and respond to us. We imagine how we appear to others and how they evaluate our appearance. Based on that, we develop some sort of self-feeling, such as pride or embarrassment. Because children's earliest interactions are typically with their parents, it is that interaction that is most important in the formation of a self-image. This helps explain why feral children and others who spend their formative years in prolonged social isolation are unlikely to form a fully developed self-image: There are no others to respond to them. It is as we interact with others, especially when we are young, that we develop a sense of our selves.

The major thinker associated with symbolic interactionism (see Chapter 2) is one of Cooley's contemporaries, George Herbert Mead (1863–1931). Mead ([1934] 1962, 7) was very concerned with the micro level (the individual, the mind, the self). He prioritized the social, including interaction, and the importance of symbols in social interaction. In fact, it is this prioritization of the social that distinguishes sociologists from psychologists in their studies of individuals and interaction.

Humans and Nonhumans

Mead distinguished between humans and nonhumans. However, both are capable of making gestures (such as by raising a limb). By **gestures**, Mead meant the movements of one individual that elicit automatic and appropriate responses from another individual.

Both animals and humans are capable of not only gestures but also *conversations of gestures*, whereby they use a series of gestures to relate to one another. Thus, the snarl of one dog may lead a second dog to snarl in return. That second snarl might lead the first dog to become physically ready to attack or be attacked. In terms of humans, Mead gave the example of a boxing match, where the

George Herbert Mead's ideas strongly influenced the development of sociological theory, especially symbolic interactionism. His most famous work, *Mind, Self, and Society*, originated as lectures from his teachings at the University of Chicago.

cocking of one boxer's arm may cause the other boxer to raise an arm to block the anticipated blow. That raised arm might cause the first boxer to throw a different punch or even to hold back on the punch. A less aggressive example can be found in the realm of flirting (Delaney 2012; Henningsen 2004), where one person's prolonged eye contact (a subtle gesture) may cause another person to return the eye contact. The returned gaze might cause the first flirter to look away and, perhaps, quickly glance again at the other person. As in the case of animals, the gestures of boxers and those who flirt (among many others) are instantaneous and involve few, if any, conscious thought processes.

In addition to physical gestures, animals and humans are both capable of vocal gestures. The bark of a dog and the grunt of a human (boxer) are both vocal gestures. In both cases, a conversation of vocal gestures is possible, as the bark of one dog (or the grunt of a boxer) elicits the bark (or grunt) of another. However, when humans (and animals) make facial gestures (such as originating eye contact in an effort to flirt), they cannot *see* their own facial gestures. In contrast, both animals and humans can *hear* their own vocal gestures. As a result, misunderstanding is more likely when people rely on facial

rather than vocal gestures. For example, men may be more likely than women to interpret making eye contact as sexual in nature.

It is the vocal gesture that truly begins to separate humans from animals. In humans, but not other animals, the vocal gesture can affect the speaker as much and in the same way as the hearer. Thus, humans react to and interpret their own vocal gestures and, more important, their words. Furthermore, humans have a far greater ability to control their vocal gestures. We can stop ourselves from uttering sounds or saying various things, and we can alter what we say as we are saying it. Animals do not possess this capacity. In short, only humans are able to develop a language out of vocal gestures; animals remain restricted to isolated vocal gestures.

ASK YOURSELF

In what ways do you interact with your pets in the same way you interact with humans? In what ways is the interaction different? Do you find it more satisfying to interact with people or with pets?

Symbolic Interaction

Of greatest importance in distinguishing humans from animals is a kind of gesture that can be made *only* by humans. Mead calls such a gesture a **significant symbol**, a gesture that arouses in the individual making it a response of the same kind as the one it is supposed to elicit from those to whom it is addressed. It is only with significant symbols, especially those that are vocal, that we can have communication in the full sense of the term. In Mead's view, ants, bees, dogs, and apes are unable to communicate by means of such symbols (Gerhardt and Huber 2002).

Over time, humans develop a set of vocal significant symbols, or language. According to Mead, language involves significant symbols that call out the same meaning in the person to whom an utterance is aimed as they do in the person making the utterance. The utterances have meaning to all parties involved. In a conversation of gestures, only the gestures are communicated. With language, both the (vocal) gestures and the meanings are communicated. One of the key functions of language is that it makes the mind and mental processes possible.

Essentials of Sociology

To Mead, thinking (and the mind; see the following discussion) is nothing more than internalized conversations individual humans have with themselves.

ASK YOURSELF

What did George Herbert Mead mean by saying that thinking is so much like talking to yourself that it is little different from talking to other people? Do you agree with him? Why or why not? Think of some examples and counterexamples.

Symbols also make possible **symbolic interaction**, or interaction on the basis of significant symbols. It also allows for much more complex interaction patterns than those that occur where interaction is based only on gestures. Because people can think about and interpret significant symbols, they can interact with large numbers of people and make complex plans for some future undertaking. They can interpret the symbolic meaning of what others say and do and understand, for example, that some of them are acting in accord with their own plans. Animals lack the ability to make and understand complex plans.

Mind and Self

Central to Mead's ideas about the development of human beings, and the differences between humans and nonhumans, are the concepts of mind and self. As pointed out previously, the **mind** is an internal conversation using words (and also images, especially, but certainly not only, for the autistic and the deaf; Fernyhough 2014; Grandin 2000). That internal conversation arises, is related to, and is continuous with interactions, especially conversations that one has with others in the social world. Thus, the social world and its relationships and interactions precede the mind and not vice versa. This perspective stands in contrast to the conventional view that prioritizes the brain and argues that we think first and then engage in social relationships. It also differs from the view that the mind and the brain are one and the same thing. The brain is a physiological organ that exists within us, but the mind is a social phenomenon. It is part of, and would not exist without, the social world. While the brain is an intracranial phenomenon, the mind is not.

The **self** is the ability to take oneself as an object. The self develops over time. Key to the development of self is the ability to imagine being in the place of others and looking at oneself as they do. In other words, people need to take the role of others in order to get a sense of their own selves. There are two key stages in Mead's theory of how the self develops over time, the **play stage** and the **game stage**:

1. *Play stage.* Babies are not born with the ability to think of themselves as having a self. However, as children develop, they learn to take on the attitudes of specific others toward themselves. Thus, young children play at being Mommy and Daddy, adopt their parents' attitudes, and evaluate themselves as do their parents. However, the result is a very fragmented sense of the self. It varies depending on the specific other (e.g., Mommy *or* Daddy) being taken into consideration. Young children lack a more general and organized sense of themselves.

2. *Game stage.* Children begin to develop a self in the full sense of the term when they take on the roles of a group of people simultaneously rather than the roles of discrete individuals. Each of those different roles comes to be seen as having a definite relationship to all the others. Children develop organized personalities because of their ability to take on multiple roles—indeed, the entirety of roles in a given group. The developed personality does not vary with the individual role that a child happens to be taking. This development allows children to function in organized groups. Most important, it greatly affects what they will do within specific groups.

Mead offers the example of a baseball game to illustrate his point about the game stage of development. It is not enough in a baseball game for you to know what you are supposed to do in your position on the field. In order to play your position, you must know what those who play all other positions on the team are going to do. In other words, a player, every player, must take on the roles of all the other players. For example, a shortstop must know that the center fielder is going to catch a particular fly ball; that he is going to be backed up by the left fielder; that because the runner on second is going to "tag up," the center fielder is going to throw the ball to third base; and that it is his job as shortstop to back up the third baseman. This ability to take on multiple roles obviously applies in a baseball game, but it applies as well in a playgroup, a work setting, and every other social setting.

The Generalized Other

Mead also developed the concept of the **generalized other**, or the attitude of the entire group or community. The generalized other includes the roles, prescriptions, and proscriptions that individuals use to develop their own behaviors, attitudes, and so forth. Individuals take the role of the generalized other. That is, they look at themselves and what they do from the perspective of the group or community. In taking the perspective of the generalized other, children begin developing more complete selves. The generalized other becomes central to the development of self during the game stage. In the baseball example, the generalized other is the attitude of the team. Having members who can take the role of the generalized other is also essential to the development of the group, especially in its organized activities. The group can function more effectively and efficiently because it is highly likely that individual members will understand and do what is expected of them. In turn, individuals can operate more efficiently within the group because they can better anticipate what others will do.

This discussion might lead you to think that the demands of the generalized other produce conformists. However, Mead argues that while selves within a group share some commonalities, each self is different because each has a unique biographical history and experience. Furthermore, there are many groups and communities in society and therefore many generalized others. Your generalized other in a baseball game is different from your generalized other in a classroom or in the family.

The "I" and the "Me"

Critical to understanding the difference between conformity and creative thinking and acting is Mead's distinction between two aspects, or phases, of the self—the "I" and the "me." The "I" and the "me" are subprocesses that are involved in the larger thinking process. An individual sometimes displays more of the "I" aspect of the self and sometimes more of the "me" aspect. In any given instance, the relative mix of "I" and "me" determines the degree to which an individual acts creatively (more "I") or more as a conformist (more "me").

The **"I"** is the immediate response of an individual to others. It is that part of the self that is unconscious, incalculable, unpredictable, and creative. Neither the person nor the members of the group know in advance what that response of the "I" is going to be. As a result of the "I," people often surprise themselves, and certainly others, with the unexpected things they say and do.

Mead greatly values the "I" for various reasons, including the fact that it is the source of new and original responses. The **"me"** is the organized set of others' attitudes and behaviors adopted by the individual. In other words, the "me" involves the acceptance and internalization by the individual of the generalized other. To Mead, the "me" involves a conscious understanding of what a person's responsibilities are to the larger group. The behaviors associated with the "me" also tend to be habitual and conventional. We all have a "me," but conformists have an overly powerful "me."

It is through the "me" that society is able to dominate the individual.

In Mead's game stage of the development of the self, we learn how to work with others by understanding their roles as well as our own. Do you think this learning process is ever complete?

In fact, Mead defines *social control* as the dominance of the "I" by the "me." Nevertheless, people and society as a whole need both "I" and "me." For the individual, the "me" allows for a comfortable existence within various social groupings. The "I" lends some spice to what might otherwise be a boring existence. For society, the "me" provides the conformity needed for stable and orderly interaction. The "I" is the source of changes in society as it develops and adapts to the shifting environment.

While the "me" generally provides the individual with some comfort and security, that is less the case in consumer society (Trentmann 2016). The reason is that consumer society is all about change, and as a result the "me" is constantly changing. For example, one might be expected to adopt a given fashion at one time, but soon an entirely different fashion comes to be expected. Instead of attaining stability, "consumers must never be allowed to rest" (Bauman 1999, 38). Of course, the "I" always impels the individual in unpredictable directions, such as making unusual fashion statements. However, in consumer society *both* the "I" and the "me" are at least somewhat unpredictable. This serves to make many people uneasy because they lack, at least as far as fashion is concerned, the comfort of a strong and stable "me."

THE INDIVIDUAL AS PERFORMER

Erving Goffman (1922–1982) is another important contributor to the symbolic interactionists' understanding of the self and how it develops (Jacobsen and Kristiansen 2015). Goffman's work on the self was deeply influenced by Mead's thinking, especially the tension between the "I" and the "me." In Goffman's work, this distinction takes the form of the tension between what we want to do spontaneously and what people expect us to do (Goffman 1959).

Goffman developed the notion of **dramaturgy**, which views an individual's social life as a series of dramatic performances akin to those that take place on a theatrical stage. To Goffman, the self is not a thing possessed by the individual but the dramatic product of the interaction between people and their audiences. While many performances of the self are successful, there is always the possibility that performances can

One of the most influential sociologists of the twentieth century, Erving Goffman, employed qualitative methods, particularly ethnography, in much of his research. One of his main research topics was the sociology of everyday life, or the way in which people manage the impressions they make on others in face-to-face interactions.

be disrupted by the actions of audiences. For example, audiences can jeer at performances or even walk out on them. Goffman focuses on these possibilities and what people can do to prevent them by improving their dramatic performances or to deal with disruptions once they occur.

IMPRESSION MANAGEMENT

When people interact with others, they use a variety of techniques to control the images of themselves that they want to project during their social performances. They seek to maintain these impressions even when they encounter problems in their performances. Goffman (1959) called these efforts to maintain certain images **impression management**.

For example, in your sociology class, you might typically project an image of a serious, well-prepared student. Then one night you might stay up late partying and not get the required reading done before class. When the instructor asks a question in class, you might try to maintain your image by pretending to write busily in your notebook rather than raising your hand. Called on nonetheless, you struggle, in vain, to give a well-thought-out, serious

Alone Together: Why We Expect More from Technology and Less from Each Other (Basic Books, 2012)

Sherry Turkle (Abby Rockefeller Mauzé Professor of the Social Studies of Science and Technology at Massachusetts Institute of Technology; PhD, Harvard University, 1976)

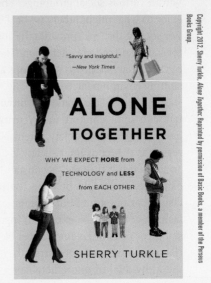

One controversial issue today is whether or not technology is contributing to a decline in meaningful social relationships. Some experts argue that technology can help us build and maintain social networks, but in *Alone Together,* Sherry Turkle offers a critical look at how different technologies are leaving us detached and afraid of face-to-face social interactions. Turkle finds that some people prefer interacting with social robots instead of real humans because they do not have to deal with unpredictable emotions that might make them feel vulnerable—robots love unconditionally, and they never die. These social robots are so technologically sophisticated that they can follow our gaze and even talk to us, making it seem like they can empathize and understand our feelings. Turkle warns that intimacy with machines is no substitute for human intimacy and that machine-human relationships cause us to reduce our expectations from other humans.

When we do engage in social interactions with other humans, many of us often do so using technology, such as smartphones or computers. These machine-mediated exchanges allow us to communicate quickly and conveniently, but not very expressively. While communicating via text, social media, and e-mail can be quite practical, it is also more impersonal and less spontaneous than face-to-face interactions. For example, announcing a pregnancy on Facebook might be efficient, but it might also be insensitive if a person has not personally told close family members and friends first. New technologies allow us to edit and manage our impressions more than face-to-face interactions, even if we cannot always verify how they are interpreted. Our online audience generally does not challenge our performances and most likely confirms our impressions of our selves by "liking" what we post (if they respond at all). Social media might provide us with thousands of virtual connections; however, most of these are weak ties that require nothing consequential from us. This is why many of us feel alone at the same time that we are digitally connected.

Supplementary Resources

- Turkle explains the key themes of her book *Alone Together* in her TED Talk, "Connected, but Alone?" (www.ted.com/talks/sherry_turkle_alone_together?language=en).
- Turkle elaborates on the social implications of the digital revolution in a *Frontline* interview (www.pbs.org/wgbh/pages/frontline/digitalnation/interviews/turkle.html).

answer to the question. The smiles and snickers of fellow students who know that you were out partying late the night before might well disrupt the performance you are endeavoring to put on. To deflect attention from you to them, you might suggest that they try to answer the question.

While the idea of impression management is generally associated with face-to-face social interaction, it also applies to interaction on social networking sites. For instance, many people constantly change the pictures on their Facebook pages to alter the images of themselves being conveyed to others (Cunningham 2013).

ASK YOURSELF

What impression management activities do you undertake? Have they generally been successful? Do you see yourself performing more of these activities as time goes on, or fewer? Why?

FRONT AND BACK STAGE

Continuing the theatrical analogy, Goffman (1959) argued that in every performance there is a **front stage**, where the social performance tends to be idealized and designed to define the situation for those who are observing it. When you are in class, as in the previous example, you are typically performing on your front stage. Your audience is the teacher and perhaps other students. As a rule, people feel they must present an idealized sense of themselves when they are front stage (e.g., by giving that seemingly well-thought-out answer). Because this performance is idealized, things that do not fit the image must be hidden (such as the fact that you were partying the night before and are now unprepared to answer questions intelligently).

Also of concern to Goffman is the back stage. In the **back stage**, people feel free to express themselves in ways that are suppressed in the front (Cahill et al. 1985). Thus, after class you might well confess to your friends in the cafeteria that you had been partying and faked your answer to a question asked in class. If somehow your front-stage audience—the instructor, in this case—sees your back-stage performance, your ability to maintain the impression you are trying to project in the classroom, in the front stage, is likely to become difficult or impossible in the future.

The existence of two stages, front and back, causes us all sorts of tensions and problems. We are always afraid that those in the front stage will find out about our back stage, or that elements of the back stage will intrude on the front stage.

While the distinction between front and back stage is important, bear in mind that these are not "real" places, nor are they rigidly separated from one another. That is, what is the front stage at one point in time can become the back stage at another. Nevertheless, in general, people are most likely to perform in an idealized manner on their front stage when they are most concerned about making positive impressions. They are likely to perform more freely back stage, among those who are more accepting of less-than-ideal behavior and attitudes.

SOCIALIZATION

Socialization is the process by which an individual learns and generally comes to accept the ways of a group or a society of which he or she is a part. It is during the socialization process that children develop a self as they learn the need, for example, to take on the role of the generalized other. Socialization almost always involves a process of interaction, as those with knowledge and experience teach those with a need to acquire that knowledge or to learn from others' experiences.

While socialization occurs throughout an individual's lifetime, it can generally be divided into two parts. Socialization during childhood sets the course for a lifetime and has been a central focus for researchers. However, researchers have increasingly pointed to a variety of ways in which adults continue to learn how to function within their society.

CHILDHOOD SOCIALIZATION

A central concern in the study of socialization is those who do the socializing, or the **agents of socialization** (Wunder 2007). The first and often most effective agents of socialization are the child's parents, as well as other family members and friends. These are defined as primary agents of socialization. In addition, broader, less personal influences, such as the educational system, the media (Prot et al. 2015), and consumer culture, are important in socialization. These are defined as secondary agents of socialization. All play a part in creating an individual who can effectively operate within and shape culture. Except for education, which will be discussed in Chapter 13, we will examine each of these various agents of socialization in the following discussion.

Primary Socialization and the Family

In a process known as **primary socialization**, newborns, infants, and young children acquire language, identities, cultural routines, norms, and values as they interact with parents and other family members (Laible, Thompson, and Froimson 2015; Lubbers, Jaspers, and Ultee 2009). This socialization lays the foundation for later personality development. Early socialization performs various functions for society, such as equipping the young to fit better into society and perpetuating the culture from one generation to the next.

In addition to a great deal of primary socialization, parents provide **anticipatory socialization**— that is, they teach children what will be expected of them in the future. Anticipatory socialization is how parents prepare children for the very important developmental changes (puberty, for example) that they will experience. Among the many other things that must be anticipated in family socialization are entrance into grade school, high school, college, the work world, and life as an independent adult. Anticipatory socialization helps prepare children not only for changes within society but also for changes within the family and changes that will affect them more directly.

Many assumptions about primary and anticipatory socialization are changing dramatically as the nature of families and the way they are understood culturally undergo major transformations. The socialization process was thought to be rather straightforward when the ideal of the nuclear family, composed of a mother, a father, and two or more children all living in the same home, predominated, as it did throughout much of the twentieth century. The lesson children were required to learn, at least as far as the family was concerned, was that when they became adults, they would go on to reproduce the same kind of nuclear family as the one in which they grew up. However, assumptions about the goodness and inevitability of the nuclear family and the ease of the socialization process now seem impossible to accept (McLanahan 1999). This is the case because of increasing public awareness of the many problems associated with the nuclear family, such as divorce, abuse, and unhappiness (see Chapter 10).

Then there is the expansion of what were at one time called "alternative family forms" (e.g., single-parent households, grandparents as primary caregivers) and the increasing centrality of day-care centers and their workers to the socialization process (Patterson, Farr, and Hastings 2015). The agencies doing the socializing today are much more complex and varied than they were in the era of the predominance of the nuclear family. As a result, socialization is not as straightforward as it once was thought to be. In addition, at one time socialization was seen as one-directional, for example, from parent to child. Current thinking sees such socialization among intimates as two-directional, even multidirectional, with, for example, parents socializing children and children socializing parents, other adults, and families (Gentina and Muratore 2012). For example, children tend to be far more familiar than their elders with the latest advances in digital technology, and they teach their parents much about both the technology itself and the digital culture. Another example is found in the large number of immigrant families in the United States and elsewhere. Children in these families are more likely than their parents to learn the language and culture of their new country (often in school). As a result, they are frequently the ones to teach, or at least try to teach, that knowledge to their parents (Mather 2009). This is **reverse socialization**, in which those who are normally being socialized are instead doing the socializing.

ASK YOURSELF

Have you experienced any instances of reverse socialization? For instance, have you taught your parents how to use their smartphones or set up Facebook pages, or has a younger relative or friend introduced you to a new smartphone app? What was this experience like?

Peers

A good deal of socialization within the schools takes place informally, through children's interaction with fellow students (see Chapter 11 for a discussion of the role of schools and teachers in the process of socialization). This is a situation where primary agents of socialization (peers) compete with secondary agents of socialization (teachers and other employees of the school system; Bukowski et al. 2015). Such informal socialization grows increasingly important as students progress through the school years, especially the high school years. Peers are also important sources of socialization in contexts outside of school, such as athletic teams of various kinds (Fine 1987). For example, researchers have found that children involved in contact sports, such as football and wrestling, are socialized to be more physically aggressive in everyday life (Kreager 2007). Male students who participate in contact sports such as football (and their friends) are more likely to get into serious fights than are nonathletic males or males involved in noncontact sports such as baseball, basketball, and tennis.

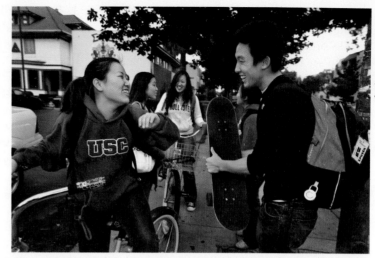

Peers are highly influential in the socialization process, especially during adolescence and early adulthood. What role do you think fellow students play in your socialization? Which ones will most influence you?

As the child matures and spends an increasing amount of time in the company of friends, peer socialization is increasingly likely to conflict with what is being taught at home and in the schools. Adolescents raised in a family with strong support tend to experience less peer pressure than those living in a weaker family climate (Pushpa and Singh 2017). Youths with less family support might find themselves susceptible to participating in risky and delinquent behavior with their peers, such as smoking, drinking alcohol, or using drugs. Although peer socialization is especially important in, and associated with, childhood, it continues to be important throughout the life course. For example, peers help us learn what we are expected to do at college (Brimeyer, Miller, and Perrucci 2006), at work (Montoya 2005), in social settings (Friedkin 2001), and in civic arenas (Dey 1997), as well as how to be sports fans (Melnick and Wann 2011).

Gender

Sociologists devote a great deal of attention to gender socialization, or the transmission of norms and values about what boys and girls can and should do

(Leaper and Farkas 2015). Even before babies are born, their parents (and many others) start to "gender" them. In the United States they do so by, for example, frequently buying blue clothing for boys and pink for girls. Parents often dress baby girls in frilly dresses and affix bows to their bald heads to signal to others that the babies are girls. These gender differences are reinforced by the toys children are often given by parents—trucks and soldiers for boys, dolls and dollhouses for girls. Boys may get toys and games organized around action, activity, and role-playing thought to be appropriate for boys. Girls may get toys and games focused on interactions, relationships, and less active play. Sociologist Emily Kane (2012) found that while parents often want to challenge gender assumptions about what constitutes appropriate toys and clothing for children, they are constrained by traditionally gendered structures and social institutions.

As children grow up, they learn from their parents and other significant others (as well as the generalized other) what behaviors are considered appropriate and inappropriate for their gender. They also learn the consequences, or sanctions, for deviating from these expectations. For example, parents may give a girl a great deal of sympathy when she cries, whereas they may tell a boy to "be a man" and not cry after an injury. Boys may be expected to have an interest in sports, to play roughly with each other, and to be unable to sit still. Girls, in contrast, are expected to display more "ladylike" behaviors, such as sitting quietly and sharing. Many children come to see these traditional gender expectations as "natural" expressions of being male or female. Parents trying to raise boys are more likely to socialize them into narrow gender roles. They cite biology, or "nature," as the reason for doing so. Parents also do so because they fear social sanctions if they socialize the boys differently.

The feminist movement of the 1970s challenged traditional notions about the socialization of boys and girls (Lorber 2000). Today, some parents pride themselves on their "gender-neutral" (Auster 2016; Martin 2005) child rearing. They socialize their children without rigid adherence to traditional binary gender roles, rejecting the ideas that boys and girls are completely different. Yet many parents continue to strongly discourage boys from expressing an interest in activities that are stereotyped as "for girls" (Kane 2006). Illustrating this difference, *tomboy* can be a positive term applied to a girl who likes physical activity and plays with boys. *Sissy*, in contrast, is a derogatory term for boys who express an interest in quieter types of play or playing with girls (Thorne 1993). Advice about the differential socialization of boys and girls continues to dominate child-rearing and parenting books, as well as other media (Martin 2005).

Historically, traditional socialization for gender roles has been reinforced in schools, sports, and the mass media. In schools, teachers and curricula once tended to support traditional gender norms, and peer groups were likely to be segregated by gender (Thorne 1993). In sports, girls and boys were channeled into different sports; for example, girls tended to play softball, while boys played baseball (Coakley 2007). When girls did play "male" sports, their efforts were often labeled differently; for instance, girls' football competitions might be called "powderpuff" football. The passage in 1972 of Title IX of the U.S. Education Amendments, which bars discrimination on the basis of gender in educationally based sporting activities receiving federal funding, has changed such views dramatically. Since the passage of Title IX, women's athletic activities in college and even in high school have become increasingly visible and, in some cases, more highly regarded as "real" sports. One of the best examples is women's

basketball at the collegiate level. More generally, both men and women are now more likely to seek to build muscular and athletic bodies.

ASK YOURSELF

Why do you think traditional ideas about gender role socialization in childhood remain strong in U.S. culture today? Do you foresee that they will ever give way entirely to more egalitarian norms? Why or why not?

The media, especially movies, TV, and video games, have also tended to reinforce children's traditional gender role socialization. However, that, too, is changing. Television programs are increasingly featuring strong female characters (e.g., *Grey's Anatomy*), and numerous shows have featured female cops and police chiefs (e.g., *Law & Order: SVU*). Female action stars (e.g., Michelle Rodriguez in *The Fast and the Furious* series and *Avatar*) are increasingly likely to play strong and aggressive characters. Young adult novels and the movies based on them often also have strong female leading characters, such as the extremely smart Hermione Granger in the *Harry Potter* series and Katniss Everdeen in the *Hunger Games* series.

Change is less obvious in other settings. Malls tend to reinforce traditional gender roles by offering separate shops for boys and girls, and for men and women. The Disney theme parks offer highly differentiated attractions aimed at boys (Pirates of the Caribbean) and girls (It's a Small World). Modern advertisements, both in print and on television, continue to feature men and women in their "traditional" roles—men are often shown fixing things around the house or doing hard labor, while women are shown cooking, cleaning, and taking care of the kids. Most video games are targeted at boys, while girls are offered computer games focused on facial makeovers and shopping. This media emphasis on female appearance is not new. Movies, television programming, and advertisements have been widely critiqued for decades for their unrealistic portrayal of women's bodies (Neuendorf et al. 2009). Magazines such as *Rolling Stone* have featured sexualized images of men on their covers, but they still use many more such images of women. More striking is the fact that the images of women have become increasingly sexualized over time (Hatton and Trautner 2011). Many of the action heroines (e.g., those in James Bond and X-Men movies) continue to embody traditional male preferences for female bodies: young, attractive, and slender. Young women comparing themselves with these versions of adult Barbie dolls become anxious about their own bodies. Media images of women may also reaffirm racial stereotypes, with young women of color often being sexualized or portrayed as poor and irresponsible (Collins 2004).

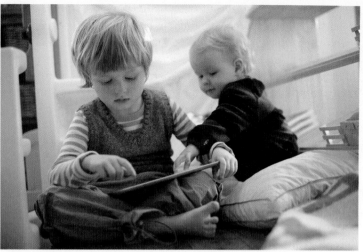

What do you think the impact will be of the increasing amount of time young children are spending looking at devices' screens?

Mass Media and New Media

Until recently, much of the emphasis on the role of the mass media in socialization has been on the effects of television and the enormous number of hours per week children spend in front of their TVs (Comstock and Scharrer 2007). TV remains an important socialization agent, especially for young children. However, it is clear that as children mature, especially in the middle and upper classes, more of their socialization is taking place via the computer, smartphones, video games, and other new and emerging technologies (Rideout, Foehr, and Roberts 2010). As the range of media devices has expanded, so has the portion of time spent using them. In 2009, children and young people between the ages of 8 and 18 spent almost 11 hours per day exposed to media of various sorts, reflecting an increase of more than 3 hours from 10 years prior (Da Silva 2015). The percentage of young people who own their own media devices is high and, for the most part, increasing.

Of course, a world of wonderful information is available to children on the computer via Google and other forms of new media. However, there are also lots of worrying things online that children can easily find or stumble upon. In addition, access to computers has changed the viewing experience considerably. Watching TV programs or movies is a passive activity. Even when "adult themes" are presented, the child is an observer, not a participant. However, on computers and other new digital media, the child can play video games such as *Pokémon Go, Grand Theft Auto V,* and *Call of Duty: Infinite Warfare.* Some of these games engage children in simulations of antisocial activities such as stealing cars and evading police chases. Clearly, the nature of the socialization implicit in such games is at odds with the lessons that parents and teachers wish to impart.

Smartphones and social networking sites play a role in socialization as well, mostly through the influence of peers. A great deal of peer socialization also takes place via sites such as Facebook, Twitter, and Snapchat (boyd 2014; Skoog, Sobring, and Bohlin 2015). All of this is so new, and new forms of media are emerging so rapidly, that it is hard to know exactly what role the new media will play in socialization in the future, but their role is likely to be increasingly powerful and pervasive.

Consumer Culture

Consistent with the emphasis on consumption in this book, and in the contemporary world, it is important to understand that children need to be socialized in order to consume, and especially in order to devote a significant portion of their lives to consumption (Atkinson, Nelson, and Rademacher 2015). Like many other types of socialization, much of this socialization takes place early on in the family (Meuleman and Lubbers 2016), in schools, and in peer groups. Of course, we must not ignore the role of marketing, especially to children, in how people learn to consume (Schor 2005).

However, much socialization now takes place in consumption sites themselves rather than in the family, in schools, or through advertisements. For example, preteens and teens spend a large amount of time at shopping malls, either with their families or, as they mature, on their own and in the company of peers. Although young people may be going to a movie in a mall's multiplex or just "hanging out" at the mall rather than shopping, the fact remains that those activities take place in a setting devoted to shopping and consumption (Cook 2004; Rose 2010). Children readily learn the nuts and bolts of how to consume. They also learn various norms and values of consumption, and especially to value the processes of consumption and shopping as well as the goods and services acquired through those processes. For example, there is a toy line produced by Moose Toys oriented mainly to selling figurines called Shopkins to children (see-www.shopkinsworld.com). More important, these products aim at promoting unbridled consumption—"Once you shop . . . you can't stop!"—both in the present and implicitly throughout the lifespan of those who first play with the toys as children. The immediate goal is to entice children into collecting as many Shopkins and as much associated paraphernalia as possible. A broader goal is implicit in the fact that the figurines are characters associated with a wide array of items that can be purchased in stores. Among them are Kooky Cookie (a chocolate chip cookie), Polly Polish (a bottle of nail polish), and Lippy Lips (a tube of lipstick). Most broadly, the goal is to encourage a lifetime of "hyperconsumption" (Ritzer 2012a).

Online consumption and shopping sites (such as Amazon and eBay) are also socializing agents. Navigation and buying strategies are learned at digital retailers, and those have an effect on consumption in the brick-and-mortar world. For instance, many younger people who have grown up with online shopping are adept comparison shoppers. They are likely to compare products online and to search out the best possible deals before making purchases. Some storefront retailers have gone out of business as a result of online competition, further reinforcing the use of online retailers. Other storefront retailers have developed new hybrids of online and storefront retailing. They offer consumers the ability to buy online and then pick up their items at local outlets. The hope is that visits to local stores will lead consumers to make unplanned purchases. These new forms of retailing offer new ways of socializing young people into our culture of consumption.

Socialization into being a consumer also reinforces lessons about race, class, and gender (Otnes and Zayre 2012). Christine Williams (2006) shows that consumer choices—where to shop, what brands to buy, what products are appropriate for whom—contribute to the maintenance of social inequalities. Girls face pressure to consume beauty products that encourage them to live up to an idealized and usually unattainable level of female beauty (Wiklund et al. 2010). For example, the Barbie doll is often presented as an ideal form of the female body—a form that is physically impossible to attain in real life. Such toys socialize children not only into a consumer culture but also into one that reproduces and reinforces harmful gender expectations.

ADULT SOCIALIZATION

A great deal of adult socialization takes place in later life as people enter the work world and become independent of their families (Ellis, Bauer, and Erdogan 2015).

Workplaces

At one time, socialization into a workplace was a fairly simple and straightforward process. Many workers were hired for jobs in large corporations (General Motors, U.S. Steel) and remained there until they reached retirement age. Especially for those who held jobs in the lower reaches of the corporate hierarchy, socialization occurred for the most part in the early stages of a career. Today, however, relatively few workers can look forward to a career in a single position within a single company. Increasing numbers of workers are changing employers, jobs, and even careers with some frequency (Legerski 2012; Pugh 2016). Each time workers change jobs, they need **resocialization** to unlearn old behaviors, norms, and values and to learn new ones. They can no longer rely (assuming it was ever possible) on what they learned as children, in school, or in their early years on the job.

The Great Recession caused a record number of workers to lose their jobs, and those who have been able to find new ones have needed to be resocialized into them. One study of more than 1 million people found that 16 percent reported having lost a job between 2007 and 2009 (Farber 2011). Furthermore, these displaced workers were more likely to remain unemployed than were previous cohorts of displaced workers. This trend continued through 2014, although over time more workers were able to find new jobs. However, among losers of full-time jobs, those new jobs were more likely to be part-time and to be lower in pay (Farber 2015).

Total Institutions

At some point in their lives, many adults find themselves in some type of total institution (Gambino 2013; Goffman 1961a). A **total institution** is a closed, all-encompassing place of residence and work set off from the rest of society that meets all of the needs of those enclosed in it.

A major example of a total institution is the prison. In 2016, 2.3 million Americans were housed in prisons and jails of various types (including, among others, military prisons and detention centers for immigrants; www.prisonpolicy.org/reports/pie2016.html; International Centre for Prison Studies 2011). On initial entry into prison, inmates undergo formal resocialization in the form of being told the rules and procedures they must follow.

However, of far greater importance is the informal socialization that occurs over time through their interactions with guards and especially with other inmates (Walters 2003). In fact, other inmates often socialize relatively inexperienced criminals into becoming more expert criminals; prisons are often "schools for crime" (Sykes [1958] 2007; Walters 2003).

Another total institution is the military. Members generally live in military housing. They often eat together, share living quarters, and have access to all necessary services on the military base. They must follow strict rules of dress, conduct, physical appearance, and organization of their time.

Other Aspects of Adult Socialization

Adult socialization and resocialization take place in many other ways and in many other settings. For example, medical schools, law schools, and graduate schools of various types socialize their students to be doctors, lawyers, nurses, and members of other professions (Becker and Geer 1958; Granfield 1992; Hafferty 2009). The students have to learn the norms that govern their appearance, conduct, and interactions with others in their professions, their patients or clients, and the public at large. Medical residents, for example, need to learn how to present their diagnoses to patients with sensitivity and confidence. They also learn to maintain and reinforce status differences between doctors and nurses.

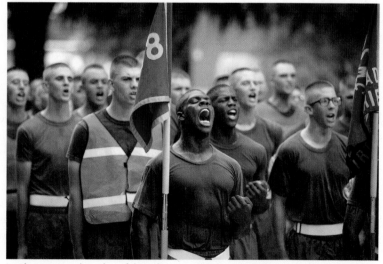

In what ways are branches of the military total institutions? Why are they set up as total institutions?

There are a number of other situations that lead to the need for adult socialization or resocialization (Brim 1968; Lutfey and Mortimer 2006; Wilson 1984):

- *Changes in societal values and norms.* Many aspects of American culture are experiencing rapid change, and people need to be socialized into the new cultural realities.

- *Family changes.* Separation, divorce, death of a spouse, and remarriage involve particularly important transitions for the adults who are involved, not just the children. They require considerable adult resocialization into new relationships, new household organization, and new public images.

- *Geographic mobility.* Job change, retirement, and migration are becoming increasingly likely. People undergoing any of these transitions must be resocialized into not only new physical environments but also new subcultures.

- *Changes associated with aging.* As people age, they gradually become disengaged from work, which has implications for relationships and financial well-being. A retired person must become resocialized into this new status.

INTERACTION

In the previous section of the chapter, we focused on the socialization of individuals. However, socialization generally involves **interaction**, or social engagement involving two or more individuals who perceive, and orient their actions to, one another (vom Lehn 2007). Interaction has generally been seen as involving face-to-face relationships among people, but in the twenty-first century, interaction is increasingly mediated by smartphones and social media. Interaction is an important topic of study in itself because of its ubiquity and its influence on individuals. It is also a key building block for more macroscopic social phenomena, such as networks and groups as well as larger organizations, societies, and the global domain, which will be explored more deeply in the next chapter.

Personal interaction occurs throughout our lifetimes. Examples include interactions between parents and children, between children and their siblings, between teachers and students, between coworkers, and between medical personnel and patients. Interactions early in the life cycle, especially in the family and in schools, tend to be long-term and intense. Later in life, many interactions tend to be more fleeting (a quick hello on the street or a brief conversation at a cocktail party), although interactions with family members tend to remain intense.

SUPERORDINATE–SUBORDINATE INTERACTIONS

Simmel saw society as being defined by interaction. Moreover, he differentiated between the forms that interaction takes and the types of people who engage in interaction. For example, one "form" of interaction is the relationship between a *superordinate* and a *subordinate* (Simmel [1908] 1971). This type of relationship is found in many settings, for example, between teacher and student in the classroom, between judge and defendant in the courtroom, and between guard and prisoner in the jail. We tend to think of this relationship as eliminating the subordinate's independence. However, a relationship between the two cannot exist unless the subordinate has at least some freedom to be an active party to the interaction. The relationship between employee and supervisor is a good example. If the employee cannot react to the supervisor's direction, there is no interaction—only one-way communication from the supervisor to the employee. Furthermore, experimental research has demonstrated that the greater the equality in an employee–manager relationship, the greater the amount of two-way communication. In such a situation, the subordinate feels less resentment, anger, and worry when conflict arises with the manager (Johnson, Ford, and Kaufman 2000).

DIGITAL LIVING

Digital Natives

Many of you reading this book are digital natives—members of the Millennial generation who have been socialized into a digital world since birth. Unlike the older generations of "digital settlers" and "digital immigrants" who had to go through a process of resocialization to adapt to the digital world, digital natives "learned in digital the first time around" (Palfrey and Gasser 2008, 4). Although digital natives possess the skills to use the internet and social media, that does not necessarily mean they are cognizant of the consequences of their online behavior. Creating and managing their identities online is complicated because they must "contend with collapsed contexts and invisible audiences" (boyd 2014, 31). For instance, teenagers in particular create their online identities for their peers, not for their teachers, parents, college admission selection committees, or future employers. But these other actors also look at teenagers' Facebook profiles and

Twitter page and judge them based on what they post, often taking the content out of its original context (boyd 2014).

Given that versions of our online identities are so accessible and persistent, it would be wise for not just digital natives but all of us who use social media to be careful of whom we "friend" or "follow" and what we post online. But digital natives tend to be reluctant to use privacy settings because they do not want to block peers with similar interests (boyd 2014, 32). Palfrey and Gasser (2008, 26) contend that digital natives share so much personal information online in order to establish group memberships, which they incorporate into their social identities. Online group memberships are types of reference groups that provide clues to an individual's preferences and values. While some online groups are secondary groups with weak ties, others approximate primary

groups for digital natives, even if they do not involve face-to-face interaction. Although digital natives can change their online identities quickly and easily, these identities are insecure because they lack the power to control how others perceive them (Palfrey and Gasser 2008, 31).

Engaging the Digital World
One criticism directed at digital natives is that they are addicted to digital technology and social media. Instead of talking to each other before class begins, they are checking their Twitter feed on their smartphones. Some have been known to text their friends even when they are sitting in the same room. How addicted are you to digital technology and social media? Try to disengage the digital world for 24 hours—no e-mails, social media, or streaming music. Explain your experience. Did you find yourself unable to leave the digital world entirely?

RECIPROCITY AND EXCHANGE

To sociologists who theorize about exchange, interaction is a rational process in which those involved seek to maximize rewards and minimize costs. Interaction is likely to persist as long as those involved find it rewarding, and it is likely to wind down or end when one or more of the parties no longer find it rewarding. An important idea in this context is the social norm of **reciprocity**, which

means that those engaged in interaction expect to give and receive rewards of roughly equal value (Gouldner 1960; Molm 2010; Mazelis 2015). When one party feels that the other is no longer adhering to this norm—that is, not giving about as much as he or she is receiving—the relationship is likely to end.

Studies of exchange relationships, like much else in sociology, are now being challenged to find ways of dealing with new forms of virtual interaction: e-mail, social networking, and interaction on Skype and WhatsApp. One researcher who has explored the effects of virtual reality on interaction in the "real" world, and vice versa, concludes that "the constantly evolving avatar [or digital representation of oneself] influences the 'real' self, who now also orients toward virtual, yet all-too-real others" (Gottschalk 2010, 522). In other words, interactions in the digital realm and those in the physical realm both influence the self. Additional research questions come to mind quite readily. For example, are people compelled to cooperate to the same extent in the digital realm (such as when using e-mail communication) as they are in the material world (such as during in-person communication; Naquin, Kurtzberg, and Belkin 2008)? However, it is important to remember that the digital and material worlds are not separate from one another, but rather interpenetrate. An important issue, then, is the connection between, for example, collaborative relationships online and offline (Ritzer 2013).

"DOING" INTERACTION

Another interactionist theory of great relevance here is ethnomethodology, which focuses on people's everyday practices, especially those that involve interaction. The basic idea is that interaction is something that people actively "do," something that they accomplish on a day-to-day basis. For example, the simple act of two people walking together can be considered a form of interaction. Engaging in certain practices makes it clear that you are walking with a particular someone and not with someone else (Pantzar and Shove 2010; Ryave and Schenkein 1974). You are likely to walk close to, or perhaps lean toward, a close friend. When you find yourself walking in step with a total stranger, you probably behave differently. You might separate yourself, lean away, and say, "Excuse me," to make it clear that you are not walking with that stranger and are not engaged in interaction with her. More complex forms of interaction require much more sophisticated practices. In the process of interacting, people create durable forms of interaction, such as those that relate to gender (West and Zimmerman 1987) and the family.

Ethnomethodology also spawned **conversation analysis**, which is concerned with how people do, or accomplish, conversations (Heritage and Stivers 2012). For example, you must know and utilize certain practices in order to carry on a successful conversation: You must know when it is your turn to talk and when it is appropriate to laugh at a comment made by someone else (Jefferson 1979). Conversation analysts have taken the lead in studying conversations, and interaction more generally, in great depth. They typically record conversations using audio or video devices so that they can study them in detail. Later, they transcribe the conversations to create written records of them.

INTERACTION ORDER

While every instance of interaction may seem isolated and independent of others, each is part of what Erving Goffman (2000) called the **interaction order** (Rawls 2015). This is a social domain that is organized and orderly. The order is created informally and governed by those involved in the interaction rather than by some formal structure, such as a bureaucracy and its constraints (Fine 2012; Jacobs 2007). One example of an interaction order is a group of students who form a clique and develop their own norms to govern their interaction. In this thinking, Goffman was following Simmel's view that society is based, in a real sense, on interaction. In many ways, society is interaction.

The interaction order can be seen in many settings and contexts. One example is the 2016 shooting of police officers in Dallas by a lone sniper, which killed five officers. Before the shooting, an orderly demonstration against police brutality was taking place, but the shooting destroyed this interaction order and replaced it with fear and confusion. Some sociologists have suggested that human interaction with animals is another area in which we can observe the interaction order (Jerolmack 2009, 2013).

STATUS AND ROLE

Status and role are key elements in the interaction order, as well as in the larger structures in which such interactions often exist. A **status** is a position within a social system occupied by people. Within the university, for example, key statuses are professor and student. A **role** is what is generally expected of a person who occupies a given status. Thus, a professor is expected to show up for class, to be well prepared, to teach in an engaging manner, and so on. For their part, students are also expected to attend class, to listen and sometimes to participate, to avoid texting and checking their Facebook pages during class, to complete the required assignments, and to take and pass examinations.

The concept of status can be broken down further into ascribed and achieved status. An **ascribed status** is one that is not chosen; it is beyond the individual's control. It involves a position into which the individual is placed or to which he or she moves, regardless of what that person does or the nature of his or her capacities or accomplishments. In some cases, individuals are born into an ascribed status—for example, the status associated with race, ethnicity, social class, sex, or gender. In contrast, an **achieved status** is a position that a person acquires on the basis of accomplishment or the nature of the individual's capacities. It may be based on merit or earned, or the person may choose it—for example, by seeking out and finding someone who will be a mate for life. Spouse, parent, and career as a "successful" entrepreneur are all achieved statuses. In addition, adults can achieve improvement in their social class or socioeconomic status (children's social class is almost always ascribed).

Whether it is ascribed or achieved, a status can become a **master status**, or a position that is (or becomes) more important than any other status, both for the person in the position and for all others involved. A master status will become central to a person's identity, roles, behaviors, and interactions. Primary examples of master statuses are those associated with race, disability, gender, and even sexuality.

The social roles connected with any statuses can be congruent; that is, the expectations attached to a given status can be consistent. Student status (achieved) may have role expectations of attending class and doing homework outside of class. But roles can also come into conflict—for example, going to class and keeping up with your social life. **Role conflict** can be defined as conflicting expectations associated with a given position or multiple positions (Merton 1957; Schmidt et al. 2014). A professor who is expected to excel at both teaching and research can be seen as having role conflict. Devoting a lot of time to research can mean that a professor is ill prepared to teach her classes. Or a professor may be torn between the expectations of being a teacher (preparing for class) and those of being a parent (playing with her children). A student may need to deal with the role conflict between being a student and studying and being a friend who spends the evening helping a close acquaintance deal with a personal problem.

Much research has been done on the role conflicts experienced by workers with domestic obligations. Each role interferes with the individual's ability to satisfactorily meet the expectations associated with the other role (Moore 1995). Research has supported this idea. For example, women who work outside the home, who still tend to be responsible for the care of children and the home, experience higher levels of stress and poorer physical health than working men (Gove and Hughes 1979; Pearlin 1989; Roehling, Hernandez Jarvis, and Swope 2005). The heavy burden of the female caretaking role inhibits women's ability to fulfill their role as caretakers of themselves.

Another role-related problem is **role overload**, in which people are confronted with more expectations than they can possibly handle (Mathews, Winkel, and Wayne 2014). Students during final exams week are often confronted with role overload in trying to satisfy the expectations of several professors and courses. One study of the American "time crunch" and mental health suggests that feeling under time pressure is likely the active ingredient in role overload, which in turn affects people's psychological well-being (Roxburgh 2004).

There is a tendency to see roles as fixed, unchanging, and constraining. However, people do have the ability to engage in **role making**. That is, they have the ability to modify their roles, at least to some degree (Turner 1978). Thus, the professor in the previous example might take his child to the office so that he can perform parent and teacher roles simultaneously. Researchers have noted that parents adopt a variety of strategies to reduce work-family conflict (Becker and Moen 1999; Bianchi and Milkie 2010). Examples of such strategies include reducing work hours, turning down promotions, and negotiating trade-offs with one's partner.

MICRO-LEVEL SOCIAL STRUCTURES

Through an accumulation of persistent patterns of interaction and social relationships, individuals contribute to the creation of social structures, which are enduring and regular social arrangements. Social structures include everything from the face-to-face interaction that is characteristic of the interaction order to networks, groups, organizations, societies, and the globe. This chapter focuses on micro-level social structures—interpersonal relationships, social networks, and groups. Chapter 5 covers larger-scale social structures.

INTERPERSONAL RELATIONSHIPS

A good place to start a discussion of social structures is with another famous set of concepts created by Georg Simmel (1950) to describe the structures common to interpersonal relationships. **Dyads** are two-person groups, and **triads** are three-person groups.

Dyads are the most basic of interpersonal relationships, but they often evolve into triads—such as when a couple welcomes a new child. It would appear on the surface that the addition of one person to a dyad, creating a triad, would be of minimal importance sociologically. After all, how important can the addition of one person be? Simmel demonstrated that no further addition of members to a group, no matter how many that might be, is as important as the addition of a single person to a dyad. A good example is the dramatic change in the husband–wife relationship caused by the arrival of a first child. Another is the powerful impact of a new lover on an intimate dyadic relationship. In cases like these, social possibilities exist in the triad that do not exist in a dyad. For example, in a triad, two of the parties can form a coalition against the third: A wife and child can form a coalition against the husband. Or one member of the triad—say, the child—can take on the role of mediator or arbitrator in disputes involving the other members.

The most important point to be made about Simmel's ideas on the triad is that it is the group structure that matters, *not* the people involved in the triad or the nature of their personalities. Different people with different personalities will make one triad different from another, but it is not the nature of the people or their personalities that make the triad itself possible.

SOCIAL NETWORKS

Simmel's work also informs the study of social networks. **Networks** are broadly defined as interconnected nodes or positions. For example, individuals can be seen as nodes in a network of people. **Social networks** involve two or more individuals, but groups, organizations, and societies can form such networks.

Network analysts are interested in how networks are organized and the implications of that organization for social life. They look at the nodes, or positions, occupied by individuals (and other entities) in a network, the linkages among nodes, and the importance of central nodes to other nodes in the network. Figure 4.1 shows a network with low centrality and one with high centrality. In the low-centrality network, one node appears in the center, but it is actually linked to only two other nodes. The central node in the high-centrality example is far more influential. Every other node is connected to it, and there is only one link that is independent of the central node. Those who occupy positions that are central in any network have access to a great many resources and therefore have a considerable ability to gain and to exercise power in a network.

A key idea in network theory is the "strength of weak ties." We are all aware of the power of strong ties between, for example, family members, or among those who belong to close-knit social groups such as gangs. However, as Mark Granovetter (1973) has demonstrated, those who have only weak ties with others (that is, they are just acquaintances) can have great power. While those with strong ties tend to remain within given groups, those with weak ties can more easily move between groups and thus provide important linkages among and between group members (see Figure 4.2). Those with weak ties are the ones who hold together disparate groups that are themselves linked internally by strong ties.

Researchers generally find that at least half of all workers in the United States have obtained their jobs through informal means, meaning referrals, rather than formal job postings (Marsden and Gorman 2001; Pfeffer and Parra 2009). It makes

FIGURE 4.1 • Social Network Centrality

Opposite Degrees of Network Centrality

Low Network Centrality   High Network Centrality

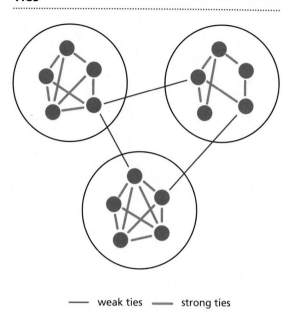

SOURCE: Social Network Centrality is reprinted by permission of S. Joshua Mendelsohn.

FIGURE 4.2 • The Strength of Weak Ties

——— weak ties   ——— strong ties

SOURCE: Adapted from *Weak Ties in Social Networks, Bokardo*, a blog about interface and product design, Joshua Porter.

sense, then, to understand the strength of weak ties. If you are looking for a job, you may want to seek out the help of friends and acquaintances who have weak ties to many groups. This is because they are likely to have many diverse and potentially useful contacts with people you *and* your strong ties do not know at a number of different employers.

One point worth underscoring in any discussion of social networks is the importance of internet networks, including Facebook, Instagram, and Twitter (Gee, Jones, and Burke, forthcoming). This is another domain where weak ties can be of great importance. On Facebook, for instance, you may have hundreds, even thousands, of "friends." However, it is clear that many of these "friendships" involve weak ties—in fact, far weaker ties than analysts such as Granovetter had in mind. It is also important to note that they leave objective traces, such as e-mail messages and writings on Facebook walls. As a result, such networks are much easier to study than, for example, those that exist in face-to-face interaction, which usually leave few material traces. This is the reason the app Snapchat was developed; it forces you to arrange for traces—such as photos—to disappear within 1 to 10 seconds (Wortham 2013).

GROUPS

We have already encountered the key sociological concept of groups at several points in this chapter, especially in Simmel's ideas on the dyad and beyond. A **group** is a relatively small number of people who over time develop a patterned relationship based on interaction with one another. However, just because we see a small number of people who appear to be together—say, in a queue waiting to board a plane—that does not mean that they necessarily constitute a group. Most people in a queue are not likely to interact with one another, to have the time or inclination to develop patterned relationships with one another, or, if they do interact, to do so beyond the time it takes to board the plane and find their seats.

Types of Groups

Several key concepts in sociology relate to groups. Consider the traditional distinction between the primary group and the secondary group (Cooley 1909). **Primary groups** are those that are small, are close-knit, and have intimate face-to-face interaction. Relationships in primary groups are personal, and people identify strongly with the groups. The family is the model of a primary group. **Secondary groups** are generally large and impersonal; ties are relatively weak, members do not know one another very well, and members' impacts on one another are typically not very powerful. Members of a local parent–teacher association would be a good example of a secondary group.

Reference groups are those groups that you take into consideration in evaluating yourself. Your reference group can be one to which you belong, or it can be another group to which you do not belong but nevertheless often relate (Ajrouch 2007; Merton and Kitt 1950). People often have many reference groups, and those groups can and do change over time. Knowing people's reference groups, and how they change, tells us a great deal about their behavior, attitudes, and values. We often think of reference groups in positive terms. An example would be a group of people whose success you would like to emulate. They also can be negative if they represent values or ways of life that you reject (say, neo-Nazis). The group to which one belongs is not necessarily the most powerful group in one's life.

Reference groups can be illustrated by the case of immigrants. Newly arrived immigrants are more likely to take those belonging to the immigrant culture, or even those in the country from which they came, as their reference group. In contrast, their children, second-generation immigrants, are much more likely to take as their reference group those associated with the new culture in the country to which they have immigrated (Kosic et al. 2004).

One final set of concepts that can help us understand the sociological importance of groups is the distinction between in-groups and out-groups (Sumner [1906] 1940). An **in-group** is one to which people belong and with which they identify, perhaps strongly. An **out-group** is one to which outsiders, at least from the perspective of the in-group, belong. Thus, from your perspective, the group you sit with at your regular table in the college dining hall or fast-food court would be the in-group, while other groups at other tables might be the out-groups. The differences between these groups may be insignificant (e.g., whether they get their food in the food court from McDonald's or Pizza Hut). However, they can also come to be so important ("jocks" versus "geeks") that each group not only accepts its own ways but also rejects those of the others. In extreme cases, this can lead to conflict between the in-group and the out-group. Research suggests that hostility often arises when members of the in-group perceive the out-group as constituting a threat to their self-interest (Rosenstein 2008). This is particularly evident in research on immigration (Schlueter and Scheepers 2010; Schneider 2008). In that case, native-born individuals (representing the in-group) may maintain discriminatory attitudes toward a growing population of foreign-born individuals (representing the out-group). In a more specific study, it was found that religious fundamentalists in Western Europe, especially Muslims, have very high levels of hostility to out-groups (Koopmans 2015).

Conformity to the Group

We have seen that group members generally conform to certain aspects of the group with which they prefer to identify. Some conformity is clearly necessary for a group to survive. If everyone "did his or her own thing," or went his or her own way, there would be no group. But too much conformity can have disastrous consequences. A central issue in the sociological study of groups has been the degree to which members conform to the expectations and demands of the group despite their own misgivings. Groups often develop informal authority. A series of experiments, conducted by Solomon Asch (1952), showed that the power of the group

FIGURE 4.3 • Solomon Asch's Conformity Experiment Cards

SOURCE: Adapted from Solomon E. Asch, "Opinions and Social Pressure," *Scientific American* 193 (1955): 31–35.

is so great that it may override an individual's own judgments and perceptions (see also Kinney 2007). In one of the experiments, groups of seven to nine students were assembled. All but one (the subject) were confederates of the researcher. All but the subject knew the details of the experiment. Only the subject believed that the experiment was investigating vision. Each group was shown two cards, one with one vertical line on it and a second with three such lines (see Figure 4.3). One of the lines on the second card was the same length as the line on the first card. The other two lines were clearly different. All the students were asked to choose the line on the comparison card that matched the single line on the reference card. As they had been instructed, each of the confederates chose, out loud, one of the wrong lines. The subjects were always positioned last in their groups.

When the subjects' turns came, about one-third of them conformed to their groups' erroneous choice and selected the same wrong line. They made the wrong choice even though they apparently knew it was the wrong choice.

There is no question that some people conform to group demands at least some of the time. Conformity is especially likely when the demands come from someone in authority in the group. However, it is important to remember that about two-thirds of the choices made by subjects in the Asch conformity experiments indicated independence from the group. This chapter has focused largely on such micro-level phenomena as individuals, interaction, and groups. In Chapter 5, we turn to the progressively more macro-level phenomena of organizations, societies, and the globe as a whole.

SUMMARY

The sociological perspective on the individual and the self focuses on the social interactions that humans are capable of having with each other. Cooley's concept of the looking-glass self, the idea that humans develop self-images reflecting the way others respond to them, is fundamental to sociology. Symbolic interactionism posits that humans use significant symbols, such as gestures and language, to develop a sense of self. George Herbert Mead defined the self as the ability to take oneself as an object. Once individuals are able to internalize the perspective of a group or community, they come to possess a sense of the generalized other. According to Mead, the self is composed of two parts, the "I" that is impulsive, and the "me" that is conformist.

Erving Goffman believed that in every interaction, or performance, individuals attempt to manage projections of themselves. On a front stage they operate in an idealized manner, but on a back stage, they can more freely express themselves.

Socialization is the process through which a person learns and generally comes to accept the ways of a group or of a society as a whole. Primary socialization

begins with newborns and infants and continues over the course of childhood during anticipatory socialization. Socialization does not end with childhood—adults continue to be socialized throughout their lives. Our families, our peers, our workplaces, and the media are important agents of socialization.

Socialization involves interaction, or social engagement between two or more individuals. Some interaction involves reciprocity, or the expectation that those involved in it will give and receive equally, while other interactions transpire between those with power and their subordinates. Interaction is deeply involved in people's statuses and their related roles.

Patterns of interaction and social relationships that occur regularly and persist over time become social structures. A group is one type of social structure that develops when individuals interact over time and develop a patterned relationship. A small, close-knit group with intimate face-to-face interactions is a primary group. Secondary groups are larger and more impersonal; their members do not know each other very well.

KEY TERMS

REVIEW QUESTIONS

1. How can we use the literature on feral children to explain the importance of interaction to human development? In what ways does this relate to the "nature versus nurture" debate?

2. According to Mead, what distinguishes humans from nonhumans?

3. How does the socialization process help individuals develop their sense of self? Why are games so important to the socialization process?

4. What is the difference between the "I" and the "me"? Why do people and society as a whole need both the "I" and the "me"?

5. According to Goffman, in what ways do we use impression management in our front-stage performances? Why would a sociologist say that racism has increasingly been relegated to the back stage? What is problematic about this development?

6. Why are families important agents of socialization? How do families from higher social classes socialize their children differently than families from lower social classes do? What effects might these differences in socialization have on children?

7. How are we socialized to be consumers? In what ways has the internet resocialized us as consumers?

8. In what ways is being a fifth grader in the United States both an ascribed and an achieved status? What does this suggest about the differences between roles attached to ascribed statuses versus those attached to achieved statuses?

9. In the realm of social networks, why are "weak ties" helpful to those who are looking for jobs? What effect has the internet had on the development of weak ties and strong ties?

10. In what ways do we use images in the mass media as reference groups? How do the mass media help define in-groups and out-groups?

PRACTICE AND APPLY WHAT YOU'VE LEARNED

▶ **edge.sagepub.com/ ritzeressentials3e**

CHECK YOUR COMPREHENSION ON THE STUDY SITE WITH:

- **Diagnostic pre-tests** to identify opportunities for improvement.

- **eFlashcards** that strengthen your understanding of key terms and concepts.

- **Post-tests** to check your progress and ensure mastery of key learning objectives.

ORGANIZATIONS, SOCIETIES, AND GLOBAL RELATIONSHIPS

Questioning Governmental Authority

Oliver Stone's 2016 biopic *Snowden* gave renewed life to the controversy surrounding U.S. Central Intelligence Agency contractor Edward Snowden and his leak of thousands of classified government documents. The clamor in the United States had become especially loud in mid-2013—and it has not died away to this day—when Snowden told the world that the U.S. government, through its National Security Agency, had been attempting to prevent terrorist acts by spying on ordinary American citizens. This was being done through the systematic accumulation of bulk data or (metadata) on routine phone calls. Public reaction was swift and divided, with some arguing that Snowden was a hero for revealing this fact and that the government had gone to unwarranted lengths in breaching its citizens' privacy. This view was upheld in mid-2015 by a federal appeals court ruling that such data collection was illegal. Others continue to argue that any and all steps, including spying on American citizens, that are necessary to uncover terrorist plots are defensible. Snowden, who

LEARNING OBJECTIVES

5.1 Describe the features of bureaucracies and informal organizations.

5.2 Discuss challenges that arise in contemporary organizations.

5.3 Contrast gemeinschaft and gesellschaft societies.

5.4 Understand global relationships and organizations.

edge.sagepub.com/ ritzeressentials3e

- Take the chapter quiz
- Review key terms with eFlashcards
- Explore multimedia links and SAGE readings

$SAGE edge™

made his revelations from Hong Kong, fled to Russia, where he received asylum and in 2014 a three-year residency permit. Snowden's revelations continue to have impacts. Some terrorist groups have altered the way in which they communicate because some of the documents Snowden released revealed information about U.S. surveillance techniques. The leaks also led to great changes in the way in which the government protects secret documents.

The events surrounding Snowden's leaks reveal the relationship between us as individuals and the different organizations and institutions that frame our lives, such as our local and national governments. These organizations cannot exist, at least for very long, without willing members. When groups of individuals begin to question the authority and rationality of the bureaucracies that govern them, they may voice concern about, seek to change, or even rebel against those bureaucracies.

Picking up where the previous chapter left off with groups, this chapter moves on to the more macroscopic levels of interest to sociologists: organizations, societies, and global relationships. These social structures are discussed here as if they were clearly distinct from one another. However, the fact is that they tend to blend together in many clear-cut ways, as well as in many other almost imperceptible ones.

The individuals, interaction, and groups of focal concern in Chapter 4 all exist within, affect, and are affected by the various macroscopic phenomena of concern here. In fact, neither microscopic nor macroscopic social phenomena make much sense without the other level. Individuals, interaction, and groups do not exist in isolation from macro-level phenomena, and organizations, societies, and global social relationships cannot exist without individuals, interaction, and groups. ●

ORGANIZATIONS

Organizations are collectives purposely constructed to achieve particular ends. Examples include your college or university, which has the objective of educating you as well as your fellow students; corporations, such as Apple, Amazon, and Walmart, whose objective is to earn profits; the International Monetary Fund (IMF), which seeks to stabilize currency exchanges throughout the world; and Greenpeace, which works to protect and conserve the global environment.

There is a particularly long and deep body of work in sociology that deals with organizations (Adler et al. 2016; Godwyn and Gittell 2011), much of it traceable to the thinking of Max Weber on a particular kind of organization, the bureaucracy. A **bureaucracy** is a highly rational organization, especially one that is very efficient. However, both Weber's own thinking and later sociological research (see the following section) make it clear that bureaucracies are *not* always so rational and are even as irrational as you undoubtedly sometimes find them to be. Nevertheless, the bureaucracy is a key element of Weber's theory of the rationalization of the Western world. For decades, the concept of bureaucracy dominated sociological thinking about organizations, and it led to many important insights about the social world.

BUREAUCRACIES

Weber created and used many "ideal types" as methodological tools with which to study the real world and conduct comparative-historical analysis (see Chapter 2). An **ideal type** greatly exaggerates the characteristics of a social phenomenon such as a bureaucracy. It is a model of how the social phenomenon is supposed to operate in some optimal sense, but rarely does. Once the model has been created, we can compare it to the characteristics of any specific example of the social phenomenon anywhere in the world. It serves to identify the ways in which the ideal type differs from the way the social phenomenon actually operates.

The ideal type of bureaucracy is primarily a methodological tool used to study real-life bureaucracies. However, it also gives us a good sense of the advantages of bureaucracies over other types of organizations. The ideal-typical bureaucracy is a model of what most large-scale organizations throughout much of the twentieth century looked like or at least tried to resemble. Figure 5.1 is an organization chart for a typical bureaucracy. A bureaucracy has the following characteristics:

FIGURE 5.1 • Organization Chart for a Typical Bureaucracy

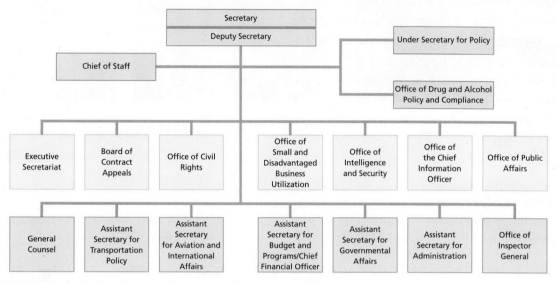

SOURCE: Organization Chart for a Typical Bureaucracy, U.S. Department of Transportation.

- A continuous series of offices, or positions, exist within the organization. Each office has official functions and is bound by a set of rules.

- Each office has a specified sphere of competence. Those who occupy the positions are responsible for specific tasks and have the authority to handle them. Those in other relevant offices are obligated to help with those tasks.

- The offices exist in a vertical hierarchy.

- The positions have technical requirements, and those who hold those offices must undergo the needed training.

- Those who occupy the positions do not own the things needed to do the job (computers and desks). The organization provides officeholders with what they need to get the job done.

- Those who occupy particular offices—chief executive officers, for example—cannot take the offices as their own; these remain part of the organization.

- Everything of formal importance—administrative acts, decisions, rules—is documented in writing.

The development of the bureaucracy is one of the defining characteristics of Western society. In Weber's view, it was a key source of the superiority of the West over other civilizations in the operation of society as a whole as well as of its major components, such as the military. Weber felt that in meeting the needs of large societies for mass administration, there is no better organizational form than, and no alternative to, the bureaucracy.

ASK YOURSELF

Have you ever been a member of a bureaucracy? How many of Weber's characteristics did it have? How well or poorly did it meet the needs of the society it was designed to serve? Why?

Authority Structures and Bureaucracy

Weber's work on bureaucracy is related to his thinking on three types of authority structures. Before getting to those types, we need two preliminary definitions. **Domination** is the probability, or likelihood, that commands will be obeyed by subordinates (Weber [1921] 1968). There are degrees of domination. Strong domination involves a high

Elected officials such as President Donald Trump (left) wield rational-legal authority, while King Salman of Saudi Arabia (center) has traditional authority based on his inherited position. Charismatic authority characterizes such revered leaders as Mahatma Gandhi (right).

probability that commands will be obeyed; domination is weak when those probabilities are low. **Authority** is a particular type of domination: legitimate domination. The key question, then, is what makes authority legitimate as far as subordinates are concerned.

Weber differentiates among three types of authority:

- **Rational-legal authority** is domination legitimated on the basis of legally enacted rules and the right of those with authority under those rules to issue commands. For example, the president of the United States has rational-legal authority to take a variety of actions, such as appointing federal officials, because the president is duly elected in accord with the country's election laws. It is also legitimate for the president in the role of commander in chief to issue various commands, such as to order the use of troops in the case of an attack on the United States.

- **Traditional authority** is based on belief in long-running traditions. For example, although the pope is elected by the college of cardinals, his authority within Catholicism is based primarily on the long traditions associated with his position.

- **Charismatic authority** is based on the devotion of followers to what they define as the exceptional characteristics of a leader. Large numbers of people believed that Martin Luther King Jr. and Mahatma Gandhi had such exceptional characteristics and, as a result, became their devoted followers.

Each type of authority can spawn its own organizational form. However, it is rational-legal authority that is most associated with bureaucracy. In comparison to the bureaucracy, organizations based on traditional and charismatic authority are less rational. They are, for example, less efficient than the highly efficient bureaucracy.

Rationality and Irrationality

Much sociological research on organizations has taken Weber's highly rational model of a bureaucracy as a starting point for the study of the ways in which bureaucracies actually work. However, much of that research has found Weber's ideal-typical model to be unrealistic. For one thing, there is no single organizational model. The nature of the organization and its degree of rationality are contingent on such factors as the organization's size and the technologies that it employs (Orlikowski 2010; Pugh et al. 1968). For another, researchers have found Weber's ideal-typical bureaucracy to be overly rational. This is not surprising, because for Weber ([1903–1917] 1949, 47) it was "not a *description* of reality." Weber purposely exaggerated its degree of rationality. The ideal-typical bureaucracy is a fiction designed to serve as a reference point for the study of real-world bureaucracies. However, researchers have often overlooked the fact that this ideal type is a methodological tool and have mistaken it for

TRENDING

Gang Leader for a Day: A Rogue Sociologist Takes to the Streets (Penguin Books, 2008)

Sudhir Venkatesh (William B. Ransford Professor of Sociology at Columbia University; PhD, University of Chicago, 1997)

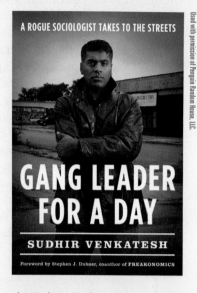

One of many provocative findings discussed in Sudhir Venkatesh's *Gang Leader for a Day* is that the organization of street gangs is similar to bureaucracies, such as corporations and the military. The original intent of Venkatesh's research was to study how African Americans experience urban poverty. But after Venkatesh is unexpectedly befriended by J. T., the charismatic leader of a Chicago gang, he learns that in order to carry out his study, he needs J. T.'s guidance and protection. Venkatesh discovers that J. T.'s gang, the Black Kings, controls the territory that includes one of Chicago's largest public housing projects, the Robert Taylor Homes. The absence of official authority, particularly law enforcement, and steady, full-time employment creates a vacuum of power and jobs that the Black Kings fill through its illegal drug trade. Like any other trade, the illegal drug trade requires a hierarchical organization to ensure that it operates efficiently. Careful bookkeeping and calculation are crucial to keeping a record of supply, wages, profits, and losses. Customer demand for a predictable product necessitates quality control measures. A clear division of labor and chain of command exists in the Black Kings. Numerous low-wage street dealers, or foot soldiers, sell the drugs, while only a few high-ranking officials, such as J. T., manage the trade within their respective territory. J. T. must report his affiliated gang's activities to a regional board of directors, who occupy the positions at the very top of the Black Kings hierarchy. While being the leader of a gang might appear to be a glamorous job, Venkatesh comments that J. T.'s daily routines are quite mundane, albeit with the potential risk of encountering violence from a rival gang.

Through J. T.'s friendship Venkatesh is able to gain access to the residents of the Robert Taylor Homes, who are mostly impoverished African American women and their children. In order for the Black Kings to conduct its illegal drug trade smoothly, the gang performs certain services for these residents, such as buying school supplies for the children or cleaning up dirty hallways. J. T. even refers to himself as a philanthropist, using drug profits to help the community survive. The gang, however, holds a monopoly of power over the residents and "taxes" activities that generate any revenue, including prostitution, child care, and selling food. Money from the drug trade and these taxes fuels the informal economy coordinated by the Black Kings in the Robert Taylor Homes. It also accounts for why street gangs such as the Black Kings are prosecuted by the federal government as organized criminal enterprises under the Racketeer Influenced and Corrupt Organizations Act (RICO).

Supplementary Resources

- Venkatesh briefly describes *Gang Leader for a Day* in this video trailer: www.youtube .com/watch?v=yRq1AhFAN-4.
- Steven Levitt uses Venkatesh's research to explain the economics of gangs in his TED talk "The Freakonomics of Crack Dealing": www .ted.com/talks/steven_ levitt_analyzes_crack_ economics?language=en
- *Dislocation* (2005) is a documentary directed by Venkatesh that portrays the demolition of the Robert Taylor Homes.

an attempt to accurately describe bureaucracies. They conclude that, at best, real-world organizations exhibit a limited form of rationality, or what is called **bounded rationality** (Simon [1945] 1976; Williamson 1975, 1985). That is, rationality is limited by the instabilities and conflicts that exist in most, if not all, organizations and the domains in which they operate (Scott 2014). It is also limited by inherent limitations on humans' capacities to think and act in a rational manner. Some members of the organization are capable of acting more rationally than others. However, none are able to operate in anything approaching the fully rational manner associated with Weber's ideal-typical organization.

The military is an example of an organization with bounded rationality. One source of instability in the military is the cycling of personnel in and out of it, especially in combat zones. Newcomers to the battle zone rarely know what to do. Their presence in, say, a platoon with experienced combat veterans can reduce the ability of the entire group to function. Another larger source of instability lies in the conflicts that exist between branches of the armed forces, as well as between central command and those in the field. In addition, military actions are often so complex and far-reaching that military personnel cannot fully understand them or rationally decide what actions to take. This phenomenon is sometimes referred to as the "fog of war" (Blight and Lang 2005).

A good deal of sociological research on bureaucracies has dealt with how the rational (that is, what is efficient) often becomes irrational (or inefficient). This is often referred to as the "irrationality of rationality"—the irrationality that often accompanies the seemingly rational actions associated with the bureaucracy (Ritzer 2017). For example, Robert Merton ([1949] 1968) found that instead of operating efficiently, bureaucracies introduce great inefficiency due to, among other things, "red tape"—that is, the rigid rules that a bureaucracy's employees are required to follow, as well as the unnecessary questions to be answered and forms to be filled out by the clients of the bureaucracy. Bureaucracies generally demand much more information than they need, often to protect themselves from complaints, bad publicity, and lawsuits. Red tape also includes the telephone time wasted by keeping clients on hold and forcing them to make their way through a maze of prerecorded "customer service" options.

"Parkinson's Law" was conceived as a humorous attempt to point to another source of irrationality in bureaucratic organizations. It was formulated by Cyril Northcote Parkinson (1955), who worked in the British civil service and thus was intimately familiar with the ways in which large bureaucratic organizations functioned. Parkinson summarized the law when he wrote that "work expands so as to fill the time available for its completion." Thus, if a bureaucrat is assigned three reports to complete in a month, it will require a month's work to complete all three. If that same employee is assigned two reports during that time, it will take a month to complete two. And the task will still take a month even if the assignment calls for completing only one report.

Another source of irrationality is what Robert Merton ([1949] 1968) called the **bureaucratic personality**, someone who follows the rules of the

Robert Merton is considered to be the founder of the science of sociology. His work, mostly in the structural-functional tradition, was influential in public policy. For instance, his research on successfully integrated communities was a key element in the U.S. Supreme Court's decision to desegregate public schools. His conceptual contributions to sociology include the bureaucratic personality, unintended consequences, and the self-fulfilling prophecy, among others.

organization to such a great extent that the organization's ability to achieve its goals is subverted. For example, an admissions clerk in a hospital emergency department might require incoming patients to fill out so many forms that they do not get needed medical care promptly.

In these and in many other ways, the actual functioning of bureaucracies is at variance with Weber's ideal-typical characterization.

The Informal Organization

A great deal of research in the twentieth century focused on the **informal organization**, that is, how the organization actually works as opposed to the way it is supposed to work as depicted, for example, in Weber's ideal-typical formal bureaucracy (Blau 1963). For instance, those who occupy offices lower in the bureaucratic hierarchy often have greater knowledge of and competence in specific issues than those who rank above them. Thus, fellow employees may seek the advice of the lower-level bureaucrat rather than the one who ranks higher in the authority structure. The informal organization can help make up for inadequacies in the formal organization (Gulati and Puranam 2009). It might lead employees to take very useful actions that are ignored by the formal organization. For example, students constitute an informal network that offers advice about which faculty members to seek out if students are looking for undemanding courses or guaranteed high grades. Most generally, it is important *not* to examine informal and formal organizations in isolation from one another. Rather, the focus should be on the many linkages between them (McEvily, Soda, and Tortoriello, 2014). Informal organizations often arise to deal with problems and failures in formal organizations, and formal organizations often change in order to take account of actions in informal organizations.

ASK YOURSELF

What specific bureaucracy came to mind when you read about Weber's definition of this type of organization? Is there an informal organization at work there? How is it different from the formal organization? In what ways is it more effective or less effective than the formal one?

Employees sometimes do things that exceed what is expected of them by the organization. However, they more often do less, perhaps far less, than they are expected to do. For example, contrary to the dictates of the formal organization, the most important things that take place in an organization may never be put down in writing. Employees may find it simply too time-consuming to fill out every form or document they are supposed to use. Instead, and contrary to the organization's rules, they may handle many tasks orally. In addition, employees handle some tasks orally so that if anything goes wrong, there is no damning evidence that could jeopardize careers and even the organization as a whole.

The problem for organizations (and individuals) is somewhat different in the digital age. Rather than too little information in writing, the danger is now that too much information is in written form, such as e-mail messages, posts on the internet, tweets, and the like. Of particular concern are posts that can exist forever and be widely and endlessly circulated. This danger was realized in 2016 when WikiLeaks, a global organization, released some of the Democratic Party's e-mails. The messages showed that the party, which is supposed to be neutral, favored Hillary Clinton over her close rival, Bernie Sanders, for the party's nomination for the presidency in 2016. The release of the e-mails arguably contributed to Clinton's losing the election (Sanger and Perlroth, 2016).

Snapchat attempts to deal with the problem of information remaining on the internet forever by automatically deleting posts and photos after a few seconds. While this seems comforting, those who receive the information and photos can save them by taking screenshots. The sender is notified about any screenshots, but there are ways for those taking them to conceal their identities. As one of the founders of Snapchat put it, "Nothing ever goes away on the internet" (Wortham 2013, A3).

While in some bureaucracies, power is meant to be dispersed throughout the offices, it often turns out that an organization becomes an **oligarchy**. That is, a small group of people at the top illegitimately obtain and exercise far more power than they are supposed to have. This can occur in any organization. Interestingly, this undemocratic process was first described by Robert Michels ([1915]

1962) in the most unlikely of organizations—labor unions and socialist parties that supposedly prized democracy. Michels called this "the iron law of oligarchy." Those in power manipulate the organization so that they and their supporters can stay in power indefinitely. At the same time, they make it difficult for others to get or to keep power. While oligarchy certainly develops in some organizations, in reality its occurrence is neither "iron" nor a law. That is, most organizations do not become oligarchical. Nevertheless, the tendency toward oligarchy is another important organizational process not anticipated by Weber's ideal-typical bureaucracy.

CONTEMPORARY ORGANIZATIONAL REALITIES

As the social world has changed, so too has sociological thinking about many things, including organizations. New concepts are supplementing the concept of bureaucracy to enrich our understanding of these new realities. These concepts include gendered and network organizations and others that help inform our efforts to deal with organizational challenges such as sexual harassment, outsourcing of jobs, McDonaldization, and globalization.

GENDERED ORGANIZATIONS

Weber's model does not account for discrimination within organizations. In the ideal bureaucracy, any worker with the necessary training can fill any job. However, as "gendered organization" theorists such as Joan Acker (1990, 2009) have shown, bureaucracies do not treat all workers the same. Jobs are often designed for an idealized worker—one who has no obligations except to the organization. Women, and sometimes men, who carry a responsibility for child rearing can have difficulty fitting this model. Women may face the "competing devotions" of motherhood and work (Wharton and Blair-Loy 2006). Some women who face inflexible workplaces due to gendered organizational practices and family obligations opt to become self-employed (Thébaud 2016). Organizations may also discriminate (consciously or unconsciously) in hiring and

promotions, with white men (who tend to populate the higher levels of bureaucracies) being promoted over women and minorities. Some women in male-dominated business organizations find that they hit a "glass ceiling"—a certain level of authority in a company or organization beyond which they cannot rise (Gorman and Kmec 2009; Wasserman and Frenkel 2015). This is also true in other contexts, such as medicine and higher education (Hart 2016; Zhuge et al. 2011). They can see the top—hence the "glass"—but cannot reach it. Within other organizations, particularly female-dominated ones, men can find themselves riding the "glass escalator" (Williams 1995). This is an invisible force that propels them past equally competent, or even more competent, women to positions of leadership and authority (Dill, Price-Glynn, and Rokovski 2016).

In a global context, American female executives face a "double-paned" glass ceiling. There is the pane associated with the employing company in the United States, and there is a second pane women executives encounter when they seek work experience in the corporation's foreign locales. This is a growing problem, because experience overseas is increasingly a requirement for top-level management positions in multinational corporations, but corporations have typically "masculinized" these expatriate positions and have thereby disadvantaged women. Among the problems experienced by women who succeed in getting these positions are sexual harassment, a lack of availability of programs (such as career counseling) routinely available to men, a lack of adequate mentoring, and male managers who are more likely to promote male rather than female expatriates. Much of the blame for this problem lies in the structure of the multinational corporations, and with the men who occupy high-level management positions within them. However, research has shown that female managers' greater passivity and lesser willingness to promote themselves for such expatriate management positions contributes to their difficulties (Insch, McIntyre, and Napier 2008).

While most of these ideas have been developed on the basis of studies of American organizations, they likely apply as well, or better, globally. For example, a recent study found that the glass ceiling exists in Durban, South Africa (Kiaye and Singh 2013). Figure 5.2 shows where women in industrialized

FIGURE 5.2 • Glass-Ceiling Index

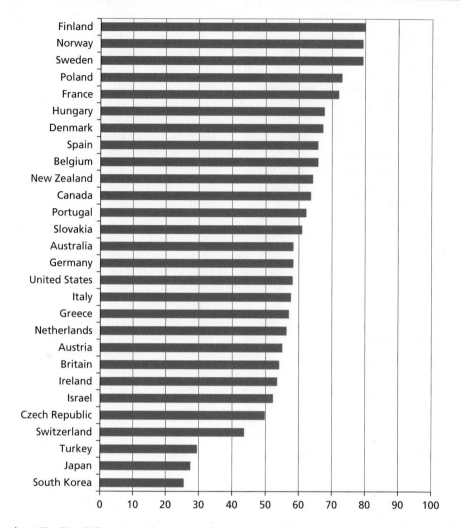

SOURCE: Data from "The Glass-Ceiling Index," *The Economist*, March 5, 2015. © The Economist Newspaper Limited, London (2015).

NOTE: 100 = best for working women.

nations have the best chance of circumventing the glass ceiling—that is, of being treated equally in the work world. New Zealand is best for working women; South Korea is the worst. The United States is in the middle of the pack.

The idea of a glass ceiling relates to vertical mobility—and its absence—for women in organizations. A related concept is the "glass cage," which deals with the horizontal segregation of women (and other minorities; Gabriel, Korczynski, and Rieder 2015; Kalev 2009). The idea here is that men and women doing the same or similar jobs operate in separate and segregated parts of the organization. As in the case of the glass ceiling, women can see what is going on in other cages, but, compared with men, they find it more difficult to move between the cages. Although the cage is made of glass, the skills and abilities of women tend to be less visible, and, as a result, stereotypes about them abound. In addition, women have less communication with those outside the cage, are less likely to learn about jobs available there, are not as likely to get high-profile assignments, and are less likely to get needed training. The situation confronting women would improve if there were more collaboration across the boundaries of the glass cage. Of course, the ultimate solution involves the elimination of the glass cage, as well as the glass ceiling. The glass ceiling and the glass cage represent barriers to the mobility of women within organizations.

The concept of the "glass cliff" describes what can happen to women who experience upward mobility when an organization is going through hard times (Peterson 2016; Ryan and Haslam 2005). The implication is that women who rise to high levels at such times end up in highly precarious positions. In such a situation, females are more likely than males to find themselves at the edge of an organizational cliff. A disproportionate number of those women are likely to be demoted or fall off that cliff (i.e., lose their jobs) and be replaced by males (Cook and Glass 2014).

OTHER PROBLEMS IN ORGANIZATIONS

Beyond the problems associated with gendered organizations, the ideal-typical bureaucracy makes no provision for an array of other problems in the organization or for problematic organizations. However, in the real world there is no shortage of either. The most heinous example of a problematic (to put it mildly) organization is the Nazi bureaucracy responsible for the murder of 6 million Jews, and others, during the Holocaust (Bauman 1989). The Islamic State, Al-Qaeda, the Mafia, and Mexican drug cartels, among many others, would also be considered by most people to be problematic organizations. In addition, many less developed countries in the world regard global organizations such as the International Monetary Fund and the World Bank as problematic because of the damaging austerity programs and other forms of "structural adjustment" they impose on recipient countries in exchange for monetary assistance and other help.

Problems also occur in organizations that in themselves are not seen as problematic. For example, a scandal broke out in the National Football League (NFL) in late 2014 when the website TMZ released a video of Baltimore Ravens star running back Ray Rice knocking out his then-fiancée (and later wife) in an elevator in an Atlantic City hotel-casino earlier in the year. The NFL claimed it did not know about the incident, although it turned out that it did. When the incident became public, Rice was at first suspended for two games, but when the public furor grew, he was released by the Ravens and suspended by the NFL. The NFL could come increasingly to be seen as a problematic organization as evidence of player spousal abuse mounts, along with alarming revelations about the disastrous long-term effects of brain-related injuries incurred by players during practices and games, including dementia and suicide, stemming from concussions. The NFL seems to have learned its lesson, as is clear in the case of another scandal known as "Deflategate." Various people associated with the New England Patriots deflated footballs before the 2015 Super Bowl game (won by the Patriots) in order to give the team an advantage over the Indianapolis Colts. A quick investigation was undertaken, and as a result the Patriots were penalized in various ways: They were fined $1 million and lost two future draft picks, and superstar quarterback Tom Brady was to be suspended without pay for the first four games of the next season (Pennington 2015a). He appealed that judgment, but dropped his appeal in mid-2016, and he was suspended for the first four games of the 2016–2017 NFL season.

Sexual harassment, another common organizational problem, consists of unwanted sexual attention, such as sexually oriented remarks and jokes, advances, and requests that take place in the workplace or in other settings (see Chapter 9). In the United States, the federal Equal Employment Opportunity Commission (2015) was informed of 6,822 charges of sexual harassment in the workplace in 2015. However, many women (and the vast majority of victims are women) are afraid to report to management that they have been subjected to sexual harassment. Even when claims of sexual harassment are reported to management, many claims never find their way into the judicial or criminal justice system.

Cases of sexual harassment also rarely get publicity, but that is changing. For example, in mid-2016, Roger Ailes, the powerful head of Fox News, was sued by a former news anchor, Gretchen Carlson, for sexual harassment (she was awarded $20 million). Other female newscasters at Fox were then emboldened to claim that they, too, had been subject to sexual harassment. In short order, Ailes was forced to resign as a result of the lawsuit and an internal investigation by Fox News of the other claims of sexual harassment by Ailes, as well as the enormous negative publicity that the case engendered (Koblin, Steel, and Rutenberg 2016). In April 2017, Bill O'Reilly was also forced to resign from Fox News because of numerous complaints of sexual harassment.

While there is a tendency to ignore it, sexual harassment is widely practiced not only in the United States but globally, and a great many women are harmed by it. The United Nations estimates that 40 to 50 percent of women in European Union countries experience some form of sexual harassment at work (Directorate-General for Employment, Industrial Relations and Social Affairs 1998, iii, cited in United Nations General Assembly 2006, 42; see also UN Women 2014).

To be considered illegal in the United States, sexual harassment must recur and/or be severe and result in a hostile workplace environment or even the firing of the harassed employment. The stereotype of the high-ranking man (e.g., Roger Ailes) demanding sexual favors from subordinates (usually women) is generally accurate, although both men and women can perpetrate and be subject to all forms of sexual harassment. About 17 percent of 2015 charges reported to the Equal Opportunity Employment Commission were filed by men (U.S. Equal Employment Opportunity Commission 2015).

In the U.S. armed forces, sexual harassment does seem to follow the stereotypical pattern of males harassing females. There have been many allegations of sexual harassment (and sexual assault) of female service members, and criticism of the armed services for failing to react adequately has been mounting. The U.S. Department of Defense reported that cases of sexual assault in the military increased almost 50 percent between fiscal year 2012 and fiscal year 2013 and continue to grow (see Figure 5.3). Military men and those at higher ranks perceived fewer barriers to reporting such assaults compared to military women and those at lower ranks (U.S. Equal Employment Opportunity Commission 2015).

One of the largest organizations in the world, the Catholic Church, has had to address a global organizational culture that enabled priests and other church officials to perpetuate a system of sexual assaults and abuses against children. This culture has been a huge problem not only because of the behavior of the priests and its impact on children, but also because church officials have not done

FIGURE 5.3 • Total Reports of Sexual Assault Made to the Department of Defense, 2004–2015

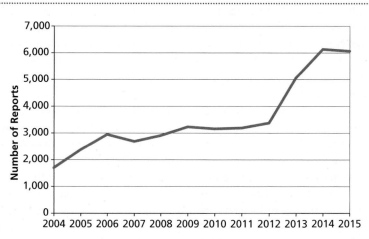

SOURCES: Data from U.S. Department of Defense, "Sexual Assault Prevention and Response," *Department of Defense Annual Report on Sexual Assault in the Military: Fiscal Year 2013* (Washington, DC: Author, 2014); data for 2014 onward from U.S. Department of Defense, "Appendix B: Statistics on Sexual Assault," Fiscal Year 2015 (Washington DC: Author, 2015).

nearly enough to dismiss those responsible and make it more difficult for such assaults to occur in the future. This problem and the difficulties involved in uncovering it, let alone dealing with it, constitute the central theme of *Spotlight,* the 2016 Academy Award winner for best motion picture.

Disasters (and other unplanned outcomes) are deeply problematic for organizations. Such events often occur as the result of rational organizational processes (Vaughan 1996). For example, in the 1980s, the National Aeronautics and Space Administration (NASA) operated on the basis of what it considered to be a highly reliable and rational plan. As a result, it focused on, among many other things, a variety of quantifiable factors to keep the space shuttle *Challenger* on schedule for its launch. In doing so, the agency cut a number of corners and engaged in various economies. These actions made sense from the perspective of NASA as a rationalized organization. However, they contributed to the disaster on January 28, 1986, in which *Challenger's* fuel tank broke apart, causing the in-flight destruction of the shuttle and the deaths of seven crew members.

CONTEMPORARY CHANGES IN ORGANIZATIONS

Bureaucratic organizations have undergone a number of important changes that do not fit well with Weber's view of organizations. For one thing, contrary to Weber's thinking on the likelihood of their growth and spread, many of the largest organizations, especially industrial organizations and labor unions, have been forced to downsize dramatically (Cooper, Pandey, and Campbell 2012). The idea that "bigger is better" is no longer the rule in most organizations. Instead of constantly adding new functions, and more employees, organizations are now likely to focus on their "core competencies." For example, the Ford Motor Company is focusing on manufacturing automobiles and not, as it once did, on making (among many other things) the steel for the frames and the rubber for the tires. Ford also sold off the Volvo and Jaguar lines to focus on the Ford brand. In essence, organizations have come to concentrate on being "lean and mean" (Harrison 1994). They have also sought to streamline their systems of production—to develop lean methods

of production using more high-tech systems and fewer employees (Janoski 2015). Many newer organizations such as Facebook and even Google have learned crucial lessons from the problems experienced by organizational giants such as Ford. They are smaller and far less hierarchical; they are increasingly flat structures with the characteristics of social networks discussed in Chapter 4. They seek to avoid ever losing their focus or becoming too large and diverse. As a result, it is unlikely that they will ever need to downsize or simplify to the degree that Ford has in order to accomplish these goals.

To adapt to a rapidly changing environment, contemporary organizations have also been forced to become more flexible and more agile than the ideal-typical bureaucracy suggests. For example, it appears that Ford has become flexible enough to compete with rising automobile manufacturers such as Hyundai. When today's organizations lack such flexibility, there is a strong likelihood that they will decline or disappear. For instance, the video store chain Blockbuster, which went bankrupt in 2010 and closed its last store in late 2013, failed to adapt to competition from Netflix and, at least initially, its movies by mail. More important, it failed to anticipate the streaming of movies to one's television or computer (and now to both smart TVs and regular TVs connected through devices such as Roku). Customers were no longer willing to travel to a video store when they could stream movies from the comfort of their homes via a cable provider such as Comcast or online from Netflix, Hulu, or Amazon.

Yet another important organizational development is the increasing trend toward **outsourcing**, or the transfer of activities once performed by one organization to another organization in exchange for money. Since the early 2000s, outsourcing has increased dramatically. Companies have become more likely to outsource functions such as those handled traditionally by human resource departments (Korkki 2012). Hospitals outsource the operation of their emergency rooms to businesses that employ people—including physicians—devoted to such work. Hospitals are also increasingly likely to outsource such activities as cleaning and food preparation to outside contractors. Local, state, and federal governments also outsource work to other organizations, especially private businesses. An example that received a lot of negative publicity after the Iraq war was the U.S. government's outsourcing of many military and paramilitary activities in Iraq to a company known as Blackwater (now Xe Services), which engaged in unwarranted killings and use of unnecessary force.

Another recent trend in organizations not anticipated by Weber's ideal-typical bureaucracy is that of turning over to clients some of the work formerly performed by officeholders. For example, we are increasingly filling out census forms on our own, thereby doing work that used to be done by census takers. We are scanning checks into our smartphones instead of handing them to tellers, reviewing restaurants and movies online rather than reading reviews by professional critics, and talking about our experiences with products or brands on social networking sites instead of passively accepting advertising messages from producers. More and more, we are scanning our own groceries; the first self-checkout machine was installed in the United States in 1992, and by 2014 it was estimated that 430,000 such machines were in operation across the country. In taking on these tasks, clients and consumers are turned into producers, at least for a time. In other words, consumers have been transformed into *prosumers,* combining the acts of consumption and production (Ritzer, Dean, and Jurgenson 2012; see Chapter 12). This is yet another wide-ranging and pervasive change that is dramatically transforming the nature of organizations and organizational life. The most recent changes are even eliminating the work performed by customers and clients and turning it over to "smart machines" (Ritzer 2015b). For example, instead of requiring a person to unload a shopping cart and scan each product at checkout, a smart machine can now scan the products in the cart as the customer leaves the store and charge the total bill to the customer's credit card.

GLOBALIZATION AND ORGANIZATIONS

Most organizations of any significant size have become increasingly global. They are affected by numerous global realities and changes and in many cases have become global forces and players themselves. The global reach of McDonald's is well known. It has more than 36,000 restaurants in 119 countries throughout the world. However, in the fast-food industry, Yum! Brands (corporate parent of Pizza Hut, KFC, and others) is in slightly more countries—140—and has more than 7,000 more restaurants than McDonald's. Walmart is another American global powerhouse, with more than 11,000 stores in 27 countries. Other organizations with a presence in the United States have their roots elsewhere in the world. Examples include IKEA, based in Sweden, with 328 stores in 28 countries; H&M, an apparel retailer from Sweden; T-Mobile, a telecommunications company originating in Germany; HSBC, a financial services provider from Hong Kong and Shanghai; and Zara International, a fashion retailer, whose home base is in Spain (Ritzer 2015a).

Globalization has also accelerated the transfer of work to organizations in other countries, known as **offshore outsourcing**. See Table 5.1 for a list of the world's top 20 outsourcing destinations. The top 8

TABLE 5.1 • Top 20 Outsourcing Destinations, 2016

RANK	COUNTRY	CITY
1	India	Bangalore
2	Philippines	Manila
3	India	Mumbai
4	India	Delhi
5	India	Chennai
6	India	Hyderabad
7	Philippines	Cebu City
8	India	Pune
9	Poland	Kraków
10	Ireland	Dublin
11	Costa Rica	San José
12	China	Shanghai
13	China	Beijing
14	Czech Republic	Prague
15	China	Dalian
16	Sri Lanka	Colombo
17	Malaysia	Kuala Lumpur
18	Vietnam	Ho Chi Minh City
19	Vietnam	Hanoi
20	South Africa	Johannesburg

SOURCE: Data from "Tholons 2016 Top 100 Outsourcing Destinations," Tholons, January 29, 2016.

david pearson/Alamy Stock Photo

One form of offshore outsourcing that has become familiar to many U.S. consumers is customer service and product support provided by Indian call centers. Why are some employees in such centers encouraged to assume American identities?

Donald Trump railed against the fact that offshore outsourcing had caused the loss of companies and the jobs they had provided. In addition, there was already a movement for *backsourcing,* or bringing businesses and jobs back into the countries that were not long ago eager to outsource them (Gylling et al. 2015). However, given the erosion and destruction of plants and equipment in those countries and the seeming paucity of workers willing to take low-wage, low-skill jobs, it remains to be seen how much backsourcing will actually occur in Europe and the United States.

destination cities are all in India and the Philippines, where a large proportion of the population is fluent in English. This is important because the United States is the world leader in offshore outsourcing. Offshore outsourcing takes many forms, but the one we are most familiar with is the outsourcing of call center work. A call center is a centralized office that handles a large volume of telephone calls from people asking an organization for information and help. At first, many U.S. organizations outsourced such work to call centers in the United States. More recently, much of that work has been outsourced offshore because it can be done outside the United States much less expensively.

India is a particularly attractive location for the outsourcing of call center work once performed in the United States. The pay of call center workers is much lower in India than it is in the United States, and many Indians speak excellent English. In fact, many call center workers outside the United States are expected to "pose as Americans" as part of their employment. In a strategy referred to as "national identity management," they adopt, among other things, American names and hometowns (Poster 2007).

Recently, there has been a backlash against offshore outsourcing. This has occurred in a number of European countries, but it has been especially strong in the United States. In the 2016 presidential campaign,

McDonaldization and Bureaucratic Organizations

During the early twenty-first century, the fast-food restaurant can be seen as the best example of the ongoing process of rationalization first described by Weber (Ritzer 2015a). While the fast-food restaurant is a relatively new and important organizational development, it is continuous with the bureaucracy and its basic principles: efficiency, predictability, calculability, control, and the seemingly inevitable irrationalities of rationality. What, then, distinguishes McDonaldized fast-food restaurants from bureaucracies?

Many fast-food restaurants, and a variety of other businesses, are franchised. In a franchise system, a large business (like McDonald's) sells various rights to franchisees, who control small, legally independent firms. The franchisees invest their own money, and much of the risk of failure falls on them rather than the big business that grants the franchise. In return for their investment, franchisees obtain the right to use, among many other things, the company name, its logo (e.g., the "Golden Arches"), its distinctive products, and its ways of operating. While each franchise is independent, it "must conform to detailed standards of operation designed and enforced by the parent company" (Dicke 1992, 2–3). Thus, a franchise system combines a small business with a large bureaucratic system in which it exists and functions. Most important, the franchise must operate on the basis of the same rational principles that characterize the large bureaucratic organization.

McDonaldization is applicable to both consumption-oriented organizations and production-oriented organizations. The bureaucratic model is most applicable, outside of government, to large production-oriented corporations. However, the United States has moved away from a society dominated by work and production to one dominated by consumption. As a result, the large corporation involved in goods production has declined in importance, at least in the United States and other developed countries. In its place we have seen the rise of similarly large corporations, such as Subway, Walmart, and IKEA, devoted to consumption. While the corporate structures of these organizations remain highly bureaucratized, their real hearts lie in the numerous smaller outlets that constitute the sources of income and profit for the organizations. Thus, of greatest importance now is the McDonaldization of those outlets and not the bureaucratization of the larger organizations in which they exist.

The key point is that bureaucratization involves a kind of rationality that is highly centralized and largely invisible to those who consume the goods and services produced by these organizations. However, McDonaldization is both very local and highly visible to those who consume in settings such as fast-food restaurants. People have a lot of direct, person-to-person contact with those who work in McDonaldized settings. This means, among other things, that the fast-food restaurant—and, indeed, almost all McDonaldized systems in the realm of consumption—needs to be much more "customer-friendly" than does the traditional bureaucracy. Counter people are trained to smile and wish you a "nice day." At Walmart there is even an employee—the greeter—whose sole task is to be warm and friendly to customers when they enter the store. Then there are those "smiley faces" that customers see throughout the store. Similarly, Mac computers maintain their physical presence through aesthetically pleasing Apple stores, which include "genius bars" staffed by friendly and knowledgeable workers who can answer questions in person and fix your laptop.

ASK YOURSELF

Why do you think being customer-friendly is more important to McDonaldized systems than to traditional bureaucracies? What is the goal of this user-friendliness, and why aren't bureaucracies more user-friendly?

Despite the spread of McDonaldization, some are speculating that it, like bureaucratization, has passed its peak. The online auction site eBay is considered by some to be a new model of organizational development in the contemporary world (Ahuvia and Izberk-Bilgin 2011). Unlike McDonaldization, the basic dimensions of eBayization include variety, unpredictability, and limited control. Millions of products are available on eBay, compared to only the few dozen offered at McDonald's. The predictable products of McDonald's are quite unlike the highly unpredictable products on eBay. Whereas eBay sellers interact directly with buyers of their products, with little involvement from the eBay organization, McDonaldized systems exercise more widespread control. McDonald's may be fast, but eBay is vast. However, it is possible to argue that eBay is a highly McDonaldized company. For example, it takes a highly rationalized company and system to offer millions of products for sale.

NETWORK ORGANIZATIONS

The bureaucracy and the fast-food restaurant both continue to be important in the early twenty-first century. However, organizations continue to change and evolve. Further, entirely new organizational forms are coming into existence. One such new form is the **network organization**, which is defined by its networks, especially those based on and linked together by information (Blaschke, Schoeneborn, and Seidl 2012). The network organization came about in the wake of the revolution in informational technology in the United States in the 1970s. Developments included the penetration of television deep into American life and the introduction of home computers, personal data assistants (PDAs), and the internet (Van Dijk 2012). The network model is also inextricably entwined with globalization. Most of the important functions and processes in the information age are increasingly dominated by these networks, and many of them are global in scope. This revolution led, in turn, to a fundamental restructuring of the global capitalist system beginning in the 1980s. For example, multinational corporations grew in importance, in part because of great improvements in the ability to communicate globally. Those corporations that were narrowly nation based experienced serious declines or were themselves transformed into multinationals.

Characteristics of the Network Organization

This new organizational form has several notable characteristics. Of greatest importance is the idea that an organization is composed of several networks, or "interconnected nodes" (see the discussion of social networks in Chapter 4). A network organization has the following characteristics:

- *Horizontal structure*. In contrast to the vertical and hierarchical structures that characterize classic bureaucracies, network organizations are flatter, meaning that there are fewer positions between the top of the organization and the bottom.

- *Fuzzy boundaries*. Network organizations are *not* seen as distinct entities with clear and definite boundaries, as would be the case with a bureaucracy. Rather, organizations intertwine with one another in many ways. Most obviously, they form strategic alliances with other organizations that have similar or complementary goals.

- *Dispersed decision making*. Many of the differences between network organizations and bureaucracies stem from a number of highly successful Japanese innovations. One such innovation is more collective decision making, or the involvement of many more people in the organization in the decision-making process.

- *Flexible production*. Manufacturing organizations with a network model have moved away from mass production and toward more flexible production methods, such as variable and limited production runs.

An organization with these characteristics is, in comparison with a bureaucracy, more open, more capable of expansion, more dynamic, and better able to innovate without disrupting the system.

In the global information economy, at least in developed nations, the nature of work is being transformed. Workers, including manufacturing employees, are dealing more with information and less with material processes. This has reduced the total number of employees needed, even as output increases. In addition, the network organization allows for new kinds of work arrangements because information can flow anywhere, especially anywhere there is a computer and a smartphone. Thus, for example, more people can work from the comfort of their homes, in transit on airplanes, and in hotels anyplace in the world.

Informationalism

The processing of knowledge, or what Manuel Castells (1996, 1997, 1998) famously calls **informationalism**, is a key feature of the network organization. Forces of production and consumption, such as factories and shopping malls, are linked through knowledge and information. Thus, for example, the stocking of shelves at Walmart is done nearly automatically. Computerized technology at the local Walmart tracks stock on hand and transmits the information to centralized warehouses. As the stock is being depleted, new shipments are sent out automatically, so that the shelves at the local Walmart will remain well stocked.

Informationalism has five basic characteristics:

- Technologies act on information, such as the depletion of stock at Walmart.

- These technologies have a pervasive effect, as information transmitted to personal computers, tablets, and smartphones increasingly becomes a part of all human activity.

- All organizations, and other systems, using information technologies are defined by a "networking logic" that allows them to affect a wide variety of processes and organizations to which they are linked. For example, Walmart has linkages to its many suppliers throughout the world.

- The new technologies are highly flexible, allowing them to adapt and change constantly.

- The specific technologies associated with information are already merging into a highly integrated system that cuts across many different organizations and areas of the world. Thus, for example, the internet, e-mail, and text messaging link innumerable global organizations.

As a result of informationalism, a new, increasingly profitable global information economy has emerged. The productivity of firms and nations depends on their ability to generate, process, and apply knowledge-based information efficiently. Global communication systems allow those involved in this economy to operate as a unit on a worldwide scale. While it is a global system, there are regional differences, even among those areas—North America, the European Union, the Asia-Pacific region—that are at the heart of the new global economy (Abdul 2015). Other regions such as sub-Saharan Africa are largely excluded, as are pockets of deprivation in the developed world, including inner cities in the United States.

The network organization, as well as the informationalism that defines it, is the latest organizational form to draw sociologists' attention, but it will certainly not be the last. New organizational forms are likely to emerge as society and the world continue to change.

Manuel Castells is well known for his research in communication and the information society, including the ways in which information is increasingly becoming a part of all human activity and how the processing of knowledge has allowed for the emergence of an increasingly profitable global information economy. He is also known for his studies of social movements.

SOCIETIES

Sociologists have traditionally defined *society* as a complex pattern of social relationships that is bounded in space and persists over time. This definition has two key characteristics: First, it is very abstract; second, this abstractness allows it to encompass the gamut of social relationships. Thus, in these terms, a triad (a three-person group) and any larger group would be a kind of society, as would the United States and other countries, as well as global organizations such as the United Nations and the International Monetary Fund.

Ferdinand Toennies ([1887] 1957) differentiated between two broad types of societies—*gemeinschaft* and *gesellschaft*. He labeled traditional societies **gemeinschaft societies** and defined them as being characterized by face-to-face relations. Toennies considered families, rural villages, and small towns to be gemeinschaft societies. Such societies tend to be quite small because they are based on intimate interaction. Relationships between people are valued for their intrinsic qualities, such as familiarity and closeness, and not, or at least not merely, for their utility. Gemeinschaft societies continue to exist in many parts of the world, including the United States.

More modern societies are **gesellschaft societies**, characterized by impersonal, distant, and limited social relationships. In such societies, people tend to enter relationships for what they can gain from them rather than for their intrinsic qualities. That is, relationships are often a means to an end. Gesellschaft societies are much more likely to be large-scale societies, or to exist within them.

Of course, gemeinschaft and gesellschaft are ideal types. In the real world, including today's world, aspects of both exist in all societies. The abstract and broad-ranging definition of society mentioned previously encompasses both gemeinschaft and gesellschaft societies, and everything in between. Furthermore, both concepts can be applied to every social relationship, from the smallest group, such as a dyad or triad, to the largest society, such as China.

ASK YOURSELF

Keeping in mind that gesellschaft and gemeinschaft societies are idealized abstractions of reality and that real societies can have characteristics of both, make a list of all the groups and communities to which you belong and decide which are more gesellschaft and which are more gemeinschaft. Why have you included each group or community in one category or the other? In which groups or communities do you prefer to spend time, and why?

Although the earlier general definition of society has its utility, society can be more narrowly and specifically—and usefully—defined as a relatively large population that lives in a given territory, has a social structure, and shares a culture. The United States, China, and Spain would be societies in this macro-level sense of the term; a triad or group or organization would not be a society. This definition also fits the thrust of this chapter, which ends with a discussion of the most macroscopic level of social organization: the global society.

One of the best-known theories of society in this sense was created by Talcott Parsons. As a structural-functionalist, Parsons had a very positive view of macro-level societies. He was concerned with the major structures of societies, including the economy, the political system, systems responsible for transmitting culture and its norms and values (e.g., schools), and the legal system, which is responsible for the integration of society. Clearly, these are key components of society in the macro sense of the term.

Sociologists who study societies often ask big questions about them and their changing nature. One of the most notable recent efforts to think

about the issues facing society as a whole is the work of German sociologist Ulrich Beck. Until recently, it was the norm to think of society as being dominated by industry. In "industrial society," the key issue was wealth and how to distribute it more evenly. However, Beck ([1986] 1992) argues that we have moved from an industrial society to a **risk society**, where the central issue is how to prevent, minimize, and channel risk. While in an industrial society a central concern is equality, in a risk society the focus shifts to how to remain safe in the face of increasing risk. Most important, there is a big difference between the two types of societies in the ways in which solidarity is achieved. In an industrial society, solidarity is achieved by people joining together for the positive goal of creating a more equal society. In a risk society, solidarity is achieved through the largely negative and defensive goal of being spared from danger. The implication is that risk society is weaker, more individualized, and less laudable than industrial society and its humanitarian goal of increased equality.

Globalization is the major reason why there are far greater risks to society than ever before. Risks in one society easily flow to many other societies. For example, because of relatively easy and inexpensive air travel, a flu outbreak in one society can quickly engulf many other societies. Thus, modern risks are not easily restricted to one locale or society. For example, the 2014 Ebola epidemic spread throughout several countries in West Africa, killing thousands of people. It also spread to the United States after an infected man from Liberia, Thomas Duncan, traveled to Dallas. Two of the nurses caring for him contracted Ebola, and though both nurses recovered, Duncan died from the virus. In addition, an American doctor working in Guinea was diagnosed with Ebola several days after he returned to the United States. Though many feared that they may have contracted the disease after being in close proximity with that doctor, there were no reported cases.

Globalization has led some sociologists to call into question the equation of society and the nation-state, arguing that in the contemporary world, it is necessary to think about a global society. Debates about the possibility of global citizenship are one example of how the idea of globalization is reshaping how we think about the boundaries of what we call society (Kivisto and Faist 2007, 138–140).

John Urry (2000) argues that because of all sorts of increased mobilities, we live in a post-society era. People, objects, and information, among many other things, move too often and too quickly to be encapsulated in societies or, perhaps, anything else. It is clear from the preceding discussion that sociologists who still analyze societies do not stop at their borders but also examine various mobilities within, among, and between societies. As a result, the focus of such scholarship in recent years has shifted beyond societies and even their interrelationships to the even more macroscopic global level and the mobilities that serve to define it.

GLOBAL RELATIONSHIPS

Most sociological work on the global level operates with a set of concepts that are different from those discussed throughout this chapter. All of these concepts are consistent with the macroscopic sense of society:

- A **nation** is a large group of people linked through common descent, culture, language, or territory. Nations can exist in contiguous geographic areas, regardless of country borders. For example, the Kurds live in Kurdistan, a region that overlaps Iraq, Iran, Syria, and Turkey. Nations can also be spread throughout much of the world, such as the Roma people (so-called Gypsies), who live throughout Europe and increasingly in the United States.

- A **state** is a political organizational structure with relatively autonomous officeholders that makes its own rules and receives its resources largely from taxes. The U.S. government would be an example of a state.

- A **nation-state** is an entity that encompasses both the populations that define themselves as a nation and the organizational structure of the state. Israel is a nation-state, because it has a state government and encompasses a nation of Jews.

Of greater importance in the global age is the idea that these entities, especially the nation-state, are losing influence because of globalization and broad global processes, including mobilities and flows of all types.

CONTROLLING GLOBAL FLOWS AND MOBILITIES

The nation-state is under siege largely because it has lost or is losing control over a number of global flows and mobilities (Ritzer and Dean 2015). In many ways, the global flow that most threatens the nation-state is informationalism. E-mail, entries on Facebook, tweets, and WhatsApp messages, to take a few examples, flow around the world readily and quickly. There is little or nothing the nation-state can do to stop or limit those flows, although China, among others, keeps trying (see Figure 5.4 for a depiction of the levels of internet freedom in countries around the world). The Chinese government has erected the "Great Firewall of China," a virtual surveillance system that censors what its citizens can access on the internet, including a block on Google and on web sources that promote free speech and other Western, democratic values (Denyer 2016). There are many economic, financial, and technological flows around the world that involve information of various kinds. Global information flows have the potential to subvert the authority of nation-states because they cover a much larger geographic area than the nation-state. This is especially true of information that would cast a negative light on the nation-state. One example would be the distribution of information throughout China about the great inequality that exists there and China's human rights abuses.

A more specific example of the decreasing ability of nation-states to isolate themselves from global processes is the economic crisis that began in the United States in late 2007 and cascaded rapidly around the world. For example, dramatic drops in the U.S. stock market (see the film *The Big Short* [2015] for a fictionalized treatment of the origins of that economic crisis) were followed by declines in many other stock markets in the world. Similarly, bank failures in the United States were quickly followed by even more ruinous bank failures in other countries, most notably Iceland and Ireland. This series of events illustrates the importance and power of global flows and demonstrates the inability of the nation-state to do much, if anything, to limit the impact of global flows on its economy and the lives of its citizens within its borders.

FIGURE 5.4 • Freedom on the Internet, 2016

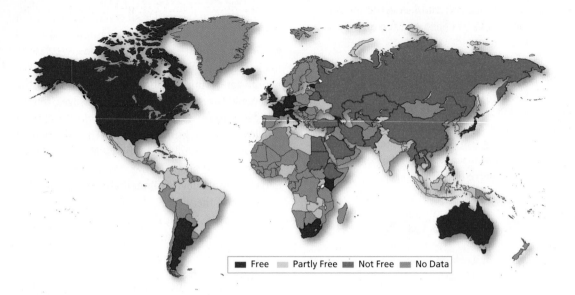

Legend: ■ Free ■ Partly Free ■ Not Free ■ No Data

SOURCE: Reprinted with permission from Freedom House.

The Islamic State (IS) organization has been very adept at using many types of media in a recruitment effort that reaches many parts of the world. Its communications are designed to transcend national boundaries in order to attract new supporters, who, the group hopes, will help force the creation of a new nation-state, a caliphate. Among other things, IS has released videos of threatened and actual beheadings, has been active on social media (including Twitter), and has made imitations of popular video games (such as *Call of Duty*) and movies (such as *Natural Born Killers* and *Saw*). Countries in which IS has been successful in finding recruits, such as France, England, and even the United States, would dearly love to stop its call to arms, but that is literally impossible given the nature of modern technology.

Information and economic flows are just two of the many global flows that nation-states cannot control. Among the others are flows of undocumented immigrants, new social movements, expertise in various domains, terrorists, criminals, drugs, money (including laundered money and other financial instruments), and human trafficking. Then there are global problems such as Zika virus, HIV/AIDS, H1N1 flu, tuberculosis, and the effects of climate change that flow around the world readily and cannot be handled very well by a nation-state operating on its own.

Thus, the largest unit of analysis in sociology has now become the globe, and especially the global flows that best define globalization today. The concept of globalization appears throughout this book in an informal sense, but it is now time for a formal definition of *globalization:* "a transplanetary *process* or set of *processes* involving increasing *liquidity* and the growing multidirectional *flows* of people, objects, places and information as well as the *structures* they encounter and create that are *barriers* to, or *expedite,* those flows" (Ritzer and Dean 2015, 2 [emphasis in original]; see also Chapter 14). Clearly, this is a view that goes beyond the nation-state and sees it as enmeshed in and subordinated to a global set of flows, mobilities, and structures.

OTHER GLOBAL FLOWS

Globalization is increasingly characterized by great flows of not just information, ideas, and images but also objects and people. For example, food now flows more quickly and to more people around the world (Inglis 2016). Examples of foods sold in locales far from their sources include fresh fruit from Chile, fresh sushi from Japan, and live lobsters from Maine. Looking at a very different kind of flow, migration within countries and from one country to another has become more common as well.

Landscapes

Although global flows and globalization contribute to some degree of homogenization of the social experience around the world, they also contribute to greater global cultural diversity and heterogeneity. A very important contribution to thinking on the latter aspects of global flows is Arjun Appadurai's (1996) work on what he calls **landscapes**—*scapes* for short. These are fluid, irregular, and variable global flows that produce different results throughout the world. As we will see in the following list, these scapes can involve the flow of many different things, including people and ideas. At the heart of Appadurai's thinking are five types of landscapes that operate independent of one another to some degree, and may even conflict with one another:

- **Ethnoscapes** allow the movement, or fantasies about movement, of various individuals and groups, such as tourists and refugees. The ethnoscape of undocumented immigrants is of particular concern these days. They are often poor people who have in the main been forced to move because of poverty and poor job prospects in their home countries. They have also moved because of the belief, sometimes the fantasy, that economic conditions will be better for them elsewhere in the world, especially in the more developed countries of the United States and Western Europe.

- **Technoscapes** include mechanical technologies such as the containerized ships now used to transport freight, informational technologies such as the internet, and the materials (e.g., refrigerators and e-mail) that move so quickly and freely throughout the world via those technologies.

- **Financescapes** use various financial instruments to allow huge sums of money and other items of economic value (e.g., stocks, bonds, and precious metals, especially gold) to move through nations and around the world at great speed, almost instantaneously. The great global economic meltdown that began in late 2007 demonstrated quite clearly the importance and the power of financescapes in the contemporary world.

- **Mediascapes** include both the electronic capability to produce and transmit information around the world and the images of the world that these media create and disseminate. Those who write blogs and download photos on Tumblr and videos on YouTube, global filmmakers and film distributors, global TV networks (such as CNN and Al Jazeera), and even old-fashioned newspapers and magazines create a variety of mediascapes.

- **Ideoscapes**, like mediascapes, include images, although they are largely restricted to political images in line with the ideologies of nation-states. Also included here are images and counterideologies produced by social movements oriented toward supplanting those in power or at least gaining a portion of that power. Thus, for example, the United States has one ideoscape that disseminates negative images and information about IS; in turn, IS has an ideoscape that responds with similarly negative images and information about the United States.

Further increasing the global heterogeneity that results from the interaction of these landscapes is the fact that the impact of one can be at variance, or even in conflict, with another. In addition, these landscapes are interpreted differently by people and groups in different parts of the world. Interpretations depend on both the cultures in which people exist and the people's own subjective perspectives on the scapes. Powerful forces create at least some of these scapes. Nonetheless, those who merely live in them or pass through them have the power not only to redefine them in idiosyncratic ways but also ultimately to subvert them in many different ways. For example, those on a guided tour designed to show a given locale in a positive light can break off from the tour and see and hear things that lead to a very different impression of the locale. When the tourists return home, they can portray that locale in a way that contradicts the image presented by the tour creators and guides.

DIGITAL LIVING: DIGITAL CURRENCY

One relatively recent addition to the global financescape is Bitcoin, a digital currency, which is popularly referred to as "digital gold." It is a universal currency that can be used in all countries, so a Bitcoin user does not need to exchange it for local currencies when he or she crosses national borders (Popper 2015). Bitcoin was created in 2008; since then, more than 41 million Bitcoin accounts have been opened around the world. Unlike national currencies that are created by central banks and controlled by national governments, Bitcoin is decentralized and overseen by volunteers, who authenticate encrypted electronic signatures on transactions (Kharif 2014; Popper 2015). Bitcoins can be accrued through extensive data mining or purchased on Bitcoin currency exchanges. These online exchanges require consumers to open an account and create a digital wallet. They can then transfer money into the digital wallet, buy and sell bitcoins, and purchase products and services from individuals and companies that accept bitcoins. Bitcoin ATMs allow users to deposit cash into their digital wallets at physical locations in their communities (Ember 2014). Concern exists, however, over the actual value of a bitcoin and whether or not this digital currency will crash eventually.

Libertarians and anarchists were early supporters of Bitcoin because of its decentralized organizational structure and the lack of government regulations for its

Bitcoin ATMs, like this one, allow users to exchange their currency for the digital money.

use (Kharif 2014). Because of the digital nature of bitcoins, they are easy to transfer and difficult to trace, especially their sources and destinations, which remain anonymous. Thus, they are favored by those involved in criminal activities, as well as by those active in the dark web, where cyberpunks challenge the dominance of large global financial institutions (Popper 2015). Criminals appreciate the anonymity of bitcoins because they can use them to buy and sell illegal goods and services on websites such as the Silk Road. The utility of bitcoins for criminals was manifest most dramatically (so far) in a May 2017 global cyberattack (Reuters 2017). Those whose computers were attacked by this "ransomware" were instructed to pay a minimum of $300 in bitcoins, or else they would lose at least some of their computerized data.

While still tainted by its association with criminality, Bitcoin has begun to move into the mainstream. Parents are using the digital currency to pay babysitters or distribute allowances to their children (Kharif 2014). It is a quick and convenient way to electronically transfer money to a friend in another country without having to wait for a bank to open or a personal check to clear. Many mass retailers and big box stores, such as CVS and Home Depot, now accept bitcoins.

Engaging the Digital World
You can find the Bitcoin ATM nearest to you at http://coinatmradar .com, and you can learn where you can use Bitcoin at www.coindesk .com/information/what-can-you-buy-with-bitcoins or https://coinmap.org.

Where would you be most likely to use Bitcoin, and what would you purchase with it? Why? How do you think using PayPal is similar to or different from using Bitcoin?

GLOBAL BARRIERS

The globe and the flows that increasingly pervade it are of central concern to sociology. However, there is another aspect of globalization that is of growing concern to sociology, and that is the various global barriers to these flows. The world is made up of not just a series of flows but also structures such as trade agreements, regulatory agencies, borders, and customs barriers. Any thoroughgoing account of globalization needs to look at the ways in which structures alter and even block flows as well as produce and enhance them. The most important and most obvious barriers to global flows are those constructed by nation-states. There are borders, gates, guards, passport controls, customs agents, health inspectors, trade regulations, and so on in most countries in the world. Although undocumented immigrants, contraband goods, and digitized messages do get through those barriers, some other phenomena that nation-states deem counter to their national interests are successfully blocked or impeded. For example, in 2016 the U.S. government prevented Philips from selling the majority stake of its lighting businesses, Lumileds, to Asian buyers for "security reasons" (Sterling 2016). Congress also cited America's national security as a reason why the federal government should block the acquisition of the Chicago Stock Exchange by a Chinese company (Rogin 2016). Some have noted that as nations focus more on "nationalism and militarism," their openness to international trade and other formalized flows across borders decreases (Acemoglu and Yared 2010). This was nowhere clearer than in Donald Trump's 2016 campaign for the presidency. He adopted nationalistic and militaristic positions in order to argue for greater barriers to international trade, a ban on Muslim immigrants, the mass deportation of 11 million undocumented immigrants, to say nothing of the building of a wall between the United States and Mexico (even though immigration from Mexico has slowed to a crawl). As president, Trump has been forced to modulate some of these actions and to postpone others, but his basic position does not seem to have changed.

Are Global Barriers Effective?

However, many of the barriers created by nation-states are not effective. For instance, it is highly doubtful that the very expensive fence (to say nothing of Donald Trump's proposed wall) that has already been constructed between Mexico and the United States, combined with the use of cameras, lights, satellites, and drones, will be able to curtail the flow of undocumented immigrants to the United States. It has become more difficult, costly, and dangerous to enter the country illegally, but the fence has not stopped such entry. Moreover, the fence has had the unintended consequence of making it harder for Mexican nationals who are already in the United States illegally to move back to Mexico. Similarly, it is not clear whether the wall between Israel and the West Bank (or the more recently erected wall between Israel and Egypt) will stop the flow of terrorists into Israel the next time hostilities in the Middle East flare up. On the positive side, the wall is not stopping Palestinians and Israelis from communicating person to person via digital media. While there is no wall around the Gaza Strip, there is a closely watched and guarded wire fence. Nevertheless, beginning in 2014, and continuing to this day (Hadid and Waheidi 2016), the Israelis have found that Hamas fighters have dug numerous tunnels that they have used to commit terrorist acts in Israel.

In the European Union, until recently, barriers to movement between member countries had been greatly reduced, if not eliminated. In creating a structure that allows people (including, unfortunately, terrorists) and products (including, regrettably, illicit drugs and weapons) to move much more freely and quickly, the EU attempted to make Europe much more a space of flows than a space of places. However, that has changed recently, as a reaction against what were perceived to be the excesses of such openness (swarms of refugees—a few of whom turned out to be terrorists—swamping a country) gained force. For example, a number of EU countries (e.g. Hungary, Bulgaria, Slovenia) began building fences in an effort to keep out refugees (Lyman 2015a, 2015b). In mid-2016, Great Britain voted to leave the EU because, in large part, of the influx of immigrants (Taub 2016). It will take several years for Great Britain's exit ("Brexit") from the EU to be finalized. When this does happen, it is presumed that one of the first things that Great Britain will do will be to create greater barriers (in terms of both number and size) to the entrance of immigrants into the country.

Globalization involves a dialectic of flows and barriers to those flows. While the barriers seem to be in ascent at the moment, it is likely that the flows will continue and find ways of breaching the new barriers.

Organizational Barriers

There are many different kinds of organizations that, though they may expedite flows for some, create all sorts of barriers for others. One example is found in the two-tier system of passport control at international airports, where citizens usually pass through quickly and easily while foreigners wait in long lines. Another example is the protectionist tariff systems that nation-states create in order to help their own farmers send agricultural products (such as wheat) and their manufacturers send goods (such as automobiles) across the borders of other nation-states while inhibiting the inflow of goods from their foreign competition. For example, in January 2017, President Trump canceled the then-pending trade accord in Asia—the Trans-Pacific Partnership (TPP), involving the United States and 11 nations on the Pacific Rim—because he believed that the elimination of tariffs among the countries involved (i.e., the creation of a free-trade zone) would adversely affect American companies. It would, in his view, lead to the further loss of American jobs as industries and jobs moved to low-wage countries involved in the TPP (Granville 2016).

Multinational corporations usually use market competition rather than trade policies to achieve global success. Toyota, for instance, is devoted to optimizing the flow of its automobiles to all possible markets throughout the world. It also seeks to compete with and outperform other multinational corporations in the automobile business. If it is successful, the flow of automobiles from competing corporations is greatly reduced, further advantaging Toyota.

Labor unions are also organizations devoted to promoting the flow of some things while working against the flow of others (Bronfenbrenner 2007). Unions often oppose the flow of undocumented immigrants because they are likely to work for lower pay and fewer benefits (e.g., health insurance) than are indigenous, unionized workers. Similarly, labor unions oppose the flow of goods produced in non-union shops, in other countries as well as their own. They do so because the success of nonunion shops puts downward pressure on wages and benefits.

Unions also tend to opposed free trade agreements such as the TPP and the North American Free Trade Agreement (NAFTA) because of the belief that jobs are lost to countries with lower wages (Kaufman 2016). Unions have a complex and complicated relationship with global flows and barriers.

ASK YOURSELF

What kinds of global flows does your college or university allow or promote? What kinds of global flows does it impede, and how?

More Open Organizations?

Organizations of many types that seek to control global flows are facing increasing competition from organizations that are becoming more fluid and open. The best-known computer operating systems are produced by Microsoft. They cost a great deal and are closed. Only those who work for the company can, at least legally, work on and modify them. In contrast, IBM, a traditional closed organization, has embraced Linux, a free computer operating system that welcomes changes contributed by anyone in the world with the needed skills to do so. IBM has also opened up more and more of its own operations to outside inputs. Another example is Apple, which has traditionally kept its Macintosh operating system closed but is now allowing outsiders to produce applications for its iPhone and iPad. Many other manufacturers of smartphones have followed suit. The free online encyclopedia Wikipedia and wikis more generally encourage virtually anyone, anywhere in the world, to contribute. In contrast, traditional and very costly dictionaries such as *Merriam-Webster's Collegiate Dictionary* and reference works such as *Encyclopedia Britannica* and *The Blackwell Encyclopedia of Sociology* (Ritzer 2007) are closed to contributions from anyone other than selected and invited experts.

Even with the new open systems, structural realities help some and hinder others. For example, to contribute to Linux or Wikipedia, one must have a computer, computer expertise, and access—preferably high-speed access—to the internet. Clearly, those without economic advantages—people in the lower classes in developed countries and people who live in the less developed countries of the Global South—are on the other side of the "digital divide" and do not have access to the tools required for making such contributions. As a result, they are unable to contribute to, or to gain from, open systems to the same degree that those in more privileged positions can. The fact that women are less likely than men to contribute to Wikipedia suggests that there are additional social factors to be considered here as well (Cohen 2011). Indeed, it is argued that women experience—and need to break through—a glass ceiling in order to contribute to Wikipedia (Jemielniak 2016). This further suggests that women in the Global South are doubly disadvantaged when it comes to access to these open systems—and much else.

Thus, despite the new openness, most organizations and systems remain closed to various flows. These barriers usually benefit some (elites, males) and disadvantage others (the poor, females).

SUMMARY

Much sociological work on organizations is based on Max Weber's model of bureaucracy. However, one criticism of this model is that bureaucracies are not as highly rational as Weber believed. The informal organization refers to how organizations actually work as opposed to how they are intended to function. While bureaucratic power is supposed to be evenly dispersed, this is not always the case. For example, an oligarchy might develop if a small group of people at the top of an organization illegitimately obtain and exercise more power than they should.

Contemporary organizations faces several challenges. Women often encounter a glass ceiling as a result of gender discrimination, which prevents them from achieving vertical mobility. They also might suffer from sexual harassment. Workers have to contend with outsourcing when corporations transfer their jobs to other countries. A new type of organization, the network organization, is emerging that is based on information and is more open and flexible than class bureaucracies are.

Two ideal-typical societies exist—gemeinschaft and gesellschaft societies. Gemeinschaft societies are characterized by face-to-face relationships, while gesellschaft societies are more impersonal and distant. Today, most of us in the Global North live in a risk society, where we are focused on trying to stay safe, as opposed to an industrial society, where individuals are more concerned about wealth distribution.

A key structure in global analysis is the nation-state, which is composed of a population that defines itself as a nation and the organization structure of a state. The nation-state as a form of social organization is under siege because of global flows over which it has little control. Consequently, sociologists are coming to focus more attention on global relationships and global flows. Manuel Castells, for instance, argues that globalization has brought a change from spaces of places to spaces of flows. Arjun Appadurai focuses on five different types of global landscapes. Some barriers to global flows include nation-states and labor unions.

KEY TERMS

authority, 118
bounded rationality, 120
bureaucracy, 116
bureaucratic
    personality, 120
charismatic authority, 118
domination, 117
ethnoscapes, 135
financescapes, 135

gemeinschaft
    societies, 131
gesellschaft societies, 131
ideal type, 116
ideoscapes, 135
informal organization, 121
informationalism, 130
landscapes (scapes), 135
mediascapes, 135

nation, 133
nation-state, 133
network
    organization, 129
offshore
    outsourcing, 127
oligarchy, 121
organizations, 116
outsourcing, 126

rational-legal
    authority, 118
risk society, 132
sexual harassment, 124
state, 133
technoscapes, 135
traditional authority, 118

1. What are the characteristics of the ideal-typical bureaucracy? What are some of the ways in which the ideal-typical bureaucracy is unrealistic?

2. It is often the case that those who occupy offices lower in the bureaucratic hierarchy have greater knowledge and competence than those who rank above them. What does this suggest about the ideal-typical bureaucracy? Can you think of examples from your own experiences where this has been the case?

3. According to Weber, what are the three types of legitimate authority? How is rational-legal authority related to Weber's concept of bureaucracy?

4. Over the last several decades, what changes have bureaucratic organizations undergone? How are these changes reflective of increasing globalization?

5. What is informationalism, and how has it affected the global economy? How is the emergence of informationalism related to the development of new communication technologies, such the internet, social networking sites, and smartphones?

6. How has the process of globalization threatened the nation-state? What sorts of barriers have nation-states developed to limit global flows? What sorts of flows have nation-states been unable to limit?

7. Explain some factors that account for the emergence of a risk society. What role does globalization play in spreading risk?

8. Discuss each of Appadurai's landscapes, with special focus on the disjunctures among and between them (including examples). What are the implications of these disjunctures for the process of globalization?

9. How are network organizations different from classic bureaucracies? What are the main characteristics of networks?

10. How are open-source technologies reflective of a more fluid and open world? What structural barriers have transnational corporations created to limit these open-source technologies? What do you think is going to be the direction of the future? Why?

PRACTICE AND APPLY WHAT YOU'VE LEARNED

▶ edge.sagepub.com/
ritzeressentials3e

CHECK YOUR COMPREHENSION ON THE STUDY SITE WITH:

- **Diagnostic pre-tests** to identify opportunities for improvement.

- **eFlashcards** that strengthen your understanding of key terms and concepts.

- **Post-tests** to check your progress and ensure mastery of key learning objectives.

⑤SAGE edge™

DEVIANCE AND CRIME

Norms, Labels, and Judgment

When he was running for president, Donald Trump labeled immigrants entering the United States from and through Mexico as criminals. He said, "They're bringing drugs. They're bringing crime. They're rapists" (Mandell 2016). As a result, he announced the need to build a wall between Mexico and the United States. Such views and plans contributed much to the support for Trump's campaign and to his eventual victory in the presidential election, even though rival Hillary Clinton received a majority of the popular vote.

In the early days of Trump's administration in 2017, he initiated steps to implement his plan to keep immigrants, especially those who are undocumented, from entering the United States from Mexico. However, as of mid-2017, no progress had been made on the wall, due to widespread opposition to it, as well as to scandals that had rocked the Trump administration. Even Trump's contention that Mexico would ultimately pay for the wall no longer seemed likely. (Needless to say, Mexico does not agree with Trump's position. Taking to Twitter, former Mexican president Vicente Fox responded repeatedly to Trump, stating, "Mexico has spoken, we will never ever pay for the #F******Wall" [Fox 2017].)

Do the data actually demonstrate the need for a wall and such enormous expenditure? Are immigrants are more likely to commit serious crimes? No. Rather, the data show that immigrants are *less* likely to commit the

LEARNING OBJECTIVES

6.1 Define deviance.

6.2 Compare and contrast theories of deviance.

6.3 Discuss the criminal justice system and different types of crimes.

6.4 Summarize the relationship between globalization and crime.

edge.sagepub.com/
ritzeressentials3e

- Take the chapter quiz
- Review key terms with eFlashcards
- Explore multimedia links and SAGE readings

kinds of crimes that cause them to end up in prison (Ewing, Martinez, and Rumbaut 2015). More specifically, census data from 1980 to 2010 show that for men between 18 and 49 years of age, immigrants were only somewhere between one-fifth to one-half as likely to be in prison as those born in the United States. In addition, among those incarcerated in federal and state prisons, a smaller percentage of them are noncitizens than are represented in the population as a whole. Further, while undocumented immigrants had crime rates higher than those who had entered the United States legally, even they had lower crimes rates than did U.S. citizens (Perez-Pena 2017). In fact, communities with large numbers of immigrants are safer than most other communities (Sampson 2008).This demonstrates a key point in the sociology of crime: Criminalization is not always based on the facts, and it does not occur of its own accord. Some interest group—or an authority figure, in the case of the proposed wall on the U.S.-Mexico border—must seek to have a type of action or a group of people criminalized. This is a political decision, and it is linked to the desire on the part of one powerful group—or its leader—to exert social control over another group. ●

DEVIANCE

What exactly is deviance, and where is the line between deviance and nondeviance? Without giving it much thought, many people would likely express the absolutist view that certain things are deviant in all places, for all groups, and at all times. However, from a sociological perspective, no act, belief, or human characteristic is inherently deviant. Thus, even genocide, while morally reprehensible and indefensible, has not been defined as deviance in some societies and at certain points in time (such as in Nazi Germany). Therefore, to the sociologist, deviance is socially defined. **Deviance** is any action, belief, or human characteristic that is considered a violation of group norms by a large number of members of a society or a social group and for which the violator is likely to be censured or punished (Ben-Yehuda 2012).

If a powerful interest group wants to have a form of behavior defined as deviant, it is likely to be so defined. At the same time, powerful interest groups are likely to use their power to resist the efforts of others to define the powerful group's behaviors as deviant (McCaghy et al. 2016). For example, in the wake of the collapse of the home mortgage market in 2008, bankers fought, largely successfully, against being seen as deviant and even as criminal for their fraudulent predatory loan policies. However, borrowers who lied about their financial situation were less successful in avoiding being seen as deviant, and they suffered far greater negative consequences. They were likely to lose their homes, often their jobs, and sometimes even their health. Those interest groups that have social, political, legal, and/or financial power have a great deal of influence over who is (or is not) defined as deviant and who suffers the negative consequences of such a definition.

SHIFTING DEFINITIONS OF DEVIANCE

In addition to being influenced by power relationships, what is thought to be deviant varies from one time period to another, from one geographic location to another, and from one group to another. For example, being tattooed used to be seen as a stigmatizing form of deviance, but for many it now seems normal, or at least far less stigmatized (Larsen, Patterson, and Markham 2014). Indeed, about 45 million Americans now have tattoos. We readily accept the sight of athletes—especially professional basketball players—covered with tattoos. Once restricted largely to men, tattoos are more and

This chapter deals with two closely related social phenomena: deviance and crime. Most forms of deviance—for example, having full-face tattoos—are not crimes. However, all crimes—theft, murder, rape—are forms of deviance. To become a crime, a form of deviance must be negatively sanctioned by the legal system, a process known as **criminalization**.

more popular today with women. Some women, such as Kat Von D, have also gained fame as tattoo artists, a historically male-dominated occupation. And tattoo parlors, once limited to the marginal areas of town, are now found on Main Street, as well as in the shopping mall. Tattoos have become just another product of our consumer society (Patterson and Schroeder 2010).

As another example of the movement from deviance to normality, consider U.S. attitudes toward premarital sex (Regnerus and Uecker 2011). Just a few decades ago, a leading textbook on the subject of deviance devoted a chapter to "premarital sex" (Bell 1971). Today, premarital sex is so common and widely accepted (or at least tolerated) that it is considered normal in most groups. In fact, it is now often the case that *not* having premarital sex, or being a "late bloomer" sexually, can be stigmatizing (Gesselamn, Webster, and Garcia 2016)

"Hooking up"—engaging in "something sexual" outside of committed romantic relationships—is common among teens and twentysomethings today, but it was considered deviant behavior by earlier generations (Lewis et al. 2012; Reay 2014; Wade 2017). Much the same can be said about cohabitation before marriage (see Chapter 10): It once was

defined as "living in sin," but today the pendulum has swung entirely in the other direction, to the point where many people might consider couples who do *not* live together before marriage to be deviant. In other words, cohabitation has become normative, and for some it occurs instead of, or at least before, marriage (Kuo and Raley 2016; Popenoe 2009; Sassler and Miller 2011). Homosexuality is another form of sexual behavior that has changed in the public's perception; many no longer consider it to be a form of deviance (see Chapter 9). Its normalization is reflected in a host of social changes, such as the inclusion of same-sex partners in family benefits offered by employers, the repeal of the military's "don't ask, don't tell" policy, the 2011 reversal of the federal government's position on the Defense of Marriage Act (Savage and Stolberg 2011), and the 2015 U.S. Supreme Court decision legalizing same-sex marriage (see Figure 6.1 for a look at the changing attitudes of U.S. adults toward same-sex marriage). Popular actors such as Ian McKellen (Gandalf in the *Lord of the Rings* movies) and Neil Patrick Harris (TV's *How I Met Your Mother* and the movie *Gone Girl*), musicians such as Adam Lambert and Lance Bass, professional athletes such as Jason Collins (basketball), Michael Sam (football), and

FIGURE 6.1 • Support of and Opposition to Same-Sex Marriage in the United States, 1996–2016

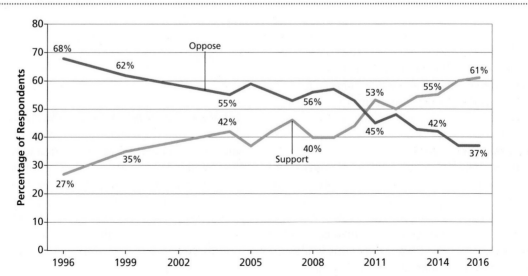

SOURCE: Data from Justin McCarthy, "Americans' Support for Same-Sex Marriage Remains High, at 61%." Gallup, May 19, 2016.

Billie Jean King and Martina Navratilova (tennis) have publicly identified themselves as gay and are (or were) able to maintain successful careers.

Of course, some members of American society cringe at the idea that homosexuality, premarital sex, and cohabitation before marriage are becoming normative. Religious fundamentalists, for example, may believe in an absolute moral standard according to which these behaviors are deviant, no matter how many other people consider them to be normal. Fundamentalists believe that only married heterosexuals should live together and have sexual intercourse with one another (Hendershott 2002; Powell et al. 2010).

There are great differences from one geographic area to another in the ways in which some behaviors are defined. At one time, smoking cigarettes was an accepted, even admired, form of behavior in the United States. Now, of course, smoking is widely considered deviant by many groups in the United States. However, it is certainly not viewed as deviant in most parts of Europe, and it is considered quite normal in China (Kohrmann 2008). Smoking marijuana in public is considered deviant by most groups in the United States, but in the Netherlands (and now in several American states, such as Colorado and Washington), marijuana smoking is quite normal.

While there are great differences in what is considered to be deviant, it is important to remember that deviance has existed for all groups, in all parts of the world, and in all times. Virtually all groups define themselves by specifying the limits of acceptable behavior for their members. Such limits, and their violation, help a group sharpen its norms and values. Without limits and at least occasional violations, norms and values might become increasingly unclear and grow weaker over time.

ASK YOURSELF

Can you think of other behaviors that were once considered deviant and are now accepted or even normative? What brought about the change in their status? Can you identify any behaviors that were once normative and are now considered deviant, such as using your cell phone while driving or failing to clean up after your dog?

GLOBAL FLOWS AND DEVIANCE

Deviance can be seen as a global flow. People who are defined as being deviant can move around the world quickly and easily. In addition, definitions of deviance flow even more easily from society to society. For example, through its "war on drugs," the United States has made a strong effort to have the use of certain drugs defined as a form of deviance throughout the world and to make drug use illegal wherever possible. Global trends toward normalizing what was defined at one time and in some places as deviant are even clearer and more pronounced. This is particularly the case with changes in the acceptability of various forms of sexuality. Ever greater portions of the world are accepting premarital sex, cohabitation before marriage, and, to a lesser degree, homosexuality. According to the International Lesbian, Gay, Bisexual, Trans and Intersex Association (ILGA), as of May 2014, "deviant" sexuality was protected by antidiscrimination laws in 76 countries, and same-sex unions were recognized in 47 countries (see Figure 6.2). However, the barriers to normalizing such forms of sexual behavior remain in place and are quite powerful in large parts of the world. As Figure 6.2 indicates, deviant sexual behavior is punishable by imprisonment in 78 countries and by death in 6. Such punishments are especially common in Islamic societies, which tend to be more absolutist on matters relating to sexual deviance and where deeply held religious beliefs serve as a barrier to normalization. In spite of the barriers, these behaviors exist, often covertly, in these societies and may well be expanding in the wake of increasing global acceptance.

DEVIANCE AND CONSUMPTION

The most obvious relationship between deviance and consumption is the use of goods and services that are illegal or considered deviant. This form of consumption often involves committing deviant, or illegal, acts in order to be able to afford to consume. For example, many of those addicted to drugs are forced into committing criminal acts such as prostitution, shoplifting, mugging, and breaking and entering in order to pay for the high cost of their illegal drugs.

FIGURE 6.2 • Lesbian and Gay Rights around the World, 2016

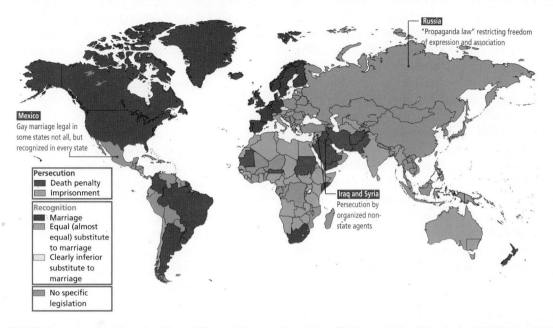

SOURCE: International Lesbian, Gay, Bisexual, Trans and Intersex Association, "Lesbian and Gay Rights in the World," June 2016. Reprinted by permission of the International Lesbian, Gay, Bisexual, Trans and Intersex Association.

Poverty drives some to commit illegal and/or deviant acts so that they can afford to consume what is necessary for survival (Edin and Lein 1997; Livermore et al. 2011). There are many reasons for engaging in prostitution, including the need to pay for illegal drugs, a history of abuse and rape, and being forced through human trafficking or other coercion, as well as simply a last-ditch effort to survive (Kennedy et al. 2007; Weitzer 2009). However, many women—and men—engage in prostitution to earn the money they need to afford to consume various conventional goods and services.

As with all sorts of deviance, definitions of what constitutes deviant consumer behavior are frequently in dispute. For instance, deviant consumers often do not see a relationship between deviance and their consumption patterns. Most of those in the United States who use the services of prostitutes or smoke marijuana may well see such consumption as justifiable and therefore not as a form of deviance. Their actions are partly due to the fact that the laws prohibiting consumption of the services of prostitutes and the use of marijuana are rarely enforced. "Johns" and "Janes" are rarely arrested, and if they are, they ordinarily get only a legal slap on the wrist. Purchasing and smoking marijuana in states where these actions continue to be illegal are treated in a similar fashion, at least for those who are white and middle-class.

However, those who consume the "wrong" drugs are more likely to be considered deviant than those who consume the "right" drugs. Thus, people who consume alcohol, even if they consume it excessively, are far less likely to be considered deviant than people who use marijuana. And the purchase and use of "harder drugs," such as crack cocaine and heroin, are dealt with more harshly (especially by the law) than the purchase of marijuana where it continues to be illegal.

THEORIES OF DEVIANCE

Deviance is a very good topic to study if you want to better understand the utility of, and contrasts between, the main types of sociological theories—structural/functional, conflict/critical, and inter/actionist. But before we get to these theories, it is important to make a key distinction between explanatory and constructionist theories of deviance:

- **Explanatory theories** seek to explain why deviance does or does not occur (Meier 2015). These theories are also thought of as being scientific, or "positivistic," because they view deviant behavior as objectively real, and they suggest that these forms of real behavior can be studied empirically. Explanatory theories assume that deviant behavior is determined by a wide variety of factors, such as the biological makeup of the person labeled as deviant and the structure of the larger society. For example, the structure of the social class system ensures that large numbers of people will live in poverty, at the bottom of the hierarchy, and that some of them will commit acts defined as deviant and criminal in order to survive.

- **Constructionist theories** are concerned with achieving a greater understanding of the process by which people define and classify some behaviors as normal and others as deviant. Whereas explanatory theories focus mainly on people labeled as deviant and what they do or embody, constructionist theories concentrate on those who are in power and the actions they take to create and define deviance in the first place. Rather than seeing deviance as "real," this perspective sees it as a social construction. For example, the Boy Scouts of America constructed transgender boys and gay boys and adult leaders as deviant by banning them from becoming members of its organization for more than a century. The organization ended its ban on gay youths in 2013 and its ban on gay adult leaders in 2015, then in early 2017, it permitted transgender boys to join (Chokshi 2017). The inclusion of these previously excluded groups demonstrates that definitions of deviance can change over time through the actions of influential organizations.

STRUCTURAL/FUNCTIONAL THEORIES

Émile Durkheim argued that because deviance and crime have existed in all societies at all times, they must have positive functions for the larger society and its structures. In other words, deviance would not have existed in the past and continue to exist were it not for the fact that it was and is functional; deviance served and continues to serve various purposes.

The most important function of deviance in Durkheim's view is that it allows societies, or groups, to define and clarify their collective beliefs—their norms and values. More important, the norms and values that limit or prohibit deviance would grow weak without the need to be exercised on a regular basis in response to deviant acts. The public as a whole, officials, and even potential deviants would grow progressively less aware of, and less sensitive to, the existence of these prohibitions. Thus, in a sense, society needs deviance. If periodic violations of standards of conduct did not occur, those standards would become less clear to all concerned, less strongly held, and less powerful (Dentler and Erikson 1959; Jensen 1988).

ASK YOURSELF
Do you agree with Durkheim that deviance is, in a sense, normal and therefore functional? To support this argument, can you think of an example of a deviant act or behavior that has helped society define its standards of conduct?

Strain

The most important structural-functional approach to deviance is known as **strain theory**, which was developed by Robert K. Merton (see Chapter 2). According to strain theory, there is a discrepancy between the larger structure and culture of society, especially regarding what is valued, and the structural means available to achieve what is valued. Strain exists when the culture values something—say, material success—but the structure of society is such that not everyone can achieve or realize that value in a socially acceptable way.

Of greatest interest is the strain placed on some people by the relationship between means and ends. Merton identified five possible relationships between means and ends and associated them with five types of adaptation:

- **Conformists** are people who accept both cultural goals, such as making lots of money, and the traditional means of achieving those goals, including hard work. Conformists are the only ones among Merton's types who would not be considered deviant.

- **Innovators** accept the same cultural goals the conformists do, but they reject the conventional means of achieving them. Innovators are deviants in that they choose nonconventional routes to success. Joaquín Guzmán, aka El Chapo, is a Mexican drug lord who rose swiftly through the ranks to achieve his financial success. By the 2010s, Guzmán had achieved a Robin Hood–like status among some for his provision of much-needed services in Mexico's Sinaloa mountains, but his illegal methods of operation saw him extradited from Mexico to the United States in early 2017.

- **Ritualists** realize that they will not be able to achieve cultural goals, but they nonetheless continue to engage in the conventional behavior associated with such success. Thus, a low-level employee might continue to work diligently even after realizing that such work is not going to lead to much economic success.

- **Retreatists** reject both cultural goals and the traditional routes to their attainment. Retreatists have completely given up on attaining success within the system. One example is the Brown family documented on the Discovery Channel reality show *Alaskan Bush People*. This family has lived off the grid for more than 20 years in the Alaskan bush.

- **Rebels** are like retreatists in that they reject both traditional means and goals. However, they substitute nontraditional goals and means to those goals. Revolutionaries such as Ernesto "Che" Guevara can be seen as fitting into the rebel category. Guevara rejected success as it was defined in Cuba during the 1950s. Instead, he chose to assist Fidel Castro in his effort to overthrow the country's dictatorial system. Furthermore, he chose unconventional means—guerrilla warfare—to attain his goals.

Adaptations of means to ends exemplify a structural-functionalist approach, because some of the adaptations are highly functional. Conformity certainly has positive consequences, in the sense that it allows the social system to continue to exist without disturbance. Innovation is functional because society needs innovations in order to adapt to new external realities. No society can survive without innovation. Even rebellion can be seen as functional because there are times when society needs more than gradual innovation—it needs to change radically.

Structural-functionalism is concerned not only with functions but also with dysfunctions. For example, ritualists and retreatists can be seen as largely dysfunctional for society, or at least as having more dysfunctions than functions. The unchanging behavior of ritualists contributes little or nothing to the requirements of an ever-changing society, and retreatists contribute even less because they are uninvolved in, and have withdrawn from, the larger society.

Social Control

Travis Hirschi's (1969) **social control theory** is also included under the heading of structural/functional theories. Hirschi's theory focuses on the reasons why people do *not* commit deviant acts. In brief, people are less likely to commit deviant acts if they have a variety of social bonds. Conversely, they are more likely to commit such acts if those bonds are weak. Social control involves the structures of society and the people who formally act on behalf of those structures. In a sense, Hirschi sees those structures and the people who work on their behalf as functional for society. People who are involved in those structures and are responsive to those who act on their behalf are more likely to be conformists and less likely to become deviants. However, those who are more likely to become deviants are not deeply involved in those structures and not responsive to their demands or to people who act on their behalf. When people lack attachments to family members, teachers, or employers and fail to internalize conventional norms and goals, there is little to prevent them from becoming deviants. The lack of other vested interests, such as owning a house, is also likely to contribute to deviant behavior. People in such a situation have little or nothing to lose in violating norms and laws.

CONFLICT/CRITICAL THEORIES

Proponents of structural/functional theories trace the source of deviance to the larger structures of society and the strains they produce or the fact that they do not exercise adequate social control. Conflict/critical theorists are also interested in those structures and their effects on people, but they adopt a different orientation toward them. A major focus is the inequality that exists in those structures and the impact that it has on individuals. In conflict theorists' view, inequality causes at least some of the less powerful individuals in society to engage in deviant—and criminal—acts because they have few, if any, other ways of succeeding in society. In this, they are similar to the innovators in Merton's taxonomy of adaptations to strain. Conversely, those in power in executive or managerial positions in organizations are more likely to commit crimes, especially corporate or white-collar crimes (Simpson 2013; Simpson and Weisburd 2009). This is the case because the nature of their high-level positions in various social structures (business, government) makes it not only possible but also relatively easy for them to do so. White-collar criminals are more likely to use deception in committing their crimes and bribery in order to conceal them; their crimes are more likely to be clandestine and to remain hidden (Van Slyke, Benson, and Cullen, 2016, ix). Further, conflict theorists argue, those in power in society create the laws and rules that define certain things as deviant, or illegal, while others are defined as normal. They do so in a self-serving way that advantages them and disadvantages those who lack power in society.

Deviance and the Poor

Conflict theories can be applied to social inequalities throughout the ages. For instance, they form the basis of research by William Chambliss (1964) on vagrancy laws in medieval England. These laws came into existence as feudalism was falling apart; the first vagrancy law was enacted in England after the Black Death, around 1348. In the feudal system, serfs were forced to provide labor for landowners, but with the end of feudalism, and therefore of serfdom, a new source of labor was needed. Not coincidentally, the former serfs now lacked permanent homes and sources of income and wandered about the countryside. Those in power saw them as a group likely to provide the needed labor at little cost, so they created vagrancy laws. Under these laws, it was illegal for those without work or a home

to loiter in public places, and some of the itinerants were arrested. As a result, many people who otherwise might not have worked for the landowners were forced to do so in order to avoid arrest and imprisonment.

Contemporary conflict theorists, heavily influenced by Marxian theory, have come to see deviance as something created by the capitalist economic system. Today's definitions of deviance serve the interests of the capitalists, especially by further enriching them. Conversely, they adversely affect the proletariat, especially the poor, who grow even poorer. Conflict theorists do not argue that have-nots never commit crimes or deviant acts. Rather, they argue that it is because of the laws created by societal elites that the actions of the have-nots are singled out for notice and for sanctions. Furthermore, the costs to society of elite deviance are much higher than the costs associated with crime and deviance among society's have-nots. Compare, for example, the approximately $65 billion the disgraced and now imprisoned Bernie Madoff cost his clients by engaging in illegal activities to the few dollars a con artist or a mugger wrests from his victims.

Furthermore, affluent people can afford to be deviant and commit criminal acts. Many poor people do not have the funds to pay fines, court fees, or monetary penalties imposed for breaking the law. This legal debt accrues interest and accumulates over time, trapping indigent offenders in the criminal justice system until it is paid in full. Impoverished individuals who are arrested and imprisoned for crimes experience difficulty finding employment and housing after serving their sentences. Legal debt perpetuates poverty and inequality (Harris 2016). How can a poor person pay the fine of a speeding ticket or a late court fee if he is placed in prison for failing to do so? Imprisoning poor people for not paying their legal debts is creating modern-day debtors' prisons, which many consider a violation of civil rights (Benns and Strode 2016). Ultimately, monetary sanctions criminalize being poor.

Deviance and the Elite

Great efforts are made to legitimate elite crimes and acts of elite deviance and, failing that, to pay little or no attention to them (Simon 2012). Those who rank high in such hierarchies as business, government, and the military have a much greater ability to commit deviant acts (such as sexually harassing subordinates), to have these acts be seen as legitimate, and to get away with them.

However, there are times when the acts are so extreme that they can no longer be hidden. They come to light and become great public issues. Once this happens, even the most elite members of society have a difficult time escaping negative judgment and perhaps even punishment and imprisonment.

There is a long list of scandals involving elite public figures of various types who have been found to have committed deviant acts. In the main, their acts were so extreme, or the revelations about them became so public, that they could not be ignored. However, what has often caused difficulties for those involved has been their awkward efforts to lie about, or cover up, their offenses once they first became public. In many cases, especially in this era of the internet, evidence is uncovered or witnesses come forward that make it clear that the public figure has been deceiving the public and the authorities. The following are a few notable examples in the U.S. context (there are innumerable others everywhere in the world):

Once powerful and widely revered, Penn State assistant football coach Jerry Sandusky was sentenced to at least 30 years in prison for his part in a scandal involving the sexual abuse of children. Conflict theorists believe that wrongdoing by elites rarely comes to light or is punished.

- In perhaps the most famous example of all, President Richard Nixon resigned in 1974 as he faced imminent impeachment for his role in the infamous Watergate break-in and for his efforts to conceal his and his associates' roles in it from the public.

- Gracious-living guru and media magnate Martha Stewart served five months in jail in 2004 and 2005 for lying about a 2001 stock sale. Stewart sold off her ImClone stock just before its price plunged, suggesting she might have benefited from insider trading.

- In 2015, New England Patriots football star Aaron Hernandez was convicted of first-degree murder. He was serving a life sentence in prison without the possibility of parole when he took his own life in April 2017, after being acquitted of

murder charges in a second case. Shortly thereafter, a Massachusetts judge vacated Hernandez's murder conviction, although the local district attorney planned to appeal the ruling.

The view of conflict theorists is that, as lengthy as the list of elite deviants and criminals might be, it is merely the tip of the iceberg. Because elites have a wide variety of means at their disposal to conceal their actions, many, many more of their acts of deviance and criminality escape detection and punishment. Such acts by elites can persist for years, decades, or even a lifetime.

INTER/ACTIONIST THEORIES

Inter/actionism can also be used to analyze deviance (Rubington and Weinberg 2016). For example, to the rational choice theorist, a person chooses deviance because it is a rational means to some desired goal. Gang members join gangs because of the camaraderie and perceived protection offered by the gang, as well as to gain access to a world in which the member can obtain money and achieve recognition and high status (Decker and Curry 2000; Melde, Taylor, and Esbensen 2009). Ethnomethodologists are concerned with the ways in which people "do" deviance—that is, the everyday behaviors in which they engage that produce deviance. People need to adopt methods of speech and forms of behavior that make their deviance invisible to most others. In a classic ethnomethodological study, Harold Garfinkel (1967) describes the painstaking steps taken by Agnes, a transgender woman, to "pass" as a woman. She not only changed her manner of dress, posture, and demeanor but also underwent bodily changes. However, there are times when those who are deviant want to talk and act in ways that make it clear that they are deviant. For example, gang members may use certain phrases, dress in certain ways, and display certain tattoos to make their allegiance clear to other members of the same gang—and to members of opposing gangs. However, when they interact with the public or the police, gang members may speak and dress in ways that conceal, or at least attempt to hide, their membership in the gang.

ASK YOURSELF

Has engaging in any form of deviance ever seemed rational to you, in the sense that inter/actionist theories use the term? If so, was the deviance visible or invisible to others? Did it help you (or would it have helped you) achieve a goal?

Labeling

Symbolic interactionism is of great utility in analyzing and furthering our understanding of deviance. One variety of symbolic interactionism—labeling theory—is particularly useful in thinking about deviance. From that perspective, at least two things are needed for deviance to occur:

- A **symbol**, or in this case a "label." In the realm of deviance, a number of labels are particularly powerful negative symbols: *alcoholic, drug addict, pedophile, adulterer,* and so on.

- Interaction between the person or group doing the labeling (the labeler) and the person or group to whom the label is applied (the labelee). During this interaction, one or more of these labels is applied to the deviant.

Those who do the defining—the labeling—are known as **social control agents**. Some of these agents (e.g., police, psychiatrists) are performing official functions, but far more often it is friends or family who label others as, for example, drunks or womanizers. When public figures are labeled as deviant, the media and their representatives are often the ones who do the labeling.

From the perspective of **labeling theory**, a deviant is someone to whom a deviant label has been successfully applied (Becker 1963; Goode 2014; Restivo and Lanier 2015). This stands in contrast to the view of the public and many sociologists, who focus on what an individual does in order to be labeled a deviant. Also of interest in labeling theory is the way in which the person labeled as deviant is affected by the label. The person can accept the label to varying degrees or make efforts to resist, reject, or shed the label. People also vary greatly in how they react to, and feel about, being labeled as deviant. For example, some might be mortified by being labeled as sex addicts, but others might take pride in it.

Labeling theory is also concerned about the actions and reactions of social control agents, as well as about their interactions with those being labeled. From the labeling perspective, "deviance is not a consequence of the act the person commits, but rather a consequence of the [creation and] application by others of rules and sanctions to an 'offender'" (Becker 1963, 9). A focus on social control agents, rather than deviants, leads to the view that deviant labels are not necessarily applied uniformly. Some people and some forms of behavior are more likely than others to be labeled as deviant. Thus, murderers and the act of murder are almost uniformly labeled as deviant (and criminal). However, in many other cases, the process is more selective and less clear-cut: "Some men who drink too much are called alcoholics and others are not; some men who act oddly are committed to hospitals and others are not; some men who have no visible means of support are hauled into court and others are not" (Erikson 1964, 11–12). Overall, people are more likely to be socially defined as deviant when they are poor, work in low-status occupations, or are in similarly devalued circumstances (Goffman 1959). A person in a more advantageous social situation often escapes being defined or labeled as deviant, despite manifesting the same forms of behavior.

Primary and Secondary Deviance

An important distinction that flows from labeling theory is that between primary and secondary deviance:

- **Primary deviance** consists of early, random acts of deviance, such as an occasional bout of drinking to excess or an isolated act considered strange or out of the ordinary. Virtually all of us commit such acts; we all have engaged in various forms of primary deviance (Lemert [1951] 2012; Wallerstein and Wyle 1947). Isolated acts of primary deviance rarely, if ever, lead to the successful application of a deviant label. Primary deviance consists of acts and behavior, not identities or labels.

- Of far greater interest to labeling theorists is **secondary deviance**, or deviant acts that persist, become more common, and eventually cause people to organize their lives and personal identities around their deviant status (Liberman, Kirk, and Kim 2014). Secondary deviance usually occurs after an individual has been stigmatized and judged for deviant behavior and possibly labeled as "deviant." In response, the individual begins to see and define him- or herself as deviant.

While labeling theory tends to focus on others labeling an individual as deviant, it is possible, or even likely, that individuals will label themselves in this way, that they will do so before anyone else does, and that they will act in accord with their self-imposed label (Lorber 1967; Thoits 1985, 2011). This is consistent with the view of the leading symbolic interactionist, George Herbert Mead, who saw the mind as an internal conversation with oneself. Such an internalized conversation may certainly lead to labeling oneself as deviant.

Key Ideas in the Labeling Process

Social control is the process by which a group or society enforces conformity to its demands and expectations. One way in which this is accomplished is through the creation and application of rules and labels. This leads to the distinction between rule creators and rule enforcers. **Rule**

Moral panics—such as the witch-hunting crazes of Renaissance Europe—rely in part on the use of labels to identify perceived threats. What might help prevent the development of a moral panic?

creators are usually elite members of society who devise its rules, norms, and laws. Without rule creators and their rules, there would be no deviance. Rule creators are usually (but not always) distinct from **rule enforcers**, who threaten to or actually do sanction the rule violators. Another important idea here is that of **moral entrepreneurs**, or those individuals or groups of individuals who come to define an act as a moral outrage, and who lead a campaign to have it defined as deviant and to have it made illegal and therefore subject to legal enforcement (Becker 1963). Drugs provide a good example, especially globally, because moral entrepreneurs (particularly those located in the United States) have taken it upon themselves to have drugs defined as illegal and their use as deviant. They have done so even though the use of many of these drugs (such as marijuana) is common and accepted, not only in many societies throughout the world but also among a large portion of the American population.

Moral Panics

Moral entrepreneurs can stir up such a fuss that they can cause a **moral panic**, or a widespread and disproportionate reaction to the form of deviance in question (Goode and Ben-Yehuda 2009; Hier 2011; Krinsky 2013). It could be argued that today we are witnessing, in Europe and to a lesser degree in the United States, concern about Muslim immigrants that is quickly becoming a moral panic (Morgan and Poynting 2012). This moral panic is related, at least in part, to the increasing threat of terrorism posed by radical Islamic groups, especially the Islamic State and al-Qaeda (among many other incidents around the world, the early 2015 murder by Islamist extremists of 12 people at the Paris satirical newspaper *Charlie Hebdo* and 4 people at a Jewish supermarket; the killing of 49 people at a nightclub in Orlando, Florida, in June 2016, as well as an attack on Ataturk Airport in Turkey in the same month that killed 45 people; and the killing of 84 people at a Bastille Day celebration in Nice, France, in July 2016). In spite of these gruesome and highly publicized attacks, it is important to remember that very few Muslims are Islamist extremists, let alone terrorists.

A good historical example of a moral panic is the witch craze that occurred in Europe between the fourteenth and sixteenth centuries (Ben-Yehuda 1980, 1985). The idea of witches had existed before this time, but it was seen as a more complex phenomenon involving both bad and good witches. In any case, no assumption had been made about a conspiracy between women and Satan to corrupt the world. However, in this era, Dominican friars took the lead in defining witchcraft as such a conspiracy and as a crime subject to corporal punishment, in this case, burning at the stake. The friars were the moral entrepreneurs in this case. They played a key role in generating a moral panic that came to involve large numbers of people. That panic, in turn, led to the painful deaths of hundreds of thousands of people, mostly women.

Moral panics are, by definition, exaggerated. Thus, the threats posed by witches in the fifteenth century, the communists in the 1950s, and immigrants and even terrorists today have been made out by many, especially moral entrepreneurs, to be greater than they really are. One of the ways to do this is to create a "folk devil" who stands for what is feared. Terrorism, for example, made Osama bin Laden a folk devil.

Stigmas

Erving Goffman's *Stigma* (1963) is a very important contribution of symbolic interactionism to our understanding of deviance. A **stigma** is a person's characteristic that others find, define, and often label as unusual, unpleasant, or deviant. Goffman begins his analysis with physically stigmatized individuals, such as those missing a nose. He then introduces a wide array of other stigmas, such as being on welfare. In the end, readers come to the realization that they have been reading not only about people who are unlike them, with major physical deformities, but also about themselves: "The most fortunate of normals is likely to have his half-hidden failing, and for every little failing there is a social occasion when it will loom large, creating a shameful gap" (Goffman 1963, 127). Goffman's idea of stigma has attracted many scholars and has been applied to many forms of deviance, such as prostitution (Scambler and Paoli 2008; Wong, Holroyd, and Bingham 2011), mental illness (Payton and Thoits 2011), Asperger's syndrome (Hill and Liamputtong 2011), and tattooing (Dickson et al. 2014).

There are two types of stigmatized individuals. The individual with a **discredited stigma** "assumes his differentness is known about already or is evident on the spot." In contrast, those with a **discreditable stigma** assume that their stigma "is neither known about by those present nor immediately perceivable about them" (Goffman 1963, 4). An example of a discredited stigma might be the bodily symptoms of having advanced AIDS, a lost limb, or being a member of a minority group viewed negatively by others, while discreditable stigmas include having done poorly in school or having a prison record. Of great importance is the symbolic nature of the stigma and the individual's interaction with others, especially those thought to be normal. Because the physical nature of a discreditable stigma is not visible to others, neither are the stigma's symbolic qualities. Nevertheless, the people with such a stigma want to make sure it remains secret and thus try to conceal the stigmatizing information during most interactions. However, in the case of a discredited stigma (such as being morbidly obese), those with the stigma must deal with the tension associated with interacting with people who view them negatively because of the stigma.

The idea of discreditable stigmas has wide applicability to the contemporary world. For example, the court records of juvenile offenders are often hidden from the public or expunged to avoid stigmatizing otherwise promising young people for a lifetime. People with mental illnesses or substance abuse problems often go to great lengths to hide the real reasons for unscheduled absences from work. Parents of mentally disabled children, especially the mildly impaired, "mainstream" their children in standard classrooms in part so that the children's disabilities will be more likely to be discreditable than discredited.

CRIME

As pointed out previously, it is the fact that the law is violated that differentiates **crime** from other forms of deviance. **Criminology** is the field devoted to the study of crime. Many, but certainly not all, criminologists are sociologists. While many criminologists are now found in university departments and schools devoted to the study of criminology, a large number work in sociology departme[nts. It] is a sociology of crime, but the field also [includes] those from many other disciplines, such as [psychol]ogists, economists, biologists, and anthrop[ologists,] as well as officials who once worked in the c[riminal] justice system. In fact, the field today has become increasingly multidisciplinary, even interdisciplinary (Wellford 2012).

While there is growing interdisciplinarity in the study of crime, sociology plays an important role in it. Clearly, a variety of sociological factors, including social class and race, are involved in who commits crimes and which crimes they commit. The same sociological factors are involved in who gets caught, prosecuted, and incarcerated, as well as how much of their sentences they actually serve. And such factors are involved in what happens to people after they serve their sentences and whether or not they are likely to end up back in prison.

The "father of criminology" is Cesare Lombroso, who published *The Criminal Man* in 1876. The title of the book reflects the fact that the focus of early criminologists was on criminals and their innate physical or psychological characteristics. In more recent years, criminology has shifted away from its focus on criminals and their defects and toward a concern with the social context of criminal actions and the effects of those actions on the larger society. A key figure in bringing a sociological perspective to criminology was Edwin Sutherland (1883–1950). His work has helped shift the focus in criminology from the criminal and his or her misdeeds to society, especially the societal reaction to those actions, including the labels placed on criminals.

Sutherland's most important contribution to the sociology of crime is **differential association** theory. The main point of the theory is that people are *not* born criminals; they learn criminal behavior. Therefore, whom a person associates with is crucial. One's family and friends—the primary group—are important sources of attitudes toward crime, knowledge about how to commit crimes, and rationalizations that help one live with being a criminal. Today, we would need to add the fact that criminal behavior can also be learned through television, songs, and especially the internet (e.g., the impact of the internet on the Islamic State's ability to recruit terrorists). Many criticisms were leveled at differential association theory; even Sutherland later came to criticize it on various grounds. For example, it did not explain why some people became criminals while others exposed to the same situations did not. One of Sutherland's own criticisms was the fact that the theory did not give enough attention to the role of opportunity in committing crimes.

ASK YOURSELF

Can you think of any reasons why some people become criminals, while others exposed to the same situations do not? Consider the theories of deviance discussed previously as you prepare your answer.

While the previous discussion focuses on the causes of crime, especially those that are sociological in nature, criminology has long had a second focus on the criminal justice system (Siegel and Worrall 2014; Wellford 2012). This interest is traceable to another early Italian scholar, Cesare Beccaria (1738–1794; McShane and Williams 2007). Beccaria was a lawyer by training and received a doctorate in law. He is best known for his 1764 book *On Crimes and Punishments* and its concern with such issues as the origins of law and the criminal justice system. His work led to an interest not only in this system as a whole but also in whether its major components—law enforcement, courts, and corrections—are fair, effective, and just. In terms of the latter, much work has been done on the (un)fairness, especially as far as race is concerned, of arrest decisions by the police, the length of sentences, and the likelihood of receiving the death penalty.

THE CRIMINAL JUSTICE SYSTEM

The criminal justice system in the United States consists of various loosely connected government agencies and the individuals who work in those agencies. It is involved in the apprehension, prosecution, and punishment of those who violate the law. It also seeks to prevent such violations before they occur. Finally, the criminal justice system has much more general responsibilities, such as ensuring public safety and maintaining social order (Culver 2007, 851). The major components of the criminal justice system are law enforcement, the courts, and the correctional system.

An enormous number of people are being held in the jail and prison system. In 2014, 2,217,947 adults were incarcerated in U.S. jails and federal and state prisons. The United States has the highest rate of incarceration (almost 1 percent of the adult population) in the world. It has approximately 568,140 more prisoners than China and almost 1.6 million more than Russia (see Figure 6.3 for the prison population around the world). Although the United States has only 4 percent of the world's population, it has about 25 percent of the world's prisoners (Cullen, Jonson, and Nagin 2011). This is a very costly system to operate. It is estimated that in 2013, local, state, and federal governments spent about $71 billion on corrections, much of it on incarceration (Schmidt, Warner, and Gupta 2010). Further complicating matters is the fact that the economic problems facing the United States in general, and state and local jurisdictions in particular, mean that fewer prisons and jails are being built while an increasing number of Americans are being sentenced to them. The growing number of prisoners creates other problems, including overcrowding of the prisons as well as increased violence among prisoners. Given the huge numbers involved, prisons have become little more than warehouses for prisoners. The ability of prisons to rehabilitate inmates has declined, and the focus on punishment has strengthened (Phelps 2011).

The millions of people in prisons, and the billions of dollars spent on them, became hot public issues in 2016. One of the concerns was mandatory minimum sentences for nonviolent offenders (Williams 2016), which have helped lead to a sharp increase in the number of nonviolent offenders (often involved in drugs) in prison. Many of those offenders—roughly 160,000—are serving life sentences. This is more than four times the number of those serving such sentences in 1984. Obviously, putting people in prison for life is very costly. In any case, such sentences are highly questionable as punishment for minor, drug-related crimes.

Beyond the more than 2 million people in prisons and jails in 2014, more than 4.7 million people were under the control of the criminal justice system because they were either on parole (856,900) or on probation (3,864,100; Kaeble, Maruschak, and Bonczar 2015). **Parole** is the supervised early release of a prisoner for such efforts as good behavior while

FIGURE 6.3 • Prison Population around the World, 2015

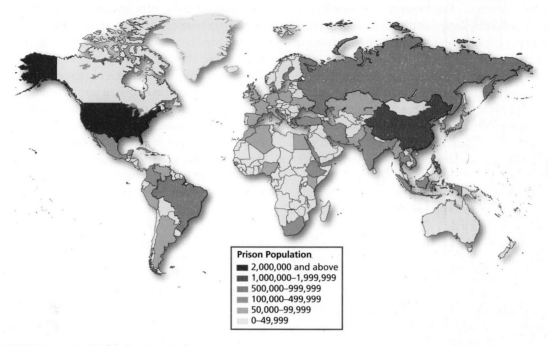

Prison Population
- 2,000,000 and above
- 1,000,000–1,999,999
- 500,000–999,999
- 100,000–499,999
- 50,000–99,999
- 0–49,999

SOURCE: International Centre for Prison Studies.

in prison. Parole officers work with those on parole to help them adjust to life outside prison and to be sure they are not violating the conditions of their release. If they do violate those conditions, they can have their parole revoked, and they can be sent back to prison. Those who are convicted of less serious crimes may be placed on **probation**, whereby they are released into the community with supervision. They are also released under certain conditions, such as that they must be enrolled in and complete a substance abuse program. If the offender does not adhere to these conditions, is arrested, or is convicted, probation can be revoked. In that case, a new, more restrictive probation can be imposed, or the offender can be sent to prison. Both parole and probation require the participation of bureaucracies, and especially the parole and probation officers who are employed by them. These systems, like the prison and jail system, are very costly.

It might be argued that the enormous cost of prisons—as well as the parole and probation systems—would be justifiable if incarceration taught people that "crime does not pay." In other words,

a case might be made for mass imprisonment if it rehabilitated prisoners so that they were less likely to commit crimes after they were released. But does a prison term serve as deterrence to the commission of crimes after an inmate is released from prison? It is obvious that prisoners are deterred from further crime while imprisoned, although some seem to be able to engage in crimes while in prison. After a prisoner is released, those involved in the criminal justice system are interested in the issue of **specific deterrence**, or whether the experience of punishment in general, and incarceration in particular, makes it less likely that the ex-prisoner will commit crimes in the future. In other words, the issue is whether an individual will be "scared straight" by punishment, especially by incarceration (Apel and Nagin 2011).

Most research in the field has shown that prisons do a poor job of rehabilitating prisoners, and as a result they do not reduce **recidivism**, or the repetition of a criminal act by one who has been convicted of a prior offense (Smith 2007). Those who serve time in prison learn new and better criminal techniques during their incarceration. In other words, prisons have a "criminogenic" effect, leading to more rather than less crime (Cullen et al. 2011). Nonetheless, no expert would argue for the elimination of punishments, including imprisonment, for most crimes. However, there is a need for more focused forms of specific deterrence (Braga and Weisburd 2012). Furthermore, important individual and situational differences can have impacts on the effectiveness of such deterrence. What is needed is a focus on what forms of specific deterrence will be effective on what types of criminals and under what circumstances (Piquero et al. 2011).

General deterrence deals with the population as a whole and whether individuals will be less likely to commit crimes because of fear that they might be punished or imprisoned for their actions (Apel and Nagin 2011). Although it is not clear how many people do not commit crimes because of fear of punishment, it is clear that such fear constitutes some level of deterrence to some who might otherwise become criminals.

The ultimate example of both forms of deterrence is capital punishment, or the death penalty (Hood and Hoyle 2015; Paternoster, Brame, and Bacon 2007). Someone who is executed clearly cannot commit another crime. However, there is evidence that even the threat of capital punishment is not a strong general deterrent to crime (Cohen-Cole et al. 2009).

Although a number of countries have abolished the death penalty, the United States is one of a handful that continue to employ it. Figure 6.4 shows the legality of the death penalty across U.S. states, as well as data on the number of people on death row per state and the number executed since 1976. The four leading countries in the world in terms of the number of people executed are China, Iran, Pakistan, and Saudi Arabia. These are countries that the United States would not like to be associated with, especially on this issue. The United States ranks fifth, with 28 executions in 2015 (Death Penalty Information Center 2016). This is far fewer than the 200 or so who were executed in each of two consecutive years in the 1930s. There have been nearly 1,437 executions in the United States since 1976. Overall, there have been more than 15,269 known executions in the United States (Paternoster 2007). There has also been a trend toward more

"humane" execution (if such a thing is possible). Prior to 1930, most executions were done by hanging. Many of these were mishandled, resulting in those who were condemned gradually choking to death. From 1930 to 1967, the majority of executions in the United States were by electrocution. This did not seem to be much of an improvement, as the initial electrical charge, at least in some cases, did not cause death or even unconsciousness and in some cases caused the condemned to catch fire. Beginning in 1977, there was a movement toward the use of lethal injections, and about 88 percent of executions are now performed in that way. However, a number of recent botched executions by injection have caused long and painful deaths.

The application of capital punishment continues to be highly controversial. In fact, many death sentences are accompanied by active campaigns against them and vigils protesting executions both before and as they occur. There are many who feel that it is morally wrong for the government to kill anyone. Others are opposed to the death penalty because it is likely that at least some wrongly convicted people are killed in the process (Aronson and Cole 2009). Finally, there is strong evidence of bias, especially racial bias, in capital punishment. Many studies have shown that blacks, and nonwhites more generally, who are convicted of killing whites are more likely to get the death penalty than are whites who kill other whites (Lee, Paternoster, and Rowan 2016).

TYPES OF CRIMES

Data on crime across the United States are found in the Federal Bureau of Investigation's Uniform Crime Reports (UCR), which include data on crimes reported to police departments and police arrest statistics. Two broad types of crime are reported. **Violent crime** includes the threat of injury or the threat or actual use of force. The violent crimes tracked by the FBI are murder and nonnegligent manslaughter, forcible rape, robbery, and aggravated assault. Figure 6.5 shows the reported violent crime rates in the United States for 1994 through 2015. In recent years, although they do not appear in the UCR, increasing attention has been paid in the United States and elsewhere to violent crimes related to terrorism, as well as globally to war

FIGURE 6.4 • The Death Penalty in the United States, 2016

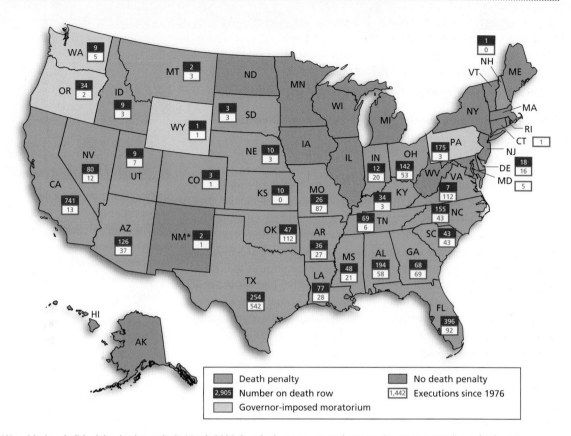

*New Mexico abolished the death penalty in March 2009, but the law was not made retroactive, so two remain on death row.

SOURCE: Data from Death Penalty Information Center, States With and Without the Death Penalty (http://www.deathpenaltyinfo.org/states-and-without-death-penalty) and State-by-State Database (http://www.deathpenaltyinfo.org/state_by_state).

crimes (Gartner 2007). **Property crimes** do not involve injury or force, but rather are offenses that involve gaining or destroying property. While there are others (such as shoplifting and forgery), the major property crimes are burglary, larceny-theft, and motor vehicle theft. About three-fourths of all U.S. crime is property crime (Copes and Null 2007). Figure 6.6 shows the property crime rates in the United States for 1994 through 2015. Another important way of categorizing crimes is by separating **felonies**, or more serious crimes punishable by a year or more in prison, from **misdemeanors**, or minor offenses punishable by imprisonment of less than a year.

- **White-collar crimes** are those committed "by a person of responsibility and high social status

in the course of his occupation" (Geis 2007b, 850; Simpson 2013).

- **Corporate crime** involves legal organizations that violate the law. It includes such illegal acts as antitrust violations, stock market violations (e.g., insider trading), and false advertisements (Geis 2007a).

- **Organized crime** can involve various types of organizations, but it is most often associated with syndicated organized crime, especially the Mafia, which uses violence or the threat of violence and the corruption of public officials to profit from illegal activities (Griffin 2007). Other examples of criminal organizations are Mexican drug cartels, the Russian Mafia, and the Islamic State.

The New Jim Crow: Mass Incarceration in the Age of Colorblindness (The New Press, 2012)

Michelle Alexander (Associate Professor of Law at Ohio State University; JD, Stanford University, 1992)

African American inmates at the Pitchess Detention Center in Castaic, California, speak to clergy and community activists. According to Alexander's research, up to 75 percent of young black men will be incarcerated in their lifetime in some communities.

Rates of incarceration have been increasing more quickly in the United States than in any other nation. In the 1980s, the federal government initiated the war on drugs, which imposed mandatory prison time for minor, nonviolent drug offenses. Drug users became criminals and subject to punishment in prisons instead of treatment in rehabilitation facilities. Today more than 2 million people are in U.S. prisons, serving time related to drug convictions. From Michelle Alexander's perspective, the most distressing aspect of mass incarceration is the high percentage of racial and ethnic minorities who are imprisoned. Poor, young black men are significantly overrepresented in U.S. prisons. In some poor communities, up to 75 percent of young black men will be incarcerated at some point in their lives. As Alexander details, this is not because they use or sell drugs more often than others, but because of racial discrimination in the criminal justice system. Law enforcement possesses enormous discretion in regard to search and seizure practices and ultimately in terms of who is arrested. In the past, police officers routinely stopped and frisked individuals without probable cause and

searched vehicles during traffic violations. Overwhelmingly, they stopped, searched, and arrested young black men more than anyone else (Alexander 2012, 6–7, 61).

Alexander argues that mass incarceration has become the new Jim Crow—a legal form of racial discrimination that aims to socially control and exclude black men from mainstream society. Social control and exclusion do not stop with the end of a prison sentence. Former prisoners are stigmatized, labeled as criminals even after they have served their sentences. Felons on parole and probation are legally barred from voting in most states. They experience difficulty finding employment because the law requires them to disclose that they have a felony conviction on job applications. They can be denied food stamps and other public benefits. Similar to the racial segregation created by the old Jim Crow laws of the early to mid-twentieth century, mass incarceration is creating an underclass that is legally prevented from achieving upward social mobility. But unlike the overt racism of the past Jim Crow era, Alexander asserts that the new Jim Crow is being practiced in a so-called colorblind society that fails to recognize the institutional

racism prevalent in the criminal justice system. Even the civil rights movement, which was fundamental in dismantling the old Jim Crow laws, neglected the impact of mass incarceration in black communities; however, the popular reception of Alexander's book may be starting to change this.

Supplementary Resources

- You can watch Bill Moyer interview Alexander about how difficult it is for those who have been incarcerated to achieve the American dream at https://www.youtube.com/watch?v=om2hx6Xm2JE.
- Read about the popular reaction to *The New Jim Crow* in *The New York Times* at http://www.nytimes.com/2012/03/07/books/michelle-alexanders-new-jim-crow-raises-drug-law-debates.html?_r=0.

FIGURE 6.5 • Reported Violent Crime in the United States, 1994–2015

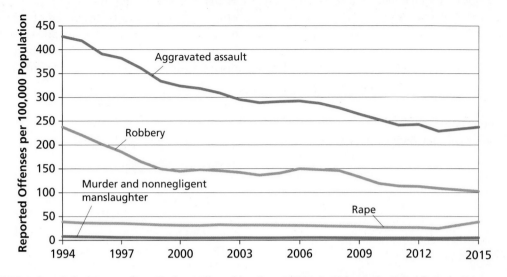

SOURCE: Data from Federal Bureau of Investigation, Uniform Crime Reports, Table 1: "Crime in the United States by Volume and Rate per 100,000 Inhabitants, 1996–2015."

NOTE: In 2013, the FBI UCR Program initiated the collection of rape data under a revised definition and removed the term "forcible" from the offense name. The 2015 data reflect offenses committed under the revised definition, which can be read in full at https://ucr.fbi.gov/crime-in-the-u.s/2015/crime-in-the-u.s.-2015/tables/table-1/table-1-data-declaration_final.

FIGURE 6.6 • Reported Property Crime in the United States, 1994–2015

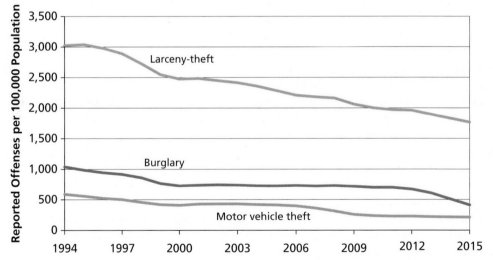

SOURCE: Data from Federal Bureau of Investigation, Uniform Crime Reports, Table 1: "Crime in the United States by Volume and Rate per 100,000 Inhabitants, 1996–2015."

- **Political crimes** can be either offenses against the state to affect its policies, such as the assassination of one of its officials, especially its leader (as in the assassination of John F. Kennedy), or offenses by the state, either domestically (e.g., spying on citizens) or internationally (e.g., state-sponsored terrorism, bribery of a foreign official; Tunnell 2007).

- **Hate crimes** are those that stem, in whole or in part, from the fact that those who are being victimized are in various ways different from the perpetrators. These differences include race, religion, sexual orientation, gender, national origin, and disability status. Victims are held in contempt by the perpetrators (Levin 2007).

- **Cybercrime** targets computers (for instance, by hacking; Hill and Marion 2016). Cybercriminals use computers to commit traditional crimes, such as stealing from a bank account or theft of a credit card number. They also use computers to transmit illegal information and images to carry out such activities as insider trading, identity theft, child pornography, plans for terrorist acts, and "cyberterrorism" (see the Digital Living box in this chapter and in Chapter 12 for more on cybercrime).

- **Consumer crimes**, or crimes related to consumption, include shoplifting and the use of stolen credit cards or credit card numbers.

Although all the offenses described previously are classified as crimes, they are not all considered equally abhorrent. In line with the idea that deviance is defined by elites, so are crimes and criminal punishments. Thus, white-collar and corporate crimes are often downplayed, while the crimes usually associated with those in the lower social classes—for example, violent crimes, especially felonies, and property crimes—receive a great deal of attention from the police, the media, and the public.

Nonetheless, violent crime is a major issue in the United States, especially murder committed with widely available and readily obtainable guns. In 2014, 8,124 Americans were killed by guns—27 per day (Quealy and Sanger-Katz 2016). That amounts to about 31 homicides per million people. In comparison, about 2 out of every million people are shot to death in Germany, the Netherlands, and Austria; in Poland and England, the number who die from gunshots is 1 per million; and in Japan, the rate of gun deaths is 1 in 10 million (about the chances of an American being killed by lightning).

ASK YOURSELF

Why are all crimes not considered equally serious? White-collar crime, for instance, can have far-reaching effects and untold numbers of victims. Consider the definitions of crime in your answer.

GLOBALIZATION AND CRIME

The amount of global, or cross-border, crime has increased with globalization (Aas 2013; Andreas and Nadelmann 2006; Shelley, Picarelli, and Corpora 2011; also see the journal *Global Crime*). Globalization makes cross-border crime increasingly possible and more likely. International crime has existed for centuries in such forms as piracy on the oceans and the African slave trade. However, today there seems to be far more of it. This may be due to the fact that, because of the increase in global criminal flows, much more public and government attention is devoted to these crimes. Fortunately, action against crime flows almost as easily as the crimes themselves.

The growth in global crime is largely traceable to increasing concern about illicit drug use in the United States in the late 1960s and early 1970s, as well as Western Europe's interest in terrorism during roughly the same period. Drugs and terrorism now top the list of concerns about the "global illicit economy" (Andreas 2015), but others include trade in weapons, counterfeit products, and human trafficking. All of these involve flows of all sorts—drugs, money, humans (e.g., prostitutes, or, more recently, terrorists and those fleeing war or oppression and trying to gain illegal entry into Europe [Glenny 2015]). They also include various illegal content that flows through the internet (e.g., child pornography, laundered funds, computer viruses, calls to commit terroristic acts).

These illegal flows have been aided by the decline of the nation-state and its increasing inability to reduce or halt such flows. Furthermore, global criminal cartels have come into existence to expedite illegal flows and to increase the profits that can

DIGITAL LIVING: DIGITAL PIRACY

Music and video piracy is undoubtedly the most widespread form of criminal activity on the internet. Many of us listen to songs or watch movies online without thinking about whether or not they have been uploaded illegally. But if these songs and movies are being shared and accessed without the permission of the individuals who created them, we are violating copyright laws. Music, movies, photographs, books, and other forms of creative expressions and innovations are considered the intellectual property of their creators, who have "exclusive ownership and rights to use, produce, and distribute" their work (Piquero 2010, 89). Every time we engage in music and video piracy, we are stealing someone's intellectual property and failing to financially compensate that person for his or her work. According to research in the Recording Industry Association of America's 2015 digital music report, 52 percent of respondents from 13 countries agreed that downloading and streaming copyrighted material without permission constituted theft, and 53 percent wanted licensed content to appear before pirated content on internet search engines (Recording Industry Association of America 2015).

Although individuals who engage in digital piracy are certainly at fault for violating copyright laws, web companies are also to blame. The 1998 Digital Millennium Copyright Act requires that web companies remove URLs that contain pirated content; however, instead of making these

Fredrik Neij, co-founder of The Pirate Bay, a site that allows users to share entertainment content and software, was convicted of enabling copyright infringement. He and the other founders were ordered to pay fines and sentenced to a year in prison. Do you think this was a fair outcome?

companies monitor possible cases of digital piracy, the Act expects the creators of their work to do so. Creators who find illegal content then have to make a request that the companies remove it. Given how fast and easy it is to upload illegal content, this is a time-consuming and burdensome chore to place on individual creators (Taplin 2016). Google, the web company with the most removal requests, received more than 20 million requests per week in 2016 (Molla and Ovide 2016). The good news is that web traffic on torrent websites that actively facilitate digital piracy appears to be decreasing. BitTorrent, a site where users can swap and watch pirated movies, saw its web traffic decrease from 13 percent of all web traffic in 2011 to only 4 percent in 2015. At the same time, YouTube, which is owned by Google, experienced an increase in total web traffic, from 10 percent in 2011 to 17 percent in 2015 (Molla and Ovide 2016). This is a worrisome trend, considering the "rampant piracy" on YouTube (Taplin 2016).

Engaging the Digital World

Do you believe that sharing music or video files online is deviant? Should it be criminalized? Who benefits, and who is harmed? What type of punishments should be established to prevent digital piracy, and who should enforce them? Conduct an online search of your favorite movie or song. How many URLs do you find? How many do you suspect might link you to pirated material? What clues do these links contain that make you think they are pirated?

be derived from them. In his book *McMafia* (2008), Misha Glenny attributes much of the cartels' success to increasingly sophisticated organizational methods (including economies of scale, global partnerships, and the opening of new markets) copied from leading legitimate businesses such as McDonald's. New technologies have also been employed to make at least some criminal flows more successful. For example, one cartel used a primitive submarine to transport drugs. The internet has made a number of illegal flows (e.g., child pornography and internet scams) much easier and is largely impervious to efforts at control by individual nation-states.

CRIMINALIZATION OF GLOBAL ACTIVITIES

As pointed out earlier, crime (and deviance) is always a matter of social definition or social construction. So, although the power of nation-states has generally declined in the global age, it continues to matter greatly as far as what come to be *defined* as global forms of deviance and crime. In the era of globalization, the nation-states of Western Europe and the United States have played the central role in criminalizing certain activities. It is *their* sense of morality and *their* norms of behavior that have come to be the rule in much of the world (Andreas and Nadelmann 2006). The global criminalization of drug use is a good case in point.

However, while there have been a number of efforts to define drug use as deviant and illegal, they have not always been successful. The global drug trade has in fact expanded in spite of great efforts by the United States and other nation-states to at least reduce it.

Much of the publicity about drugs and the ways in which they are implicated in globalization involves cocaine and heroin. Great attention is devoted to, for example, the growing of poppies in Afghanistan and drug production in Guatemala, and the ways in which drugs from those areas and many others make their way around the world. A more recent global drug is methamphetamine (meth), made easily and cheaply in home-based "cooking facilities" from pseudoephedrine, the main ingredient in a number of cough, cold, and allergy medications. The AMC television show *Breaking Bad* dealt with the cooking of meth by a former high school

chemistry teacher in New Mexico and meth's often violent relationship to the drug trade in nearby Mexico. Once largely an American phenomenon, the production and use of methamphetamine is beginning to expand globally. For example, it is the drug of choice in Indonesia, and there was fear as long as a decade ago that it would spread throughout the European Union (Kulish 2007; Reuters 2016b).

Several aspects of cross-border crime, especially as it relates to drugs, help account for why global as well as national efforts to counter it have been largely unsuccessful. First, those who commit the crimes do not require a great many resources. Second, they do not need very much expertise to commit the crimes. Third, such crimes are easy to conceal. Fourth, in many cases, the crimes are not apt to be reported to the police or other authorities. Finally, the crimes are those for which great consumer demand exists and for which there are no readily available alternative products (e.g., drugs) or activities (e.g., prostitution; Andreas and Nadelmann 2006).

However, it would be wrong to judge global efforts to control drugs and other illegal substances and activities as complete failures. The fact is that while drugs continue to flow readily throughout the world for the reasons suggested previously, the United States has had considerable success in internationalizing its views, laws, procedures, and efforts at enforcement. As mentioned earlier, powerful societies are often able to get weaker societies to adopt their ways of doing things. Foreign governments have

- Altered their laws and methods of law enforcement to more closely match U.S. laws on drugs

- Acceded to demands by the United States to sign law enforcement treaties

- Adopted American investigative techniques

- Created specialized drug enforcement agencies

- Stationed law enforcement representatives in other countries

- Enacted various laws on conspiracy, asset forfeiture, and money laundering related to drugs

- Provided greater assistance to the United States and changed their laws on financial secrecy

In other words, we have seen an Americanization of law enforcement throughout much of the world. However, a wide variety of failures, most notably in the so-called "war on drugs," in both the United States and globally, has led to more questioning of many of these changes in law enforcement (*New York Times* 2016).

GLOBAL CRIME CONTROL

The growth in global crime has been met, of course, by the expansion of international policing and of the role of the police in international relations (Bowling and Sheptycki 2012). In addition to its role regarding drug trafficking, the United States has taken the lead in countering other forms of global crime and in influencing other nations to work against these crimes. In the early twentieth century, its focus was on "white slavery" (prostitution); during the Cold War, it was the control of weapons and advanced technology; and in the mid-1980s, the focus shifted to the regulation of securities markets, especially insider trading. Following the onset of the Great Recession, the focus shifted again to abuses in the global financial system as well as illegal economic activities. These include the existence of secret bank accounts in other countries, especially Switzerland, as well as the creation of shell companies in, among other places, Panama. (Shell companies have few assets and exist mainly to evade taxes.) An international scandal arose in 2016 when the leak of more than 11.5 million documents from a Panamanian law firm revealed its involvement in the creation of shell companies, as well as the names of many of them (Semple 2016).

Since 9/11, there has been a dramatic erosion of distinctions in the world of criminal justice in an effort to forestall further terrorist attacks and to catch or kill people defined as terrorists. For example, the distinction between law enforcement and intelligence operations has eroded as law enforcement authorities seek to gain intelligence on potential terrorists. The distinction between law enforcement and security has also eroded. The USA PATRIOT (Uniting and Strengthening America by Providing Appropriate Tools Required to Intercept and Obstruct Terrorism) Act, signed into law on October 26, 2001, has played a key role in this erosion by, for example, extending the concern of

law enforcement agencies to domestic terrorism. In addition, surveillance of the border between the United States and Mexico, and in immigrant communities in the United States, has increased. In the process, many immigrants have been defined as criminals, apprehended, and then returned to Mexico. It is important to note that far less attention is devoted to surveillance on the much longer border with Canada, and those who do cross that border illegally are much less likely to be defined, or apprehended, as criminals.

Some European countries have recently instituted a similar toughening of border controls and surveillance. However, within the European Union, border law enforcement has become more homogeneous as criminal justice norms and procedures have become more similar and law enforcement contacts and exchanges of information among member states have become more regular. Of great importance has been the formation of Europol, the EU's law enforcement agency, which enables better and increased communication and cooperation among national police agencies.

While these efforts have improved global crime control, they have a variety of downsides. Democracy and civil rights may be threatened by these efforts. Crime control efforts are not always as transparent as they should be, and the officials involved often need to be more accountable. For another, tougher border and immigration controls have led to more daring and dangerous efforts to cross borders, leading to more deaths in the process. Those who have been denied entry often suffer in poorly constructed and overcrowded border camps. Efforts by the United States to deal with trafficking in women and children have focused more on criminalizing that traffic than on protecting the human rights of the women and children being trafficked. Finally, the attention and money devoted to international crime and its control have tended to distract attention, and to take money away, from efforts to deal with a wide range of fundamental issues within nation-states, including the welfare of large portions of society.

Public efforts to control global crime have been far from totally successful. For example, in 2014, 43 Mexican college students were murdered by a drug gang. The murders were committed at the behest of the mayor of Iguala, who was later arrested, as were some members of the gang (Archibold 2015). Between 2007 and 2011, approximately 40,000 people were killed in the wars between drug gangs, and the wars continue (although, as noted previously, to a declining degree) to ravage Mexico, and they have spread across the border into the United States. The police in Mexico have failed to halt the carnage, and even the use of the Mexican military has not been met with much success. The news media, often intimidated by the gangs, have often failed to provide needed and accurate information about criminal activities.

SUMMARY

Deviance is any action, belief, or human characteristic that violates the norms of a group or society. Deviance changes over time—certain actions that were considered norm violations in the past, such as cohabitation, are not anymore. Norm violations are an important way in which groups and societies define acceptable behavior and form cohesion.

Explanatory and constructionist theories are two different ways to understand deviance. Explanatory theories attempt to explain why deviance does or does not occur. Constructionist theories are more concerned with the process of how some behaviors are defined and classified as deviant. Structural/functional theories are explanatory. Strain theory, for example, posits that deviance is a caused by a discrepancy between the larger structure and culture of society. Social control theory suggests that deviance is a result of weak social bonds, while broken windows theory suggests that deviance is a result of social disorder. Conflict/critical theories are also explanatory and focus on how the elite are less likely to be defined as deviant than the poor. Inter/actionist theories are constructionist, highlighting how social control agents label certain behaviors as deviant. Individuals who are stigmatized by social control agents organize their lives and identities around their deviant status.

Crime is a form of deviance that violates criminal law. The major components of the criminal justice system are law enforcement, the courts, and the correctional system. There are a number of different types of crime, but the broadest distinction is between violent crimes that involve the threat or use of force and property crimes that involve gaining or destroying property.

Globalization has been associated with increases in cross-border crime, particularly the international drug trade. Illegal flows are aided by nation-states' declining ability to halt them. International policing has expanded to contend with the growth in global crime.

KEY TERMS

conformists, 148
constructionist theories, 148
consumer crimes, 162
corporate crime, 159
crime, 155
criminalization, 144
criminology, 155
cybercrime, 162
deviance, 144
differential
    association, 155

discreditable stigma, 155
discredited stigma, 155
explanatory theories, 148
felonies, 159
general deterrence, 158
hate crimes, 162
innovators, 149
labeling theory, 152
misdemeanors, 159
moral entrepreneurs, 154
moral panic, 154

organized crime, 159
parole, 156
political crimes, 161
primary deviance, 153
probation, 157
property crimes, 159
rebels, 149
recidivism, 157
retreatists, 149
ritualists, 149
rule creators, 153

rule enforcers, 154
secondary deviance, 153
social control, 153
social control agents, 152
social control theory, 149
specific deterrence, 157
stigma, 154
strain theory, 148
symbol, 152
violent crime, 158
white-collar crimes, 159

1. What do sociologists mean when they say that deviance is socially defined? Given a sociological approach, in what ways is tattooing deviant, and in what ways is it not?

2. How can we understand deviance as a global flow? How do countries differ in terms of their interpretations of what is deviant? In an increasingly globalized world, what are the consequences of these differing interpretations?

3. How does consuming the "wrong" products and services make someone a deviant? What does this suggest about the relationship between power and deviance?

4. Adolescents value a certain level of independence from their parents, often wanting more control over their own lives. They want to be able to do what they want to do without needing permission from their parents. Apply Merton's strain theory to an understanding of how adolescents might behave, given this desire for more independence.

5. Why do those who rank high in such hierarchies as business, government, and the military have a much greater ability to commit deviant acts, to have those acts seen as legitimate, and to get away with them? What does this suggest about the "fairness" of deviance?

6. What are the differences between a discredited stigma and a discreditable stigma? What is an example of each?

7. How is crime different from deviance? Why do some forms of deviance become criminalized, whereas others do not?

8. How do you explain the fact that the United States has so many people in prison? Why is the U.S. incarceration rate the highest in the world?

9. Is the death penalty useful as a form of general deterrence? Are you in favor of the death penalty? If so, for what crimes?

10. What sorts of barriers have countries attempted to implement to limit the global flow of drugs? Why have these been relatively unsuccessful?

SOCIAL STRATIFICATION IN THE UNITED STATES AND GLOBALLY

Student "Haves" and "Have-Nots" in Higher Education

The world of higher education is stratified in various ways. For example, a status hierarchy is formed by graduates of high-ranking Ivy League universities, middle-level state universities, and lower-level community colleges. Whatever the level of the higher education system from which you graduate, another aspect of stratification, and one that undoubtedly interests and may even trouble you, is the high cost of your education. Cost is not much of a problem for the very wealthy or those brilliant (or athletically gifted) enough to earn full scholarships. However, for most students, it is a major issue, and for many (and likely their parents), it can be a hardship if not an overwhelming barrier to attending and ultimately graduating from college. The ability to afford a college degree is closely related to social class position.

Students from the middle and lower classes deal with the cost of education in various ways, such as by holding part-time jobs, attending lower-cost state and especially community colleges, and taking out loans, either on their

LEARNING OBJECTIVES

7.1 Describe the three dimensions of social stratification.

7.2 Identify factors contributing to economic inequality.

7.3 Identify different types of social mobility.

7.4 Discuss theories of social stratification.

7.5 Explain the relationship between consumption and social stratification.

7.6 Understand the characteristics of global stratification.

edge.sagepub.com/ ritzeressentials3e

- Take the chapter quiz
- Review key terms with eFlashcards
- Explore multimedia links and SAGE readings

own or through their parents. Whatever route they take, they are disadvantaged in comparison to those who have no problem affording whatever college they wish to attend.

Student loans represent an especially big problem for many students. Private loans are likely to have variable interest rates and offer little protection in case of default. This stands in contrast to federal student loans, which have fixed rates and many protections, including against default. Total student loans in the United States amount to more than $1.36 trillion, a fourfold increase between 2000 and 2016. Many students leave college owing $35,000, or more, and they are then likely to find themselves unemployed or with low-paying jobs. As a result, many are unable to make the payments due on their loans, and they may remain saddled with college debt for a large part of their lives, perhaps even into old age.

Of great and particular concern is debt incurred by students who attend for-profit colleges such as the University of Phoenix, as well as institutions that don't even deserve to be thought of as colleges (or universities), such as the scandalous Trump "University" where students lost tens of thousands of dollars (Carey 2016). Such colleges are most likely to be attended by those who are underprepared for higher education, are economically disadvantaged, and rank low in the stratification system. These students may receive a poor education, have a lower-than-average graduation rate, and incur higher-than-average student debt, even if, as is often the case, they do not complete their degrees. For-profit colleges enroll only 11 percent of all college students in the United States, but they account for almost 35 percent of student defaults on loans (Douglas-Gabriel 2016; Shen 2016). Further complicating matters for such students is the fact that they are preyed upon by debt-relief companies that charge high fees and/or often do not deliver on their promises to cut or eliminate the debt. These students' debt is high both because they have fewer economic resources with which to avoid or repay the debt and because for-profit colleges are often more expensive than other colleges.

The educational experience is just another example of the highly stratified character of many areas of U.S. society in which the poor pay more—and get far less. ●

We often hear that American society, as well as the world as a whole, is unfair. This is generally taken to mean that a relatively small number of people have way too much, while most of the rest of us have far too little. In the United States, this unfairness is made abundantly clear when we see news reports about the excesses of the super-rich, such as multimillion-dollar bonuses, private jets, and mansions or condos in New York or London worth tens or hundreds of millions of dollars. At the other extreme, the gap is just as clear when we encounter homeless people begging on street corners and at turn lanes on heavily traveled roads.

What is it that some people have, or are thought to have, and others lack? The most obvious answer is money and what money buys. However, **social stratification** involves hierarchical differences not only in economic positions but also in other important areas, such as status, or social honor, and power. Social stratification has a profound effect on how monetary and nonmonetary resources are distributed in American society and around the globe.

DIMENSIONS OF SOCIAL STRATIFICATION

Any sociological discussion of stratification draws on an important set of dimensions derived from the work of the great German social theorist Max Weber ([1921] 1968; Bendix and Lipset 1966). These three dimensions are social class, status, and power.

SOCIAL CLASS

One's economic position in the stratification system, especially one's occupation, defines one's **social**

class. A person's social class position strongly determines and reflects his or her income and wealth. Those who rank close to one another in wealth and income can be said to be members of the same social class. For example, multibillionaire entrepreneurs such as Bill Gates and Warren Buffett belong to one social class; the janitor in your university building and the mechanic who fixes your car at the corner gas station belong to another. Terms often used to describe a person's social class are *upper class* (for example, large-scale entrepreneurs and many large investors, especially in hedge funds), *middle class* (nurses, teachers, veterinarians, air traffic controllers, travel agents, and firefighters), *working class* (manual, clerical, and full-time service workers in industries such as fast food), and *lower class* (part-time service and other workers and the unemployed). Figure 7.1 illustrates the relationships among occupation, income, and social class in the United States (Gilbert 2015). Its teardrop shape represents the percentage of Americans in each class; there are substantially more people in the working and lower classes than there are in the upper class. As we will soon see, the United States is even more stratified than Figure 7.1 suggests.

STATUS

The second dimension of the stratification system, status, relates to the prestige attached to a person's positions within society. The existence and importance of this dimension demonstrate that factors other than those associated with money are considered valuable in society. For example, in a 2015 Harris Poll of 2,223 U.S. adults, the well-paid doctor was ranked the most prestigious, followed by the less well-paid scientist, and in third place the

FIGURE 7.1 • Social Classes, Occupations, and Incomes in the United States

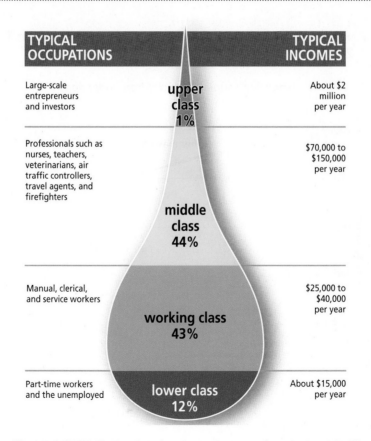

SOURCE: Adapted from Gilbert, D. L. (2015). *The American class structure in an age of growing inequality.* Thousand Oaks, CA: SAGE.

comparatively modestly paid firefighter. However, the often exorbitantly paid and rewarded corporate executive was not even in the top 10 occupations in terms of prestige (Harris Interactive 2016).

POWER

A third dimension of social stratification is **power**, the ability to get others to do what you want them to do, even if it is against their will. Those who have a great deal of power rank high in the stratification system, while those with little or no power are arrayed at or near the bottom. This is clearest in the case of politics, where, for example, the president of the United States ranks very high in power, while millions of ordinary voters have comparatively little political power.

Greater income is generally associated with more power, but there are exceptions to this rule. In the late 2000s, an increasing number of media stories focused on the phenomenon of "breadwinner wives" and "breadwinner moms," or those wives and moms who are the sole or primary providers of income for their families. Only 11 percent of households with children under 18 had breadwinner moms in 1960, but that had risen to 40 percent in 2011 (Mundy 2012; Wang, Parker, and Taylor 2013). Then there are "alpha wives and moms"— women who earn more than their husbands (Chae 2015). As shown in Figure 7.2, only 4 percent of wives in 1960 had income greater than that of their husbands, but by 2011, 23 percent of wives earned more than their husbands.

In spite of their greater income, breadwinner wives and moms may not have greater power in the marital relationship, and in many cases, they are compelled to be content with sharing power with their husbands (Cherlin 2010).

ECONOMIC INEQUALITY

A major concern in the sociological study of stratification is **inequality**, a condition whereby some

FIGURE 7.2 • Percentage of Married Women Who Earn More Than Their Husbands, 1960–2011

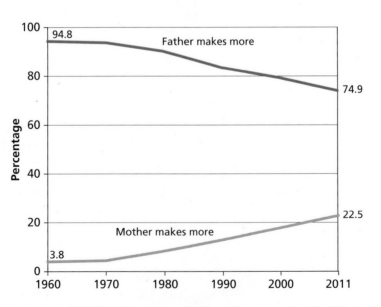

% based on married couples with children under age 18

SOURCE: Who Makes More in the Family? 1960–2011, from p. 12 in *Breadwinner Moms*, May 29, 2013. Reprinted by permission of Pew Research Center, Washington, DC.

NOTE: The category of father and mother having the same income is not shown.

positions in society yield a great deal of money, status, and power, while others yield little, if any, of these. While other bases of stratification exist, the system of stratification in the United States, and in much of the contemporary world, is based largely on money.

Money can take the form of income or wealth. **Income** is the amount of money a person earns from a job, a business, or returns on various types of assets (e.g., rents on real estate) and investments (e.g., dividends on stocks and bonds). Income is generally measured year by year. For example, you might have an income of $25,000 per year. **Wealth**, on the other hand, is the total amount of a person's financial assets and other properties less the total of various kinds of debts, or liabilities. Assets include, among others, savings, investments, homes, and automobiles, while debts include home mortgages, student loans, car loans, and amounts owed to credit card companies. If all your assets total $100,000 but you owe $25,000, your wealth (or net worth) amounts to $75,000.

Wealth can be inherited from others, so that a person can be very wealthy yet have a modest income. Many elderly widows and widowers find themselves in this position. Conversely, people can earn substantial incomes and not be very wealthy because, for example, they squander their money on expensive vacations or hobbies, or on alcohol or drugs.

INCOME INEQUALITY

Sociologists are interested in inequality in status and power, but they tend to be most concerned about economic inequality. In many parts of the world, incomes became more equitable from the late 1920s until the 1970s. However, since the 1970s, there has been a substantial increase in income inequality in many countries, with a few individuals earning a great deal more and many earning little, if any, more. Even in the United States, which we historically and erroneously regard as an egalitarian society, income inequality has been rising since the 1970s and now rivals levels that existed in the late 1920s (Reich 2016). That was at the peak of the boom years of the Roaring Twenties and just before the bursting of the economic bubble that heralded the beginning of the Great Depression. In 1928, the top 1 percent of families, the main beneficiaries of the economic boom of the 1920s, received almost 24 percent of all pretax income, while the bottom 90 percent of families earned only about

Jean Baudrillard's idea of "symbolic exchange" laid the basis for thinking about an alternative to the system of stratification in capitalist society. This and other ideas of Baudrillard's, as well as his published works, earned him noted recognition and made him one of the most famous social theorists of the twentieth century.

51 percent of that income. The Depression and World War II altered the economic landscape and led to greater equality. By 1944, the top 1 percent were receiving *only* about 11 percent of income, while the bottom 90 percent were earning more than 67 percent of that income. However, the situation began to change again in the 1970s, and by 2015, the top 1 percent of American families earned nearly 17 percent of all income, up from 10 percent in 1960 (see Figure 7.3)—this was almost as much (in percentage terms) as in 1928. At the same time, the share of the bottom 90 percent was below 50 percent, even less than in 1928. While the upper and lower classes have grown over the past two decades, the middle class has contracted. A recent Pew study found that the middle-class households in the United States declined from 62 percent to 59 percent between 1991 and 2010 (Schwartz 2017).

FIGURE 7.3 • Income Share of the Top 1 Percent of Families in the United States, 1950–2015

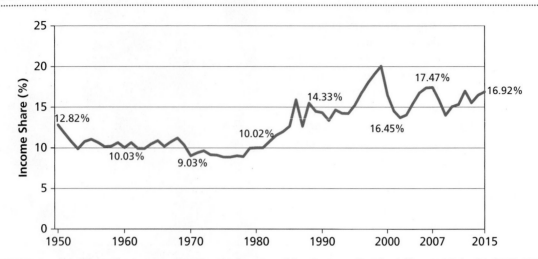

SOURCES: Dennis L. Gilbert, *The American Class Structure in an Age of Growing Inequality,* 9th ed. (Thousand Oaks, CA: SAGE, 2015); personal communication with Dennis L. Gilbert.

Income inequality today is even greater if we focus not on the top 1 percent but on the elite of the elite, the top 0.1 percent of households. In 2012, the average annual household income for the top 0.1 percent was a whopping $6,373,782. By comparison the top 1 percent had to make do with an income of *only* $1,264,065. How about the bottom 90 percent? Their average household income was $30,997. In other terms, the top 0.1 percent earned 206 times as much as the bottom 90 percent, while the top 1 percent made 41 times the income of those at the bottom. This gap, too, has worsened over time. In 1980, the multiples were 47 and 14; in 1990, they were 87 and 21 (Lowrey 2014). Thus, it's a great time to be rich, but it is an even better time to be uber-rich.

Several broad reasons have been put forth to explain recent increases in income inequality:

- *Deindustrialization.* The decline of U.S. industry, as well as of industry in other developed countries, has led to the loss of many higher-paying industrial jobs (Bluestone and Harrison 1984; Goldstein 2017; Kollmeyer and Pichler 2013). Deindustrialization is also related to the decline in the power of labor unions, which had helped many industrial workers obtain higher pay and generous benefits.

- *Technological advances.* The highest-paying new jobs in recent years have been created in high-tech, high-skill areas such as information technology (IT). Many Americans have not received the training necessary to shift from industrial to high-tech work.

- *Political climate.* A variety of political decisions help explain the increase in income inequality. There is, for example, political opposition in the United States (mainly from Republicans and their wealthy supporters and backers) to raising the federal minimum wage (currently $7.25 per hour) at all, or to raising it very much (Ritzer 2015b). In addition, tax policies benefit homeowners, not renters, who are more likely to be poor (Desmond 2017).

ASK YOURSELF

Which of the proposed reasons for the steady increase in income inequality do you think has had the greatest impact on those you know? What about in society at large? Why?

WEALTH INEQUALITY

As unfair as income inequality may seem, the greatest disparities in society—the largest differences

FIGURE 7.4 • Wealth Share of the Top 0.01 Percent to 1 Percent of Households in the United States: 1960–2012

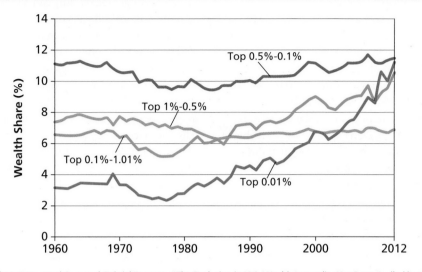

SOURCES: Data from Emmanuel Saez and Gabriel Zucman, "The Explosion in U.S. Wealth Inequality Has Been Fuelled by Stagnant Wages, Increasing Debt, and a Collapse in Asset Values for the Middle Classes," London School of Economics and Political Science, 2014; and Emmanuel Saez and Gabriel Zucman, "Wealth Inequality in the United States Since 1913," October 2014.

between the haves and the have-nots—are found in the enormous differences in wealth (that is, economic assets) in society. Wealth inequality tends to be much greater than income inequality The two are linked, however, because wealth tends to produce various sources of income, such as dividends and interest. Those with significant amounts of income from such sources are far more likely to rank toward the top of the stratification system in terms of income than are those who rely mainly on wages and salaries. Thus, wealth itself is important, as is the seemingly endless stream of income that wealth tends to produce.

Like income inequality, wealth inequality has tended to increase in recent years in the United States and other Western countries (and the U.S. tax system is of *decreasing* utility in reducing that inequality [Looney and Moore 2016; Reich 2016]). More than 80 percent of the wealth gain in the United States between 1983 and 2009 went to the wealthiest 5 percent of the population. Over the last three decades, the wealth of the top 0.1 percent of households has increased from 7 to 22 percent of the total. In contrast, the poorest 60 percent of the population saw a 7.5 percent *decline* in wealth. Their wealth has eroded because of such factors as the decline of many housing values and stagnant

wages, as well as the large number of people who have given up and left the labor force, thus earning no income and acquiring no wealth (Appelbaum 2014; Saez and Zucman 2014).

As with income inequality, the super-rich (the top 0.01 percent in terms of wealth) are becoming dramatically better off in terms of wealth. The share of the wealth for the top 0.01 percent grew from about 3 percent in 1960 to about 11 percent in 2012.

Wealth brings with it a wide range of advantages:

- It can be invested to generate income and ultimately even greater wealth.

- It can be used to purchase material comforts of all sorts: large homes, vacation retreats, and luxury cars, as well as the services of housekeepers, gardeners, and, personal trainers.

- It can afford a high level of financial security, allowing the wealthy, if they wish, to retire at an early age.

- It purchases far more freedom and autonomy than less wealthy individuals can acquire, such as the freedom to leave unsatisfactory employment without worrying about how the bills will be paid.

- Most wealth can be passed on to offspring, even generations away, guaranteeing that they live a similarly privileged lifestyle.

Wealth and the growing disparities in wealth received enormous academic and media attention with the publication of economist Thomas Piketty's *Capital in the Twenty-First Century* (2014; see also Antonio 2014). Piketty sees wealth as being of greater importance than income. Rather than relying on pay or a salary (even though it might be high) for their labor, those with wealth rely much more on the income their wealth produces, such as earned interest, rental from properties, dividends on stocks and bonds, and royalties. Overall returns from such sources have historically outstripped increases in salaries and pay.

Status, Power, and Wealth

Perhaps of greatest importance is the fact that wealth not only accords a high-level position on one dimension of stratification, social class, but it is also an important factor in gaining similar positions on the other dimensions of stratification, status and power. Those who have great wealth tend to rank high in social class because class is, to a considerable degree, defined economically, and wealth is a key indicator of it. Those with great wealth are also generally able to buy or to otherwise acquire what gives them high status and great power. In terms of status, the wealthy can afford more and better-quality education. They can, for example, send their children to very expensive and exclusive prep schools and Ivy League universities. In some elite universities, being a "legacy" applicant—the son or daughter of an elite who attended the same school—can increase the chances of gaining admission, perhaps by as much as 45 percent (Mandery 2014). The practice of favoring legacy applicants is sometimes called "affirmative action for the rich" (Kahlenberg 2010). The wealthy can also achieve recognition as philanthropists by, for example, attending $1,000-per-ticket charity balls or even donating the money needed to build a new wing of a hospital.

Power over employees is a fact of life for wealthy individuals who own businesses or run other organizations. Their needs for financial, household, and personal services give the wealthy another source of power. They have the ability to direct the activities of many charities and civic groups. And if that weren't enough, the wealthy can buy more power by bribing political officials or making generous campaign contributions to favored politicians. In some cases, the wealthy choose to use their money to run for public office themselves; if successful, their families may come to occupy positions that give them great power. For example, Prescott Bush made his money on Wall Street and became a U.S. senator. His son, George H. W. Bush, became president of the United States, as did his grandson, George W. Bush. Another grandson, Jeb Bush, former governor of Florida, was a (failed) candidate for the Republican nomination for president in 2016.

The Perpetuation of Wealth

One of the great advantages of the wealthy is their ability to maintain their social class across generations. Their ability to keep their wealth, if not expand it, often allows the members of the upper class to pass their wealth, and the upper-class position that goes with it, to their children. The wealthy are able to perpetuate their wealth in large part because they have been able to use their money and influence to resist taxation systems designed to redistribute at least some of the wealth in society. For example, the wealthy have fought long and hard against the estate tax, which places a high tax on assets worth more than a certain amount that are left behind when an individual dies. Many of the wealthy prefer to refer to the estate tax in more negative terms, as a "death tax."

THE DECLINE OF THE AMERICAN MIDDLE CLASS

Much has been written in recent years about the decline, or the hollowing out, of the American middle class (Frank 2013; Schwartz 2017). While there is no clear economic dividing line that separates the middle class from the upper and lower classes, we can say that to be considered part of the middle class, a family of four must have earnings (adjusted for inflation) between $35,000 and $100,000 per year (Searcey and Gebeloff 2015). The proportion of the U.S. population in the middle class *declined* from 53 percent in 1967 to 50 percent in 2015 (Parlapiano, Gebeloff, and Carter 2015). Some of

Stratification in the New Sharing Economy

In the sharing economy, instead of buying or renting in the usual ways, we share goods and services—at a low cost or free of charge—with others (Gansky 2010; Stein 2015). Instead of renting a hotel room, we can get a room in a private home, or even an entire home, through the online site Airbnb. Instead of hailing a taxi, we can use Uber's smartphone app and get a pre-paid ride in a private automobile. Instead of waiting for a table at a "hot" restaurant, we can hire someone online to do so through TaskRabbit.

The sharing economy is clearly the wave of the future. But while some sharing is free of profit making and the exchange of money (Atsushi 2014), big businesses have become deeply engaged, and the sharing economy is growing highly stratified.

At the top are the founders, executives, and financiers of the most successful companies. Uber is now valued at about $68 billion (Austin, Canipe, and Slobin 2015), and its founders are likely to be millionaires or even billionaires. But for most of the drivers, the job is part-time and the pay is low. Drivers use their own cars, pay their own expenses, and lack benefits and job security. As a result, they are likely to land in or near the lower class. Worse, their success is costing traditional taxi drivers their jobs. Uber cars now outnumber yellow taxis in New York City by more than three to one (Hu 2017; Pramuk 2015).

Smartphone apps such as those of Uber and Airbnb create a divide between those who control the sharing economy and those who work in it. Is such increased stratification inevitable?

Airbnb, valued at about $25 billion, has created a similar stratification system, with founders and executives on top and many who list their apartments and homes nearer the bottom. However, few of those participants are actually individuals sharing space with others. While New York City is attempting to crack down on this, commercial operators supply more than one-third of Airbnb rental units and earn more than one-third of the profits; 6 percent of the hosts earned 37 percent of the revenue, and one had 272 units earning revenue of $6.8 million. Some critics argue that at least in this case, "the very term 'sharing economy' is ridiculous" (Austin, Canipe, and Slobin 2015; Streitfeld 2014, A1).

Belk (2014) argues that in all these cases and many others, sharing is being transformed into "pseudo-sharing" by, among others, profit-making organizations that have found this to be a way to grow rich. As Ritzer (2017) puts, there is "woefully little sharing" in the sharing economy. The sharing economy is creating a new stratification system, or at least new positions in the current system. Many will be at or near the bottom.

Engaging the Digital World

Do you think the stratification taking place in the sharing economy is inevitable? Why or why not? Should consumers avoid participating in this economy, even if the services offered are desirable and affordable? Why or why not? If you participate in the sharing economy, explain what types of services you use (or provide) most often and what the alternatives would be to each of them.

those in the middle class have been able to rise into the upper class, which grew from 7 percent to 21 percent of the U.S. population between 1967 and 2015. However, many have dropped into the lower class (which, nonetheless, dropped from 40 percent to 29 percent of the population in that period).

The major reason for the decline of the middle class is the decline of middle-income jobs such as better-paid, often unionized, positions in manufacturing, usually owing to technological change (Ford 2015). In other cases, those jobs have been lost to successful companies elsewhere in the world. Some displaced workers have been able to get better-paying jobs and thereby move up the stratification hierarchy. However, many more have had to take lower-paying service jobs, such as in the fast-food industry. They have likely dropped into the lower class, as have those unable to find jobs or unwilling to accept poorly paid work. Another major factor in the decline of the middle class is wage stagnation in the kinds of jobs that members of this class are likely to continue to hold (Greenhouse 2015; Wisman 2013). They may still have the same jobs they had a decade or two ago, but the wages associated with them have tended to increase little, and more likely have tended to decline in real terms, over that time. As a result, they may no longer be able to afford the things usually associated with a middle-class lifestyle.

The Great Recession badly hurt the middle class. For example, many lost their homes because they could no longer afford their mortgage payments. Government efforts in the wake of the recession (such as bailing out banks and investment companies) greatly aided the upper class, but they did little or nothing for the middle class (the government bailed out few homeowners in danger of losing their homes; Hacker and Pierson 2010).

The decline of the middle class is of great concern, especially to those who are no longer in it, or who can no longer aspire to be part of it. From a large-scale perspective, this decline creates a stratification system that splits into the upper and lower classes, with an increasingly massive hole in the middle. This leads to growing inequality and to increasingly less hope for those in the lower classes of finding middle-income positions that will allow them to rise in the stratification system.

POVERTY

While some in the middle class have become poor and dropped into the lower class, poverty is obviously a problem mainly for the much more numerous and often long-term members of that class. Poverty and the many problems associated with it are of great concern both to sociologists and to society as a whole (Desmond 2016; Edin and Schaefer 2015; Iceland 2013).

Poverty is troubling for many reasons, the most important of which is its negative effect on the lives of the poor themselves. The lack of a job, or having one that does not offer a living wage, is likely to be associated with many troubling conditions. Those suffering from poverty are likely to suffer from food insecurity; that is, they have difficulty getting enough to eat. They are also likely to be in poor physical and mental health and, as a result, to have a lower life expectancy. In fact, the poor are falling increasingly behind the rich as the gap between the rich and poor in life span has widened dramatically over the years. For men born in 1920, those in the top 10 percent of earners could expect to live six more years than those in the bottom 10 percent of earners. For men born in 1950, the gap had more than doubled to 14 years. For women over the same time period, the gap had grown from 4.7 years to 13 years (Tavernise 2016). Major causes of these growing disparities in life span are significant class differences in smoking, obesity, and involvement in the prescription drug epidemic, especially among poor whites.

The great disparity between the rich and the poor is considered by many to be a moral problem, if not a moral crisis, for society as a whole. The poor are often seen as not doing what they should, or could, to raise themselves out of poverty. They are seen as disreputable, which makes them objects of moral censure by those who have succeeded in society (Damer 1974; Matza 1966; Shildrick and MacDonald 2013). However, some see poverty as an entirely different kind of moral problem. They argue that the poor should be seen as the "victims" of a system that impoverishes them (Ryan 1976). The existence of large numbers of poor people in otherwise affluent societies is a "moral stain" on those societies (Harvey 2007). Something must be amiss in the economic and political systems in societies that perpetuate so much poverty (Rank 2014).

How are poverty and social class related? Is poverty inevitable in a stratified society?

ASK YOURSELF

Do you believe the poor are victims? If so, of whom? Or do you believe the poor have chosen not to raise themselves from poverty? If so, what sociological factors would explain this choice?

ANALYZING POVERTY

It may be tempting to blame the poor for the existence of poverty, but a sociological perspective notes the larger social forces that create and perpetuate poverty. To the sociologist, poverty persists for three basic reasons:

- Poverty is built into the capitalist system. Capitalist businesses seek to maximize profits. They do so by keeping wages as low as possible and by hiring as few workers as possible. When business slows, they are likely to lay people off, thrusting most of them into poverty. It is in the interest of the capitalist system to have a large number of unemployed, and therefore poor, people. This population serves as what Marx called the "reserve army of the unemployed." This is a readily available pool of people who can be drawn quickly into the labor force when business booms and more workers are needed.

- Competition among social classes encourages some elite groups of people to seek to enhance their economic position by limiting the ability of other groups to maintain even their economic positions. The elites do so by restricting the poor's access to opportunities and resources such as those afforded by various welfare systems.

- Government actions to reduce poverty, or ameliorate its negative effects on people and society, are generally limited by groups of people who believe that the poor should make it on their own and not be afforded the aid of the government. They also believe that government aid reduces people's incentive to do on their own what they need to do to rise above the poverty line.

There are two broad types of poverty:

- **Absolute poverty** is a measure of what people need in order to survive. No matter the standard for measuring poverty, absolute poverty remains constant over time, although its level is revised to take inflation into consideration.

- **Relative poverty** is defined not by some objective standard but rather by the fact that some people, irrespective of income, are, or feel themselves to be, poor relative to others to whom they relate. Thus, even middle-class people (especially those who have experienced wage stagnation or have lost their jobs) and some upper-class people can see themselves as poor in comparison with those around them.

POVERTY IN THE UNITED STATES

To measure poverty, the U.S. government uses an absolute measure, a **poverty line**, or threshold, in terms of a set income. A household whose income falls below the threshold is considered to be poor. The formula used involves multiplying the cost of what is deemed to be a nutritionally adequate food plan by three. This is because a family is assumed to spend one-third of its budget on food. It is worth noting that many people criticize this calculation for not considering other necessary expenses, such as child care, housing, and transportation. The poverty line in 2017 for a family of four was a pretax income of $24,600, and $12,060 for a single adult (U.S. Department of Health and Human Services 2017). In 2014, 15 percent of the U.S. population, or 46.7 million people, lived below the poverty line and were therefore officially categorized as poor (DeNavas-Walt and Proctor 2015).

Of course, millions who exist at or slightly above that line would also be considered poor by many people in society. In the wake of the Great Recession's lingering effects, there have been calls for a stronger focus on the "near poor" (DeParle, Gebeloff, and Tavernise 2011; Hokayem and Heggeness 2014). Those who have income that is less than 25 percent above the poverty line would

be included in this category. Using this measure, it has been estimated that in 2014, almost 15 million people in the United States were considered to be near poor. If we combine that number with the number of the poor, we see that almost 60 million Americans are poor or very close to it. There is no question that poverty is a huge problem in the United States, but it is almost certainly far greater than most of us imagine.

Looking at the longer-term trends shown in Figure 7.5, we can see that there has been considerable variation in the numbers of people living in poverty from year to year since 1959. What is striking, however, is the sharp increase in poverty that coincided with the beginning of the Great Recession; 6 million more households were below the poverty line in 2015 as compared with 2009.

As you might expect, given their disadvantages in income and wealth, minorities suffer disproportionately from poverty. The poverty rate in 2014 for non-Hispanic whites was 10 percent. The 12 percent poverty rate for Asians was down significantly from 16 percent in the mid-1980s, but still higher than the rate for non-Hispanic whites. Even more telling, the poverty rate was more than 20 percent for both blacks (26 percent) and Hispanics (24 percent; DeNavas-Walt and Proctor 2015; U.S. Census Bureau 2014).

THE FEMINIZATION OF POVERTY

A central issue in the study of poverty is the degree to which women and children are overrepresented among the poor (Abercrombie and Hastings 2016). In 2014, 15 percent of U.S. women were below the poverty line, whereas only 12 percent of men lived in poverty (U.S. Census Bureau 2015). Poverty levels vary by age: Women between the ages of 45 and 64 are less likely to be poor than are those 18 and below and 65 and above. Female poverty levels also vary based on race and ethnicity: Both black and Latino women are more than twice as likely to be poor as are white women. Also, as noted previously, female-headed households with no husband present have far higher rates of poverty than do families headed by married couples.

The **feminization of poverty**, first framed as a concept in 1978, means that those living in poverty are more likely to be women than men

FIGURE 7.5 • **Poverty in the United States, 1959–2015**

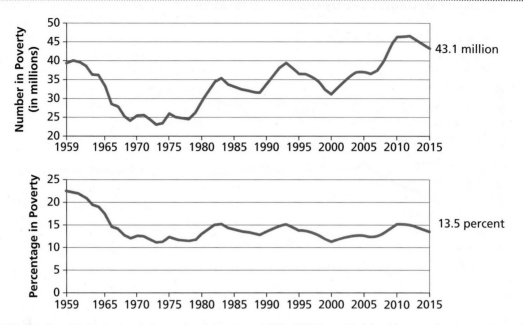

SOURCES: Data from U.S. Census Bureau, Current Population Survey, 1960 to 2015 Annual Social and Economic Supplements; Bernadette D. Proctor, Jessica L. Semega, and Melissa A. Kollar, Figure 4: "Number in Poverty and Poverty Rate: 1959 to 2015," in *Income and Poverty in the United States: 2015,* Current Population Reports P60–256(RV), U.S. Census Bureau, September 2016.

(Goldberg 2010; Pearce 1978). Although in recent years the improved position of women in the work world, and increases in women's earnings, would seem to indicate that the poverty gap is narrowing, the gender gap persists (McLanahan and Kelly 1999). One of the reasons for that persistence is the fact that the trend toward gender wage equalization has been more than offset by the increasing tendency for a greater proportion of men to raise their earnings through "overwork"—that is, by working more than 50 hours per week (Cha and Weeden 2014).

A variety of demographic factors and changes help explain the feminization of poverty:

- Women are more likely than men to live alone; single women marry later than single men, divorced women are less likely to remarry than are divorced men, and women have longer life spans than men.

- Women have lower average earnings than men do. More children are being born to unmarried women, who tend to earn less than married women and who are more likely to be fully responsible for dependents.

Economically, women suffer from a variety of disadvantages. Historically, males were considered to be the main breadwinners, and women, if they worked, were thought of as secondary earners. Women today exist in a sex-segregated labor force in which the best and highest-paying positions go largely to men. The subordinate economic position of women is reinforced by the systematic wage discrimination practiced against them. They are routinely paid less than men, even for the same work. In regard to income, women are also adversely affected by the fact that they are more likely than men to work part-time, to hold temporary jobs, or to work at home (Presser 2005). Female workers have gained some ground in recent years: They earned about 61 percent of male earnings in 1960 but 79 percent in 2014 (DeNavas-Walt and Proctor 2015), in part because of stagnation in male earnings. In spite of the improvement, the gender gap in earnings persists to this day (see Figure 7.6).

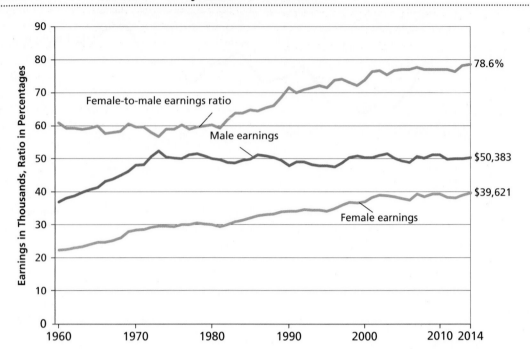

SOURCES: Data from U.S. Census Bureau, Current Population Survey, 1961 to 2014 Annual Social Economic Supplement, Figure 2; Carmen Denavas-Walt and Bernadette D. Proctor, Table A-4: "Number and Real Median Earnings of Total Workers and Full-Time, Year-Round Workers by Sex and Female-to-Male Earnings Ratio: 1960 to 2014," in *Income and Poverty in the United States, 2015,* Current Population Reports P60–252, U.S. Census Bureau, September 2015.

SOCIAL MOBILITY

Those who live in poverty are understandably eager to improve their lot. However, virtually everyone in a stratified system is concerned about **social mobility** (Hout, 2015; van Leeuwen and Maas 2010), or the ability or inability to change one's position in the hierarchy. *Upward mobility,* the ability to move higher (Kupfer 2012; Miles, Savage, and Bühlmann 2011), is obviously of great personal concern to many Americans. In addition, the possibility of such mobility for most is what lends legitimacy to the U.S. stratification system, indeed the entire U.S. economic system (Leventoğlu 2014). Recent research has shown that people throughout the stratification system greatly overestimate the amount of upward mobility in U.S. society, although such overestimation is greater among those who rank lower in the system (Kraus, Davidai, and Nussbaum 2015). The poor tend to end up in about the same place in

the stratification system as where they started; they have little upward mobility (Alexander, Entwisle, and Olson 2014).

People in all social classes are also concerned about *downward mobility* (Wilson, Roscigno, and Huffman 2013). That is, people worry about descending to lower levels within their social class or to lower classes. Downward mobility causes people real hardships, and even its mere possibility is a great cause of concern. Immigrants and refugees who move to a new country almost always experience serious difficulties, such as language differences (Guo 2013), and as a result, they are likely to experience downward mobility during the first generation in their new locale. This is especially true of those who held high-level occupations in their countries of origin (Gans 2009). Given the current economic problems in the United States and Europe, it is likely that many people will experience downward mobility relative to their parents' status.

ASK YOURSELF

Why should the public be concerned about the prospect that young people today will be less well off in the future than their elders? What negative effects could this future reality have on social institutions, such as schools, workplaces, and industries like banking and real estate? Would it be likely to have any positive effects, perhaps on consumerism or the natural environment? How might it affect the world standing of the United States as a society? Explain your answers.

TYPES OF SOCIAL MOBILITY

To this point, we have discussed upward and downward mobility, but there are a number of other types of social mobility as well. Upward and downward mobility are the key components of the general process of **vertical mobility**. Also of interest is **horizontal mobility**, or movement within one's social class. For example, the chief executive officer (CEO) of a given corporation may experience horizontal mobility by becoming the CEO of a different corporation. At the other end of the spectrum, the taxi driver who becomes a driver for Uber also exhibits horizontal mobility (Ultee 2007).

Sociologists are also concerned about two other types of mobility. One is **intergenerational mobility**, or the difference between the parents' position in the stratification system and the positions achieved by their children (Corak 2013; Park and Myers 2010). Children who rise higher in the stratification system than their parents have experienced upward intergenerational mobility. Those who descend to a lower position on the ladder have experienced downward intergenerational mobility. Chetty et al. (2014) found that children today have about the same chance of upward mobility as did children born in 1970.

Intragenerational mobility involves movement up or down the stratification system in one's lifetime. It is possible for some to start their adult lives in the lower class and to move up over the years to a higher social class. However, it is also possible to start out in the upper class and to slide down the stratification ladder to a lower class in the course of one's lifetime (Corak, Lindquist, and Mazumder 2014).

Much of the concern about mobility relates to the work that people do or the occupations they hold. All the previously discussed types of mobility are concerned with individual mobility. **Structural mobility** describes the effects of changes in the larger society on the positions of individuals in the stratification system, especially the occupational structure (Gilbert and Kahl 1993; Miller 2001). For example, China under communism offered people little mobility of any type. Now that China has a booming capitalist economy, the country has experienced a vast increase in structural mobility, because many more higher-level positions (especially occupations) are now available (Lui 2014; Vogel 2011). Millions have moved out of the peasantry and into an expanding hierarchy of nonagricultural occupations and thus higher social positions.

ACHIEVEMENT AND ASCRIPTION

Thus far, we have been describing a system of social stratification defined by status, power, and class—especially economic class. This, however, is but one type of stratification system. A chief characteristic of this system is the idea that social positions are based on **achievement**, or the accomplishments—the merit—of the individual. For example, a person becomes a physician, and thereby attains a high-level position in the stratification system, only after many years of education, hard work, and practical experience. Conversely, some people believe that a person at or near the bottom of the stratification system is there because he or she lacks the necessary accomplishments. These people might suggest that a homeless person is homeless because that individual has not worked hard enough to earn a living wage. The idea that achievement determines social class is accurate to some extent, but the fact is that where a person ends up in the stratification system may have little or nothing to do with achievement. Instead, it can be explained by external factors over which the individual has little control.

A person's status usually has a great deal to do with **ascription**, or being born with, or inheriting, certain characteristics such as race, gender, wealth, and high status (or, conversely, poverty and low status; Bond 2012). Thus, a person's position in the social hierarchy may be due to nothing more than the accident of being born a man or a woman, or black or white. At the extremes, ascribed status has little or nothing to do with a person's accomplishments, skills, or abilities.

THEORIES OF SOCIAL STRATIFICATION

Within the sociology of social stratification, the dominant theoretical approaches are structural/functional theory and conflict/critical theory. Also to be discussed here are inter/actionist theories of stratification.

As in all areas of the social world, different theories focus on different aspects of social stratification. Instead of choosing one theory over another, it may make more sense to use all of them. Structural/functional and conflict/critical theories tell us much about the macro structures of stratification, while inter/actionist theories offer great detail about what goes on within those structures at the micro levels.

STRUCTURAL/FUNCTIONAL THEORIES

Within structural/functional theory, it is structural-functionalism that offers the most important—and controversial—theory of stratification. It argues that all societies are, and have been, stratified. Further, the theory contends that societies need a system of stratification in order to exist and to function properly (Davis and Moore 1945). Stratification is needed, first, to ensure that people are motivated to occupy the less pleasant, more difficult, and more important positions in society. Second, stratification is needed to ensure that people with the right abilities and talents find their way into the appropriate positions. In other words, society needs a good fit between people and the requirements of the positions they occupy.

The structural-functional theory of stratification assumes that higher-level occupations, such as physician and lawyer, are more important to society than such lower-level occupations as laborer and janitor. The higher-level positions are also seen as being harder to fill because of the difficulties and unpleasantness associated with them. For example, both physicians and lawyers require many years

of rigorous and expensive education. Physicians are required to deal with blood, human organs, and death; lawyers have to defend those who have committed heinous crimes. It is argued that in order to motivate enough people to occupy such positions, greater rewards, such as prestige, sufficient leisure, and especially large amounts of money, need to be associated with them. The implication is that without these high rewards, high-level positions would remain understaffed or unfilled. As a result, structural-functionalists see the stratification system as functional for the larger society. In this case, it provides the physicians and lawyers needed by society.

CONFLICT/CRITICAL THEORIES

Conflict/critical theories tend to take a jaundiced view of stratified social structures because they involve and promote inequality. These theories are especially critical of the structural-functional perspective and its view that stratification is functional for society. Conflict/critical theories take a hard look at who benefits from the existing stratification system and how those benefits are perpetuated.

ASK YOURSELF

Do you agree with the structural-functional perspective that stratification provides an important function for society? Or do you believe, as conflict/critical theorists do, that stratification exists to perpetuate benefits for the elite and expand their control? Justify your choice.

Social Rewards and Status

Conflict theorists ridicule the idea that higher-level positions in the social structure would go unfilled were it not for the greater rewards they offer (Huaco 1966; Tumin 1953). They ask, for example, whether higher-level positions in the stratification system are less pleasant than those at the lower end of the continuum. Is being a surgeon really less pleasant than being a garbage collector? The argument being made by structural-functionalists seems preposterous to conflict theorists and to many others.

Conflict theorists accept the idea that higher-level positions, such as being a lawyer, may be more difficult than lower-level positions, such as being a garbage collector. However, they wonder whether higher-level positions are always more important. Garbage collectors, after all, are importance to society because they help prevent the spread of diseases that could develop if waste were left to accumulate.

Conflict theorists also criticize the idea that those at the upper levels of the stratification system require the large rewards offered to them. Many people would be motivated to occupy such positions as CEO of a multinational corporation or hedge fund manager without such extraordinary rewards. Fewer economic rewards for those at the top, and more for those on the bottom, would reduce the economic gap and make for a more equal society. Conflict theorists also argue that providing huge sums of money is not the only way to motivate people to pursue an advanced education or whatever else is necessary to occupy high-ranking positions. For example, the status or prestige associated with those positions would be a strong motivator, as would the power that comes with them.

Gender, Race, and Class

Operating from another variant of conflict/critical theory, feminist theorists tend to focus on the issue of stratification in the work world. Because men owned the means of production in the development of capitalism, they gained positions of great power and prestige that yielded major economic rewards (Hartmann 1979). Women, by contrast, were relegated to subordinate positions. Over the years, women's position in the U.S. stratification system has improved with the entrance of more women into the workforce and greater legal protections against workplace gender discrimination. There are now many more women in such high-ranking positions as executive, physician, and lawyer. Yet, compared with men overall, women still occupy a subordinate position in the stratification system. They can also find it harder to rise very high in that system.

Further, while males have been advantaged by their ability to engage in overwork and earn extra income (see above), females, especially in male-dominated occupations, are likely to be disadvantaged, and even forced to leave the labor

Despite some notable exceptions, such as Indra Nooyi, CEO of PepsiCo, women are still vastly underrepresented in the executive suite. How does feminist theory explain this imbalance?

force entirely, because of excessive work-related demands (Cha 2013). While the occupational situation for women has improved in recent years, the occupational world remains segregated on the basis of gender (Gauchat, Kelly, and Wallace 2012). For example, women face a "motherhood penalty" (Budig, Misra, and Boeckman 2012, 2016) in the workplace that limits upward mobility among women with children. Mothers seeking jobs are less likely to be hired, are offered lower salaries, and are seen by others as less committed to the workplace. Illustrating how pervasive this penalty is, the wage gap between women without children and mothers is greater than the wage gap between men and women (Boushey 2008; Hausmann, Ganguli, and Viarengo 2009). Even women at the highest levels of the corporate world continue to face barriers unique to their gender. Recent research finds that women tend to boast less about their accomplishments and to give themselves lower self-ratings than do men. This internalized modesty about work performance contributes to lower upward mobility over and above external factors such as the glass ceiling (Smith and Huntoon 2014).

Critical theorists focus on the control that those in the upper levels of the stratification system exercise over culture (Kellner and Lewis 2007; Lash and Lury 2007). Elites are seen as controlling such important aspects of culture as television and movies, and as seeking to exert increasing control over the internet and such major social networking sites as Facebook and Twitter. Elites use the media to send the kinds of messages that further their control. Furthermore, the amount of time that those lower in the stratification system are led to devote to TV, video games, movies, and the internet is so great that they have little time to mobilize and oppose, let alone overthrow, those in power.

INTER/ACTIONIST THEORIES

From an inter/actionist theory perspective, social stratification is not a function of macro-level structures but of micro-level, individual actions and interactions. While both structural/functional and conflict/critical theorists see stratification as a hierarchical structure, inter/actionists see it as much more of a process or a set of processes. As a process, stratification involves interactions among people in different positions. Those who occupy higher-level positions may try to exert power in their interactions with those below them, but the latter can, and usually do, contest such exertions of power.

To the symbolic interactionist, inequality ultimately depends on face-to-face interaction. It is what happens in face-to-face interaction that leads to inequality. One symbolic interactionist approach identifies four processes that produce and reproduce inequality (Schwalbe et al. 2000). First, the dominant group defines the subordinate group into existence. Second, once in existence, the subordinate group finds ways of adapting to its situation. Third, efforts are made to maintain the boundaries between the two groups. Finally, both groups must manage the emotions associated with their positions in the stratification system. For example, those at the top must not show too much sympathy for those below them, and those at the bottom must not display too much anger toward those above them.

Ethnomethodologists note that people may exist within a stratified structure, but what really matters is what they *do* within such a structure. As in other aspects of the social world, people use commonsense procedures to operate and make their way in such structures. These procedures are used by elites and the downtrodden alike to "do" their positions in the system. For example, elite members of society are likely to carry themselves with authority and self-importance. In contrast, those at the bottom rungs of the stratification system are more likely to appear overburdened and to slouch throughout the day. In other words, one of the ways in which people do stratification is through their body language.

CONSUMPTION AND SOCIAL STRATIFICATION

Much of this chapter relates to issues of production and work, but social stratification is also related to consumption in various ways. For one thing, different positions in the stratification system involve differences in consumption. Most obviously, those in the upper classes are able to afford to consume products (such as yachts, Maserati automobiles, and Dom Pérignon champagne) and services (such as those provided by maids, chefs, and chauffeurs) that those in the middle and especially the lower classes cannot even contemplate. For another, the nature of consumption itself forms a stratification system. The consumption of certain sorts of things accords a higher position than does consumption of other kinds of things.

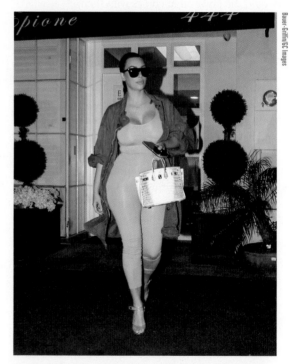

Kim Kardashian West epitomized the concept of conspicuous consumption when she carried a Hermès bag worth $120,000 to a casual lunch.

TRENDING

Evicted: Poverty and Profit in the American City (Crown Publishers, 2016)

Matthew Desmond (John L. Loeb Associate Professor of the Social Sciences at Harvard University; PhD, University of Wisconsin–Madison, 2010)

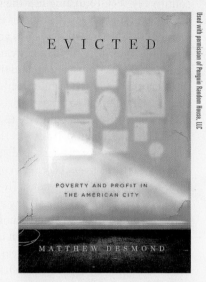

Lack of access to safe and affordable housing is a serious problem in the United States, especially for poor families who are forced into the private rental market. Though many of us might assume that these families live in public or government-subsidized housing, most (67 percent) receive no federal assistance (Desmond 2016, 303). Matthew Desmond lived in a trailer park on the south side of Milwaukee and a rooming house on the north side of the city to better understand the relationship between renters who live at or below the poverty line and their landlords. He discovered that landlords can make a substantial profit from impoverished renters. Landlords hold considerable power over their poor tenants, charging them high rents for properties that have broken toilets or are infested with cockroaches. Tenants are reluctant to complain, because they fear that if they do, they will then be evicted. Even if they do not complain, millions of families across the country are evicted every year because they do not have enough income to make their rent payments on time.

Once a person is evicted, it can be difficult to find a new place to live; many landlords refuse to rent to someone with an eviction record, deeming it too risky.

The feminization of poverty is evident in Desmond's study: Women of color and their children are most likely to be evicted. But they are not alone. Whites, the elderly, widowers, the physically and mentally disabled, and those addicted to opioids join their ranks. Many of these poor renters spend up to 70 or 80 percent of their income on housing, so they have little left for food, clothing, or utilities. The few personal possessions they do own are often lost when they are evicted—unless they can afford to put them in storage until they find new housing. In terms of stratified consumption, Desmond describes how landlords judge their tenants in terms of their personal possessions. If a tenant who is behind on her rent buys herself a new pair of shoes, the landlord might feel slighted and demand that the rent be paid immediately or threaten eviction. Tenants, however, also judge their landlords this way. A landlord who drives around in an expensive truck or wears what tenants consider to be too much jewelry might be viewed as greedy and not in need of rent payments. Yet landlords can also be generous, purchasing groceries for their tenants or letting them miss rent payments for a few months. This generosity, however, is mitigated by tenants' enduring substandard housing, living in dangerous neighborhoods, and, most important, eventually paying their late rent. In sum, impoverished renters suffer from a variety of injustices because of a lack of affordable, quality housing in the United States.

Supplementary Resources

- You can watch Desmond discuss *Evicted* on C-SPAN BookTV at http://www.c-span.org/video/?405981-1/book-discussion-evicted.
- Sociologist Barbara Ehrenreich explains the social significance of *Evicted* in her book review that appeared in *The New York Times:* http://www.nytimes.com/2016/02/28/books/review/matthew-desmonds-evicted-poverty-and-profit-in-the-american-city.html?_r=0.

STRATIFIED CONSUMPTION

Fashion is a good example of a stratified form of consumption. Georg Simmel ([1904] 1971) argued that those in higher levels of the stratification system continually seek to distinguish their consumption from that of those below them. This is evident in the realm of fashion, where the elites adopt new fashions, thereby displaying that they can afford the latest styles. However, elites soon find that those below them have copied their fashions with cheaper, if not cheap, imitations. Thus fashion, as well as other choices by elites, has a tendency to "trickle down" the social stratification ladder to the middle and eventually the lower classes. To distinguish themselves from the masses, elites must continually move on to new and different fashions. This phenomenon most obviously applies to fashions in clothing, but there are fashions in many other things as well, such as cars, homes, vacations, and even ideas.

Simmel's contemporary Thorstein Veblen ([1899] 1994) also theorized about stratification and consumption. In Veblen's view, the elite members of society want to be "conspicuous." In the past, they had been conspicuous about their accomplishments in the work world, but over time, these feats became less and less visible as they came to be concealed by the walls of factories and office buildings. As a result, elites shifted more toward *conspicuous consumption,* wanting others to see what they were able to consume, especially things that served to differentiate them from those in lower social classes (see Chapter 2). Thus, their money came to be invested in mansions, fancy furnishings, fine riding horses, expensive automobiles, designer dresses, and exquisite jewelry, because such things can easily be seen and admired by others.

ASK YOURSELF

Do you think Simmel's concept of trickle-down fashion or Veblen's notion of conspicuous consumption is a more accurate description of the relationship between consumption and social stratification? Why? Can you provide examples to support your answer?

SOCIAL CLASS AND TASTE

A person's taste in consumption also helps indicate the social class to which that person belongs. For example, if you read the *New York Times,* you are likely to be classified as being in the middle or upper class. However, if you read *USA Today* or don't follow the news at all, you would be classified by most as standing lower in the stratification system. While taste can be demonstrated in the purchase and display of expensive consumer goods, it also can be shown much more subtly in the way one talks, the kind of music one listens to, and the books one reads. Good taste in these and other areas demonstrates and enhances the position of elite members of society. It supposedly shows that they have good breeding, come from a good family, and have a good education, and especially that they value things according to their merit and not simply because of how much they cost. Those without such taste, who have a taste for the necessary rather than the good taste of elites, are likely to be relegated to the lower reaches of the stratification system (Bourdieu 1984; Prior 2011).

A more contemporary sociologist, Pierre Bourdieu (1930–2002; 1984), argued that the desire for **distinction**, or the need to distinguish oneself from others, motivates the consumption and leisure habits of elites. In particular, elites seek to distinguish themselves from others by their good taste.

Distinction and taste are closely related to struggles for power and position within the stratification system. On the one hand, elites use culture to obtain and maintain their position. They might do this by focusing on high culture, such as opera or art (see Chapter 3). Such taste helps elites gain high-level positions in the stratification system and makes those below them accept their lesser positions in that system. Even those from the lower classes who manage to acquire considerable wealth are often not likely to have or to develop the level of cultural sophistication needed to appreciate something like ballet.

The idea of *cultural omnivores* (Katz-Gerro and Jaeger 2013; Peterson and Kern 1996) offers a very different view of the relationship among social class, consumption, and taste. From this perspective, elites are not seen as refined and exclusive in their tastes, but as having very diverse tastes, ranging from those that are highly refined to those that are unrefined, even coarse. Their tastes are not exclusive but rather wide-ranging and inclusive. Thus, elites might attend both the opera and kickboxing matches, and they might buy both opera arias and country and western music from iTunes. In contrast, those in lower classes have been seen as having more limited tastes, which might be more oriented toward kickboxing and country and western music; in other words, those in the lower classes are less likely to be omnivores.

GLOBAL STRATIFICATION[1]

So far, this chapter has focused on social stratification in the United States. In this section, we shift to the global level to understand how wealth, income, status, and power are distributed unevenly throughout the world. As is clear in the theories of Immanuel Wallerstein (1974), to be discussed later in this chapter, nations of the world form a stratified system. At the top are those that tend to be better off economically, to wield great power in many parts of the world, and to be looked up to around the globe. Conversely, the nations at the bottom of the global stratification system are likely to be very poor, to have little power outside (and perhaps even inside) their borders, and to be looked down upon by many throughout the world. Global stratification is a macro-level phenomenon that has profound effects at the micro level of individuals and their relationships and opportunities.

POSITIONS IN GLOBAL STRATIFICATION
The Global North and South

Stratification on the global level is often seen as a divide between those nation-states located in the Northern Hemisphere (more specifically, the north temperate climate zone), or the Global North, and those located in the tropics and Southern Hemisphere, or the Global South (Williams, Meth, and Willis 2014). For centuries, the North has dominated, controlled, exploited, and oppressed the South. Today the North encompasses the nations that are the wealthiest and most powerful, and that have the highest status in the world, such as the United States, China, Germany, France, Great Britain, and Japan. The South, on the other hand,

Pierre Bourdieu was a major intellectual figure of the twentieth century. His research in part focused on people's practices and developing theory related to those practices, which reflected some Marxist ideas that Bourdieu rejected early in his career but continued to express in his work. For instance, among his contributions is the idea that society's elites define high and low culture because they have won a power struggle with the masses.

has a disproportionate number of nations that rank at or near the bottom in terms of global wealth, power, and prestige. Most of the nations of Africa and South America would be included here, as well as others, especially in Asia, such as Yemen.

A society's position in the global stratification system greatly affects the stratification within that society. A nation that stands at or near the top of the global stratification system, such as the United States, has a large proportion of middle- and upper-class positions. In contrast, a low-ranking nation, such as Somalia, is dominated by lower-class positions and the poverty associated with them. While the terms *Global North* and *Global South* are widely used to describe positions within the global hierarchy, they do not always clearly relate to positions on the world map. For example, Australia is in the Southern Hemisphere, but is clearly part of the Global North economically. Similarly, there are several very poor countries (e.g., Afghanistan) in the Northern Hemisphere that are economically part of the Global South.

---

[1] Paul Dean coauthored this part of the chapter.

High-, Middle-, and Low-Income Countries

The wide variation among and between countries is hidden when they are simply categorized as part of either the Global North or the Global South. For example, countries in the same category may have more or less inequality. The United States and France are generally placed in the same category (Global North, high income), but the United States has a greater percentage of people at the bottom of the stratification system living in poverty. Similarly, Vietnam and Nigeria are in the same category (Global South, middle income), but Nigeria has a larger number of wealthy elites than does Vietnam. In other words, the level of income inequality within Nigeria is far greater than that in Vietnam. Argentina has a high standard of living compared with the immense poverty found in many African countries, such as Sudan. However, both countries are considered to be part of the Global South. The Global North–South dichotomy ignores many of the important economic (and political) differences between nations within each category.

A slightly more nuanced category system focuses on low-income, middle-income, and high-income economies (and their countries; see Figure 7.7; Ferrarini and Nelson, 2016). As a general rule, low-income countries are concentrated in the Global South, while high-income countries are found in the Global North. Middle-income countries exist in both parts of the world, but a disproportionate number of them are in the Global South.

High-income economies exist in countries with the highest incomes in the world. Countries with gross national income (GNI) per capita of $12,476 are in this category (World Bank 2015a). Currently, 79 countries have GNI that high or higher. As a result, they occupy lofty positions in the global hierarchy. They include countries long considered part of the Global North. However, they also include countries that are traditionally thought of as part of the Global South, including Chile and Uruguay (South America), Equatorial Guinea (Central Africa), and Oman (Middle East). Some of these countries have been considered to have high-income economies since the Industrial Revolution, while others (e.g., Japan) have industrialized—and grown wealthy—more recently. Still other high-income countries are not yet highly industrialized but derive their income from natural resources such as oil (e.g., Equatorial Guinea and Oman).

FIGURE 7.7 • High-Income, Middle-Income, and Low-Income Economies

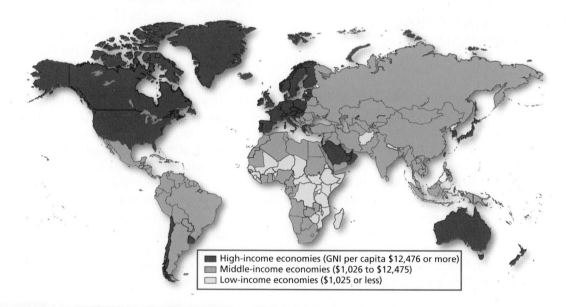

■ High-income economies (GNI per capita $12,476 or more)
■ Middle-income economies ($1,026 to $12,475)
□ Low-income economies ($1,025 or less)

SOURCE: Data from World Bank, "Country and Lending Groups," 2016.

Middle-income economies are found in countries that have average levels of income on a global level. Countries are placed in this category if they have a GNI per capita between $1,026 and $12,475. This encompasses a significant range that begins at or near the bottom of per capita income, with the Kyrgyz Republic in central Asia (average GNI of $1,200 per capita), and includes Sudan (Africa), Nicaragua (Central America), and Vietnam (Asia). Toward the top of this range are upper-middle-income countries including Argentina and Brazil (South America), Cuba (Central America), South Africa, and Thailand (Asia). The World Bank considers 108 countries to be in the middle-income category. Many countries in this range, such as China (and most of Asia), began industrializing relatively recently (the 1970s or later). Other middle-income countries were formerly communist countries. They were highly, albeit primitively, industrialized, but they declined industrially and economically after the collapse of the Soviet Union in the late 1980s.

Low-income economies are in countries that are home to many of the world's poorest people, have very little of the world's wealth, and are largely agrarian societies with low levels of industry. The World Bank counts 31 low-income countries with GNI per capita below $1,025. They include many of the countries in sub-Saharan Africa, North Korea, Afghanistan, and Haiti (Caribbean). People in these countries are much more likely to experience disease, hunger, and malnutrition and have a lower life expectancy. Increasingly, they are moving into densely populated cities in search of economic opportunities, only to find themselves in very crowded and unsafe living conditions.

The Global Concentration of Wealth

There is certainly great inequality between the North and the South, or between high-income and low-income countries, but a focus on such relationships

While social stratification involves the relative positions of people within a society, global stratification demonstrates that widespread poverty and lack of opportunity can leave an entire nation near the bottom of the global pecking order. This boy is on his way to collect water in an encampment in Madagascar.

tends to obscure the full extent of global inequality. A recent report by the global charity Oxfam offers a stunning picture of the concentration of wealth in the world (Hardoon 2015): As of 2015, the richest 1 percent of people in world owned 50 percent of the wealth. That left only exactly half—50 percent—for the other 99 percent of the world's population. Furthermore, Oxfam has projected that the top 1 percent may soon have *more wealth* than everyone else in the world combined. The 62 richest people in the world (among the top are four U.S. men, Bill Gates, Warren Buffett, Jeff Bezos, and Mark Zuckerburg) are worth $1.76 trillion, about the same as the poorest 3.6 billion people in the world combined.

Also worth considering is the broader category that includes the world's poorest people—the "bottom billion" of global residents (Murphy and Walsh 2014). The vast majority (70 percent) of the people in the bottom billion are in Africa.

Wherever they live, the bottom billion have not only low incomes but also many other serious problems, such as

- A low life expectancy of about 50 years
- A high infant mortality rate
- A higher likelihood of malnourishment

GLOBAL ECONOMIC INEQUALITIES

The Global Digital Divide

According to the most recent statistics, there were about 3.5 billion internet users worldwide at the end of 2016, and that number will certainly continue to grow (www.statista.com/statistics/273018/num ber-of-internet-users-worldwide). At least theoretically, the internet allows for participation by anyone, anywhere in the global, digital economy. However, in reality there is a daunting and persistent global digital divide (Drori 2006, 2012; Pick and Sarkar 2015). The International Telecommunications Union found that the percentages of individuals using the internet in 2016 remained very low in many low-income countries in the Global South, such as Ethiopia (4 percent), Iraq (13 percent), and Haiti (12 percent). Compare these figures with the Global North where internet usage is usually above 80 percent, including in the United States (89 percent), Australia (85 percent), and Sweden (93 percent). Figure 7.8 shows the difference in internet access between households in the Global North and the Global South.

The main barrier to global equality in access to, and use of, the internet, and information and communications technology (ICT) more generally, is the lack of infrastructure within the less developed countries of the Global South. Also important are the low incomes in those areas that make complex digital technologies prohibitively expensive (Wakefield 2013). Language represents another source of inequality on the internet. Most websites are in English, and increasingly in Chinese, as well as eight other languages; comparatively few sites are in the world's other languages (Bowen 2001; EnglishEnglish.com n.d.). Clearly, those who do not speak any of these 10 languages—the overwhelming majority of whom live in the Global South—are at a huge disadvantage on the internet.

However, there are signs that the digital divide is being reduced. This was clear, for example, in the wide-scale use of social media during the 2010–2011 Arab Spring revolutions in Tunisia, Libya, and especially Egypt. More recently, the narrowing of the digital divide has been evidenced by the adept use of the internet by the terrorist organization calling itself the Islamic State of Iraq and Syria (ISIS) to, for example, disseminate video of people being beheaded and, in 2015, being burned alive in cages. ISIS is also adept at using social media to recruit supporters throughout the world (Shane and Hubbard 2014). The United States has struck back by using social media to lure people away from ISIS (Cooper 2016).

FIGURE 7.8 • Percentage of Households with Internet Access by Level of Development, 2002–2016

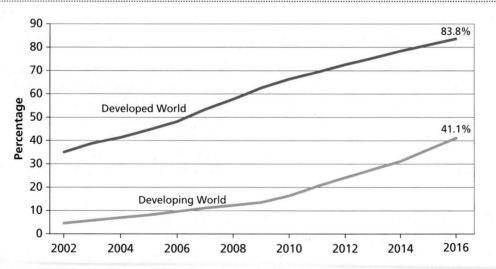

SOURCE: ITU. 2016. "ICT Facts and Figures 2016," p. 4.

The digital divide is beginning to be bridged by the rising accessibility of relatively simple and inexpensive smartphones, laptops, and tablets that are essentially minicomputers. An important reason for the rapid expansion of mobile access is that mobile devices are not only relatively inexpensive, but they also do not require the expensive, hardwired infrastructure needed by traditional computers and computer systems. Cellular signals provide internet access at increasingly high speeds. Some nations have avoided having to build fixed phone line systems by moving straight to mobile phone technology.

Global Health Inequality

While globalization has been associated with increased aggregate life expectancy throughout the world, it also has tended to widen global disparities in life span and in health (Vogli et al. 2014; Winchester 2016; see also Chapter 13). For example, Johns, Cowling, and Gakidou (2013) found that the widening gap between the world's rich and poor is continuing to increase differences in life expectancy. According to the World Health Organization (2016), the average life expectancy of newborns in high-income countries is at least 80 years old. In contrast, newborns in sub-Saharan African counties will live less than 60 years on average. Economic inequality drives many of these health disparities.

Those in poor nations tend to have poorer health as a result of limited access to health services, education, sanitation, adequate nutrition, and housing. In turn, the poor health of residents tends to limit economic growth in those nations mainly by adversely affecting productivity. The Global South has a disproportionate share of mortality and morbidity, much of which could be prevented inexpensively and treated effectively if the money were available to do so. Of the total burden of disease in the world, 90 percent is concentrated in low- and middle-income countries, which account for only 10 percent of health care expenditures. Furthermore, the Global South has lower levels of education, which lessens the likelihood of residents' knowing about preventive strategies and obtaining knowledge about how to control their own health (Rinaldo and Ferraro 2012).

Countries in the Global South also suffer disproportionately from hunger and malnutrition (Serra-Majem and Ngo 2012). Recent political catastrophes have led to hunger crises in 2016 in Syria, the Ukraine, Chad, Mali, the Central African Republic, and South Sudan, among others. Environmental crises such as droughts and hurricanes are other major causes of people going hungry. Hunger involves inadequate or almost totally unavailable food supplies and a lack of assured and continual access to food, as well as poor and unbalanced diets. These problems are especially important for children, who are likely to die young from malnutrition. Poor nutrition causes nearly half of all child deaths in the world (Reuters 2016a). Furthermore, those children who survive, even though their growth is stunted because of a lack of food, are likely to be less physically and intellectually productive when they become adults, and to suffer more chronic illnesses and disabilities. This pattern carries on intergenerationally, as the ability of such adults to provide adequate nutrition for their children is compromised.

To complicate matters, there is a dramatic increase in obesity among other segments of the poor in the Global South (Global Nutrition Report 2016; McNeil Jr. 2016). It is estimated that there are 41 million overweight children under five years of age in the world today, an increase of 10 million from 1990 (Reuters 2016a). Those in the Global South therefore now increasingly likely to suffer from a "double nutritional burden"—that is, some do not have enough to eat, and others eat too much, especially the wrong kinds of foods (e.g., foods that are high in fat and cholesterol).

Finally, poor countries are less likely to provide extensive health care for their populations. Low-income countries tend to have fewer hospitals, less capacity for research on health and disease, and fewer people covered by medical insurance programs. These problems can be addressed through economic growth when national governments prioritize spending on health care.

It is worth noting that a society's wealth does not always correspond to health coverage or better health outcomes. For example, the United States spends the most in the world on health care, but it ranks significantly lower than other high-income countries on a number of public health indicators. Compared with their counterparts in other high-income countries, Americans tend to live shorter lives, to be more likely to experience violent deaths, to be more likely to be obese, and to have

The extent of inequality in access to health care around the world was made starkly apparent by the 2015 outbreak of the deadly and highly contagious Ebola virus in Africa. While stricken medical workers evacuated to the West were likely to survive, inadequate diagnostic and treatment facilities and even a lack of information and transportation were blamed for the thousands of deaths that occurred in Africa before the epidemic subsided. Here a health worker sprays a dying man with disinfectant on a Liberian road while a crowd looks on.

higher rates of many diseases. Unlike the residents of all other countries in the Global North, many Americans (particularly those with low incomes) do not have health coverage.

Global Gender Stratification

While men's labor force participation rates worldwide have decreased slightly over the last several decades, a notable increase has occurred in women's labor force participation around the world (Elborgh-Woytek et al 2016; Moghadam 1999). While the progress in women's employment status is linked at least in part to gender equality movements, the key factor in this change is the better integration of an increasing number of areas into the world economy through trade and production. Nevertheless, in no part of the world (see Figure 7.9) are women as involved as men in the labor force. In some areas—South Asia and the Middle East and North Africa—women's labor force participation is markedly lower than that of men.

In much of the Global North, educated middle-class women have made inroads into professional and managerial employment. In the global paid labor market, women predominate as service and clerical workers and in elementary occupations, such as agriculture and manufacturing (United Nations Department of Economic and Social Affairs 2015a). They are likely to work as teachers and university professors, as nurses and doctors in public hospitals, and as workers and administrators in government offices (Moghadam 1999). Women have also made inroads in professional services such as law, banking, accounting, computing, and architecture.

However, according to the World Bank, women earn less and participate in the labor force less than men. Globally, Gallup polling finds that men are twice as likely as women to have full-time jobs. The wage gap found in the United States is also a global phenomenon, and the gap is especially large in the Middle East and in North Africa. Mothers' wages are lower than fathers' in many countries (Misra and Strader 2013). The historical belief persists that fathers are supporting entire families (and thus need a higher wage) and mothers are not. Despite the gains made by women, high-pay and high-status occupations continue to be dominated by men in both the Global North and the Global South. Even in countries such as the United States and those in Western Europe, men still have easier access to, and therefore hold a much larger percentage of, professional and managerial jobs.

At the same time that some women are finding success in the paid labor force, others are being limited by the nature of their arrangements with employers. Women are more likely than men to have informal jobs (Limoncelli, forthcoming). Informal employment, which has increased in many countries, includes temporary work without fixed employers, paid employment from home, domestic work for households (de Regt 2009), and industrial work for subcontractors. Informal sectors are characterized by low pay and a lack of secure contracts, worker benefits, and social protections. Workers in the informal economy do not have wage agreements, employment contracts, regular working hours, or health insurance

FIGURE 7.9 • Men's and Women's Labor Force Participation Rates by World Region, 2014

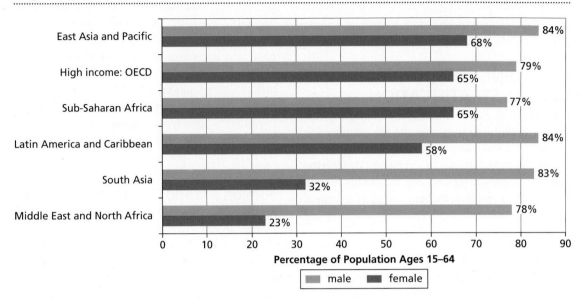

SOURCE: Data from World Bank, "World DataBank: Gender Statistics."

or unemployment benefits (Kabeer, Sudarshan, and Milward 2013). They often earn below legal minimum wage and may not be paid on time. While greater informal employment characterizes the entire labor force globally, women and men are concentrated in different types of informal work (Vanek et al. 2014). Men are concentrated mainly in informal wage-based jobs and agricultural employment, while women are typically concentrated in nonagricultural employment, domestic work, and unpaid work in family enterprises. Compared with men's informal employment, women's employment is much more likely to have lower hourly wages and less stability. To reduce labor costs, most multinational corporations establish subcontracting networks, with local manufacturers employing low-paid workers, mostly women, who can be laid off quickly and easily. In these production networks, women are more likely to work in small workshops or from home. Many women accept the lower wages and less formal working arrangements of home-based work in order to be able to continue to carry out household responsibilities.

Another form of global gender inequality occurs within families through caregiving work. As men and women from low-income countries migrate to find better-paying jobs, women especially find employment in domestic work. Arlie Hochschild (2000) argues that the migration of domestic workers creates **global care chains** that involve a series of personal relationships between people across the globe based on the paid or unpaid work of caring (Yeates 2012). Care includes social, health, and sexual care services, and usually involves menial tasks such as cooking, cleaning, and ironing. In global care chains, women supply their own care labor to their employers while consuming other women's care labor, both paid and unpaid. Thus, instead of care chains, it might be better to think of this as "care circulation" (Lutz and Palenga-Mollenbeck 2016). Migrant domestic workers often rely on female relatives, neighbors, and daughters as well as paid domestic workers for the care of their children back in their home countries. For instance, while a mother works as a nanny in a high-income country, her young children may be cared for by an older daughter or by a nanny who migrated from a middle- or low-income country. For example, affluent Kuwaitis hire female domestic workers from relatively poor countries, including the Philippines, Sri Lanka, Nepal, and Indonesia (Fahim 2010). Attracted to Kuwait by higher wages than they could earn elsewhere, these workers can send large sums of money home, but power relations between them and their employers are starkly unequal (Fernandez 2010). In this sense, women's labor force participation does not necessarily result in a change in traditional gender roles, but rather in the greater exploitation of immigrant women by middle- and upper-class women.

CHANGING POSITIONS IN GLOBAL STRATIFICATION

Despite the several forms of global inequality discussed previously, it is possible for countries to develop economically and change their positions within the global stratification system. This section examines the risky strategy of a race to the bottom in offering cheap labor, the importance of industrial upgrading, and the controversial use of foreign aid as a means of development.

Race to the Bottom

Those countries that rank low in the global stratification system often have to engage in a so-called economic race to the bottom in order to have a chance of eventually moving up the global hierarchy. The basic method is to offer lower prices than the competition—usually other low-ranking countries. Such nations may lower prices by reducing costs, which they do by offering their citizens lower wages, poorer working conditions, longer hours, ever-escalating pressure and demands, and so on. Figure 7.10 shows wage disparities among countries; pay special attention to the disparities between the Global North and South. An especially desperate nation will go further than the others to reduce wages and worsen working conditions in order to lower costs and attract the interest and investments of multinational corporations. However, the "winning" low-income nation remains a favorite of the multinationals only until it is undercut by another low-ranking country eager for jobs.

ASK YOURSELF

What could the Global North do to reduce other countries' need to engage in the race to the bottom? Why have such efforts so far been few and generally ineffective? How would slowing or even ending the race to the bottom affect the trend toward consumerism in the countries of the Global North?

In actuality, winning the race to the bottom might mean that a country remains at or near the bottom. For example, some countries compete in the world economy by focusing on agricultural exports and by employing cheap, local labor to plant and harvest crops. As countries battle with one another by paying workers less money, they make their agricultural goods cheaper on the global market. But if these export sectors do not eventually transition to other types of goods and services, with higher wages, the countries might never lift themselves off the bottom.

Foreign Aid and Development[2]

Another way in which global economic inequality can be addressed is through the use of foreign aid to improve a poor country's position within the world economy. **Foreign aid** is defined as economic assistance given by countries or global institutions to a foreign country in order to promote its development and social welfare. In the form that we now know it, foreign aid began following the economic devastation of World War II with the United States' Marshall Plan to help struggling European economies. Foreign aid has continued to expand since that time, totaling $131.6 billion in 2015, according to the Organisation for Economic Co-operation and Development (OECD 2016).

The OECD states that aid may take the form of grants or subsidized loans and must promote development and welfare. This can include funding or other resources for education, health, debt relief, social or economic infrastructure, humanitarian assistance, or other development projects. To qualify as "aid," loans must be given with interest rates at least 25 percent below market rates. Most aid is bilateral, or given directly from one country to another. Aid can also be multilateral, where resources of many donors are pooled through a third party such as the World Bank, which then distributes the aid. The 34 members of the OECD, which include much of the Global North, provide the majority of foreign aid. Other providers of significant aid are Brazil, China, India, and the United Arab Emirates (Williams 2014). The United States is by far the largest donor

---

[2] Miranda Ames made significant contributions to this section.

FIGURE 7.10 • Minimum Wage Rates for Selected Countries, 2013

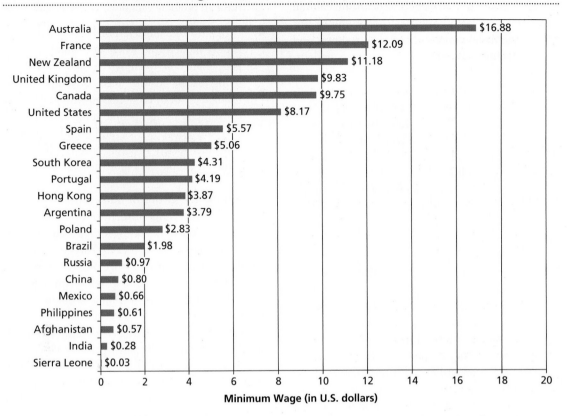

Country	Minimum Wage (in U.S. dollars)
Australia	$16.88
France	$12.09
New Zealand	$11.18
United Kingdom	$9.83
Canada	$9.75
United States	$8.17
Spain	$5.57
Greece	$5.06
South Korea	$4.31
Portugal	$4.19
Hong Kong	$3.87
Argentina	$3.79
Poland	$2.83
Brazil	$1.98
Russia	$0.97
China	$0.80
Mexico	$0.66
Philippines	$0.61
Afghanistan	$0.57
India	$0.28
Sierra Leone	$0.03

Minimum Wage (in U.S. dollars)

SOURCE: Data from Matthew Boesler, "Here's How America's Minimum Wage Stacks Up against Countries Like India, Russia, Greece, and France," *Business Insider*, August 19, 2013.

in terms of dollars, giving more than $31 billion in foreign aid in 2015 alone. However, when measured as a percentage of gross national income, the United States gives only 0.17 percent, which is considerably short of the target of 0.7 percent set by the United Nations (OECD 2016).

Critics of foreign aid express concern about its effectiveness and the political agendas of donors and recipients. Donors often seek to promote the economic growth of nations to enhance their own economic interests, preserve access to natural resources, and benefit their political positions. Foreign aid is also frequently tied to very specific stipulations about how countries may spend it. Donor countries often provide aid for specific purposes, some of the most common of which are education, transportation and communications infrastructure, and the development of government and civil society institutions. Issues can arise concerning such stipulations when the intentions of

the donor country are not in line with those of the receiving country. Causes of this can be anything from miscommunication to blatant corruption, and the end result can be the misuse or misdirection of billions of dollars. In addition, countries receiving loans may redirect their own funds toward the military.

THEORIES OF GLOBAL STRATIFICATION

As noted previously, the dominant theoretical approaches to social stratification are structural/functional theory and conflict/critical theory. These approaches are useful for examining social stratification not only in the United States but also globally.

Structural/Functional Theories

A dominant structural/functional theory of global stratification is **modernization theory**, which explains unequal economic distributions based on the structural (especially technological) and cultural differences between countries. According to this theory, the development of certain structures and cultural realities is essential for societies to modernize (Jacobsen 2015).

One of the thinkers best known for articulating and promoting modernization theory is Walt Rostow (1960, 1978), an economic theorist who served as an adviser to President John F. Kennedy. Rostow argued that low-income countries must abandon their traditional values and ways of life in order to improve their economic standards of living. He saw countries as progressing through four stages in a very linear path on their way to economic development:

1. *Traditional stage.* People in traditional societies have lived their lives the same way for many generations and know only the lives of their ancestors. Such societies are characterized by hardship and a lack of material comfort, conditions that they accept as inherent and inevitable features of life. With traditional values, people are encouraged to follow the paths of others in their families and communities. This acceptance of one's position in life, and a cultural focus on family and community, does not give people the incentive to work harder, save money, and acquire more material goods.

2. *Takeoff stage.* When people in poor countries begin to abandon their traditional values, they think more ambitiously about the future. They start to save and invest, trading with others to acquire profit, and new markets are developed for these exchanges. This stage is marked by greater individualism and a growing desire for material goods, with less emphasis placed on family and community.

3. *Drive to technological maturity.* A country in this stage continues to experience economic growth with the development of more advanced industries, high levels of investment, increasing urbanization, and higher standards of living. Institutions and societal values become more oriented toward production and consumption, with individualism trumping traditional values and norms. As people demand more material

comforts and gain more education, they continue to promote economic advancement.

4. *High mass consumption.* For Rostow, a country is fully modernized when large numbers of its people are able to enjoy the high standard of living associated with mass consumption and brought about by economic growth. In the mass consumption stage, people come to expect the everyday conveniences, and even luxuries, of consumer society. Absolute poverty falls significantly as people have more material comforts.

Among the critics of modernization theory, some have argued that it focuses too narrowly on economic production. Putting forth a theory of **neo-modernization**, Tiryakian (1991) argues that technological and cultural differences between countries are important for explaining both economic and social development. He notes that economic modernization can come at a high cost to forms of political and social life. A thriving civic culture, in which people can meaningfully participate in political processes, is also important for a country to be considered modern. The emphasis on cultural values is, therefore, extended beyond ideas such as individualism and competition to include democratization.

Conflict/Critical Theories

At the global level, world-systems theory is one of the most influential conflict/critical theories used to study global stratification. **World-systems theory** focuses on the current stratification system by viewing the world as a single economic entity (Wallerstein 1974). It envisions a world divided mainly between the *core* and the *periphery*. The core includes the wealthiest industrialized countries, such as Western European countries, the United States, Australia, and Japan. The nation-states associated with the periphery are dependent on, and exploited by, the core nation-states. The periphery includes most of Africa and parts of Asia (Indonesia, Vietnam, Afghanistan), the Middle East (Iran, Syria), and South America (Peru, Bolivia). There are also a number of states in the middle, the *semiperiphery*, including much of Eastern Europe, India, China, South Africa, and Argentina.

The core has been able to benefit from the periphery in a number of ways. Core nation-states have helped keep the countries of the periphery focused on narrow export-oriented economies rather than on developing their industrial capacity. The "race to the bottom" discussed previously benefits the core by providing the periphery's cheap labor and helps keep profits flowing back to the core. The core can also make loans to peripheral countries, but because of the power imbalance, the core is able to dictate the terms of the loans. Currently, poor countries owe the United States and other core countries more than $4 trillion in debt, leaving them in a weak economic position relative to the core.

World-systems theory argues that we can understand an individual nation's wealth today only by examining its current relationship to other countries. Of course, countries in the core, periphery, and semiperiphery can shift positions over time. At one time, Great Britain was the dominant core nation-state in the world, but by the time of World War II, it had been replaced by the United States. Today, the United States is slipping, and China, at one time a peripheral country, shows every sign of moving to the core.

ASK YOURSELF

In the context of world-systems theory, could a time come when the United States is in the semi-periphery or even the periphery? What do you think would make this result more likely? What could perhaps prevent it?

SUMMARY

Social stratification results in hierarchical differences and inequalities. Three important dimensions of stratification are social class, status, and power. In the money-based stratification system in the United States, wealth and income are the main determinants of social class. Since the 1970s, the United States has experienced increasing income inequality. However, the greatest economic differences in U.S. society are due to differences in wealth. People with great wealth often have high class, status, and power and can usually pass most of these advantages to future generations. Those who have little have a difficult time amassing their own wealth. The middle class in the United States has declined in recent decades, leaving a large "hole" in the stratification system between the lower and the upper classes. In the United States, the measure of absolute poverty is the poverty line, or the level of income that people are thought to need in order to survive in our society. Members of minority groups, women, and children are overrepresented among the poor.

While individuals in the United States have generally experienced intergenerational upward mobility, it seems likely that young people in the twenty-first century will experience more downward mobility. Sociologists are also concerned about structural mobility, or changes in the occupational structure.

Structural-functional theories of stratification argue that societies need a system of stratification in order to function properly. Conflict theorists challenge this assumption, particularly the idea that positions at the higher end of the stratification system are always more important. Finally, symbolic interactionists view stratification as a process or set of interactions among people in different positions.

Social stratification is related to consumption in a number of ways. Those in the higher classes can afford expensive items that those in the lower classes cannot. Elites use their patterns of consumption to distinguish themselves, sometimes conspicuously, from those beneath them.

Global stratification refers to the hierarchical differences and inequalities among countries and individuals across the world. This stratification is evident in the oppression of the Global South by the Global North, the differences among upper-, middle-, and low-income countries, and the differences between the richest and poorest people in the world. While global inequalities are highly persistent, it is possible for countries to develop economically and to change their positions within the global stratification system. The dominant structural/functional theory of global stratification is modernization theory, which argues that technological and cultural factors explain countries' varying levels of economic and social development. In contrast, conflict theorists argue that rich countries oppress and exploit poor countries, thus keeping them poor.

KEY TERMS

absolute poverty, 180
achievement, 183
ascription, 183
distinction, 188
feminization of
    poverty, 180
foreign aid, 196
global care
    chains, 195

high-income
    economies, 190
horizontal mobility, 183
income, 173
inequality, 172
intergenerational
    mobility, 183
intragenerational
    mobility, 183

low-income
    economies, 191
middle-income
    economies, 191
modernization
    theory, 197
neomodernization, 198
poverty line, 180
power, 172

relative poverty, 180
social class, 170
social mobility, 182
social stratification, 170
structural mobility, 183
vertical mobility, 183
wealth, 173
world-systems
    theory, 198

REVIEW QUESTIONS

1. According to Max Weber, what are the various dimensions of social stratification? What are some examples of people who rank high on each of these dimensions? Other than the examples discussed in the chapter, can you identify individuals who are status-inconsistent?

2. What is the difference between income and wealth? Which is more important to explaining the differences between the haves and the have-nots? Why?

3. How has inequality in the United States changed since the 1970s? In what ways are the explanations for these trends related to globalization?

4. What do we mean when we refer to the feminization of poverty? What factors help explain the position of women in the system of social stratification?

5. According to structural-functional theories, how is inequality beneficial to society? How can the

income and wealth of celebrities and sports stars be used as a criticism of this model?

6. Compare and contrast the different ways of classifying countries in the global stratification system. What does each classification emphasize?

7. How does access to the internet and new technologies relate to the global system of stratification? How can the internet be used to alter this system?

8. How are men and women affected differently by the global economy? Do you expect these differences to change significantly in the future? Why or why not?

9. According to structural/functional theories, how is culture related to global stratification?

10. Is foreign aid an effective way of addressing global poverty? How might conflict theories explain the role of foreign aid in global stratification?

PRACTICE AND APPLY WHAT YOU'VE LEARNED

▶ edge.sagepub.com/ritzeressentials3e

CHECK YOUR COMPREHENSION ON THE STUDY SITE WITH:

- **Diagnostic pre-tests** to identify opportunities for improvement.

- **eFlashcards** that strengthen your understanding of key terms and concepts.

- **Post-tests** to check your progress and ensure mastery of key learning objectives.

RACE AND ETHNICITY

Minorities Acquire Political Power

Evo Morales, a widely popular union leader and political activist, was elected president of Bolivia on the basis of an unorthodox leadership style and a reformist agenda. He was reelected in a landslide in 2009, and he won a third term, once again by a wide margin, in 2014. However, in 2016, a referendum thwarted his effort to run for a fourth term. A pioneer in many respects, Morales not only brought the democratic republic of Bolivia a new socialist mandate and a reformed constitution, but as an Aymara, he also became the developing nation's first indigenous president.

The Aymara are a racially and ethnically distinct people who have lived in central South America for more than 2,000 years. Conquered first by the Incas and then by Spanish colonists, they lived as an indentured minority group until Bolivia won its independence in 1825. Despite achieving legal freedom, however, the Aymara continued to be stereotyped, discriminated against, and marginalized by the country's Spanish-descended majority.

After nearly two centuries of marginalization, the Aymara rose via a number of social movements to achieve social equality and political power for Bolivia's indigenous populations. Organizations such as the militant Tupac Katari Guerrilla Army and Evo Morales's own Movimiento al Socialismo (MAS) challenged racist norms and championed sweeping reform. Running on a string of successful

LEARNING OBJECTIVES

8.1 Understand historical and recent views of racial categories and ethnic identities in the United States.

8.2 Describe majority–minority relations.

8.3 Discuss the foundations of racism.

8.4 Explain race and ethnicity in a global context.

MAS actions (including the ousting of the previous president) and a populist platform of farmers' rights and antimilitarism, Morales transcended old stereotypes and expectations, rising to his country's highest office.

Like Nelson Mandela before him in South Africa and Barack Obama, his U.S. contemporary, Evo Morales is a living symbol of a particular culture's ongoing struggle with prejudice, racism, and institutional discrimination. His presidency marks an important step in Bolivia's social evolution, but it by no means signifies that the Aymara have achieved social equality. Racism and ethnic discrimination have permeated Bolivia for hundreds—if not thousands—of years. During that time, the country's dominant groups have accumulated wealth, power, and prestige—assets they have been reluctant to share.

It took roughly eight generations for Bolivia to elect its first indigenous president and slightly longer for the United States to elect its first biracial one. These accomplishments have led some to suggest that we have achieved a postracial, or "color-blind," world. Racism, xenophobia, ethnic conflict, and ethnocentrism are sensitive topics for most people. However, denying that these difficult problems persist will only perpetuate them. ●

A discussion of race and ethnicity flows naturally from a discussion of social stratification. Racial and ethnic differences per se are not a problem. Problems arise when these differences are defined in such a way that people are ranked at or near the bottom of the stratification system *because* of their race or ethnicity. In addition, those in these groups confront prejudicial, often racist, attitudes and discriminatory conduct. **Racism** consists of defining a minority group as a race, attributing negative characteristics to that group, and then creating the circumstances that keep that group at a disadvantage relative to the majority (Law 2012).

While many scholars and citizens have come to believe that racism is on the wane and that the chances for racial integration and a postracial society have improved (Khanna and Harris 2015), others contend that racism not only continues to exist but also remains highly virulent (Bonilla-Silva 2015; Feagin 2012). To understand the conflicting claims, we need to put the issue of race into a broader context and define concepts basic to a sociological understanding of race, ethnicity, and majority–minority relations.

THE CONCEPTS OF RACE AND ETHNICITY

Globally, many groups of people have been singled out for differential treatment on the basis of "race." They include people whose complexions or skin colors are different—white, black, brown, red, and yellow—as well as those who share a lineage, such as Roma, Jewish, Arab, Navajo, Tibetan, Finnish, and Serbian. You may notice a difference between these two sets of groups. The reason is that **race** is a *socially constructed* definition based on some real or presumed physical, biological characteristic, such as skin color or hair texture, as well as on a shared lineage. However, races are usually defined according to social and historical ideas about what has been deemed biologically important. While race is often based on real or presumed bodily characteristics, it is more about what people define it to be than about any meaningful physical differences. **Ethnicity** is also socially defined, but on the basis of some real or presumed cultural characteristic such as language, religion, traditions, or cultural practices. Ethnic groups may define themselves on the basis of their ethnicity, or they may be so defined by others. **Ethnic groups** have a sense of shared origins and relatively clear boundaries, and they tend to endure over time. These boundaries may be recognized by both insiders and outsiders (Carter and Fenton 2010).

While races and ethnic groups have been defined separately, the line between race and ethnicity is not always clear. Races are often considered ethnic groups, and ethnic groups are often considered races. For instance, *white* is a racial category that is frequently subordinated to ethnic categories such as Italian American or White Russian. Similarly, *black* has become "ethnicized." For example, Davis (1991) argues that blacks in the United States are now a self-conscious social group with an "ethnic identity." The creation of Kwanzaa, soul food, and the development of hip-hop all speak to the significance of *African American* as a cultural identity—not just a racial one. On the other hand, Jews, most notoriously in Nazi Germany during the Holocaust, have frequently been thought of not simply as an ethnic group but, as mentioned previously, also as a race. However, Jews do not all come from the same genetic stock; some have Semitic features, and others have European features. They do tend to have some ethnic characteristics in common, most notably a religion and a shared cultural history. Thus, as you read this chapter, which at times discusses race and ethnic groups separately, bear in mind the strong overlap between race and ethnicity.

What is race, and what is ethnicity? This Ethiopian boy, newly arrived in Israel, is a member of an ancient Jewish community.

HISTORICAL THINKING ABOUT RACE

The concept of race has an ancient history. It has taken many different forms over the centuries, but it always serves as a way of differentiating among groups of people and creating hierarchies that empower some and disempower, or disadvantage, others (Song 2007). Race has also played a key role in most imperial conquests, often with whites imposing their will on, and then exploiting, other races. During the peak of the British Empire, for example, the British controlled India, the West Indies, and West Africa, all of whose dark-skinned populations were subordinated to the British. The rationalizations for this pattern of dominance included both "scientific" and cultural explanations.

"Scientific" Explanations

Following the Enlightenment, and especially in the nineteenth and early twentieth centuries, folk ideas about race were supplemented with "rational" (which today are seen as pseudoscientific) justifications for treating people of other races differently (Blatt 2007). While Enlightenment thinkers believed in the unity of humankind, they also believed in classifying people along a continuum from primitive to modern. One result was classification schemes based on race (Arthur and Lemonik 2007).

A more ominous result was the use of allegedly fixed biological characteristics not simply to differentiate among groups of people but also to "scientifically" justify the unequal distribution of wealth, power, prestige, access to resources, and life chances to subordinate racial groups. In 1795, a German naturalist invented the idea of the Caucasian race as the first and most perfect race. In 1800, a French scientist argued that race was involved in social hierarchies and that whites stood on top of those hierarchies.

Evolutionary thinking spurred interest in racial categories. The idea of social Darwinism, associated with sociologist Herbert Spencer, was taken to mean that racial differences were the result of evolutionary differences among the races. One race was better off, and another was worse off, because of evolution. Further, society was not to try to tamper with, reduce, or eliminate these differences; it was not to interfere with a natural process. Spencer (1851, 151) defined this in terms of the "survival of the fittest."

Also during the nineteenth century, Gregor Mendel's work on genetics and heredity led to the idea that the races could be distinguished from one another on the basis of their genetic makeup. This idea played a role in the development of the eugenics movement, which notoriously argued that the human population could be improved genetically through scientific manipulation. Especially in the first half of the twentieth century and during the Nazi era, eugenicists defended racial segregation, opposed interracial marriage, and sought the restriction of immigration and the compulsory sterilization of those considered "unfit."

ASK YOURSELF

Do you think the ideas behind the eugenics movement would be widely accepted by many people today? Why or why not?

Others criticized these extreme ideas while still arguing the existence of genetically based racial differences in behavior. With the creation of the IQ test in the early 1900s, IQ was used not only to differentiate among races but also to demonstrate racial superiority and inferiority. Later scholars argued that it is possible to make predictions based on race about intelligence (Herrnstein and Murray 1994), the likelihood of inheriting certain diseases (Hatch 2009), and the propensity to engage in criminal activities (Duster 2003). Contemporary sociologists typically reject single-minded "scientific" explanations of race, including the view that genetic differences are responsible for socially significant differences among racial groups (Hatch 2016; Hughey and Byrd 2015). Rather, most see the historical, structural, institutional, and oppressive contexts of race as explanations for observable differences among racial groups. Sociological research focusing on genetics tends to take the stance that genes matter, but so does environment. Conceptualizations by sociologists of race (and ethnicity) acknowledge that socially constructed racial categories overlap with some biological/genetic differences among racial groups. However, biological/genetic differences within racial groups are often as important as those between such groups.

Cultural Explanations

Even though "scientific" explanations of race continue to exist, explanations based on social and cultural factors such as religion, language, and national origin are more prevalent today. In the second half of the twentieth century, ideas of cultural superiority and inferiority increasingly replaced those associated with biological superiority and inferiority. For example, African Americans have been described as having a "culture of poverty," which suggests that they have a sense of learned helplessness and powerlessness (Cohen 2010). While this argument has been used against poor people more generally, it has often been racialized to explain the disproportionately high rates of black poverty. According to the U.S. Census Bureau, in 2015 about 24 percent of African Americans were poor, while about 14 percent of all people living in the United States were impoverished (Proctor, Semega, and Kollar 2016).

As is the case with "scientific" explanations, there are often problems with cultural explanations. For instance, the concept of the culture of poverty has been used to legitimate racial differences in class position rather than to explain these differences in terms of the structural lack of economic opportunity that African Americans have faced throughout their history. Very recently, there has been a revival of interest in serious cultural explanations that avoid the excesses of the culture of poverty argument yet deal critically with aspects of black culture (e.g., the tendency to devalue traditional coparenting). However, such cultural explanations must not ignore the structural problems facing the black community (Patterson and Fosse 2015; Sanneh 2015). Racial differences, like poverty, are complicated and multivariate in cause, effect, and scope. Needless to say, biological, cultural, and structural explanations should not be used, on their own or collectively, to legitimate racial (or ethnic) differences in positions in the system of social stratification.

THE FLUIDITY OF RACIAL CATEGORIES

Sociologists point to the fact that racial categories are often blurred and subject to change; race is a dynamic and fluid social concept. There are many examples of the fluidity and variability of the race concept in the United States. For example, former president Barack Obama is the offspring of a white mother and a black African father. However, he is referred to as black or African American, not "half black" or "half African American." This is a legacy of the **hypodescent rule**, also known as the "one drop" rule or the "one Black ancestor rule" (Davis 1991). In Virginia, people with as little as one-sixteenth

TABLE 8.1 • Race in the U.S. Census, 1790–Present

RACIAL CATEGORY	YEAR(S) USED IN CENSUS	DESCRIPTION
White or black	1790–1850	Only *white* and *black* categories used (*mulatto* also used if not "fully" black); *black* was divided into "free" and "slave"
Mulatto	1850–1870, 1890, 1910, 1920	Mixed race, one mixed parent and one white parent
Quadroon	1890	Mixed race, one-quarter African ancestry
Octoroon	1890	Mixed race, one-eighth African ancestry
Hindu	1910–1940	South Asian Indian
Mexican	1930	First and only time listed as a race, if parent or individual was Mexican born
Hispanic	1980–present	Anyone of Spanish-speaking descent, regardless of race or physical appearance
More than one	2000–present	First time in U.S. history when a person could identify with more than one specific racial category

SOURCE: Race in the U.S. Census, 1790–Present is reprinted by permission of Lisa Speicher Muñoz.

African ancestry were considered by law to be black; in Florida, this was one-eighth, and in Louisiana, this was one-thirty-second. In the early twentieth century, several states, including Tennessee and Alabama, adopted the rule that a person with the slightest trace of African ancestry was considered to be black. While its effect is muted today, the one-drop rule continues to affect how at least some black Americans think of themselves (Guo et al. 2014; see Table 8.1).

The fluidity and variability of the race concept are even clearer when we adopt a global perspective. In South Africa during apartheid (1948–1994), there were three racial categories: white, black, and colored. Whites were descended from Europeans and blacks from Africans. The colored category was more complex, including both those with mixed racial backgrounds (who might also have been labeled black) and those descended from Asians. In many Caribbean and Latin American countries, especially Brazil, race is a matter of gradations between black and white, with indigenous descent and social status factored in as well. In this case, it is especially clear that the color of an individual's skin does not determine whether that person is "black" or "white." It is also true that someone defined as

black in the United States might be considered white in, say, Peru. Clearly, racial categories embrace far too much variation to claim a scientific basis. As pointed out previously, variation within racial categories is often as great as, or greater than, variation between racial categories.

Race data have been collected by the United States since its first census in 1790. However, the categories have changed across time, reflecting the social, economic, and political climate of the era. It wasn't until 1970 that individuals were allowed to choose their own race in responding to census questionnaires. Prior to that time, census takers had filled in the race category, based at times on asking the individuals and at other times on their own assumptions (Passel 2010). Although many people have identified as "mixed race" for generations, it wasn't until the 2000 census that such individuals were allowed to identify officially with two or more races.

Table 8.2 shows the racial composition of the U.S. population based on data from the 2000 and 2010 censuses. Of great interest in this table is the strong increase between 2000 and 2010 in the Hispanic or Latino and Asian populations and the slow growth of the Black or African American population.

TABLE 8.2 • Racial Composition of the U.S. Population, 2000 and 2010

	2000		2010		CHANGE, 2000 TO 2010	
	NUMBER	PERCENTAGE OF TOTAL POPULATION	NUMBER	PERCENTAGE OF TOTAL POPULATION	NUMBER	PERCENTAGE
Hispanic or Latino	35,305,818	12.5	50,477,594	16.3	15,171,776	43.0
Not Hispanic or Latino	246,116,088	87.5	258,267,944	83.7	12,151,856	4.9
White Alone	194,552,774	69.1	196,817,552	63.7	2,264,778	1.2
One Race	274,595,678	97.6	299,736,465	97.1	25,140,787	9.2
White	211,460,626	75.1	223,553,265	72.4	12.092,639	5.7
Black or African American	34,658,190	12.3	38,929,319	12.6	4,271,129	12.3
American Indian and Alaska Native	2,475,956	0.9	2,932,248	0.9	456,292	18.4
Asian	10,242,998	3.6	14,674,252	4.8	4,431,254	43.3
Native Hawaiian and Other Pacific Islander	398,835	0.1	540,013	0.2	141,178	35.4
Some Other Race	15,359,073	5.5	19,107,368	6.2	3,748,295	24.4
Two or More Races	6,826,228	2.4	9,009,073	2.9	2,182,845	32.0

SOURCE: From "Overview of Race and Hispanic Origin: 2010," Table 1, p. 4. *Census Briefs,* March 2011. United States Census Bureau, U.S. Department of Commerce.

RACIAL AND ETHNIC IDENTITIES

Because oppression and subordination are often based on race and ethnicity, many individuals from racial and ethnic minorities go to some lengths to identify with the dominant group. They might adopt the cultural values and practices of the dominant culture. For instance, linguistic assimilation—adopting English, perhaps leaving the old language behind—has almost been inevitable among nearly all ethnic minority groups in the United States. In the past it was common for individuals to change

their names to have a more "Anglo" sound; some did this when they immigrated to the United States (Cannato 2009). Some individuals defined as part of a minority racial or ethnic group may physically resemble the dominant race or ethnic group, and they may go so far as to straighten, curl, or color their hair or lighten their skin to increase that resemblance (Campbell 2010). They might even undergo cosmetic surgery (Luo 2013).

At the same time, many members of minority groups have strong and positive attachments to their racial or ethnic identities. They make this evident in various ways, including by supporting racial or ethnic organizations, participating in group-specific celebrations, taking pride in the achievements of highly successful members of their groups, and resisting dominant cultural expectations, such as those regarding beauty (Lloréns 2013).

MAJORITY–MINORITY RELATIONS

Race and ethnicity can be understood in the context of a wide range of relationships that can be subsumed under the heading of *majority–minority relations* (Farley 2011; Yetman 1991). The focus in work on such relations is often on the difficulties experienced by minority groups, especially racial

and ethnic minorities. Many of these problems are traceable to majority group prejudice and discrimination. Those in a dominant group are prone to exploiting and marginalizing members of subordinate groups.

However, the distinction between *majority* and *minority* raises a number of questions. How can the white race, to take one example, be considered a majority group when it is outnumbered by a wide margin in the world by those in other races? Whites are still numerically dominant in the United States, but the U.S. Census Bureau has projected that by 2044 the non-Hispanic white population in the country will be in the minority when compared with the combined nonwhite population groups, although whites will still outnumber any single racial/ethnic group (Colby and Ortman 2015). The 2010 census terms this demographic situation a **majority-minority population**, defined as a case

FIGURE 8.1 • Majority-Minority Counties in the United States, 2012

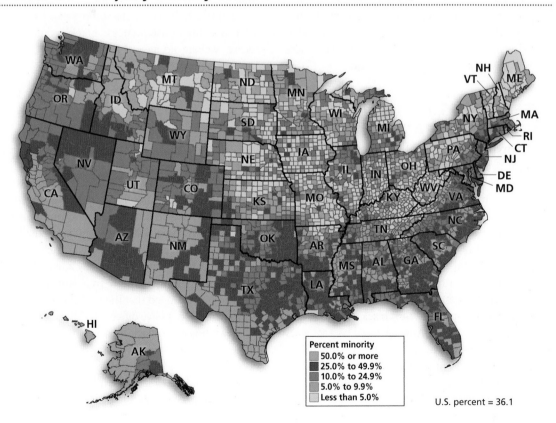

Percent minority
- 50.0% or more
- 25.0% to 49.9%
- 10.0% to 24.9%
- 5.0% to 9.9%
- Less than 5.0%

U.S. percent = 36.1

SOURCE: U.S. Census Bureau, Population Division, Vintage 2012 Population Estimates.

"where more than 50 percent of the population is part of a minority group" (U.S. Census Bureau 2011). Majority-minority populations already exist in California, Texas, Hawaii, New Mexico, and the District of Columbia. Figure 8.1 shows the percentage of minorities residing in each county in the United States in 2012.

Similarly, the Kaiser Family Foundation (2015a) reports that there are 157 million women (51 percent) and 151.8 million men (49 percent) in the U.S. population. How can women be a minority when they outnumber men? The answer to this question lies in the sociological definitions of *majority* and *minority*, which do not rely on the numerical size of groups. Rather, these definitions are concerned with differences in levels of money, prestige, and power possessed by groups. As the classic social theorist Max Weber defined the terms, a **minority group** is in a subordinate position in terms of wealth, power, and prestige (status), while a **majority group** is in a dominant position on those dimensions. While these three factors often vary together, a higher ranking in only one or two areas can be enough to accord a group majority status and, by implication, define another as a minority group. Women are a minority group because, although they are in the numerical majority, as a group they have less wealth, power, and prestige than men do.

STEREOTYPES, PREJUDICE, AND DISCRIMINATION

A **stereotype** is a generalization about an entire category of people that is thought to apply to everyone in that category. Stereotypes are frequently manifested in daily social interaction. For example, people might assume that a clean-cut, young, white student-athlete at the elite Stanford University would be highly trustworthy. In contrast, stereotypes about racial and ethnic minorities tend to work against them. In department stores, security guards may follow black customers without apparent cause, salespeople may view black shoppers with suspicion, cashiers may avoid physical contact with black customers when giving change, and white customers may exhibit nervousness when joined by a black man in an elevator (Staples 1986). This all occurs because of a stereotype relating black people with criminal behavior. Stereotypes are the basis for prejudice and discrimination. **Prejudice** consists of preconceived negative attitudes, beliefs, and feelings toward minorities, typically derived from unfounded opinions or stereotypes. **Discrimination** is the unfavorable, unjust treatment of minorities arising from the negative stereotypes associated with prejudice. Racial discrimination is unequal treatment based on race. Discrimination occurs both formally (e.g., on the job) and informally (e.g., in interpersonal situations). It can occur in any social realm, including in schools, workplaces, health care institutions, housing, and the criminal justice system. Members of the majority group unfairly deny minority group members access to opportunities and rewards that are available to the majority. In the United States today, much overt discrimination has been outlawed.

Discrimination and prejudice do not necessarily occur in concert with one another. People can be prejudiced without discriminating; they need not act on their prejudices. However, stereotypes, prejudice, and discrimination often interact with one another. For example, black women often face stereotypes that identify them as overly sexual and financially irresponsible (Collins 2004; Rosenthal and Lobel 2016). These stereotypes can have negative real-life consequences. Black women who receive welfare aid have at some points in U.S. history been compelled to undergo compulsory sterilization. The assumption in these cases is that black women will have too many children and be unable to support them financially.

The stereotype of black men as dangerous criminals has persisted from the end of slavery to the present and has created grave difficulties for black citizens (Dow 2016; Ferguson 2001). Recent examples of those difficulties were evident in the 2012 acquittal of a Florida man accused of murdering a black man, Trayvon Martin, whom he claimed was a suspicious person. Then there was the killing in late 2014 of an unarmed young black man, Michael Brown, in Ferguson, Missouri, by a white police officer who had assumed that the young man was dangerous. In 2016, police officers in Chicago shot and killed an unarmed black teen fleeing on foot from officers; he had allegedly stolen a car. Those killings and resulting demonstrations led to and fueled the development of a powerful new social movement, "Black Lives Matter" (see the Digital Living box in this chapter). It focuses on dealing with the prejudice and discrimination facing black people throughout the United States and other parts of the world. More specifically, it is concerned with the phenomenon of black lives that are "systematically and intentionally targeted for demise." It involves an "affirmation of Black folks' contributions to this society, our humanity, and our resilience in the face of deadly oppression" (blacklivesmatter.com). Black Lives Matter became more visible in 2014 after helping mount protests over the deaths of several black men at the hands of the police, including Michael Brown in Ferguson, Eric Garner in New York City in 2014, and Freddie Gray in Baltimore, Maryland, in 2015. The killings and protests continued in 2016, most notably involving the murder, also by police officers, of Alton Sterling in Baton Rouge, Louisiana, and Philando Castile in St. Anthony, Minnesota. Blacks and other racial minorities are legally entitled to receive fair treatment from the police, as well as in jobs, housing, and education. While they may get fairer treatment in at least some of these areas, prejudice has been harder to root out. Many minorities still face negative stereotypes. They are constantly reminded that their social group has been defined as "different" from the majority group. George Yancy has described lingering prejudice as being reinforced on a daily basis through "the white imaginary," a "perspective that carries the weight of white racist history and everyday encounters of spoken and unspoken anti-Black racism" (2008, 5). This white imaginary, or racist social construction of "difference," has a cumulative effect that can alienate, disempower, and psychologically oppress blacks (Trepagnier 2010).

Members of the majority group do not experience discrimination or prejudice on a regular and ongoing basis and thus may have trouble empathizing with members of minority groups (Croll 2013). Members of the majority do not have to consider repeatedly whether their daily experiences reflect or do not reflect discrimination and prejudice. Peggy McIntosh (2010) sees this freedom from daily consideration of such issues as "white privilege," which she defines as obliviousness to the sorts of challenges that minorities experience on a regular basis.

INTERSECTIONALITY

Many groups may be described as minority groups. Individuals may belong to more than one such group—for instance, gay Filipinos or Native Americans with disabilities. People's experiences as one type of minority may overlap and intersect with other experiences common to another type of minority. *Intersectionality* is the idea that members of any given minority group are affected by the nature of their position in other systems or other forms of social inequality (P. Collins 2000; Collins and Bilge 2016). This concept was developed initially to analyze the situation confronting women of color, who face discrimination along both gender and racial lines. It has subsequently been expanded to include other variables, such as age, disability, and sexual orientation. Minority group members are seen as being enmeshed in a "matrix of oppression" that involves not only race but also gender, ethnic group, sexual orientation, age, social class, religion, ability status, and the part of the globe, North or South, in which they live. The problems associated with being a member of multiple oppressed minority groups are not simply additive; rather, the disadvantages multiply, as do their effects (Kivisto and Croll 2012, 66). The converse is also true. That is, a person who holds a number of statuses that are highly valued by society is likely to be extremely advantaged. One of the most esteemed groups consists of people who are male, white, Anglo-Saxon, upper-class, heterosexual, and adult. This could be seen as a "matrix of power and advantage."

A dramatic example of how gender and race intersect is provided by black transgender men—individuals who were categorized as "female" at birth but who physically transition, with the aid of hormones and surgeries, to become men. They find that their lives as black men are radically different from their previous lives as black women. They come to realize that many white women are afraid of them when they pass on the street, an experience they did not face as black women. As men, they face the experience of being pulled over by police for "driving while black." Whereas white transgender men find that they gain some social privileges as white men that they did not enjoy as white women, black transgender men can experience greater social constraints and discrimination (Schilt 2010).

PATTERNS OF INTERACTION

When members of majority and minority groups interact, the outcomes tend to follow one of four patterns: pluralism, assimilation, segregation, or genocide.

Race in Cyberspace

Although whites, blacks, and Hispanics use social media at similar rates, recent findings from a Pew Research study indicate that whites and minorities tend to prefer different platforms. Facebook is the most popular social media site for all races, with about 70 percent of all people using the platform. Twitter users are roughly equally distributed, with 25 percent of Hispanics, 27 percent of blacks, and 21 percent of whites using this social media site. But people of color use Instagram more frequently than do whites, and whites are most likely to use Pinterest (Krogstad 2015). Another Pew study found that the viewing of race-related content on social media platforms was significantly different depending on a person's race. Twenty-four percent of blacks reported that most of the content they viewed on social media was about race or race relations, compared to only 6 percent of whites (Anderson and Hitlin 2016). While social media has been lauded as having the potential to transcend racial differences (Kang 2000), research has found that racial segregation offline is often replicated online (boyd 2014). For example, boyd (2014, 168) discovered that teenagers were more likely to be friends both online and offline with other teens of the same race—though the teens themselves understood their behavior through a lens of personal preference rather than racism.

One of the most significant instances of race on social media is

The #BlackLivesMatter (or #BLM) hashtag spread quickly on Twitter, calling attention to the injustices faced by African Americans and prompting in-person protests. When did you first hear the phrase "Black Lives Matter"?

the Black Lives Matter movement, which began as a hashtag on Twitter in 2013. #BlackLivesMatter centers on exposing injustices experienced by African Americans, including police brutality, incarceration, and poverty. Pew Research has found that social media platforms, especially Twitter and tweets associated with #Ferguson and #BlackLivesMatter, have brought greater awareness to racial inequality in the United States. While most of the tweets associated with #BlackLivesMatter have been supportive, following the July 2016 shooting of police officers in Dallas, there was a significant increase in comments critical of the movement and a rise of tweets from followers of #AllLivesMatter and #BlueLivesMatter (Anderson and Hitlin 2016). Some scholars argue that #BlackLivesMatter needs to be more inclusive in regard to gender and sexuality, calling for a greater presence of digital intersectionality (Tynes, Schuschke, and Noble 2016). *Digital intersectionality* refers to the connections between myriad social categories, such as race, ethnicity, gender, sexual orientation, socioeconomic class, and religious affiliation, that an individual or group may identify with online.

Engaging the Digital World

How racially diverse are your online social networks? Do they mimic your offline social networks? If yes, in what ways? How often does content related to race and racial inequality appear on the social media platforms that you frequently use? Do you think this influences your limits on, or expands your understanding of, race in the United States?

Pluralism exists in societies where many groups are able to coexist without any of them losing their individual qualities. For example, in pluralistic societies, there may be multiple races, ethnic groups, and religions and many languages spoken.

Assimilation occurs when a minority group takes on the characteristics of the dominant group and leaves its old ways behind. In the United States, assimilation has occurred when immigrant groups have chosen to give up their native languages for English or when they have adopted mainstream American cultural values and customs. Sometimes, however, assimilation has been forced on certain groups. During the late nineteenth and early twentieth centuries, many Native American children were forced into boarding schools where they were given new names, forced to speak English (and punished for speaking their native languages), and taught Christianity.

The United States has leaned more at times toward pluralism and at other times toward assimilation. Even when minorities feel that their differences are respected, all majority–minority relations are fraught with at least the potential for conflict. Members of the majority group act to maintain or enhance their positions, and minority group members struggle to improve theirs, or at least to prevent them from declining any further. These conflicts, potential or real, are generally resolved in favor of the majority group, because it has far greater resources (money, power) than the minority group does.

This issue was in the news during the 2016 presidential campaign, when then Republican candidate Donald Trump suggested that Muslim communities within the United States (representing about 3.3 million people, roughly 1 percent of the population) constituted a potential source of danger to the country. He also attacked American pluralism and urged at least a temporary "total and complete shutdown of Muslims entering the United States." He proposed that customs agents ask travelers to the

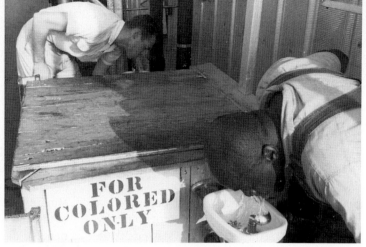

While segregation still exists informally in the United States, especially in schools, it is no longer supported by the law, as it was when this photo was taken in the American South.

United States if they were Muslim; if they said yes, the agents were to turn them away (Rappeport and Haberman 2016).

In the early days of Trump's presidency in 2017, he followed through on these proposals by prohibiting, at least initially for 90 days, entry into the United States of those coming from Syria, Iran, Iraq, Somalia, Sudan, Libya and Yemen. Christians were to get priority when—and if—refugees from those countries would be permitted to enter beyond that deadline (Walsh 2017). Within hours of the announcement of this new policy, people from those countries began to be refused to be allowed to board planes bound for the United States. Trump's views and initial actions as president were so outrageous that they led to an outcry from not only Muslims but also many in the majority group in the United States, as well as many people throughout the world.

ASK YOURSELF

If your parents or grandparents came to the United States from another country, did they arrive during a period when pluralism or assimilation was the norm? How did this prevailing norm affect their experience as immigrants? Do you think it has had an effect on your life, or on the life of your family?

Segregation is the physical and social separation of majority and minority groups. Historically, segregation was mandated by law in the United States (and elsewhere). As a result, whites and minorities were not able to attend the same schools, live in the same neighborhoods, or share the same public facilities (such as restrooms, theater seating areas, swimming pools, or courtrooms). *Brown v. Board of Education* (1954) is seen as the beginning of the end of legally mandated segregation in the United States. While levels of segregation have declined, such history set into motion practices that continue to segregate majority and minority groups. Residential segregation is key to majority-minority, especially racial, stratification (D. Massey 2016). Schools are generally still segregated, a reflection of the persistence of residential segregation (Logan, Minca, and Adar 2012).

Genocide—an active, systematic attempt at eliminating an entire group of people—is a fourth outcome of majority–minority group relations. A genocidal campaign was conducted against Native Americans from the early days of European settlement in the United States through the 1800s. This was committed even though an official governmental policy of extermination did not exist. In this regard, the tragedy of the Native Americans is not the same as the genocide experienced by Jews, the Roma, and homosexuals during the Nazi reign of terror known as the Holocaust or the Tutsi ethnic group during the genocide in Rwanda. In those cases, genocide *was* official government policy.

RACISM

As noted at the beginning of this chapter, racism involves defining a group as a race and attributing negative characteristics to that group (Elias and Feagin 2016). It also involves creating the circumstances that keep that group at a disadvantage relative to the majority. Racism can be seen as a subtype of xenophobia, or "fear of strangers." **Xenophobia** involves the beliefs, attitudes, and prejudices that reject, exclude, and vilify groups who are not part of the dominant social group.

Note that the definition of racism used here allows us to discuss negative attitudes and treatment based on either race or ethnicity. Cultural characteristics that are different from the mainstream, the hallmark of ethnic identity, are almost always associated with racial groups, so cultural discrimination is central to racial discrimination. In short, racism is based on ethnocentrism, or the belief that the norms, values, and customs of one's own group are superior to those of other groups (Sumner [1906] 1940).

If you were to ask any American on the street whether he or she is racist, you would almost certainly be told that the person is not prejudiced and considers people of all races and ethnicities to be equal. Yet racist attitudes and behaviors persist. Minority members are likely to have experienced, or to know someone in their group who has experienced, discrimination at the hands of a white person or within the structure of an organization or society as a whole. A Pew Research Center poll of U.S. adults found that blacks are far more likely than whites to say there is "a lot of discrimination" against blacks (Doherty 2013): 46 percent of black respondents agreed with this statement, while only 16 percent of whites agreed (see Figure 8.2).

Erving Goffman's ideas on dramaturgy can be used to analyze this disparity (Slatton and Feagin 2012). Whites often quite unconsciously conceal or play down their racism in their *front stage*. However, when they are *back stage* with those they are confident hold similar views, they are quite comfortable making overtly racist comments or telling racist jokes (see Chapter 4 for a discussion of the concepts

FIGURE 8.2 • How Much Discrimination Is There against African Americans?

% saying ...

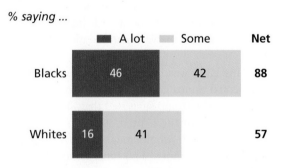

SOURCE: For African Americans, discrimination is not dead, by Carroll Doherty. June 28, 2013. Reprinted by permission of Pew Research Center, Washington, DC.

NOTE: Blacks and whites include only those who are not Hispanic.

The Cosmopolitan Canopy: Race and Civility in Everyday Life (W. W. Norton & Company, 2011)

Elijah Anderson (William K. Lanman, Jr., Professor of Sociology at Yale University; PhD, Northwestern University, 1976)

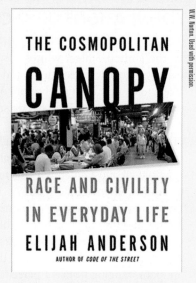

W.W. Norton. Used with permission.

Elijah Anderson explores public spaces in the city of Philadelphia in order to observe the everyday interactions between individuals from different racial and ethnic backgrounds. He finds that most urban residents act with civility and coexist peacefully in what he calls "cosmopolitan canopies," or "settings that offer respite from the lingering tensions of urban life and an opportunity for diverse peoples to come together" (Anderson 2011, xiv). Cosmopolitan canopies are relaxed environments that encourage "people watching" without fear of offending strangers because "ethnocentric feelings" are kept in check (2001, xvii). Two places in particular exemplify cosmopolitan canopies: Philadelphia's Reading Terminal Market and Rittenhouse Square. Reading Terminal Market is a crowded public space with a variety of shops, kiosks, and restaurants, where interracial interactions and cross-cultural exchanges are common and do not engender anxiety or conflict. Rittenhouse Square is a historic public park where a diverse population gathers to observe others and be observed without feeling self-conscious. Though Anderson discovers that interracial eye contact, or "eye work," can be complicated here, most "people watching" across color lines and other social categories, such as gender and sexuality, is understood as a form of entertainment and as harmless fun.

Outside of cosmopolitan canopies, racial and ethnic differences are more likely to be emphasized and can result in discomfort and tension. In these spaces, individuals often form racially homogenous "clumps" and avoid interracial interactions (Anderson 2011, 226). For example, many whites will not sit by young black males on public transportation because they look "ghetto" and are perceived as possibly dangerous (2011, 217). The black middle class often experiences uncomfortable encounters outside of cosmopolitan canopies because the dominant white society views them as lower class. This is one reason why, Anderson argues, they conspicuously display their wealth by wearing expensive clothes or driving luxury cars. Anderson finds that middle-class blacks feel the color line acutely in upscale restaurants, where they clearly confront racial prejudice and discrimination. They are stereotyped as "difficult, demanding customers, who don't tip" and are often seated at the worst tables (2011, 235–236). Many instead prefer to patronize chain restaurants, where they feel they receive better service—if they choose to eat out at all. Anderson argues that we need to extend the civility and openness of cosmopolitan canopies to not just racially segregated public spaces but also our neighborhoods and workplaces in order for all of us to become more comfortable with diversity.

Supplementary Resources

- Listen to a free podcast of Anderson delivering a talk on his book *The Cosmopolitan Canopy* at https://libwww .freelibrary.org/podcast/ episode/650.
- You can read an article by Anderson based on his popular ethnographic study *Code of the Street* in *The Atlantic* at http:// www.theatlantic.com/ magazine/archive/1994/05/ the-code-of-the- streets/306601.

of front and back stage). If they happen to be in a place where outsiders, especially minority group members, might intrude, they may use code words or symbols instead of overt racial slurs.

FOUNDATIONS OF RACISM
Social Structure and Racism

In the United States, whites disproportionately occupy higher-level positions, and blacks are more likely to be near or at the bottom of the racial hierarchy. However, this is an overly simplistic picture of U.S. racial stratification. There are blacks (and other minorities) scattered throughout every level in that hierarchy, even in its highest reaches, as exemplified, most notably, by the recent presidency of Barack Obama (2009–2017). Undocumented immigrants to the United States are predominantly Latino, and they are much more likely than blacks to exist at the lowest rungs in the racial hierarchy. About 21 percent of Hispanics in the United States are poor, ranging from 42 percent in Kentucky to 15 percent in Virginia and the state of Washington and 12 percent in Washington, DC. Large numbers of whites also exist at or near the bottom rungs in that hierarchy: About 13 percent of whites in the United States are poor (Kaiser Family Foundation 2015b).

As is clear in the preceding discussion, one of the main indicators of racial stratification is the extent to which poverty is linked to race. Figure 8.3 shows the relationship between race/ethnicity and poverty between 1959 and 2015. The fact that 24 percent of blacks and 21 percent of Hispanics were below the poverty line in 2015—compared with 12 percent of whites and 11 percent of Asians—is a strong indicator of economic disadvantage for the first two groups. Also worth noting is the strong increase in poverty among blacks and Hispanics beginning in 2008, right after the onset of the Great Recession. The historical influences of segregation and legal discrimination in generations past, coupled with the economic benefits of white privilege, help link economic disadvantage and racism.

Culture and Racism

Some sociologists argue that a part of the larger culture of the United States involves a "white racial frame" through which whites, and to some degree blacks, view race (Feagin 2013). The **white racial frame** includes an array of racist ideas, racial stereotypes, racialized stories and tales, racist images, powerful racial emotions, and various inclinations that discriminate against blacks (as well as other minorities, including Latinos [Feagin and Cobas

FIGURE 8.3 • Poverty Rates in the United States by Race and Ethnicity, 1959–2015

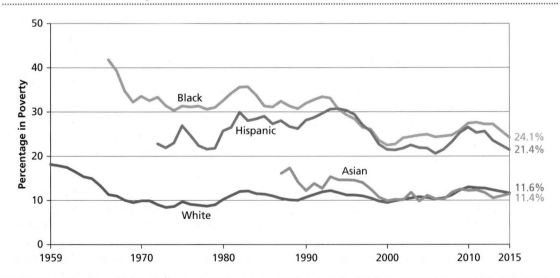

SOURCE: Data from Bernadette D. Proctor, Jessica L. Semega, and Melissa A. Koller. 2016. "Income and Poverty in the United States: 2015." Current Population Reports, P60–256(RV). September.

2014]). To a certain extent, blacks themselves have adopted elements of this frame. This is exemplified in "gangsta" style being identified as black culture. It is also found in measures of success—such as graduating from college, gaining a professional job, or living in the suburbs—being seen by black culture as selling out, or "acting white." This white racial frame is largely responsible for perpetuating racial stereotypes, as is seen throughout movies, music videos, and television shows.

Racism has often been, and can still be, a matter of physical domination of minorities by, for example, the state. However, racism is now more a matter of **hegemony**. That is, one race now subordinates another more on the basis of dominant ideas, especially about cultural differences, than through force.

Throughout this discussion, whiteness as a racial category has either been ignored or, especially in the case of the white racial frame, dealt with negatively as the source of prejudice and discrimination against blacks and other minorities. However, white is a "racial category," and whites can be considered a "racial group" (Hartigan 2014; Smangs 2016). Whiteness can be, and for some people is, a positive source of identity. Many whites are antiracist, and large numbers embrace other races. In any case, as we saw earlier in this chapter, in not too many decades, whites will be a numerical minority in the majority-minority United States. The relationship of whites to minorities and the role of whiteness in prejudice and discrimination need to remain the focus of attention in work on majority–minority relations, as well as in efforts to create a more equitable society.

INSTITUTIONAL RACISM

While there is a general tendency to emphasize individual prejudice and discrimination in discussing racism, from a sociological perspective, it is institutional discrimination—more specifically, institutional racism (Bonilla-Silva 2009; Carmichael and Hamilton 1967; Ward and Rivera 2014)—that is the far bigger problem. **Institutional racism** is race-based discrimination that results from the day-to-day operation of social institutions and social structures and their rules, policies, and practices. In other words, racism is more than attitudes (prejudice) or behavior (discrimination); it is "systemic"

within society, especially American society, and within its most important and powerful social structures (Feagin 2006).

Institutional discrimination is found in many settings:

- Educational systems, where schools in which the student body is disproportionately black or Latino are often underfunded (Lee 2012).

- Labor markets, where equally qualified black candidates are less likely than their white counterparts to obtain interviews and jobs. A study of Muslim women who applied for jobs while wearing headscarves (*hijab*) found that they were less likely to receive callbacks (Ghumman and Ryan 2013).

- The courts and prison system, where drug laws and enforcement heavily penalize the selling and possession of the kinds of drugs, especially narcotics, that young black and Latino men are more likely to use or sell (Alexander 2012).

- The health care system, where blacks and Latinos are likely to receive no treatment at all or are more likely to receive poorer-quality treatment in, for example, emergency rooms rather than in the offices of physicians in private practice (Lara-Millán 2014).

ASK YOURSELF
What type of workplace layoff policy might be less racially and ethnically discriminatory than "last hired, first fired" when minorities lack seniority? Do you think the setting of such policies should be up to employers or mandated by law? Why?

The "Invisibility" of Institutional Racism

Individual acts based on racism are often out in the open and easier for all to see than institutional racism. However, institutional discrimination is far subtler—often even invisible. Individual acts that are reflective of prejudice (shouting a racial epithet) or discrimination (a taxi driver refusing to pick up a black passenger) are easy to discern. However, the mundane operations of a large organization are often difficult to see.

In addition, large numbers of whites benefit from the racism of larger structures by being awarded higher-paying jobs, better working conditions, and power over others, including over blacks and other minorities. These beneficiaries have a deep, if perhaps unacknowledged, interest in seeing institutions continue to operate to their benefit but to the detriment of blacks and other racial minorities.

Because their day-to-day operations are largely invisible, institutions that operate in a racist manner are much less likely to be seen as a problem than individual acts of prejudice or discrimination. This is the case in spite of the fact that institutional racism and discrimination represent a far greater problem for blacks and other minorities than individual discrimination and prejudice do. In addition, the comparative invisibility of institutional racism makes it far more difficult to find ways of combating it.

SOCIAL MOVEMENTS AND RACE

Hate Groups

Most hate groups in the United States are white supremacist movements, with the Ku Klux Klan (KKK) being an archetype. It is best known for its antiblack positions and activities, but the KKK originated as a nativist, anti-Catholic, and anti-Semitic group. KKK activity began at a time of high European immigration from places such as Ireland, Italy, and other non-WASP (white Anglo-Saxon Protestant) nations. These new arrivals were seen as a threat to national identity.

Other well-known racist hate groups include the neo-Nazis and skinheads. In 2016, the Southern Poverty Law Center (SPLC) identified 892 active hate groups in the United States (www.splcenter .org/hate-map). The SPLC has cited a rise in ethnic-based hate crimes following 9/11. It reports that an increasing number of hate crimes are directed toward immigrant populations, thus reflecting continued xenophobia in American society. Activities of hate groups include rallies, speeches, marches, leafleting, publishing, the maintenance of websites, and criminal activities including vandalism, arson, sexual assaults against immigrant women, and other

violence. Figure 8.4 reports the breakdown of hate crimes in 2014 and shows that almost half of them were motivated by race.

Participation in racial hate groups was long considered to be the domain of white men. When white women participated in such movements, they were assumed to have been brought into the movement through husbands and boyfriends. However, sociologist Kathleen Blee (2002), one of the first researchers to study gender in racist hate movements, found that these women have a variety of reasons for joining that do not include the influence of men. She conducted in-depth interviews with 34 women involved in several groups. Some women had joined after experiencing life tragedies that they, rightly or wrongly, blamed on another racial group. Others had moved into social circles that supported and propagated racist views, often attributing a variety of social ills to blacks, Hispanics, and Jews.

FIGURE 8.4 • Breakdown of the 5,922 Single-Bias Hate Crime Incidents Reported in 2014

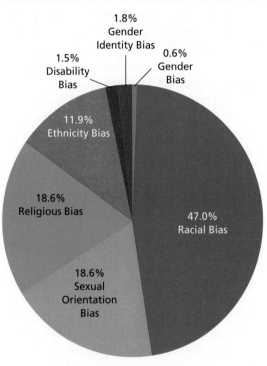

SOURCE: Data from Federal Bureau of Investigation, *Uniform Crime Reports, 2015.* "Latest Hate Crime Statistics Available," November 16.

Blee showed that white women are not just auxiliary members but rather are integrated into positions of power within many of these organizations.

The Civil Rights Movement

While we have focused here on various forms of oppression of blacks and other minority groups, there also has been, and continues to be, resistance to this oppression by blacks and others. One major example is, of course, the modern civil rights movement, which arose in the mid-1950s and 1960s, largely in the South, to deal with black oppression maintained by the Jim Crow system (Morris 1984, 2007). Under Jim Crow laws, instituted after the Civil War and Reconstruction, blacks were denied political and social rights and were exploited economically. (See the Trending box in Chapter 6.)

Blacks and progressive allies had long opposed and fought against this system. However, it was the civil rights movement that brought Jim Crow to an end. It did so by honing a variety of techniques, such as "boycotts, mass marches, mass arrests, sit-ins, freedom rides, attempts to register at all-white schools, lawsuits, and other unruly tactics" (Morris 2007, 510). For their part, racist whites and their representatives often responded with "bombings, billy clubs, high-pressure water hoses, and attack dogs" (Morris 2007, 510). These responses often took place in front of TV news cameras, and the national coverage served to put pressure on the federal government and white public opinion to reform the system.

As a result, between 1955 and 1965, Jim Crow was dismantled. The civil rights movement of that era led to the passage of the Civil Rights Act of 1964 and the Voting Rights Act of 1965, formally striking down legal discrimination in various aspects of public life. While blacks today tend to suffer from many of the same problems they did before the civil rights movement, the problems are now caused more by institutional racism than by the law or racial hatred of individuals.

Collective Identity and "Power" Movements

After the successes of the civil rights movement in the mid-1960s, several social movements arose in the late 1960s and early 1970s that sought to

Bettmann/Getty Images

The civil rights movement eventually brought the Jim Crow era to an end, but racism and discrimination are still with us. Why?

energize racial minorities. Winning legal rights was one thing, but many individuals continued to feel belittled and oppressed. The Black Power movement was the best-known attempt to raise a racial minority out of its sense of inferiority. Its slogan was "Black is beautiful."

The visibility of the Black Power movement contributed to racialization among Hispanics. The Brown Berets saw themselves as analogous to the Black Panthers. The Brown Berets adopted the slogan "Brown Power" (and later "*Viva la raza*," or "Long live the race"). The 1968 East L.A. Chicano Student Walkout was an important historic event. More than 2,700 students walked out of schools to protest institutional racism that included prohibitions against speaking Spanish in class and guidance counseling that pushed Latino students to consider menial labor instead of college. Police beat and arrested some students and arrested some of the teachers who helped students mobilize (Global

Nonviolent Action Database 2011). More recent politicized racial identities among American Latinos include the *indigena* movement, which elevates South American Indian ancestry to a matter of pride.

RACE AND ETHNICITY IN A GLOBAL CONTEXT

Historically, ethnic identities have been closely tied to nation-states. For instance, until the modern era, the population of Ireland embraced almost exclusively the Gaelic language and Irish culture. However, nation-based ethnic identity has declined over time. One major factor in this decline is **diaspora**, or the dispersal, typically involuntary, of a racial or ethnic population from its traditional homeland and over a wide geographic area. In recent years, mass migration in an age of globalization has had a powerful impact on ethnic identities and has reduced their association with given nation-states.

Such population movement has led to the existence of multiple identities on the global stage. This, in turn, has increased the possibility of people having hybrid ethnic identities. That is, an increasing number of people identify not only with, say, the ethnic group into which they were born, but also with other ethnic groups in geographic areas to which they may have migrated. Thus, migrants from India to China may see themselves as both Indian and Chinese.

ETHNIC IDENTITY AND GLOBALIZATION

Some see globalization as a threat to ethnic identity; they see globalization as leading toward a world of homogeneous identities. However, others disagree, citing the following reasons:

- Ethnic identities are not nearly as fragile as is often believed. Ethnicity is inculcated from birth, within the family, and then often in school and by the surrounding culture. Thus, it usually becomes part of a person's core identity.

- Globalization can be a force, maybe the most significant force, in the creation and proliferation of ethnic identity (Tomlinson 2000).

Ethnic groups and many aspects of their culture flow around the globe, creating new pockets of ethnic identity and reinforcing that identity in particular locales. Global pressures toward a homogenized identity may also stiffen a person's resolve to maintain ties to an ethnic culture.

- Ethnic identity and globalization are part of the same modern process. For example, through the development of advanced forms of communication, globalization allows ethnic group members to stay in touch with one another for the express purpose of maintaining familiar traditions. This more powerful sense of ethnic identity can be exported back to the home country through the same global media. This is part of the broader process of transnationalism (Faist, Fauser, and Reisenauer 2013).

ASK YOURSELF

Do you believe that globalization threatens ethnic identity by making the world more homogeneous through information and cultural flows? Or do you feel that ethnicity is a strong enough identity factor to survive globalization, and that global communication flows can help preserve ethnic identities by keeping emigrants in touch with their home countries? Explain your answer.

GLOBAL PREJUDICE AND DISCRIMINATION

To this point, we have focused on majority–minority relations within specific nation-states, especially the United States. But we can also examine majority–minority relations in a global context. The North–South distinction is a key factor. Most of the "bottom billion," or the poorest billion people in the world, are minority group members in the Global South. Few from the bottom billion are in the North. In fact, the richest billion people in the world are largely in the Global North and are mainly members of the majority groups.

It has long been the case that the Global North and its majority groups have dominated, controlled, exploited, and oppressed the Global South and its minority groups. Historically, imperialism, colonialism, economic development, Westernization, and Americanization have worked in large part to Northerners' advantage and to the disadvantage of Southerners. The system that dominates globalization today—neoliberal economics—helps those in the advantaged categories in the Global North and hurts, often badly, those in the disadvantaged categories in the Global South (Harvey 2005).

Majority groups from the Global North have often "invented" minority groups in the Global South. One example is the creation of "Indians" as an oppressed minority group after the British colonized India. Until that point, Indian society had had its own highly developed system of majority and minority castes. Another example derives from **Orientalism**, a set of ideas and texts produced by the Global North that served as the basis of systems designed to dominate, control, and exploit the Orient (the East) and its many minority groups (Said [1979] 1994).

Racism is not exclusive to the West in general, or to the United States in particular, but exists in many societies throughout the world. For example, in Japan, differences in skin color, hair, and even body odor have been used to distinguish among races such as the Ainu and Buraku. Japanese citizens whose ancestry is partly Caucasian or African are also subject to prejudice within their own country. China has 56 officially recognized ethnic groups, totaling about 105 million people; nearly 92 percent (1.2 billion) of all Chinese are in the Han ethnic group. Figure 8.5 shows the geographic distribution of ethnolinguistic groups in China; note the concentration of Han in the heavily populated coastal areas. Uyghurs, a Muslim, Turkic-speaking minority in northwestern China, are discriminated against—job listings specify that applicants must be ethnic Han or be Mandarin Chinese speakers (A. Jacobs 2013). Uyghurs have held many protests against the Chinese government (Holdstock 2014).

GLOBAL FLOWS BASED ON RACE AND ETHNICITY

One way to think about globalized majority–minority relations is in terms of global flows. Both race and ethnicity can be said to flow around the world. One manifestation is the migration of people of various races and ethnic groups, who move around the world today with greater ease and rapidity than ever before. People from the North are more likely to be tourists or

retirees who visit or take up residence in the nations of the South because of the good weather and low cost of living (Croucher 2009). In contrast, residents of the South typically migrate to wealthy nations in the North in search of employment, be it in low-skilled or high-skilled positions (Kivisto and Faist 2010, 49–54).

Another form of global flow involves the social and cultural aspects of race and ethnicity. As we have seen, neither race nor ethnicity is defined by objective characteristics such as "blood," genes, or skin color. Rather, both are defined socially and culturally. As social constructions—as ideas—race and ethnicity flow across borders and around the world effortlessly. A good example is the global spread of anti-Muslim prejudice today. Globalized mass communication helps spread these ideas, but they are also carried by people who are taking advantage of inexpensive means of travel, especially by air.

Paul Gilroy's *The Black Atlantic: Modernity and Double Consciousness* (1993) is an important work on majority–minority relations that stresses global flows. As the title makes clear, Gilroy is particularly interested in the flows that relate to blacks in the Atlantic region (Figure 8.6 shows those flows, as well as another flow of slaves from Africa to Asia): "I have settled on an image of ships across the spaces between Europe, America, Africa and the Caribbean as a central organizing symbol. . . . The image of a ship . . . in motion" (Gilroy 1993, 4). This image encompasses the flow of slaves from Africa to the eastern coast of the Americas and the later return of some blacks to Africa. It also encompasses the circulation of activists, ideas, books, works of art, and the like that relate to blacks and race relations. All are seen as involved in "displacements, migrations, and journeys" (Gilroy 1993, 111). Gilroy argues that in trying to understand global flows based on race, we should focus not on national boundaries but rather on the "Black Atlantic," which he portrays as a transnational space.

Positive and Negative Flows

Those in the Global North are able to create structures that greatly enhance positive or protective flows. For example, in the United States, the 911 phone system quickly summons help, and medical alert systems are available that allow elderly people and others who may not be able to get to a telephone to call for aid by pressing a button. Setting up the complex networks to

FIGURE 8.5 • Chinese Ethnolinguistic Groups

SINO-TIBETAN
- Miao-Yao
- Sinitic
  - Mandarin Chinese (Han)
    1. Eastern
    2. Northern
    3. Southern
  - Southern Chinese (Han)
    1. Gan
    2. Hakka
    3. Min
    4. Wu
    5. Xiang
    6. Yue (Cantonese)
- Tibetan-Burmese
  - Tibetan
    1. Amdo
    2. Kham
    3. Ü-Tsang
  - Yi

ALTAIC
- Korean
- Manchu-Tungus
- Mongolian
- Turkic
  - Kazakh
  - Kyrgyz
  - Uyghur

TAI
- Kam-Tai (Zhuang)

INDO-EUROPEAN
- Iranian
  - Tajik

AUSTRO-ASIATIC
- Mon-Khmer

AUSTRONESIAN
- Taiwan-Austronesian
- Sparsely populated

SOURCE: Courtesy of the University of Texas Libraries, The University of Texas at Austin.

handle these emergencies is expensive. In the Global South, minorities have little or no access to such networks and therefore to the positive flows expedited by them. Those in minority categories are far less likely to participate in the globe's positive flows of money, commodities, food, health care, technologies, and the like. Conversely, those in the majority categories are likely to be in the thick of these positive flows, both as creators and as beneficiaries.

On the other hand, the structures that expedite negative flows are more likely to dump into, and to be found in, areas dominated by minority groups. For example, illegal structures allow the relatively free flow of weapons into and through many poor areas of the world. Much stronger structures are in place to prevent their flow into the wealthier regions of the globe. Another example is the tendency for people in the Global South to live in close proximity to disease vectors, such as malaria-bearing mosquitoes and chickens carrying avian flu. The result is that they are at greater risk of contracting vector-borne diseases. In contrast, majority group members in the Global North are far more likely to live at some distance from, or to be heavily protected from, disease-carrying mosquitoes or live chickens, to say nothing of the vectors for many other diseases.

FIGURE 8.6 • Slave Trade Routes, 1518–1850

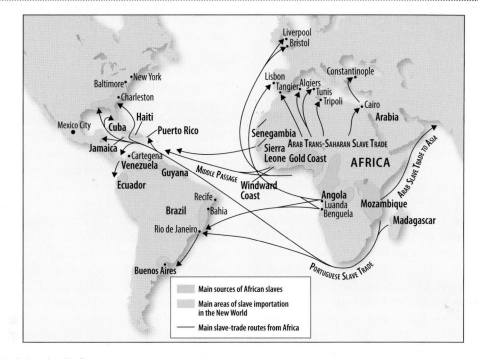

SOURCE: LatinAmericanStudies.org.

Racism itself can be seen as having wide-ranging negative consequences for minority group members as the ideas and practices associated with it flow around the world (Goldberg 2009). This flow of racism around the world has been referred to as the "racialization of the globe" (Dikötter 2008; Treitler 2016). Nevertheless, racist ideas and practices are certainly not the same throughout the world, but rather are adapted and modified in each locale. They are affected by local ideas as well as by local economic, political, and military realities. As a result, racism as it involves blacks is not the same in Great Britain as it is in Ghana or the United States. Racism also changes over time, as reflected today in the flow of anti-Islamic racism through many parts of the world, especially the United States and much of Europe.

ETHNIC CONFLICT WITHIN NATION-STATES

Greater ethnic diversity has increased the possibility of ethnic conflict within many nation-states. Of course, such ethnic conflict is not new. Among the most notable examples in the twentieth and twenty-first centuries have been conflicts between Turks and Armenians in Turkey; between Germans, especially Nazis, and Jews in Germany; between Tamils and the Sinhalese in Sri Lanka; between the Tutsi and Hutu in Burundi and Rwanda; between Arabs and ethnic Africans in Darfur; and between various ethnic groups—Slovenes, Croatians, Serbs, Bosnians, Montenegrins, Macedonians, and Albanians—after the breakup of Yugoslavia in 1991.

The possibility of ethnic conflict within nation-states has reached a whole new level in recent years with the vast migration of various peoples from the Middle East and North Africa to Europe. The sheer number of migrants has challenged many countries and locales. Migrants bring with them cultures, religions, and practices that are greatly at variance from those that exist in their destinations. These migrants compete with local populations for jobs, creating further tension. As a result, there has been a tendency to ghettoize these migrants, thereby increasing polarization between groups and creating greater alienation among both migrants and nationals (Fisher 2016).

The most disturbing examples of ethnic conflict tend to involve the majority group's efforts to "deal" with ethnic minorities through expulsion, ethnic cleansing, or genocide.

Expulsion

Expulsion, or the removal of a group from a territory, may seem relatively benign because minorities are not purposely injured or killed in the majority's efforts to get rid of them. Expulsion can take two forms: direct or voluntary (Costalli 2016; Simpson and Yinger 1985). In *direct expulsion*, minority ethnic groups are ejected by the majority through military and other government action. In *voluntary expulsion*, a minority group leaves "of its own volition" because its members are being harassed, discriminated against, and persecuted. Of course, in the real world, these two forms of expulsion occur in concert with one another. And although physical harm may be relatively light, social and economic harm can be considerable. The people who are forced to leave typically lose much of their property, and their social networks are often irretrievably broken.

Many of the racial and ethnic groups involved in diasporas have experienced both forms of expulsion. This has been particularly true for Jews and the Roma, who have often been forcibly ejected (e.g., Jews from Jerusalem by the Romans in the second century and from Spain and Portugal in the fifteenth century) or have moved voluntarily (e.g., some Jews left the Stalinist Soviet Union because of harassment).

Ethnic Cleansing

Ethnic cleansing is the establishment by the dominant group of policies that allow or require the forcible removal, abuse, and even murder of people of another ethnic group (Oberschall 2012; Sekulic 2016). Nazi actions against Jews and the Roma fit the definition of ethnic cleansing.

Ethnic cleansing achieved more recent notoriety during the wars associated with the dissolution of Yugoslavia in 1991. The ethnic groups that dominated various regions sought to create areas that were ethnically homogeneous, and they did this by expelling and even killing members of other ethnic groups. For example, Croatians were expelled from parts of Croatia inhabited by Serbs. Bosnia, which declared independence in 1992, was composed of three major ethnic groups—Slavic Muslims (the largest single group), Serbs, and Croats. Serbian armed forces created ethnically homogeneous enclaves by forcibly removing and murdering members of the other ethnic groups, especially Muslims.

In situations of ethnic cleansing, women and girls often have been targeted for physical violence and murder, as well as, in many cases, sexual violence. In Bosnia in the 1990s, Serbian men systematically raped an estimated 50,000 Muslim and Croatian women as part of their campaign of terror. Because the Serbian police were in positions of power, it was difficult, if not impossible, for the women who were victims of rape to get help or to prosecute their attackers. As of 2010, only 12 of as many as 50,000 cases had been prosecuted (Cerkez 2010).

Mass rape as a weapon of war has also occurred in the region of Darfur within Sudan, with the government-supported Janjaweed militiamen raping Darfuri women and girls held in refugee camps. In 2008, Sudan's president, Omar Hassan Ahmed Bashir, was accused

U.S. citizens of Japanese descent were forced into internment camps during World War II in actions that were upheld by the Supreme Court but are now seen as discriminatory. Contrast these camps with steps the government is taking today to try to ensure national security.

(and later indicted) by the prosecutor of the International Criminal Court (ICC) of the Hague of not only mass genocide but also propagating rape as a weapon of war and terror (Scheffer 2008). Bashir has yet to be tried by the ICC, but the accusations and the indictment did not prevent him from being reelected president of Sudan in 2015 with 94 percent of the vote (Kushkush 2015). Sudanese armed forces have continued to carry out mass rapes (and killings) in Darfur to this day (Gladstone 2015).

Genocide

The most extreme cases of ethnic conflict involve an active, systematic attempt at eliminating an entire group of people, or genocide. *Genocide* was defined in 1948 by the United Nations Convention on the Prevention and Punishment of the Crime of Genocide as "acts committed with the intent to destroy, in whole or in part, a national, ethnic, racial, or religious group" (cited in Karstedt 2007, 1909–1910). It is seen as the crime of the twentieth century, and it shows every sign of continuing to define the twenty-first century.

Figure 8.7 shows select genocides of the twentieth and twenty-first centuries. The earliest genocide depicted here dates back to 1914, but there were many other instances of genocide long before that. The 1948 UN convention on genocide was prompted by the Nazi Holocaust. At first, the Holocaust occurred within the confines of Germany, but it later spread to the European countries allied with, or conquered by, Germany. It was in that sense transnational, and it would have undoubtedly become far more of a global phenomenon had the Nazis achieved their goal of world conquest. For example, had the Nazis succeeded in conquering the United States, we would undoubtedly have seen the genocide of American Jews.

In the main, however, genocide continues to be practiced within nation-states. Examples include the murder of nearly 2 million people by the Khmer Rouge in Cambodia in the mid- to late 1970s, the killing in 1974 of as many as 1 million people (mostly minority Tutsis) by the majority Hutus in Rwanda, the murder of tens of thousands of Bosnians and Croats in the 1990s by Bosnian Serbs, and the killing of hundreds of thousands of ethnic Africans in Sudan since 2003 by ethnic Arabs.

The global age has brought with it the globalization of genocide, as instances of it have flowed

FIGURE 8.7 • Select Genocides around the World, 1914–Present

SOURCE: Adapted from Online Resources from The Choices Program, Brown University.

around the world (Karstedt 2016). That is, genocide has become another negative flow making its way from one part of the world to another. Genocide may become more likely in the future because of proliferating and accelerating global flows of ideas, agitators, and arms. Added to this is the increased inability of nation-states to block many of these flows.

SUMMARY

Race has historically been defined on the basis of a shared lineage and some real or presumed biological characteristic. In the second half of the twentieth century, race began to be defined more as a cultural phenomenon, making it a more fluid than fixed type of identity. Ethnic groups are typically defined on the basis of some real or presumed cultural characteristic, such as language, religion, traditions, or cultural practices.

Race and ethnicity have always served as a way of stratifying individuals into groups with more or less power. The majority group, even if it has fewer members, has the power to act on its prejudices and discriminate against members of minority groups. Intersectionality, or belonging to more than one type of minority (for example, being black and female), often compounds disparities.

Majority–minority relations devolve into racism when the majority defines a group as a race and attributes negative characteristics to that group. It is the combination of xenophobia and ethnocentrism that makes racism so powerful. Current racism is also a matter of hegemony, or the majority group foisting its culture on minority groups and the persistence of institutional racism.

Putting majority–minority relations in a global context, the North has more majority group members and dominates and oppresses those in the South. Majority groups are better positioned than minority groups to create structures that enhance positive or protective global flows. Greater ethnic diversity within nation-states has opened up more possibilities for internal ethnic conflicts. At the extreme, ethnic conflict leads to expulsion, ethnic cleansing, and genocide of minorities by the majority within a territory.

KEY TERMS

diaspora, 220
discrimination, 210
ethnic cleansing, 224
ethnic group, 204
ethnicity, 204
expulsion, 224

genocide, 213
hegemony, 217
hypodescent rule, 206
institutional
    racism, 217
majority group, 210

majority-minority
    population, 209
minority group, 210
Orientalism, 221
pluralism, 213
prejudice, 210

race, 204
racism, 204
segregation, 214
stereotype, 210
white racial frame, 216
xenophobia, 214

REVIEW QUESTIONS

1. What is the difference between race and ethnicity? What are the similarities? How have biological and cultural explanations helped create racial and ethnic differences?
2. Barack Obama is the child of a white mother and a black African father, but more often than not he is referred to as black. What does this suggest about the nature of race in the United States? What are the consequences of this perception?
3. What criteria do sociologists use to define a majority group? How do majority groups maintain their positions of privilege?

4. What is the difference between prejudice and discrimination? Explain the interaction between stereotypes, prejudice, and discrimination.
5. What is intersectionality? Provide an example of how intersectionality oppresses a member of a minority group.
6. What are some mechanisms that minorities have used to resist racism?
7. What is institutional racism, and what are some examples of institutional racism? In what ways is institutional racism more problematic than individual racism?
8. How would you characterize majority–minority relations on a global level? What sorts of advantages do majority groups have on the global level?
9. Why has greater ethnic diversity within nation-states increased the possibility of ethnic conflict? How do you think we can prevent future ethnic conflicts?
10. In what ways can ethnic groups use digital technologies and social media to retain their ethnic identity?

GENDER AND SEXUALITY

Challenging Gender Stereotypes

In a *favela* (slum) in Rio de Janeiro, Brazil, a thoughtful, handsome man named Marcio talks about his life. "My dream was to be a father," he says, standing with his son and wife. Sending a kite into the gray sky, he continues, "For some people, maybe it's a career, for others maybe to travel somewhere, but my dream was always to be a father. And to give my son something I never had." Marcio explains that his childhood was marked by constant violence; his father beat his mother, and the community stood by and accepted it. "He had to show he was a man," he says of his father. Marcio learned from his father that manhood meant having many women, drinking, partying, and staying out all night.

As he cries at the memory of his father's absence and lack of attention, Marcio explains how he managed to avoid becoming like his father by founding a group of men who had had similar experiences. As they met, talked, and cried together, Marcio saw how traditional cultural gender stereotypes of masculinity and femininity had been harmful. He came to be willing to challenge his culture's sex and gender norms in order to create a better life for himself, his wife, and his son. With the help of a global organization

LEARNING OBJECTIVES

9.1 Understand gender identities and inequalities.

9.2 Describe how social forces influence sexuality.

9.3 Explain the effects of globalization on gender and sexualities.

9.4 Examine global flows related to gender.

edge.sagepub.com/
ritzeressentials3e

- Take the chapter quiz
- Review key terms with eFlashcards
- Explore multimedia links and SAGE readings

$SAGE edge™

Phil Clarke Hill/Corbis Historical/Getty Images

called Promundo, he now works with other men to support their efforts to challenge traditional gender expectations. As Marcio puts it, "The rain doesn't come all at once; it comes a drop at a time. And then it becomes a strong river." Change in the lives of a few can lead to change in the lives of many and, indeed, even in an entire nation or culture.

Beliefs and attitudes about gender and sexuality differ across countries as well as over time. Globalization, technological advancements in communication, and growing awareness of the consequences of gender inequalities are among the factors changing what we think about gender and sexuality. As the founders of Promundo listened to accounts of men committing violence against women and children around the world, they saw an opportunity and a need for reform. Promundo now works with local community stakeholders and agencies such as the World Health Organization in 22 countries, helping men and boys change themselves and their communities. For the people involved in Brazil—and elsewhere—the ongoing struggle between tradition and freedom is exhilarating and terrifying, joyful and heart-wrenching. For sociologists, it's a testament to the intricate beauty of a living, breathing culture that is always changing. ●

*S*ex and *gender* are terms that are often used interchangeably and confused with one another. However, it is important that they be distinguished clearly. **Sex** is principally a biological term, usually expressed as *female* or *male*. Sex is typically reflected in a person's chromosomes, gonads, genitalia, and hormones. **Gender** is a cultural term, connected to societal definitions of expected behaviors, attitudes, and personalities, and is usually reflected in terms like *woman* or *man, girl* or *boy*. Gender consists of the physical, behavioral,

---

NOTE: The author thanks Rebecca Plante for her help in revising this chapter.

and personality characteristics that are defined as appropriate for one's sex. The key difference is that sex is based mainly on biology, whereas gender is based on social distinctions. Western conceptualizations of gender assume that there are strong, clear gender differences based on sex. Westerners often assume that genitalia are "not only the primary marker of gender identity, but indeed, the underlying *cause* of that identity" (Helliwell 2000, 797; emphasis added). But bodies and biology are socially constructed as the basis for gender. "Gender builds on biological sex, but it exaggerates biological difference, and it carries biological difference into domains in which it is completely irrelevant" (Eckert and McConnell-Ginet 2013, 2). There is nothing in human biology to explain why, for example, we think that only women should wear high heels, or men should not paint their nails.

ASK YOURSELF

Why is gender so important in many cultures? Do you think we could make gender less important in the United States? Should we make gender less important? What would need to happen in order to minimize the importance of gender in our interactions with others?

GENDER AND SEX

Gender and sex are examples of a master status, or a position that is more important than any others, both for the person in the position and for all others involved. Master statuses dominate all other statuses, including achieved (such as education) and ascribed (such as age), and are therefore of great consequence (see Chapter 4).

Biological sex has long been linked with gender as a social construct, but the two are not as neatly entwined as we have been taught. Furthermore, sex and gender, especially gender, are *not* simply natural, biological processes. They are both—again, especially gender—strongly affected by social and cultural forces.

Although we tend to think in terms of only two biological sexes, in fact, there is a continuum of sex (Fausto-Sterling 1999). **Intersex** is a "general term used for a variety of [medical] conditions in which a person is born with a reproductive or sexual anatomy that doesn't seem to fit the typical definitions of female or male" (Intersex Society of North America 2008). Only a few intersex conditions represent "true medical emergencies," in that the genitalia are a sign of an underlying metabolic medical issue needing immediate treatment. The majority of intersex conditions do not require hasty or immediate medical interventions. Until quite recently, intersexed people were stigmatized with the label *hermaphrodite,* and doctors often surgically altered infants' and children's genitalia to attempt to match more typical male or female anatomy (Coventry 2006). Thanks to intersex advocacy and increased awareness among medical personnel, today intersexed people who may have been subject to surgery in the past have much more choice about whether, and how, to proceed (Zeiler and Wickstrom 2009).

These Lebanese men walked a mile in women's shoes during a 2015 event calling for an end to violence against women. Men have routinely worn high-heeled shoes in the past—for instance, during the time of King Louis XIV (1638–1715) of France. Why don't they do so now?

Most aspects of maleness and femaleness are on a continuum as well. For example, both males and females have the hormones estrogen and testosterone. However, the amounts vary greatly from individual to individual within and between sexes, as well as over time (Liaw and Janssen 2014). Both sexes also have breasts, so although breast cancer is largely a female disease, some males develop it. Facial hair is usually thought of as a male characteristic, but some females grow enough facial hair to need to shave regularly. Biologically, the differences between males and females are few, but much of U.S. culture is based on assumptions about sex (and gender) differences. Unfortunately, we rarely encounter "separate but equal" social structures based on notions of such differences. Instead, beliefs about difference are often translated into constructions of superiority and inferiority.

FEMININITIES AND MASCULINITIES

The terms *femininities* and *masculinities* refer to the cultural definitions of the traits associated with being a "woman" or a "man" acquired during the socialization process (Laurie et al. 1999; Lind 2007). They are plural because there are many forms of both, connected to other characteristics such as race, ethnicity, age, nationality, and social class (see Chapter 8 for a discussion of intersectionality). Cultural interpretations of femininities and masculinities are subject to change, depending on place and historical era. There is a tendency to develop stereotypes about what it means to be a woman and to be feminine (mother, nurturant, emotional) and to be a man and masculine (father, tough, unemotional). However, in reality, these stereotypes are not natural or biological; rather, they are socially constructed. As Simone de Beauvoir famously put it, "One is not born, but rather becomes, a woman" ([1952] 1973, 301). The same is true, of course, for a man. Yet the distinction between masculine and feminine persists.

Sociologist Raewynn (née Robert W.) Connell (1944–; 1987, 1997, 2009; Gough, forthcoming) coined the terms *hegemonic masculinity* and *emphasized femininity* and analyzed the roles that these ideas have played in global gender inequalities. *Hegemonic* means dominant. Therefore, **hegemonic masculinity** refers to the dominant form or most idealized vision of masculinity. We take this form for granted as "natural." It is linked to patriarchy, a form of society that is dominated by men and focused on men and hegemonic masculinity (Johnson 2005). Hegemonic masculinity is the vision of masculinity that underlies patriarchal systems. **Emphasized femininity** is a set of socially constructed ideas about "model womanhood." These ideas are organized around accommodating the interests of men and patriarchy. Emphasized femininity focuses on social ability rather than intellect, ego stroking, and acceptance of the roles of mother and wife (Spade and Valentine 2011). It represents a subordinate heterosexual femininity. Specific manifestations of femininity and masculinity are measured against these dominant forms.

Hegemonic masculinity and emphasized femininity adversely affect both men and women. Men who do not live up to the stereotype of hegemonic masculinity, including gay and working-class men, as well as men of color, are negatively affected. Generally, the rigid expectations of hegemonic masculinity mean that many men, even heterosexual, white, middle-class men, will be viewed, and will view themselves, as falling short of the ideal. Many women are adversely affected because they do not and cannot live up to the ideals associated with emphasized femininity (Butler 1990).

While some men benefit greatly from hegemonic masculinity, their advantages have, at least until recently, been largely invisible to them. Not having to think about masculinity, or what it means to "be a man," has been one of the dividends (or privileges) of gender inequality. In contrast, women often think a great deal about the disadvantages of masculinity and gender stereotypes, because they are oppressed by the system of gender inequalities in many different ways.

Masculinities and femininities can be detached from biological sex, the body, and gender. Men can act in socially defined "feminine" ways by nurturing others, and women can behave in a socially defined "masculine" manner by competing aggressively. As is true of the continuum of male and female sexes, we should not think in simple, either/or terms about gender. There is a continuum of masculinities *and* femininities, resulting in part from the variety of socialization patterns that we experience over the life course. People adapt throughout their lives, emphasizing different aspects of gender and interpreting the gender role expectations constructed by society. We merge gendered expectations with those of other intersectional statuses, including race, class, and sexual orientation. Gender performance is fluid, not static, and allows room for individuals to make some choices about how to perform gender within socially defined roles (Fields, Copp, and Kleinman 2007; Goldschmied and Kowalczyk 2016).

Photographed by Dianne Reggett; used with permission by Raewyn Connell

Raewynn (née Robert William) Connell has made important contributions to the study of social stratification and the study of gender, including the idea that gender is a large-scale social structure, not just a matter of personal identity. She frequently uses biographical interviewing in her research and was one of the first people to study the social construction of masculinity.

ASK YOURSELF

What did Simone de Beauvoir mean by saying, "One is not born, but rather becomes, a woman"? Do you agree with her view? Why or why not? Do you think she would say the same thing today?

TRANSGENDER AND NONBINARY GENDERS

As is the case with sex, we often think of gender in binary terms. We think of a *gender binary* involving only two genders, man and woman. But just as sex, most notably in the case of the intersexed, is not a simple binary, gender has multiple aspects, forms, and expressions; it is not a simple, neat binary. It is socially constructed and variable across cultures, times, and places. Individuals who might identify themselves as one of the two dominant genders— namely, as a man or a woman—enact a wide range

Gender-Swapping in Online Games

Virtual reality allows individuals a variety of opportunities to experiment with their identities, including their gender. **Gender-swapping,** or gender-switching, occurs when an individual represents him or herself online as a gender that is different from his or her offline gender. Gender-swapping is particularly evident in massive multiplayer online role-playing games, such as World of Warcraft and Second Life, which require players to create avatars to play the games (Hussain and Griffiths 2008; Martey et al. 2014). An avatar "marks" a player's identity and offers a "visual representation of the player" (Song and Jung 2015, 435). Players are free to construct their visual representations by selecting skin, hair, and eye color, hairstyle, body type, clothing, and accessories such as glasses for their avatars. While some players choose to create avatars that closely mimic their offline appearances, others opt to create fantasy avatars—for fun and aesthetic or strategic purposes. For example, some male players create female avatars because "they prefer the esthetic of watching the female avatar form," particularly from behind, which is where most role-playing games visually position the gaze of their players (Martey et al. 2014, 289). Other male players explain that they create female avatars because other players treat them better and more readily give them gifts or hints that they need to advance to subsequent game levels (Hussain

Participants in online gaming may choose an avatar that bears no physical resemblance to their actual appearance or even one of the opposite gender.

and Griffiths 2008; Song and Jung 2015). Thus, gender-swapping may be less an expression of one's identity than a "rational choice based on practical benefits" (Song and Jung 2015, 435).

Even if gender-swapping is not necessarily an extension of an individual's offline identity, studies have found that players who engage in this practice find themselves adopting the gendered behaviors of their avatars during online play. Song and Jung (2015, 444) discovered that gender-swapping males acted more feminine and displayed "socially amiable behaviors" when playing as female avatars. Martey et al. (2014, 295) found that they adopted female linguistic behaviors, such as using more emotional phrases, than men who did not gender-swap. Other research has revealed that the avatars of

females who gender-swap tend to display more aggressive, achievement-oriented behaviors (Song and Jung 2015, 238). Interestingly, gender-swapping appears to be reinforcing heteronormativity and traditional gender stereotypes instead of encouraging gender diversity.

Engaging the Digital World

Create a virtual avatar "superhero" that is different from your offline gender at http://marvel.com/games/play/31/create_your_own_superhero. Describe the appearance of this avatar (eyes, hair, body type, accessories) and how it conforms (or not) to traditional gender stereotypes. Explain how the options available to you on this website constrained or enabled you to adhere to or deviate from traditional gender stereotypes.

of gender portrayals, roles, and identities, including being transgender.

Most basically, **transgender** is an umbrella term for people whose gender identity and/or gender presentation differs from the gender assigned to them at birth or in infancy. **Gender identity** is a person's internal sense of gender (Wood and Eagly 2015). Trans individuals may have **gender roles**—the social presentation of gender that includes clothing, hairstyle, and attitudinal and behavioral traits—that differ from or correspond with their gender identities.

Trans individuals do not follow a single path. They may or may not locate themselves somewhere in the broad matrix of gender. They may or may not identify with either of the two culturally dominant genders. They may or may not wish to use hormones or obtain surgeries to change aspects of their physical sex. Trans individuals may choose identities and/or create self-applied labels—such as *genderqueer, agender,* or *gender fluid*—that do not fit neatly within the gender binary. People who are *agender* may not identify with any gender, while those who are *gender fluid* may feel that their identities change depending on the context. *Genderqueer* is a broad umbrella term that encompasses a range of gendered identities, feelings, and self-determined labels.

The official number of Americans who identify as transgender is 1.4 million, which is double previous estimates based on a smaller federal database (Hoffman 2016). Although only about 8 percent of U.S. adults say they personally know someone who is trans, general awareness of trans people has increased in recent years (Pew Research Center 2013). Not long ago, *Time* magazine ran a cover story, "The Transgender Tipping Point," featuring actor Laverne Cox, a "proud African-American transgender woman" (K. Steinmetz 2014). Kye Allums is a "queer fluid trans artist and athlete" who played Division I college basketball and was the first NCAA player to come out as trans (see http://time.com/3537849/meet-the-first-openly-trans-genderncaa-athlete). Cox and Allums do advocacy work and education across the United States; Cox has appeared in many venues, working tirelessly on behalf of trans people, especially trans youth. *Dancing with the Stars* featured Chaz Bono, a trans man whose parents are entertainers Sonny and Cher, and in 2015, Olympic gold medalist Bruce Jenner—now Caitlyn Jenner—came out as transgender.

Trans history and context runs deeper than is suggested by a few years of increased public visibility. Sylvia Rivera (1951–2002), a "drag queen [and] bisexual transgender activist," was a "loud and persistent voice for the rights of people of color and low-income queers and trans people" (Sylvia Rivera Law Project 2015). She was among those who clashed with police in the 1969 New York Stonewall bar riot, in which gay, queer, and trans people resisted police harassment. That riot is often seen as the start of the modern U.S. lesbian, gay, bisexual, and trans rights movement (see Chapter 15). The Transgender Day of Remembrance (TDOR) began in 1999, when trans woman of color Rita Hester was the victim of a hate murder. Between January 2008 and December 2015, 2,016 trans people were murdered around the world; most of these crimes occurred in Central and South America (Trans Murder Monitoring Project 2016). Life is particularly hellish for trans individuals who find themselves in prison, where rape is an ever-present danger (Sontag 2015). Trans women of color in the United States—and elsewhere—are disproportionately targeted and beaten, abused, or murdered (National Coalition of Anti-Violence Programs 2014). Violence is only one of many issues trans people face in a society that remains largely inflexible about gender diversities. However, one exception to this is the official policy of the U.S. military, which was changed in mid-2016 to allow transgender Americans to serve openly (Rosenberg 2016).

ASK YOURSELF

What might explain hate-based violence against trans people? Do you think there is a connection between this violence and the recent increase in the visibility of trans people? Why or why not?

GENDER DIVERSITY

Globally, there are many cultures with various nonbinary genders. Some North American Native and First Nations tribes include roles for *two-spirit* individuals. They are socially defined as truly distinct, neither man nor woman nor a combination of the two, and are respected in their tribes (Roscoe 1998). Another kind of gender diversity can be found in some mountain villages in Afghanistan (Nordberg 2014), where a rigidly constructed culture dictates that sons are necessary for families hoping for prestige (Arbabzadah 2011). In order to gain such prestige, some families without male children present young girls as boys (called *bacha posh*), with the clothing, haircuts, and behavioral shifts common to boys. At puberty, they are "changed" into girls. In southern Oaxaca State in Mexico, there is a group of people—"muxes"—who do not identify as male or female, although they were born with male bodies. There is a long tradition of a mixed-gender way of life in Mexico. Muxes have been widely accepted and their "embroidery, hairstyling, handicrafts and cooking" are greatly admired (Burnett 2016, A4). Nevertheless, in recent years, protests have arisen about muxes' use of women's restrooms.

LGBTQ advocate Laverne Cox, a star of the Netflix series *Orange Is the New Black*, is the first openly transgender actor to be nominated for a Primetime Emmy Award. She has been named one of *People* magazine's most beautiful women of the year and one of *Time*'s 100 most influential people.

GENDERED INEQUALITIES

As a master status and a primary basis for the persistence of structural, institutional inequalities, gender is a key variable in understanding life chances in the United States. Gender is structured into all our social institutions or systems—education, families, the economy, the law, and so on. Social institutions are powerful established sociocultural pathways that exist to meet our collective needs (Acker 1992). In the United States, we socialize people into the binary gender system through our social institutions and then channel them into differently valued activities, attributes, and pursuits. Gender inequality is not just a problem in the United States; it is also a global problem (see the discussion of global stratification in Chapter 7). The World Economic Forum (2016) measures gender inequality in terms of gender gaps in health care, education, economy, and politics. Statistics on men's and women's salaries, participation in paid labor, access to education, representation in political bodies, and life expectancy contribute to the score. No country in the world has a score of one; no country has full equality between men and women. Scores closer to one indicate that a country has a relatively narrow gap between men and women—that women are doing nearly as well as men. As you can see in Figure 9.1, Iceland is the most equal country in the world in terms of gender, with a score of 0.881, while Yemen is the least, with a score of 0.484. The United States, with a score of 0.74, ranks 28th.

There are global differences in the way societies deal with gender differences and inequalities. Change.org petitioners in the United Kingdom and Ireland seek to send a message to toy retailers: Stop labeling some toys for boys (construction sets, cars, and the like) and others for girls (princess outfits, play kitchens). Some Swedes strongly support the idea that traditional gender norms enhance inequalities. They argue for gender-neutral pronouns as a way of promoting equality. Swedish preschools and elementary schools have begun to use the gender-neutral pronoun *hen* (Braw 2014).

GENDER AND EDUCATION

Educational systems constitute an important site and source of gender inequality throughout American society and across the globe. Historically, families invested relatively little in the education of girls because they were expected to grow up to stay at home as wives and mothers. Thus, there has long been a gender gap in education in many countries, including the United States.

FIGURE 9.1 • Global Gender Gap Index, 2015

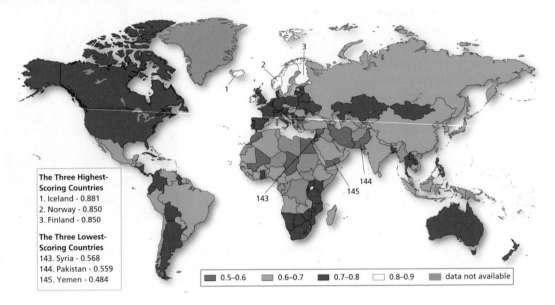

The Three Highest-Scoring Countries
1. Iceland - 0.881
2. Norway - 0.850
3. Finland - 0.850

The Three Lowest-Scoring Countries
143. Syria - 0.568
144. Pakistan - 0.559
145. Yemen - 0.484

0.5–0.6   0.6–0.7   0.7–0.8   0.8–0.9   data not available

SOURCE: Data from World Economic Forum, *The Global Gender Gap Report 2015* (Geneva: World Economic Forum, 2016).

Clearly the formal educational system, especially at the primary and secondary levels, has been a major cause of that gap, and it continues to pose some persistent problems for women. One aspect of that system, and a root cause of the gender gap in education, is often the **hidden curriculum**, or a school's unofficial norms, routines, and structures that transmit dominant cultural norms and values (De Lissovoy and García 2013; Giroux and Purpel 1983). Schools reproduce unquestioned social norms such as obedience to authority, hard work, and the value of hierarchy. Because boys are socialized from infancy to enact these preferred values, they are likely to get more attention in class from teachers, to be asked more questions, to get more constructive criticism, and, at least in the early years of school, to monopolize class discussions (Sadker and Sadker 1994; Sharp 2012).

There is a deeply hidden curriculum regarding gender conformity and norms (Surtees 2008). Analyses of elementary teacher training materials and in-depth studies of elementary school classrooms suggest that most teachers are not well trained to deal with gender (or sexuality) issues at school. A small, exploratory study found that elementary school teachers were afraid of the prospect of having a transgender student (Payne and Smith 2014). A lack of formal training, education, and institutional support, combined with individual-level discomfort, creates this fear. Institutional policies against discussing sexuality, and the mistaken perception that gender identity is linked to sexuality, hamper teachers' ability to deal with transgender students.

ASK YOURSELF

Think back to your elementary and high school years. Did the schools you attended have a hidden curriculum? You may have been unaware of it at the time, but can you now identify any specific examples of the way in which it manifested itself?

Increasing awareness of the gender gap in education has led to significant efforts to overcome it and subsequently to great educational gains for women (Dorius and Firebaugh 2010). Nevertheless, a gender gap in education persists. In spite of this continuing gender gap, some girls, especially those who are white, experience success in primary and secondary schooling due, in part, to gendered socialization. They are more engaged in school and more likely to comply with school rules, such as doing homework and responding to teacher requests (Buchmann and DiPrete 2006). Such "non-cognitive" skills are strong predictors of academic success. They partly explain why girls outperform boys on most academic indicators.

Another explanation for girls' success in primary and secondary school is structural, related to long-term job success. Many occupations continue to be segregated by sex. The most consistently male-segregated occupations (e.g., truck driver, auto mechanic, firefighter) do not require postsecondary schooling, whereas several of the most consistently female-segregated occupations (e.g., preschool teacher, registered nurse, dental hygienist) do require schooling beyond high school. Young women therefore must maintain some success in high school in order to get into the college programs needed for future job training. This occupational segregation is increasingly responsible for women's advantages in educational attainment (Jacobs 1996).

Changing societal attitudes about gender roles and declining sexism have had dramatic effects on women's educational attainment as they advance through the educational system. Women are significantly more likely than men to graduate from high school and to attend either a two- or four-year college (Carbonaro and Covay 2010). In 1960, women represented less than 40 percent of college undergraduates in the United States; today, roughly 56 percent of students at both two- and four-year colleges are women (Goldin, Katz, and Kuziemko 2006). Women are more likely than men to receive bachelor's or master's degrees (Bauman and Ryan 2015). Figure 9.2 depicts the dramatic gap between men and women enrolled as undergraduates in the United States, which is expected to remain large. By 2025, women are projected to be almost 57 percent of undergraduates, while men will be 43 percent. We can also see this trend in the dramatic increases in law and medical degrees earned by women. However, men continue to be more likely to be trained in the most prestigious colleges and universities and to obtain doctoral degrees. In part this is because elite institutions have traditionally highly valued SAT scores, and men continue to perform better on the SAT (Bielby et al. 2014).

FIGURE 9.2 • Gender Differences in Undergraduate Enrollment in the United States, 1970–2025 (projected)

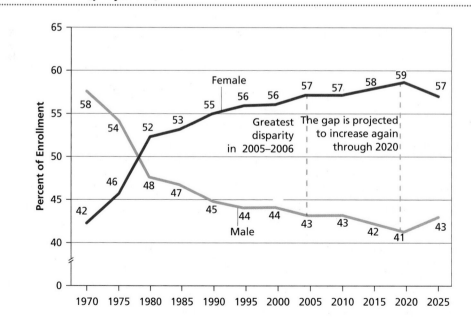

SOURCE: National Center for Education Statistics. "The Condition of Education 2016."

Even with women's gains in higher education, a significant pay gap exists between men and women once they leave school and begin their careers (Brown and Patten 2017). While women are in college, they are more likely to major in sex/gender-segregated academic fields, such as education, English, and psychology, which tend to lead to jobs that do not pay as well as jobs dominated by men. While there are differences among the fields, women continue to be less likely to major in science, technology, engineering, and math (STEM fields) in college. Majoring in these fields tends to lead to higher-paying jobs. Figure 9.3 shows that women now earn a majority of degrees in biology, and they have shown strong gains in the physical sciences and mathematics/statistics. However, they continue to be less likely than men to earn degrees in STEM fields. Worse, women lag far behind men in bachelor's degrees in computer science and information sciences, as well as in engineering. Part of the reason for this underrepresentation is the fact that women continue to be likely to be stereotyped as being less capable scientifically and technically.

GENDER, FAMILY, AND WORK

The relationship between gender and work is one of the most studied issues in the field of gender (Mills 2015). A primary concern has been documenting the intersections of gender, work, and family. As you can see in Figure 9.4, heterosexual families with men and women in the paid labor force earn more than all other family types. Even when their wives are not in the paid labor force, married men earn more than unmarried men (Ahituv and Lerman 2007; Ashwin and Isupova 2014). However, unmarried women's household income is far below that of all men and of married women. Many of these inequities are based on historical, traditional gender roles in families.

Separate Spheres

Industrialization brought about the separation of the public and private spheres. Men tended to become the breadwinners, venturing forth into the public world of work; women were less likely to work outside the home and were apt to be relegated to the private sphere (Kerber 1988).

FIGURE 9.3 • Percentage of Bachelor's Degrees Awarded to Women in Select STEM Majors in Postsecondary Institutions in the United States, 1949–2014

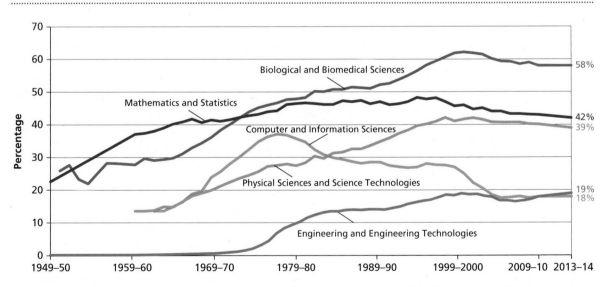

SOURCES: Data from U.S. Department of Education, National Center for Education Statistics, Higher Education General Information Survey (HEGIS), "Snapshot Report—Degree Attainment," January 26, 2015 (http://nscresearchcenter.org/snapshotreport-degreeattainment15/) and "Degrees and Other Formal Awards Conferred" surveys, 1970–71 through 1985–86; Integrated Postsecondary Education Data System (IPEDS), "Completions Survey" (IPEDS-C:87-99); and IPEDS fall 2000 through fall 2012, completions component.

FIGURE 9.4 • Median Income of Families in the United States, by Family Type, 1950–2015

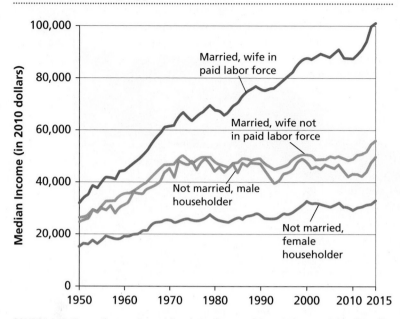

SOURCE: U.S. Census Bureau, Current Population Surveys, Selected Characteristics of Families by Total Money Income.

The once clear-cut, gender-based differentiation between the public and private spheres in the United States has been breaking down since the mid-twentieth century. Now women are more likely not only to be in the work world but also, increasingly, to be the principal—or even the only—wage earner in the family (England 2010). The family characterized by a division between male/breadwinner and female/homemaker has increasingly given way to more blended roles, and even to role reversals, especially in dual-earner families (McClelland, Mok, and Pierce 2014). Figure 9.5 shows the steadily increasing percentage of mothers who earn most of the family income (breadwinners), along with those who are co-breadwinners.

Dual-Earner Households and the Stalled Revolution

A key issue in the study of gender, work, and family is the difference between heterosexual men and women in the ways they use their time in the era of dual-earner families. Arlie Hochschild (1989, 2012) argues that in U.S. dual-earner families with children, wives who work outside the home tend to be saddled with additional labor—the traditionally gendered tasks of child care and housework—when they get home from their paid work. Such women can be said to be working a "second shift." Figure 9.6 presents 2015 data on gender differences in performing three household tasks: cleaning the house, preparing and cleaning up after meals, and caring for and helping children. On an average day, 70 percent of women did meal preparation or cleanup, while only 43 percent of men performed these tasks. More extremely, 50 percent of women cleaned the house on an average day, while only 22 percent of men did such work. In terms of caring for and helping household children, 26 percent of women perform these tasks, compared to only 16 percent of men.

While the second shift continues to exist for women, they are now spending more time at work and less at home. Thus, they have less time for, and are less involved in, the second shift. Between 1965 and 2015, the amount of time American women spent per week on housework decreased, on average, from 32 to 16 hours (Liss 2014). Men are spending less time at work and more time at home, participating more in the tasks associated with the second shift. Between 1965 and 2015, their average weekly time devoted to housework increased from 4 to 10 hours.

ASK YOURSELF

Did your mother or grandmother work a "second shift"? How many women who you know are doing so now? Do you know any men who could be said to be working a "second shift" to the same degree as women?

FIGURE 9.5 • Share of Mothers Who Are Breadwinners or Co-Breadwinners in the United States, 1967–2012

SOURCE: Sarah Jane Glynn, "Breadwinning Mothers, Then and Now," Center for American Progress, June 2014: 6.

FIGURE 9.6 • Division of Household Labor in the United States, by Gender, 2015

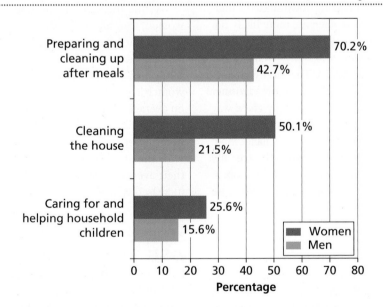

SOURCES: Data from U.S. Department of Labor, Bureau of Labor Statistics, "Daily Household Labor in the United States by Gender," in *American Time Use Survey Summary,* June 18, 2014; 2015 data from "American Time Use Survey—2015 Results," June 24, 2016: 9.

Men's tendency to do less domestic work than women has been attributed to a "stalled [gender equality] revolution," especially in the United States (Coontz 2013; England 2010). Explanations for the stalled revolution are complex and extend beyond the bounds of individual families (Thébaud and Pedulla 2016). The gender equality revolution has stalled, at least in part, because work-life policies lag behind domestic realities. For example, the United States has no federal maternity leave policies. The Family and Medical Leave Act grants 12 weeks of unpaid maternity leave, but only for full-time employees who have worked at least 1,250 hours in the year preceding the leave and who work in companies with 50 or more employees. Thus, part-time employees and full-timers in workplaces that employ fewer than 50 people are not covered. Even full-timers may not be able to afford time off without pay for the responsibilities associated with childbirth and beyond. Papua New Guinea and the United States are the only countries that do not have federally supported paid time off for mothers. Unlike Sweden (which offers a total paid leave of 60 weeks), Germany (58 weeks), and Canada (52 weeks), the United States offers zero paid leave days. In fact, the United States ranks at the bottom globally in government-supported time off for new parents (see Figure 9.7).

Gender Inequality at Work

In nearly every kind of job and work setting, gender inequalities persist and begin to intersect with racial inequalities. Perhaps the most widely cited inequality is the wage gap, the difference between men's earnings and women's earnings, usually expressed as a percentage of men's earnings. In the United States in 2016, the wage gap was 80 percent. According to the U.S. Bureau of Labor Statistics, overall, women earn (on average) 80 cents for every dollar earned by white men. As is evident in Figure 9.8, a wage gap exists at all levels of the occupational ladder. Women in entry-level jobs or positions (for example, cashiers and food preparers) earn much less ($407) per week than similarly employed young men ($471). The gap between well-educated men in white-collar jobs and similarly situated women is large. For example, female financial managers earn $1,130 per week, while male financial managers earn $1,732. Of the 30 best-paying jobs, 26 are dominated by males. On the other hand, 23 of the 30 lowest-paying jobs are dominated by females (Miller 2016).

Some explanations for the wage gap are structural and institutional. Women remain strongly clustered in some relatively low-paid occupations (e.g., nursing, elementary school teaching), although they have made inroads into historically male-dominated fields, such as law, medicine, and business (Blau, Brummund, and Liu 2012). Occupations and specialties within certain occupations that are male-dominated tend to have higher salaries than occupations and specialties that are, or have been, female-dominated. The higher the percentage of women in an occupation, the lower the average wages. Another explanation is more personal or family based. Historical gender roles and stereotyping, particularly in the middle class, have led to the expectation that women who have children will take time off from their paid employment to care for them. Such career disruptions certainly contribute to the wage gap. Women who take time away from the paid labor force lose ground in terms of salaries and the rate of advancement into higher-paying positions.

GENDER AND CONSUMER CULTURE

In consumption, as in many other aspects of the social world, gender matters (Casey 2015). Since the Industrial Revolution, production has been centered outside the household and has primarily been the function of white men. White middle- and upper-class women, largely relegated to the home, were assigned the role of consumers. This is both different and unequal, because historically production has been far more highly valued than consumption.

Consumption, Work, and Family

Women were not just defined as the prime consumers—their consumer practices were also closely tied to their domestic practices and their roles in the home. Women consumed goods and services to care for, and on behalf of, their families (De Laat and Baumann 2016; DeVault 1991). Much of women's shopping was related to love, especially their love of family members (Miller 1998);

FIGURE 9.7 • Government-Supported Paid Leave for New Parents in Select Countries

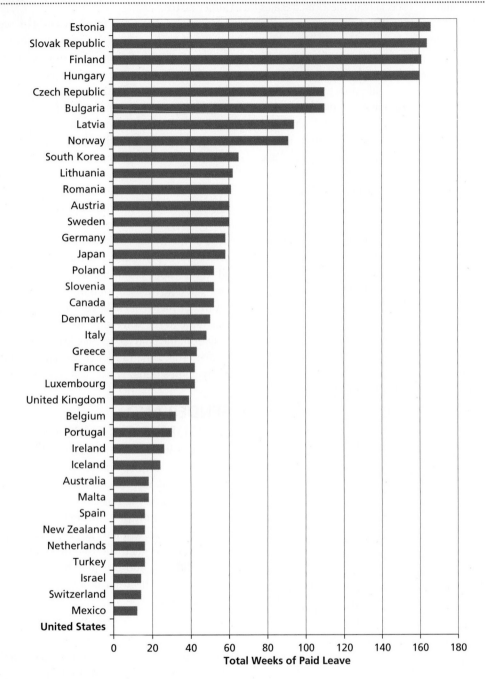

SOURCE: Data on paid leave from Organisation for Economic Co-operation and Development, "PF2.1: Key Characteristics of Parental Leave Systems," OECD Family Database, Table PF2.1.A, p.3, February 28, 2016.

NOTE: Total paid leave represents maternity, parental, and home care leave available to mothers. The data do not address paid leave or other accommodations that individual employers make available to employees or guarantees provided by a few individual states.

FIGURE 9.8 • Median Weekly Earnings of Full-Time Wage and Salary Workers by Occupation in the United States, 2015

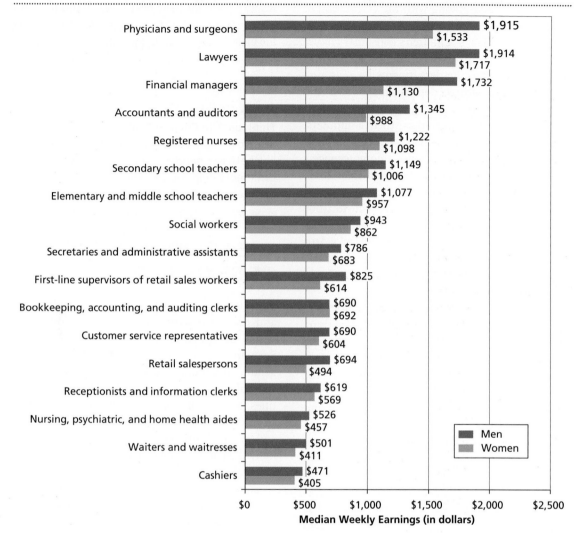

SOURCE: Data from U.S. Department of Labor, Bureau of Labor Statistics, Table 39: "Household Data: Annual Averages," 2015.

it was an instrumental way of showing caring and affection. In one way or another, women generally made purchases for their families and to fulfill their responsibilities in the home and to those who lived there. Women are still thought to constitute a "multiple market"—they purchase things for significant others, family members, and friends. As women have entered the paid working world in increasing numbers, their consumption patterns have changed. They are now more likely to consume an array of subcontracted services, such as cleaning and child care. Much of this work is done by other women—women are subcontracting work to other women (Bowman and Cole 2009). In addition, they are increasingly more likely to consume for themselves than for others. For example, greater involvement in the work world requires the use of a wider variety of clothing: business casual options, conservative office work wear, and uniforms, to name a few. This certainly contributes to what U.S. women spend on clothing—$116 billion in 2013 (Madhok 2014).

Several historical events mark the development of greater interest in girls, and children more generally, as consumers (Cook 2007). One was the emergence of the department store in the middle and late 1800s, along with the celebration of Christmas, and its associated gifts, by department stores such as Macy's. Children's consumer culture gained further impetus when department stores began to have separate departments for toys and, more important, separate departments for boys' and girls' clothing. Now, of course, all children, including girls, are being targeted on their computers, their smartphones, and myriad other new technologies that have a ready audience among teenagers and younger children (Kahlenberg and Hein 2010; Sheldon 2004). Some teen women court others in the form of shopping "haul" videos, "the YouTube equivalent of calling a best friend and gushing about a recent shopping spree" (Khrais 2013). Haul videos help drive young women's consumption—about 4 in 10 buy a product after seeing it discussed in a haul video (Parker 2012).

This focus on consumption is particularly clear in the efforts made by the cosmetics and clothing industries to sell to young women by advertising in magazines aimed at them (e.g., *Seventeen, Teen Vogue*) and through pop-up advertisements on the internet. "Women/girls . . . are expected to consume their way into attractiveness" (Deutsch and Theodorou 2010, 234). One of the unfortunate consequences of this for young girls is increased rates of eating disorders and body dysmorphia—an obsession with perceived flaws in one's body—as well as the hypersexualization of their lives (Hesse-Biber 1996; Kimmel 2012). Hypersexualization has become such a concern globally that the Norwegian minister of family affairs urged chain stores to remove sexualized clothing (for example, string bikini underwear; Rysst 2008).

Gendered stereotyping has inhibited the recognition that boys and men are important consumers. Heterosexual men are thought to be wary of paying too much attention to their looks and appearance (Brosdahl and Carpenter 2012). Thus, we develop other labels for them—hipster, lumbersexual (Compton and Bridges 2014)—and define their consumption habits accordingly. Currently, one of the most stereotyped narratives about men's consumption is that of the "man cave," which is room or space in a house reserved for a man to engage in his hobbies. Female partners and children are discouraged from entering this exclusive masculine zone. There are stores designed specifically to cater to men who want to shop for their man caves. Mantiques and More, in Corpus Christi, Texas, is designed as a store for men, because "an antique store can be seen as anything but cool, hip, and manly" (Salinas 2014).

ASK YOURSELF

Think back to Chapter 2, about sociological theory. How might sociological theorists explain the link between gender and social inequalities? How can theory help you see why gender and inequalities persist in most of the world?

THE SOCIOLOGY OF SEXUALITY

Sexuality is the way in which people think about, and behave toward, themselves and others as sexual beings (Kimmel, 2014; Plummer 1975). Sexuality is, of course, related to both sex and gender, and includes sexual attitudes, behaviors, sensuality, values, anatomy, biochemistry, identities, and orientations. It is of central interest to sociologists, perhaps because of its complicated and seemingly opposed elements. Sexuality is both individual and personal *and* collective and public; it is biological and biochemical as well as cultural, social, and historical. There is variation in degrees of sexuality among individuals and across cultures and time periods.

There is now a large and growing body of literature on the sociology of sexuality (Plummer 2012). While bodies and biology are involved, the bulk of this work deals with the social, social psychological, and cultural aspects of sexuality. Sociologists have become increasingly interested in sexuality for a number of reasons:

- The growing number of sexually linked social problems, including sexual violence and sexually transmitted diseases

- Social changes in attitudes and behaviors, including the increase in "hooking up" (see the section later in the chapter) and casual sexual relationships

- The greater visibility of sexuality-related social movements, especially those associated with LGBTQ people

- Technological changes, such as the popularity of erectile dysfunction (ED) drugs

- The media's presentation of sex in its many forms

- The globalization of sexuality, for example, through sex tourism and sex trafficking (Frank 2012; Lerum and Brents 2016)

- The increase in overt expressions of sexuality in consumer culture

- The increasing popularity of the internet, especially its prevalent commercial sex culture (Waskul 2015)

Sexuality is rarely simply a matter of sexual release or so-called reproductive imperatives. It is complex, contradictory, and often confusing (Plante 2015). For example, we are told that "having sex"—meaning, usually, engaging in heterosexual activities (Seidman 2003)—is "natural" and that reproduction is the key goal of these activities. Similarly, we are told that people "naturally" have hormones, sexual urges, and needs that must be fulfilled. However, we are also told that people should control themselves for religious, social, or cultural reasons (Plante 2014). Culture gives us patterns, rules, and codes to manage our sexualities and sexual identities. Laws and formal sanctions, along with informal sanctions, are intended to regulate cultural and individual sexualities. Culture provides the big picture for our sexualities by communicating our shared attitudes, values, goals, and practices. However, the existence of a wide variety of subcultures means that there is great diversity in our sexualities.

SEXUAL SELVES

Sexual Identities and Orientations

In the United States we believe in the concept of **sexual identity**, an internal sense of one's sexual self (Manning 2015). The idea that people have sexual orientations and identities is fairly new in human history. Until as recently as 1923, one could still find *heterosexual* defined in the dictionary as a

medical term (it was not an *identity* term) meaning "morbid sexual passion for one of the opposite sex" (Katz 2004, 44). In the past 125 years or so, we have begun to classify and label people according to culturally powerful decisions about what is "normal." One element of sexual identity is **sexual orientation**, which identifies whom you desire (fantasies), with whom you want to have sexual relations (behavior), and with whom you have a sense of connectedness (feelings; Scott and Schwartz 2008). Sexual orientation is actually quite complicated. We have tended to oversimplify it by assuming that there are only a few orientations—gay or lesbian, bisexual, and heterosexual.

Although there are cultural, social, and historical contexts for our sexualities, sexual expression varies among individuals. For example, someone may define herself as bisexual and may be sexual with men and women but may prefer romantic relationships with women. Another person may define himself as an asexual heteroromantic, someone with no sexual attractions but who is interested in a romantic relationship with a woman (DeLuzio Chasin 2011). Like sex and gender, sexualities and identities are also on continua. In fact, it may be most accurate to conceive of these aspects of ourselves as a matrix. And our interests, fantasies, tastes, and desires may change quite a bit through the life course (DeLamater 2012).

Our attitudes about sexual identities reflect changes in the larger society. Recently the changes have been profound, as have their effects. The best-known example today is the increasing openness many people feel about identifying as gay, lesbian, bisexual, or transgender. In many settings, it is no longer necessary to hide those identities. It is increasingly possible to be very public, and to feel very good, about having such an identity (Plummer 2007a). The Pew Research Center (2013) conducted a nationally representative survey of 1,197 lesbian, gay, bisexual, and transgender adults, and found that 92 percent of respondents said that, compared to 10 years ago, U.S. society is now more accepting of LGBTQ people. But the increasing multiplicity of sexualities and sexual communities makes conflicts over the boundaries of sexualities increasingly likely (Köllen 2013). Thus, while LGBTQ individuals are more accepted, it is also the case that more hate crimes are now aimed at them than at

African Americans, Jews, and Muslims (Park and Mykhyalyshyn 2016).

Some of the conflicts *seem* individual and interpersonal, as you can see in Figure 9.9. For example, nearly 40 percent of the Pew survey respondents reported that they had been rejected by a close family member or friend; 30 percent had been physically threatened or attacked, and almost 60 percent had been verbally attacked. These statistics have social and historical roots in homophobia and heterosexism. **Homophobia** is defined as "the fear of being, appearing, or seeming gay; fear of anyone or 'anything' gay. . . . At its most virulent, homophobia inspires hate crimes, murders, assaults (sexual, physical, and emotional), rapes, batteries, and other forms of violence" (Plante 2015, 212). **Heterosexism** is the belief that heterosexuality is superior to other sexual orientations, along with individual and institutional discrimination against those with other orientations. Heterosexism and homophobia combine to drive some of the alienation and aggression experienced by LGBTQ people.

Spotlight on "Hooking Up"

What exactly is hooking up? It is *not* a clearly socially defined relationship such as dating, seeing someone, having a boyfriend or girlfriend, or being engaged to be married. It *can be* somewhat committed or somewhat casual, emotionally and physically intense or not, sporadic or fairly regular, sober or intoxicated; it can involve friends or strangers (Plante 2014). Hooking up involves the occurrence of some sort of sexual event—very broadly defined—usually between only two people, and sometimes including alcohol or other drugs. It may include only kissing and making out, or it may involve a range of behaviors, from touching to oral sex, penile–vaginal sex, and/or anal sex. The lack of rules or expectations for hookups makes this concept quite ambiguous. Researchers have observed that hooking up maintains the heterosexual gendered double standard (Hamilton and Armstrong 2009). The **heterosexual double standard** describes a cultural belief system in which men are expected to desire and seek sex from whomever, whenever, while women are expected to be sexual only within committed,

FIGURE 9.9 • Discrimination against LGBTQ People in the United States

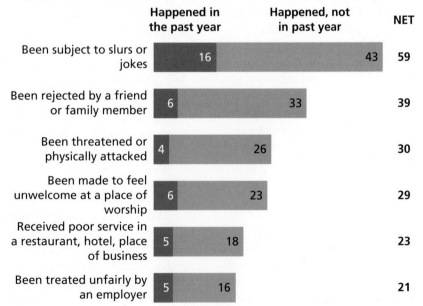

% saying this . . . because of their sexual orientation or gender identity

	Happened in the past year	Happened, not in past year	NET
Been subject to slurs or jokes	16	43	59
Been rejected by a friend or family member	6	33	39
Been threatened or physically attacked	4	26	30
Been made to feel unwelcome at a place of worship	6	23	29
Received poor service in a restaurant, hotel, place of business	5	18	23
Been treated unfairly by an employer	5	16	21

SOURCE: From "A Survey of LGBT Americans: Attitudes, Experiences and Values in Changing Times," June 13, 2013. Reprinted by permission of Pew Research Center, Washington, DC.

TRENDING

Dude You're a Fag: Masculinity and Sexuality in High School

(University of California Press, 2012)

C. J. Pascoe (Associate Professor of Sociology at University of Oregon; PhD, University of California, Berkeley, 2006)

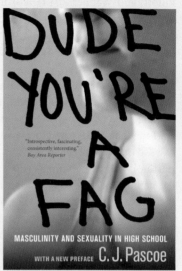

A common assumption is that the word "fag" is a derogatory term for the sexuality of gay boys and men. However, after spending 18 months observing and interviewing teenage boys at a high school in North Central California, C. J. Pascoe found that there was more to fag discourse than simply denoting sexuality. It was directed not just at gay males, but also at heterosexual males. Many of the heterosexual teenage boys in Pascoe's study called other heterosexual teenage boys "fags" if their behaviors were viewed as feminine and weak. Thus, calling someone a "fag," whether or not that person is gay, reaffirms hegemonic masculinity. Another way in which the heterosexual boys in Pascoe's study asserted their masculinity was through sexualizing teenage girls and women. The boys were expected by their peers to brag about their sexual exploits with females—or at the very least publicly express their heterosexual desires. These practices served to protect them from being called fags and thereby having their masculinity questioned (Pascoe 2012, 85–87). When Pascoe experienced being objectified sexually

as a desirable female during her study, she attempted to adopt a "least-gendered identity" by wearing baggy pants, smiling less, and talking about her athletic interests, including weight-lifting (2012, 181).

Heterosexual normativity, or the assumption that heterosexuality is the norm, is reinforced at the institutional level by schools through curriculum, pedagogy, informal teacher-student interactions, and rituals. For instance, Pascoe witnessed a classroom discussion about state laws and marriage that ignored same-sex marriage. She also heard homophobic jokes between teachers and students in stereotypically male spaces (e.g., the weight room and auto shop class). She observed only one teacher reprimanding students for voicing homophobic slurs (Pascoe 2012, 35, 38). School rituals, including dances, assemblies, and football games, that Pascoe attended were rife with what she calls compulsive heterosexuality. Most of these rituals "naturalized heterosexual pairings" and gave boys the opportunity to publicly perform their masculinity by watching, "getting," and touching girls (2012, 41). These rituals also provided the occasion

for boys who had been labeled as "fags" to renounce this identity by being seen kissing or touching a girl. Interestingly, when these boys engaged in one-on-one, private interactions, they were less likely to objectify girls sexually or to feel compelled to prove their masculinity (2012, 107).

Supplementary Resources

- Pascoe discusses bullying, masculinity, and the "spectre of the fag" in this microLECTURE: https://www.youtube.com/watch?v=5Ha2kSDJ9dY.
- This article from the *New York Times* Opinion Pages situates Pascoe's findings in the context of sexual identity and adolescent socialization: http://opinionator.blogs.nytimes.com/2009/04/16/who-are-you-calling-gay/?_r=0.

romantic relationships. Those who hold this double standard may also believe that women's sexual behavior is different from men's and should be judged differently (Allison and Risman 2013; Reid, Elliott, and Webber 2011). For instance, they may judge women negatively for seeking sex and pleasure outside relationships, while they judge men less harshly, if at all, for the same behavior (Armstrong, England, and Fogarty 2012).

Although there is some evidence that belief in the double standard is weakening, we still see it in heterosexual hooking up. For instance, it may lead to what Hamilton and Armstrong (2009, 594) call "sexual dilemmas," in which young women in particular find that social rules and expectations for gender and social class contradict each other. Heterosexual women are told they should be sexual only in romantic, committed relationships, but also that they should avoid the baggage (and feelings) of committed relationships in favor of self-development and the achievement of academic and career goals. Researchers have explored the sexual dilemmas of hooking up by examining the ways in which heterosexual young women are expected to look and act appropriately sexy—the "just right," or Goldilocks, amount (Plante 2015)—while also "distanc[ing] themselves from the troubling figure of the 'drunken slut'" (Griffin et al. 2012, 187).

SOCIAL CONSTRAINTS ON SEXUALITY

There is a growing sense, not without reason, that sexuality has become increasingly free of social constraints. This seems especially true in the way the media treat sexuality. The last 15 years have seen an abundance of increasingly relaxed, open-minded portrayals of sexual experiences and attitudes. TV series from *The Good Wife* to *Orange Is the New Black* to *Unbreakable Kimmy Schmidt* are obvious examples. The popularity of *Fifty Shades of Grey* and its sequels, which depict bondage and sexual domination, suggests that we have become more open about sexuality. Examples of changing consensus about sexualities and social constraint are abundant in modern culture. In 1969, only 21 percent of Americans said that sex between unmarried men and women was morally acceptable (Pennington 2003). By 1973, 43 percent were saying that it was acceptable morally. A majority of Americans (68 percent) now say that sex between unmarried men and women is morally acceptable (Riffkin 2014). The rapid shift in perceptions of the morality of premarital heterosexual sex is an excellent example of changing consensus. Surprisingly, perhaps, American attitudes about heterosexual marital monogamy remain stable. For decades, Gallup has found that 93 percent of Americans believe that "married men and women having an affair" is "morally unacceptable" (Riffkin 2014). While there is much to support the idea of increasing sexual freedom, human sexuality is never totally free from social and cultural constraints and regulatory attempts. For example, a public school in Mississippi canceled its senior prom because a lesbian student wanted to bring her girlfriend as a date (Joyner 2010). The school was afraid of the message it would send if it allowed a same-sex couple to attend. Generally speaking, culturally oppressed minorities' relationships and sexualities are more likely to be constrained than those of the hegemonic, or dominant, group. Sodomy laws, which loosely defined acts of sodomy as "crimes against nature" or "unnatural copulations," were intended to punish sexual activities and romantic relationships between gay men. People of color have been subject to numerous dehumanizing laws, customs, and discourses that constrain their sexualities (Garcia 2012; Rousseau 2011).

CULTURE AND CONSENT

Important to a discussion of social constraints on sexuality are the concepts of consensual sexual activities, sexual assault, and rape. All involve issues of the relative power of the individuals involved, along with complicated sociocultural histories and contexts regarding gender and sexualities. **Consensual sexual activities** are those agreed on by the participants, any of whom have the right to decide to stop at any point and for any reason. **Informed, or "effective," sexual consent** has been in the news recently, as hundreds of college campuses have been investigated for poor enforcement of rape and sexual assault laws. Informed, effective consent can be defined as follows:

- Informed: Both parties demonstrate a clear and mutual understanding of exactly what they are consenting to.

- Freely and actively given: There is no coercion, force, threats, intimidation, or pressuring.

- Mutually understandable: Consent is expressed in words or actions that indicate a clear willingness to do the same thing, at the same time, in the same way, with each other. Silence does not equal consent.

- Consent is not indefinite; furthermore, consent may be withdrawn at any time, and at that time all sexual activity must cease unless and until additional effective consent is given (Reed College 2015).

Under such informed consent, consenting to one behavior does not obligate an individual or imply consent to any other behaviors. Consenting to a person or an act on one occasion also does not obligate an individual or imply consent on any other occasion.

Sexual assault encompasses sexual acts of domination, usually enacted by men against women, other men, and children. Such assaults can occur between strangers, but they usually occur between acquaintances or intimates. **Rape**, also a form of domination, is defined as "penetration, no matter how slight, of the vagina or anus with any body part or object, or oral penetration by a sex organ of another person, without the consent of the victim" (Federal Bureau of Investigation 2014).

Communities vary in the probability of sexual violence and the effectiveness of legal, social, and moral constraints on the kinds of behaviors that often lead to such violence. In many religious communities, strong expectations for modesty and sexuality only within marriage keep sexual violence to a minimum. In contrast, the nature of residential colleges' sexual climates can promote a "rape culture" (Boswell and Spade 1996; Plante and Smiler 2014), an environment conducive to sexual assaults and rape. Rape cultures tend to be prevalent in and around college campuses due to several factors, including gender imbalances (more women than men enrolled), the routine presence of alcohol and other drugs at social events and parties, the

age of the population, and the relatively unsupervised nature of life "at college." Structural aspects of college campuses that can reproduce gender imbalances include party systems controlled by fraternities and social life environments that actively or passively promote settings combining alcohol use with assumptions about sexuality (Corprew and Mitchell 2014; Flack et al. 2007).

Sexual assaults and rapes have, to put it mildly, very serious consequences. According to the Rape, Abuse, and Incest National Network (RAINN), the largest anti–sexual violence network in the United States, survivors are more likely to suffer from depression and posttraumatic stress disorder, contemplate and attempt suicide, and use illicit drugs than the general public. Sexual violence is endemic in the United States, where it has been estimated that 17.7 million women have been victims of completed or attempted rapes, along with 2.78 million men. Most sexual assault victims (54 percent) are under the age of 30. Men and women of color are disproportionately likely to be victimized, particularly Native Americans (RAINN, n.d.). The mental and physical consequences of assaults combined with systematic racism are profound (McGuffey 2008).

SEX AND CONSUMPTION

Regardless of constraints on sexuality, everyday life has been sexualized to a large degree—the world has been "made sexy" (Rutherford 2007). In our consumer society, sex is used to encourage consumption of all sorts of things that are not inherently sexual. Advertisements use sexualized images to promote innumerable products, from cars to toothpaste and from clothing to soft drinks. The implication in many of these ads is that use of the products leads to sexual relationships. The well-known media adage that "sex sells" shows no signs of going out of fashion, and it is certainly applied to sexual products, such as Viagra. However, researchers have found that women usually have a strong negative reaction to explicit sexual content in advertising and are less likely to buy merchandise promoted with these types of ads, unless the sexual content is promoting an expensive item (Vohs, Sengupta, and Dahl 2014). In comparison, men tend to feel positively about such ads.

AP Photo/Matt Rourke

These Penn State students and supporters are protesting a campus fraternity's depiction on Facebook of sleeping or unconscious women in the nude. Why are women victimized in this way more often than men?

More blatant than the use of sexual images to sell products and services is the way in which human sexualities have been increasingly turned into commodities and marketed (Sanders 2013; Y. Taylor 2007). Of course, the consumption of sex is nothing new—after all, prostitution is often referred to as the "oldest profession" (Bazelon 2016). What is new since the mid-twentieth century is the rise of a huge sex industry, one whose reach and influence spans the globe. This sexual marketplace may be described as being composed of five interlocking markets. These markets are characterized as (1) bodies and sexual acts, such as stripping; (2) pornography and erotica; (3) sexualized objects, such as sex toys and lingerie; (4) sexualized technologies, including contraceptives and genital reconstructive surgery; and (5) sexualized relationships (Plummer 2007b).

SEXUALITY, GENDER, AND GLOBALIZATION

SOCIAL CHANGE AND THE GLOBALIZATION OF SEXUALITY

Globalization is one of a number of forces that are affecting and interacting with sexuality in the twenty-first century. The globalization of sexuality is linked to a variety of social changes that are altering not only sexuality but also much of what transpires in the social world:

- *The globalization of media and technologies.* The global media, including movies, advertising, television, and the internet, have been sexualized; they can even be said to have undergone a process of "pornographication" (McNair 2002; Ogas and Gaddam 2012; Tyler and Quek 2016).

- *Increasing urbanization.* Urbanization is a key trend across the globe, and it has contributed both to increased freedom of sexual expression and to the globalization of sexuality (Bell 2007; Hubbard, Gormley-Murray, and Nash 2015). Cities are at the center of freedoms of all sorts, including sexual freedoms. Sex trafficking and sex tourism take place primarily in the world's cities. The world's major cities, including London, Ho Chi Minh City, and Shanghai, are nodes in global "sex-scapes" (Hoang 2015; Maginn and Steinmetz 2015).

- *Globalized social movements and social change.* Women's and LGBTQ movements (see Chapter 15), as well as more specific social change efforts focused on repressive sex laws, are global. Activists, change agents, and ideas flow, spread, and adapt to their specific contexts (Parker, Garcia, and Buffington 2014).

- *Increased mobility.* It is relatively easy now for people to travel to locales far from home. Thus, travel for sex itself is a global and commercial phenomenon, in the form of sex tourism and sex holidays (Altman 2001; Frank 2012).

GLOBAL FLOWS RELATED TO SEX AND SEXUALITY

Sexuality "flows" around the world in many other ways, such as via sex trafficking, sex work, gay global parties, and the sexual diaspora, as members of various sexual subcultures move around the world (especially via the internet.) Globalization has had a real effect on sexual interactions, identities, and relationships (Wieringa and Sívori 2013). There are now a number of globally applied sexuality laws, such as those attempting to outlaw the sexual exploitation of children. Organizations like UNICEF monitor these laws and seek to protect the vulnerable from sexual abuse and violence. Laws dealing with sexual crimes, such as rape, have grown increasingly similar (DiMaggio and Powell 1983).

Some norms and values have grown increasingly similar in many parts of the world. For example, there has been a general movement away from trying to control sexuality and procreation while attempting to maintain the collective order. At the same time, there has been a movement toward viewing sexuality as a series of acts that are mainly about pleasure and self-expression. Premarital (or nonmarital) sex has also become increasingly normative in many (but certainly not all) parts of the world.

Another example of global cultural change involves the global diffusion of such sexual identities as straight, gay, and bisexual. The terms *gay, lesbian,* and *transsexual,* as well as the idea that they refer to identities, are exports from the Global North. Almost anywhere you go in the world, you may be able to find similar identities, norms, and values relating to sexuality.

Lesbian, Gay, Bisexual, Transgender, and Queer Sexualities in a Global Context

A key issue for lesbian, gay, bisexual, transgender, and queer (LGBTQ) people consists of the barriers that inhibit their movement around the world or encourage their movement from one place to another (Carrillo and Fontdevila 2014; Lewis 2014). Such barriers may be erected within the home country as well as between countries. Barriers at home that might *push* LGBTQ people to migrate include legal prohibitions of consensual sex acts and relationships with same-sex partners, lack of equal opportunity in the workplace, and bans on same-sex marriages. State-sanctioned physical assaults and even murders of LGBTQ people can force them to seek better lives elsewhere in the world. They can also be *pulled* elsewhere in the world by better conditions, such as more opportunities to work, marry, and live more freely with less fear. Urban environments are attractive, because large and visible groups of other LGBTQ people often create communities and neighborhoods in cities around the globe (Nash and Gorman-Murray 2014).

Other aspects of globalization, such as inexpensive air travel, the internet, and sex tourism, have made it easier for LGBTQ people to communicate and be together anywhere in the world. Globalization has also contributed to the rise of gay and lesbian global social movements and to the increasing acceptance in large parts of the world of same-sex sexual relationships (Stone and Weinberg 2015).

Yet while globalization has aided sexual minorities, it has also facilitated the spread of homophobia and other forms of prejudice and discrimination

Homosexuality remains a highly controversial subject in Uganda, spurring protests on both sides of the issue. Some opponents of gay rights view homosexuality as an unwelcome import from the United States.

(Binnie 2004; Kaoma 2014). Globalization clearly has not been an unmitigated good as far as LGBTQ people are concerned.

The Global Sex Industry

Industries based on sex have become increasingly important to global capitalism. Bars, dance clubs, massage parlors, pornography, sex work establishments, international hotel chains, airline companies, and the tourist industry create, and help meet, the demand for sexual labor around the globe. **Sex trafficking**, a commercial sex act that includes force, fraud, or coercion and transporting and obtaining a person for sex acts, is truly a global issue. It is one sector of human trafficking, which the U.S. State Department calls "modern slavery" or forced labor, and includes child soldiers, debt bondage, and domestic servitude. The International Labour Organization (2017) estimates that 21 million people are victims of human trafficking around the world; 4.5 million of these victims are involved in forced sexual labor, which generates $99 billion in revenue annually. According to the U.S. State Department's annual *Trafficking in Persons Report* (2016), in 2015, there were 18,920 prosecutions for human trafficking but only 6,609 convictions.

The flow of people in the global sex industry moves not only from the South to the North but also in the other direction. Over the past 30 years, the global sex tourism industry has grown to be a multibillion-dollar enterprise (Weitzer 2012; Wortmann 2007). **Sex tourism** occurs when individuals travel to other countries specifically for the purpose of buying sex from men, women, and sometimes children; sex is the primary or sole purpose of these trips. These encounters can be complicated by the fact that locals and tourists usually do not have the same levels of economic privilege. For one thing, tourists have the disposable income needed to take such trips (Dewey 2015). While some sex tourism involves people traveling to the developed countries of the Global North, most of it involves customers traveling from the Global North to the Global South (Katsulis 2010). For example, Thailand receives millions of sex tourists every year from the United States, Western Europe, Australia, and Japan, bringing in billions of dollars (Hepburn and Simon 2013).

Several factors have contributed to the rise of sex tourism. The internet expedites it, as information about destinations is readily available through websites, chat rooms, e-diaries, blogs, promotional videos, and guidebooks (Wortmann 2007). Websites offer advice on the best tourist sites to visit, the best sex workers at those sites, how to arrange visits, and even how to negotiate with sex workers to get the lowest prices (Katsulis 2010). It is even possible to buy a customized package tour of the best locations in the world for sex tourism, joining other sex tourists from the Global North. Low-cost travel has permitted more sex tourists to circle the globe in search of sexual relations (Brennan 2004). Many sex tourists believe that their money, attention, and transactions are welcome to residents in the Global South because it provides them with a source of income.

GLOBAL FLOWS RELATED TO GENDER

THE FEMINIZATION OF MIGRATION

The global economy has contributed to an unprecedented increase in women's migration (Ehrenreich and Hochschild 2002). Some have referred to this trend as the "feminization of migration" (Gabaccia, forthcoming). Much of this flow involves women from the Global South moving, legally and illegally, to the Global North to handle work that was historically performed by Northern women. Large numbers of women are emigrating from China, India, Indonesia, Myanmar, Pakistan, the Philippines, Sri Lanka, Thailand, and Bangladesh. The migrants often become nannies, maids, or sex workers (Brennan 2002; Eckenwiler 2014; Ehrenreich 2002; Gündüz 2013). Most immigrant women are in service occupations (33 percent) and business/managerial positions (33 percent; see Figure 9.10).

This migrant labor enriches the Global North and enhances its already elevated lifestyle. Domestic work is now considered to be the largest labor market for women worldwide. Many female labor immigrants clean the homes and care for the children of affluent families while trying to send money (remittances) to their own families in their home countries (Faist, Fauser, and Reisenauer 2013; Hondagneu-Sotelo 2000). They believe that this work will bring with it better pay and improved working conditions, increasing the immigrants' quality of life and that of their families.

Undocumented and informal migration, which is common for women migrating to the North for domestic work, exposes women to the worst forms of discrimination, exploitation, and abuse (Adams and Campbell 2012; Jones 2008; United Nations 2006). They can be held as debt hostages by recruitment agencies until their transportation and placement fees are paid, imprisoned in the houses of their employers, treated inhumanely, and sometimes murdered. Increasing numbers of migrant women are victims of sexual abuse (including rape), sex trafficking, and prostitution, as discussed previously.

FIGURE 9.10 • Occupational Fields of Female Immigrants in the United States, 2015

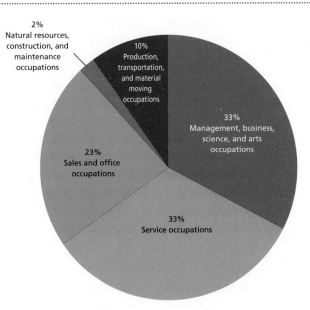

SOURCE: Ariel G. Ruiz, Jie Zong, and Jeanne Batalova, "Immigrant Women in the United States," Figure 7, Migration Policy Institute, March 20, 2017.

NOTE: Data may total more than 100 percent due to rounding.

THE FEMINIZATION OF LABOR

There has been a notable increase in women's labor force participation rates worldwide, particularly in the Americas and Western Europe. In the United States, 57 percent of women 16 years and older were employed in 2015, compared to 69 percent of men. In 1948, only 31 percent of women were employed, in comparison to 84 percent of men. Even though there are significant variations within and across regions, women's labor force participation has also risen substantially in sub-Saharan Africa, North Africa, Eastern Europe, Southeast Asia, and East Asia over this period (Cagatay and Ozler 1995; Heintz 2006; Kivisto and Faist 2010; Moghadam 1999). As noted in Chapter 7, while the progress in women's employment status is linked at least in part to gender equality movements, the key factor in this change has been the better integration of an increasing number of areas into the world economy through trade and production.

The increasing participation of women in the labor force has been termed the **feminization of labor** (Standing 1989). This refers to the rise of female labor participation in all sectors and the movement of women into jobs traditionally held by men. This global trend has occurred in both developing and developed countries (Hawkesworth 2006).

The feminization of labor, especially in the developing economies, is often accompanied by **female proletarianization** as an increasing number of women are channeled into low-status, poorly paid manual work. Female proletarianization is closely related to the feminization of poverty (see Chapter 7; Brady and Kall 2008). Globally, more women are being drawn into labor-intensive and low-paying industries, such as textiles, apparel, leather products, food processing, and electronics (Chen et al. 2013; Villareal and Yu 2007). Jobs in these industries are characterized by the flexible use of labor, high turnover rates, part-time and temporary employment, a lack of security and benefits, and often dangerous working conditions. Female employees are preferred in these industries because they are considered to be more docile and to have more dexterity than men in performing standardized and repetitive work.

ASK YOURSELF

What is the relationship between the feminization of labor and the feminization of poverty? Is this relationship inevitable? What social, structural, and gender-related factors might account for it?

GENDER, WAR, AND VIOLENCE

Men are certainly more likely than women to be killed or wounded in warfare. However, a 2015 Human Rights Watch report describes the ways in which women bear the brunt of war, violence, and failed peace efforts. More specifically, women are more likely to be the noncombatant victims of wars and other forms of organized collective violence, including being raped and killed (Human Rights Watch 2015; Sanford, Stefanos, and Salvi 2016). Rape and sexual assault have long been used to weaken and demoralize the nation-states and ethnic enclaves in which victims live. Rape as a tool of war is used to traumatize its victims and humiliate the enemy by "taking" their women. For example, the Islamic State proclaims that it is legal for males to rape the women that they have captured, and ISIS has forced ethnic Yazidi women and girls into sexual slavery (Callimachi 2016). As is true of rape in general, rape in warfare is not a sexual act, but rather an act of power (Brownmiller 1975). Women are also likely to suffer as a result of local and global terrorism and political violence (Gentry and Sjoberg 2015).

Several changes have made it more likely that women will be the victims of international violence. One is the change in the nature of warfare. For example, "asymmetric warfare," or warfare involving forces of unequal capabilities, often takes the form of shootouts in the streets. Obviously, civilians—women, children, and the elderly—are more likely to be victims in such cases than they are when conventional ground battles take place. This is evident, for example, in the brutal civil wars that continue to engulf Syria, Iraq, Libya, and Yemen at the time of this writing. In addition, more women are in the armed forces and in terrorist groups, which greatly increases their chances of being the victims of violence. In some cases, terrorist groups use women to carry concealed explosives and to detonate them in or near targets, killing themselves and those in the vicinity (Gentry and Sjoberg 2015).

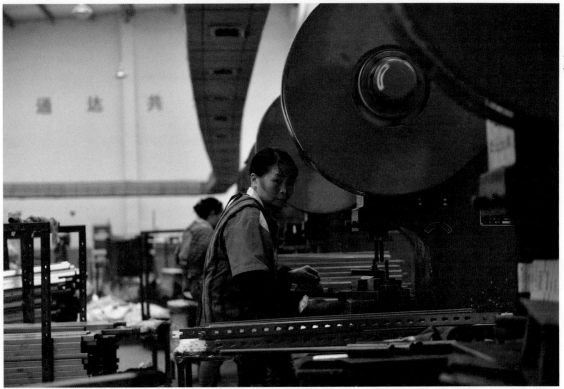

Women in the Global South, such as these workers in China, are much more likely than their counterparts in the more industrial Global North to be employed in assembly line work or other low-wage labor. Why does this situation persist?

One unintended consequence of war is that women can sometimes benefit from warfare and its disruption of business as usual. Among other things, they can gain greater economic independence, more freedom to act, and greater mobility. With the norms and values of society disrupted, women can do things they could not do before: acquire a more public role in the community and society, gain greater responsibility for decision making, and generally acquire more power. Such was the case during World War II, when labor shortages caused by the mobilization of men for military service resulted in work opportunities for women. The iconic image of Rosie the Riveter working in a factory reflected this new reality, as women entered the blue-collar workforce that had been dominated by males.

THE GLOBAL WOMEN'S MOVEMENT

As you have seen, globalization and the rise of a global economy have created or exacerbated a variety of inequalities faced by women. One response has been expansion of the international women's movement (see Chapter 15). It has grown dramatically in recent years because of problems created for women by globalization. It has also expanded because of the increased ability of those working on behalf of the movement to travel globally and to communicate with one another. The international women's movement has a long history, traceable to the late 1800s. It has focused on issues such as sexual violence, reproductive rights, labor issues, sexual harassment, and the right to vote in countries around the world (Antrobus 2004).

The larger global movement is concerned with a variety of issues: human rights, economic concerns, the environment, health care, and violence against women. The movement has also come to focus on the adverse effects of global capitalism (e.g., increased global trafficking in women), the lack of women's voices in global civil society, the growth of antifeminist fundamentalist movements (e.g., the

Taliban, IS, Boko Haram), and the HIV/AIDS epidemic. More generally, the international women's movement has focused attention on issues of global justice for women and other minorities. It has had a strong impact on the United Nations and has helped create strong linkages among the UN, national governments, and nongovernmental organizations.

Women throughout the world have not only been active in the global women's movement but have also responded at local and regional levels to common problems caused by globalization. They also localize global political activities undertaken by the international women's movement and global human rights groups. In addition, they organize against global activities such as militarism and conflict and use global organizations (such as the UN and international nongovernmental organizations) to help in local and regional activities (Naples and Desai 2002). However, even the activities that have been primarily or exclusively local in nature have had profound effects globally. Even with all the local variations, feminism can be seen as "a truly global phenomenon" (Ferree and Tripp 2006, viii).

SUMMARY

Sex is principally a biological concept, while gender is a cultural term connected to societal definitions of expected behaviors, attitudes, and personalities. Femininities and masculinities are socially constructed and subject to change and variation. Transgender and intersexed individuals confront the difficulties of living in a society that is still based on binary understandings of gender and sex. Gendered inequalities persist in numerous domains, including in education, at home and in families, and at work.

Sexuality is related to both sex and gender and is experienced both individually and collectively. A person's sexual orientation is an important aspect of one's sexual identity. Sexual orientation is more complicated than the few categories we typically use to express it, such as heterosexual, gay, or lesbian. Heterosexism refers to the belief that heterosexuality is superior to other types of sexual orientation. Social constraints exist that shape what types of sexual expressions and activities are appropriate (or not). Consensual sexual activities are those agreed on by the participants, in contrast to those that are not, such as sexual harassment and rape.

Globalization reinforces but also destabilizes preexisting gender structures on a global scale. The greater flow of people creates more opportunity for traffickers to transport women and children for sexual exploitation and for people to travel for sex tourism. Globalization is linked to the increasing number of women working in the Global South, although many are drawn into low-status, poorly paid, and sometimes dangerous manual work. Women are often victims of international violence, including being subjected to rape as a weapon of war.

KEY TERMS

consensual sexual activities, 248
emphasized femininity, 232
female proletarianization, 254
feminization of labor, 254
gender, 230

gender identity, 234
gender roles, 234
gender-swapping, 233
hegemonic masculinity, 231
heterosexism, 246
heterosexual double standard, 246

hidden curriculum, 236
homophobia, 246
informed (effective) sexual consent, 248
intersex, 230
rape, 249
sex, 230
sex tourism, 252

sex trafficking, 252
sexual assault, 249
sexual identity, 245
sexuality, 244
sexual orientation, 245
transgender, 234

REVIEW QUESTIONS

1. What is the difference between sex and gender? How does sex affect gender? How does gender affect sexuality?

2. What do sociologists mean when they say that there are no clear-cut biological differences between men and women?

3. What are the differences in the ways that men and women experience "hegemonic masculinity" and "emphasized femininity"? How do these constructs help create and reinforce gender stratification?

4. How do men and women differ in terms of their educational experiences? In what ways does the hidden curriculum of educational systems reinforce gender stratification?

5. Why are women and men treated differently as consumers? What events in recent decades have changed the way in which women are thought of as consumers?

6. What are the differences in the ways in which men and women approach sexuality? How are the differences related to the socialization process? Do you think increasing equality between men and women will affect sexualities?

7. In what ways has the sex industry become increasingly important to global capitalism? How is this sex industry reflective of gender stratification? How is it reflective of inequalities between the Global North and South?

8. In what positive and negative ways have LGBTQ people been affected by globalization?

9. What do sociologists mean by the "feminization of poverty"? By "female proletarianization"? How are these related to one another and to the more general process of the "feminization of labor"?

10. What types of violence are women most likely to experience when they live in places experiencing war and other types of armed conflict?

FAMILIES

Fictional Families Get Real

The family has been a staple on television since the medium's early years. Fictional, very traditional families were a staple, perhaps most notably on the long-running and top-rated shows *I Love Lucy* (1951–1957) and *The Adventures of Ozzie and Harriet* (1952–1966). Interestingly, while these shows were fictional, the actors playing husband and wife in both cases were married in real life. The best-known early series to deal with a real family in a nonfictional way, and TV's first reality show, was the groundbreaking *An American Family,* which aired on public television in the 1970s. It was intended simply to chronicle the happy, mundane lives of a husband and wife and their five children, but over the course of the series, cracks in the family's calm and stable facade became apparent, exposing events never before seen on U.S. television. The public witnessed the husband and wife's real-life separation and subsequent divorce, for example, and the eldest son's coming out as television's first openly gay person.

Since then, family-based television shows, both fictional and nonfictional, have flourished and become increasingly "real," going far beyond the kinds of problems depicted in *An American Family.* The fictional *Transparent* (2014–) portrays a family with an array of difficulties, most notably drug addiction and challenges traceable to the discovery that the father is transgender and frequently appears in public wearing dresses. The reality show *Keeping Up with the Kardashians* (2007–) depicts the family and a number

LEARNING OBJECTIVES

10.1 Explain the concepts of the family, marriage, and intimate relationships.

10.2 Describe current trends that are changing marriage and the family.

10.3 Apply structural/functional, conflict/critical, and inter/actionist theories to the family.

10.4 Describe current problems associated with the family.

10.5 Identify the effects of globalization on the family.

edge.sagepub.com/
ritzeressentials3e

- Take the chapter quiz
- Review key terms with eFlashcards
- Explore multimedia links and SAGE readings

 SAGE edge™

of relatives who deal with divorce, have numerous affairs, perform in a sex tape, are arrested for drunk driving, and so on. The popular sitcom *Modern Family* (2009-) features several different types of families, including a heterosexual couple with three children, a same-sex white couple with an adopted Asian daughter, and a heterosexual couple that consists of an older male married to a much younger woman from Colombia, her son from a previous relationship, and their own son. Compared to early TV shows about the family, those on the air today are not only more honest (the stars of *I Love Lucy* in reality had a troubled marriage, which led to divorce) but also reflect the dramatically changing nature of the family.

It should come as no surprise that family-based TV shows are enormously popular. The family, after all, is a universal social institution. It constitutes a person's first group and primary socializer, and, for many, a lifelong source of companionship and security. Because the institution of family is such a central part of life, it is natural that we are fascinated by—and even feel connected to—the intimate relationships, conflicts, and problems experienced by families.

Family-based TV shows paint a picture of domestic dynamics and realities that is captivating and intriguing but by no means complete. These shows largely sidestep issues critical to sociology, such as poverty, gender inequality, and the prevalence of domestic abuse. Also, unlike sociology, most shows in the United States have not adopted a global perspective, choosing instead to focus on American families. That leaves us with much to learn and study. ●

FAMILY, MARRIAGE, AND INTIMATE RELATIONSHIPS

The U.S. Census Bureau defines the **family** as "a group of two people or more (one of whom is the householder) related by birth, marriage, or adoption and residing together." Families are especially important in socializing children so that they are able to fit into the larger society. Although families often fail in this and many other things, sociologists continue to view the family as a universal social institution that is central to social life. Sociologists are interested in such issues as the relationship between family and marriage, the different forms taken by families, and how families are formed and maintained, expand and contract, and even dissolve (Cohen 2014; Coontz 2016; Farrell, VandeVusse, and Ocobock 2012; Gerson 2011).

SOME BASIC CONCEPTS

In this section, we will define such basic concepts and ideas as marriage, intimate relationships, and love and explore their roles in the family.

Marriage

Marriage is the socially acknowledged and approved and often legal union of two people, allowing them to live together and to have children by birth or adoption. Families govern various issues that relate to marriage, such as the "meanings of marriage" as well as "the number of marriage partners" (Shaw and Lee 2009, 378). **Monogamy** has traditionally been defined as marriage between one wife and one husband. However, given changing laws related to gay marriage, monogamy today might involve two wives or two husbands. There are also many other forms of marriage, such as **polygamy**, which allows multiple spouses. **Polygyny**, in which a single husband has multiple wives, is a more common form of polygamy than **polyandry**, in which a single wife has multiple husbands. **Cenogamy** is group marriage.

Historically and around the world, rules, customs, and laws have been created to define and control marriage. Key to understanding marriage (and thus most families) is the concept of **endogamy**, or marriage to someone with similar characteristics in terms of race, ethnicity, religion, education level, social class, and so on (Penn, forthcoming). In contrast, **exogamy** involves marriage to someone with characteristics that are dissimilar on these dimensions. Throughout history, families have been defined much more by endogamy than by exogamy. In recent years, endogamy has declined in importance, and there is more exogamy. For example, there has been an increasing tendency of Americans to marry persons of other races (Qian and Lichter 2011). However, as a general rule, families continue to be characterized more by endogamy than by exogamy.

In the last several decades, the nature of family and marriage has undergone a series of rapid and dizzying changes. It is less and less clear exactly what constitutes marriage or a family. One thing is clear, however: The close linkage between marriage and the family has been greatly weakened, if not broken. Nevertheless, most people in the United States end up being married one or more times during their lifetimes. And those who marry often create families, although they may not stay together as long as families did in the past. Being married and in a family does not mean that the marriage or the family will remain the same for decades, or even years. Nevertheless, while marriage and the family will remain important intimate relationships, they will not be the only, or even the dominant, forms of intimacy in the future.

Endogamy, or marriage to a partner who is culturally, socially, and racially similar, is still much more common in the United States than exogamy, or marriage to someone who is different on these dimensions. Do you think this situation will change in the future?

Intimate Relationships

An **intimate relationship** occurs between partners who have a close, personal, *and* domestic relationship with one another. This intimate relationship is a byproduct of courtship rituals in which two people are attracted to each other, develop intimacy, enjoy each other's company, and identify as a couple after a period of dating.

The nature of intimacy is not static, but changes over time. Fifty or one hundred years ago, couples could be intimate without necessarily sharing very much about themselves with each other, especially their most private thoughts. However, in Western culture today, intimacy increasingly involves disclosing much, if not everything, about oneself to one's partner (Jamieson 2007). Levels of disclosure tend to be gendered (Kimmel 2012). Women tend to function as emotional caretakers within heterosexual relationships. They do so because they are generally socialized to engage in communication in which they express their emotions, whereas men are socialized to suppress their emotions and communicate little about them. In other words, women tend to be the ones to share first and to help males share by drawing out their emotions. The assumption made by most women is that such self-disclosure will strengthen a relationship because there are no secrets and therefore there will be no surprises, or at least there will be fewer of them, as the relationship develops.

Love

Intimacy in domestic relationships is, of course, often associated with love. **Passionate love** has a sudden onset, inspires strong sexual feelings, and tends to include idealization of the one who is loved (Hatfield, Bensman, and Rapson 2012). Passionate love brings with it great intimacy, but it is an intimacy very likely to be short-lived. In contrast, **companionate love** develops more gradually, is not necessarily tied to sexual passion, and is based on more rational assessments of the one who is loved. Companionate love is more likely than passionate love to lead to long-lasting intimate relationships. However, these two types of love are not clearly distinguished from one another. This is clearest in the fact that long-term intimate relationships often start out with passionate love, but in those that succeed over time, it tends to be combined with, or even supplanted by, companionate love.

Passionate love, also known as romantic love, has a long and interesting history. For example, some of our more recent senses of love are traceable to 1950s consumer culture (Shaw and Lee 2009). It was then that love became closely associated with consumption and travel. The movie, automobile, fashion, and makeup industries capitalized on, and disseminated ideas about, romantic love. Each of these industries, in its own way, glamorized romance and conveyed the message that romance was associated with commodities that were available for a price.

Zygmunt Bauman has sought to get at the essence of love in the contemporary world in his book *Liquid Love* (2003). To Bauman, love, like everything else in today's liquid society, is fleeting. This clearly applies to passionate love, but to Bauman, even companionate love is today constantly at risk of erosion and disappearance. This represents a major challenge to all intimate relationships, especially marriage, and to all of those involved in them. However, liquid love can also be seen as offering people freedom from lifelong loveless relationships. It also offers the possibility of innumerable experiences with love and the possibility of many different relationships built on love.

ASK YOURSELF

What do you think of Bauman's concept of "liquid love"? Do you agree that love is fleeting, and that this impermanence is a reflection of a society in which nothing lasts? Why or why not? Would you find the experience of liquid love troubling, or liberating? Why?

It can be argued that our main concerns in this chapter—family and marriage—are also increasingly liquid. Because they are now so liquid, the borders of marriage and the family are increasingly difficult to define. More important, many traditional forms of marriage and the family are confronting the possibility of being washed away. As a result, many sociologists have moved away from a focus on the family and marriage and prefer to discuss vaguer phenomena such as "relationships" and "personal life." Nevertheless, most people, including most sociologists, continue to think in terms of marriage and the family (Powell et al. 2010). We will do the same in this chapter, but with an understanding that both are changing dramatically and refer to phenomena that are far more liquid than they were in the past.

BROAD CHANGES IN MARRIAGE AND THE FAMILY

We will discuss two major changes in this section: the decline of marriage and changes in the family household.

DECLINE IN MARRIAGE

In 1970, married couples constituted 71 percent of all U.S. households (see Figure 10.1); by 2012, only 49 percent of all households were married couples. Similarly, the traditional **nuclear family** consisting of two adults and one or more children dropped from 40 percent of all households in 1970 to not quite 20 percent of all households in 2012.

Another way to get a sense of the dramatic change in marriage and the family is to look at the percentage of those who have never been married. Figure 10.2 shows that, in 2016, 28 percent of men and 24 percent of women in the United States ages 25 and older had never been married, compared to 10 percent of men and 8 percent of women in 1960.

However, it remains the case that as people age, they are more likely to marry. Figure 10.3 shows that in 2016, 43 percent of men and 33 percent of women had never been married by age 35. And by age 45, 17 percent of men and 12 percent of women had never married. In comparison, in 1960, only 7 percent of men and 6 percent of women had never married by the age of 45. Further declines are expected in most, if not all, age categories.

PERSPECTIVES ON THE DECLINE IN MARRIAGE

Many sociologists have observed that the norms relating to marriage have weakened in the United States and other countries around the world (Brown, Manning, and Payne 2015; Cherlin

FIGURE 10.1 • U.S. Households by Type, 1970 to 2012

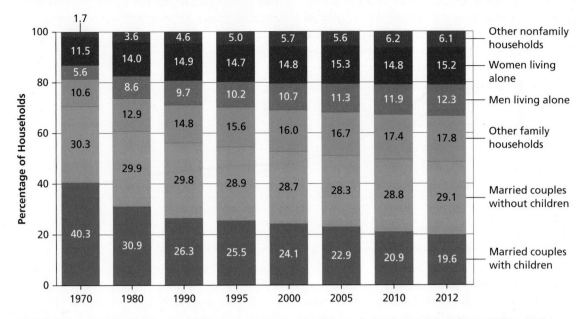

SOURCE: U.S. Census Bureau, Current Population Survey, Annual Social and Economic Supplement, Selected Years, 1970 to 2012.

FIGURE 10.2 • Share of Never-Married Adults in the United States, by Gender, 1960–2016

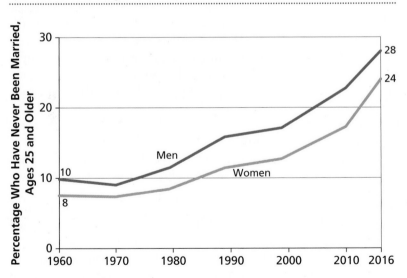

SOURCES: Pew Research Center analysis of the 1960–2000 decennial census and 2010–2012 American Community Survey, Integrated Public Use Microdata Series (IPUMS), September 24, 2014. Data for 2016 from U.S. Census Bureau, "America's Families and Living Arrangements: 2016: Adults," Table A1.

2004; Davis and Friedman 2014; Treas, Lui, and Gubernskaya 2014). This is referred to as the **deinstitutionalization** of marriage; as a result, people increasingly question their actions, or those of others, as they relate to marriage. In the mid-twentieth century, especially in the United States, few questioned marriage and the creation of a nuclear family. Because of this, most plunged into both, sometimes successfully, but more often with dubious or even disastrous results. Now, with marriage and perhaps the nuclear family and the family household deinstitutionalized, it is much easier for people *not* to rush into such arrangements. They are freer to experiment with many other arrangements.

Five factors have been influential in the deinstitutionalization of marriage:

- First, as more women entered the labor force, the clear division of labor in the family between

FIGURE 10.3 • Share of Never-Married Adults in the United States, by Age, 2016

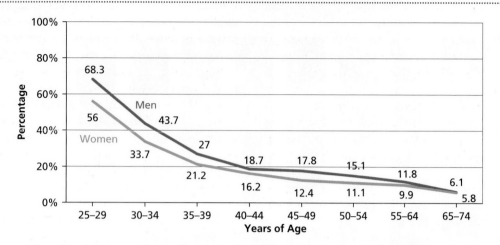

SOURCE: U.S. Census Bureau, "America's Families and Living Arrangements: 2016: Adults," Table A1.

homemaker and breadwinner began to break down. This helped weaken the once clear norms about what men and women were to do in a marital relationship.

- Second, the norms about having children within the context of marriage and the family have also weakened, demonstrated by the dramatic increase in childbirth outside of marriage since the late 1970s.

- Third, the high and increasing divorce rate between 1960 and 1980 changed attitudes about the stability and longevity of marriage.

- Fourth has been the growth in cohabitation, which began in the 1970s and accelerated as the twentieth century ended.

- Finally, same-sex marriage became more common in the 1990s and has grown even more prevalent in the twenty-first century.

These ideas on deinstitutionalization are embedded in a long-term model of change. In the early twentieth century, **institutional marriage** was the predominant form. The focus in such a marriage was on the maintenance of the institution of marriage itself. There was less concern that those involved would love or be good companions to one another.

By the middle of the twentieth century, a model of **companionate marriage** had become predominant (Amato et al. 2007; Burgess and Locke 1945). Companionate marriage meshed well with the nuclear family. It involved a clear division of labor between the single-earner breadwinner—almost always the male—and the female homemaker. In spite, or perhaps because, of the strict division of labor, husbands and wives were held together by bonds of sentiment, friendship, and sexuality. They were supposed to be each other's companions, which included being each other's friends, confidants, and lovers. Romantic love was an essential component of companionate marriage.

In the 1960s, a dramatic shift began to take place in the direction of **individualized marriage** (Lauer and Yodanis 2011). The goal of companionate marriage was the satisfaction of the couple, the family as a whole, and the roles the couple played in the family. However, that focus began to shift increasingly in the direction of the satisfaction of each individual, as well as toward individuals' ability to develop and express themselves. In addition, instead of being as rigid as companionate marriage, individualized marriage became increasingly open and flexible. Furthermore, couples were becoming more open with each other in communicating about and dealing with problems. Many couples, as well as many observers, applauded the greater freedoms and sensitivities associated with individualized marriage, although the changes may not be as clear-cut as was first believed (Yodanis and Lauer 2014).

A major factor in the rise of individualized marriage was the changing place in society of women, especially middle-class women. For example, as more women went to work, they were no longer restricted to the homemaker role and reliance on the male breadwinner. As more women obtained higher education, their occupational prospects were enhanced. This put them in a context where the ideas associated with companionate marriage were increasingly open to question. Greater access to contraception and to abortion enabled more women to plan their reproductive lives, releasing them from some of the constraints of companionate marriage as they related to producing and socializing children.

As a result of all these changes, people today feel freer to never marry, to marry later, to end unhappy marriages, and especially to engage in many other types of intimate relationships. Yet in spite of these changes, the vast majority of people—as many as 90 percent or more—will eventually marry, although many of their marriages will end long before they reach the "till death do us part" stage. Thus, even though marriage may be more deinstitutionalized today than in the past, most of us still believe in it enough to get married.

Self-Disclosing Intimacy and Pure Relationships

The deinstitutionalization of marriage has encouraged the conception of new individualized forms of marriage and relationships (Giddens 1992). The key to these new forms of relationship is "self-disclosing intimacy" (Duncan 2014; Giddens 1992; Funk and Kobayashi 2016). Couples are disclosing much more to each other. As a result, much more intimate relationships are likely to develop. However, intimate relationships based on full disclosure are made much more fragile by such disclosures, especially as the disclosures continue and proliferate over time. The more weaknesses someone reveals to a partner, the more likely that partner is to become disappointed with the relationship. Despite this, intimate relationships are likely to be more mutually satisfying, equal, and

democratic than institutional or companionate marriages (Giddens 1992). Because marriage of any kind can be confining and limiting, some couples prefer a **pure relationship** that is entered into for its own sake, or for what each partner can get from it; those in the relationship remain only as long as each derives enough satisfaction from it (Giddens 1992). While pure relationships can exist within marriage, they are more likely to exist outside such legal relationships. As a result of the increasing predominance of this idea, at least among young people, a relationship is likely to be ended when the couple no longer find it satisfying. This fits with the increasing individualization of contemporary society as well as the closely related phenomenon of individuals wanting more choices and greater freedom of choice. In whatever type of intimate relationship people find themselves today, the possibility that it will dissolve is never very far from their consciousness. This may be one of the reasons why young adults are putting off developing intimate relationships (Rauer et al. 2013).

NONFAMILY HOUSEHOLDS

A **nonfamily household** is one in which a person lives either alone or with nonrelatives. Of greatest interest is the growth of one-person households, or people living alone. As is clear in Figure 10.4, the United States has witnessed an increase in such households, from 13 percent in 1960 to more than 28 percent of all households in 2016.

One-person households, or "singletons," are the subject of Eric Klinenberg's *Going Solo: The Extraordinary Rise and Surprising Appeal of Living Alone* (2012). (See the Trending box in this chapter.) Detailed in this work is the long-term increase in the number of people living alone. Overall, 31 million Americans now live alone. The fastest-growing segment of the population going solo consists of young adults between the ages of 18 and 34. In 1950, only a half-million of those in this age group lived alone, while today the total of 5 million is 10 times the number in the mid-twentieth century. Among those who are middle-aged (35 to 64), 15 million live alone, while 10 million of the elderly are singletons. More women (17 million) than men (14 million) live alone. Going solo is mainly an urban phenomenon; more than half of dwellings in Manhattan are one-person residences.

FIGURE 10.4 • Percentage of U.S. Households with One Person, 1960–2016

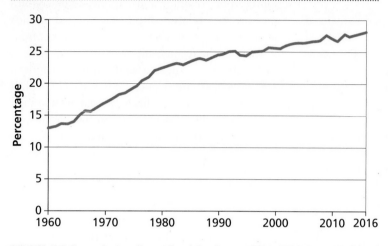

SOURCE: U.S. Census Bureau, Current Population Survey, 1960 to 2011, Annual Social and Economic Supplements; data for 2016 from U.S. Census Bureau, "America's Families and Living Arrangements: 2016: Households," Table H1.

ALTERNATIVE FORMS OF FAMILIES

Recent social changes have made it possible for people to choose nontraditional family structures for themselves, such as cohabitation, single-parent families, families with nonresident parents, stepfamilies or blended families, or lesbian or gay families (Few-Demo and Demo 2016).

Cohabitation

Cohabitation is defined as an arrangement in which a couple shares a home and a bed without being legally married. There are clearly more cohabiting couples today than there were previously, although they still compose only a small proportion (about 6 percent) of all U.S. households. The United States ranks low among developed countries in terms of cohabitation. For example, cohabitation is much more common in France, Estonia, Denmark, and the United Kingdom (see Figure 10.5).

It is unclear exactly how many people are living in such relationships, because cohabitation is not a formally constituted relationship and it leaves no legal records. Furthermore, it is not clear how many nights, weeks, months, or years a couple must be together to be categorized as cohabiting. It is clear, however, that more young

FIGURE 10.5 • Percentage of Cohabiting Households in Selected Countries, Couples Aged 20 Years and Older

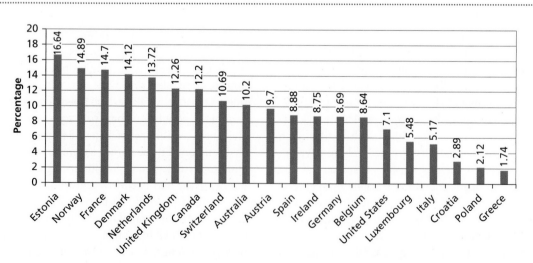

SOURCE: Data from Organisation for Economic Co-operation and Development, 2011.

TRENDING

Going Solo: The Extraordinary Rise and Surprising Appeal of Living Alone

(Penguin Books, 2012)

Eric Klinenberg (Professor of Sociology and Director of the Institute for Public Knowledge at New York University; PhD, University of California, Berkeley, 2000)

An interesting trend—the rise of singletons, or individuals who live alone—is changing the dynamics of family, marriage, and intimate relationships around the world. Today, 27 percent of all U.S. households contain only one occupant. At 47 percent, Sweden has the largest percentage in the world of single-person households. In contrast, India has one of the smallest percentage of households with only one occupant, at 3 percent. Klinenberg explains that relatively affluent people in the Global North are choosing to live alone because they have the economic wealth and social security needed to do so.

There are several reasons for the increase in singletons. First, increasing economic affluence has made it possible for more people to afford the greater costs associated with living alone. Second, living alone is consistent with the growth of individualism in the United States and much of the developed world. Third, the rising status of women and their higher levels of education and higher-paying jobs enable more of them to live alone (although their wages continue to be lower than men's, and they are more likely than men to be poor). With greater independence, they are more likely to marry later, separate, or divorce. Fourth, the communications revolution has allowed people to communicate with other people, and to be entertained, while they are home alone. Fifth, mass urbanization has made the active social life of the city available to more people. Finally, the population is aging, and as people live longer, they are more likely to find themselves alone.

Klinenberg and his research assistants spent seven years conducting in-depth interviews with more than 300 singletons, finding some demographic differences in why and how individuals live alone. Younger singletons prefer to live alone because it provides them with the opportunity to be independent and to focus on self-discovery. Most have strong social networks that they can rely on if they feel lonely or need support. Older, widowed singletons prefer to live alone rather than remarry or move in with family members; however, they face social isolation if they do not develop robust social networks.

In general, women are stigmatized more than men for being single and must more often defend their singleton status. Even though women are achieving higher status in society, their femininity may be questioned if they choose to remain single and not have children. For those who do not have good financial resources, being single can be extremely difficult due to the lack of affordable housing. The infirm elderly who need to live alone in nursing homes or assisted living facilities also suffer from a lack of quality care and services. To address these social changes and challenges, Klinenberg suggests that we need to redesign our cities and suburbs to better integrate all singletons into society, for example, by building more apartments instead of houses for nuclear families (2012, 207).

Supplementary Resources

- You can read an interview with Klinenberg that appeared in the *New York Times* at http://www .nytimes.com/2012/02/12/ fashion/America-Single-and-Loving-It.html.
- You can watch Klinenberg discuss his book at a presentation he gave for Talks at Google: https:// www.youtube.com/ watch?v=C8E8usVe7-s.

Online Dating

In the past, a person was likely to be introduced to a potential partner by family members or friends or to meet him or her at school, work, or church. Today one can use an additional intermediary: online dating websites and mobile apps. Match.com claims that one in five relationships begin on online dating sites. eHarmony commercials boast that matches made on its website have resulted in more marriages than those formed through other online dating services. Unlike traditional intermediaries, online dating sites require us to actively participate in finding and selecting our own partners (Shepherd 2016, 29). eHarmony users, for example, have to complete the site's 29 Dimensions of Compatibility questionnaire, which asks them to provide information about such topics as their family background, personality traits, communication skills, and appearance (Shepherd 2016, 44–46). After these data have been collected and analyzed via a set of algorithms, compatible users are "matched" to each other. Match.com operates in a similar manner, although it also allows users to state their preferences about their ideal partners (Shepherd 2016, 57). Perhaps the most important difference between eHarmony and Match.com is that eHarmony does not permit its users to browse the profiles of all of its members—only profiles that the service has officially "matched" together (Shepherd 2016, 49). Both, however, charge members for their services.

While eHarmony and Match.com cater to heterosexuals interested in eventually getting married, mobile apps connect people more interested in a quick hook-up or in a gay or bisexual relationship. Tinder users can swipe right on their smartphones to find a willing partner for a quick sexual encounter. Grindr, which has 2 million daily users, connects gay and bisexual men looking for a partner. Though Tinder and Grindr are free of charge, paid subscriptions for premium services on Tinder are available. Paying for dating assistance has been a subject of debate, with critics arguing that it commodifies love. Others wonder whether meeting someone online is as authentic as unexpectedly finding love through a chance encounter in real life. Being "matched" with a potential partner through an online dating service might take the romance out of getting to know someone over time, because you can read a profile to discover a person's hobbies or favorite color (Rosewarne 2016). Many Americans are not troubled by these concerns. The use of online dating sites and mobile apps has increased from 10 percent in 2013 to 27 percent in 2015 for young adults (18–24 years old) and from 6 percent in 2013 to 12 percent in 2015 for middle-aged adults (55–64 years old; Smith 2016).

Engaging the Digital World

Have you ever used online dating sites or mobile apps? If yes, state which ones, describe how they work, and describe your experience, including whether you eventually went on a real date with a person to whom you were "matched." If no, would you consider using one? Why or why not?

men and women (especially those between 25 and 35) are living together outside marriage, even if they are not considered, or do not consider themselves, to be cohabiting couples (Manning and Cohen 2015). Living together in this way has come to be considered a common tryout for, and pathway to, marriage, although few people plan to marry when they begin cohabiting. Then again, marriage may never occur or even be discussed, and cohabiting couples may break up and move on to other relationships. A declining number of cohabiting couples—less than 40 percent—end up getting married.

At one time, cohabitation was associated with being poor, less educated, or in the lower classes;

it was seen as the "poor man's marriage." More recently, cohabitation has become increasingly common among those with advanced education, even college degrees. In the past, black women were more likely to cohabit than white women, but in recent years, the cohabitation rates for white women have increased dramatically, and they are now more likely to cohabit than black women (Manning 2013). There are differences between these groups in the function of cohabitation. For instance, for blacks, cohabitation is more likely to be an alternative to marriage; for whites, it is more likely to serve as a prelude to marriage (England and Edin 2009; Smock and Manning 2004).

Three major reasons why couples choose to cohabitate are to spend more time with each other, to save money by sharing expenses, and to assess a partner's compatibility (Huang et al. 2011). Gender differences exists in terms of how men and women view the ways in which cohabiting has enhanced a relationship: Women focus on love, while men focus on sex. In addition, women see cohabitation as less legitimate and as entailing less commitment than marriage, while men worry about the decline in freedom compared with being single (Huang et al. 2011).

Rates of cohabitation vary greatly around the globe. Sweden has a long history of cohabitation, and the process is well institutionalized there. In excess of 90 percent of first partnerships are cohabitations, and more than 40 percent of all first births are to cohabiting couples (Perelli-Harris and Gassen 2012). The legal status, or the rights and privileges, of those who cohabit is virtually the same as that of married couples in terms of such things as social security and taxes (Wilk, Bernhardt, and Noack 2010). Other, mainly Catholic, European countries—Italy and Spain—have much lower rates of cohabitation. There is evidence of the spread of cohabitation throughout much of Europe, including Eastern Europe, and elsewhere.

Single-Parent Families

Among the developed countries, the United States has the highest rate of single-parent families (30 percent of all households with children), while Japan has the lowest (10 percent). In Europe, the northern countries—for example, the United Kingdom

(25 percent), Ireland (23 percent), and Denmark and Germany (both 22 percent)—have the highest rates of single-parent families. It is mainly the southern European countries—Greece and Spain (5 percent), Portugal (6 percent), and Italy (7 percent)—that have the lowest rates of such families. Though children who grow up in single-parent households are more likely to live in poverty, suffer from mental health problems, and have higher rates of drug use, many of them view their family life as "normal" and experience stability in their homes (Nixon, Greene, and Hogan 2015).

Nonresident Parents

Nonresident parents are fathers and mothers who live apart from their children (Smyth 2007). Most nonresident parents are fathers, although the number of mothers in this category is increasing. Historically, there have been many reasons for fathers to be absent from their families, including work, war, and incarceration. Today, although those reasons continue to exist, the major reasons are nonmarital childbearing (with the parents never having lived together), the breakdown of cohabiting relationships, and marital dissolution.

The issue of nonresident parents is highly related to globalization and to the tendency for at least one parent to migrate in search of work. The physical distance created by work migration makes it difficult to adequately perform the role of mother or father, although that is ameliorated by the internet and interaction through e-mail, Skype, Facebook, and text messaging via services such as WhatsApp. Such services have helped create new "cyberparents." While much of the focus has been on the negative effects of globalization on both nonresident parents *and* their children, it is possible that we are seeing a restructuring of global parenting—and the creation of a new category of transnational parent—with a number of benefits, especially for the children. For example, parents who emigrate for work may end up being better off economically. This is especially true for mothers who may be empowered and better able to take on the "breadwinner" role. They are likely to be better able to send remittances and "care packages" back to their families (Cohen 2015).

Some nonresident parents are in the armed forces. This Air Force servicewoman marches with her son during a Memorial Day parade in Indiana. How are the stresses on military families different from those faced by others with nonresident parents?

Stepfamilies and Blended Families

A **stepfamily** consists of two adults who are married or cohabiting, at least one of whom has a child or children from a previous marriage or cohabitation living with him or her (Ganong and Coleman 2017). A **blended family** includes some combination of children from the partners' previous marriages or relationships, along with one or more children of the currently married or cohabiting couple (Martin-Uzzi and Duval-Tsioles 2013). Stepfamilies and blended families have become very common in the United States, because about half of all marriages include a partner who was previously married. According to a 2011 Pew Research Center survey, 42 percent of all U.S. adults have at least one step-relative. The U.S. Census Bureau estimates that 50 percent of children under the age of 13 live with one biological parent and that parent's partner (Stepfamily Foundation, n.d.). Stepfamilies are complex because the children are likely to spend time with a stepparent as well as with the mother or father from their first-marriage family. In addition, stepfamilies often have insufficient time to develop the family routines and rituals that are likely to have existed in first families. Children may well have difficulty adapting to these new, nonroutinized ways of living.

Lesbian and Gay Families

Gay and lesbian couples have various similarities with, as well as differences from, straight families. One important difference is that gay and lesbian couples tend to be more reflexive and democratic in their family decisions and practices than straight couples. This is particularly the case concerning housework and other domestic duties, which are contentious issues for heterosexual couples who both work outside the home. Gay and lesbian couples are less constrained by social and institutional gender roles, with the result that they are freer in their negotiations over relational and family practices. Norms for sexual relationships are less institutionalized among gay and lesbian couples as well, leading to some creative adaptations. Although monogamy is often assumed (but often violated) by straight couples, same-sex male couples are not as wedded to the idea or practice of sexual exclusivity. They negotiate over this issue and develop clear ground rules for nonmonogamous sexual relationships (Adam 2006; Barrett and Pollack 2011). Gay male relationships tend to be more fragile, while lesbian relationships tend to be far more stable. Some of the reasons for these gender differences are related to gender socialization patterns (Kimmel 2012).

The polar views on same-sex marriage are, on the one hand, that it is an expression of greater tolerance in the population as a whole and, on the other hand, that it is yet another threat to religion, morality, and heterosexual marriage. Whatever the perceived dangers, same-sex marriage has become increasingly common in the United States and in many other countries (Biblarz and Stacey 2010; Heaphy 2007). As recently as the 1990s, there was no legal recognition of such marriages *anywhere in the world,* and the prospect of such marriages faced considerable hostility and intolerance. A key event

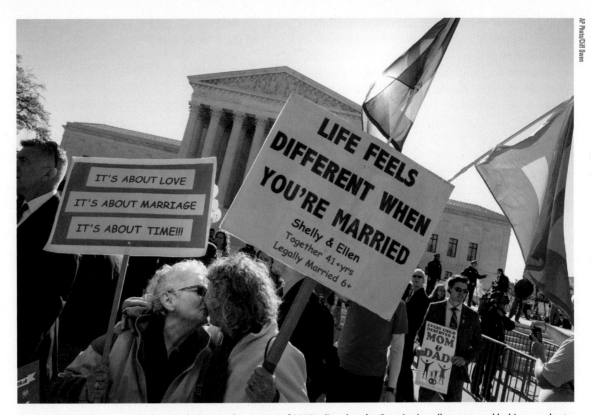

The U.S. Supreme Court issued a historic decision in the summer of 2015 ruling that the Constitution allows gay and lesbian couples to marry.

occurred in September 2000, when the Netherlands extended the right to marry to same-sex couples. In the ensuing decade, a number of other countries throughout the world came to permit same-sex marriages, including Argentina, Canada, Spain, and South Africa.

After same-sex marriage had been legalized in a number of U.S. states, the U.S. Supreme Court finally declared same-sex marriage constitutional in mid-2015, making it legal in all 50 states.

ASK YOURSELF

Why do you think it took the Supreme Court as long as it did to declare same-sex marriage constitutional? What factors finally changed the Court's position?

THEORIZING THE FAMILY

Whatever the family form, the main types of theories outlined in Chapter 2 and used throughout this book—structural/functional, conflict/critical, and inter/actionist theories—can be used to think about and shed light on the family.

STRUCTURAL/FUNCTIONAL THEORIES

Writing in the mid-twentieth century, in the heyday of marriage, the nuclear family, and the family household, Talcott Parsons, the preeminent structural-functionalist, saw the family as a structure with very important functions for society as a whole. The nuclear family was especially important in the America of Parsons's day. Its structure freed family members from the obligations of an **extended**

family—two or more generations of a family living in the same household or in close proximity to one another—and allowed them the mobility needed in the industrial society of the time. Of greatest concern to structural-functionalism is the need for order in society. A very important source of that order is the socialization of children into how they are supposed to act, as well as the process by which they learn the norms, values, and morality of society. The family, especially in the heyday of the nuclear family, played a crucial role in socialization. Furthermore, such a family was more likely than any other family form to communicate a coherent sense of society's culture and morality. This kind of thinking has been picked up by those sociologists who emphasize the functions of the family:

- First, society must at least replace those who die. This is accomplished through childbearing, which traditionally has been preferred to occur within the family.

- Second, the family fulfills the need to provide physical and emotional care to children.

- Third, the family fulfills the socialization function discussed previously.

- Fourth, the family shares resources to meet its economic needs.

- Fifth, the family provides intergenerational support as parents continue to support their adult children economically, emotionally, and in many other ways.

- Sixth, the family has traditionally served to control sexual behavior.

- Finally, the family is a mechanism for helping children find a place in society, especially in its stratification system.

There are many criticisms of the structural-functional theory of marriage and the family, not the least of which is that it applied best to the realities of the 1950s and is increasingly out of touch with today's realities. It simply "doesn't take into account the diversity of family structures and roles found in American marriages and families" (Scott and Schwartz 2008, 349). Moreover, structural-functional theory has a conservative bias that aims to maintain and reproduce the status quo, including that of marriage and the nuclear family. Furthermore, it tends to "understate disharmony and conflict" and, more generally, the array of family-related problems that will be discussed in the following section (Scott and Schwartz 2008, 349).

CONFLICT/CRITICAL THEORIES

Unlike structural-functionalists, conflict theorists have never seen the family as a coherent unit or as contributing in an unambiguously positive way to the larger society. For one thing—as pointed out previously, and as we will discuss later in this chapter—the family itself is riddled with stresses, strains, and conflicts that lead to all sorts of problems for the family, its members, and society as a whole (Noller and Karantzas 2012). The family is an especially rich arena for conflicts based on gender and age (e.g., sibling rivalries, children versus parents). Such conflicts are closely related to the issue of power within the family—who has the most power, how it is used (and abused), and so forth. Above all, conflict can arise when one or more family members seek to wrest power from those who possess it.

Was structural/functional theory more relevant to nuclear families of the 1950s than it is to today's socially diverse families?

In contrast to structural functionalists' harmonious view of the family, conflict theorists see the family as an arena of gender conflict in which males have historically been the winners, leaving female family members in an inferior positions (Collins 1975). Similarly, when it comes to age-based conflict within the family, parents are generally victorious and children relatively powerless.

A key issue in looking at inequality and conflict within the family is found in the resources possessed by the various parties involved. In terms of the conflict between adults and children, parents have a variety of resources, including greater size, strength, experience, and ability to satisfy the needs of the young, and as a result, the young are likely to be dominated by the adults. Among the few resources possessed by the young are their physical attractiveness and physical prowess (Kimmel 2012). However, as children mature, they acquire other resources and are better able to resist adults.

Feminist Theory

Feminist theory tends to be critical of the dominant family model—male-dominated, white, middle-class, heterosexual, with dependent children. Feminist theorists see the family as being internally stratified on the basis of gender: Men and women possess different economic and social positions and interests, and they struggle over those differences (Allen and Jaramillo-Sierra 2015). Males have been able to create and to impose a gendered division of labor within the family that benefits men and adversely affects women. The family is seen as a patriarchal structure in which males exercise power and oppress women. Male control is enhanced by an ideological mechanism whereby traditional family norms are upheld. For example, girls tend to learn to accept the idea that they should put family responsibilities ahead of everything else, including their personal development and satisfaction. This tends to engender and support masculine power and privilege. According to the staunch feminist Emma Goldman, "the institution of marriage makes a parasite of woman, an absolute dependent" (cited in Shaw and Lee 2009, 298).

INTER/ACTIONIST THEORIES

The inter/actionist theories discussed in this section, symbolic interactionism and exchange theory, look at the family from a more microscopic perspective than either structural/functional or conflict/critical theories do.

Symbolic Interactionism

Symbolic interactionism focuses on the meanings attached to identities, roles, and social relationships, treating meaning as socially constructed. This approach has long been used in family research (Stryker 1959). For example, men may attach different levels of significance to the role of father, and marital partners may redefine their relationship over time. Recent research on the family carried out from a symbolic interactionism perspective includes how the offspring of anonymous sperm donors construct their identities and the challenges gay fathers encounter when trying to secure health insurance for their families (Harrigan et al. 2015; Potter and Allen 2016).

Exchange Theory

Exchange theorists look at the family from the perspective of choices made on the basis of rewards and costs. People enter marital relationships because they think the rewards associated with marriage will outweigh the costs. They also tend to think that marriage will be more rewarding than the alternatives to it: remaining single or becoming involved in other kinds of intimate relationships. Heterosexual marriage benefits men and women; however, men generally benefit the most. However, both married men and married women live longer, have fewer health problems, have more sex, save more money, and have fewer psychological problems, such as depression, than do unmarried men and women.

PROBLEMS IN THE FAMILY

There are a wide variety of family troubles, but we will focus on a few of the major ones in this section.

FAMILY CONFLICT

Conflict is endemic to family life, with numerous flash points between husband, wife, and children in a traditional nuclear family, and innumerable other possibilities for conflict in the wide array of other forms of intimate relationships. While divorce is usually seen as the major result of family conflict, conflict often exists long before a divorce, and it may not even lead to divorce. Much conflict simmers below the surface in many families, surfacing only now and then. Family conflicts may arise over such issues as the family's objectives, resources, and the need to protect the interests of various family members (Kellerhals and Widmer, forthcoming).

ABUSE AND VIOLENCE WITHIN THE FAMILY

Heightened conflict within the family can lead to abuse and violence. This can take various forms, but the most common are parental abuse of children and violence by husbands against their wives (who are considered "battered women"; Dunn 2005; LaViollete and Barnett 2014). Far less common is women abusing and behaving in a violent manner toward their children and even their husbands. Violence within the family can take emotional or psychological forms (Ellin 2016). It can also involve physical and sexual abuse (Pennington 2015b). Although norms that relate to the acceptability of such behavior have changed in recent years, such abuse and violence are still common and accepted in some groups and parts of the world. In such cases, parents feel justified in abusing children, and husbands think it is acceptable to batter their wives. While there are exceptions, we should remember that the vast majority of those who engage in such behavior are not considered to be criminals (Straus 1980).

Child Abuse

Hundreds of millions of children throughout the world are abused, maltreated, and exploited (Bell 2011; Whittier 2016). According to the World Health Organization, "child abuse or maltreatment constitutes all forms of physical and/or emotional ill-treatment, sexual abuse, neglect, or negligent treatment or commercial or other exploitation, resulting in actual or potential harm to the child's health, survival, development, or dignity in the context of a relationship of responsibility, trust, or power" (cited in Polonko 2007, 448). In the United States alone, reports indicate that several million children (15 percent) are severely maltreated, but this number reflects only official reports—the actual number is much higher. Furthermore, the official number includes only those who have been the victims of severe abuse and who clearly have been injured. The most common forms of child abuse are parents hitting their child with an object (20 percent), kicking or biting their child or hitting their child with their fists (10 percent), or physically beating up their child (5 percent) (Kimmel 2012). Fathers and father surrogates are most likely to commit these offenses.

The impact of child abuse is great, especially for the children involved, but also for the parents (or other adults) and the larger society. Physical and emotional abuse and violence experienced in childhood can lead to an increased likelihood of cognitive impairment (lower IQ and levels of educational attainment), impaired ability to reason morally (a weakly developed conscience), and a greater likelihood of engaging in violence and crime. Children who have been abused are themselves more likely to be violent toward other children, including siblings, and later in life to abuse their own children, their spouses, and even elderly parents.

There is often a cycle of violence and abuse toward children that stretches across several generations (Steinmetz 1987). Many of the parents who mistreat and abuse their children were themselves victims as children and, as a result, may have developed mental and substance abuse problems that can increase their own likelihood of mistreating others.

There is also a cost to society. The Centers for Disease Control and Prevention (2012) has estimated that in the United States alone, the economic cost of child abuse is more than $124 billion. This cost is traceable to such things as social services provided to families, the lesser contributions of victims to society, and related criminal justice and health care activities. While there are things that can be done to deal with the adults involved in terms of intervention and prevention, the structure of society as a whole needs to be addressed in various ways to reduce this problem. Of greatest importance is the need to change a culture where children are viewed as property that parents and other adults can treat, and abuse, in any way they want. Children also need to be seen as having human rights. In addition, children need to be better protected, helped, and treated by the various agencies involved. More generally, society and the government need to believe in and support a wide range of policies that are of benefit to children, such as more and better child care.

Domestic Violence

Domestic violence entails the exertion of power over a partner in an intimate relationship through behavior that is intimidating, threatening, harassing, or harmful (Carmody 2007). The partner can be harmed physically and/or sexually, emotionally, and psychologically; the violence can occur multiple times (Goodlin and Dunn 2011). A debate in this area is whether the concept of domestic violence should be restricted to physical violence, or whether abuse in all of these areas qualifies as domestic violence.

A great deal of research has been done on domestic violence, and several general conclusions can be drawn from this work:

- Women are about five times more likely than men to be victims.

- Women are about six times more likely to be assaulted by those they are intimate with (partners or former partners) than by strangers.

- One of the leading causes of injury to women is domestic violence.

- Among minority groups, blacks have the highest rate of such violence.

- Most likely to be victims are poor females between 16 and 24 years of age.

- It is difficult to leave a violent relationship, and the risk of serious, even fatal, injury is greatest when one does try to leave such a relationship.

- Domestic violence is a major cause of homelessness.

Conflicts in some families can turn violent. This boy's father was arrested for beating and torturing his wife and children.

- About one-third of all female homicide victims are killed by those who are intimates.

Figure 10.6 shows that from 1994 to 2011, intimate partner violence dropped by more than 60 percent for both males and females. From 1994 to 2011, such violence was down 49 percent for females and 46 percent for males. From 2000 to 2005, the rate of intimate partner violence against females dropped an additional 31 percent, while male victimization rates remained nearly steady. The rate of intimate partner violence against females remained almost stable from 2005 to 2011, while males experienced a decline from 1.7 to 1.5 victimizations per 1,000 males age 12 or older.

Because gender socialization often leads men to see violence as an appropriate means of communication, it follows that most abusers tend to be male. Heterosexual men and gay men can suffer intimate partner violence, however, as can lesbian, bisexual, and queer people (Dutton and White 2013; Messinger 2014). Men who experience such violence are often discouraged from reporting the crime or seeking social support. Societal assumptions that domestic violence cannot be perpetrated against men, combined with masculine socialization, can make male victims reluctant to report it.

In addition to being very costly to victims and their families, domestic violence is costly to society. Those abused are not likely to be able to function as well in the larger society as those who are not victimized. For example, the abused have higher levels of absenteeism from work. Furthermore, society often needs to pay the costs associated with medical treatment, police involvement, court expenses, and shelters for those who have been victimized.

FIGURE 10.6 • Intimate Partner Violence, by Sex, 1994–2011

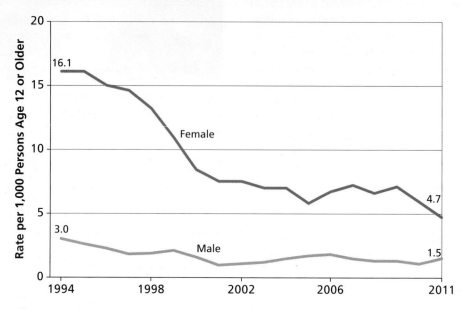

SOURCE: Data from Bureau of Justice Statistics, *National Crime Victimization Survey, 1993–2011*, Appendix Table 1.

NOTE: Estimates based on two-year rolling averages beginning in 1994. Includes rape or sexual assault, robbery, aggravated assault, and simple assault committed by current or former spouses, boyfriends, or girlfriends.

Elder Abuse

The elderly do not escape abuse merely because of their advanced age. This is certainly an ancient problem, although it has come to wide-scale public attention only in the last half-century. In a large national study, about 10 percent of elderly respondents reported some type of abuse (Acierno et al. 2010). The elderly are abused in various ways, including physically, psychologically, financially, sexually, and through neglect. Among other things, we know that elderly women are more likely to be abused than men, the very elderly (over 80 years of age) are most likely to be victims, and adult children and spouses are most likely to perpetrate the abuse. Beyond the elder abuse committed by family members, such abuse also takes place in residential care facilities for the elderly (Burns, Hyde and Killett, 2013).

POVERTY AND THE FAMILY

There is a close relationship between family structure and poverty, especially for female-headed households (Edin and Kefalas 2011). For example, the poverty rate in 2015 in the United States for married-couple families was 5 percent, but for female-headed families, it was 28 percent—almost five times as much. The likelihood of poverty for female-headed families is much lower in many other developed countries, largely because of more generous social welfare programs. The concentration of poverty among female-headed households tends largely to reflect the consequences of gender inequality.

The big debate here is not over the facts, but over whether the family structure causes poverty or poverty causes problems within the family. On the one hand, the argument is made that a weak family structure—one, for example, where women are left alone to raise children—causes poverty. Such women are apt to be poor because they are unlikely to be able to work, and the children are poor because they are not adequately supported by these women or their absent fathers. On the other hand, it is contended that poverty causes families to crumble. Women are left alone to raise children as the men leave because they cannot support them or because the mothers are more likely to qualify for welfare if the father is absent. The emotional and economic stresses associated with being poor are likely to put intolerable strains on the family.

Being unmarried is likely to be associated with poverty for women with children. Divorce is also likely to drive women, especially those who are already in a marginal economic situation, into poverty. More generally, divorce is likely to affect almost all women adversely. The only debate in this area concerns how badly women are affected and how much they are hurt economically, as well as in other ways.

GENDER INEQUALITIES

Intimate relationships, especially marriages, are unequal as far as the men and women involved are concerned. Marriages can be so different from the points of view of men and women that they seem like completely different systems. These inequalities take several forms.

The first is inequality in the amount of time devoted to household and childcare tasks (Patton and Choi 2014). Figure 10.7 shows the average number of hours per week mothers and fathers spent on paid work, housework, and child care in 1965 and 2011. In 2011, mothers on average spent almost twice as much time (18 hours per week) on housework as fathers (10 hours). Mothers also spent 7 hours more per week on child care than did fathers. Although the gap has been shrinking since 1965, gender inequalities are still clearly prevalent in the home, even as women's hours of paid work have increased dramatically. In addition, men spend more time on tasks that are discretionary, at least to some degree, while women are more likely to perform regular, repetitive labor. Mothers are more likely to maintain the children, while fathers are more likely to engage in recreational activities with the children. The disparity is even greater when it comes to the care of the ill and the elderly; this is almost always the near-total responsibility of females.

Then there are various gender inequalities in power and decision making. This can involve forcing a spouse to do something or to define a situation in a particular way. In heterosexual marriages, men are favored in terms of power within the marital relationship because of their greater size and strength. They are likely to earn more money, and they are likely to dominate conversations, thereby swinging decisions their way. In addition, male power tends

to be institutionalized and supported by religious groups and their customs (especially by Evangelical Christians, Hasidic Jews, Muslims, the Amish, and Mormons) as well as by governments and their policies. The latter often assume that husbands are the household heads and are responsible for the support of wives and children, and that wives are supposed to take care of the household and the children.

As we saw previously, women are more likely than men to be the victims of intimate partner violence, even though men are more likely to be victimized by violence in general. In 1993, the United Nations adopted the Declaration on the Elimination of Violence against Women. Within the United Nations, UN Women (previously UNIFEM) is particularly concerned with the violence perpetrated globally against women and girls, especially in the family (www.unwomen.org/en/about-us). There is a strong preference for male children throughout much of the world, with the result that female embryos are more

FIGURE 10.7 • Hours per Week Mothers and Fathers Spend on Paid Work, Housework, and Child Care, 1965 and 2011

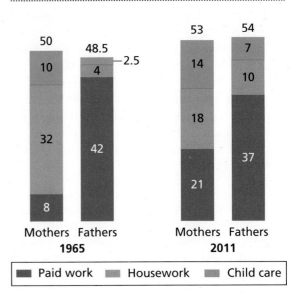

SOURCE: *Modern Parenthood: Roles of Moms and Dads Converge as They Balance Work and Family,* March 14, 2013. Reprinted with permission of Pew Research Center, Washington, DC.

NOTE: Based on adults ages 18–64 with their own child(ren) under age 18 living in the household. Total figures (at the top of each) may not add to component parts due to rounding.

likely to be aborted, female infants are more likely to be the victims of infanticide, and female children are more likely to be the victims of violence.

Globally, wife beating is the most common form of family violence. In some parts of the world, this is taken to extreme lengths, with wives beaten to death. Brides may be burned to death because of (supposed) infidelity, because the bride's family was unable to pay the dowry in full to the husband, or even because a pregnant 14-year old bride refused to work in the fields, in one specific case (Mashal 2016). In some parts of the world, women are stoned to death for such offenses. Some cultures support so-called honor killings, or killings of females because they have engaged in such "dishonorable" behaviors as infidelity, same-sex sexual relations, wanting out of arranged marriages, seeking marriage on their own, or even refusing to adhere to the dress code. There has been a good deal of publicity about, and public uproar over, honor killings in places such as Pakistan, Egypt, Turkey, and Iran.

DIVORCE

Rates of divorce increased in Western nations during the twentieth century. The United States has one of the highest divorce rates in the world (Amato and James 2010). However, the often-repeated "statistic" that half of all U.S. marriages end in divorce is inaccurate.

The divorce rate per thousand in the United States in 2014 was 3.2 (www.cdc.gov/nch/fastats/marriage-divorce/htm). The once dramatic differences in divorce rates between the United States and Europe have declined, mostly because of increases in divorce across Europe; Europe has become more like the United States in terms of divorce (Amato and James 2010).

Factors in Divorce

Regardless of how prevalent or rare it is, divorce is the best-known way of leaving a marriage. Divorce is a formal and legal mechanism that relates to legal marriages. Many marriages end with separations that become permanent without divorce. Other intimate relationships, even those that last a long time, do not require divorce; they end as informally as they began.

Divorce is often the result of a litany of family problems—for example, violence and abuse—that may have occurred over a long period of time before a divorce was ever contemplated. Divorce itself can be seen as a problem, as well as one that creates many other problems, but it also can be seen as a solution to many problems. Divorce allows a spouse to get out of a bad, even disastrous, relationship. In fact, to some, it is the relationship, especially a "bad" marriage, that is the problem and not the divorce. Thus, we should not simply assume—as many do—that divorce is in itself a problem.

An important factor in divorce today in the United States, and in the Global North in general, is the increasing emphasis on the self and individualism. This is also linked to the idea of the pure relationship discussed previously. As we have seen, in such a relationship, including a marital relationship, the partners do not necessarily feel that they are locked into it for a lifetime, or even an extended period of time. Rather, they feel that they are in a relationship as long as it continues to work for *them*. Once individuals come to the conclusion that the relationship is no longer working for them, they are free to leave. Indeed, some take the view that they have an obligation to themselves to leave because they should not jeopardize their own need to have a satisfying life.

In the past, there was a tendency to value positively all marriages that remained intact—that did not end in divorce or in other ways. In many ways, a bad marriage can be a far greater problem than one that ends in divorce. For example, children in unhappily married families tend to feel highly neglected and humiliated (Kimmel 2012, 179). As acceptance of divorce has spread, the negative attitudes and social sanctions aimed at those who divorce have declined. Thus, remarried adults are more accepting of divorce and more likely to take steps toward it when experiencing marital distress than those in first marriages. This indicates a weaker commitment to marriage among those married more than once (Whitton et al. 2013).

ASK YOURSELF

What are some of the reasons why divorce has become more socially acceptable? What specific norms and values about individuals, families, and the institution of marriage have changed to make this acceptance possible? Do you think the increase in the number of divorces has had an impact on society at large? If so, what sort of impact?

Not only have negative attitudes, norms, and values as they relate to divorce declined, but the material circumstances and barriers surrounding divorce have declined as well. Of prime importance is the fact that women today are likely to be better equipped materially to handle divorce than were women in the past. Among other things, they are better educated and more likely to be in the labor force. Thus, they may be more willing to seek divorce because they can better afford to be on their own. Furthermore, dissatisfied husbands are more likely to leave their marriages when they know that their wives can not only survive economically without them but will be financially independent after divorce. Changes in the law are another important material factor that has followed from changes in the norms and values that relate to divorce. One important example is no-fault divorce (i.e., where there is no need to show that either party has been guilty of wrongdoing), which not only has made it easier for people to divorce but also seems to be associated with an increase in the divorce rate. No-fault divorce laws have also acted on the larger culture, helping it become even more accepting of divorce.

GLOBAL FAMILIES

Just as the nation-state is eroding in the face of globalization, it could be argued that the traditional family, deeply embedded in a national context, is also declining. It is no longer necessary for family members, especially those who are relatively well off, to live in the same country, have the same passport, be of the same ethnicity, or share a household in a given locale. Characteristics that used to separate people and made creating global families difficult or impossible are less important in the global age. National hostilities, religious differences, and even great geographic distances matter less to family formation today than they did in the past (Beck and Beck-Gernsheim 2012).

On the one hand, this clearly makes possible, and even highly likely, a wide range of new family types and configurations. For example, it is increasingly possible for family members, even spouses, to live in different countries, even on different continents, and to function quite well as a family (Nobles 2011). Of course, this again is true for those with the means to

As negative attitudes toward divorce have declined, many of the barriers to divorce have eased.

afford such a family life—means that are well beyond the capacities of most people in the world.

On the other hand, these new realities also create many new possibilities for conflict within the family. That is, family members are now bringing to the family new and far broader stresses and strains of various types; clashes of different languages, cultures, religions, and races create new points of potential conflict and hostility. However, these differences are also likely to enrich the family, as well as the larger society, in various significant ways. As globalization increases, new hybrid forms of the family will be created, resulting in innovative and interesting differences within and between families. Families are subject to global flows of all types, and they and their members are increasingly part of those global flows.

GLOBAL FLOWS THAT INVOLVE THE FAMILY

Global flows that involve the family take four major forms. First, entire families, even extended families, can move from one part of the globe to another with relative ease (assuming they have the resources to do so). They can do so on vacation, in relationship to temporary job changes, or permanently.

Second, individual family members can move to a different part of the world and then bring the rest of the family along later. It is ordinarily the case that males are those doing the initial moving. Once they are secure enough economically in their new locations, they are then able to bring over the rest of their family members. Of course, it sometimes happens that males make new lives for themselves in the new locales and leave their families behind in their countries of origin. With increasing economic independence, women are now moving first more often, and then bringing the remainder of their families over (or not). However, many women move globally into low-paying, low-status jobs—for example, as care workers—or are moved, by force, into the global sex trade. Such women are unlikely to be in a strong enough economic position to enable other family members to join them.

Third, individuals can immigrate to create new families. For example, there are many marriage bureaus in developed countries that are in the business of bringing together men from those countries with women who are usually from less developed countries. Various differences between such men and women often create enormous problems for their relationships, however. For one, there is great economic disparity between the spouses. For another, the women often come from societies that are unstable politically and economically, and this makes it difficult for them to adapt to a more stable environment. Finally, marriage bureaus often portray the women as fitting traditional gender expectations, but when they arrive, it may turn out that they do not really measure up to those expectations. Overall, these differences put females in a weak position vis-à-vis males, and they are therefore more vulnerable to abuse of various kinds.

Chris and Cori Schmaus of South Dakota have adopted three children from Africa. Couples in the United States lead the world in adopting children from abroad. What do such children gain from the adoption process? What do they lose?

Fourth, transnational adoptions generally involve the flow of children from less to more developed countries (Briggs 2012; Marre and Briggs 2009; Seligmann 2013). The United States is the world leader in the adoption of children from other countries, while very few American children are adopted elsewhere. Adopting a child from another part of the world transforms the family in many ways. There are also various problems associated with such adoptions, such as the health risks associated with being born in, and having spent at least some time in, less developed countries. There are also stresses involved in the differences between the culture from which the children came and the culture of the country to which they are sent. This is especially a problem if the adopted children are not infants.

GLOBAL FLOWS THAT AFFECT THE FAMILY

As a liquid phenomenon in a liquid world, the global family is affected by, and affects, all of the other liquid phenomena that make up the global world. We will examine just a few of them in this section.

Global Economic Flows

Families are likely to be affected in various ways by global shifts in the economy. For example, a weak economy at home and a boom in another part of the world can lead or even force family members to seek work in the locale that is booming. They are likely to be compelled to leave the rest of the family behind, at least temporarily. This movement of workers can take many forms, such as low-wage male construction workers moving from India or Bangladesh for work in Dubai, female care workers in the Philippines being drawn to Singapore to care for young children, or mostly male workers from between 75 and 90 countries who are drawn to the many low-status, often seasonal jobs available in the American cruise line industry (Oyogoa 2016). In such cases, families can be broken up for long periods at a time, and the stress of those periods can have permanent negative effects on the marriage, as well as on the children. This has been

AP Photo/Argus Leader, Elisha Page

reduced somewhat in the contemporary world of cell phones, the internet, and social networking, which help maintain family relationships or at least reduce the possibility of them fraying or breaking.

Global Migration

The global family is affected by population flows of various kinds. Of utmost importance is the high rate of global migration (Castles 2013), both legal and illegal (see Chapter 14). Among other things, this means that very different people from very different parts of the world are coming together in greater numbers than ever before. Some will settle and marry in diasporic communities composed of people like them; many others will not. Those who do not are likely to create families with mates who are very different from themselves in terms of place of origin, race, ethnicity, religion, and the like (Qian and Lichter 2011). As you recently learned, those entering hybrid families are likely to encounter various difficulties and hostilities. Such problems are likely to be greatest for undocumented immigrants, whose family problems are compounded by the fact that they are in the country illegally. This became a major issue during the 2016 U.S. presidential campaign, when then Republican candidate Donald Trump threatened, if elected, to have deported the approximately 11 million undocumented immigrants in the United States and their children, many of whom were born in the country and are therefore U.S. citizens. Most recently, in late 2017, Trump vowed to phase out the Deferred Action for Childhood Arrivals (DACA) program—also known as the "Dreamers" program—enacted by former president Obama. Under DACA, minors who immigrated with their parents illegally can receive renewable two-year work and education permits to remain in the United States and avoid deportation.

Global Trafficking

Human trafficking involves selling and buying humans as products. It is likely to affect the family in many ways (Jakobi 2012). Children are sometimes trafficked for the purpose of illegal adoption. As with legal adoption, the children generally flow from poor, weak countries to those that are rich and powerful. Recall from Chapter 9 that women are trafficked for purposes of prostitution and forced marriage, both of which have the potential to disrupt family life. Then there is the illegal global traffic in human organs. People in developed countries who need organ transplants but cannot obtain the organs locally are better able to survive because of this traffic. Poor people in less developed countries sell organs not critical to their lives, which are then transported to developed countries and implanted into well-to-do recipients (Negri 2016; Scheper-Hughes 2001). Although the poor in less developed countries do receive some money for their organs, this is but another form of exploitation of the global poor by the global rich. It is a particularly heinous form of exploitation, because the poor must sacrifice one or more of the things that make them human in order to survive.

Global Conflict

Global conflict can affect the family in a number of ways. For one thing, family members, if not entire families, can be forced to flee, sometimes to neighboring countries or even to other parts of the world. For example, after the Vietnam War, more than 2 million people fled Indochina. Many families did not survive intact; in fact, almost 60,000 of the survivors were unaccompanied children. They often not only were traumatized but also suffered from neglect and abuse in the camps in which they found themselves.

For another, there is the impact of the fact that it is young combatants who are the most likely to die in war. This can create a "marriage squeeze," leaving women without a sufficient number of suitable males from which to choose partners (Akers 1967; Bethmann and Kvasnicka 2013). Such a squeeze occurred in Vietnam in the 1970s and 1980s. Another has occurred in Lebanon, which has been afflicted with armed conflict for decades (Karraker 2013). Although it is not necessarily true for all wars, the deployment of American troops in Iraq and Afghanistan has also been associated with higher divorce rates (Negrusa and Negrusa 2014; Negrusa, Negrusa, and Hosek 2014). It is also likely that civilians in countries that have experienced armed conflict will have higher rates of divorce.

Then there is the reality of life for military families, especially those associated with the U.S. military. Many can become "military nomads," moving from bases throughout the world over the course of their military careers (Ender 2002). While the U.S. military has put a lot of supports in place, such perpetual movement can wreak havoc on families, especially in times of deployment during warfare.

The family today is an integral part of globalization, which it is both affecting and being affected by. There is no such thing as a typical global family; at best, there are many global families. More to the point, the people involved in today's families are part, and at the intersection, of innumerable global flows, and as a result, they are enmeshed in constantly changing intimate relationships of all sorts.

SUMMARY

The family is a crucial social institution that is central to social life. Marriage is a legal union of two people, which typically involves monogamy. In an intimate relationship, partners have a close, personal, and domestic relationship with one another. Some relationships are characterized by passionate love with short-lived intimacy, while others are involve long-term companionate love based on rational assessment.

Marriage has declined over the years, and so has the traditional nuclear family, which now accounts for only about one-fifth of all households. The social norms associated with marriage have weakened, resulting in a loss of institutional and companionate marriages and the growth of individualized marriages. Many households today are nonfamily households with a single person who lives alone or are cohabiting households comprised of couples who are not legally married. Other contemporary households include single-parent families, blended families, and lesbian and gay families.

Structural/functional theorists posit that the family is important to society because of its ability to control adult behavior and socialize children. Conflict/critical theorists see the family primarily as a relationship involving inequality and conflict, particularly between those of different ages and genders. Inter/actionists focus on the meanings associated with the family and how individuals choose to enter relationships based on costs and rewards.

Family life is not always harmonious, and conflicts are likely to occur. At the extreme is conflict that involves domestic violence, such as spousal and child abuse. Gender inequality in families is visible by how much time each partner devotes to household and childcare tasks. Spouses who find themselves unhappy in their marriages may choose to get divorced.

Global flows affect the family in a variety of ways. For example, entire families can move from one part of the globe to another, or individual family members can move to a different part of the world and bring the rest of the family later. Global migration and human trafficking all affect the family.

KEY TERMS

blended family, 270
cenogamy, 260
cohabitation, 266
companionate love, 261
companionate marriage, 264
deinstitutionalization, 263

domestic violence, 275
endogamy, 260
exogamy, 260
extended family, 271
family, 260
individualized marriage, 264

institutional marriage, 264
intimate relationship, 261
marriage, 260
monogamy, 260
nonfamily household, 265
nonresident parents, 269
nuclear family, 262

passionate love, 261
polyandry, 260
polygamy, 260
polygyny, 260
pure relationship, 265
stepfamily, 270

1. What is marriage? What are the different types of marriage?

2. What factors account for the deinstitutionalization of marriage over the past few decades? Which one do you think is most significant? Why?

3. According to structural/functional theorists, why are families so important to society? What criticisms do conflict/critical theorists have of structural/functional theories?

4. What forms can intimate relationships take? Do you think that some forms of relationships in the United States are valued more highly than others? Do you think these values will change in the future? Why or why not?

5. Recent studies show that many people are using internet dating sites to start intimate relationships. How could you use exchange theory to explain this trend?

6. Explain the growth of nonfamily and cohabiting households. Do you find either of these household arrangements to be more desirable than a family household? Why or why not?

7. What are the causes and consequences of divorce? What are the benefits and disadvantages of divorce?

8. What are some general conclusions that sociologists have made about domestic violence? Where is there still debate concerning such violence? What are some other common problems that arise within families?

9. Many sociologists see a close relationship between family structure and poverty. What is this relationship? What role does gender play? What are some contrasting viewpoints?

10. In what ways has globalization affected the family?

EDUCATION AND RELIGION

Science versus Religion in the Public Schools

Proposed by Charles Darwin in 1859 and affirmed by countless twentieth-century biologists, the theory of evolution has achieved consensus as an explanation of the natural origin of humankind over time. In contrast, proponents of the idea of intelligent design see the overwhelming complexity of the universe, including the creation of humankind, as the work of a rational, omnipotent designer, such as a god or other supernatural entity. In the United States, debate has arisen over whether these competing explanations of the origin of humans and the universe should be taught in public schools.

Since 1925, U.S. laws and court cases have challenged the teaching of evolution, creationism (the belief that the biblical God created the universe), and intelligent design in public schools. Advocates of evolution-only science programs cite the First Amendment's Establishment Clause, which supports the separation of church and state and the imperative to teach scientifically valid ideas in the classroom. Many advocates of the teaching of evolution contend that intelligent design has no place in educational courses dedicated to evidence-based knowledge. Intelligent design proponents argue that evolution and

LEARNING OBJECTIVES

11.1 Understand the purpose of education and its benefits.

11.2 Describe inequality in education, its sources, and its effects.

11.3 Compare the educational system in United States to the system in other countries around the world.

11.4 Define religion and its major components.

11.5 Identify different types of religious organizations.

11.6 Describe the relationship between globalization and the world's major religions.

edge.sagepub.com/ritzeressentials3e

- Take the chapter quiz
- Review key terms with eFlashcards
- Explore multimedia links and SAGE readings

intelligent design should be taught equally and that students should be encouraged to decide for themselves which one is valid.

Some religious beliefs are at odds not only with scientific knowledge that is taught in public schools but also with social issues that might be discussed, such as same-sex marriage and abortion. Parents who feel strongly about not exposing their children to ideas and practices that contrast with their religious beliefs often opt to send their children to religious schools or homeschool them. In some U.S. states, parents can use government-issued vouchers, funded by public tax dollars, to pay for their children's tuition at private religious schools. Critics of voucher programs question the constitutionality of this practice, asserting that it violates the separation of church and state.

Teaching evolution and other controversial topics in schools is not a problem exclusive to the United States. The radical organization the Islamic State recently banned the teaching of evolution in schools it controls. Globally, however, religious schools play an important part in education, particularly where there are few if any alternatives. The most recent World Values Survey found that, with the exception of Europe, higher levels of education are not significantly associated with a decline in the importance of religion in people's lives. ●

EDUCATION

Education is closely related to the process of socialization discussed in Chapter 4, because both involve the learning process. As a general rule, socialization tends to be a more informal process, while education takes place more formally in schools of various types. Much socialization—for example, learning not to eat with one's hands—takes place largely within families in children's early years. Children also usually learn to talk and in many cases to read before they begin formal schooling. By the time most U.S. children are five years old, the focus has shifted

from the highly informal process of socialization in the family to the more formal educational process in schools. Formal educational settings, such as preschools, elementary and high schools, colleges, and universities, build on and expand the base of knowledge acquired through the early socialization process. In addition, classroom rules teach children about order, respect for authority, and the benefits of conformity. In adulthood, much new learning takes place during socialization processes, such as when starting a new job, but adults also increasingly participate in adult education programs.

While five years of age is the norm for starting school in the United States and other developed countries, much younger children are increasingly entering preschools. Of course, preschool is only the beginning of the educational process. In the United States, as in all other advanced industrial countries, education continues for many years, through grade school, high school, college, graduate school, and professional school, and even beyond in formal adult socialization programs. Most people do not progress through all these stages, though the stage at which someone's formal education ends has profound implications for that person's future.

Clearly, educational attainment is closely related to employment and earnings. Figure 11.1 shows the correlation between educational attainment and employment and income in 2015. Individuals age 25 and over with less than a high school diploma were almost three times more likely to be unemployed than those with a bachelor's degree; they were five times more likely to be unemployed than those with a doctorate. A person's likelihood of being unemployed decreases as he or she ascends the educational ladder.

Higher levels of education serve as a protection against unemployment, especially in hard economic times. During the Great Recession that began in late 2007, the hardest-hit segment of the population was people with less than a high school diploma. The recession's smallest negative effect was on those with doctoral and advanced professional degrees. According to the U.S. Department of Labor's Bureau of Labor Statistics (see Figure 11.1), the unemployment rate in 2015 for individuals with doctoral degrees and advanced professional degrees was nearly 2 percent. At the same time, the rate for individuals with less than a high school diploma was

FIGURE 11.1 • Unemployment Rates and Earnings by Educational Attainment in the United States, 2015

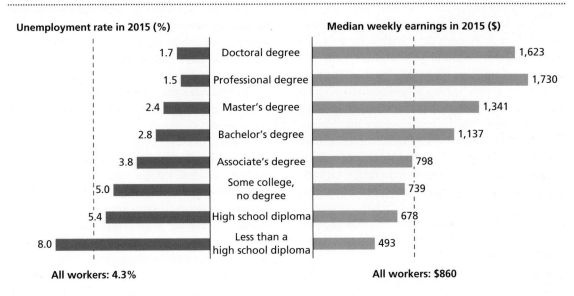

Unemployment rate in 2015 (%)

1.7	Doctoral degree
1.5	Professional degree
2.4	Master's degree
2.8	Bachelor's degree
3.8	Associate's degree
5.0	Some college, no degree
5.4	High school diploma
8.0	Less than a high school diploma

All workers: 4.3%

Median weekly earnings in 2015 ($)

Doctoral degree	1,623
Professional degree	1,730
Master's degree	1,341
Bachelor's degree	1,137
Associate's degree	798
Some college, no degree	739
High school diploma	678
Less than a high school diploma	493

All workers: $860

SOURCE: U.S. Department of Labor, Bureau of Labor Statistics, Employment Projections.

NOTE: Data are for persons age 25 and over. Earnings are for full-time wage and salary workers.

8 percent, whereas it was 5 percent for people with no more than a high school diploma.

Individuals' median weekly earnings increase significantly with level of education, although there is a slight decrease for those with a doctoral degree compared to those who hold a professional degree. Those with a professional degree have the highest median weekly earnings, at $1,730, nearly four times the earnings of those without a high school degree and almost three times the earnings of individuals with a high school degree. While there are many other measures of success in life, levels of education and earnings are obviously of great importance (Blau and Duncan 1967). Other individual benefits of having more education include being less likely to commit a crime and being better off in terms of overall health (Brennan, Durazzi, and Séné 2013; Smith et al. 2015); those with more education are also more open politically (Osborne and Sibley 2015).

Education makes a huge difference not only at the individual level but also at the level of the nation-state. Thus, if we compare nation-states on a global basis, nations with strong educational systems and high levels of education tend to be more economically prosperous.

INEQUALITY IN EDUCATION

A **meritocracy** is a system based on a dominant ideology involving the widely shared belief that all people have an equal chance of succeeding economically based on their hard work and skills. A meritocratic social system also requires that people's social origins, such as class background, and ascribed characteristics, such as race and gender, be unrelated to their opportunities to move up in the social system. Education is a centrally important institution in a meritocracy because it has the potential to level the playing field and provide equal opportunities for students to learn, work hard, and compete to move up in the social hierarchy.

WHO SUCCEEDS IN SCHOOL?

In a meritocratic society, we would expect to find that social origin and ascribed status (see Chapter 4) have little effect on how much students learn and how far they go in school. However, there is a clear pattern of inequality in the United States that suggests that our educational system is not meritocratic.

Students with the highest reading and math scores at the end of high school are those whose parents have the most education. The same pattern is evident if we look at family income and parental occupational status. In terms of race/ethnicity, we see in Figure 11.2 that Asian and white students, both male and female, are more likely than black or Hispanic students to complete high school and attain either a bachelor's or master's degree, or higher. Looking at sex differences in the figure, we see that females generally have better high school completion rates than their male counterparts and are also more likely to obtain a bachelor's or master's degree (or higher).

Clearly, social origins and ascribed (race, gender) characteristics are strongly related to educational outcomes. To many observers, this suggests that American society is decidedly unmeritocratic.

THE COLEMAN REPORT: HOW MUCH DO SCHOOLS MATTER?

The first large-scale study of American schools was conducted in the 1960s by James Coleman. Coleman's study was commissioned by the U.S. Congress, and everyone anticipated that the findings would support the conventional wisdom of the time: Differences in student learning reflect inequalities in school quality. Coleman's findings, published in what has become known as the Coleman Report, were a surprise, and they changed the way in which sociologists understand educational inequality. They led to a rethinking of the assumption that educational institutions can create equal opportunities that will overcome existing class and racial inequalities in the larger society.

First, Coleman (1966) estimated how much schools differ in "quality." He collected data on teachers' salaries, teacher quality, the number of books in the library, the age of school buildings, the curriculum, and numerous other features of schools. On average, schools were much more similar in these respects than was commonly believed. Subsequent research has supported this finding, and reforms in the past half-century have made schools even more similar than they were when Coleman conducted his study.

Second, Coleman found few school characteristics that were related to student learning. School resources, such as per-pupil spending, the books in a library, and so on, did not predict student

FIGURE 11.2 • Educational Attainment of Persons 25 to 29 Years Old, by Race/Ethnicity and Sex, 2016

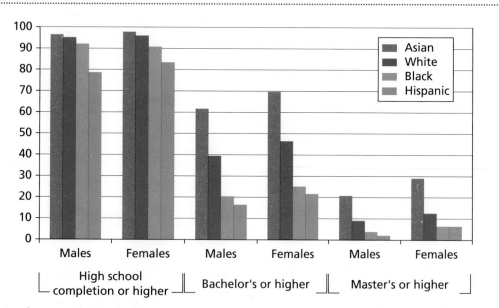

SOURCE: Data from National Center for Education Statistics, Table 104.20, Percentage of Persons 25 to 29 Years Old with Selected Levels of Educational Attainment, by Race/Ethnicity and Sex: Selected Years, 1920 through 2016.

achievement. In terms of achievement, Coleman found that the most important school characteristics were teacher quality and the family background and racial composition of the students attending the school. Students learned more in schools with better teachers and white, middle-class peers. Finally, Coleman found that the most important predictor of student learning was a student's family background.

ASK YOURSELF

What resources—social, material, and other—does the institution of the family provide to account for Coleman's finding that family background is the most important predictor of student learning? Does it surprise you to learn that schools are very similar in terms of their physical and material features? Why or why not?

Recent research on "school effects" has generally been supportive of Coleman's conclusion that school differences in resources contribute less to educational inequality than has often been assumed. The key point is that schools play a role secondary to that of the different levels of cultural capital students bring to the classroom due to their socioeconomic backgrounds. There have been many studies of the importance of school funding for student learning, and generally the results have been mixed. Numerous studies of public–private differences in student learning have indicated at best only a small advantage in learning for Catholic high school students, mostly due to more rigorous coursework (Carbonaro and Covay 2010; Elder and Jepsen 2014). In elementary and middle school, public school students actually outperform private school students in math, and they do equally well in reading (Lubienski 2006).

In addition, recent large-scale surveys indicate that socioeconomic and racial and ethnic differences in student ability are sizable when children *begin* kindergarten. Furthermore, these differences can be detected when children are as young as two years of age (Aud and Hannes 2011). Clearly, schools cannot be blamed for producing educational inequalities if the inequalities are present *before students even enter school*. In short, Coleman's study and subsequent research undermine the simplistic explanation that educational inequality merely reflects unequal opportunities available to students while they are in school.

This is not to argue, as some have, that family backgrounds are determinative and schools are irrelevant. They are not. Indeed, they play a significant role. Coleman conducted his study during the height of the civil rights movement, and one of his concerns was the impact of segregated schools. Using standardized test results, he observed that blacks did not do as well as whites. However, he found that black students did best when they were in integrated schools rather than in predominantly black ones. Integration, in other words, was a resource, just like teacher quality was. Unfortunately, efforts aimed at school integration led to massive "white flight." The integration of public schools peaked in the 1980s, and since then the nation has witnessed the resegregation of schools (Orfield 2001). Figure 11.3 shows that in Boston during the 2014–2015 school year, 77 percent of the public school student population was black and Hispanic and only 13 percent was white. In Washington, D.C., public school enrollment was 84 percent black and Hispanic, and in Atlanta the figure was 82 percent. In Los Angeles, where 74 percent of public school students were Hispanic, only 10 percent were white. The educational achievement gap between blacks and whites narrowed between the 1960s and 1990s, but since that time it has remained basically unchanged (Camera 2016; Condron et al. 2013; Gamoran and Long 2006).

While it is certainly not the last word on the debate over the Coleman Report, Downey and Condron (2016) have recently made the case for a more nuanced and balanced position on the relationship between inequality and schools. That is, some inequalities might be reproduced or even increased by schools, but others (e.g., disparities in cognitive skill) may be reduced.

INTELLIGENCE AND SCHOOL SUCCESS

One possible explanation for Coleman's findings, and those of others, focuses on what are hypothesized as innate differences in intelligence. Richard Herrnstein and Charles Murray (1994) offered the most detailed and widely cited argument in support

FIGURE 11.3 • Racial Composition of U.S. Public Schools in Selected Cities, 2014–2015

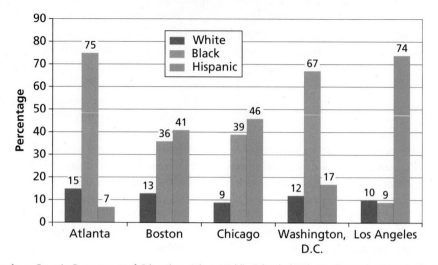

SOURCES: Data from Georgia Department of Education, Atlanta Public Schools (761), Enrollment by Ethnicity/Race, Gender and Grade Level (PK-12)—Fiscal Year 2015–3 Data Report (https://app3.doe.k12.ga.us/ows-bin/owa/fte_pack_ethnicsex.entry_form); Boston Public Schools, Boston Public Schools at a Glance 2014-2015 (http://www.bostonpublicschools.org/cms/lib07/MA01906464/Centricity/domain/187/publications/At%20a%20Glance/BPS%20at%20a%20Glance%202014-1030.pdf); Chicago Public Schools, School Data: Demographics (2015-2016 school year) (http://cps.edu/Performance/Documents/DataFiles/FY15_Racial_Ethnic_Survey.xls); District of Columbia Public Schools, DCPS at a Glance: Enrollment (http://dcps.dc.gov/page/dcps-glance-enrollment); Education Data Partnership, Los Angeles Unified.

of this thesis in their controversial book *The Bell Curve.* They argued that educational inequalities are due mostly to "natural" differences in intelligence in human populations, rather than systematic differences in educational opportunities. Far more troubling were their claims that whites had discernibly higher intelligence levels than blacks and Latinos. However, the consensus of the social scientific community is that there are not grounds for contending that there are innate intelligence differences along racial lines (Fischer et al. 1996). Indeed, students' self-discipline, including their study habits and perseverance, has been found to have a greater impact on grades than intelligence (Duckworth and Carlson 2013; Duckworth and Seligman 2005).

CLASS DIFFERENCES IN EARLY CHILDHOOD

If both school-based and "natural" explanations of educational inequality fail, what remains? Many social scientists have turned their attention to inequalities in children's earliest experiences—the home environment. Betty Hart and Todd Risley

(1995) did a fascinating in-depth study of 42 families with children. Each child studied was seven to nine months old when the study began. The researchers visited each family once every month until the children were three years old. For each hour-long visit, Hart and Risley recorded every spoken word and took notes on what happened. They found that the three types of families in their study—professional, working-class, and welfare—differed markedly in how they spoke to and interacted with the children. By the time the children were three years of age, there were massive differences in the numbers of words that had been addressed to them among these different families: 35 million words in professional families, 20 million in working-class families, and fewer than 10 million in welfare families. Hart and Risley also found that children in professional families experienced the most encouragement and fewest discouragements by their parents, as well as the greatest diversity in language. In terms of interaction styles, parents in professional families tended to use questions rather than commands to direct children's behavior. They were also more responsive to their children's requests.

Did these differences in home environments matter for early learning outcomes? By age three, children's exposure to differences in parenting practices and styles is highly correlated with vocabulary growth, vocabulary use, and intelligence. These effects persist when intelligence is measured at ages nine and ten. In addition, class differences in early cognitive outcomes are explained almost entirely by differences in parenting. A recent study that reanalyzed Hart and Risley's data found that it was not the parents' socioeconomic status (SES) but the quality of education given by the parents that mattered most in the children's cognitive development (Rindermann and Baumeister 2015).

PRESCHOOL

Can we change children's educational outcomes by changing the cognitive culture that they experience when they are very young? Several intensive preschool programs have shown impressive results. From 1962 to 1967, 123 black children whose families were living in poverty in Ypsilanti, Michigan, participated in a fascinating policy experiment (Heckman et al. 2010; Schweinhart, Barnett, and Belfield 2005). Half of the children were assigned to an enriched preschool program (High/Scope Perry Preschool), while the other half—the control group—received no preschooling (Stoolmiller 1999). By the time the program ended, children who had attended the Perry Preschool program for two years were experiencing larger gains in intelligence than the control group. However, this IQ advantage faded only a few years after the program ended. The Perry students performed better in school because they were more motivated to learn. Researchers followed these two groups of students well into adulthood (age 40) and found that the Perry students did substantially better as adults than did members of the control group. The Perry students were more likely to finish high school and college and to hold steady jobs, and they had higher earnings than the control group. Those in the control group were more likely to be arrested, to use public assistance, and to have out-of-wedlock children.

James Heckman (2006) has estimated that in the long run, every dollar spent on the Perry Preschool program saved $7 in tax revenue. Because the differences in cognitive ability between the two groups were negligible, he attributed the success

Students who learn more may have higher IQs, but even more important to their academic success are their solid work habits, self-discipline, and perseverance, as well as mastery of the "hidden curriculum." How do these conclusions reflect the propositions of structural/functional and conflict/critical theories?

enjoyed by Perry students as adults to the better social skills they learned in preschool.

ASK YOURSELF

How strong do you think the connection is between social skills learned in preschool and adult success? Why? What advice would you give educational policy makers based on your conclusions?

INEQUALITY WITHIN SCHOOLS: TRACKING AND STUDENT OUTCOMES

Many studies have examined whether students who attend the same school receive similar learning opportunities. It is common at all levels of schooling in the United States to group students by ability, which is typically measured by standardized test scores and/or grades. This is commonly known as **tracking**. Barr and Dreeben (1983) examined first-grade reading groups in which students were grouped by their reading abilities at the beginning of the year. Students in higher-ability groups learned more new words and improved their reading skills more rapidly than did students in low-ability groups. Better readers were placed in high-ability groups at the beginning of the year. They received more instructional time, were exposed to more new words, and experienced a faster pace of instruction than did students who were placed in low-ability groups. In short, higher-performing students received more learning opportunities than did lower-performing students. Consequently, the gap between high- and low-achieving students grew larger during the year. This process is known as **cumulative advantage**—the most advantaged individuals are awarded the best opportunities, and this increases inequality over time (DiPrete et al. 2006).

As students progress through middle and secondary school, curricular differentiation takes the form of different classes with different content. Traditionally, these curricular tracks are aligned with students' future ambitions: The "high" track entails coursework that prepares students for four-year colleges and professional careers, and the "low" track focuses on basic and/or vocational skills for semiskilled occupations that do not require a college degree. Research consistently finds that high-track classes offer better learning opportunities to students because they are taught by more experienced, higher-quality teachers who have higher expectations of their students (Kelly 2004). Higher-track classes cover more material, and students receive higher-quality instruction (Gamoran et al. 1995). Students in high-track classes are more engaged and exert greater effort in school, which also helps them learn at a faster rate (Carbonaro 2005). Research consistently shows that otherwise similar students learn more when placed in a higher-track class because of higher expectations (Karlson 2015), greater effort, and better learning opportunities. Ultimately, high-track students are more likely to attend college than low-track students.

What determines how students are assigned to different ability groups, tracks, and classes? In a meritocracy, achieved characteristics—hard work and prior academic success—should determine which students have access to high-track classes. Most studies show that prior achievement and grades are indeed the most important predictors of track placement. Because students from high-SES families are more likely to be high achievers, they are much more likely than low-SES students to take high-track classes. However, when students with the same test scores and grades are compared, students from higher-SES families are still more likely

than their low-SES counterparts to be enrolled in high-track classes (Gamoran and Mare 1989). Thus, high-SES students are doubly advantaged in the track placement process. This is because high-SES students are more likely to have college-educated parents who are knowledgeable about curriculum and the process of course placement. Their parents also have more integrated social networks in schools and use these connections to obtain information about teachers and classes (Useem 1992).

ALTERNATIVES TO TRADITIONAL PUBLIC SCHOOL

Not everyone attends public schools. For one thing, elite families often send their children to private boarding schools where they can interact with members of their own upper-class stratum and remain apart from members of other classes (Khan 2011). For another, members of some religious groups opt to send their children to parochial schools to reinforce particular worldviews. In general, three alternatives to public school have emerged in the past few decades: vouchers, unschooling and home-schooling, and charter schools. Proponents of the various alternatives are highly critical of existing public schools, either for what they claim are shortcomings in educational achievement or for promoting values at odds with their particular beliefs.

Vouchers

School **vouchers** are government-issued certificates that allow students to use public tax dollars to pay tuition at private schools. Parents seeking to remove their children from underperforming public schools find vouchers to be an attractive alternative. As of 2013, 17 U.S. states offered 33 programs relying on vouchers (Santos and Rich 2013).

Many voucher schools are religious schools. This raises constitutional issues about the separation of church and state and using public money to support religious schools. Moreover, whereas public schools are required by law to accept all students, this does not apply to private schools. Thus, private schools are not required by law to provide special education services if they would have to make major adjustments to do so.

Proponents of school vouchers argue that voucher programs provide parents—particularly poor parents—with options for their children's education that they otherwise would not have (e.g., the chance to avoid inadequate public schools). (Betsy DeVos, confirmed as Secretary of Education in early 2017 under the Trump administration, is a major advocate of these vouchers [Stewart, 2016].) In addition, proponents contend that under voucher programs, the increased competition the local public schools face from private schools stimulates them to enact changes to improve their educational programs (Figlio and Hart 2014). Opponents counter that vouchers encourage the creaming off of the best students from public schools. They question the constitutionality of voucher programs on the basis of the First Amendment (Harris, Herrington, and Albee 2007). They also express a concern that vouchers will reduce funding levels for already underfunded public schools.

There has been limited research on whether students in voucher schools do better than their counterparts remaining in public schools. In a study in Florida, a state that has been very active in promoting vouchers, Rudolfo Abella (2006) found that over a two-year period, voucher students did about as well as students remaining in public schools (the exception was math, in which they performed more poorly).

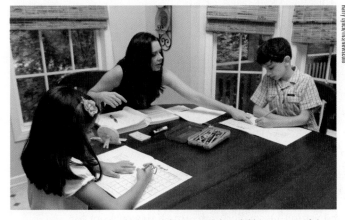

Is religious education as relevant in the United States today as it was in the past?

Andrea Forte conducts the day's math lesson with her children as part of their homeschooling. Should homeschooling be more heavily regulated by the government, or less?

Homeschooling

The popularity of homeschooling has grown over the years (Rich 2015). About 3 percent of the U.S. school-age population was homeschooled in 2011–2012. The vast majority of these approximately 2 million children were white (68 percent). Among the minority children being homeschooled, 15 percent were Hispanic, 8 percent were black, and 4 percent were Asian or Pacific Islander (U.S. Department of Education, National Center for Education Statistics 2014). Homeschooling is also growing in many other countries (Lois 2013; Stevens 2001, 2007), but the United States has the largest percentage of school-age children currently being taught at home (Kunzman and Gaither 2013).

As shown in Table 11.1, many parents of children who are homeschooled (74 percent) are dissatisfied with the quality of the instruction offered in the public schools and believe that their children are not adequately challenged in those schools. Even more parents (91 percent) express concern about environmental factors in schools, such as safety, drugs, and negative peer pressure. However, a large number of parents homeschool their children to ensure that they receive religious (64 percent) and moral (77 percent) instruction that the parents do not think can be found outside the home and in traditional schools. Many parents (44 percent) desire a nontraditional approach to their child's

TABLE 11.1 • School-Age Children Who Were Homeschooled, Ranked by Reasons Parents Gave as Important and Most Important for Homeschooling, 2011–2012

REASON	IMPORTANT[a]		MOST IMPORTANT	
	NUMBER	%	NUMBER	%
A desire to provide religious instruction	692,299	64	176,338	16
A desire to provide moral instruction	831,842	77	51,210	5
A concern about environment of other schools[b]	986,643	91	268,628	25
A dissatisfaction with academic instruction at other schools	799,336	74	204,312	19
A desire to provide a nontraditional approach to child's education	474,545	44	56,045	5
Child has a physical or mental health problem	166,878	15	50,652	5
Other reasons[c]	404,313	37	226,423	21

SOURCE: U.S. Department of Education, National Center for Education Statistics, Parent and Family Involvement in Education Survey of the National Household Education Surveys Program (NHES), 2012.

NOTE: Homeschooled students are school-age children (ages 5–17) in a grade equivalent to at least kindergarten and not higher than grade 12. This excludes students who were enrolled in public or private school more than 25 hours per week and students who were homeschooled only because of temporary illness.

a. Respondents could choose more than one reason.

b. Based on the response to the question "Are you concerned about the school environment, such as safety, drugs, or negative peer pressure?"

c. Parents homeschool their children for many reasons that are often unique to their family situation. "Other reasons" parents gave for homeschooling included family time, finances, travel, and distance.

education. A smaller number (15 percent) opt for homeschooling because their child has a physical or mental health problem.

As the numbers of homeschooled students have risen, universities have begun to address the need to assess such students as they apply for admission. Based on standardized tests, homeschooled children may on average perform slightly better than their public school counterparts, but this is not the case in all regions of the country. Critics point to limitations in much of the research in this area, but, more important, they identify two topics that standardized tests do not address. The first has to do with whether homeschooled students have the social skills to function in a diverse society. The second raises concerns about the critical abilities of homeschooled students and whether they look at the world unreflectively, embracing their parents' worldviews.

ASK YOURSELF

Why might homeschooled children be at risk of lacking the social skills and worldviews necessary to succeed in a diverse society? Is it important for homeschooling parents to address this risk? Does your answer to this question agree with your thoughts about the connection between social skills learned in preschool and adult success? Why or why not?

Charter Schools

Charter schools began in 1992, but they have grown dramatically in recent years. In the 15 years between 1999 and 2014, they almost quadrupled in the United States, to well over 6,000 such schools, serving about 2.5 million children (Berends 2015). Charter schools are a hybrid: They are intended to be alternatives to traditional public schools, but nevertheless they remain part of the public school system. They receive funding from public tax dollars, although they can also receive private funding. However, they are not run by the government (although they are accountable to it); they have a separate governance structure that can include parents, teachers, and community and private groups. Charter schools were intended to be schools of choice, alternatives for parents dissatisfied with the local public schools and interested in sending their children to schools over which they have greater control. Unlike private or parochial schools, charter schools do not charge tuition. One of the things that distinguishes them from mainstream public schools is that their teachers are not members of teachers' unions. The ideal of charter schools is that they would be more responsive to the concerns of parents and more accountable in terms of ensuring solid student outcomes.

Given the fact that public schools have not managed to provide students in poor communities with the education necessary to become upwardly mobile, a great deal of the interest in charter schools has revolved around assisting the poor—in particular racial minorities living in neighborhoods characterized by concentrated poverty. These schools are granted greater autonomy than traditional public schools. They define their own missions and establish criteria for determining whether or not they achieve their objectives. Charter schools have sponsors, and they are accountable to those sponsors and to the states in which they are located. One of the chief objectives of early proponents of charter schools was to reduce racial segregation in schools by bringing together people who shared a vision of what they wanted for their children's education. At the same time, because the traditional public schools would end up competing with charter schools, proponents argued that the traditional schools would be forced to improve in order to remain viable.

The results from a quarter-century of experience with charter schools are mixed at best (Berends 2015). For one thing, the schools have experienced managerial problems. Somewhere between 10 percent and 15 percent of charter schools have failed and closed. This has led some to propose larger-scale administrative organizations that would

overcome some of the shortcomings of existing local charter management (Farrell, Wohlstetter, and Smith 2012). Second, the evidence does not support the idea that racial segregation is being reduced by charter schools. On the contrary, it appears that the self-selection process built into the idea of choice actually increases levels of racial segregation (Garcia 2008; Roda and Wells 2013). Third, there is no clear evidence supporting the idea that charter school competition results in the improved performance of traditional public schools (Silvernail and Johnson 2014; Zimmer and Buddin 2009).

A 2013 study conducted by the Center for Research on Education Outcomes at Stanford University found that charter schools are improving. But the findings reveal wide differences across states. Table 11.2 shows the performance of charter schools relative to that of the traditional public schools in their markets. Students in 25 percent of charter schools demonstrated significantly stronger academic growth than their public school counterparts in reading, 56 percent were not significantly different, and 19 percent had significantly worse growth than students in public schools. In math, 29 percent of students in charter schools had stronger academic growth than their public school counterparts, 40 percent had growth that was not significantly different, and 31 percent had growth that was significantly worse. Overall, this is a decidedly mixed picture and does not represent a clear case for or against charter schools. Berends (2015) offers a slightly more positive position. In his view, while

TABLE 11.2 • Academic Performance of Charter Schools Compared to Local Noncharter Schools

	READING (%)	MATH (%)
Significantly better	25	29
No significant difference	56	40
Significantly worse	19	31

SOURCE: Center for Research on Education Outcomes, Stanford University, "National Charter School Study 2013." © 2013 CREDO.

the evidence is mixed on student achievement in charter schools, charter school students seem to do better in terms of graduating from high school and attending college.

WHO GOES TO COLLEGE?

Student learning is an important outcome of schooling, but successfully obtaining educational credentials is critically important for numerous life outcomes, such as income, occupational status, health, and well-being. Figure 11.4 shows that students with more advantaged family backgrounds are more likely to graduate from high school and to enroll in college. Although college enrollment for students from low-income households rose from 31 percent in 1975 to nearly 58 percent in 2014, these students still lagged far behind middle-income students. In 2014, middle-income students were 16 percent more likely than low-income students to enroll in college, and high-income students were 26 percent more likely to enroll in college.

Family background is important not only in regard to college enrollment but also in regard to graduation from college. Studies from the 1950s through the 1980s found that students from high-income families had a greater likelihood of receiving a college degree. More recent studies, however, suggest that virtually all students—regardless of family background—want and expect to complete a college degree (Schneider and Stevenson 1999). This trend reflects a "college for all" mentality on the part of policy makers, school counselors, and the general public (Rosenbaum 2001, 2011). This is not just true in the United States; it is a global trend (Marginson 2016).

Students from high-income families are more likely to attend and to graduate from college because they encounter a "college-going habitus" at home and in school; they learn and internalize the "rules of the game" in terms of getting into the right colleges and how to succeed in them (Lareau 2015). A **habitus** is an internalized set of preferences and dispositions that are learned through experience and social interactions

FIGURE 11.4 • College Enrollment in the United States, by Income Level, 1975–2014

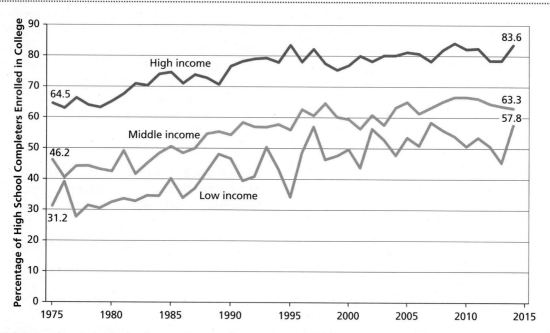

SOURCE: Data from National Center for Education Statistics, Percentage of Recent High School Completers Enrolled in 2-Year and 4-Year Colleges, by Income Level: 1975 through 2014.

NOTE: *Low income* refers to the bottom 20 percent of all family incomes, *high income* refers to the top 20 percent of all family incomes, and *middle income* refers to the 60 percent in between.

Essentials of Sociology

TRENDING

Paying for the Party: How College Maintains Inequality (Harvard University Press, 2013)

Elizabeth A. Armstrong (Associate Professor of Sociology and Organizational Studies at the University of Michigan; PhD, University of California, Berkeley, 1998) and Laura T. Hamilton (Associate Professor of Sociology at the University of California, Merced; PhD, University of Indiana, 2010)

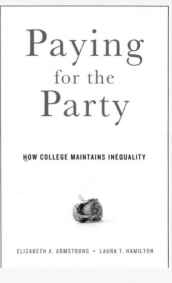

Historically, the purpose of four-year public universities was to help disadvantaged in-state students achieve social mobility by providing affordable, quality education. This purpose has been compromised over the past few decades as these schools have suffered from a drop in federal and state funding at the same time that their budgets have increased. In order to cover their costs, public universities not only raised tuition but started to enroll more affluent out-of-state students. These students are from families that have the financial resources to pay full tuition rates—and they are "primed to party." Such students may often be less interested in education than in the social activities that these schools offer, especially Greek life. Elizabeth Armstrong and Laura Hamilton argue that catering to these privileged students has shifted the purpose of public universities away from the social mobility of disadvantaged groups and toward providing pathways for the elite to party. Unfortunately, less affluent students suffer when these schools prioritize the "partying" of their elite students rather than paying for quality educational programs, advising assistance, and investments in teaching.

Armstrong and Hamilton spent five years studying 53 women at a large public university in the Midwest, which we will refer to as MU. During the first year of their study, they lived in a residence hall with the students, observing their initial reactions to university life as freshmen. Armstrong and Hamilton quickly learned how the socioeconomic positions of these students shaped their motives for attending MU and their expectations for what they would achieve after they graduated. Affluent students, many from out-of-state, attended MU to party and socialize; many majored in easy subjects and assumed that they would marry a successful man to support them. A few affluent students chose MU for academic reasons. They pursued the "professional pathway" in higher education and envisioned themselves as independent career women after they graduated. Women from lower-income backgrounds were motivated to attend MU to achieve social mobility and escape their hometowns. Unlike their affluent peers, the lower-income women had to depend on student loans and part-time work instead of their families to fund their educations. Most felt isolated at MU and transferred to smaller, regional campuses near their hometowns. Few achieved secure upward mobility—some ended up working minimum-wage jobs that did not require a college degree. Armstrong and Hamilton argue that unless public universities eliminate the party pathway, such as by abolishing the Greek system, they are culpable for reproducing class inequality.

Supplementary Resources

- You can read an interview with Hamilton that appeared in the *New York Times* at http://www.nytimes.com/2013/08/04/education/edlife/elizabeth-a-armstrong-on-her-book-paying-for-the-party.html.
- You can learn more about the cost of higher education and the student loan crisis, and also watch a clip of the documentary *Ivory Tower* (2014), at http://www.takepart.com/ivorytower.

in specific social contexts (Bourdieu and Passeron 1977). For example, children raised in families with highly educated parents may constantly be exposed to justifications of the importance of education in adult life. They may also hear dismissive and derogatory comments that devalue people with less education. It may become clear that education is a critical part of being accepted as a member of the group. Ultimately, children in this situation may not see the pursuit of a college degree as a "choice"; rather, they may see it as an obligation. As students experience different social contexts that correspond with their family backgrounds, they form different ideas about the importance of college and the role it plays in their lives.

GLOBALIZATION AND EDUCATION

We have spent much time discussing educational inequality in learning outcomes in the United States.

Is the American system typical? How do other school systems around the world differ, and with what consequences?

PISA RANKINGS

The Program for International Student Assessment, or PISA, is a worldwide study of student educational performance (Meyer and Benavot 2013). The Organisation for Economic Co-operation and Development (OECD) created the program in 1997. Since 2000, it has measured the proficiency of 15-year-olds in reading, math, and science every three years. Critics have pointed to shortcomings in the assessment, but it remains the best comparative portrait we have today. Figure 11.5 shows the top-performing nations in 2015, when the most recent test was carried out. Students in Asian countries consistently garnered the highest scores in math, reading, and science. Especially worrisome for the United States is the fact that American

FIGURE 11.5 • PISA Scores for Math, Reading, and Science, Top Countries, 2015

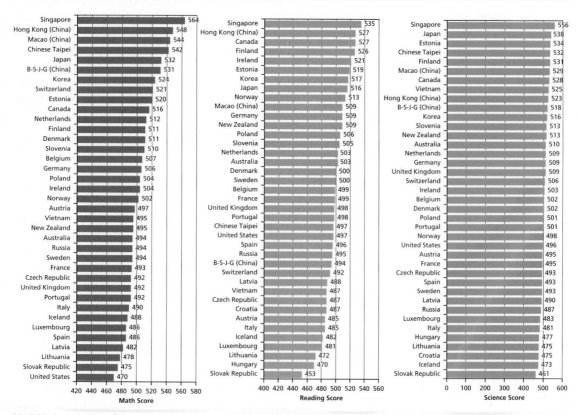

SOURCE: Organisation of Economic Co-operation and Development (OECD), PISA Results in Focus: 2015.

students ranked toward the bottom of the list of countries—38th in math, 25th in reading, and 30th in science (Weisenthal 2013).

Educational experts have been especially fascinated by Finland's consistently high rankings over the years and have pondered whether it may be possible to translate the lessons of the Finnish case to other countries. What does the Finnish educational system look like? First, teachers are well trained. Gaining acceptance into teacher-training programs in universities is competitive. Teachers are not extravagantly paid, but they are paid well, and the teaching profession remains highly respected. Teachers are unionized, a fact that undercuts the argument of conservatives in the United States and elsewhere that teachers' unions have been detrimental to the delivery of quality education. Indeed, there is evidence that teachers in Finland exhibit a high level of accountability, not because of imposed standards but because of their commitment to their profession.

Second, Finland has not embraced any of the policies pursued in recent decades in the United States, including charter schools, vouchers, merit pay for teachers, and evaluation of teachers and schools in terms of how well they perform on standardized tests (Ravitch 2012, 19).

Third, Finnish schools perform at remarkably similar levels. In other words, there is less variation in achievement across the educational system than there is in other countries (Sahlberg 2011). This has led educational reformer Diane Ravitch (2012, 19) to conclude that Finland comes "closest to achieving equality of educational opportunity." This commitment to equal opportunity means, among other things, that school funding is uniform and equitable. The school system reflects the larger national culture, which has been shaped for many decades by a social democratic commitment to equality and to a welfare system that promotes it.

U.S., GERMAN, AND JAPANESE EDUCATION SYSTEMS

As we have seen, the U.S. schooling system does not create inequality in student learning outcomes. Sometimes it compensates for other inequalities, sometimes it reinforces these inequalities, and sometimes it increases educational inequality. Other nations have structured their educational systems differently. These institutional differences have important implications for inequalities in learning among students.

Three schooling systems—those in Germany, Japan, and the United States—are compared here to illustrate how different nations allocate learning resources to students who will occupy different positions in the social hierarchy.

In Germany, all elementary school students attend *Grundschule,* which does not practice ability grouping; all children are exposed to the same curriculum. At the end of fourth grade, teachers make a recommendation to each child's family regarding the type of secondary school the child should attend based on his or her test scores and the teachers' subjective assessments of the student's ability. There are three types of schools that represent academic and vocational tracks: lower-level *Gymnasium* (the college track), *Realschule* (the middle track), and *Hauptschule* (the lowest track). Each of these has its own curriculum, which is designed to correspond with the future occupational trajectories of its students. Only 30 percent of students are placed in the *Gymnasium* level. Transferring to a different track is possible, but it is difficult and rare. Between-school tracking continues at the next level of schooling, and only students who attend upper-level *Gymnasium* can proceed to the university system and attain the equivalent of a baccalaureate degree.

Japan has a very different system of educational stratification. From school entry through ninth grade, there is little or no ability grouping among students, either between or within schools. For the first nine years of school, Japanese students are exposed to a remarkably uniform curriculum. At the end of ninth grade, Japanese students take a high-stakes test that determines which type of high school they will attend. About 75 percent of students attend *futsuuka*, which has a college preparatory curriculum. The remaining 25 percent of students attend a variety of technical and vocational schools. Family background still plays an important role in educational success for Japanese students because of a "shadow education" system, in which informal schooling opportunities outside school give more advantaged students better preparation for both high school and college entrance exams.

The German and Japanese systems highlight key features of the U.S. public schooling system. Education in the United States has always been organized around the "common school" ideal: All American students, regardless of their class origins and their future aspirations, attend the same types of schools. In the United States, tracking occurs within schools, not between schools. The United States also has more variability in school quality by geographic region. The German and Japanese systems are much more centralized than the United States. The United States has 50 different educational systems (one run by each state) with different levels of funding and varying curricula. In the United States, more so than in Japan and Germany, the quality and character of a student's education is likely to be affected by where the student's family lives.

These differences have implications for achievement outcomes in each nation (Montt 2011). Germany has the highest levels of achievement inequality because of its highly stratified system. Japan has higher average achievement than Germany but much less inequality in outcomes because it does not practice curricular differentiation until very late. The United States actually has the lowest average achievement and the least variability of these three nations.

Two features of educational systems are significant for student outcomes. First, nations with highly differentiated school systems—with between-school tracking—have more unequal learning outcomes for students, and family background tends to matter more for student outcomes (Van de Werfhorst and Mij 2010). Second, standardization—the degree to which the curriculum and examinations are the same across schools—produces less inequality in student outcomes and a weaker correlation between family background and achievement. Thus, institutions do matter greatly, and the choices nations make have important consequences for how learning is distributed within society.

RELIGION

Religion is of great importance to billions of people throughout the world. Similar to education, religion is related to socialization. Religious institutions and organizations teach their members particular beliefs and rituals that shape their identities and influence their behaviors. Some of this religious socialization occurs within educational institutions run by religious groups, such as madrassas (Muslim schools) and parochial schools. Furthermore, as the opening vignette of this chapter illustrates, religious beliefs can influence what is taught even in public schools.

The definition of religion employed here is largely derived from Émile Durkheim's ([1912] 1965) classic statement: **Religion** is a social phenomenon that consists of beliefs about the sacred; the experiences, practices, and rituals that reinforce those beliefs; and the communities that share similar beliefs and practices (Kurtz 2016).

COMPONENTS OF RELIGION

Three of the major components of religion are beliefs, rituals, and experiences.

BELIEF

Every religion has a set of interrelated **beliefs**, or ideas that explain the world and identify what should be sacred or held in awe—that is, the religion's ultimate concerns. Religious beliefs have been shaped over thousands of years; they are embedded in religious traditions and also serve as the "raw material" for new religions.

Durkheim ([1912] 1965, 14) argued that all human experience could be divided into two categories. The **sacred** is extraordinary, set aside, and of ultimate concern and leads to awe and reverence. The **profane**, in contrast, *is* the ordinary and mundane. People can come to *believe* that virtually anything is sacred—a deity, a place (Jerusalem, Mecca), a particular time or season (Ramadan, Diwali), an idea (freedom), or even a thing (an animal, a mountain, a tree, a canyon, a flag, or a rock). The sacred is treated with respect, and one's relation to it is often defined in rituals: You might genuflect when passing in front of an altar or take off your shoes when entering a temple. People believe that anything that is not considered sacred is profane.

Beliefs are often presented in sacred stories and scriptures. They address questions about the origin and meaning of life, theories about why the world was created, and explanations of suffering and death. They first express a **worldview**, that is, a culture's most comprehensive image of the ways in which life—nature, self, and society—is ordered (Geertz 1973). That worldview, in turn, shapes an *ethos,* which "expresses a culture's and a people's basic attitude about themselves and the world in general" (Geertz 1973, 173). Thus, beliefs are at the same time both models of and models for reality. They provide believers with information and a framework for interpreting the world around them.

One of the most difficult dilemmas for any religion is to explain why good people suffer and bad people sometimes flourish. While the suffering of the righteous is problematic, most religious explanations suggest that ethical behavior will eventually be rewarded. Most mainstream religions suggest that suffering is just part of the way the universe functions, so that everyone is subject to it at one time or another. It is how you deal with suffering that is most important.

RITUAL

In most religious traditions, simply believing is never enough; one also has to act. The belief systems of religious traditions are loaded with rituals that reinforce those beliefs, serve as reminders, and help believers enact their beliefs in the world. A **ritual** consists of regularly repeated, prescribed, and traditional behaviors symbolizing a value or belief. Rituals are enacted during ceremonies and festivals, such as funerals, weddings, and baptisms. Rituals are a central part of the **rites of passage** that accompany major transitions in life, such as birth, puberty, marriage, economic crises, and death (O'Loughlin et al. 2016; van Gennep 1961). Also included under the heading of rituals are ongoing spiritual practices, such as personal prayer and attending worship services of faith communities, as well as elements of everyday language that serve as religious reminders for many people.

Rituals come in many forms. Some, such as prayer, chanting, singing, and dancing, help

The waters of the Ganges are considered sacred to the pilgrims who bathe there. What do you consider sacred?

people communicate with or show devotion to the gods. Some, such as mantras and meditations, help believers organize their personal and social lives. Some frame daily life, such as those relating to diet, hygiene, and sexual practices, while others celebrate cycles of nature and build community, such as holidays, seasonal festivals, and processionals.

Rituals solve problems of personal and collective life by providing time-tested actions, words, and sentiments for every occasion. When addressing a serious problem, such as death, violence, a natural disaster, or a social crisis, people often use rituals to

1. Identify the source of the problem

2. Characterize it as evil

Makeshift memorials, like this one at the site of a shooting at an elementary school in Connecticut, are a form of ritual that can provide comfort after a tragedy. Do you participate in any religious rituals?

3. Mark boundaries between "us" and "them"

4. Arrive at some means of working toward a solution, or at least the satisfaction that they are doing something about the problem

In times of crisis, rituals can help people deal with tragedy and offer an opportunity to strengthen social bonds. Consider the ways in which people create and repeatedly visit memorials at the sites of tragedies. Recent examples include memorials at the site of the 2015 attack on the Bataclan concert venue in Paris, France, and the 2016 shooting at the Pulse nightclub in Orlando, Florida. These memorials often involve prayer candles and services with clergy, similar to what one would find in a house of worship. Such rituals build a sense of solidarity that provides support for the suffering and reinforces the authority of the social order and the institutions that sponsor the rituals, especially when they are being threatened. Rituals can also provide a theory of evil and focus participants' attention on some abstract issue, a personified devil or mythical figure, or a human enemy who needs to be denounced or attacked.

ASK YOURSELF

Which religious rituals have you been involved in or witnessed in your life? Consider those of your own religion, if any, and those of other religions to which you have been exposed through friends or relatives. What was the stated purpose of these rituals? Were there other reasons for these rituals that were less obvious? If so, what were they?

Religious rituals often mark a **liminal period**, or a special time set apart from ordinary reality (Turner 1967). The sacred time during a religious ceremony may involve an inversion of apparent reality, giving hope for the oppressed that they will be liberated, for the sad that they will be comforted, and for the last that they shall be first. In the traditional Catholic Carnival ritual preceding Lent (a period of penitence), the norms of appropriate behavior appear to be suspended as the celebrants sing, dance, and drink to excess.

FIGURE 11.6 • The Importance of Religion Worldwide

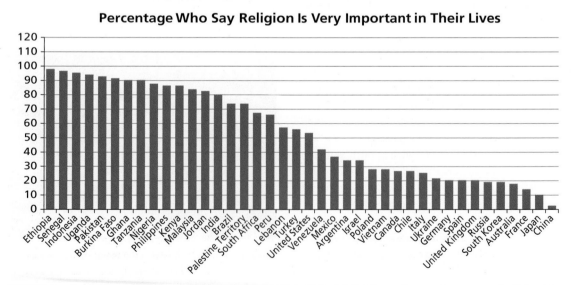

Percentage Who Say Religion Is Very Important in Their Lives

SOURCE: Angelina E. Theodorou, "Americans Are in the Middle of the Pack Globally When It Comes to Importance of Religion," Pew Research Center, Washington, DC, December 23, 2015.

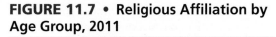

FIGURE 11.7 • Religious Affiliation by Age Group, 2011

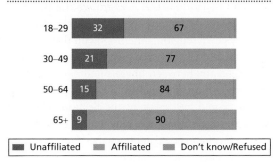

18–29	32	67
30–49	21	77
50–64	15	84
65+	9	90

■ Unaffiliated   ■ Affiliated   ■ Don't know/Refused

SOURCE: "'Nones' on the Rise," Pew Research Center, Washington, DC (October, 2012), http://www.pewforum.org/2012/10/09/nones-on-the-rise.

EXPERIENCE

The combination of beliefs, rituals, and other practices forms the variety of religious experiences for believers, regardless of which tradition they celebrate. Much of the human community views the world through a religious lens and constructs an identity around religious affiliation and experiences, such as prayer or attendance at religious services. In a survey of 40 countries, large numbers of people, especially in sub-Saharan Africa, the Middle East, and parts of Asia, reported that religion is very important in their lives (see Figure 11.6). Interestingly, a negative relationship exists between wealth and religiosity, with people living in poorer nations being more religious than those in wealthy countries. The major exception is the United States, where 53 percent of respondents report that religion is very important to them. Religion is much more important to Americans than it is to people living in other wealthy nations, such as Germany and Britain (21 percent), Japan (11 percent), and France (14 percent). In many sub-Saharan countries, no fewer than eight in ten people report religion as very important. Nine in ten of those in the predominantly Muslim countries (such as Indonesia and Pakistan) view religion as very important.

While religion remains important to most Americans, young people do not necessarily accept this view. They—and many others—are increasingly religiously unaffiliated. Almost one-third of those between 18 and 29 years of age are unaffiliated (see Figure 11.7). However, this does not mean that religion is completely unimportant to them; more than two-thirds say that they believe in God. In comparison, only 9 percent of those over 65 report being unaffiliated.

SECULARIZATION

Secularization is defined as the declining significance of religion (Bruce 2013). It occurs at both the societal and individual levels. At the societal level, it can involve the declining power of organized religion as well as the transfer of functions such as education from religion to the state. At the individual level, secularization means that individual experiences with religion are less intense and less important than other kinds of experiences.

Secularization includes historical developments in the modern world that undermine the authority of religion. Among the mechanisms that are seen as contributing to it are the following:

1. The rise of scientific thinking as an alternative way of interpreting the world (the scientific perspective encourages skepticism and doubt, thereby challenging the certainty of religious belief)

2. The development of industrial society, particularly when it results in relative affluence and thus encourages materialism and downplays otherworldly concerns

3. The rise of governments that do not mandate or promote an established religion

4. The encouragement of religious tolerance, which leads to a "watering down" of religion in general and religious differences in particular

5. The existence of competing secular moral ideologies, such as humanism (Smelser 1994, 305–306)

Given the combined impact of these developments, by the 1960s, proponents of secularization theory assumed that religion would continue to decline (Berger 1969; Wilson 1966). It was thought that people would be less likely to believe in God, attend religious services, join religious institutions, or embrace religious beliefs. This was already happening in the wealthy industrial nations of Western Europe, the first to become "modern," and it was believed that it would inevitably happen elsewhere, too, at some point in the future. But religion continues to be vibrant in most of the world, and the United States remains a religious nation. A recent poll, which found that 79 percent of Americans still believe in God, makes it clear that the United States is an exception to the secularization thesis (see Figure 11.8). In fact, given this reality, as well as the rise of Islam in much of the world, it is the more secularized Europe that increasingly looks like the exception.

Two examples of secularization are civil religion and how religion is becoming a form of consumption. While both challenge the authority of conventional religions, they do not necessarily reject the components of religion: beliefs, rituals, and experiences.

CIVIL RELIGION

Civil religion consists of the beliefs, practices, and symbols that a nation holds sacred (Turner 2014). Robert Bellah (1967) argued that civil religion has existed in U.S. society since the nation's founding. Examples include presidential addresses, the Constitution, revered geographic locations, and community rituals, such as parades and fireworks on the Fourth of July (Gorski 2011). Civil religion becomes especially prominent and important in difficult times, such as after 9/11. Civil religion provides a sense of a collective national identity. It

FIGURE 11.8 • Percentage in the United States Who Believe in God, 2016

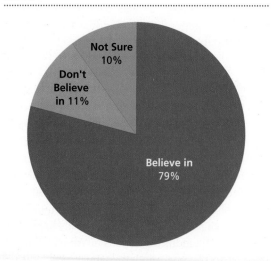

SOURCE: "Most Americans Still Believe in God," Gallup, June 29, 2016.

does so by promoting and reaffirming shared ideas and ideals. It reinforces a sense of solidarity, defining who constitutes the "we" in "we the people." While many Americans continue to believe in the country's civil religion, others contend that it is less important today. Divisions within American society, especially between liberals and conservatives (expressed most extremely in the 2016 presidential campaign and spurred on by the election of Donald Trump), suggest that there may no longer be a consensus on the major components of America's civil religion. This lack of consensus is not surprising, given that the existence of competing worldviews is one mechanism that contributes to secularization.

RELIGION AS A FORM OF CONSUMPTION

Oddly, secularization can be connected to the development of an extensive religious marketplace in societies that have a great deal of religious diversity and in which people are free to choose their religion (Roof 2011). Roger Finke and Rodney Stark (2005) describe religious institutions in terms of a "religious economy" that operates like commercial economies. In this view, religious institutions are like business firms seeking to serve a market, and in so doing, they enter into competitive relationships with other "firms" in order to maintain or expand market share and attract more "consumers" (believers).

Consumers of religion have different tastes, which can be influenced by class, race, gender, educational attainment, age, region, and similar factors. When consumers "purchase" religious institutions, they do so for different reasons. Some might seek a family-friendly place with quality child care on the premises, some might emphasize worship that is very traditional, others may value contemporary worship formats, and still others might place a premium on the religious leaders' stances on various social and moral issues.

Like all other aspects of consumer culture, religions need to respond to the demands of those who consume them and advertise what they have to offer (Roof 2001). Among the more obvious examples, which are certainly not new phenomena, are efforts to sell all sorts of goods and services linked to religion (Moore 1997). All major holidays are associated with one form of consumption or another, but this is most clearly true of Christmas (Belk 1987, 2013). As another example, in Orlando, Florida, near Disney World, the Trinity Broadcasting Network runs the Holy Land Experience. At this theme park, customers can visit such places as the Garden of Eden, Bethlehem, and the Garden of Gethsemane.

Many churches, especially large megachurches, are increasingly oriented to making themselves consumer-friendly (Sanders 2014). In these churches and others like them, the founders "have created sanctuaries that can only be intended to be entertainment spaces, complete with stages, lighting, and even theater-style seats" (Drane 2012, 105). The fanciest megachurches may have Christian rock music (Bowler and Reagan 2014), aerobics classes, food courts, and bowling alleys, as well as multimedia Bible classes presented in ways that resemble MTV videos (Niebuhr 1995). Ironically, secular forms of entertainment might help recruit and retain worshippers and increase attendance at religious services.

While religion has become increasingly like much more secular forms of consumption, it can be argued that consumption has become our new religion. As a result, shopping malls and fast-food restaurants, among many other settings, have become places where people go to practice their consumer religion. A trip to Disney World has been described as the "middle class hajj, the compulsory visit to the sunbaked city" (Garfield 1991). Similarly, the shopping mall has religious qualities and therefore can truly be considered a "cathedral of consumption" (Ritzer 2010a). It is in such cathedrals, and in the process of consumption, that many people have what can only be described as religious experiences.

TYPES OF RELIGIOUS INSTITUTIONS

Various typologies describe the most common religious institutions. Much of this work begins by distinguishing between two basic kinds of religious organizations, the *sect* and the *church*. These two terms are appropriately conceptualized as poles on a continuum, from the sect at one end to the church on the other (Ren 2007).

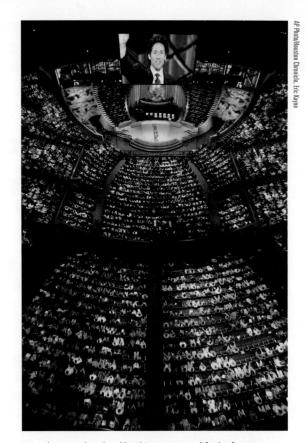

How do megachurches like this one exemplify the features of McDonaldization—efficiency, predictability, calculability, and control? What are the advantages for the church? For its congregation? Are there any disadvantages?

SECT

A **sect** is a small group of people who have joined the group consciously and voluntarily to have a personal religious experience. They see themselves as the "true believers" who have privileged access to religious truths, which makes them critical of other religious institutions. The members' religious experiences and general behavior tend to be spontaneous and unregimented. A sect's leadership is usually composed of laypersons rather than those with specialized training. As such, the organizational structure is nonbureaucratic and nonhierarchical. Leaders often arise because they are seen as possessing charisma and thus should be obeyed without question. Sects tend to be antiestablishment, and the members often feel alienated from, and as a result are prone to reject, society and the status quo. In fact, sects can be seen as breakaway,

DIGITAL LIVING

Practicing Virtual Faith

Instead of being threatened by new technologies like the internet, many religious institutions are finding that their success, even their continued existence, is dependent on these technologies. Virtual religious services help recruit and sustain members, especially the infirm, those without access to transportation, or students or military personnel who temporarily move away. Catholics can attend a virtual mass officiated by Pope Francis, Buddhists can follow the blog of a Tibetan monk, and Muslims can listen to an imam's prayer service on YouTube. Some churches rely on virtual tithing via PayPal and credit cards for financial support. Facebook pages and internet chat rooms can be a source of spiritual sustenance and a means of building virtual religious communities. One recent study found that evangelical Christians use religious internet chat rooms to expand their sexual knowledge and improve their nonvirtual sex lives within the confines of heterosexual marriage (Burke 2016).

To generate revenue and sustain followers, many religious institutions use the internet to sell traditional religious objects, such as rosaries, yarmulkes (or skullcaps), and prayer beads. In addition,

Many religious institutions have increasingly accepted technology, including social networks. Pope Francis joined Instagram in 2016 and tweets regularly. Do you ever use the internet in the practice of religion?

GABRIEL BOUYS/AFP/Getty Images

they even sell more commercial items, such as religiously themed T-shirts and bumper stickers. The selling of actual religious rituals also occurs and may become more common as religious diasporas, such as the Hindu diaspora, grow. For instance, the religious market in India is a multibillion-dollar industry that profits from the sale of online pujas, or religious ceremonies, to Hindus who live in India and abroad. Companies like Shubhpuja.com hire Hindu priests to perform virtual pujas, which customers purchase to pray for a variety of things, such as getting a promotion at work, celebrating a wedding, or healing from an illness. Prices for a puja range from $10 to $500, and the ceremonies are typically conducted via Skype (Bengali 2016).

Engaging the Digital World

Learn more about a religion of your choice by visiting the following website: http://www.bbc.co.uk/religion/religions.

Write a brief report that describes what you have learned about the history, beliefs, rituals, and practices of the religion you have selected.

dissident groups that leave established religious institutions. They do so because they think such institutions have compromised too much with "the world" and therefore have polluted the religion's teachings.

Sects tend to set themselves apart from the larger society and admit only those who rigorously conform to the group's norms. There is a demand for high levels of commitment on the part of members. Likewise, doctrinal purity is emphasized, and diversity of opinions within the group about such matters is not permitted. Sect members frequently set themselves apart from society in terms of such things as how they dress and what they eat. In addition, they might even segregate themselves physically and live in isolated areas.

Numerous sects within the Christian tradition have long histories in the United States, including the Amish, Hutterites, Seventh-day Adventists, and Jehovah's Witnesses. Sects with twentieth-century origins include the Soldiers of the Cross and Pentecostal churches that practice snake-handling. Sunni and Shia are the major sects in Islam. Within Judaism, Hasidic Jews are an example of a sect.

The Puritans were a sect that had enormous influence in the American colonies and in the development of the United States. With what other sects are you familiar? Have you been actively involved in any of them?

CHURCH

A **church** is a large group of religiously oriented people into which members are usually born (rather than joining consciously and voluntarily). The church's leadership is composed of professionals who have highly specialized training. The church as a whole tends to have a highly bureaucratic structure and a complex division of labor. Churches tend to draw members from throughout society and across all social classes. While a sect tends to restrict membership to true believers, a church seeks to include as many people as possible. Churches often actively seek out new members, sometimes by employing missionaries. A church's belief systems tend to be highly codified, and rituals are often elaborate and performed in a highly prescribed manner. In comparison with members of sects, church members tend to have a lower level of commitment, and much less is expected of them. While sects tend to reject the status quo, churches accept it.

While *sect* and *church* are presented here as if they are totally distinct, in reality there is no clear dividing line between them. In fact, over time there is a tendency for a sect to become transformed into something that takes on the organizational features of a church. As sects become larger, they need, among other things, ever-larger bureaucratic structures with less charismatic leadership and more leadership based on expertise. The behavior of sect members becomes less spontaneous and more formal.

DENOMINATIONS

Like a church, a **denomination** is an organized form of religious expression that is usually supportive of the social order and of other religious forms.

Denominations are hierarchical and bureaucratic. Local organizations are not independent but part of larger regional or national institutional structures. They rely on specialized, professionally trained, full-time clergy. The clergy are generally trained in seminaries run by the denominations to ensure conformity to doctrines.

Among major Christian denominations today are a long list of Protestant groups, including American Baptist, Assemblies of God, Church of Christ, Episcopal, Evangelical Lutheran, Lutheran, Presbyterian, Southern Baptist, United Church of Christ, and United Methodist (Figure 11.9 shows

FIGURE 11.9 • Protestant Christian Groups with the Largest Number of Adherents, by County, 2010

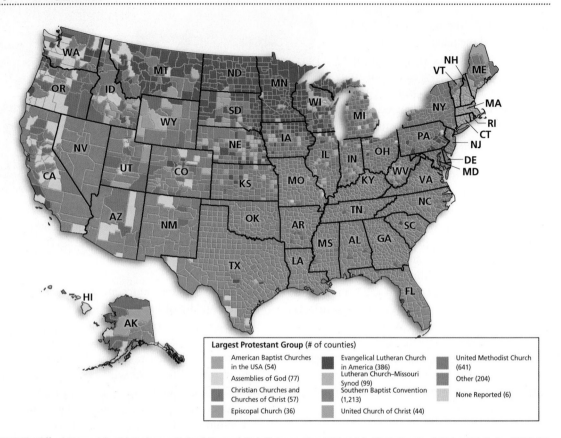

Largest Protestant Group (# of counties)

- American Baptist Churches in the USA (54)
- Assemblies of God (77)
- Christian Churches and Churches of Christ (57)
- Episcopal Church (36)
- Evangelical Lutheran Church in America (386)
- Lutheran Church–Missouri Synod (99)
- Southern Baptist Convention (1,213)
- United Church of Christ (44)
- United Methodist Church (641)
- Other (204)
- None Reported (6)

SOURCE: Clifford Grammich, Kirk Hadaway, Richard Houseal, Dale E. Jones, Alexei Krindatch, Richie Stanley, & Richard H. Taylor. *2010 U.S. Religion Census: Religious Congregations & Membership Study.* Nazarene Publishing House, Kansas City, Missouri. 2012. © Association of Statisticians of American Religious Bodies (ASARB).

NOTE: The "Other" category includes 37 groups with less than 20 counties each. Six of these had at least 10 counties where each was the largest group: Lutheran Congregations in Mission for Christ (16 counties), Wisconsin Evangelical Lutheran Synod (16), Church of the Nazarene (15), Amish Groups, undifferentiated (13), National Baptist Convention, USA, Inc. (12), and African Methodist Episcopal Church (10).

the largest Protestant Christian groups at the county level). But this list would also include Roman Catholics and the Eastern Orthodox Church.

CULTS AND NEW RELIGIOUS MOVEMENTS

A cult resembles a sect in many ways, but it is important to distinguish between the two (Stark and Bainbridge 1979). While a sect is a religious group that breaks off from a more established religion as a result of a schism in order to revive it and rediscover the original beliefs and practices of that organization, a **cult** is a new, innovative, small, voluntary, and exclusive religious tradition that was never associated with any religious organization. A cult is often at odds with established religions as well as the larger society. Those who found cults tend to be religious radicals, and because they are new, cults, even more than sects, tend to be led by charismatic figures. Like sects, cults demand high levels of commitment and involvement on the part of members. Among the better-known cults are Baha'i, the International Society for Krishna Consciousness (Hare Krishnas), Rastafarians, and the Unification Church, founded by the Reverend Sun Myung Moon. The term *cult* has fallen out of favor in sociology because it is has come to be associated in the popular mind and press with such destructive groups as Charles Manson and his "family," who murdered a number of people, including actress Sharon Tate, in 1969. The Manson cult was not actually a religious organization, but a number of religiously based cults have proved to be very destructive. These include Jim Jones's People's Temple, David Koresh's Branch Davidians, and Heaven's Gate. All of these groups ended in tragedy. In the case of the People's Temple, the end involved the 1979 mass suicide and murder of 918 of Jones's followers in their jungle compound in Guyana. In the case of the Branch Davidians, the leader and members died in a controversial confrontation in Waco, Texas, with federal officials from the Bureau of Alcohol, Tobacco, and Firearms. And in the case of Heaven's Gate, a charismatic leader convinced his followers that Comet Hale-Bopp was hiding a mother ship that would take them to a better world. The result was that 39 members committed suicide.

More than 900 people died as part of Jim Jones's People's Temple, including Jones himself, when he ordered his followers to drink cyanide-laced grape Flavor Aid.

Given the negative connotations associated with the term *cult,* some sociologists prefer the term **new religious movements** to encompasses sects, cults, and a wide array of other nontraditional religious groups (Bromley 2016; Lewis and Tollefson 2016). New religious movements tend to be typified by their zealous religious converts, their charismatic leaders, their appeal to an atypical portion of the population, their tendency to differentiate between "us" and "them," a distrust of others, and a proneness to rapid fundamental changes (Barker 2007). Use of the term *new religious movements* is intended to eliminate or reduce the negative connotations associated with cults. It also emphasizes the idea that each unconventional religious organization should be examined objectively based on its own characteristics.

RELIGION AND GLOBALIZATION

Every major religious tradition was originally a local, even tribal, expression of faith that grew out of a specific environment and then diffused across certain regions and eventually the globe. The study of the relationship between religion and globalization is relatively recent, but it is clear that religion globalized before anything else.

Today, as Figure 11.10 shows, Christians make up 33 percent of the world's population (Britannica 2012; Kurtz 2016, 46). About 22 percent are Muslims, 14 percent are Hindus, and smaller proportions are followers of Buddhism (7 percent), Sikhism (0.36 percent), Judaism (0.21 percent), and the Baha'i faith (0.11 percent). Atheists (those without any religious belief) account for 2 percent of the world population.

Two issues are of particular importance in regard to the relationship between globalization and religion. First, transnational migration brings different religion to new locales, making those places more multireligious. Migrants also generate in those locales new and different versions of the local religions. This, in turn, can alter religion in the migrants' homeland. Thus, transnational migration globalizes religion spatially and contributes to the further pluralization of religion around the world. Migrants help unify various parts of the world by, for example, making pilgrimages to religious sites such as Mecca and the Wailing Wall, posting prayers in cyberspace, and sending money to religious centers in their homelands.

Second is the spread of religious organizations and movements through independent missions.

FIGURE 11.10 • The World's Dominant Religions, by Percentage of Believers

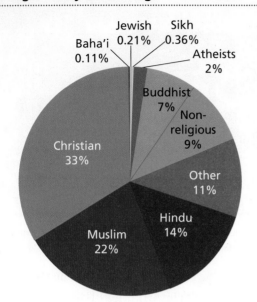

SOURCE: CIA World Factbook. (2013). *World*.

Here the Christian Church, especially the Roman Catholic Church, has played a central role through its missionaries. In fact, Christianity became the first worldwide religion. Messengers for Islam created the most global system prior to the modern era (see the discussion of Islam in the following section).

ASK YOURSELF

Have any other social institutions spread as widely as religion? What do you think accounts for religion's staying power in the places to which it has been transported? Why are religions still expanding globally today?

THE MOST SIGNIFICANT GLOBAL RELIGIONS

In this section we will deal with several globally important religions—Judaism, Buddhism, Hinduism, Islam, and Christianity. Although Mormonism is not a large global religion, and debate continues about whether it should be defined as a Christian denomination or a new religion, we will also examine it here because of its very contemporary efforts to become a global religion. However, as is clear in Figure 11.11, many of the world's dominant religions, despite their spread, are still to a large extent concentrated in particular parts of the world.

Judaism

Founded more than 3,000 years ago, Judaism is today one of the smallest of the world's religions, with roughly 14.3 million people in the world defining themselves as Jews (Goldberg 2007; Goldscheider 2012). However, for a variety of reasons, Judaism's importance both historically and contemporarily has been far greater than one would think by simply looking at the numbers involved. By the late nineteenth century, there were 12 million Jews in the world, many of whom had migrated from the Middle East and were spread in mostly small enclaves across many countries. There was and continues to be a large concentration of Jews in Europe, but migrations to North America, as well as to Palestine (then under Ottoman control), began during this period. By the onset of World War II, the number of Jews in the world had grown to 16.6 million, but the atrocities of the Nazis led to a reduction in the population to about 10 million. The founding of Israel in 1948 marked an important turning point for Jews, and that nation's population is now more than 6 million people. Another large concentration of Jews—approximately 6 million—is found in North America, mostly in the United States. The vast majority of the more than 14 million Jews alive today live in either North America or Israel, with fewer than 2 million living elsewhere, mostly in Europe. Just a few of the factors that give Judaism great global significance are the spread of Jews throughout the world, Zionism (which helped lead to the founding of Israel), the Holocaust, anti-Semitism, and the conflict between Israel and its Arab neighbors over Palestine.

Hinduism

Although no precise starting date can be determined, Hinduism began sometime between 800 and 200 BCE (Abrutyn 2012). While it has ancient origins, Hinduism became firmly established in India as the country opposed foreign occupation by Muslims (999–1757) and later the British (1757–1947). Today, the vast majority of Hindus (about 966 million) live in India. Hinduism is strongly defined by the *Vedas*, which are

FIGURE 11.11 • The World's Dominant Religions

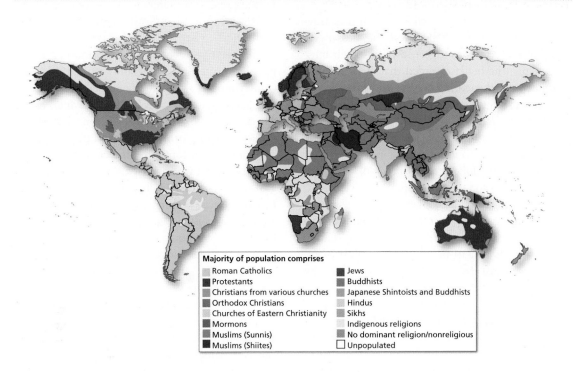

Majority of population comprises

- Roman Catholics
- Protestants
- Christians from various churches
- Orthodox Christians
- Churches of Eastern Christianity
- Mormons
- Muslims (Sunnis)
- Muslims (Shiites)
- Jews
- Buddhists
- Japanese Shintoists and Buddhists
- Hindus
- Sikhs
- Indigenous religions
- No dominant religion/nonreligious
- Unpopulated

both historical documents and enumerations of incantations needed for successful rituals. Hinduism is also closely associated with India's caste system.

While it continues to be heavily concentrated in India, Hinduism is a global religion spanning six continents. It has been spread by both migrants and itinerant religious teachers (Madan 2007). Although it is heavily concentrated geographically, Hinduism has been important as part of the "Easternization of the West" (Campbell 2007) in, for example, the spread of yoga (including now "he-man" yoga; Bluestein 2014), Transcendental Meditation, and so on. (And, of course, there has been a parallel, but much stronger, Westernization of the East [Sander and Cavallin 2015]). However, Hinduism has not been nearly as expansionistic as Christianity, Islam, or even Buddhism.

Buddhism

Buddhism arose in the Indus Ganges basin in about the sixth century BCE and began to have a transnational influence about three centuries later (Nichols 2012; J. L. Taylor 2007). Today there are somewhere around 488 million Buddhists across the globe, although the vast majority are in Asia. China has the largest number of Buddhists, followed by Japan. Other Asian countries with majority Buddhist populations include Thailand, Cambodia, Myanmar, Bhutan, Sri Lanka, Laos, and Vietnam. Thus, while Buddhism moved out from its origins in India, it has remained primarily concentrated on the Asian continent.

Islam

Islam was founded by the Prophet Muhammad, who was born on the Arabian Peninsula and lived between 570 and 632 CE. The lands encompassed by Islam were seen as the center of the world, with all else subordinate to it. Important to Islam's spread was its universalistic worldview; Muslims did not view themselves as a chosen people but believed that they and all of humanity had a common destiny. Islam's universalistic ideas (God-given standards that lead everyone to search for goodness) had to be diffused throughout the world. Such beliefs led to a global mission to rid the world of competing idea systems, such as idolatry and superstition. On the other hand, Islam saw itself as building on, but going beyond, Judaism and Christianity. Thus, "Islam was the first of the world's great religious civilizations to understand itself as one religion among others" (Keane 2003, 42).

Believers in Islam, as well as their armies, traveled with the belief that they were the messengers and that everyone was eagerly awaiting their message. Thus, the belief emerged that "Islam would prevail among the world's peoples, either by willing acceptance, or by spiritual fervour, or (in the face of violent resistances) by conquest" (Keane 2003, 42). Because there was only one God and therefore only one law according to Islam, such a view—and mission—meant that followers of Islam took no notice of nation-states and their borders.

In the end, the efforts of Islam's early missionaries were thwarted. One factor in this failure was the effort of alternative religions, especially Christianity and its various militaristic campaigns against Islam. Another was that the principle of *jihad,* or the duty to struggle on behalf of God against those who doubt him or are his enemies, was rarely pursued unconditionally. Furthermore, Muslims believed that contact, trade, and traffic with nonbelievers was acceptable, even encouraged. Efforts to globalize Islam remain strong among many devotees of Islam and helps inform the contemporary thinking of jihadists and Islamic fundamentalists (Sayyid 2012).

Christianity

Christianity and Islam are the two fastest-growing religions in the world today. Christianity spread in the Middle East following the death of Jesus of Nazareth. By 1000 CE, a schism had developed between Roman Catholicism in the West and Orthodoxy in the East, with more Christians living in the East than the West. A major series of events in the history of globalization was the Crusades, which began in 1095 CE and lasted for centuries. The Crusades were designed to liberate the Holy Land from Muslims and others who had gained control of Jerusalem in 638 CE. This is still a sensitive issue for Muslims, as reflected in protests that erupted when President George W. Bush used the word *crusade* in a speech shortly after the 9/11 terrorist attacks.

Christianity today is declining in Europe, but that is more than compensated for by strong growth in the Global South, including parts of Asia, Africa, and Latin America. Growth is so strong in the Global South that it is predicted that by 2050,

80 percent of the world's Christians will be Hispanic. Furthermore, Christianity is different in the Global South—"more . . . morally conservative, and evangelical" (Garrett 2007, 143). Pentecostalism, a charismatic movement, offers another example of the spread of Christianity around the globe (Anderson 2013). This religion had its origins in revivals attended by poor blacks and whites in Los Angeles in 1906. It is now the second-largest and fastest-growing form of Christianity, with about 280 million adherents, and has come to exceed in size all forms of Christianity except Catholicism. Its growth has been especially great in Asia, Africa, and Latin America (Lechner and Boli 2005). Similarly Mormonism, or the Church of Jesus Christ of Latter-Day Saints, has shown substantial growth in the last 60 years. Founded in the United States in the nineteenth century, Mormonism had fewer than 2 million members in 1960, but today the number has risen to approximately 15 million (McCombs 2013).

The Church of Jesus Christ of Latter-Day Saints is centrally controlled from its headquarters in Salt Lake City, Utah. Once almost exclusively an American religion, today Mormonism has more members outside the United States and thousands of churches and meetinghouses in most of the world's countries and territories. Eighty thousand missionaries spread Mormonism across the globe.

In contrast to other globally successful religions, Mormonism has not significantly adapted to local customs and realities. For example, unlike the far more rapidly expanding Pentecostalism, Mormonism has *not* incorporated a variety of indigenous customs into its African Sunday services. Through watching Salt Lake City services via satellite, worshippers elsewhere in the world can easily see that the services and the teachings are the same—or at least very similar.

FUNDAMENTALISM

Religious **fundamentalism** is a strongly held belief in the fundamental or foundational precepts of any religion (Stolow 2004). It is also characterized by a rejection of the modern secular world (Kivisto 2012). Fundamentalists see the world in stark terms (Koopmans 2015), dividing it into true believers (the in-group), who are saved, and the rest of the world's population (the out-groups), who are damned. There is often hostility between the in-group and out-groups. Fundamentalists seek to replace doubt and ambiguity with crystal-clear certainty. All of the major world religions have fundamentalist elements, as do many smaller religions. One example of fundamentalism is strict adherence to *sharia,* or traditional Islamic law. This includes modest dress for women, abstention from alcohol, and public prayers. Sharia law has been seen as the basis of a governmentally enforced legal structure among Islamic fundamentalists, most notably the Taliban in Afghanistan and more recently the terrorist organization the Islamic State (IS) in Iraq and Syria.

Fundamentalism can be seen as being involved in globalization in at least two major senses (Brouwer, Gifford, and Rose 2013; Lechner 1993). First, it is often expansionistic, seeking to extend its reach into more and more areas of the world and to extend its power in those areas. Second, it is profoundly affected by various globalizations. For example, the globalization of one fundamentalist religion, such as Islamic militants, is likely to lead to a counterreaction by another, such as Hasidic Jews. Another important reaction involves movements against various forces seen as emanating from the modern world, including secularism, popular culture, rationalization, and the United States and the West in general. Much of the momentum for the recent rise of fundamentalism can be seen as traceable to a reaction against such forces. For example, IS is reacting against artificial borders in the Middle East drawn and imposed by the West largely after World War I, as well as the West's military involvement and cultural imperialism in that region.

FAITH ON THE MOVE

The globalization of religion—and the growing diversity of religions around the globe—is also the result of the movement of people. While the number has probably grown, the United Nations estimates that in 2010, there were 214 million immigrants globally. This figure represents just over 3 percent of the total population of the world. The Pew-Templeton Global Religious Futures Project provides a broad overview of the movement of major world religions in a study led by Phillip Connor (2012). Figure 11.12 summarizes the findings. It is perhaps not surprising that the world's two largest religions—Christianity and Islam—contribute the largest numbers of immigrants. Christians account for 2.3 billion

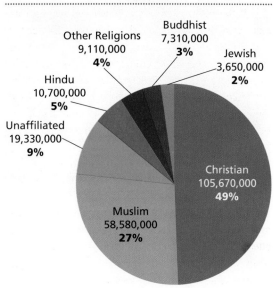

FIGURE 11.12 • Religious Composition of International Migrants

SOURCE: "Faith on the Move—The Religious Affiliation of International Migrants," Pew Research Center, Washington, DC (March 2012), http:// www.pewforum.org/2012/03/08/religious-migration-exec.

adherents worldwide, and nearly half of all immigrants. Islam has 1.6 million adherents, and Muslim immigrants amount to 27 percent of all immigrants. Hinduism is the third-largest religion, but only 5 percent of Hindus are migrants. Jews, though the smallest of the world's religious groups, contribute 2 percent of all immigrants. Buddhists contribute 3 percent of all migrants, even though their religion has many more members than Judaism. Because of the rise of anti-Semitism, especially in Europe, we are likely to see an increase in Jewish immigration, especially to Israel and the United States. In fact, in light of the *Charlie Hebdo* massacre in 2015 (and similar and even more recent events elsewhere in France and Europe more generally), the prime minister of Israel encouraged the mass immigration of Jews from Europe (Kershner 2015).

In terms of country of origin, more Christian immigrants are from Mexico than from any other nation. For Muslims, the largest point of origin is the Palestinian Territories. Most Palestinians are not recent migrants, but rather became refugees after the establishment of Israel in 1948. For Jews, the largest point of origin is Russia; for Hindus, it is India; and for Buddhists, it is Vietnam. China, a

The growing Muslim population in Europe has sparked controversy, including over the modest attire of some Muslim women. Some cities have even attempted to ban the "burkini" swimsuit.

major country of emigration, is the top country for both "other religions" and the unaffiliated.

Turning to destination countries, the United States is the number one country for Christians. The United States is also the number one country for Buddhists and the primary destination for the unaffiliated. Israel is the main destination for Jews, while Saudi Arabia is the main destination for Muslims. India is a rather curious case, for it is both the number one country of origin for Hindus and the number one destination. In general countries with long histories of immigration, like the United States, Australia, and Canada, are especially popular destinations.

SUMMARY

Education is closely related to the process of socialization, although it most often takes place more formally in schools. Both individuals and society benefit from the social institution of education. Higher levels of education are correlated with lower rates of unemployment, higher levels of income, better health, and more political openness. Unfortunately, education does not provide equal opportunities for all students to learn and achieve social mobility. Research has found that inequalities exists in the educational system that prevent many from succeeding. Coleman found that teacher quality, family background, and racial composition of the student body were the most important factors affecting student achievement. In addition, the use of tracking in schools often leads to cumulative advantage for students placed in higher tracks. Students with more advantaged family backgrounds are more likely to graduate from high school and to enroll in and graduate from college.

Educational inequality also exists around the world. Countries vary greatly in their ability to educate students and educate them well. The Program for International Student Assessment (PISA) measures the proficiency of

15-year-olds in reading, math, and science every three years. Students in United States fall near the bottom, while students in Singapore rank at the top.

Like education, religion is also involved in the process of socialization. Religion consists of shared beliefs, rituals, and experiences. Beliefs are ideas that explain the world and identify what should be sacred (or extraordinary) and profane (or mundane). Rituals are repeated behaviors that symbolize beliefs and are often a central part of weddings and other rites of passage. Secularization refers to the declining importance of religion. Civil religion consists of the beliefs, rituals, and symbols that a nation holds sacred.

Sociologists have identified different types of religious organizations, including churches, sects, cults, and new religious movements. A church is hierarchically organized with professional leaders and members are typically born into it. A sect is a small group of "true believers" who voluntary join together to have a personal religious experience. Cults are small, voluntary groups that are newer and more innovative than sects. Both sects and cults are part of the new religious movement.

The spread of religion is not new, but it has accelerated with increased globalization. The most significant global religions are Christianity, Islam, Hinduism, Buddhism, and Judaism. Christianity and Islam are the two largest religions in the world and are growing, while Judaism is the smallest. One factor contributing to growing global religious diversity is global migration.

KEY TERMS

beliefs, 300
church, 307
civil religion, 304
cult, 308
cumulative
  advantage, 292

denomination, 307
fundamentalism, 312
habitus, 296
liminal period, 302
meritocracy, 287

new religious
  movements, 309
profane, 300
religion, 300
rites of passage, 301
ritual, 301

sacred, 300
sect, 305
secularization, 303
tracking, 291
vouchers, 292
worldview, 301

REVIEW QUESTIONS

1. What is a meritocracy, and why is the educational system an important component of a meritocratic society? In what ways is the U.S. education system meritocratic, and in what ways is it not meritocratic?

2. According to the Coleman Report, how important is the quality of schools to student achievement? What other factors affect student achievement? What factors have not been found to affect student achievement to any great extent?

3. Homeschooling has grown in popularity in recent years. What are the main reasons why parents opt to educate their children at home rather than sending them to either public or private schools? What are some of the drawbacks to homeschooling?

4. What is the relationship between income of parents and the ability of their children to enroll in and graduate from college? How does this relationship challenge the idea that the U.S. educational system is meritocratic?

5. Compare and contrast the U.S., German, and Japanese educational systems. How do these systems' differences affect achievement outcomes in these countries? How do their attitudes toward grouping reflect the countries' respective cultural norms and values?

6. How do we define religion? What are the basic elements and components of religious institutions? In what ways have religions changed over time?

7. What are the major religions of the world? How are people distributed among the major religions of the world? In what ways are religions global?

8. What is a ritual? Why is it an important component of religion? Provide an example of a ritual practice from a new religious movement.

9. What does it mean to speak of a religious or spiritual marketplace? Provide examples that illustrate how religion is marketed to consumers.

10. Provide a definition of civil religion and discuss its function. Is civil religion important to you? Why or why not?

12 POLITICS AND THE ECONOMY

The Interrelationship of Government and the Economy

"It's the economy, stupid" is a phrase attributed to Democratic political consultant James Carville and offered as advice in 1992 to successful presidential candidate Bill Clinton. The phrase was specific to the campaign against sitting Republican president George H. W. Bush, who was saddled with an economic recession. It was designed to remind Clinton to address the economy whenever he could, because that was what was most on people's minds and was likely to attract the most votes. However, it is a phrase—and a reality—that has lived on and continues to be applicable to most, if not all, political campaigns. Except in the rare case of an economic boom, it is almost always the economy that is key as far as politics is concerned and, conversely, economies are always deeply political.

We were reminded of that once again in 2016 as the political landscape in several countries was drastically altered by a series of dramatic developments. The most extreme example was Brexit, or the British exit from the European Union (EU). The EU is a political organization that, at least in part, grew out of the European Economic Community (EEC), or "Common Market," which was

LEARNING OBJECTIVES

12.1 Contrast democracy and dictatorship.

12.2 Outline who rules the United States using the perspectives of structural/functional and conflict/critical theories.

12.3 Explain how global politics affect war and terrorism, geopolitics, and the nation-state.

12.4 Describe the U.S. economy's transition from industrialization to deindustrialization.

12.5 Discuss how work, consumption, and leisure shape our understanding of the economy.

12.6 Describe the effects of globalization on the world economy.

edge.sagepub.com/ritzeressentials3e

- Take the chapter quiz
- Review key terms with eFlashcards
- Explore multimedia links and SAGE readings

$SAGE edge™

created in 1957. As the name suggests, the EEC was created to bring about economic integration among member nations. It was absorbed into the political European Union (EU) in 1993.

Many Europeans, however, grew dissatisfied with both the centralized political control exerted by the EU, which mandated open borders between EU member countries, among other things. That contributed to massive flows of immigrants from poorer countries, threatening those with well-paying jobs in the richer countries of the EU. Other economic problems included the inability of poorer countries in the EU to devalue their currencies because they were all using the euro. Historically, poorer countries have been able to compete economically in times of recession by devaluing their currencies, thereby making their products cheaper and therefore more competitive.

In the context of this dissatisfaction with the EU, Britain engaged in what was considered to be a *pro forma* vote on whether or not it should remain in the EU. To the surprise of many, however, the British public voted against remaining in the EU, and unless something dramatic happens, Britain will leave the organization in a few years. Brexit could have dire economic consequences for Great Britain (and much of Europe), but it had great, immediate political consequences for British Prime Minister David Cameron, who had opposed Brexit and felt compelled to resign as a result of the vote.

Surprisingly, the decision by the British reverberated in the United States, especially among a large number of lower- and middle-class people who were suffering economically. They had never really recovered from the Great Recession and had few prospects of ever recovering fully. Republican presidential candidate Donald Trump appealed to that population, its economic frustrations, and its fear of the Other, especially in the form of undocumented immigrants from Mexico, including the idea that they would work for less than American workers.

This led, among other things, to Trump's famous call to build a great wall between the United States and Mexico . . . and to make Mexico pay for it.

Politics is economics . . . economics is politics. Sociology looks at how people make political and economic choices and how societies deal with the personal, national, and global consequences of those choices. ●

POLITICS: DEMOCRACY OR DICTATORSHIP

Society can be seen as a collection of groups that compete to determine whose members get what, as well as when and how they get it (Lasswell 2012). When groups operate through established governmental channels to do so, this competition is referred to as **politics**. The state is the political body organized for government and civil rule. By putting pressure on the state, a group can advance a given position or promote policies that benefit its members. Therefore, politics is one way of exercising power in society.

DEMOCRACY: CITIZENSHIP AS A RADICAL IDEA

A **democracy** is a political systems in which people within a given state vote to choose their leaders and in some cases vote on legislation as well. In modern democracies, people vote to choose their legislators rather than actually managing their own political affairs and directly making decisions about the things that affect their lives. Nevertheless, contemporary theorists of democracy often suggest that the power to rule in democracies comes from the *consent* of the people.

Sometimes these systems are called representative democracies. The people, as a whole body, do not actually rule themselves but rather have some say in who will best represent them in the state. In direct democracies, by contrast, the people have a say in decisions that directly affect them.

Democratic states are organized into bureaucracies (see Chapter 5), with clear hierarchies as well as established and written codes, laws, and rules. The authority that legislators have under democracies is based on legal codes that confer this authority on them. Democracies tend to extend rights to citizens, the people represented by the state and most often born within its territories. **Citizenship** means that the people of a given state can vote for their representatives and that they have rights and responsibilities as citizens (Soysal 2012; Turner 2011). Under *universal citizenship,* the rights of citizenship are generally conferred on most people residing in a given state's territory. At times, however, citizenship is still denied to groups of immigrants residing within that territory. In the United States, citizens have certain rights and can vote on who will be president and on who will represent them in Congress.

Most democratic states guarantee citizens the right to freely express dissent, the right to due process and equality before the law, the rights of freedom of speech and of the press, and the right to privacy. These rights and others are sometimes extended to noncitizens. Freedom House, an organization committed to monitoring democratic trends and human rights around the world, publishes an annual survey on 195 countries rating political rights and civil liberties (Figure 12.1). In 2016, of the 195 countries assessed, 86 (44 percent) were rated "free," 59 (30 percent) were rated "partly free," and 50 (26 percent) were rated "not free." Ratings for the Middle East and North Africa were the worst in the world, followed by Eurasia. Syria, a dictatorship mired in civil war, ethnic division, and uncontrolled terrorism, received the lowest score of any country in more than a decade. The other "worst of the worst" countries are North Korea, Saudi Arabia, Somalia, Sudan, and Uzbekistan.

Democracies are not without their critics, even from within. Some have argued that voters are typically uninformed about many political issues. For example, many of those in Great Britain who voted for Brexit were not fully aware of its implications for them. Many working-class voters in the United States did not anticipate that Donald Trump would appoint billionaires and millionaires to his cabinet who would likely be unresponsive to their needs and interests (Duhigg 2017). Other critics argue that liberal democracies extend *too many* rights and tend to allow too much diversity of thought and interest, making them unstable.

FIGURE 12.1 • Freedom in the World, 2015

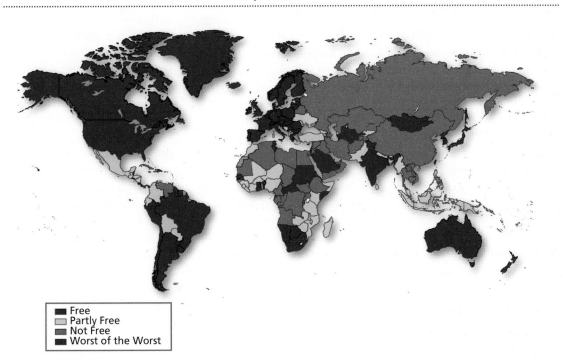

Legend:
- Free
- Partly Free
- Not Free
- Worst of the Worst

SOURCE: Data from Freedom House (2015). Freedom in the World. *Issues.*

Hacktivism and State Interference

Digital technologies have enabled hackers to access private computer servers and leak or sell personal information, such as Social Security numbers, credit card accounts, and e-mails. Hackers target not only individuals but also governments, corporations, universities, and internet search engines such as Yahoo and Google. While some hackers engage in such behavior to prove that they have the technical skills to do so, others profit from selling information they obtain to the highest bidder. Some so-called hacktivists view themselves as digital activists who can change the world with the information that they hack and target powerful individuals and organizations. The website WikiLeaks permits hackers to post leaked information, which it archives for the public to access.

Recently, U.S. political figures and organizations have been targeted by hackers, which has had a profound effect on the political process. For example, in the summer of 2016, more than 30,000 e-mails from Hillary Clinton's private server when she served as secretary of state were leaked and posted on WikiLeaks. Thousands of leaked e-mails from the Democratic

Wikileaks, an organization led by Julian Assange, has posted thousands of hacked documents, including personal e-mails of politicians and campaign workers.

National Committee were also posted on WikiLeaks that summer, leading to the resignation of its chair, Debbie Wasserman Schultz. According to American intelligence agencies, Russian hackers interfered in the 2016 U.S. presidential election and leaked documents from Democratic Party organizations to WikiLeaks, in the process possibly influencing the election in favor of Donald Trump (Sanger and Shane 2016). Russian hackers also targeted Democratic House candidates in the election, leaking documents from the Democratic

Congressional Campaign Committee to journalists in Florida (Lipton and Shane 2016).

Engaging the Digital World

How concerned are you about hackers accessing and leaking your personal information? What do you think the U.S. government's response should be to international hackers leaking e-mails and documents of politicians and government agencies to WikiLeaks? Is using our "cyberarsenal" against the Russian government an appropriate action? Why or why not?

DICTATORSHIP: THE SEIZURE OF POWER

Dictatorships are states that are usually totalitarian and ruled either by a single individual or by a small group of people. Dictatorships are governments *without* the consent of the people being governed. In the modern period, dictatorships are often formed in formerly democratic states that have been seized by small groups of political fanatics.

In the years just before and during World War II, the world saw an alliance of dictatorships based on fascist principles. These dictatorships shared some very basic institutional arrangements and principles. They

- Were totalitarian in that they attempted to control every facet of social life

- Saw conflict and war as natural states and methods for human betterment

- Were viciously opposed to liberalism, anarchism, and any form of socialism or communism

Dictatorships did not end with the defeat of the fascist powers in World War II. Indeed, in the post-war era, the Soviet Union and its satellites in the Eastern Bloc were often organized as dictatorships, with small groups of Communist Party officials controlling society. Latin America has had a number of dictatorships since World War II. Among dictatorships elsewhere in the world today, North Korea is arguably the most dangerous, given its fraught relationship with South Korea and its frequent testing of nuclear weapons. The United States has often sponsored dictatorships and fought against democracy. This has occurred particularly where democratically elected leaders might turn toward political orientations (such as socialism or Islamism) that would make their governments problematic for American political and business interests (Chomsky 1985).

WHO RULES THE UNITED STATES?

Even though the United States is a democracy, the issue of who rules the nation is a source of continuing debate among sociologists (and political scientists).

THE STRUCTURAL/FUNCTIONAL PERSPECTIVE: PLURALISM

Within structural-functionalism, the typical position put forward regarding who rules America is pluralism. This is the view that the United States is characterized by a number of powerful competing interest groups, and no one of them is in control all of the time. In other words, there is a kind of balance of power among these interest groups. In addition, there is a separation of powers in the government. That is, the three major branches of government—legislative, executive and judicial—are separate and counterbalance one another so that there is little danger that any one branch of government can wield too much power.

Among pluralists, there are two major strands of thought. **Group pluralism** focuses on society's many different interest groups and organizations and how they compete for access to political power to attempt to further their interests (Drache 2008; Fung 2004). For group pluralists, this jockeying for power by various organizations provides stability for society. They see a balance of group power, where no one group retains power indefinitely and any group can always be challenged by another group. Further, there are crosscutting group memberships, with group members belonging to a variety of organizations that see to their needs and interests. This allows people to be political actors in a variety of collective processes. Group pluralists also believe that there tends to be a general consensus of values in society. As a result, the state is expected and pressured to legislate for the common good.

Elite pluralism focuses specifically on how political elites form similar interest groups and organizations that vie for power (Higley and Burton 2006; Lipset 1981; Rose 1967). While voters may decide which elites represent them, the ultimate decision-making power rests in the hands of those elites. Similar to group pluralists, elite pluralists look at political elites as a diverse social body that organizes into groups to compete with one another for votes. This competition for votes ensures that no one group retains political power indefinitely. Stability is achieved in the system because these political elites must forge agreements with one another in order to pass legislation. This allows for a diversity of interests to be satisfied through those agreements, which tend to represent the common values of the larger society.

THE CONFLICT/CRITICAL PERSPECTIVE: THE POWER ELITE

Pluralism is often juxtaposed to a theory produced by conflict/critical theorists: C. Wright Mills's (1956; Maclean, Harvey, and Chia 2010) **power elite theory**. This theory holds that power is not dispersed throughout a stable society—either among citizen groups or among elite groups. Rather, power is concentrated among a small number of people who control the major institutions of the state, the corporate economy, and the military. The powerful people who make up these institutions may have minor disagreements about policy, but for the most part they are unified in their interests and in the business of owning and operating much of American society.

These elites develop a common worldview. First, they undergo a process of co-optation, whereby they are taught the common ideology of the elite. Further, they forge a shared ideology through their common class identity. That is, members of the power elite tend to come from wealthy families, go to similar schools, and belong to similar clubs. The clubs provide private spaces where friendships and common policies are forged (Clogher 1981; Domhoff 1974, 2013).

In his college days, George H. W. Bush (standing nearest the clock, on the left) belonged to the elite and secret Yale University society called Skull and Bones. How does membership in such groups confer advantage on members later in life?

The power elite within the military, the state, and the corporate world are also often interchangeable. That is, the people who hold leadership positions within these three major institutions play a sort of institutional "musical chairs," switching from one powerful institution to another.

GLOBAL POLITICS

Politics has long been global, but it is convenient to trace modern political globalization to the end of World War I in 1918 (Heywood 2014; Kaarbo and Ray 2010). After the war, efforts at peace led to the creation of the League of Nations in 1920. Of course, peace failed, leading to the start of World War II in 1939. That war had disastrous consequences for much of the world, but it did lead to the formation of several important global organizations, including the International Monetary Fund and the World Bank in 1944 and the United Nations in 1945. While far from unmitigated successes, these organizations persist to this day as important sites and sources of political globalization.

However, global organizations have not led to world peace. Since the formation of the UN, there have been several major interstate wars—conflicts fought between different countries—including the Korean War, the war in Vietnam, the various wars involving Israel and its Arab neighbors, and the conflicts in Iraq, Afghanistan, and Syria. However, the number of interstate warfare has decreased significantly since the UN's founding, but internal conflicts such as civil wars continue to endure, as shown in Figure 12.2.

GEOPOLITICS

Geopolitics entails political relationships that involve broad geographic areas, including the globe as a whole (Black 2016; Steinmetz 2012). On the one hand, geopolitics is concerned with how politics affect geography. One example is the ways in which national borders are redrawn after the end of a war. On the other hand, geopolitics is concerned with the ways in which geography affects politics. One example is the (usually) constant

FIGURE 12.2 • Civil Wars and Interstate Armed Conflicts, 1946–2012

SOURCE: Trends in Armed Conflict, 1946–2014, PRIO Conflict Trends, 01, 2016, Figure 1, p. 2. © Peace Research Institute Oslo.

low-level warfare between Israel and its neighbors. After World War II, much of geopolitics focused on the relationship between the United States and the Soviet Union and their allies. There was great concern over the global expansion of communism. The United States and the Soviet Union clashed, usually indirectly, over their political influence in Germany, Korea, Cuba, Vietnam, and so on. While the Soviet Union sought to expand geopolitically, the United States followed a policy of containment of Soviet efforts to expand communism. For decades, the United States acted based on what was known as the domino theory: If one nation was allowed to fall to communism, many neighboring nations would also fall. For example, the United States feared that if Vietnam fell to the communists, neighboring countries such as Laos and Cambodia would be next. The United States and its relationships with Russia, China, and the Islamic world are at the center of geopolitics today.

THE NATION AND THE NATION-STATE

Geopolitics relates to core concerns in the global age: the future of the nation and the nation-state. A *nation* is a group of people who share, often over a long period of time, similar cultural, religious, ethnic, and linguistic characteristics (Chernilo 2012). Jews are a nation by this definition, and, ironically, so are their

frequent geopolitical enemies, the Palestinians. While many Jews and Palestinians live in the Middle East, many others, especially Jews, are spread throughout the world. They are scattered or dispersed; they exist in a diaspora (Fiddian-Qasmiyeh 2012). The people in the diaspora retain a collective and idealized memory of the homeland that they transmit to their offspring as well as to other members of the diaspora. (Cohen 1997). Many of those involved in a nation, especially those in the diaspora, may have no direct contact with the homeland or with those who live there. Their linkages to them may be largely or purely imaginary. They exist in what Benedict Anderson (1991) calls **imagined communities**, or communities that are socially constructed by those who see themselves as part of them. Thus, Jews who have never been to Israel, or who may never even want to visit there, may still be part of an imagined community rooted in Israel.

Nation-states exist within a global context, but they are affected, even threatened, by globalization in various ways (Hershkovitz 2012). First, global flows of various kinds—undocumented immigrants, drugs, terrorists, and so on—easily pierce the borders of nation-states and serve to erode their national sovereignties. Second, globalization serves to alter the nation-state's structure and functions. For example, corporations have become increasingly important on the global stage and have come to operate more autonomously from states. Third, the government itself has to change to adjust to global changes. For example, the United States created the Department of Homeland Security in 2002 to deal with, among other things, the global threat of terrorism. Fourth, there is the possibility that global flows can strengthen the nation-state. For example, external threats can lead citizens to put their differences aside, at least for the time being, and rally around the government and the nation-state more broadly. In spite of changes such as those described previously, we continue to think of nation-states as being all-powerful. However, a number of them have failed, or are on the verge of failing, to fulfill the "basic conditions and responsibilities" of sovereign states (Boas 2012, 633). Among the characteristics of a failed state are a "lack of control over [its] own territory, widespread corruption and criminality, huge economic recession and/or hyperinflation, failure to provide basic services, and large flows of refugees and internally displaced persons" (Boas 2012, 633). Failed states tend to exploit one segment of society (the middle and lower classes, for example) for the benefit of another

subset, especially the rich (Acemoglu and Robinson 2012). The Fragile States Index, an annual ranking of 178 nations, highlights weak and failing states around the world based on their levels of stability (Figure 12.3). In 2016, the countries that received the worst scores were Somalia, South Sudan, Central African Republic, Sudan, Yemen, and Syria.

War

War occurs when a nation uses its military in an attempt to impose its will on others outside the nation (Malesevic 2010). It also occurs when a nation uses its military to impose its political will within its borders—the case of civil war. War is one method of "doing politics," or dealing with political disagreements.

Why does war occur? First, there needs to be a cultural tradition of war. Second, a situation must exist in which two political actors have objectives that are incompatible. Finally, a "fuel" must bring the situation from thinking about war to actually making war (Timasheff 1965).

FIGURE 12.3 • Fragile States Index, 2016

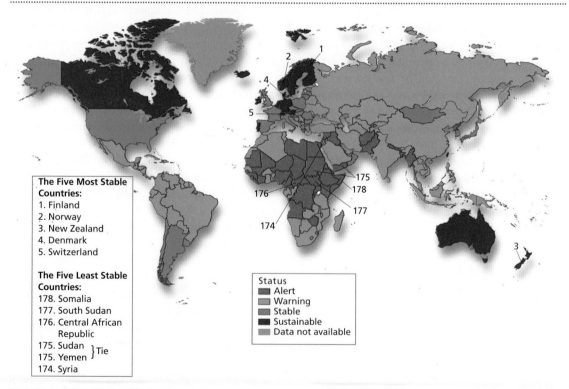

The Five Most Stable Countries:
1. Finland
2. Norway
3. New Zealand
4. Denmark
5. Switzerland

The Five Least Stable Countries:
178. Somalia
177. South Sudan
176. Central African Republic
175. Sudan } Tie
175. Yemen
174. Syria

Status
- Alert
- Warning
- Stable
- Sustainable
- Data not available

SOURCE: Data from The Fund for Peace, "Fragile States Index 2016."

In the United States, the cultural tradition of war is all around us. We are often taught in our history classes about U.S. involvement in foreign wars, in which we are depicted as saviors, the bringers of democracy, and so on. In our own history, we can see antagonistic situations that brought us into military conflict with other nations or peoples. Acts of aggression, such as the Japanese attack on Pearl Harbor and the September 11 terrorist attacks, have served as the fuels that ignited war.

Terrorism

Terrorism typically involves nongovernmental actors engaging in acts of violence targeting non-combatants, property, or even military personnel in order to influence politics (Vertigans 2011). The term *terrorism* is often controversial, because it is usually the powerful who define who is and who is not a terrorist. Consider, for example, that if property destruction as a way to express political grievances constitutes terrorism, the people who were part of the Boston Tea Party fit the description. And where is the line between terrorists and revolutionaries fighting against invading or occupying armies? Who gets to draw that line and why? Can states be terrorists?

Nevertheless, all over the world, people refer to acts such as suicide bombings and the targeting of civilians of enemy nations or groups as examples of terrorism. More specifically, in the West today, a group is likely to be labeled terrorist if it has a history of engaging in violence against the citizens of a government (Beck and Minor 2013). Terrorist attacks are quite common in the early twenty-first century and do not seem to be on the decline. While terrorism is particularly likely when one nation occupies another and attempts to police its population, many acts of contemporary terrorism, especially those committed by the Islamic State, are far more wide-ranging and not limited by national

FIGURE 12.4 • Deaths from Terrorism Worldwide, 2000–2015

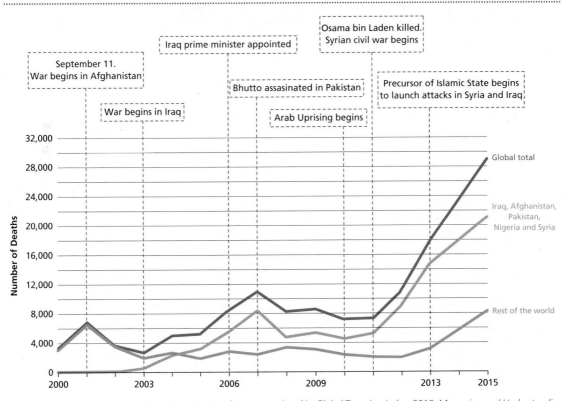

SOURCE: Based on data from the Global Terrorism Database, as reprinted in *Global Terrorism Index, 2016: Measuring and Understanding the Impact of Terrorism,* The Institute for Economics and Peace.

FIGURE 12.5 • Timeline of the Industrial Revolution, 1712–1903

1712
Thomas Newcomen patents the atmospheric steam engine.

1764
James Hargreaves invents the spinning jenny.

1785
Edmund Cartwright invents the power loom.

1807
Robert Fulton begins steamboat service on the Hudson River.

1710 1720 1730 1740 1750 1760 1770 1780 1790 1800 1810

1733
John Kay invents the flying shuttle.

1779
Samuel Crompton invents the spinning mule.

1793
Eli Whitney patents the cotton gin.

SOURCE: Adapted from Industrial Revolution: Timeline, Facts, and Resources, Research by B. Sobey, TheFreeResource.com.

borders. Figure 12.4 shows that the number of people who have died from terrorist activity each year has increased fivefold since 2000. In 2015, approximately 29,000 deaths resulted from terrorist attacks. The vast majority of these incidents (72 percent) occurred in Iraq, Afghanistan, Pakistan, Nigeria, and Syria. Not included in these numbers are acts lacking a political, economic, religious, or social goal, thus they may exclude domestic, or home-grown, terrorism such as school shootings (Kellner 2008).

ASK YOURSELF

It is often pointed out that those revered in U.S. history as the instigators of the American Revolution could be characterized as terrorists in another light. Do you agree with this characterization? What is the difference between a terrorist and a revolutionary hero?

THE U.S. ECONOMY: FROM INDUSTRIALIZATION TO DEINDUSTRIALIZATION

The **economy** is the social system involved in the production, consumption, and distribution of goods and services. The devastating effects of the Great Recession reminded us, if we ever really need a reminder, that the economy is of overwhelming importance to everyone (Orr 2012; Smith et al. 2011). While the economy in the United States and elsewhere has strengthened significantly, and stock markets have boomed, there is always the danger of another recession or even a Depression like the one that began in 1929.

Over the last 200 years, the U.S. economy has moved from reliance on industrial employment and mass production to the decline of manufacturing

1837
Samuel Morse invents the telegraph.

1876
Alexander Graham Bell invents the telephone.

1879
Thomas Edison invents the incandescent light bulb.

1900
The zeppelin invented by Count Ferdinand von Zeppelin.

1903
The Wright Brothers make the first successful airplane flight.

1820 1830 1840 1850 1860 1870 1880 1890 1900 1910

1830
George Stephenson begins passenger rail service between Liverpool and London.

1866
Cyrus Field lays the first successful transatlantic cable.

1892
Rudolf Diesel invents the diesel-fueled internal combustion engine.

1896
Henry Ford manufactures his first motorcar.

and a corresponding increase in the service and information sectors.

THE INDUSTRIAL REVOLUTION

The key development in the emergence of the modern economy was the nineteenth-century Industrial Revolution (see Figure 12.5), which introduced the factory system of production (Hobsbawm and Wrigley 1999). Instead of making products alone at home or in small groups in workshops, large numbers of workers were brought together in factories. Eventually, manual factory work with hand tools gave way to work in conjunction with machines. In addition, human and animal power were replaced by power supplied by steam and other energy sources. While there were skilled workers in these early factories, they tended over time to be replaced, because skills were increasingly likely to be built into the machinery. This meant that less skilled or even unskilled workers, less well-trained and lower-paid workers, and even children could be—and were—hired to do the work. They tended to work increasingly long hours in harsh working conditions and at ever lower pay. Another defining characteristic of this factory system was an elaborate division of labor by which a single product was produced by a number of workers, each performing a small step in the overall process.

The factories of the early Industrial Revolution were quite primitive, but over time they grew much larger, more efficient, more technologically advanced, and more oriented toward the mass production of a wide variety of goods. **Mass production** has a number of defining characteristics, including large numbers of standardized products, highly specialized workers, interchangeable machine parts, precision tools, a high-volume mechanized production process, and the synchronization of the flow of materials used in production, with the entire process made as continuous as possible. The logical outcome of this was the assembly line, which came to fruition in the early twentieth century in the mass production of Ford automobiles. By the mid-twentieth century, these systems had reached their fullest application in the United States and had spread to many other parts of the world. Today, it is China that leads the world in many forms of mass production.

FROM FORDISM TO POST-FORDISM

Fordism consists of the ideas, principles, and systems created by Henry Ford and his associates at the beginning of the twentieth century. Ford is generally credited with the development of the modern mass production system, primarily through the creation of the automobile assembly line. Among the characteristics associated with Fordism are the mass production of homogeneous products, reliance on inflexible technologies such as the assembly line, the use of standardized work routines, economies of scale, and the creation of a mass market for products, such as automobiles, that flow from the assembly line (Bonanno 2012).

Fordism dominated much of the twentieth-century American automobile industry and many others. It coincided with, and played a major role in, the "golden age of capitalism" (Vidal 2016). It declined in the 1970s, especially with the 1973 oil crisis and the rise of the Japanese automobile industry. It was also done in by the fact that consumers were no longer content with homogeneous products. They demanded greater choice in their automobiles and their components. **Post-Fordism** is associated with smaller production runs of more specialized products, especially those high in style and quality; more flexible machinery, made possible by advances in technology largely traceable to the computer; more skilled workers with greater flexibility and autonomy; less reliance on economies of scale; and more differentiated markets for those more specialized products (Amin 1994; Beynon 2016; Janoski and Lepadatu 2013).

SOCIALISM, COMMUNISM, AND CAPITALISM

From its inception, the Industrial Revolution was capitalist in nature, but it eventually gave rise to the opposing and alternative systems of socialism and communism.

Socialism and Communism

The terms *socialism* and *communism* are often used more or less interchangeably. However, it is important to differentiate between them. Both concepts are often associated with Karl Marx. **Socialism** is an economic system oriented to the collective, rather than the private, ownership of the means of production. The means of production are the tools, machines, and factories that in capitalism are owned by the capitalists and are needed by the workers—the proletariat, in Marx's terms—in order to produce. Marx hoped that the exploitation of the proletariat would lead them to revolt against the capitalist system. That, in turn, would lead to collective rather than private ownership of the means of production, resulting in a socialist economy. Control of the economic base would lead to control of everything else of importance, including the political system.

From a Marxian perspective, **communism** can be seen as a historical stage following socialism. It involves the effort by society to plan and organize production consciously and rationally, so that all members of society benefit from it (Cox 2007; Shevchenko 2012). The collective control of the means of production in socialism is a first step, but in itself it is not enough to run a society. Once in control of the means of production, the collectivity must set about the task of creating a rational centralized economy (and society) that operates for the good of all and creates social and economic equality.

The ideas associated with socialism and communism are less important today than they were only a few decades ago, before the fall of the Soviet empire in late 1991. There is little that passes for communism in the world today, except in North Korea ("North Korea Country Profile" 2015) and possibly Cuba. China continues to see itself as a communist society, even though it is on the cusp of becoming the most powerful capitalist country in the world. In China, a political commitment to communism coexists uncomfortably with a highly capitalistic economic system.

Welfare States

In the contemporary world, socialism is more vibrant than communism. Although there are no fully socialist societies in the world today, many societies have socialistic elements. Many Western European countries have become "welfare states." They have powerful social welfare programs that are socialistic in nature in that they are run consciously and rationally by centralized authorities. **Welfare states** seek both to operate their economic markets efficiently, as capitalism does, and to do so equitably, which capitalism does *not* do (Esping-Anderson 1990; Lessenich, forthcoming). Their goal is to provide for the welfare—the well-being—of their citizens. There are many examples of social welfare programs, including national health plans, old-age plans, childcare and parental leave systems, and social safety nets of various kinds (e.g., unemployment insurance).

Even the United States has social welfare programs such as unemployment insurance, Social Security, and Medicare. However, the United States lags far behind leaders in Western Europe and Canada in these kinds of programs. There are powerful forces in the United States aligned with capitalism that strongly resist efforts to expand social welfare programs. Bernie Sanders, an avowed socialist (although he played that down during the 2016 campaign), garnered enormous support in his failed effort to defeat Hillary Clinton for the Democratic nomination for president. However, the defeat of Sanders and Clinton and the victory of Donald Trump does not auger well for the future, at least in short run, of socialistic programs in the United States.

While the United States struggles to implement more social welfare programs, the most developed social welfare states in Europe are experiencing something of a crisis and finding it difficult to maintain existing programs (Kangas 2007). In fact, some, especially Great Britain, are retrenching in various ways, such as offering less generous benefits and programs, making it more difficult for people to qualify for them, and making people take greater responsibility for providing for their own welfare. Threats to, and declines in, social welfare programs have spread throughout Europe as a result of both the Great Recession and the euro crisis (see the discussion later in the chapter) that threatened the European economies. Those countries worst hit by the latter—Greece and Spain—had to cut back dramatically on these programs.

Тов. Ленин ОЧИЩАЕТ землю от нечисти.

This Russian poster of 1920 depicts Soviet leader Vladimir Lenin sweeping the exploiting classes off the Earth. Would a social change as radical as that depicted in the cartoon ever be likely?

Welfare states have been threatened before. However, they are being threatened much more today than ever before by the realities of the global economy. With today's markets for virtually everything becoming increasingly global and highly competitive, the lion's share of global business is very likely to go to the countries, and the industries in them, where costs are lowest (see Chapter 7). The costs of production in Western European countries are far higher, in part because of the extraordinary social welfare expenses that must be factored into the cost structure. This has made Western Europe, and the United States to a lesser degree, less competitive or even uncompetitive in various global markets. Some argue that these countries must reduce social welfare expenditures to compete in the global marketplace. Others contend that the more generous welfare states lower costs of business in some sectors and help make the workforce more productive (Hall and Soskice 2001). They assert that greater spending on social welfare programs can contribute to a more educated, healthier, and more flexible workforce.

Capitalism

Karl Marx lived during the era of **competitive capitalism**, characterized by a large number of relatively small firms. No single firm or small subset of firms could completely dominate and control a given area of the economy. The capitalism of Marx's day was highly competitive. However, in the late nineteenth century and into much of the twentieth century, this situation changed. Huge corporations emerged and, alone or in combination with a few other similarly sized corporations, came to dominate, or monopolize, certain markets. This was **monopoly capitalism** (Baran and Sweezy 1966). Perhaps the

best example is the American automobile industry, which for much of the twentieth century was dominated by three huge corporations—General Motors, Ford, and Chrysler.

Of course, capitalism has changed once again, and a number of foreign companies (Toyota, Honda, Nissan, Hyundai, BMW, Mercedes) now compete successfully with the U.S. firms. We may have seen the end of monopoly capitalism in the United States, but it is likely that we will see the emergence of a global system of monopoly capitalism in which a small number of corporations come to dominate a global, not just a national, market.

Whether or not capitalism once again becomes monopolistic, in recent years it has certainly become increasingly global. This can be seen as **transnational capitalism**, where it is no longer national but transnational economic practices that predominate (Kauppinen 2013; Sklair 2002). Thus, the global flow of automobiles and even money has become far more important than their existence and movement within national boundaries.

It could also be argued that the center of capitalism no longer lies in production, but rather in consumption. That is, the focus is on inducing large numbers of people throughout the world to consume at high levels. While the capitalism of Marx's day was described as producer capitalism, we now live more in an era of consumer capitalism. Within the realm of consumption, some of the leading transnational corporations are Walmart, IKEA, H&M, and McDonald's.

Ritzer (2015b) has recently argued that we are living in yet a later stage of capitalism—"prosumer capitalism." While the producer produces and the consumer consumes, the **prosumer** is *both* producer and consumer, often at the same time. Producer and consumer capitalism will continue to exist, but they will gradually be subsumed and supplanted by prosumer capitalism. Prosumption is occurring increasingly in all of the businesses mentioned at the end of the previous paragraph (e.g. the consumer's putting together—"producing"—a bookshelf purchased—"consumed"—at IKEA), but it is most notable on the internet, where there is virtually no distinction between producer and consumer. For example, one must produce the order for what one wants to consume on Amazon.com or eBay.

IKEA exemplifies the idea of prosumer capitalism. Customers are not only consumers but producers, assembling the furniture themselves—often with difficulty!

An even better example is Facebook, which exists only because prosumers perform the work of posting comments and photos, "liking" particular products, and following their favorite celebrities. All this "work" is highly profitable to Facebook in the form of "Big Data," which it can sell to corporations that can then use it to target just the right consumers for their goods and services (Lazer, forthcoming). If Ford is a model of producer capitalism, and McDonald's is a paradigm of consumer capitalism, Facebook is likely the model of the coming predominance of prosumer capitalism.

DEINDUSTRIALIZATION IN THE UNITED STATES

Industry and industrial employment were clearly crucial to economic development in the United States and other developed nations. However, a number of developed nations, especially the United States, have been undergoing a process of deindustrialization (Porter 2016b). **Deindustrialization** involves the decline of manufacturing as well as a corresponding increase in various types of services (Bluestone and Harrison 1984; Koistinen 2013; Wren 2013).

We tend to think of deindustrialization in the United States as a process that has been going on for decades, is now far advanced, and may even be near completion. The focus tends to be on the Rust Belt in middle America and the demise, beginning in the 1960s, of such steel cities as Pittsburgh, Youngstown, and Bethlehem, Pennsylvania, as well as Akron, Ohio, the heart of the rubber industry (see Figure 12.6). These industries are all but gone, and these cities have suffered greatly, although in a few cases, such as Pittsburgh, they have been able to reinvent themselves. The decline of the auto industry began a bit later, but it, too, has clearly undergone massive deindustrialization (Goldstein 2017). This is reflected in the decline of many American cities, but in no city is it more evident than in Detroit, Michigan (Silver 2015). In early 2013, conditions had gotten so bad in Detroit that the state of Michigan appointed an emergency manager to take control of the city's finances. The city filed for bankruptcy in mid-2013, but a plan to eliminate billions of dollars of debt allowed it to begin exiting bankruptcy in late 2014. However, while Detroit is now slowly revitalizing, it is highly unlikely that its economic woes are over. Deindustrialization in the United States has not yet run its course, and other industries, such as the glass industry, are now experiencing this process.

Factors in Deindustrialization

Several factors were (are) responsible for deindustrialization in the United States. First was the aging technology in many American industries. This made them vulnerable to foreign competitors, which were often building new, state-of-the-art factories. Another technological factor was the rise of automation, which greatly reduced the need for many blue-collar workers and, more recently, in the form of robotization, many other types of workers (Ford 2015; Noble 2011). Furthermore, the increased efficiency of automated technologies made it possible for corporations to close unnecessary factories, thus cutting many more jobs.

Second was globalization, which brought with it industrial competition from low-wage workers in less developed countries. This was especially true in the early years of the emergence of China as an industrial power. Now, of course, China is developing rapidly, but its low wages and seemingly endless stream of workers will make it nearly impossible for American industries to compete with Chinese industries. For example, most of the work that goes into manufacturing Apple's iPhone is done in China at Longhua Science and Technology Park (Duhigg and Bradsher 2012). At least 230,000, and maybe many more, people work there, often six days per week and for as many as 12 hours per day. Workers sleep in onsite barracks provided by the company, and only a few years ago, many earned less than $17 per day. However, as the wages—and living standards—of Chinese workers rise, we may also see an increase in the price of Chinese goods (Schuman 2016). Another aspect of globalization as it relates to deindustrialization is the closing of American factories and, in some cases, their movement, or at least their jobs, elsewhere in the world, especially to Mexico. For example, great controversy arose in 2016 when Carrier announced that it was closing its Midwestern plant that made furnaces and heating equipment and shifting many of its 1,400 jobs to Carrier plants in Mexico. The move made

FIGURE 12.6 • **The U.S. Rust Belt**

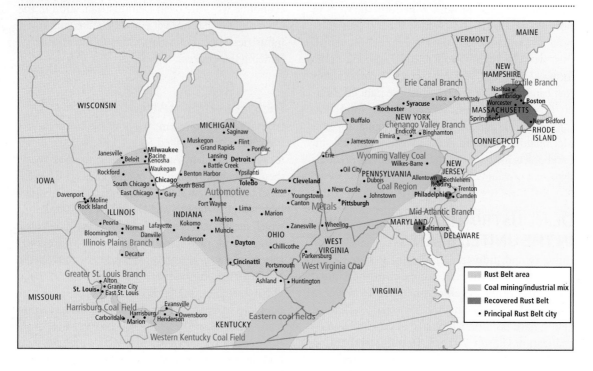

economic sense for the company. Permanent workers in the Carrier plant in Mexico earn about $19 *per day*, while comparable workers in the U.S. earn between $15 and $26 *per hour* (Schwartz 2016). However, under pressure from Donald Trump, in late 2016, Carrier announced that it would *not* close its Midwestern plant and that it would keep the majority of the 1,400 jobs there. It remains to be seen whether in the long run politics will continue to "trump" economics.

A third factor in deindustrialization was the rise of consumer society and the increasing demand for goods of all types. This should have helped American industries, but it led many more foreign manufacturers to become eager to sell products to that consumer market. American industries have had great difficulty competing with them. In terms of the demand for goods, there arose, partly as a result of the low prices offered by foreign manufacturers, a mania among American consumers for ever lower prices. This worked to the advantage of foreign manufacturers because of their much lower cost structures, especially their lower labor costs. A fourth factor responsible for deindustrialization was the rise of the service sector in

the United States (Wren 2013). In the last half of the twentieth century, an increasingly affluent U.S. population demanded not only more and cheaper goods but also a dramatic increase in services of all types (Kollmeyer 2009). Increasingly wealthy Americans seemed to prefer spending their newfound money on services rather than on industrial products. Among other things, this led to the expansion of service industries, such as the health, education, and personal and social services industries. More recently, other service industries have increasingly come to the fore, such as the financial, real estate, tourism, and hospitality (hotels, cruise ships) industries.

Service jobs proliferated, and some proved to be not so desirable. Millions of such jobs have been created for U.S. workers of all age groups, even seniors, in the retail sector, most notably at Walmart and Target. Women are disproportionally represented in these service occupations. The best example of less-than-desirable jobs is provided by the fast-food industry (Leidner 1993; Ritzer 2015a). Fast-food workers generally earn the minimum wage and often are not allowed to work a 40-hour week (Allegretto et al. 2013). As a result, they frequently do not earn enough to rise above the poverty line and are able to survive only with the help of government assistance. It costs taxpayers almost $7 billion per year to pay for this assistance for workers in the fast-food industry. McDonald's alone costs U.S. taxpayers $1.2 billion annually (Sauter, Frohlich, and Hess 2013).

ASK YOURSELF

How would a structural/functionalist explain deindustrialization in the United States? What about a conflict/critical theorist? Are there factors in this development about which they would agree?

The Decline of American Labor Unions

Closely related to deindustrialization is the decline of labor unions in the United States (Rosenfeld 2014; Western and Rosenfeld 2012). The American labor movement grew from 3 percent of the labor force in 1900 to 23 percent by the close of World War II. A decline began in the 1960s, at about the same time as the onset of deindustrialization and the rise of the service sector. As of 2015, only 11 percent of the U.S. labor force belonged to labor unions (see Figure 12.7).

There are a number of reasons for this decline in unionization, although deindustrialization, the decline of manufacturing, and the loss of blue-collar jobs rank at the top of the list. Many of those jobs either left the United States or were automated out of existence. Prosumers are now doing work for nothing (e.g., doing the work of bank tellers at ATMs), or for comparatively little pay (e.g., Uber drivers)—work that many people were paid pretty well to do not too long ago. The great increase in service and white-collar work involved a population that, in the main, had been hostile to unionization.

Today, the union movement is dramatically smaller, but its membership seems, at least for now, to have stabilized, buttressed by some successes, especially in the public realm. In fact, in 2009, for the first time, a majority of union members were employed by the government (Greenhouse 2011). One area of success has been teachers and

their unions, especially the nearly 3-million-member National Education Association (NEA) and the 1.6-million-member American Federation of Teachers (AFT). However, even that outcome has been threatened by movements in some states (Ohio, Wisconsin, and Illinois) to eliminate collective bargaining by teachers, as well as by public-sector employees more generally (Goldfield and Bromsen 2013).

THE POSTINDUSTRIAL SOCIETY

Clearly, deindustrialization and the decline of labor unions set the stage for the emergence of postindustrialism in the United States and in the developed world in general. An increasing emphasis on consumption and the dramatic growth in service jobs pushed the United States even toward a truly postindustrial society (Bell 1973; Smart 2011; Vogt 2016).

A **postindustrial society** is one that was at one time industrial, but the focus on the manufacture of goods has been replaced by an increase in service work. The latter is work in which people

FIGURE 12.7 • U.S. Union Membership among All Wage and Salary Workers, 1973–2015

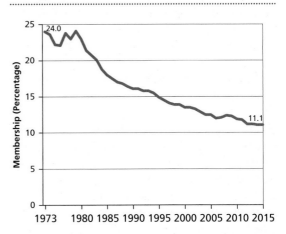

SOURCES: Data from Barry T. Hirsch and David A. Macpherson, "Union Membership and Coverage Database From the Current Population Survey: Note," *Industrial and Labor Relations Review* 56 (January 2003), 349–354; Hirsch and Macpherson (Current Population Survey); U.S. Historical Tables: Union Membership, Coverage, Density and Employment, 1973-2015, http://unionstats.gsu.edu/All-Wage-and-Salary-Workers.htm. © 2002, 2015 by Barry T. Hirsch and David A. Macpherson.

provide services for one another rather than producing goods. It encompasses a wide range of service-oriented occupations, including lawyer, physician, teacher, financial adviser, and computer programmer as well as salesperson, clerk, and counter person at a fast-food restaurant. Employment in such occupations has increased dramatically in the United States in the last century, while there has been a similarly dramatic decline in work relating to goods production. Agricultural work declined earlier and even more steeply.

WORK, CONSUMPTION, AND LEISURE

Much of the preceding discussion has dealt with the economy in terms of general trends and developments. However, most people connect to the economy either through their work or through the process of consumption, to be discussed shortly. The relationship between people and their work is undergoing rapid change.

William Julius Wilson has published research on race, social class, and the city and is particularly known for his contributions regarding the reasons for the persistence of poverty and inequality for African Americans. He has received many awards and holds 44 honorary degrees.

EMPLOYMENT, UNEMPLOYMENT, AND UNDEREMPLOYMENT

Not long ago, we tended to think of people as taking jobs, perhaps in large and stable organizations, and embarking on lifelong careers. Those careers entailed at least some upward mobility, sufficient earnings for workers and their families to live on, and retirement with ample pensions—perhaps in sunny Florida or Arizona—when workers reached their early 60s.

However, there are several problems with this romantic scenario. First, even in its heyday from about 1950 to 1990, it applied to only a very small proportion of the population. Employment has ebbed and flowed over time. It has always been the case that a number of people have been unable to get any jobs at all. In the United States, **unemployment** is defined as being economically active and in the labor force (e.g., not retired), able and willing to work, and seeking employment but unable to find a job (Nordenmark 2007). The unemployment rate in the United States has generally run at about 5 percent of the labor force.

However, in the midst of the recession in 2009, it reached 10 percent, although by April 2017 it had dropped to 4 percent (see Figure 12.8). Many observers believe that is an underestimate, because many people have given up searching for work and are therefore not included in the unemployment statistics (see the discussion of discouraged workers that follows).

William Julius Wilson (1997) focuses on long-term unemployment and the problems it creates for black Americans. Many observers have traced these difficulties (e.g., children without involved fathers, drug abuse) to social structural problems (e.g., institutional racism) that are difficult, if not impossible, to solve. However, Wilson links them directly to unemployment and thus sees them as solvable through a number of reforms, including the creation of more work for all black Americans. At the moment, black Americans experience not only greater unemployment but also a long list of additional difficulties associated with being unemployed, not the least of which is a higher incidence of poverty. In 2015, the unemployment rate for black

The Tumbleweed Society: Working and Caring in an Age of Insecurity

(Oxford University Press, 2015)

Allison J. Pugh (Associate Professor of Sociology at the University of Virginia; PhD, University of California, Berkeley, 2006)

Deindustrialization has helped create a culture of insecurity—a "tumbleweed society"—that affects not just the economy and our jobs, but also our personal relationships and our self-identity. Allison Pugh discovers through her interviews with 80 mothers and fathers that this culture of insecurity profoundly shapes their expectations of commitment, loyalty, and obligation. Flexibility in the workplace has weakened employer commitment, but not the work ethic of the labor force. Some workers value flexibility because it gives them more freedom and mobility. This is especially true for well-educated professionals, who are better positioned financially to relocate for a new job. Women in general have also gained more independence in the labor force as a result of deindustrialization. But others, particularly unskilled males, feel angry that their hard work does not guarantee stable employment. Interestingly, this anger is directed not against their bosses, but at themselves for being too dependent on their jobs. Pugh describes this as a "one-way honor system" that holds individual workers responsible for their job successes and failures, not employers.

Job insecurity transcends the workplace, influencing what kinds of expectations we have about commitment in our personal relationships. More affluent workers and their spouses try to protect their homes from the unpredictability of the economy and commit to stable, long-term relationships with each other. Less affluent workers more often take a stance of either independence or duty in their commitment to others. Low commitment expectations in the labor force parallel low commitment expectations in intimate relationships for those who pursue independence. Though extremely loyal to their children, these individuals, particularly women, do not expect their intimate relationships to endure. In contrast, those who feel angry about job insecurity, especially men, possess a strong of sense of duty in maintaining constancy in their personal lives to compensate for the instability that they experience in the labor force. These individuals desire enduring relationships with their significant others, and feel betrayed and abandoned when this does not occur. Pugh argues that we need to move beyond the tumbleweed society and establish a coral society based on "radical pluralism" that supports stable employment, committed personal relationships, and diverse types of families.

Supplementary Resources

- You can listen to Pugh discuss *The Tumbleweed Society* in a Podcast posted on the Society Pages: https://thesocietypages.org/officehours/2015/09/01/allison-pugh-on-the-tumbleweed-society.
- Read an interview with Pugh that appeared in *The Atlantic* at http://www.theatlantic.com/business/archive/2015/05/work-is-about-more-than-money/392342.

FIGURE 12.8 • U.S. Unemployment Rate, 2005–2016

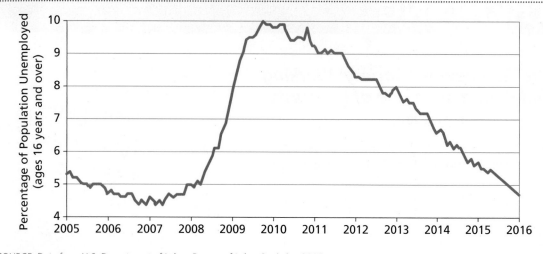

SOURCE: Data from U.S. Department of Labor, Bureau of Labor Statistics, 2016.

Americans was double the rate for whites and Asians and three percentage points higher than the rate for Hispanics (Figure 12.9).

ASK YOURSELF

The government's reported rate of unemployment includes those who are actively seeking employment. Why do you suppose it does *not* include those who have given up looking for work, or who have settled for less employment than they need or would like, such as part-time instead of full-time work? What would happen to the unemployment picture if the reported unemployment rate did include these people?

The statistics on unemployment understate the problem of a lack of work, because they deal only with those who are in the labor force and who are actively seeking work. Another large group of people who are marginally attached to the workforce includes **discouraged workers** (Heslin, Bell, and Fletcher 2012). To be categorized as such, people must have sought work within the last year or since their last job ended, if that was less than a year previous, and must have not sought work in the last four weeks.

A large number of Americans must also cope with the problem of **underemployment** (Dooley and Prause 2009). This involves (a) being in jobs that are not up to one's training and ability, such as a college professor driving a taxi at night; (b) being an involuntary part-time worker, that is, working part-time because one cannot find full-time work; or (c) working in jobs that are not fully occupying, such as in a seasonal industry like agriculture, where work slows down dramatically or disappears in the off-season.

Being without a job is a major problem. However, as pointed out previously, most Americans who want jobs have them, although they might not always have the jobs that they want. An even bigger problem is that many jobs (especially service jobs) do not pay a **living wage**, an income that is high enough to meet the most basic family expenses. This has led, among other things, to a call for a national minimum wage of $15 per hour, a call that is unlikely to be met any time soon, although it has been promised in several locations in the United States, such as New York and California, where it will be phased in by 2023.

FIGURE 12.9 • U.S. Unemployment Rate by Race/Ethnicity, 2015

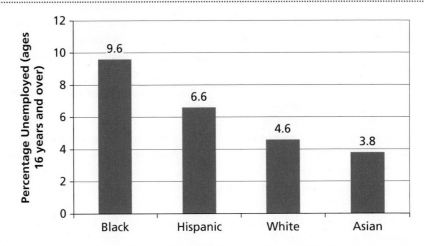

SOURCE: Data from U.S. Department of Labor, Bureau of Labor Statistics, *Labor Force Statistics from the Current Population Survey.*

CONSUMPTION AND THE POSTMODERN SOCIETY

Recall from Chapter 1 that consumption is the process by which people obtain and utilize goods and services (Cook and Ryan 2015; Wiedenhoft Murphy 2017b). More specifically, it is a process involving the interrelationship among consumer objects and services, consumers, the consumption process, and consumption sites (Ritzer, Goodman, and Wiedenhoft 2001). First, consumption involves what is to be consumed, largely consumer objects (clothes, cars, electronic gear) and services (help from computer experts, medical services). Second, consumption requires consumers, or people who do the consuming. Third, there must be a process of consumption. Fourth, this process often takes place at consumption sites, such as farmers' markets, shopping malls, theme parks, cruise ships, and, increasingly, Amazon.com and other online sites.

These sites can all be seen as **cathedrals of consumption** (Ritzer 2010a; Ostergaard, Fitchett, and Jantzen 2013). These are the large, sometimes lavish, consumption sites created mostly in the United States in the last half of the twentieth century and into the early twenty-first century. The use of the term *cathedrals* is meant to indicate the fact that consumption has in many ways become today's religion. We go to the cathedrals of consumption to practice that religion. Thus, for example, many middle-class children make a pilgrimage to Disney World at least once in their lives.

Outdoor strip malls are traceable to the 1920s, and the first indoor malls were built in the 1950s, but it is the megamall, which arrived in the 1980s and 1990s (e.g., the Mall of America in Minneapolis in 1992), that is the crucial innovation here. What defines the megamall is the combination under one roof of a number of cathedrals of consumption, especially a shopping mall and a theme park. The theme park itself is a second cathedral of consumption—the first landmark development for theme parks was the opening of Disneyland in Southern California in 1955. Third is the modern cruise ship, the first of which set sail in 1966 (Clancy 2012). The final major cathedral of consumption is the hotel-casino, most notably of the type that defines Las Vegas. The first of these—the Flamingo—was built in 1946. It was the idea of the mobster Bugsy Siegel.

Of course, there are many other important cathedrals of consumption—superstores such as Bed Bath & Beyond and Best Buy, huge discounters such as Walmart and Costco, and online retailers and malls such as Amazon.com and eBay. These cathedrals, along with other consumption sites, especially chain stores such as McDonald's and Starbucks, have come to define not only the sites themselves but also much of consumption as a whole.

In the past we had to travel, sometimes long distances, to cathedrals of consumption such as department stores (Howard 2015), but now many of them are available via the internet on our home computers or on the smartphones in our pockets or bags. As a result, brick-and-mortar cathedrals of consumption such as department stores, shopping malls, and casinos are in decline. Nevertheless, consumption continues to grow, even though much of it has shifted from offline to online cathedrals.

Consumption is generally considered to be the hallmark of postmodern society. That is, while modernity is defined by production and work, postmodernity is defined by consumption. This change is best seen in the United States, which moved from being the preeminent industrial society in the world in the mid-twentieth century to being the world's most important consumer society in the late twentieth and early twenty-first centuries. This is reflected in, for example, the fact that consumption accounts for approximately 70 percent of the U.S. economy today.

Consumption is central to the idea of a postmodern society precisely because it represents a shift from the focus on production in modern society. However, in another sense, there is such a thing as postmodern consumption that is different from, and stands in contrast to, modern consumption (Hamouda and Gharbi 2013; Venkatesh 2015). In modernity, consumption is seen as a secondary activity, as well as something to be avoided as much as possible so that people can focus on the far more important activities of production and work. This, of course, is the view associated with Max Weber's ([1904–1905] 1958) famous conception of the Protestant ethic. According to this ethic, people are to concentrate on work because it is there (especially in terms of being successful in one's work) that the signs of religious salvation can be found. People are expected to consume minimally, to be frugal, to save their money, and to reinvest what they earn from productive activities.

ASK YOURSELF

Why is a farmers' market not a cathedral of consumption? What other places in which you can engage in consumption are not cathedrals of consumption?

Postmodern consumption is best thought of as **consumerism**, an obsession with consumption. We have become consumed by consumption. This reflects the view, outlined in Chapter 2, that postmodern theory can be seen as a new kind of critical theory. For example, Baudrillard ([1970] 1998) argues against the conventional view that consumption is about the satisfaction of needs. He contends that if that were the case, consumption would cease when one's needs were satisfied. However, in contemporary consumerism, as soon as one need is satisfied, a new and different need comes to the fore, requiring additional consumption. Baudrillard further argues that consumption is really about difference. That is, it is through consumption that people seek to demonstrate that they are different from others in, for example, their taste in clothes or in cars. In the postmodern world, where an endless and ever-expanding set of differences is created, consumption becomes a never-ending process of demonstrating those differences.

Postmodernists are very prone to appending the prefix *hyper-* to many things (Lipovetsky 2005). Appending *hyper-* to any modern characteristic tends to turn it into something associated with, and critical of, the postmodern world. For example, the postmodern world is associated with hyperconsumption, or buying more than you want, need, and can afford (Ritzer 2001). Related to the idea of hyperconsumption, especially consuming more than you can afford, is the idea of **hyperdebt**, or borrowing more than you should, thereby owing more than you will be able to repay (Ritzer 2012a).

However, some postmodernists have a more complex view of consumption, whereby a more positive perspective coexists with this critical orientation (Venkatesh 2015). For example, they tend to see consumption as an aesthetic undertaking, or

Is it possible not to consume in a society that values consumption so much that it offers innumerable shopping malls, theme parks, and casino hotels? What would happen to the economy if large numbers of people consciously limited their consumption?

as a form of art. Consumers are seen as artists in, say, buying and putting together, in highly creative ways, the various elements of different outfits. This is particularly related to the postmodern idea of pastiche, or the mixing together of various elements, especially those that most people would not see as fitting together. While a modern consumer might purchase an outfit composed of matching elements (e.g., skirt and top) predesigned and preselected by the manufacturer, the postmodern consumer is seen as creatively and artistically putting together components from a wide range of manufacturers and styles. Furthermore, new and used clothing, or clothing from different time periods, is combined in unique ways to create outfits that can be seen as works of art.

LEISURE

One of the dominant trends of our time is that more and more of our leisure time is devoted to consumption. For example, in golf, consumption includes acquisition of the equipment and proper clothing, payment of greens fees, and perhaps even the purchase of membership in a country club. Leisure time also takes place in settings that are entirely devoted to consumption, such as cruise ships or online casinos. Furthermore, for many people, consumption is leisure. Going to the shopping mall, on- and offline, and making a variety of purchases can be very relaxing for some.

Leisure is defined as a means of escape from the obligations associated with work and family. It involves social activities that are not coerced. They are relaxing, perhaps informative, and set apart in time and often in space (Rojek 2005, 2007). People engaging in leisure are not just free from their usual obligations; they are also free to think differently and to do different things. It is presumed that when people are at leisure, they have much more freedom of choice than they have at work or at home.

Chapter 12: Politics and the Economy

However, much leisure activity takes place in settings that are designed to control and to limit the thoughts and actions of those at leisure. The best example is Disney World, where all sorts of conveyances are provided to lead people to move around the park and its attractions quickly, efficiently, and in given directions. Even during the times when visitors seem to be wandering around the park on their own, subtle kinds of controls are being exercised over them. Examples include preset paths, directional arrows, and signs. Most interesting from this perspective is what Walt Disney called "weenies," or highly visible attractions—mountains, castles, and the like—to which virtually all visitors will be drawn. Thus, they move in the direction of the weenies, the way that Disney management wants them to move. They do so without anyone telling them where they should go and how they should get there. This allows for the efficient movement of large numbers of visitors. On the way, they are led past many kiosks, shops, restaurants, and the like, where they can spend even more money.

Leisure time is strongly affected by social class. Many leisure activities (cruises, golf, etc.) are very expensive. Those in the lower rungs of the stratification system in the Global North, and most of those in the Global South, are largely excluded from them. Of course, there are many inexpensive and even free forms of leisure available to virtually everyone, but these are not generally deemed the most desirable forms in today's world. Furthermore,

the demands of work, and even of survival, make it difficult for the have-nots of the world to have much time for, or to get great enjoyment from, leisure-time activities.

Women's leisure, in comparison with men's, has also tended to be more constrained by economic factors (Holland 2013). That is changing somewhat, as women in the middle classes are increasingly likely to have substantial incomes associated with occupations of their own. These occupations also tend to give them more demarcated time for leisure (e.g., vacation time), something that historically has been the province of men. Yet, because women still spend more hours a week on child care and household maintenance than men do, a gendered leisure divide remains.

GLOBALIZATION AND THE ECONOMY

Globalization is associated with many changes in the economy. One of the most remarkable changes has been in **macrofinance**, or globalization as it relates to money and finance. Not long ago, money and finance were closely tied to the nation-state that issued the money and to the financial transactions that took place therein. Moving money and financial instruments—for example, stocks and bonds, as well as new instruments such as derivatives—from one part of the world to another was difficult and cumbersome. Travelers needed to change their own country's currency into the currency of the country to which they were traveling. And if they were going to many different countries, they needed to repeat this transaction for each one. Now, however, all a traveler needs is a debit card, which can be used in most nations in the world to rapidly and efficiently pay for goods and services with the currency of each of the nations visited. As Dodd (2012, 1446) puts it, "We are witnessing the end of money's geography."

As a result, money is increasingly liquid, and it flows around the world quite readily. This is clearly true for tourists and businesspeople, but it is true in other ways as well: Substantial

A mah jong game takes place in a home in Kunming, China. What is it that makes leisure time desirable? What makes it possible?

flows of money are associated with the informal economy, criminal networks, the international drug trade, and money laundering. For example, a 2016 scandal involved Panamanian law firm Mosseck Fonseca, which, among other things, was involved in the proliferation of shell companies and tax havens for the very rich that allowed them to evade taxation in their home country (Semple, Ahmed, and Lipton 2016). This became a global scandal that even resulted in the resignation of Iceland's prime minister.

To take another, more mundane example of the fluidity of money globally, much money flows in the form of remittances, largely from migrants in the Global North to family and friends back home in the Global South. In fact, in 2015, recorded remittances totaled $432 billion—though much more probably went unreported (www.worldbank.org; Ratha and Mohapatra 2012). While this sounds like a great deal of money, it pales in comparison with other types of global financial transactions. For example, in only one aspect of the global financial market, the market for the world's currencies, about $5 trillion changes hands *every day* (Knorr Cetina 2012; geta-firstlife.com/forex-trading).

The largest amounts of money by far flow easily and quickly through electronic transmissions associated with global financial markets. People and businesses are increasingly dependent on electronic transfers for the credit they need, or think they need, in today's world. Individuals usually need credit to purchase such things as homes and automobiles. Credit is also central to the growth and investments of corporations and governments.

Even more important is global trade in a series of obscure financial instruments. Questionable banking practices and speculative financial instruments tied to the U.S. housing market set off a global chain reaction in 2007–2008 that devastated international economic flows and triggered a global recession. Central to these problems was the fact that financial markets in both the United States and much of the rest of the world were deregulated to a great degree. Without governmental oversight, many of these markets were allowed to run wild. For example, rampant speculation in exotic financial instruments produced an economic bubble that burst violently, causing the recession to develop and gather momentum.

The bursting of the bubble created a global liquidity crisis because nations and their banks were reluctant to lend to one another. They were afraid that the economic crisis would render other nations and banks unable to repay their loans. Without these loans, many nations were plunged into deep recessions. This was especially true in the European countries that constitute the eurozone (the 19 of 27 European nations that use the euro as a common currency).

Over the years, this led to the euro crisis, which grew particularly intense in late 2011 and early 2012 (Riera-Crichton 2012). The wealthier European societies, especially Germany, were able to deal with the recession well. Other countries, especially Greece, Portugal, Ireland, Spain, and later Italy and Cyprus, were not (Stewart 2013). They suffered huge economic problems, such as the collapse of their housing markets and high unemployment. Several of these countries had their credit ratings diminished. In such a situation, the typical course of action for a country is to devalue its currency, thereby reducing its costs. This makes its products cheaper and more competitive in the global economy, allowing its economy to begin to grow again. However, because those troubled countries were part of the eurozone, they were unable to devalue their currency. The troubled European economies were left without the traditional method of dealing with recessions and depression.

Further worsening the situation for these countries was the fact that it became more difficult for them to borrow money to keep their economies functioning. Lenders increasingly believed that the troubled nations might not be able to repay those loans. The result was that the troubled eurozone countries had to pay ever-higher interest rates to get loans. Countries such as Ireland, Cyprus, and Greece had to get bailouts from European sources. In exchange for those bailouts, they had to agree to practice greater austerity. For example, they fired government employees and cut back welfare programs. Paradoxically, this austerity further weakened their economies, at least in the short run, because many people had less money to spend. As of this writing in 2017, Greece continues to suffer badly from the economic crisis and from the austerity it promised to practice in order to get needed bailouts.

There were many catastrophic fears associated with the euro crisis. While the worst of them did not occur, the underlying problems remain. For example, the huge economic differences between prosperous northern European countries such as Germany and comparatively impoverished southern countries such as Greece—and, to a lesser extent, Spain and Italy—remain a reality. In the event of another economic crisis, it seems less likely—if not unlikely—that the northern European countries will bail out those in the south. Furthermore, southern European countries remain locked into the shared euro currency. That means that those countries will not be able to help themselves in times of economic crisis by devaluing their national currencies in order to make their goods and services more competitive.

SUMMARY

Politics is one way to advance a given position or policy through the use of, or by putting pressure on, the state. Democracy is a political system in which people within a given state vote to choose their leaders and, in some cases, to approve legislation. This is in contrast to dictatorships, which are usually totalitarian governments operating without the consent of the governed.

The question of who rules the United States is a source of continuing debate. In analyzing politics, structural-functionalists emphasize pluralism, which is characterized by a balance of power among interest groups. Conflict theorists view power as concentrated among the elite, particularly the state, corporations, and the military.

Nation-states, nations, and nongovernmental actors are involved in global politics. One extreme way in which nation-states might deal with political disagreements is through war. Terrorism is more likely to involve nongovernmental actors engaging in violence targeting noncombatants, property, or military personnel.

The economy ensures the production and distribution of goods and services. In the last 200 years, the capitalist U.S. economy has transitioned from industrialization to deindustrialization. Industrialization was characterized by a factory system based on mass production. In contrast, today there are fewer manufacturing jobs and a growth of service jobs, which pay low wages and offer few, if any, benefits.

Consumption and leisure are becoming increasingly important as we transition to a postmodern society. Many of us spend our leisure time in cathedrals of consumption, such as shopping malls and theme parks, and even purchasing products online. Consumerism, or an obsession with goods, can result in hyperdebt.

Capitalism has become increasingly global in that transnational, not national, economic practices predominate. Substantial flows of money move easily and quickly through electronic transactions around the world. The eurozone has faced, and may again confront, a euro crisis that threatens to destabilize Europe and possibly the world.

KEY TERMS

cathedrals of consumption, 337
citizenship, 319
communism, 328

competitive capitalism, 330
consumerism, 338
deindustrialization, 331

democracy, 318
dictatorships, 321
discouraged workers, 336

economy, 326
elite pluralism, 321
Fordism, 328
geopolitics, 322

REVIEW QUESTIONS

1. What factors help explain the emergence of democratic political systems? How is democracy related to bureaucracy and rational-legal concepts that you learned about in previous chapters?

2. In what ways is citizenship an important component of a democratic political system? Do you think low voter turnout in the United States is due to a failure of the nation's citizens? Or do non-voters in the United States express their political interests in other ways? In what ways could new technologies facilitate political involvement?

3. The question of who rules the United States is still being debated. In what ways does a pluralist understanding of power and politics in the United States differ from the power elite perspective? Do you think globalization has an effect on who rules the United States? Why or why not?

4. How are socialism and communism alternatives to capitalism? What elements of welfare states are socialistic, and what forces in the United States are resistant to social welfare programs?

5. What factors help explain deindustrialization in the United States, and how does deindustrialization relate to the decline of labor unions? What effects has deindustrialization had on other countries?

6. In what ways has the internet changed the nature of work? What are some examples of the ways you use the internet as a prosumer?

7. How is our society characterized by rampant and insatiable consumerism? How do we use consumption to satisfy our needs in the world today? Do you agree that we tend to consume beyond our needs?

8. In what ways might consumption today be described as the new religion?

9. How do leisure activities create distinctions between groups of people? In what ways are these distinctions reflective of the system of social stratification?

10. What was the euro crisis? In what ways was it an economic crisis? In what ways did it show the linkage between the economy and government? Were the great fears associated with the crisis well founded?

$SAGE edge™ **Want a better grade?**

Get the tools you need to sharpen your study skills. Access practice quizzes, eFlashcards, video, and multimedia at **edge.sagepub.com/ritzeressentials3e.**

THE BODY, MEDICINE, HEALTH, AND HEALTH CARE

The Debate over Medical Marijuana

As of early 2017, 28 states and the District of Columbia had legalized marijuana for medical use. That means that as of this writing, 22 states continue to ban the drug. In addition, eight states and the District of Columbia have legalized pot for recreational use. Nevertheless, the federal government continues to define marijuana as a dangerous Schedule I drug (along with heroin and LSD), making it illegal nationally. We are in the odd situation where marijuana is legal in more U.S. states than not while still being considered illegal at the federal level.

Many fear that federal legalization allowing unlimited medical use of the drug would lead to the legalization of recreational marijuana use throughout the United States. Their opposition is motivated by a fear that the use of marijuana can be harmful, especially addictive, and that it is a portal to the use of other illegal and more dangerous drugs. This concern is amplified by worry that we have insufficient knowledge of marijuana's effects. Research on pot's effects has been greatly limited because of the federal government's definition of it as an illegal substance.

These limitations have prevented research scientists from ascertaining whether marijuana is a useful medical treatment for a long list of diseases and medical problems,

LEARNING OBJECTIVES

13.1 Discuss sociological concepts that relate to the body.

13.2 Outline the issues studied in medical sociology.

13.3 Describe the influence of globalization on health and health care.

edge.sagepub.com/ ritzeressentials3e

- Take the chapter quiz
- Review key terms with eFlashcards
- Explore multimedia links and SAGE readings

including cancer, HIV/AIDS, hepatitis C, multiple sclerosis, seizures, severe nausea, glaucoma, and chronic pain. Yet there is consensus among the medical community that the drug *is* beneficial for such medical problems. About 1 million people in the United States now use medical marijuana. However, even in states where such use is legal, patients fear, at least theoretically, prosecution by the U.S. government for violating federal narcotics law. In addition, in the states where marijuana use is legal, there is wide variation in the diseases that qualify for treatment with the drug. The quality and potency of marijuana also goes largely unregulated by those states.

Some who smoke marijuana for medical reasons are concerned about the fact that doing so exposes them to carcinogens. Others are disturbed by the psychoactive effect—the high—that is the great attraction for most other users. Said one ophthalmologist, "None of my 60-year-old patients are interested in being stoned to treat their glaucoma." However, the cause of the high—tetrahydrocannabinol (THC)—can be removed, especially when the drug is given in pill form, which also removes various contaminants.

Because of the great demand for marijuana and its apparent utility in the treatment of many medical problems, there have been strong efforts to ease federal prohibitions on its medical use. In early 2015, a bill was introduced in Congress to remove it from the most dangerous drugs category and make it a Schedule II drug. This change would have acknowledged that marijuana is medically useful but with high potential for abuse. However, in late 2016, the Drug Enforcement Agency (DEA) decided not to change marijuana's categorization. ●

The central concerns of this chapter—the body, medicine, health (including mental health), and health care—are at the top of the social, as well as almost everyone's personal, agenda. Globally, there is much concern about epidemics such as AIDS, malaria, the flu, Ebola, and Zika, as well as the great inequalities in health and health care that exist throughout the world. At the societal level, the United States has been—and may well continue to be—wracked by an acrimonious debate over reforming health care. Among other things, reformers have sought to address flagrant inequalities and increasing costs in health care. Some changes in health care (to be discussed later in this chapter) have been instituted, although they have been far less significant than many had hoped. Millions of Americans still do not have health care, even though governmentally mandated reforms took effect in 2014. These global and societal issues affect the health and health care of individuals. Among those most concerned about such issues are those who are, or will be, patients—that is, virtually everyone—as well as the large and growing number of people who work in health care.

Ultimately, much of the interest in health comes down to a growing focus on, and concern about, the state of our bodies. However, interest in the body manifests itself in different ways for various social groups. If you are young, your main concerns, and those of your friends, are likely to be how to remain good-looking, healthy, and fit through diet, exercise, and perhaps even a nip or a tuck here or there. These are likely to be lifelong concerns. However, as you age, your focus will shift to the increasing likelihood that you may develop various diseases—breast cancer for women and prostate cancer for men, as well as heart disease for both men and women. You will also become increasingly concerned about how to avoid those diseases, if possible. If you are diagnosed with one, your focus will be on how to deal with it—*if* it can be dealt with. Gender affects the types of health-protective behaviors that you employ. Women tend to be more active participants in their health maintenance than men. Health-protective behaviors include screenings, self-examinations, and regular checkups.

Some of you will fall ill, be hospitalized, and perhaps die in middle age (or even earlier). However, most of you will face health-related issues with increasing frequency and intensity as you move into old age. New health-related concerns will then emerge, such as the possibility of developing Alzheimer's disease. As shown in Figure 13.1, it is estimated that the number of people age 65 and older with Alzheimer's disease will almost triple between 2010 and 2050. The number of people 85 years of age and over with the disease—and there will be many more in that age group in the coming years—will quadruple. As you age, you may wonder whether you are going to have the funds, or the insurance, needed to pay the often astronomical health care costs associated with the inevitable illnesses of your last years, and you may worry about how you will die and whether you will be able to do so with dignity.

For these reasons as well as others, the body has emerged in recent years as a major concern in sociology (Adelman and Ruggi 2015; Garlick 2014; B. Turner 2008). However, before we turn to a discussion of the body, it is important to remember that the mind and mental processes have long been of concern and of interest to many sociologists. (For example, see the discussion of Mead's work on these topics in Chapter 4.) Mental illnesses such as depression, schizophrenia, and attention-deficit/hyperactivity disorder (ADHD) are major concerns at the global, national, and individual levels (Clark 2014; Koivusalo and Ollila 2014). There is no clear line between the mind and the body. The brain, which houses the mind, is, after all, a body part. Mental processes affect the body (such as through psychosomatic illnesses), and the body affects the mind. One example of the latter is postpartum depression,

which is caused, at least in part, by hormonal imbalances (Mollard 2014). Another is depression that develops following a diagnosis of breast or prostate cancer, as well as heart disease (Love, Thompson, and Knapp 2014). However, it is important to remember that mental processes can also have positive effects on the body and its well-being. A strong sense of self-efficacy can be helpful to an individual who is recovering from a heart attack, among other things.

THE BODY

While sociology has always had some interest in the body, the recent explosion of such interest is largely traceable to the work of French social theorist Michel Foucault (1926–1984).

THE THINKING OF MICHEL FOUCAULT

In *Discipline and Punish: The Birth of the Prison*, Foucault ([1975] 1979) is concerned, at least initially, with the punishment of the criminal's body. The book opens with a description of the punishment inflicted on a condemned murderer in 1757:

> [His flesh was] . . . torn from his breasts, arms, thighs and calves with red-hot pincers,

FIGURE 13.1 • Number of People Age 65 and Over in the U.S. Population with Alzheimer's Disease, 2010–2050 (projected)

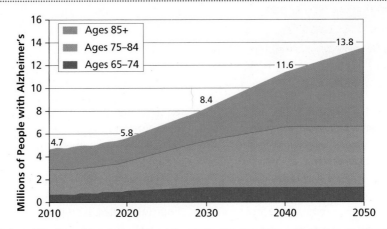

SOURCE: Figure 4, Projected Numbers of People Age 65 and Over in the U.S. Population with Alzheimer's Disease, 2000–2050, p. 23, from *2016 Alzheimer's Disease Facts and Figures.* Reprinted with permission from the Alzheimer's Association.

his right hand ... burnt with sulphur, and, on those places where the flesh will be torn away, poured molten lead, boiling oil, burning resin, wax and sulphur melted together and then his body drawn and quartered by four horses ... when that did not suffice, they were forced to cut off the wretch's thighs, to sever the sinews and hack at the joints. (Foucault [1975] 1979, 3)

Clearly, at this point in the history of punishment, the focus was on the body.

Between 1757 and the 1830s, the abysmal treatment of criminals and their bodies gave way to the rise of what seemed to be more humane treatment in prison. There, prisoners' bodies were contained and controlled rather than tortured. However, Foucault argues that in some ways, the prison system was far *less* humane than the earlier systems of physical torture. Imprisonment, as well as the continual surveillance associated with it, involved constant

Frenchman Michel Foucault is perhaps best known for his research on disciplinary power and governmentalities, particularly the idea of the panopticon, an all-seeing surveillance tower whose existence tends to control behavior. Much of Foucault's work focused on the relationship between power and knowledge—how knowledge leads to power and how those in power are better able to gain knowledge. He also studied the body and its relationship to society and culture.

mental torture of what Foucault called the "soul" of the prisoner. Today, it can be argued that the souls of prisoners and nonprisoners alike are being tortured to an increasing degree because surveillance is so much more pervasive (Bauman and Lyon 2012; Smith 2015). We are being watched by omnipresent video cameras, through scanners at airports, and on the computer, where Google and others keep tabs on the websites we visit (Andrejevic 2009). Most of us are not aware of much of this surveillance. Even when we are, we may not mind it, and we may even enjoy doing the things that allow us to be watched, such as posting a selfie on Instagram. However, all this surveillance, especially when taken together, has the potential to be used in ways we might not want, including gathering the information needed to exert great control over us.

In *The Birth of the Clinic* (1975), Foucault begins with an analysis of medicine prior to the nineteenth century. At this time, in order to diagnose a disease, doctors focused on lists of diseases and their associated symptoms. However, in the nineteenth century, the gaze of doctors shifted from such lists to human beings, especially their bodies and the diseases that afflicted them. Of great importance was the ability to see and touch diseased or dead bodies. In terms of the latter, the focus shifted to performing autopsies—cutting into bodies and body parts—to learn about diseases, their courses, and their effects on bodies and their organs. The medical gaze often depersonalizes patients by viewing them as objects. Instead of treating the whole patient, the gaze reduces him or her to localized pains or diseases that affect specific parts of the body. The medical gaze ignores not only personal problems but also social issues that may contribute to a patient's suffering (Holmes 2013, 115).

In *The History of Sexuality,* Foucault (1978) emphasizes the importance of sexuality and the role of the body in obtaining sexual pleasure. He asserts that society uses sexuality, and restrictions on it, to gain access to the body in order to control, discipline, and govern it. He suggests that people reject such constraints on the body as well as constricted forms of sexuality. Instead, Foucault (1978, 157) argues, people should focus on sexuality that is about "bodies and pleasures." One way to do that, Foucault writes, is to push one's body to the limit in sexual experiences—to make sexuality a limit experience. While most people do not come close to

Blood Sugar: Racial Pharmacology and Food Justice in Black America

(University of Minnesota Press, 2016)

Anthony Ryan Hatch (Assistant Professor of Science in Society at Wesleyan University; PhD, University of Maryland–College Park, 2009)

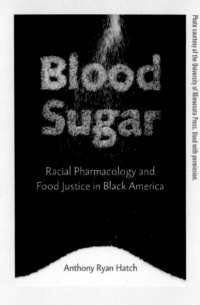

Anthony Ryan Hatch became a subject of "the political forces that aim to manipulate, control, and profit from the metabolic processes within [his] body" (2016, ix) after he was diagnosed with type 1 diabetes as a teenager. He likens his regime of monitoring his blood sugar several times per day to the self-surveillance of prisoners who learn to discipline themselves because they internalize the gaze of authority figures. In Hatch's case, he internalized the scientific discourse on metabolism constructed by biomedical researchers, pharmaceutical corporations, and the government. Diabetes is one biomarker of metabolic syndrome, which refers to a combination of high blood sugar, high blood pressure, high cholesterol, and high body mass index. According to Hatch, metabolic syndrome is a measurement or a "statistical construct" of how likely an individual is to develop one of the biomarkers that could lead to a metabolic disease. Over the past 30 years, not only has biomedical research on metabolic syndrome increased in the United States, so has the number of individuals diagnosed with it and the amount of money spent on pharmaceutical drugs to prevent and treat it.

Hatch describes metabolic syndrome as an endemic problem instead of an epidemic one, because it is a discriminating and long-term phenomenon (2016, 7). In contrast, epidemic problems are more widespread and occur at specific times, like the seasonal flu. Focusing on the discriminating aspect of metabolic syndrome, Hatch uses genealogy as a methodology to uncover the racial inequalities associated with how it is constructed and regulated. African Americans and other racial minorities, for example, have higher death rates and complications from metabolic diseases like diabetes than do whites (2016, 10). Genetics and racial food preferences for sugar are often blamed for these higher death rates and complications instead of structural factors, such as access to access to health care, health insurance, and prescription drug coverage. Biological explanations for the cause of diseases, such as genetics, fail to take into account social and environmental factors. Those who argue a person's lifestyle can cause certain diseases assume that individuals are voluntarily choosing to become sick and therefore can easily make different choices and prevent their own suffering. Blaming

individuals for metabolic syndrome allows powerful actors, such as the corporate food industry that produces unhealthy food, to remain unsullied in spite of their role in the syndrome. It also encourages an individualistic approach to treating metabolic syndrome through pharmaceuticals instead of changes in society as a whole.

Supplementary Resources

- You can watch Hatch discuss the findings from his book *Blood Sugar* in an interview on *Rising Up with Sonali* at https://vimeo.com/167320079.
- Learn more about the role of food deserts and public health and explore the Food Access Research Atlas at this website maintained by the United States Department of Agriculture: https://www.ers.usda.gov/data-products/food-access-research-atlas/about-the-atlas.

what Foucault means by "limit experiences," there is today much more openness and freedom as far as sexuality is concerned.

With the work of Foucault and many others as a base, the study of the body has become increasingly important. It is defined by a general focus on the relationships among the body, society, and culture (Turner 2007a, 2007b, 2012). It also includes a wide range of more specific concerns, including the gendered body, sexuality, body modifications such as tattooing, bodily pain, and abominations of the body. Of course, the issue of the body is also central to the main focus of this chapter, the sociology of health and medicine.

THE HEALTHY BODY: LIFESTYLE, BEAUTY, AND FITNESS

We live in an increasingly reflexive society. In the context of health, reflexivity creates a heightened awareness of the body and of ourselves more generally. Nevertheless, many of us engage in risky behaviors (for example, basking for hours in the summer sun) that endanger our health as well as the way we look and our physical fitness. However, reflexivity can lead us to be more likely to avoid risky situations, protect ourselves when we are in them (for example, by using sunblock), and seek out more beneficial ones. More generally, many of us focus on creating lifestyles that we hope will make us fit, attractive, and healthy. We may feel a responsibility to take care of ourselves, and especially to do everything possible to avoid becoming sick and dying. Our bodies, and our health, have become "projects" to be worked on continually. In spite of this, there is no shortage of times—that trip to the fast-food restaurant, one too many beers on Saturday night—during which health and the body take a backseat.

ASK YOURSELF

Do you view your body and health as "projects" you work on? Do you know others who do? What beliefs and activities can you identify that characterize this outlook on the body and health?

Reflexivity often leads to dissatisfaction with the body, especially as a result of the influence of peers and the media. We live in what might be called an "appearance culture," that is, one in which appearance is of central importance to peers and in the media. That culture includes ideas about what makes an appearance "attractive," and such ideas can negatively affect people's feelings about their own appearance. This is particularly true for adolescents, especially young women. Derogatory comments about their bodies and appearance-related teasing, among other influences, can have profoundly damaging effects on young people (Webb, Zimmer-Gembeck, and Donovan 2014). This is also true of derogatory comments about images of body parts (breasts, penises) derived from sexting and circulated to others (Ringrose and Harvey 2015).

More generally, both boys and girls have concerns about their bodies, although the nature of those concerns is often different. For example, little boys tend to want strong bodies in order to engage in sports, while little girls are apt to want bodies that "look good" (Tatangelo and Ricciardelli 2013). Boys who do not have strong bodies and girls who do not look good are likely to feel dissatisfied with their bodies. However, beliefs about the body are socially contextualized and socially constructed, and they vary by, among other things, race. For example, Latina college students report more dissatisfaction than their white and black counterparts with specific areas and features of their bodies (Warren 2014). Even desired skin tone and complexion have cultural and social determinants. In one study, adult British whites were found to want darker skin tones, while British South Asians and British African people from the Caribbean wanted lighter skin tones (Swami et al. 2013).

Beauty: Cultural Contexts

The social construction of beauty made it onto more people's radar after the publication of Naomi Wolf's book *The Beauty Myth* ([1991] 2002). Wolf argues that the media present the vast majority of people with an unattainable standard of beauty. The "objectifying gaze," rooted in patriarchal and Eurocentric ideals of beauty and attractiveness and expressed through media, includes a narrow standard for beauty and desirability (Gervais, Holland, and Dodd 2013). Heterosexual men and women report feeling more positive toward women who meet that

The Advertising Archives/Alamy Stock Photo

This Calvin Klein ad was banned in Britain by the Advertising Standards Authority because of the models' "unhealthily thin" appearance. In what ways does this billboard reveal the influence of the "appearance culture"?

standard—for example, women who have a typical hourglass shape (small waist, curvy chest and hips).

Some argue that the elevation of the importance of beauty has its roots in evolution (Singh and Singh 2011). That is, beauty may be an indicator of health and fertility. As a result, beautiful heterosexual women are more likely to be selected for mating. They are also more likely to have children who are beautiful and who have a greater chance of survival and success. Regardless of the potential biological roots of beauty, we use beauty as a means of determining who is attractive and as a way to distribute socially valuable resources. Economist Daniel Hamermesh (2011) has studied the economic effects of beauty, finding that those deemed beautiful earn more and are more successful at work. It even matters in choices made among candidates for the House of Representatives. Those who are less informed politically are more likely to choose candidates who are physically attractive (Stockemer and Praino 2015). We often are not even consciously aware of the ways in which stereotypical beauty matters in the decisions we—and others—make (Kwan and Trautner 2011).

Race, ethnicity, and class are implicated in stereotypical conceptualizations of beauty. One study compared satisfaction with body shape and skin tone, finding that biracial women were most satisfied with their skin tone, while Afro-Caribbean and African women were more satisfied with their body shapes compared to African American women (Mucherah and Frazier 2013). In addition, beauty ideals differ across cultures; however, global media are increasingly exporting Western preferences, such as thin bodies and light skin tones, to other countries, as portrayed in the documentary *The Illusionists* (2015).

Efforts to attain a high standard of stereotypical beauty may include excessive dieting, bingeing, and purging. Women are particularly susceptible to these actions. However, such actions often lead to failure, negative self-image, and low self-esteem. Some gay men feel compelled to diet excessively in order to fit the "twink" body type, a very slender physique deemed particularly attractive by some within the gay male community (Jones 2015; Kimmel 2012). Similarly, increased media attention to men's bodies leads to a preoccupation with ideas about the ideal

Chapter 13: The Body, Medicine, Health, and Health Care   351 male form. Internalization of ideals about the supe-riority of muscular bodies influences some men's drive to develop muscular physiques (Pritchard and Cramblitt 2014). However, male desire for a mus-cular body is not universal. For example, some men prefer a "refined and sophisticated" or a "trendy and cool" ideal male form (Tan et al. 2013).

The Quest for the Ideal, the Consumption of Beauty, and the Fit Body

The rewards for being beautiful are so great for women (and for men, for being muscular) that many try to at least approximate the mythic ideal. In consumer culture, beauty has become a commod-ity that can be bought (or at least we think it can) through great effort, often pain, and almost always expenditures of large sums of money. This is clear, for example, in the hundreds of billions of dollars spent in the United States on cosmetics, fitness, and clothing. The global beauty product industry is, of course, much larger. Most of the American and global consumers of beauty products are women.

The most extreme efforts to become beautiful involve cosmetic surgeries of all sorts (Gimlin 2007; also see *The Illusionists* 2015). Beauty is deemed so important in Brazil that cosmetic surgeries are offered to all who can pay for the anesthesia. Poor and rich Brazilians alike can thus buy procedures to create the culturally ideal physique. For women, that physique features small breasts, a small waist with a large derriere, and a slim nose and lips (Edmonds 2010).

About 90 percent of cosmetic surgical proce-dures in the United States (and the United Kingdom) are undergone by women (Tranter and Hanson 2015). As Table 13.1 shows, the most popular mod-ifications are breast augmentation, nose reshaping, eyelid surgery, liposuction, and facelift. Some people have genital cosmetic surgeries intended to enhance sexual response (clitoral hood reduction, vaginal tightening) or to improve genital aesthetics (vulv-aplasty; Braun 2010).

Interest in the way we look, while not new, has grown dramatically in the current era of increasing reflexivity. We are more aware of how we (and oth-ers) look. We are more conscious not only of the steps we can take to improve our appearance but

TABLE 13.1 • The Five Most Popular Cosmetic Procedures in the United States, 2015

PROCEDURE	NUMBER
Breast augmentation	279,000
Nose reshaping	222,000
Eyelid surgery	218,000
Liposuction	204,000
Facelift	128,000

SOURCE: American Society of Plastic Surgeons, "2015 Top Five Cosmetic Surgical Procedures." Reprinted with the permission of the American Society for Aesthetic Plastic Surgery.

also of the many means available to us for doing so. The increase in pure relationships (see Chapter 10) may add greater importance to this focus on appearance, because others are more likely to leave relationships with us if they are dissatisfied with the way we look (and vice versa). Our good looks are seen as a resource, or a form of capital, that is socially constructed (Hakim 2011).

Fitness and the Healthy Body

Closely related to the emphasis on beauty is the focus among both females and males on physical activity, physical fitness, sports, and bodybuilding (Klein 1993; Scott 2011). All these are seen, at least in part, as ways of obtaining a body that is not only more beautiful but also healthier—or at least one that appears that way. Hutson (2016) recently dis-cussed the results of such efforts as "bodily capi-tal." That is, the work involved in becoming fitter, more muscular, healthier, and more beautiful can all be seen as efforts to accrue more "bodily capi-tal." People invest much time, energy, and money in order to acquire—and to retain—bodily capital. More bodily capital can, in turn, be used to increase people's status.

The increasingly competitive nature of many sports may actually have adverse effects on health and appearance. Such sports require great exertion and are often violent. They can be damaging, even dangerous, to the body. Consider the increasing alarm over the effect of concussions and other brain traumas on those involved in various sports, especially professional football (Belson 2014; also see the 2015 movie *Concussion*). Attention is now also being focused on youth football, with a lawsuit being filed in late 2016 against Pop Warner for ignoring the risk of head traumas to children involved in the league (Belson 2016).

Some contact sports, such as wrestling and boxing, require competitors to qualify for, and remain in, very restrictive weight classes. This requirement can lead participants to engage in bouts of starvation and dehydration in order to "make the weight." Such practices, in turn, can evolve into "manorexia," a male analogue of the mainly female disorder of anorexia, by which women strive to attain slimmer bodies (Kershaw 2008). There is also a phenomenon known as "bigorexia," or the Adonis complex (Kimmel 2012; Mosley 2009), which may affect men who have grown up with G.I. Joe action figures or photos of bodybuilders and who aspire to have similar physiques. They might be led to lift weights obsessively and to consume mainly, or only, proteins. Such practices are especially rampant among competitive bodybuilders. Some sports, taken to extremes, can have a variety of deleterious effects on the body in both the short and the long term.

Exercise, sports, and physical activity often take as their goal the improvement of the body and of health more generally. They are increasingly oriented toward *outcomes,* such as losing weight and strengthening muscles. However, such a focus means that people often overlook the enjoyment associated with exercise (Wellard 2012). As a result, people do not explore the full potential of various kinds of physical activities.

ASK YOURSELF

Consider any sports you have played in your life so far. What was your goal? Were you forced to play during gym or fitness class, or did you play for fun, or to earn a college scholarship? What effect did your motives have on your level of engagement and the outcomes for your health? Do you still play?

BODY MODIFICATIONS

Practices of body modification have been nearly universal across societies and throughout history (Ferreira 2014; Pitts 2003). However, in recent years, there has been something of a boom in such practices in the United States and elsewhere. There are several major forms of body modification, including tattooing (Atkinson 2003; Dukes and Stein 2011), scarification (scarring or cutting of the skin; see Dargent 2014), piercing (Vail 2007; Wessel and Kasten 2014), and even intentional self-injury (Adler and Adler 2011). At one time, body modification was associated with deviants (see Chapter 6) of various types, including gang members, prisoners, and prostitutes. It was also associated with certain conventional groups, such as those in the military, particularly the navy.

Today, some body modifications, especially tattoos, have become so widespread and common that they are now mainstream (Adams 2009). For example, tattooing occurs these days in tattoo parlors found in shopping malls. The media are full of images of movie stars and especially star athletes

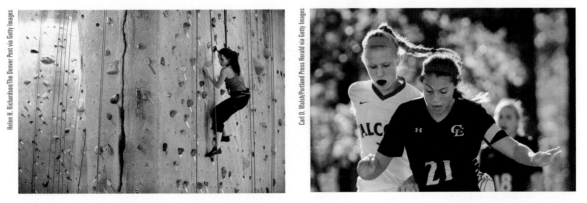

Fitness is possible at any age, indoor or out, alone or in groups. Does your fitness routine improve or adversely affect your body?

adorned, if not covered, with tattoos. Consider, for example, former soccer player David Beckham, football player Chris Johnson, and basketball players Kevin Durant, LeBron James, and J. R. Smith. Historically associated with men, body modifications now seem to be much more common among women (Botz-Bornstein 2013; Thompson 2015), including professional basketball player Brittney Griner and actress Ruby Rose. In many ways, body modification is now in fashion and is itself a fashion statement. Figure 13.2 shows the percentages of U.S. adults with one or more tattoos, grouped by age and sex. In 2015, more than one in five adults had at least one tattoo (29 percent), an increase of 13 percentage points from 2003. Adults ages 30–39 are most likely to have a tattoo (55 percent), compared to those both younger (42 percent of those 25–29 and 35 percent of those 18–24) and older (33 percent of those 40–49, 13 percent of those 50–64, and 11 percent of those 65 and older). Women are now more likely than men to have a tattoo (31 percent versus 27 percent).

Body modification reflects the increase in reflexivity. Ever-greater reflexivity is required with each succeeding decision about which new form or style of body modification to have. Among the issues to be decided are whether the modification—say, a new tattoo—should be visible, where it should be placed, and how traditional or creative and unique it should be. Furthermore, a variety of different tastes in tattooing have emerged, many of which are gendered (Anastasia 2010; Atkinson 2003), raced, and classed (Santos 2009).

As tattoos have grown more mainstream and even common among some groups, the people originally drawn to them have sought other ways of distinguishing their bodies from those of others. Many have been drawn to piercings of various types (Schorzman et al. 2007). Most popular are tongue and eyebrow piercings. However, as those, too, have become more common, more people are piercing other parts of the body, even the genitals (Thomas, Crosby, and Milford 2015), and people are getting more body piercings in general.

ASK YOURSELF

Thinking back on the definition of deviance, can you identify body modifications that you think are deviant, if any? What about modifications others might see as deviant that are normal to you? What makes the difference between these two categories?

FIGURE 13.2 • **Percentage of the U.S. Population with One or More Tattoos, by Age and Sex, 2015**

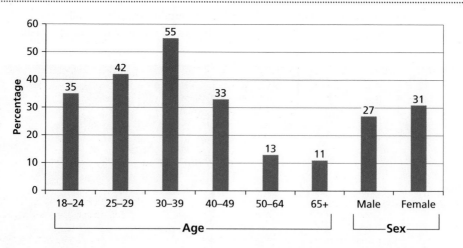

SOURCE: Larry Shannon-Missal, "Tattoo Takeover: Three in Ten Americans Have Tattoos, and Most Don't Stop at Just One." *The Harris Poll,* February 10, 2016. Harris Interactive.

RISKY BEHAVIOR

Ulrich Beck ([1986] 1992) argues that we live in a "risk society." The idea of risk has become a central concern in many areas of sociology, and one of those is the way in which it relates to the body and to health. Interestingly, this meshes well with Foucault's ideas on limit experiences, because it is in such experiences that risks are greatest. Indeed, it is the risks that draw at least some people to these experiences (Lupton 2007).

People take a wide range of risks that have the potential to jeopardize their health. On the one hand, there are the things people do *not* do, such as see their physicians, have regular medical checkups, or take prescribed medicines. Another example is

the failure, or refusal, to be vaccinated against various diseases. This was made clear in the 2015 outbreak of measles in the United States caused, at least in part, by the refusal of some parents to have their children vaccinated (Grady 2015).

On the other hand, people engage in many behaviors that they know pose health risks, such as smoking cigarettes, taking illegal drugs, drinking alcohol to excess, having unprotected sex, and texting while driving.

In some cases, the nature of work is risky. One example is the exposure to radiation risked by nuclear weapons workers, which can make them ill and perhaps kill them (Cable, Shriver, and Mix 2008). Of course, there are many occupations,

FIGURE 13.3 • Number and Rate of Fatal Occupational Injuries, by Industry Sector, 2015

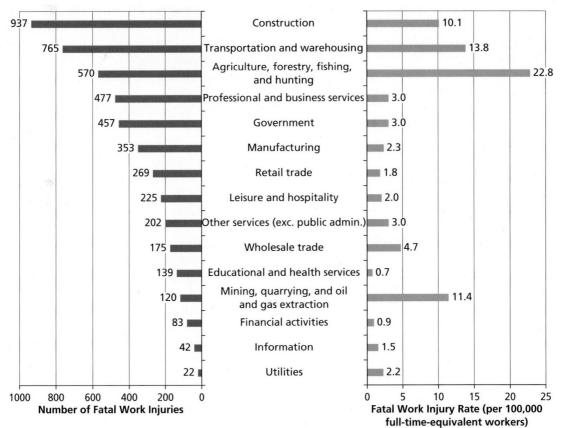

SOURCE: Data from U.S. Department of Labor, Bureau of Labor Statistics, "National Census of Fatal Occupational Injuries in 2015," December 16, 2016.

NOTE: Fatal injury rates exclude workers under the age of 16 years, volunteers, and resident military.

such as coal mining (Chen and Zorigt 2013), that carry with them a variety of health risks. Figure 13.3 shows the total number of fatal work injuries and the fatal work injury rate by industry. In 2015, construction workers accounted for the most fatalities (937); transportation and warehousing came in second, with 765 fatalities. The agriculture, forestry, fishing, and hunting industries had the highest injury rate, at 22.8 fatalities per 100,000 full-time workers. Mining, quarrying, and oil and gas extraction also had a high fatal work injury rate, with 11.4 deaths per 100,000.

There is, however, another side to engaging in risky behavior. It may well be that taking some risks makes some people happier and mentally (and perhaps even physically) healthier. This connection may help account for the growing interest in extreme sports such as surfing and snowboarding. Of course, these positive outcomes do not negate the fact that participants in such sports are exposed to extraordinary physical and health risks, as borne out by the death of snowmobiler Caleb Moore after he attempted a backflip during the 2013 Winter X Games (Branch 2013).

THE SOCIOLOGY OF HEALTH AND MEDICINE

Medical sociology is the largest specialty area within sociology (Cockerham 2016). It is concerned with the "social causes and consequences of health and illness" (Cockerham 2007, 2932). Social factors are also deeply involved in the delivery of health care. This has become an increasingly important issue in the United States and much of the rest of the world. Medical sociology addresses a wide variety of specific issues, including the following (Hankin and Wright 2010):

- Racial/ethnic differences in health care
- The basic causes of health inequalities by social class, gender, and race/ethnicity
- The linkage between stress and health
- The relationships between patients and health care providers
- The increasing use of advanced medical technology

- The astronomical cost of medical care
- The changing nature of the medical profession

Among the changes taking place in the medical profession are its declining status, the trials and tribulations of obtaining reimbursement from insurance companies and government agencies for medical services rendered, the more active role of patients as prosumers of their own health care, the more complicated relationships between patients and health care providers, and the fact that those relationships are likely to last longer because people are living longer and suffering from more chronic ailments.

THE MEDICAL PROFESSION

In the mid-twentieth century, a great deal of power was accorded to the health care system and especially to the medical profession, the key player in that system. Physicians exercised significant power over virtually everyone else involved in the health care system—nurses, hospital administrators, and so on (Hafferty and Castellani 2011). They also gained and retained great power over birth and death. This was an era in which the professions of medicine, law, and other fields not only exercised great power but also acquired great autonomy. In fact, a **profession** is distinguished from other occupations mainly by its high level of power and considerable autonomy. Other characteristics often associated with the professions are advanced education, mastery of knowledge and skills, the need to be licensed, and high prestige (Young and Muller 2014).

Historically, physicians in the United States have been disproportionately male (and white). However, that profile has changed dramatically, at least in some ways, in the last half-century. For example, women earned only 7 percent of medical degrees in 1966, but by 2016 they earned 46 percent (down slightly from 2014) of those degrees (see Figure 13.4; Williams, Pecenco, and Blair-Loy 2013). However, white male physicians' historical power continues to be evident in their starting salaries, which are consistently higher than those of their female counterparts. In fact, a salary gap exists even for physicians who teach at medical schools. On average, with the exception of radiology, female academic physicians at medical schools earn 80 percent ($206,600) of the earnings of their male counterparts ($258,000). Women earn less than men in every medical specialty, including those they dominate, such as pediatrics, where they earn only 66 percent of what male pediatricians earn.

The professions generally, and the medical profession in particular, continue to enjoy considerable power, autonomy, and high status. However, there has been a marked decline in all of those dimensions in the last half-century. In fact, in the last several decades the professions have been characterized by a process of **deprofessionalization**. That is, their power and autonomy, as well as their high status and associated wealth, have declined, at least relative to the exalted position they once held (R. Brooks 2011; Epstein 2014). A variety of factors are involved in the declining power of the medical profession, especially the increasing power of patients, particularly their ability to use the internet to inform themselves about their medical problems and options; third-party payers, such as the government through Medicare and Medicaid; and the pharmaceutical industry. However, while the medical profession is weaker than it once was, it remains a powerful force in the practice of medicine and in the larger society. In other words, the medical profession has proven itself to be quite resilient (Timmermans and Oh 2010).

How do we account for the deprofessionalization of physicians? First, they simply had acquired too much power a half-century ago to be able to sustain it at that level for very long. Second, the public, which had granted (or at least ceded to) the medical profession that power and autonomy, came to question the medical profession. One basis of this increasing doubt was a growing awareness of the extraordinary wealth and power acquired by many physicians. Another was the revelation of medical malpractice, which demonstrated that physicians did not always adhere to their own code of ethics (Ocloo 2010). The growth in malpractice suits was aided, if not instigated, by the other major profession, law, which reaped great economic rewards from medical malpractice lawsuits. Third, the government came to exert more power over the medical profession through, for example, Medicare and Medicaid. Fourth, as discussed in the coming pages, patients became much more active and aggressive consumers of physician services as well as of other aspects of the medical system. Fifth, and perhaps most important, private health insurance companies such as UnitedHealthcare became the most powerful players in the medical care system. Among other things, the insurance companies (along with Medicare and Medicaid) squeezed physicians' incomes by reimbursing them for office visits and medical services at much lower rates than the amounts billed.

FIGURE 13.4 • Percentage of Women among Medical Student Graduates in the United States, 1966–2016

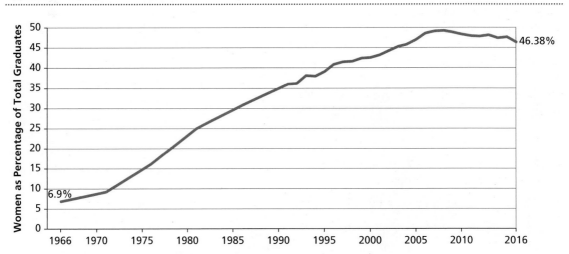

SOURCES: Data from the Association of American Medical Colleges (https://www.aamc.org/download/170248/data/2010_table1.pdf); Associate of American Medical Colleges, Table B-2.2 Total Graduates by U.S. Medical School and Sex, 2011–2012 through 2015–2016 (https://www.aamc.org/download/321532/data/factstableb2-2.pdf).

Of course, there are many other kinds of workers in the health care system—physicians assistants (PAs) are increasingly ubiquitous (Cockerham and Hinote 2015), but most notable and important are nurses. Historically, nursing was often thought of as a semiprofession (Etzioni 1969). It lacked anything approaching the power, status, income, and autonomy of the medical profession. Much of this failure had to do with the enormous power wielded by physicians and their desire to keep occupations that had the potential to compete with theirs in a subordinate position (Ocloo 2010). However, a more important factor was the fact that nursing is an occupation that was—and still is—dominated by females (Apesoa-Varano 2007, 250–253). Males in powerful positions, not only as physicians but also as high-level executives such as hospital administrators, were generally opposed to according professional status to occupations dominated by women. Nevertheless, doctors have come to rely heavily on nurses because they engage in, among many other things, "emotion work," or the emotional maintenance of patients (Lorber and Moore 2002; Rees 2013). The result has been that while physicians have almost all of the formal power and do not deal with nurses as co-equals, nurses often have a great deal of informal power over the day-to-day decisions and operation of hospitals and doctors' offices.

WEAKNESSES IN THE U.S. HEALTH CARE SYSTEM

There has been a broad consensus that the U.S. system of health care is badly flawed, and it remains to be seen whether it will improve substantially as a result of the changes associated with the Affordable Care Act (ACA; Galston, Kull, and Ramsay 2009). One major problem is the high cost of care. In 2015, health care spending in the United States reached $3.2 trillion, almost $9,990 per person (Centers for Medicare and Medicaid Services 2015).

The United States spent almost 18 percent of its gross domestic product on health care in 2014—the highest percentage among Organisation for Economic Co-operation and Development (OECD) countries by a considerable margin (see Figure 13.5). In percentage terms, the United States spends more on health care than any other country in the world (World Bank 2016).

Costs of health insurance are rising rapidly. Many Americans are forced into bankruptcy because of their inability to pay their medical bills (Sanger-Katz 2016). Among the reasons for the high cost of American medicine are

- The American love affair with expensive advanced medical technologies

- The profit motive at the base of decisions by for-profit hospitals, large medical equipment and pharmaceutical manufacturers, and physicians in private practice

- These entities' use of lobbyists in Washington to resist efforts to cut costs and reduce profits

- The cultural notion that Americans have a right to the best health care possible

- An aging population that spends more proportionately on health care than other age groups

While many men have entered the nursing profession in recent years, nursing is still seen as a female occupation. Why?

Hero Images Inc./Alamy Stock Photo

ASK YOURSELF

Why does the U.S. health care system achieve such comparatively low-quality outcomes, considering the huge financial costs it imposes on U.S. society? Why do Americans accept such poor-quality health care? What can be done to remedy this situation?

In spite of spending more than almost any other country absolutely and per capita, the U.S. health care system fares poorly in

DIGITAL LIVING

Telemedicine

Americans spend 2.4 billion hours visiting their doctors every year (Frakt 2016). Most of this time is not actually spent with doctors, but on travel and in waiting rooms. A patient who has to take off time from work for a medical appointment can lose wages. As a student, your grade in a course might drop if you have to miss class to visit a doctor. **Telemedicine**, that is, using technology to consult with doctors rather than going to their office, has the potential to save us time and make health care more convenient, especially for people who live in rural areas. E-mails and video chats are popular ways in which we can communicate with health care providers without having to leave the comfort of our homes, workplaces, or schools. Some workplaces and schools have installed telemedicine kiosks for their employees and students. One recent review of telemedicine research found no

health care outcome differences between video conferencing and face-to-face delivery for patients experiencing mental health issues, substance abuse problems, and dermatological conditions (Flodgren et al. 2015). This same review also found that telemedicine helped diabetics control their blood sugar levels better than traditional doctor visits.

Telemedicine is not without obstacles. While video chatting with our therapist when we are experiencing anxiety or e-mailing our dermatologist a photo of a bug bite that looks infected might seem like reasonable issues to manage with telemedicine, not all health care problems can be handled by distance health care delivery. Telemedicine may prove more beneficial in helping us manage chronic health conditions than in diagnosing initial symptoms. The digital divide prevents those without internet access from taking advantage of telemedicine, and not all

insurers cover e-visits. In addition, telemedicine requires our active participation. We are required to inspect, monitor, and care for our bodies more closely than required for face-to-face medical visits. This increases our own responsibility over the state of our health—and perhaps self-blame if we fail to monitor it adequately.

Engaging the Digital World

Imagine that you have the following set of health symptoms:

1. Fever, sore throat, and a runny nose
2. Irregular heartbeat, shortness of breath, and a headache
3. Profuse sweating, dizziness, and anxiety

If given the choice between telemedicine and a face-to-face doctor's visit, which one would you prefer for each set of symptoms? Why? What do you think are the future promises and limits of telemedicine?

comparison to the health care systems in other countries. Life expectancy in the United States is among the lowest of the high-income nations in the world, ranking 43rd globally. The infant mortality rate is higher in the United States than in most other industrialized countries and, startlingly, it is worse than that of many less developed countries (e.g., Mexico, Bangladesh, Ethiopia) and even war-torn nations (e.g. Iraq, Syria, Libya; Central Intelligence Agency 2015). Although there is hope that the situation will improve

in the future, more than 25,000 Americans still die each year because of a lack of medical care (Wilper et al. 2009).

Inequalities in U.S. Health Care

There are great inequalities in the American health care system. The well-off in the United States can afford any medical care they wish (including that offered by concierge medical practices). They are also able to purchase "Cadillac" health insurance

FIGURE 13.5 • Total Expenditures on Health as a Percentage of Gross Domestic Product, OECD Countries, 2015

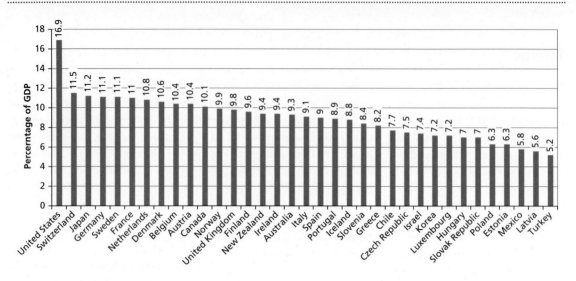

SOURCE: Data from OECD Health Statistics 2016, Health Expenditure and Financing.

policies that pay a large proportion of medical costs. In contrast, millions of Americans have no health insurance, and many others are underinsured.

The inequalities in health and health care that exist in the United States—and everywhere else in the social world—are unjust, artificial, undesirable, and likely avoidable (Lahelma, forthcoming). Among the major inequalities are those based on social class, race, and gender.

Social Class and Health. There is a largely constant relationship—the "health inequalities invariance"—between social class and health. That is, the lower one's social class, the poorer one's health is likely to be (Elo 2009; Warren and Hernandez 2007). This relationship holds across countries (although there are variations from country to country) and over time (Pascoe et al. 2016). In fact, inequalities based on social class have generally increased over the years.

There are a number of causes of social class differences in health. First, the conditions in which children live matter a great deal, because early differences may have long-lasting health consequences. Thus, living in poverty or in a broken home can contribute to ill health in childhood and therefore later in life (Duncan, Ziol-Guest, and Kalil

2010). Second, conditions in the adult years also affect health. Contributors to poor physical and mental health among adults include poor living conditions, low-wage jobs that offer little creativity or autonomy, and high levels of stress (Cockerham 2012). Third, a variety of health-related behaviors contribute to inequalities in health. These include the greater likelihood that those in the lower classes will use illegal drugs, smoke, drink to excess, and be obese as a result of poor eating habits and a lack of sufficient exercise. Finally, the presence or absence of health care in general, and high-quality health care in particular, can play a huge role in health inequalities. Those who see physicians regularly are likely to have better health than those who get no health care or get it sporadically from hospital emergency rooms.

A good example of the relationship between social class and health is found in the adverse health consequences associated with smoking. In the 1950s, those in the upper social classes were more likely than those in the lower classes to be smokers. However, by the 1960s, those in the lower social classes were more likely to smoke. It was during this period that medical knowledge about the adverse health effects of smoking became better known and publicized. While that knowledge was disseminated quickly in the upper classes, it had a much harder time working its way to and through the lower classes (Phelan et al. 2004, 269; Phelan, Link, and Tehranifar 2010). A key factor here was the lower educational level among members of the lower classes, who thus had less ability to access and understand the research and data available on the negative effects of smoking (Layte and Whelan 2009).

Race and Health. The relationship between race and health is similar to that between social class and health. In the United States, whites are more likely to be in the middle and upper classes, while blacks and Hispanics are disproportionately in the lower classes. Overall, whites tend to have better health than blacks and Hispanics. As a result, blacks in 2014 had a life expectancy 3.6 years shorter than that of whites (Centers for Disease Control and Prevention 2016a). Why do blacks have poorer health than whites? Racism, both today and as a legacy of the past, plays a major role. Given the history of experiments on black women's bodies during slavery, as well as notoriously unethical clinical trials such as the Tuskegee experiments, many black women and men have great distrust of the American medical system because of what they see as its practice of medical racism (Westergaard et al. 2014).

Blacks continue to have great difficulty getting the education they need to gain higher-status occupations and the higher incomes associated with them. Even with such education, they may still be unable to obtain those jobs. As a result, they remain in the working class and are less likely to have the best health insurance, or they may have none at all. They are also less likely to have the money to visit health care professionals, at least on a regular basis. The health care they do get from hospital emergency rooms, public hospitals, or more marginal physicians is likely to be inferior. Even if they can afford better care, offices and centers that offer such health care may be far from their homes, in forbidding white middle- and upper-class neighborhoods.

Blacks are also more likely to be poorly treated, or even mistreated, by the health care system, even if they are suffering from life-threatening diseases such as cancer (Merluzzi et al. 2014; Perloff et al. 2006; Quach et al. 2012; Wasserman, Flannery, and Clair 2007). As a result, they are likely to underutilize that system, to not utilize it at all, or to use alternative medicines (such as folk and faith healers). They are also likely to be put off by the underrepresentation of blacks in high-status health care positions and occupations—only about 5 percent of physicians are black (Tweedy 2015).

Working-class and lower-middle-class blacks are more likely to be relegated to neighborhoods and conditions that adversely affect their health. Examples include living near waste dumps where the land, air, and water are contaminated and in apartments or houses with lead-based paint that poses a health risk, especially to young children (Crowder and Downey 2010). And stress associated with racism throughout the life course increases the mortality rates of black adults and infants (David and Collins 2014; Nuru-Jeter et al. 2009).

Recently, the U.S. Department of Health and Human Services (2014) put a plan in place to reduce racial and ethnic health disparities. Also pointing in the direction of such improvement is the fact that unless researchers receive a special dispensation, research funded by the National Institutes of Health must now include proportionate numbers of racial minorities. In part, this is a result of outcries from sociologists, minority activists, and others (Epstein 2009). Knowing more about the health problems of blacks should lead to improved prevention and treatment.

ASK YOURSELF

What could social institutions such as schools, employers, the insurance industry, the medical profession, and local governments do to reduce the racial disparities in health that we observe in the United States? Does anyone benefit from these health disparities? If so, who, and how?

Gender and Health. On the surface, inequality in health does not appear to be a problem that afflicts females, because their life expectancy throughout the Western world exceeds that of males by a significant margin. While women live longer, there is a widespread, although not fully accepted, view that they have poorer health than men during their lifetimes (Shinberg 2007).

A good example of an area in which women *are* disadvantaged in comparison to men is coronary heart disease. Men are more likely to have this disease than women, but the gap is narrowing as a result, in part, of the fact that more women are smoking. Heart disease is the leading killer of *both* men and women. Medical care helps in the prevention and treatment of coronary heart disease, but it has reduced the disease more for men than for women. Doctors are less likely to give women with coronary symptoms close attention and the needed diagnostic tests (Adams et al. 2008; Ayanian and Epstein 1991). Women are more likely not to get treatment until the disease is well advanced. Less is known about heart disease in women because in the past epidemiological studies and clinical trials tended not to include female subjects. Even though the disease is somewhat different in women and men, the medical profession has simply treated women based on the findings from research on men.

Coronary heart disease is related to stress, and women appear to experience more stress (Wiegner et al. 2015). This is largely because they are less likely than men to be in control of the settings in which they find themselves. At work, they are more likely to be in lower-status jobs that give them less control over what they do as well as offer less security and fewer financial rewards. Many women who work outside the home have the additional stress of having to continue to handle household responsibilities, including child rearing (see Chapter 9).

Women have experienced the medicalization of aspects of their lives that are specific to them. **Medicalization** is the process of labeling and defining aspects of life as medical problems that were not previously so labeled and defined (McHugh and Chrisler 2015). It also involves a tendency to exaggerate the ability of medicine to deal with certain phenomena or syndromes (Conrad 1986; Conrad, Mackie, and Mehrota 2010; Conrad and Schneider 1980). Medicalization is particularly clear in the case of childbirth, a natural process now defined as a medical problem that can be dealt with only by physicians in hospital settings. Many other aspects of women's health have been medicalized in recent years, including premenstrual syndrome (PMS), infertility, and menopause. Overall, it could be argued that women receive too little medical attention in some crucial areas (such as coronary care) and too much medical attention in others (such as reproductive health).

Health Care Reform in the United States

In the wake of the kinds of problems discussed previously, especially those that relate to social class differences, new health care legislation—the Patient Protection and Affordable Care Act of 2010 (ACA, or "Obamacare")—was enacted into law. The law has been fully in effect since 2014. Initially, it was expected that the law would extend health insurance coverage to an additional 32 million people. However, by late 2016, only about 20 million people had enrolled in it. Nevertheless, one of the desired goals was achieved as the have-nots—especially immigrants and minorities—experienced the sharpest rise in health care coverage under the law (Tavernise and Gabeloff 2016), as did those with

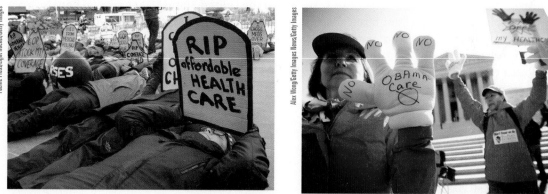

What are some of the arguments for and against the Affordable Care Act? Which arguments are most persuasive for you? If the Affordable Care Act is repealed, what—if anything—should replace it?

preexisting conditions who could not previously receive coverage. Nevertheless, by late 2016, 24 million Americans still lacked health care coverage.

In addition to providing health care to millions of Americans, the ACA expanded Medicaid coverage for the poor, established an individual mandate that fined people who refused to purchase insurance, required employers with more than 50 employees to provide health insurance, and forbade health insurance companies from rejecting applicants because of preexisting conditions (Cockerham 2012).

By 2016, an array of problems with the ACA had become clear. Premiums were rising, making the insurance less affordable for many who needed it. Major health insurance companies (e.g., Aetna, UnitedHealthcare) were exiting—or threatening to exit—the program in some states because their outlays there were higher than expected. This was due, in part, to the fact that too many of the "wrong" kind of people (the elderly and those among the poor who were more likely to become sick and therefore were most costly to the system) were signing up. Conversely, not enough younger, healthier, and therefore less costly people were enrolling.

After Donald Trump was elected president, there was a strong and immediate effort to repeal the ACA. In May 2017, the House of Representatives repealed the ACA and replaced it with the American Health Care Act (AHCA). Some key differences between the AHCA and the ACA included the use of tax credits to purchase health insurance, the elimination of the individual mandate, and the reduction of Medicaid spending. However, in July the Senate subsequently voted against passage of the bill, preventing its implementation. As of this writing, in late 2017, some Republicans and Trump himself have vowed to push for another proposal to repeal the ACA, but it remains to be seen exactly what that will entail, as well as what sort of response any revised legislation would get in Congress. For the time being, the ACA remains in place.

CONSUMERISM AND HEALTH CARE

Historically, thinking about health care involved a tendency to focus on the "producers" of health care, especially physicians, nurses, other health care workers, hospitals, and government agencies. Also included here are the insurance companies, Medicare, and Medicaid. While much attention continues to be paid to all of those producers of health care, the focus began to shift several decades ago in the direction of the consumers of that care. Larger numbers of patients began to realize that they did not simply have to accept what was offered to them by physicians, hospitals, and others. They came to the recognition that they were consumers of those services in much the same way they were consumers of many other services (and goods).

This was due, in part, to the deprofessionalization of physicians. As physicians came to be seen as less powerful professionals, it was increasingly easy for patients to question them. At the same time, the increasing questioning furthered physicians' decline in status and power. The entry of consumerism into medicine meant that more patients began to shop around for physicians and to question doctors' diagnoses and treatment recommendations.

The best example of increasing consumerism in contemporary medicine is associated with pharmaceutical companies' decision to improve sales of prescription drugs through direct appeals to consumers using catchy advertisements in newspapers and magazines, online, and on television. The avalanche started in 1997 when the U.S. Food and Drug Administration (FDA) began to relax restrictions on direct-to-consumer prescription drug advertisements. Since that time, the pharmaceutical companies have increasingly used direct-to-consumer advertising to supplement their marketing to physicians through advertisements in medical journals, salespeople, and free samples. Direct marketing targets the ultimate consumer of pharmaceuticals—the patient (Morgan 2007). The irony is that, in general, patients cannot go out and obtain the advertised drugs on their own; they need prescriptions from their physicians. Thus, the idea is to motivate patients to ask their doctors for, and in some cases demand, the desired prescriptions. The evidence is that this works, and as a result, the pharmaceutical companies have become increasingly ubiquitous presences in the media (Singer 2009). We are all now familiar with endless advertisements for the leading and most profitable prescription drugs, such as Lipitor (to treat high cholesterol), Nexium (for heartburn), and Viagra (for erectile dysfunction).

Medical Tourism

Some Americans (and others around the world) are choosing to consume medical care in other countries, or to engage in what is known as medical tourism. Medical tourism has increased dramatically, and it is estimated that it has now become a $100 billion industry (Fetscherin and Stephano 2016) Medical tourists travel to other, usually less developed, countries for medical care, often nonemergency surgery. The main reason is that such care can be had at a fraction of the cost of similar care in more developed countries. In addition, the quality of that care is deemed by many to be as good as or better than the quality obtainable at home (L. Turner 2007). Medical tourism is also attractive because such trips can be combined with vacations, which are easily paid for with the savings associated with overseas medical care. Thailand, to take one example, is now a major tourist destination both because of its affordable, high-quality health care and because of its weather and sites of interest.

From the point of view of consumption, medical treatment is increasingly seen as a service to be consumed as cheaply (assuming high quality) and in as pleasant a locale as possible. It is not unusual for less developed countries and the medical facilities associated with them to market themselves as destinations for medical tourists. For example, Argentina promotes itself as a destination for cosmetic surgery (Viladrich and Baron-Faust 2014). It is primarily the well-to-do from developed countries who are able to avail themselves of these medical services and the associated vacation opportunities. And only the wealthy from less developed countries can afford to travel to developed countries for medical care and pay the high costs associated with it.

ASK YOURSELF

Overall, do you think the shift to consumerism is a positive or a negative development for patients? What about for the medical profession? Would a structural-functionalist see medical consumerism as functional for society? Why or why not?

The Internet and the Consumption of Health Care

The internet has become implicated in the consumption of health care (e-health) in various ways. The first, and most obvious, way is by allowing people to find health care providers of all sorts more easily. The internet is a vast resource for finding providers by specialty, on the local, national, and even global levels.

One can get rankings of health care providers as well as information from previous patients about their experiences and recommendations. There is also a wealth of information and evaluation available on pharmaceuticals, medical technologies, and alternative treatments.

The increasing amount of health care–related data of all sorts on the internet allows people to become much more knowledgeable consumers of health care services and products. Consumer-patients can comparison shop for medical care on the internet in much the same way they shop for automobiles, TVs, hotels, and airfares (Konrad 2009). For example, there are sites where people can compare prices on everything from flu vaccines and annual physicals to mastectomies and bowel surgeries. Health insurance companies are also increasingly providing information online about benefits, stating, for example, what they pay out for office visits and various medical procedures. However, it is often difficult for consumer-patients to compare medical procedures because there are no standard terminological codes, available information is highly jargonistic, and the same procedure may have a dozen different prices at the same hospital because of separate negotiations with different health insurers.

A patient who uses online resources can become a much more sophisticated, knowledgeable, and independent consumer of medical services and products. For example, consumers can obtain many products and services legally or illegally—and often more inexpensively—through the internet without going through intermediaries associated with the health care system (Krauss 2004; Napoli 1999). Also available online are a variety of tests that can be done at home, such as a DNA tests. Individuals and couples can use such tests to discover on their own whether they are carriers of life-threatening diseases, such as cystic fibrosis, that could show up in their children. But there are concerns that these tests may not be reliable, that the privacy of the test results may not be ensured, and that those who rely on these tests will not get the expert advice of trained medical professionals (Brody 2009).

Other problems associated with using the internet for health-related consumption include the possibility of getting counterfeit, and perhaps ineffective, medications, as well as bogus services and information of various types (Lavorgna 2015). While consumers may become more sophisticated by exploring medical information on the internet, they are often not trained in medicine and therefore are likely unable to fully understand the advantages and disadvantages of what is available. As a result, they are more likely to be duped in various ways.

GLOBALIZATION AND HEALTH

A nearly endless array of issues could be discussed under the heading of globalization and health. We can do little more than touch on a few of them in this section.

GROWING GLOBAL INEQUALITY

While globalization has been associated with increased aggregate life expectancy, it also has tended to widen global disparities in health (Hashemian and Yach 2007; McMichael 2013). Women and children tend to be the most vulnerable populations globally, due to such things as economic inequality (Goli, Doshi, and Perianayagam 2013) and poor access to health care (Fillipi et al. 2006). As noted in Chapter 7, people in poor nations tend to have poorer health as a result of limited access to health care services, poor education, inadequate sanitation, and inadequate nutrition and housing. In turn, poor health tends to limit economic growth in those nations, mainly by adversely affecting productivity. Developing countries have a disproportionate share of mortality and morbidity, much of which could be prevented inexpensively and treated effectively if the money were available.

For the reasons mentioned previously, and others, there is a significant gap in life expectancy between developed and less developed, or between high- and low-income, countries. Figure 13.6 shows life expectancy at birth for select countries around the world. Note the 35-year age difference in life expectancy between highly developed Japan at the top of the list and the far less developed Chad at the bottom. The greatest increases in life expectancy have occurred in developing countries such as Brazil, Egypt, and Malaysia, which have tended to be increasingly and successfully involved in economic globalization. However, for most of the rest, especially the least developed, low-income countries in the Global South, globalization has been accompanied by a decline in economic growth, an increase in poverty, and, as a result, a decline in health.

Disease

The vast majority of not only acute but also chronic diseases occur at younger ages and in low- and middle-income countries. The rising cost of dealing with chronic diseases in developing countries will adversely affect their ability to deal with acute infectious diseases. Of special importance from the point of view of globalization is the increasing global marketing of tobacco, alcohol, sugar, and fat—the latter two especially aimed at children—and the consequent global spread of the diseases (lung cancer, cirrhosis of the liver, diabetes, heart disease) associated with these products.

Malnutrition

As discussed in Chapter 7, countries in the Global South suffer disproportionately from hunger and malnutrition (Van de Poel et al. 2008). Roughly 795 million people there are affected by these problems, which are the result of inadequate, or totally unavailable, food supplies and poor and unbalanced diets (www.wfp.org/hunger/stats). Dealing with hunger and malnutrition is especially important for children, because those who are underweight are, as adults, likely to be less physically and intellectually productive and to experience more chronic illnesses and disabilities. This carries on across generations as the ability of such adults to provide adequate nutrition for their children is compromised.

Undernutrition is a form of malnutrition involving an inadequate intake of nutrients, including calories, vitamins, and minerals. The other form of malnutrition involves obesity, which is caused by an excessive intake of nutrients, especially

FIGURE 13.6 • Life Expectancy at Birth among Select Countries, 2016

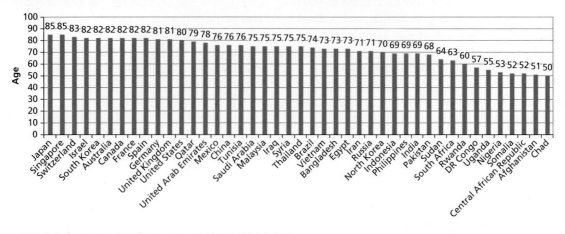

SOURCE: Data from Central Intelligence Agency, *The World Fact Book*.

calories. Developing countries now increasingly suffer from a "double nutritional burden," with some people not having enough to eat and others eating too much, especially of the wrong kinds of food (e.g., food that is high in fat and cholesterol; Vogli et al. 2014). Although obesity is increasing in the less developed world, undernutrition remains the greatest problem there, particularly for mothers and children. Undernutrition creates difficulties that continue throughout the life cycle and is responsible for stunted growth, lower levels of schooling, lower productivity, and chronic diseases; undernourished women also give birth to low-weight infants (Serra-Majem and Ngo 2012).

Undernutrition is related to problems not only for individuals but also for societies as a whole. It leads to underdevelopment and tends to perpetuate poverty. Without adequate nutrition, the human capital needed for economic development cannot develop.

Food insecurity is a major cause of undernutrition in less developed countries, and it is even an important issue in developed countries like the United States and the United Kingdom (Purdam, Garratt, and Esmail 2015). Such insecurity exists when people do not have sufficient access to safe and nutritious food—a condition necessary for leading a healthy and productive life. There are many causes of food insecurity. Poverty is a centrally important cause everywhere, but an especially important cause

in less developed countries is the lack of adequate agricultural development. A number of global programs have been undertaken to help deal with this problem through the creation of agricultural diversification programs, community gardens, farmers' markets, and the like.

SMOKING

Smoking is an important cause of health problems around the world. In spite of those health problems, however, a highly profitable tobacco industry continues to be central to the global economy (Fulbrook 2007). According to a World Health Organization (2017) estimate, about 6 million people die each year from tobacco use, and unless there are dramatic changes, that number will rise to 8 million by 2030. It is also projected that 1 billion people will die in the twenty-first century from smoking-related diseases.

With the Western market for cigarettes shrinking because of growing awareness of the risks associated with smoking, the tobacco corporations have shifted their focus to Africa and Asia. India accounts for almost one-third of the world's tobacco-related deaths. China is now the world's biggest market for cigarettes (Gu et al. 2009), with 2.5 trillion cigarettes smoked every year. The Chinese consume about 30 percent of the world's cigarettes, although China has about 20 percent of the world's population. There are about 300 million Chinese smokers. Many appear to have little knowledge of the health hazards associated with smoking (World Health Organization 2010a). For their part, the Western powers are the major exporters of cigarettes to the rest of the world. The United States is the single largest exporter of cigarettes as well as of globally recognized cigarette advertisements and brands.

ASK YOURSELF

The hazards of smoking are well known in the United States. Should it be legal for tobacco companies to export their products to markets where such information is not widely known or is disregarded? Why or why not? What would a conflict/critical theorist say is happening here?

BORDERLESS DISEASES

Another negative aspect of globalization as far as health is concerned is the flow of borderless diseases (Ali 2012). While borderless diseases have become much more common in recent years, they are not a new phenomenon. Tuberculosis (TB) was known in ancient times. Today the World Health Organization (WHO) estimates that more than one-third of the world's population are infected with the cause of the disease—the TB bacillus (Linn and Wilson 2012). Almost 10 million people in the world have the disease, and a little over 1 million of them are expected to die from it (World Health Organization 2015a). Sexually transmitted infections (STIs) of various types have long diffused globally. A specific example of the latter is syphilis, which has spread globally and continues to circulate, especially throughout a number of less developed countries. However, the roots of the disease were probably in Europe, from which it spread through colonialism and military exploits.

Then there is the increasing prevalence of other borderless diseases, many of them relatively new. Examples include severe acute respiratory syndrome (SARS), bovine spongiform encephalopathy (BSE, or "mad cow disease"), avian flu, Ebola, Zika, and HIV/AIDS. The pathogens that cause these diseases

While China has become the world's biggest market for cigarettes, only one in five people there are aware of smoking's dangers. What would it take for this situation to change? Who would benefit, and who would be harmed?

flow, or have the potential to flow, readily throughout the globe.

Several factors help explain the increasing global mobility of borderless diseases (Zhou and Coleman 2016):

- The increase in global travel and the increasing rapidity of that travel (Rosenthal 2007). Tourists both carry borderless diseases and can be infected by them in tourist destinations throughout the world (Baker 2015).

- Growing human migration and the ease with which people can cross borders. As a result, they often bring with them diseases that are not detected at national borders.

- The expansion of massive urban areas, such as Lagos, Nigeria. This has created vast mixing bowls where large numbers of people in close and frequent proximity can easily infect one another. Until 2014, outbreaks of Ebola were limited to relatively small African villages, but the explosion of cases in late 2014 was traceable to the fact that the virus had found its way

FIGURE 13.7 • Ebola Outbreaks in Africa as of January 2016

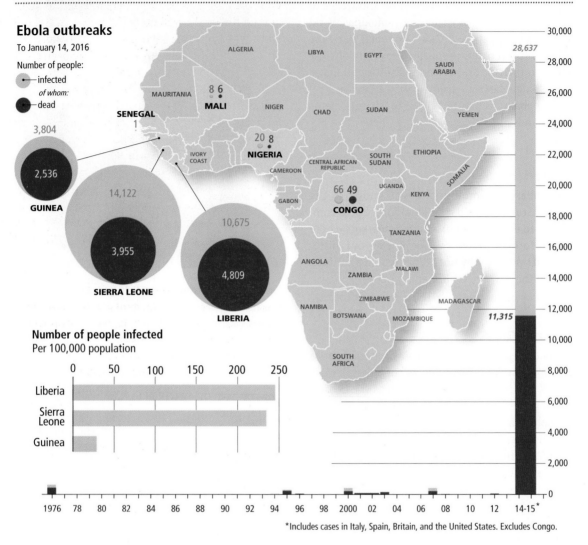

Ebola outbreaks

To January 14, 2016

Number of people:
— infected
of whom:
— dead

GUINEA: 3,804 / 2,536
SIERRA LEONE: 14,122 / 3,955
LIBERIA: 10,675 / 4,809
SENEGAL: 1
MALI: 8 6
NIGERIA: 20 8
CONGO: 66 49

28,637
11,315

Number of people infected
Per 100,000 population

	0	50	100	150	200	250
Liberia						
Sierra Leone						
Guinea						

1976 78 80 82 84 86 88 90 92 94 96 98 2000 02 04 06 08 10 12 14-15*

*Includes cases in Italy, Spain, Britain, and the United States. Excludes Congo.

SOURCE: © *The Economist* Newspaper Limited, London (2016).

into more densely populated areas. Figure 13.7 shows the African nations affected by Ebola. This disaster could have been more severe if the disease had spread to, and grown out of control in, a huge city like Lagos.

- The increasing human presence in previously untouched natural habitats. There, people can have contact with pathogens for which they have no immunity and that can spread rapidly throughout the world (Ali 2012).

The flow of efforts to deal with these diseases must be equally global. That is, there is a need for global responses to the increasing likelihood of the spread of various diseases. However, some nations have proven unable or unwilling to respond to this global need. For example, there has been widespread criticism of the slowness of the global response to Ebola and the relatively small amounts of money committed to fighting the disease.

Could medical practitioners or governments have anticipated the possibility that viruses might begin to flow more easily around the world, along with people, goods, and information? Does the Global North bear any particular responsibility for dealing with potential outbreaks? Why or why not?

HIV/AIDS

HIV/AIDS was first recognized in the United States in 1981 and has since been acknowledged as a scourge throughout not only the United States but also much of the world (Whiteside 2008, 2012). In 2015, it was estimated that 39 million people worldwide had died from AIDS since the first diagnosis. Nearly 37 million people were living with AIDS in 2015. The numbers of people infected with HIV and living with AIDS vary widely around the globe. Table 13.2 shows that Africa has been hit hardest, with nearly 70 percent (24.7 million) of the world's HIV population living on this continent. Of the 2.1 million people newly infected in 2015 around the world, 960,000 million live in Eastern and Southern Africa. About 2 million people live with HIV in Latin America and the Caribbean combined, including 100,000 newly infected in 2015. Eastern Europe and Central Asia, with an adult HIV prevalence rate of 0.9 percent, is the third-hardest-hit region in the world, after Eastern and Southern and Western and Central Africa. An estimated 5.1 million people are living with HIV in Asia and the Pacific. The huge population of this region means that even relatively low prevalence rates translate into large numbers of people infected with HIV. In contrast, people in the Middle East have the lowest rate of HIV, at 0.1 percent, or less than 230,000 HIV-infected persons.

HIV/AIDS cannot be contracted through casual contact with people who have the disease. The disease spreads only through intimate human contact with body fluids, especially through unprotected sex and intravenous drug use. Thus, in spite of the large numbers of people with AIDS, it is *not* an easy disease to contract. For instance, fellow passengers

TABLE 13.2 • HIV Prevalence and Incidence by Region, 2015

REGION	TOTAL NUMBER (%) LIVING WITH HIV	NEWLY INFECTED	ADULT PREVALENCE (%)
Global total	**36.7 million (100%)**	**2.1 million**	**0.8%**
Eastern and Southern Africa	19.0 million (52%)	960,000	7.1
Western and Central Africa	6.5 million (18%)	410,000	2.2
Asia and the Pacific	5.1 million (14%)	300,000	0.2
Western and Central Europe and North America	2.4 million (7%)	91,000	0.3
Latin America and the Caribbean	2.0 million (5%)	100,000	0.5
Eastern Europe and Central Asia	1.5 million (4%)	190,000	0.9
Middle East and North Africa	230,000 (<1%)	21,000	0.1

SOURCE: The Global HIV/AIDS Epidemic, January 19, 2017, Kaiser Family Foundation.

on an international flight will not contract AIDS simply because they sit next to, or talk with, a fellow passenger with the disease.

The spread of AIDS is linked to globalization, especially the increased global mobility associated with tourism (notably, sex tourism), the greater migration rates of workers, increased legal and illegal immigration, much higher rates of commercial and business travel, the movement (sometimes on a mass basis) of refugees, military interventions and the movement of military personnel, and so on.

People who have the disease can travel great distances over a period of years without knowing they have been infected. They therefore have the ability to transmit the disease unknowingly to many others in widely scattered locales.

The disease, as well as the many burdens associated with it, is having an adverse effect on all aspects of social and economic life throughout Africa. Some observers predicted the failure of African states and the complete economic collapse of some as a result of the spread of the disease. The economies of many African nations have already contracted as average life expectancy has declined, and it has become harder to find healthy adults to perform basic tasks.

The prevalence of HIV/AIDS in Eastern and Southern Africa is just one example of the greater vulnerability of the world's have-nots to this and many other borderless diseases. Compounding the problem is the fact that it is precisely this *most* vulnerable population that is *least* likely to have access to the high-quality health care and the very expensive drugs that can slow the disease for years, or even decades. However, there is now hope that the worst of the AIDS epidemic is over. Part of this hope is traceable to the increasing availability of highly active antiretroviral treatments (HAARTs), which were first discovered in the mid-1990s. In addition, a number of improved prevention and coping strategies have been developed to deal with the disease (Simooya 2016).

New Forms of Flu

In 2009 and 2010, the world witnessed an avian flu pandemic (H1N1), but it proved to be a relatively mild form of the disease. Prior to that, there had been fear of a pandemic of a potentially far more deadly strain of avian flu. Because we live in a global age, the spread of the flu would be faster and more

extensive than that of earlier pandemics. However, it is also the case that the ability to deal with such a pandemic is enhanced as a result of globalization. For example, global monitoring has increased, and there is greater ability to get health workers and pharmaceuticals rapidly to the site of an outbreak.

Some flu subtypes can spread through casual human contact with an infected animal, but there is little evidence of human-to-human spread of the avian flu virus. The relatively small number of humans in the world who have gotten the disease, including the even smaller number who have died from it, contracted it through direct contact with infected birds. Those in less developed nations are more likely to have direct contact with birds because birds and their eggs are central to their food supply. In contrast, in the developed world, relatively few people have direct contact with birds, and so contracting bird flu in this way is highly unlikely.

There is some fear, however, that the virus that causes bird flu might eventually transform itself into a strain that can be spread by casual human-to-human contact. This fear stems from the fact that viruses have taken this route before and caused global human pandemics, such as the infamous "Spanish flu" of 1918–1920, which killed a half-million people in the United States and tens of millions worldwide (Kolata 1999).

Superbugs

There is growing concern in the United States and globally about superbugs, or bacteria that are resistant to all known drugs. These are garden-variety germs rather than the more exotic ones like Ebola already discussed. Superbugs are often picked up during hospitalizations and have been cured easily in the past with antibiotics. Bacteria that are resistant to certain drugs can pass that resistance on to other germs that may already be resistant to other drugs. Over the years bacteria—for example, the one associated with TB—have grown resistant to more and more overused drugs (e.g., penicillin). For example, in the United States, we are down to the last drug, Colistin, that can treat "carbapenem-resistant-bacteria" (CRE). When bacteria become resistant to that drug, CRE bacteria will be unstoppable. According to the director of the Centers for Disease Control and Prevention, this is one of many indicators that we are entering a "post-antibiotic world" (cited in

Tavernise and Grady 2016). Just as diseases of all sorts can move readily around the world, so, too, can bacteria (and their associated diseases) that are resistant to all known drugs.

GLOBALIZATION AND IMPROVEMENTS IN HEALTH AND HEALTH CARE

We have focused in the last few sections on the negative effects of globalization on health. It is clear, however, that globalization has also brought with it an array of developments that have improved, or at least should improve, the quality of health throughout the world. One example is the growth of global health-related organizations, such as the World Health Organization (WHO), the Red Cross, and Médecins sans Frontières (Doctors without Borders). Of course, as with much else about globalization, the effects have been uneven and affected by a variety of local circumstances.

Increasing interpersonal relations among and between various regions throughout the world means that positive developments in one part of the world are likely to find their way to most other parts of the world, and quite rapidly. In the era of the internet and online journals, information about new medical developments flows around the world virtually instantaneously. Of course, how those ideas are received and whether, and how quickly, they can be implemented vary enormously. Surgeons in the developed world might be able to implement a new surgical technique almost immediately, but those in less developed countries would find it harder to learn about and utilize such a technique. Furthermore, the institutions where such ideas can be implemented vary greatly. Thus, hospitals in developed countries would be able to implement changes to reduce the risks of hospital-based infections, but those in less developed countries would find such changes difficult or impossible because of the costs involved.

CHARLES LOMODONG/AFP/Getty Images

A worker for Doctors without Borders helps children in South Sudan, where the World Health Organization hopes to carry out a massive vaccination campaign against cholera. What challenges does this effort face, given that unrest in that country has displaced almost 1 million people?

New medical products clearly flow around the world much more slowly than new ideas, but because of global improvements in transport, they are much more mobile than ever before. Included under this heading would be pharmaceuticals of all types.

Of course, the drugs that are most likely to be produced and distributed globally are those that are considered likely to be most profitable. Those are the drugs that address the health problems of the wealthier members of global society, such as hypertension, high cholesterol, arthritis, mental health problems, impotence, and hair loss.

Conversely, drugs that might save many lives are not apt to be produced (Moran et al. 2009). Few, if any, of the pharmaceutical companies surveyed in the United States, Europe, and Japan devote research and development money to creating drugs that would help those in less developed countries who suffer from diseases such as sleeping sickness and malaria. Such drugs are unlikely to yield great profits because those who need them are mainly the poor in less developed countries Thus, as we have seen, Africa is a hotbed of many diseases, such as malaria, some of which kill millions of people each year. To be fair, we are beginning to see a glimmer of hope for drugs to treat sleeping sickness and malaria (Kennedy 2013; Willyard 2014), but they are a long way from mass production and distribution. In the meantime, millions continue to die from these diseases.

Similar points can be made about the flow of advanced medical technologies, including MRIs and CAT scans, throughout the world. These are extraordinarily expensive technologies found largely in the wealthy developed countries of the Global North. The machines are not only more likely to exist in these developed countries but also more likely to be used extensively there because patients, either on their own or because of health insurance, are able to afford the very expensive scans and tests associated with them. Also concentrated in developed countries are the highly trained personnel needed to administer and interpret the results of, say, an MRI. In contrast, relatively few of these technologies flow to less developed, Southern countries; they are used there less extensively; and there are relatively few trained people there capable of conducting the tests and interpreting the results (Debas 2010; World Health Organization 2010b).

In terms of networks of people, much the same picture emerges. Medical and health-related personnel in the North are tightly linked through an array of professional networks. As a result, personnel can move about within those networks. More important, the latest findings and developments in health and medicine are rapidly disseminated through those networks. The problem in the Global South is not only that fewer professionals are involved in these networks but also that the flow of new information to them is more limited (Godlee et al. 2004; Horton 2000). More important, even if they are able to get the information, they generally lack the resources and infrastructure to use it, or to use it adequately.

SUMMARY

The growth of sociological interest in the body can be traced to Michel Foucault, whose work focused on the relationship between the body and society and culture. The field encompasses a wide range of concerns, such as sexuality, bodily pain, and body modifications.

The medical profession has gone through a process of deprofessionalization, characterized by a decline in power and autonomy as well as a decline in status and wealth among its members. Challenges to the authority of physicians include the threat of medical malpractice, the creation of government medical programs and policies, and the rise of private health insurance programs. Patients have become more active prosumers in the health care system, too, using the internet to shop for the lowest prices on medical procedures and reading fellow patients' reviews.

Disparities in health and health care have often been tied to globalization. Individuals in the Global South suffer disproportionately from hunger, forms of malnutrition, and food insecurity. The spread of diseases such as HIV/AIDS and Ebola is linked to increased global mobility and urbanization in the Global South.

The ability to implement new medical technologies and afford new treatments varies by region, with the Global South lagging far behind the Global North, but the rise of antibiotic-resistant superbugs poses a danger to the treatment of some diseases in all parts of the world.

KEY TERMS

deprofessionalization, 357

food insecurity, 366
medicalization, 362

medical sociology, 356
profession, 356

telemedicine, 359
undernutrition, 365

REVIEW QUESTIONS

1. We live in an increasingly reflexive society with a heightened awareness of our bodies. According to Naomi Wolf, how does the beauty myth perpetuate such reflexivity?

2. How is risk-taking behavior related to Michel Foucault's idea of limit experiences? What satisfaction do people get from risk-taking behavior?

3. What are the pros and cons of our obsession with our appearance and the fitness of our bodies?

4. What are the characteristics of a profession? What factors can help explain why physicians have become increasingly deprofessionalized?

5. What are the weaknesses of the health care system in the United States? How are these weaknesses related to systems of stratification?

6. Explain the increasing medicalization of society. How has it affected women in particular?

7. How have the internet and new social media technologies affected the consumption of health care? What are some of the disadvantages of having access to more information about health care?

8. In what ways are patients increasingly prosumers of health care? How has this change affected the power of physicians?

9. How has globalization tended to widen global disparities in health care? What kinds of health problems are you most likely to find in the Global South? What could be done to avoid some of these problems?

10. What are the major borderless diseases? In what ways are they made worse by globalization? Can globalization also play a role in curing them, or at least in reducing their prevalence?

14

POPULATION, URBANIZATION, AND THE ENVIRONMENT

Reaching a New Global Milestone

At two minutes to midnight on October 30, 2011, the world's population reached 7 billion; by early 2017, the number was approaching 7.5 billion. While it would have been impossible to identify the actual 7-billionth human born among the several hundred who came into the world at that moment in 2011, Danica May Camacho, born in Manila, Philippines, was the first of several babies chosen by the United Nations to represent this major milestone. A series of media events and press conferences were held throughout the following "Day of 7 Billion" to draw attention to the challenges posed by an ever-growing population.

For media outlets around the world, reaching the 7-billion mark proved a fascinating but passing diversion. Some reports were celebratory, others contemplative, but most were over once the next big news story broke. For sociologists, demographers, ecologists, and other scientists, however, the growing global population is a major and ongoing social phenomenon that has had—and will continue to have—enormous consequences for where and

LEARNING OBJECTIVES

14.1 Explain the causes and effects of population growth and decline.

14.2 Describe the growing urbanization of the world's population.

14.3 Summarize the development of global cities.

14.4 Discuss major environmental problems and responses to solve them.

edge.sagepub.com/
ritzeressentials3e

- Take the chapter quiz
- Review key terms with eFlashcards
- Explore multimedia links and SAGE readings

how we live. Along with environmentalists, these scientists have voiced serious concerns about what continued population growth means for the planet's finite and fragile resources.

Population growth and other demographic changes over the last 150 years, such as shifts in the proportions of young and old in many countries and the increasing concentration of people in urban environments, have helped give rise to new patterns of living. Urbanization, for instance, has brought with it the emergence of megacities, edge cities, and megalopolises. The rising global consumption that accompanies population growth has contributed to serious environmental problems on a worldwide scale, such as climate change, unchecked pollution, the rapid accumulation of human and manufactured waste, and a new scarcity of potable water. These effects will further challenge the way we perceive and interact with our environments, both natural and social.

While Danica May Camacho's birth had no direct effect on urbanization trends or the environment, the rapid growth of the global population that her arrival represented certainly has. As long as new births outpace deaths and the population climbs, Earth's cities and its environment will be challenged, and we will need to adapt. Bear in mind that the challenges will only increase as the global population continues to grow in the coming years. ●

This chapter covers three broad topics—population, urbanization, and the environment. While each is important in its own right, they are covered together here because of the many ways in which they interrelate. For example, population growth leads to more densely populated cities, and an increased population is likely to wreak ever more havoc on the environment.

POPULATION

Demography is the scientific study of population, especially its growth and decline, as well as the movement of people. Those who study these population dynamics are **demographers**. Demography is both a distinct field of study and a subfield within sociology.

POPULATION GROWTH

A great deal of attention has been devoted to population growth and the idea of a population explosion, or the "population bomb" (Ehrlich 1968). Some of that fear has dissipated in recent years. This has happened, at least in part, because of the ability of the world's most populous country, China, to slow its population growth through, among other things, its one-child policy. Although that policy was discontinued at the beginning of 2016, China's population is already huge and will continue to grow, although it will soon be surpassed by India's in size. Population increases are important because of the need for greater resources to support a growing population. Also of concern is the strain such increases place on national and city services, as well as on the environment.

While overall fertility rates are dropping globally, the world's population continues to increase, although at a declining rate. It was not until the early 1800s that the global population exceeded 1 billion people; it reached 2 billion in just one century (1930), then 3 billion by 1960. In the next 14 years, it reached 4 billion (in 1974); 13 years more, and it was 5 billion (in 1987); in another 12 years, it reached 6 billion (in 1999; Roberts 2009). As pointed out in the introduction to this chapter, in 12 more years, the world's population exceeded 7 billion people—with 37 percent of them in China and India alone (Population Reference Bureau 2010). It will likely take only another decade—to the spring of 2026—to achieve the next milestone of 8 billion people (Worldometers 2015). This recent slowdown in population growth is in stark contrast to the rapid growth after World War II. It was the latter that led to dire predictions about the future of population growth. However, it is now estimated that *only* about

9.4 billion people will be in the world by 2050 (see Figure 14.1; Bianchi and Wight 2012). While this is a dramatic reduction in future estimates, it still represents a major increase in the world's population (an additional 2 billion more people in the next three-plus decades). This growth is occurring, and will continue to occur, in spite of high death rates in many parts of the world due to high infant mortality, war, starvation, disease, and natural disasters. The death rate may increase dramatically in the twenty-first century if, as many expect, the disastrous effects of climate change accelerate, although that increase is unlikely to have much of an impact on overall population projections. Nevertheless, although there is less talk these days about a population explosion, there is little doubt that the world's population is increasing, perhaps at an unsustainable rate.

Taking a longer time perspective, it is estimated that by the year 2100, there will be as many as 12.3 billion people in the world (Gerland et al. 2014). The reason for the significant increase is largely that in many countries (such as Ethiopia and Niger), population growth continues to be very rapid. In fact, in spite of the ravages of warfare and of diseases such as malaria, AIDS, and Ebola, the population of Africa as a whole is expected to double by 2050 (United Nations Department of Economic and Social Affairs 2015b).

POPULATION DECLINE

Historically, population decline has not been considered as important as growth, but it has recently come to the fore in various parts of the world, especially in a number of European countries (Italy, Germany, Russia) and Japan (Coleman and Rowthorn 2011). By 2050, the population of Germany is projected to *drop* from 82.4 million to 81 million, while Japan's population is projected to decline from 127.7 million to 100.6 million (Coleman and Rowthorn 2011, 220; U.S. Census Bureau 2012). Also of concern is the decline expected to occur in Russia, from 142.8 million to 136.4 million in 2050. A variety of problems, such as high alcoholism rates and greatly unequal development across the country, have led to predictions of the "depopulation" of Russia. Similar declines, and problems, are expected in a number of former Soviet Bloc countries such as Ukraine, Bulgaria, and Latvia. Population decline can be caused by a low **birthrate**, the number of childbirths per 1,000 people per year. A birthrate of 2.1 is needed to replace an existing population. It can

FIGURE 14.1 • World Population, 1950–2050 (projected)

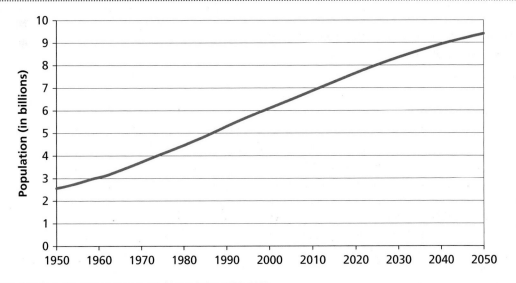

SOURCE: Data from U.S. Census Bureau, World Population 1950–2050.

also be caused by a high death rate, more emigration than immigration, or some combination of the three. In countries with aging populations, birthrates are often below the level needed to maintain the population.

Of interest here are not only the various causes of such declines but also their impact on society as a whole. For one thing, population decline can weaken nations in various ways, including militarily (Yoshihara and Sylva 2011). This is because the power of nations is often associated with having large populations; a smaller population generally translates into a smaller military (Israel is an exception). For another, population decline can weaken a nation's economy because the total number of productive workers declines. Third, the fact that population decline is generally accompanied by an aging population brings with it various problems, including a "financial time bomb." This is because of the high costs associated with caring for the elderly—especially government pensions and health-related expenses. A parallel decline in the number of younger people in the labor force means that there are fewer people who are able to help pay those costs through taxes (Singer 2010). Among other things, this financial time bomb will bring with it a great increase in national debt. This, of course, is already a concern in many countries. However, there are actions that can be taken to mitigate this problem, such as raising the retirement age so that older people can support themselves longer. Another possibility, although it is difficult politically, is for nations to reduce pensions and medical coverage, especially for the elderly.

ASK YOURSELF

What are some of the problems nations would face in reducing expensive government benefits in attempts to defuse the "financial time bomb" of an aging population? Who would benefit from such reductions? Who would be harmed, and how could governments protect them?

It would be wrong to conclude that population decline brings with it only a series of problems. Among the gains would be a reduction of the ecological problems caused by a growing population. For example, a smaller population would produce fewer automobile emissions and create less pollution. In addition, the pressure on the world's diminishing supplies of oil and water would be reduced.

While some nations will be hurt by an aging population, others, especially developing countries, will get a "demographic dividend" (Desai 2010; Lee 2007) because they have a favorable ratio in terms of those who are able to work versus those who are dependents, such as the aged and children. The dividend results, in part, from the presence of a large younger population able to work and earn money. At the same time, there are relatively few in need of their support. A significant part of the dividend is traceable to education and the greater productivity associated with a better-educated younger generation (Cuaresma, Lutz, and Sanderson 2014).

THE PROCESSES OF POPULATION CHANGE

Beyond some of the specific issues outlined previously, three basic processes are of concern to demographers. The first is **fertility**, or people's reproductive behavior, especially the number of births. Key to understanding fertility is the birthrate. Second is **mortality**, or deaths and death rates within a population. Finally, there is **migration**, or the movements of people, or *migrants,* and the impact of these movements on both the sending and the receiving locales (Bianchi and Wight 2012; Faist, Fauser, and Reisenauer 2013).

Fertility

On average, a woman could have as many as 16 births throughout her reproductive years. In reality, women rarely reach that number. In 2014, the global fertility rate was 2.45 births per woman. However, fertility levels vary widely around the globe. In 2014, they ranged from 1.2 births per woman in Macao and the Republic of Korea to 6 or more per woman in several African countries; Somalia was the highest, at 6.5 births per woman (World Bank, n.d.). In this section, we deal with the economic and social factors affecting fertility, regional differences in fertility, and fertility trends in the United States.

Economic Factors. Fertility is affected by a variety of economic factors. For example, we know that record low points in population growth were associated with the Great Depression. Low points were also recorded in the 1970s, when an oil crisis led to a dramatic jump in oil prices and rampant inflation.

Social Factors. Fertility is also affected by a variety of social factors. For instance, there is the obvious impact of age on fertility. Most childbearing involves women between the ages of 15 and 45. Especially important in the context of age is the fertility and childbearing of adolescents (younger than 20 years old). Globally, adolescents give birth to an estimated 16 million babies per year: The rate is as high as 200 per 1,000 births in some African countries, 24 per 1,000 in most developed countries, and only 7 or fewer per 1,000 in China, Japan, and Korea (Cooksey 2007). The United States has the highest rate of births to teenage mothers of all industrial nations; it is more than 4 times the rate of many Western European countries (World Health Organization 2014). However, the teenage birthrate in the United States has been declining dramatically in recent years. The peak year was 1957, with a birthrate of 96.3 per 1,000 teenage women ages 15 to 19. By 2015, the birthrate for such women had reached a record low of 22.3 (see Figure 14.2).

A second, and related, issue involves the broader category of nonmarital fertility (Musick 2007). Nonmarital fertility has increased dramatically in the United States, rising from only 5 percent of all births in 1960 to one-third in 2000, and it now accounts for almost 44 percent of all births (Bianchi and Wright 2012; Centers for Disease Control and Prevention 2016b). The United States is not unique among Western industrialized countries in this: Its rate of nonmarital fertility is higher than some countries' rates, such as Germany's and Ireland's; on a par with others' rates, such as Austria's, Spain's, and Finland's; and lower than others' rates, such as Mexico's and Iceland's, where almost two-thirds of children are born outside marriage (Haub 2013).

U.S. Fertility Trends. When the United States was founded, the average birthrate was slightly lower than 8 per woman; that rate declined throughout the nineteenth century and throughout most of the first half of the twentieth century. Then World War II led to an increase in the birthrate, and it remained high throughout the 1950s. In fact, the rise in the birthrate between 1946 and 1960 is referred to as the *baby boom.* The peak in fertility in the United States was reached in 1957, after which the birthrate declined for almost two decades, reaching a low of 1.7 in 1976. Today the birthrate is 1.84 (see Figure 14.3; Centers for Disease Control 2017). In other words, fertility in the United States is just below the 2.1 "replacement level"—the number needed to replace the population.

Mortality

As an indicator of change, a population's mortality—or death rate—is certainly as important to demographers as its birthrate. A population's **death rate** is measured as the number of deaths per 1,000

FIGURE 14.2 • Teenage Birthrate in the United States, 1940–2015

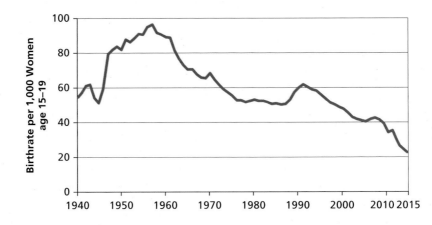

SOURCE: Data from CDC/NCHS, Division of Vital Statistics.

FIGURE 14.3 • Number of Children per Woman in the United States, 1911–2015

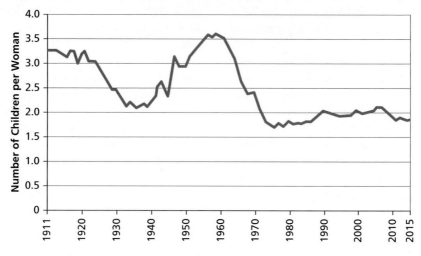

SOURCE: Data from CDC/NCHS, National Vital Statistics System.

people. **Life expectancy** is the number of years an individual can be expected to live.

Life Expectancy. In prehistoric times, life expectancy in the world ranged between 20 and 30 years; by 1900, that number had increased slightly, and today it has reached an average of 69 years. Nearly half of the decline in mortality in developed countries took place in the twentieth century. Life expectancy is now 77 years in the more developed countries, 67 years in less developed countries, and 56 years in the least developed countries (Bianchi and Wight 2012). Life expectancy in Africa is only 60 years (World Health Organization 2015b). The highest life expectancy is found in Japan, where women live an average of 88.5 years and men are apt to live 81.7 years. Life expectancy for women in the United States is about 82.1 years; for men it is 77.5 years (Central Intelligence Agency 2016). By 2050, U.S. women can expect to live between 90 and 95 years, while men can expect to live between 80 and 85 years.

Macro-social Factors. Increased life expectancy and lower death rates in a population can be affected by a variety of macro-social factors, including the following (Elo 2007):

- A general improvement in standards of living (better housing quality, improved nutrition)

- Better public health (improved sanitation, cleaner drinking water)

- Cultural and behavioral factors (stronger norms regarding healthy lifestyles)

- Advances in medicine and medical technologies (antibiotics and newer drugs, immunizations, improved surgical techniques)

- Government actions (control of diseases such as malaria)

Of course, important factors that keep death rates high continue to exist (including infectious diseases such as malaria, Ebola, and AIDS), and other factors that could increase the death rate, including global flu epidemics, loom on the horizon.

Mortality is greatly affected by one's position in the system of social stratification (see Chapter 7). In the United States, those in the lower classes are likely to have shorter life spans than those who rank higher in the stratification system. As for race, blacks have a lower life expectancy than whites, but black males are more disadvantaged in comparison to white males than black females are compared to white females. Lower life expectancies among black men are the result of the fact that they are more likely to live in rural areas, where life expectancy in general is lower, are less likely to seek health care, are at higher risk of death by homicide, and are more likely to engage in substance abuse (Sabo 1998; Singh and Siahpush 2014).

In terms of gender, women have a longer life expectancy than men, in spite of the various disadvantages they confront stemming from the system of gender stratification (see Chapter 9). This difference is due, in part, to the fact that women engage in more health-protective behaviors than men, such as visiting physicians more often. Gender roles also tend to protect women from fatal disease and injury (Rieker and Bird 2000). For example, women are less likely than men to engage in potentially disabling or deadly activities such as using illegal drugs, driving dangerously, and engaging in violent behavior. Higher death rates for male fetuses, as well as for male infants in the first four months of life, suggest that females may be more viable organisms than males. However, in general, "women now live longer than men not because their biology has changed, but because their social position and access to resources have changed" (Weitz 2010, 52). Nevertheless, in some parts of the world, such as Swaziland and Botswana, females have a lower life expectancy than males. This is traceable, at least in part, to the fact that females in some regions are more likely to die in infancy, perhaps because of parental neglect or female infanticide, or when giving birth to their own children.

Micro-social Factors. Mortality is also affected by a number of micro-social factors, especially those associated with poor lifestyle choices, including smoking, failing to exercise, overeating, and eating unhealthy foods. Obesity has long been related to higher death rates from heart disease and stroke. A more recent discovery is the linkage between obesity and death from various forms of cancer, including breast and endometrial cancer. More than 100,000 new cases of cancer per year in the United States can be traced to obesity. Conversely, healthy lifestyle choices can lead to longer lives. For example, religious groups that restrict the use of tobacco products, alcohol, coffee, and addictive drugs, such as the Mormons, tend to have longer life expectancies. In this context, special mention must be made of the increasing role of drug abuse (and addiction)—especially of heroin and prescription opioids—in mortality (Kolodny et al. 2015). Opioids killed more than 28,000 Americans

in 2014 (including the music superstar Prince in 2016). That is quadruple the number of such deaths in 1999, and it represents a 14 percent increase from the year before. Heroin use and abuse, once largely a low-income, minority, inner-city problem, occurs increasingly throughout society. Many recent users are middle-class whites who live outside major cities. At least some of these people started on opioids prescribed by their physicians, but eventually graduated to the more accessible and less expensive heroin. Opioid and heroin overdoses and alcoholic liver disease are the two causes for an *increase* in the mortality rates of white Americans between the ages of 45 and 55 who have only a high school education (Case and Deaton 2015).

The Demographic Transition

The issues of fertility and mortality are central to a major theory of population: demographic transition theory. According to this theory, population changes are related to the shift from an agricultural society to a more industrialized and urbanized society (Davis 1945; Weeks 2007). Four stages are associated with the **demographic transition** (see Figure 14.4).

In the first, or preindustrial, stage, there is a rough balance between high death rates (mortality) and high birthrates (fertility). As a result, the population growth rate, while high, is fairly stable.

In the second, or transitional, stage, the death rate declines dramatically, while the birthrate remains high (although it begins to decline slowly toward the end of this stage). The total population grows rapidly under these circumstances. In this stage, death rates decline first in developed countries for various reasons, including improvement in food production, a higher standard of living, a better-informed population, improved hygiene, and better health care. This was the situation in most of the developed countries of Europe beginning in the eighteenth century.

In the industrial stage, the death rate drops more slowly over time, to its lowest level. The deep decline in the death rate leads to more children in the family and the community. As a result, people begin thinking about limiting the number of children. Women begin to have greater access to, and are more likely to use, birth control. In addition, fewer children are required because not as many workers are needed on the family farms. Many

FIGURE 14.4 • The Demographic Transition Model

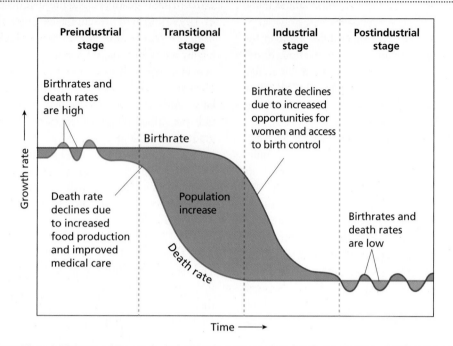

SOURCE: Adapted from *A Dictionary of Geography,* 2nd edition by Susan Mayhew (1997). By permission of Oxford University Press.

family members move into the cities and take jobs in industries and other organizations. Thus, another main cause of the decline of the birthrate in the industrial age is the fact that women have increased work-related opportunities. For these and other reasons, it is to the family's advantage to limit family size. Eventually, the birthrate drops to a level roughly equal to the low level of the death rate.

In the postindustrial stage, while there is some variation over time, birthrates and death rates remain low. As a result, in the postindustrial stage, as in the latter part of the industrial stage, population growth remains slow or stabilizes.

In Western Europe, the entire demographic transition took about 200 years, from the mid-1800s until the mid-twentieth century. The process continues today in much of the rest of the world. However, in recent years, in less developed countries, the process has taken significantly less time. This is traceable to the much more rapid decline in the death rate because of the importation of advanced, especially medical, technologies from developed countries. Because birthrates have remained high while

death rates have declined, population growth in less developed countries has been extraordinarily high.

Given this recent rapid population growth in less developed countries, the issue becomes what can be done about it, especially in the areas of the world where fertility remains high. In other words, how can the birthrate be reduced in those areas?

Reducing Fertility. Adopting the view that development is the best contraceptive, one approach to reducing fertility is to stress economic development. This follows from what has been learned from the demographic transition in Europe and the United States, where economic development did lead to lower fertility. A second approach is voluntary family planning. This includes providing people with information about reproductive physiology and the use of contraceptive techniques, providing birth control pills and condoms, and developing programs to support the use of contraception and the ideal of small(er) families. A third approach involves a change in the society as a whole, especially where large numbers of children have been considered both advantageous and desirable. In many societies, children are still needed to work to help the family survive and to provide for the parents in their old age. Changes such as compulsory childhood education and child labor laws can counter the fact that these realities lead families to have large numbers of children. Another important step is to ensure that women acquire public roles beyond the family realm. When women have greater educational and occupational opportunities, their fertility declines, and families have fewer children (Fillipi et al. 2006; Hwang and Lee 2014).

ASK YOURSELF

What happens to families who depend on children's earnings for survival when those children are required to attend school instead of working? Should companies that hired child workers in the past be responsible for these families' survival? Why or why not?

The practice of infanticide is an unfortunate reality in some parts of the world, and the selection of females for infanticide is especially problematic for various reasons, including its impact on fertility. The selective killing of female fetuses ("female infanticide") subsequently affects fertility because males end up outnumbering females in a population and there are fewer potential mothers (Bhatnagar, Dube, and Dube 2006). Infanticide is most common in South and East Asia, although it is also found in other areas of the world, including North Africa and the Middle East (United Nations 2006).

A Second Demographic Transition. In the 1980s, some scholars began thinking in terms of a second demographic transition to describe the general decline in the fertility rate and of population growth, especially in developed countries (Lesthaeghe 2010; Ochiai 2014). This decline is linked to parents' coming to focus more on the quality of life of one child, or a few children, as well as on the quality of their own lives. Better occupational prospects, and therefore a more affluent lifestyle, have come to be associated with having fewer children.

The second demographic transition is seen as involving three stages. The first stage, between 1955 and 1970, is of greatest importance. The key factor during this period was the end of the baby boom, aided by the revolution in contraception that made it less likely that people would have unwanted children. Also beginning at this time was the gender revolution, which meant, among other things, that women began to marry later and to divorce more. They also entered the work world in greater numbers. This tended to reduce the birthrate, as did the fact that there were fewer women at home to care for children. This transition has also been accompanied by the proliferation of a variety of living arrangements other than marriage and an increasing disconnect between marriage and procreation (Klinenberg 2012).

Migration

Although migration certainly takes place within national borders, our primary concern here is cross-border, international, or global migration. In the United States, the issue of illegal migration through and from Mexico has been a central concern of President Trump, who contends that he will build a much larger and stronger wall between Mexico and the United States (and force Mexico to pay for it). However, the flow of illegal immigration through Mexico to the United States has slowed dramatically, largely because of improved economic conditions in Mexico (Porter 2016a).

Globally, concern about migration reached a crescendo in 2015 and 2016 as massive numbers of people fled their home countries because of warfare, failed states, and hostility to minority groups. Syria, Iraq, Libya, and Yemen were sites of catastrophic warfare and can be considered failed, or at least failing, states. In the seas around Europe and Southeast Asia, many rickety boats (some of which sank) carried people to what they thought would be safe havens in other countries. However, at least some countries did not welcome these people or even rejected them—fearing, among other things, the cost of maintaining them until they could be integrated into those countries.

Controlling Migration. As late as the end of the nineteenth century, people moved across borders rather freely, most notably in the great Atlantic migration to the United States from Europe. It is estimated that about 50 million people left Europe for the United States between 1820 and the end of the nineteenth century (Moses 2006). Prior to 1880, entry into the United States was largely unregulated—virtually anyone who wanted to could get in. World War I changed attitudes and the situation dramatically; nation-states began to impose drastic restrictions on the global movement of people.

Unlike much else in the modern world (trade, finance, investment), legal restrictions on the migration of people, especially labor migration, have *not* been liberalized (Tan 2007). The major exception has been within the European Union, and only for the citizens of member nations. In 2017, President Trump began his tenure by seeking to impose new and severe restrictions on Mexico and several predominantly Muslim countries. In mid-February, he announced measures to enforce existing immigration laws. All unauthorized immigrants, criminal or not, may now be subject to deportation.

The borders in some European locales have been sealed (e.g., between Hungary and Croatia [Lyman 2015b]; between Greece and Macedonia; around the entrance in France to the Chunnel). There is also talk of walls being constructed in other places throughout Europe to stem, if not totally block, the flow of unwanted migrants. Beyond the physical barriers, the president of the European Council issued a stark warning to illegal migrants: "Do not come to Europe" (Kanter and Chan 2016).

Thousands of migrants have died attempting to reach Europe, including this child and the 33 others whose boat sank on the voyage from Turkey to Greece. What impact does increased control on migration have?

However, the sheer numbers of such people make control extremely difficult. According to one estimate, "tens of millions of people cross borders on a daily basis" (Hollifield and Jacobson 2012, 1390). The greatest pressure is on the United States and Europe, which are the most desirable destinations for migrants, both legal and illegal. For another thing, controls are very costly, and few nations can afford to engage in much more than token efforts.

Then there is the fact that attempts to control migration inevitably lead to heightened and more sophisticated efforts to evade those controls. A lucrative market opens up for those, such as smugglers, who are in the business of transporting people across borders illegally (Alderman 2016).

ASK YOURSELF

What social function do restrictions on immigration serve? What would a conflict theorist say about the privatization of immigration controls?

Explaining Migration. Migration is influenced by a combination of push and pull factors. Among the *push* factors are the desire of migrants for better or safer lives; problems in the home country, such as unemployment and low pay, making it difficult or impossible for migrants to achieve their goals; and major disruptions, such as war, famine, political or religious persecution, and economic depression.

Pull factors include features of the host country, such as its being a liberal nation at peace and having a favorable immigration policy, a prosperous economy, higher pay and lower unemployment, a strong social welfare program, available food, a good educational system, formal and informal networks that cater to immigrants, labor shortages, and language and culture similar to those of the home country.

Types of Migrants. **Refugees** are migrants who are forced to leave their homeland, or who leave involuntarily because they fear for their safety. The Office of the United Nations High Commissioner for Refugees is charged with determining whether migrants will be defined as refugees.

Asylum seekers are people who flee their home country, usually in an effort to escape political oppression or religious persecution. They seek to remain in the country to which they flee and are in a state of limbo until a decision is made on their request for asylum (Schuster 2012). If and when that claim is accepted, the asylum seeker is considered a refugee. If the claim is rejected, it is likely that the asylum seeker will be returned to the home country.

Labor migrants are those who move from their home country to another country because they are driven by push and pull factors (Schwartzman 2013). Examples of labor migrants are the Mexican and South American women who immigrate to the United States to find employment as domestics. Among the push factors for such women are "tenuous and scarce job opportunities," civil wars, and economic crises in their home countries (Hondagneu-Sotelo and Avila 2005, 308). The major pull factor is the existence of jobs that pay higher wages than those back home.

Undocumented immigrants are those residing in a receiving country without valid authorization (Holmes 2013). This category overlaps with some of the previously discussed types of migrants; both asylum seekers and labor migrants may be undocumented immigrants. There are three broad types of undocumented immigrants. The first are those who manage to gain entry without passing through a checkpoint or without undergoing the required inspection. The second type comprises those who gain entry legally but then stay beyond the period of time permitted by their visas. Third are those who immigrate on the basis of false documents. As shown in Figure 14.5, the number of undocumented immigrants to the United States increased from about 3.5 million in 1990 to a high of 12.2 million in 2007, before declining to about 11.1 million in 2014. Immigrants from Mexico account for the majority of undocumented immigrants. Of the 11.1 million undocumented immigrants in 2014, just under 6 million were of Mexican descent (Krogstad, Passel, and Cohn 2016). Many undocumented Mexican immigrants work on U.S. farms picking fruits and vegetables and suffer from working long hours and living in substandard housing (Holmes 2013; see Chapter 15).

FIGURE 14.5 • Undocumented Immigration to the United States: Total Number versus Mexican Immigrants, 1990–2014

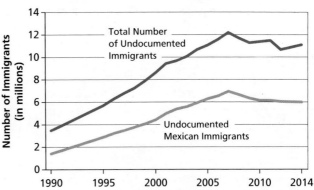

SOURCES: Data from Jeffrey Passel, D'Vera Cohn, and Ana Gonzalez-Barrera, "Population Decline of Unauthorized Immigrants Stalls, May Have Reversed," Pew Research Center, September 23, 2013; Jens Manual Krogstad, Jeffrey S. Passel, D'Vera Cohn. 2016. "5 Facts about Illegal Immigration in the U.S." Pew Research Center, November 3.

Another reason why many immigrants enter the United States is for educational opportunities that are not available in their home countries. Many become undocumented students. The U.S. Supreme Court holds that states cannot deny undocumented students access to primary and secondary education (Harmon et al. 2010: 75).

URBANIZATION

Urban areas are the destinations for many migrants and the locales most affected by population changes of various types. Until very recently, the world was predominantly rural; even in 1800, there were only a handful of large urban areas in the world. As late as 1850, only about 2 percent of the world's population lived in cities of more than 100,000 residents. Urban areas have, of course, grown rapidly since then. In the first decade of the present century, "the urban population of the Earth" outnumbered the rural population (Davis 2007, 1). However, there are great differences among the nations of the world in terms of their degrees of urban development: In the United Kingdom, 83 percent of the population is urban, and in the United States 82 percent is, while only 29 percent of Rwanda's population is urban (World

People fleeing violence, like these members of the minority Yazidi sect walking toward the Syrian border, are usually considered refugees rather than simply migrants. War and fighting in the Middle East and Africa have forced millions of people from their homelands in the last few years. What obligation toward them do the rest of the world's people have?

Bank 2015b). It is projected that by 2050, 66 percent of the world's population will live in urban areas (54 percent do today; United Nations 2014). In the more developed areas of the world, 86 percent of the population will live in cities. The greatest growth will be in developing areas, where 67 percent of the population will be urban dwellers.

The importance of **cities**, or large, permanent, and spatially concentrated human settlements, has progressively increased. Even when there were not very many of them, cities were at the heart of many societies. Max Weber ([1921] 1968) accorded great importance to the rise of the city in the West in the Middle Ages. The term *urban* generally refers to city dwelling. To be considered **urban** in the United States, an area must have more than 50,000 inhabitants. In comparison, to be classified as urban in Iceland, an area needs to have only 200 residents. **Urbanization** is the process by which an increasing percentage of a society's population comes to be located in relatively densely populated urban areas. It is clear that urbanization occurred even in

ancient times when large numbers of people moved to Rome, Cairo, and Peking; however, it has accelerated greatly in the modern era. **Urbanism** is the way of life that emerges in urban areas, including distinctive lifestyles, attitudes, and social relationships (e.g., the greater likelihood of relating to strangers; Elliott 2012).

EVER-LARGER URBAN AREAS

Cities have grown considerably larger in recent decades and have become part of even larger spatial forms. After 1920 in the United States (and later elsewhere), there emerged a new urban form—the **metropolis**—a large, powerful, and culturally influential urban area that contains a central city and its surrounding communities, known as **suburbs**, that are economically and socially linked to the center but located outside the city's political boundaries (Lacy 2016). Suburbs often create band-like structures around cities. While suburbs in the United States have tended, at least until recently, to be populated by the middle class, suburbs in other societies, such as France and South America, are more likely to be dominated by the lower class, including many recent immigrants. A **megalopolis** is a cluster of highly populated cities that can stretch over great distances (Gottman 1961). There are currently 11 megalopolises in the United States, with the area ("BosWash") between Boston and Washington, D.C. (including northern Virginia), being the classic example. Another now stretches from San Diego to San Francisco and ultimately may extend as far as Seattle and even Vancouver. The cities that surround the Great Lakes constitute another megalopolis.

Skyscrapers distinguish New York City's financial district in lower Manhattan. New York is one of the world's largest megacities.

SUBURBANIZATION

The process of **suburbanization** has traditionally occurred, at least in the United States, when large numbers of people move out of the city and into nearby, less densely populated environs. They are often impelled by urban problems such as crime, pollution, poverty, homelessness, and poor schools. The "American dream" of the last half of the twentieth century of an affordable one-family home was more likely to be found in the suburbs than in the city. Suburbanization was first associated with the United States, although it has become a global phenomenon. However, there is considerable variation around the world in this process and the nature of suburbs. It would be a mistake to assume that the American model fits suburbs elsewhere in the world (Clapson and Hutchison 2010; Herzog 2015).

Various criticisms have been directed at suburbanization. One is that it led to the creation of vast areas characterized by a seemingly endless sprawl of tract houses and the businesses created to serve them (Duany, Plater-Zyberk, and Speck 2010). More recently, many others have noted the problem of suburban sprawl promoting high levels of traffic congestion and environmental degradation.

In the past few decades, suburban development has seen the emergence of **gated communities**. In gated communities, gates, surveillance cameras, and guards provide residents with a feeling of security

from the dangers they think, sometimes wrongly, they have left behind in the city (Atkinson and Blandy 2005; Blakely and Snyder 1997). For example, there are fewer burglaries in such communities, although some gated communities offer better protection than others (Addington and Rennison 2015; Breetzke, Landman, and Cohn 2014). Nevertheless, no matter the reality, such communities tend to produce a heightened sense of fear and insecurity among residents.

Recently, a variety of new developments have affected suburbanization in the United States (Lacy 2016). First, we are witnessing the suburbanization of poverty; the number of the poor in the suburbs has increased more rapidly than in urban areas. Second, increasing numbers of immigrants have made their way into the suburbs and are making these areas their home. Third, more blacks, especially those in the middle class, are living in the suburbs.

Exurbia. Cities and suburbs continue to push outward into rural areas, where land and housing costs are lower (Taylor and Hurley 2016). These outlying areas constitute **exurbia**. The houses there are less expensive, as is the land on which they are built. Those houses exist on larger, low-density, tracts of land, often in scenic areas. The people who live in these areas are seeking a more rural lifestyle, but still require most, if not all, modern conveniences. Many are seeking a closeness to nature that they believe has been lost in both the cities and suburbs.

A POSTSUBURBAN ERA?

Suburbanization peaked in the United States in the late twentieth century. Today, there is much talk about the decline of American suburbs. Instead, some argue that we live in a postsuburban era (Phelps and Wu 2011). This is related to the growing realization that a way of life that includes large, energy-devouring private homes and vast thirsty lawns is ecologically unsustainable. High gasoline prices and home heating and air-conditioning costs further help make the cost of a suburban home prohibitive for many. Renting an apartment in or close to the city is back in vogue. While postsuburbanization is not a well-defined era, and it is taking different forms, it is clear that many of the old boundaries—between cities and suburbs, and between suburbs and exurbia—are eroding.

ASK YOURSELF

What do you think of gated communities? What is their impact on those who live in them as well as those who are excluded from them? Could you ever see yourself living in such a community? Why or why not?

THE CHANGING NATURE OF MAJOR U.S. CITIES

While there has been much talk about the decline of major American cities, and much of that decline continues, it is also the case that at least some American cities (e.g., New York, Chicago, San Francisco, Los Angeles, San Diego, and Seattle) have been booming in recent years (Kimmelman 2016).

Nevertheless, many major American cities (e.g. Detroit, Michigan; Akron, Ohio) that developed with the industrialization of the nation have experienced substantial deterioration as a result of deindustrialization, or the decline in the manufacturing sector (see Chapter 12). This decline was accompanied by *white flight*—the exodus of whites from cities—which led not only to highly segregated urban areas but also to areas that had declining tax bases and deteriorating infrastructure (roads, water and sewage systems, and public transportation) and thus declining ability to provide basic services for residents (Fitzsimmons 2016; Williams 1999).

In some cities, the water supply is compromised in various ways. One notable example is the contamination of the water in Flint, Michigan. This is a city whose population is predominantly black, and many residents are poor. The contamination occurred in early 2014 when, in a cost-saving measure, the city switched from a satisfactorily treated water supply drawn from Lake Huron to water it was supposed to treat itself from the Flint River. The city's treatment was inadequate (due mainly to lead leaching from ancient pipes) and the water was eventually deemed undrinkable, even dangerous to the health of those who drank it. As of late 2017, the city's water was still undrinkable and remained a health hazard.

In some cases, cities have realized urban renewal through the process of **gentrification**, in which real estate capital is reinvested in blighted inner-city areas to refurbish housing for the upwardly mobile middle class (Lees, Slater, and Wyly 2010; Patch and Brenner 2007). A prominent example is the borough of Brooklyn, New York, which in the 1940s and 1950s was largely shunned by New Yorkers because of its industrial-era slums. Today, much of Brooklyn, with its famous brownstones, has been transformed into a model postindustrial landscape. Town houses and condominiums have been renovated, and many are ultraexpensive. Brooklyn has become the least affordable home ownership market in the United States (Gopal 2014). Restaurants, bars, and other businesses catering to the new residents have sprung up all over the borough (Osman 2011). Pioneers in the process of gentrification are often young professionals, hipsters, younger gay men, and artists (Zukin 1982). Gentrification allows the wealthier residents (the "gentry") who grew up in the suburbs to return to the city. The expectation is that they will rebuild its depressed areas not only physically but also economically, socially, and culturally. In the process, working-class and poor residents are often forced out.

ASK YOURSELF

Does gentrification serve a social purpose? If so, what is it? Does conflict theory apply to the fate of the working class and the poor in this process? If so, how?

CITIES AND GLOBALIZATION

From the beginning, cities have been central to both scholarly and popular work on globalization (Sassen 2012). Cities are seen as being **cosmopolitan**, or open to a variety of external and global influences (Beck 2007). In contrast, small towns and rural areas are more likely to be viewed as **local**, or inward rather than outward looking. Cities therefore came to be seen as inherently global, and they grew more so as they came to encompass a range of populations, cultures, ethnicities, languages, and consumer products from around the world. Cities also exerted a powerful influence over surrounding areas.

Cities today are part of global flows of people, products, information, and more. This has been described as "mobile urbanism" (McCann and Ward 2011). Urban policies and ideas on how to improve the city flow easily throughout the world's urban areas. The many city-based organizations are linked through elaborate networks to organizations in other cities throughout the home country and the world. Furthermore, the people in those cities are themselves involved in a wide range of global networks and are linked to people throughout the globe.

GLOBAL AND WORLD CITIES

At the top of the world's hierarchy of cities are the global cities. New York City, London, and Tokyo are generally included in this elite category. Saskia Sassen (1991) embeds her notion of global cities in the process of economic (capitalistic) globalization. In this context, she accords priority to the three cities mentioned previously on the basis of their place in the world economy. Specifically, they are **global cities** because they are

- The key locations for leading industries and marketplaces and the high-level management and specialized services they require

- The centers of the production and creation of innovative, cutting-edge financial services

Detroit's return to prosperity may be a long and slow process. Vacant homes like this one have become a common sight after years of declining tax revenues and population flight. What are some possible effects of blight on those who remain behind?

- The homes of new financial, legal, and accountancy products

- The settings from which businesses and organizations exercise global command and control

Much of what global cities achieve is made possible by a wide range of new electronic technologies. In light of the history of the Great Recession, we also know that these cities, with their great financial centers, are likely to be at the epicenter of monumental collapses in the global economy and, presumably, of economic renaissances.

Global cities are central nodes in a new international division of labor. Of great importance are the linkages among and between these global cities and the flows, both positive and negative, among and between them. In many ways, the global cities have more in common with one another than with the smaller cities and the hinterlands within their own countries. They are also more integrated into the global economy than those hinterlands. The direct linkages between global cities point to the fact that nation-states are less important in the global age than they were previously. They are unable to control the flows between global cities. As Sassen (2012, 189) puts it, the global city "engages the global directly, often bypassing the national."

In addition, the nation-state is unable to stem such global flows as undocumented immigrants and illegal drugs.

MEGACITIES (AND BEYOND)

Megacities are defined as cities with populations greater than 10 million. Of course, the global cities discussed previously meet that criterion, but what is striking is the large and growing number of cities in the less developed world that can be defined as megacities (Krass 2012). In 2016, there were 31 urban areas qualifying as megacities (up from 10 in 1990), led by Tokyo, with almost 38.1 million people (see Figure 14.6). China alone has six megacities, and both it and India will likely have seven by 2030 (United Nations 2016). Extant cities are expected to grow dramatically in the coming years.

Such population concentrations bring with them enormous problems associated with the large numbers of very poor people living in these cities, especially those in less developed countries.

These megacities, even the most blighted of them, have wealthy residents as well. Thus, they are sites of some of the most profound inequalities in the world. A stunning example of this inequality is found in Mumbai, where Mukesh Ambani, the richest person in India, built a 27-story, single-family home that may be valued at as much as $1 billion. Among other things, it has nine elevators, a six-level garage, helipads, "airborne swimming pools," a spa, hanging gardens, a 50-person theater, and a grand ballroom. To function, the structure requires hundreds of servants and staff. All this is found in a city noted for its poverty, where about 60 percent of the population lives in slums (Yardley 2010).

The wealthy from various countries (Russia, for example) are paying astounding prices for these sorts of lavish residences in New York and London. The resulting flow of global money is driving up other housing prices in those cities, making it increasingly difficult for ordinary people to live in them. For instance, a residence in the Belgravia area of London can cost between $7.5 million and $75 million. In New York City, $8 billion is spent each year on residences that cost more than $5 million each; in 2015, one New York condo sold for more than $100 million (Story and Saul 2015).

THE MAIN SITE OF GLOBAL PROBLEMS

Global and world cities are home to the rich and powerful, the main beneficiaries of globalization. However, it is also the case that cities, including the global and world cities, are especially hard-hit by a wide range of global problems. Among other things, some of the world's great cities—New York, London, Madrid, and especially Paris—have been the targets of major terrorist attacks; they are the destinations for large numbers of immigrants, many of them undocumented; they are the settings where large numbers of those affected by global health problems are likely to end up and in need of medical help; and so on. This has led Zygmunt Bauman to contend that "cities have become dumping grounds for globally begotten problems" (2003, 101).

In spite of their global nature and source, dealing with these problems becomes a local political problem, and city officials often lack the economic resources needed to address them. For example, the mayor of London is limited in what he can do to deal with the forces that lead many to migrate to his city—the roots of Islamic State–inspired terrorism, the global HIV/AIDS epidemic, and climate change generated elsewhere. To take a very recent example, the Zika virus arrived in Miami from South America in late 2016, but in the long run the city may be unable to afford the costs of dealing with the mosquitos that carry the disease and those, especially babies, who are victimized by it.

THE CENTER OF CULTURE AND CONSUMPTION

In spite of their problems, cities have played a highly positive role in the development of societies throughout the world. Compared with rural areas, cities tend to have better-educated residents, are more tolerant, are more likely to generate new ideas, have the best hospitals, offer more jobs, and so on. Much of what we think of as culture, especially "high culture," has its origins, and has become centered, in the city. Thus, a great number of the world's great universities, museums, symphony orchestras, opera companies, theaters, and restaurants are found in the world's great cities. It is also the case that much of pop culture—such as hip-hop and rap—emanates from the city.

FIGURE 14.6 • The World's Megacities, 2014

- All world cities with 5 million or more inhabitants.
- Projected growth by the year 2030.

SOURCE: United Nations, Department of Economic and Social Affairs, Population Division (2014). *World Urbanization Prospects: The 2014 Revision, Highlights (ST/ESA/SER.A/352).*

The city is also the source of many developments in the world of consumption. For example, shopping arcades (Benjamin 1999), world's fairs, and department stores had their origins in nineteenth-century Paris and other European cities (Williams [1982] 1991). In the twentieth century, U.S. cities became the world leaders in such consumption sites, most notably New York City, with its world-famous department stores (Macy's and Gimbels) as well as the 1939 and 1964 World's Fairs. When those who lived outside the city could afford to travel and wanted to consume, they often made regular treks to the city to shop, go to the theater, and so on. Cities like Paris and New York also played other key roles in consumption, for example, by serving as national and global centers of fashion (Lipovetsky [1987] 2002; Simmel [1904] 1971). Furthermore, cities, especially New York and its famed Madison Avenue, became centers for the advertising industry, which functions to drive consumption. A number of cities have become more specialized centers of consumption, the most notable examples being gambling centers such as Las Vegas and Macau. Dubai has undergone a massive building boom in an effort to become the commercial and consumption center for a good part of the world, stretching from Cairo to Tokyo.

Fantasy City. A **fantasy city** is one in which great emphasis is placed on creating a spectacle, especially in the areas of consumption, leisure, tourism, and real estate, dominated by impressive buildings and other developments.

Fantasy cities are characterized by infrastructure dominated by such "cathedrals of consumption" (Ritzer 2010a) as "themed restaurants, nightclubs, shopping malls, multiplex cinemas, virtual reality arcades, casino-hotels . . . sports stadiums and arenas, and other urban entertainment centers" (Hannigan 2007, 1641). The whole idea is to draw people, especially tourists, to fantasy cities, and once they are there to lure them into the various cathedrals of consumption, where they will spend large sums of money. Like many developments in the realm of consumption, the fantasy city was largely a U.S. creation, but it has now become increasingly global, and it is possible to identify fantasy cities in

Children of Katrina (University of Texas Press, 2015)

Alice Fothergill (Associate Professor of Sociology at the University of Vermont; PhD, University of Colorado–Boulder, 2001) and Lori Peek (Associate Professor of Sociology and Co-director of the Center for Disaster and Risk Analysis at Colorado State University; PhD, University of Colorado–Boulder, 2005)

In August 2005, Hurricane Katrina made landfall in the United States, causing storm damage that devastated areas in the Gulf Coast, especially the city of New Orleans. Eighteen hundred people died as a direct result of the disaster, and more than 1 million became environmental refugees, dislocated from their homes, families, and friends—some temporarily, others permanently. Children's lives were particularly disrupted when their homes, schools, and churches were destroyed. Alice Fothergill and Lori Peek spent 7 years studying 650 children and youth who were between the ages of 3 and 18 at the time Katrina hit. They used multiple methods to study these children, including observations, focus groups, and interviews. They discovered that creative techniques, such as drawing and molding playdough, encouraged the children to talk about their experiences. Because many of the children and their families were forced to leave their homes in New Orleans and relocate, Fothergill and Peek traveled to other cities in Louisiana, Dallas, Texas, and Denver, Colorado, to conduct their research. Their observational sites included disaster relief centers, FEMA trailers, playgrounds, and restaurants. To develop trust with the children and their families Fothergill and Peek offered to take them out for lunch or dinner, sent gifts, and took the effort to maintain longstanding contact by phone, e-mail, or even letters.

Fothergill and Peek were interested in learning about the long-term effects of a disaster like Katrina for children. They selected seven children to investigate in depth because these children represented three distinctive post-disaster trajectories: declining, finding equilibrium, and fluctuating. The lives of children experiencing a declining post-disaster trajectory were worse after Katrina, while the lives of children on the equilibrium trajectory remained the same. Some children fluctuated between the stability of equilibrium and the disruption of decline. These trajectories were influenced by several key spheres in each child's life, including family, housing, peers, physical and mental health, and extracurricular activities. Children with limited financial and social resources before Katrina encountered the most difficulties and were most likely to face continuous disruptions in the key spheres of their lives on the declining post-disaster trajectory. But even children who had these types of resources pre-Katrina could end up on the declining trajectory because of multiple displacements that isolated them from their friends and social networks back home. Katrina caused an initial disruption for some children, but those whose families had financial and social resources recovered equilibrium and stability in their lives. Children in families that had extended social networks outside of New Orleans, for example, could stay in homes with family members or friends instead of temporary shelters. Other children in Fothergill and Peek's study were located on the fluctuating trajectory, suffering disruptions in some but not all key spheres.

Fothergill and Peek warn that we should not assume that all children are resilient and "bounce back" after disasters; many have continuing needs years after the initial response period. Equally important, they stress that we should not view children as passive victims but as active agents who are capable of preparing a parent or sibling for an imminent disaster and helping others during the response and recovery process.

Supplementary Resources

- Read more about the children of Katrina in this article from *The Atlantic:*
- http://www.theatlantic.com/ education/archive/2015/04/ the-lost-children-of-katrina/389345.
- This short clip from the *CBS Evening News* portrays children affected by Katrina 10 years after the disaster: https://www.youtube.com/ watch?v=RqCP0-z11fg

Australia, Singapore, Malaysia, and China, as well as the United Arab Emirates.

Although people are drawn to fantasy cities to consume, what they find especially attractive is the spectacle of the city. For example, many American cities have built huge and spectacular sports arenas and concert halls as places in which to spend large sums of money (Hoffman, Fainstein, and Judd 2003). In Las Vegas, the spectacle is the famous Strip, Las Vegas Boulevard, with its themed hotel-casinos such as Paris Las Vegas (with its replicas of both the Eiffel Tower and the Arc de Triomphe), the Venetian (with its canals and gondolas), and the Bellagio (including its famous fountains).

THE ENVIRONMENT

In recent years, there has been an explosive growth of a wide range of environmental problems. Because of concern over—and even fear of—those problems, many sociologists have been drawn to and have even led the study of the environment, especially the study of environmental problems (Kolbert 2015; Lidskog, Mol, and Oosterveeer 2015). There is now even a journal entitled *Environmental Sociology,* which had its inaugural issue in 2015. The field was inspired, as was public interest as a whole, by such highly influential books as Rachel Carson's *Silent Spring* (1962), which focused on poisons such as insecticides and weed killers and the threats they posed to the food supply. This interest has expanded exponentially, and for some it has grown to alarm, as the public has been exposed to, and made aware of, the threats posed by environmental problems.

THEORIES OF THE ENVIRONMENT AND ITS PROBLEMS

Sociological approaches to the environment differ depending on the theoretical perspective employed. Structural/functional theories tend to focus on large-scale structures and systems and their impact on environmental problems, as well as on the ability to deal with them. For example, one line of thinking is that because large-scale structures are differentiated functionally (politically, economically, legally), they have difficulty coming together to deal with environmental problems. The conflict/critical perspective focuses on free market capitalism and the need for corporations to grow and to show ever-increasing profits (Klein 2014). In other words, capitalism creates a treadmill of production whereby everyone in the system depends on continuous productive growth (Gould, Pellow, and Schnaiberg 2008). Such capitalistic needs lead to the exploitation of nonrenewable natural resources and other negative effects on the environment. Among the inter/actionists, symbolic interactionists focus on the ways in which we come to define various environmental issues as problems. We also define ourselves in relationship to environmental issues. This can include our views of ourselves if we engage in sustainable (e.g., green) consumption, as well as how others view such consumption (Noppers et al. 2014). Rational choice theorists focus on the fact that there have been great rewards, such as high profits and pay, for those who adversely affect the environment. Clearly, from this perspective, the reward and cost structures need to be changed if we hope to induce people to change their behavior and to take actions that help, rather

This energy plant in Cattenom, France, is nuclear powered. Sociologists study the way we define and grapple with the environmental consequences of our actions.

than hurt, the environment. We need to see, for example, that we can live better by consuming less and, at the same time, have the rewards associated with being more responsible as far as the environment is concerned (Jackson 2014).

GLOBALIZATION AND THE ENVIRONMENT

The environment performs three general functions for humans and other species (Dunlap and Catton 2002; Dunlap and Jorgenson 2012). First, the environment is a kind of "supply depot" that provides us with the natural resources needed for life to exist. Among the renewable and nonrenewable resources provided are air, water, food, shelter, and the materials needed for industries to operate. However, overuse of such renewable resources as water and such nonrenewable resources as fossil fuels can deplete, if not empty, the supply depot.

Second, in consuming those resources, humans produce wastes of various kinds. The environment serves as a "sink" to absorb or dispose of the waste. However, it is possible to produce so much waste that the environment cannot absorb it all. For example, too much sewage can lead to water pollution. There are ongoing efforts to find various uses for the waste we produce. For example, human excrement is being converted into fuel for everything from buses to rockets (Buck 2014; Sullivan 2014).

Third, the environment provides us with living space, or a "habitat—where we live, work, play, and travel" (Dunlap and Jorgenson 2012, 530). However, having too many people in a living space creates numerous problems associated with overcrowding and overpopulation.

In terms of all three functions, it could be argued that humans are beginning to exceed the "carrying capacity" of Earth. There is great global inequality in these three functions. Basically, the developed nations adversely affect the ability of the less developed nations to perform these functions. For example, they use less developed nations as supply depots for natural resources for which they have historically underpaid. In the process, they often adversely affect the ability of the less developed nations to continue to produce these resources. Developed nations also often ship e-waste—that is, discarded electronic equipment—to developing countries, polluting them and their people with the minerals and chemicals in this dangerous debris. This, in turn, despoils the living spaces and the ecosystems of those developing countries.

Although many environmental problems *are* global issues, this view has been challenged in various ways:

- Not everyone or every part of the world is equally to blame for the most pressing global environmental problems. Those from the most developed countries are disproportionately responsible for them, but those in developing countries also play a major role (Olivier, Janssens-Maenhout, and Peters 2012).

- Such problems do not, and will not, affect everyone and all areas of the world in the same way. For example, the rise of the level of the seas as a result of climate change will mostly affect those who live in coastal areas or on islands. Such areas will also be most affected by the expected increase in the number and severity of hurricanes. Tornadoes are also expected to increase, although they are likely to affect some geographic areas, such as the American Midwest, more than others. In addition, because of their greater wealth, those in the Global North will be better able than those in the Global South to find ways of avoiding or dealing with all but the most catastrophic of the problems caused by climate change.

- There are global differences in the importance accorded to, and the dangers associated with, these problems. For example, many in the developed North are highly concerned about climate change, while many in the Global South feel that they are faced with many more pressing problems, such as health problems related to disease and malnutrition as well as the decline of available drinking water.

- The main sources of environmental problems change. For example, the center of manufacturing, with its associated pollutants, has been moving from the United States to China.

ASK YOURSELF

Do you think environmental problems are local, global, or both? Why? Do you think it matters who is responsible for creating them, if we are to solve them? Why or why not?

THE LEADING ENVIRONMENTAL PROBLEMS

There are many important environmental problems, and we have touched on several in the preceding sections. In this section we deal with a few in more depth: the destruction of natural habitats, adverse effects of human activity on marine life, the decline in freshwater, and global warming.

Brazil's rain forest continues to be depleted. However, the country's minister for the environment reports that this depletion, a process that threatens untold numbers of plant and animal species, has begun to slow down. How can sociologists contribute to the protection and preservation of Earth's natural habitats?

Destruction of Natural Habitats

Natural habitats such as the "forests, wetlands, coral reefs, and the ocean bottom" are being destroyed across the globe, often as the result of population growth and the conversion of some of those natural habitats into human habitats (Diamond 2006, 487; Mackay 2014). The forests that have not yet been destroyed are being divided into smaller and more isolated, less self-sufficient fragments surrounded by human environments. Both their smaller size and their human surroundings threaten their continued existence (Haddad et al. 2015). The most notable deforestation in the world has been taking place in the Amazon rain forest (mostly in Brazil), where more than half of the tree species are under threat (St. Fleur 2015), but other parts of the world are also destroying or losing their forests. In fact, more deforestation may now be occurring in Indonesia than in the Amazon basin (Margono et al. 2014). The Amazon forest is being decimated to allow the area to be "developed"—to create farms and areas for livestock to graze—and for the creation of more human settlements. Brazil's forests are so huge, and they play such a large role in the global ecology, that their destruction will have negative effects on the world as a whole. For example, the burning of all those felled trees releases huge amounts of carbon dioxide, which drifts into the atmosphere and flows around the globe, contributing to climate change The loss of the forest leads to other problems for humans, including a diminished supply of timber and other raw materials. This is of great concern also because, especially in the areas undergoing deforestation, forests protect against soil erosion, they are essential to the water cycle and prevention of drought, and they provide habitats for many plants and animals.

Adverse Effects on Marine Life

A large fraction of the protein consumed by humans comes from fish. Marine life in the world's oceans has been greatly diminished by overfishing. According to the United Nations Food and Agricultural Organization, 69 percent of the world's most important fisheries can be considered either "fully exploited" or "overexploited." An early twenty-first-century study concluded that industrial fishing had led to a 90 percent decline in "big fish" such as swordfish, tuna, and marlin populations (Khatchadourian 2007). Aquaculture, which involves growing seafood under controlled conditions such as fish farms, is not an adequate replacement for the loss of natural fishing areas because it causes a whole series of ecological and other problems (de Kerckhove et al. 2015).

A major culprit in the decimation of marine life is industrial fishing. As the amount of sea life declines, the fishing industry compensates by using much more industrialized and intensive techniques. Among these industrial techniques is the use of huge nets that catch large numbers of fish, including many that are not wanted and are discarded. Modern industrial fishing is also characterized by the use of factory ships that process the fish on board rather than waiting until the ships return to port. These technologies contribute to overfishing and in the process destroy complex ecosystems.

The Decline in Freshwater

Water is becoming an increasingly critical global issue (Newton 2016). Many observers have expressed concern about the "water crisis" in some parts of the world, including California and Nevada in the United States (Nagourney 2015; Subramaniam, Whitlock, and Williford 2012). However, the less developed countries in the world are most likely to be negatively affected by a water crisis as water-dependent manufacturing industries locate themselves within their borders. In addition, they are the least likely to have environmental regulations to prevent problems or to be able to do very much about problems once they begin. Among the concerns about water are the following:

- *Water inequality.* The United States has a water footprint double that of the world average and four times that of China. While many in the world have little access to water, many Americans have a large water footprint, often wasting large amounts of water on lawns and golf courses to keep grass green (Hoekstra 2012, 2207).

- *Water pollution.* Humans contribute to the pollution of water through manufacturing processes, mining, agriculture, and inadequate treatment and management of waste. One result of this pollution is an increase in waterborne diseases, especially those that affect children (Jorgenson and Givens 2012).

- *Marine pollution.* One of the most important causes of marine pollution is the dumping of the herbicides, pesticides, and fertilizers used in modern industrial agriculture into the oceans.

- *Flooding.* Experts contend that because warmer air holds more moisture, heavy precipitation is expected to increase in some regions as a result of climate change.

- *Increasing scarcity of water.* There is a possibility that the flow of water could slow or stop completely, at least in some locales (Veldkamp et al. 2014). Some nations are forced to choose between essential uses of water, such as drinking and irrigating crops. There are tensions within nations and between nations—and even the possibility of war—over increasingly scarce water supplies (Dunn 2013).

Desertification is the decline in the water supply as a result of the degradation and deterioration of soil and vegetation (Glantz 1977; Reed and Stringer 2016). Water, once considered a public good, is increasingly becoming a valuable and privatized commodity as many places run low on drinkable water. Another preventable decline in water supply is caused by the wasting of those supplies; for example, nearly two-thirds of all water used for irrigation, in addition to as much as half of city water supplies, is wasted due to leaky pipes.

Although we usually think of water as abundant and readily accessible, the fact is that more than 1 billion people do not have reliable sources of safe drinking water, and more than 2.5 billion do not have adequate sanitation systems (World Health Organization 2015c). The poorest areas of the globe and the poorest people within those areas experience a disproportionate share of water-related problems. The situation is apt to grow worse in coming years; it is possible that half the world's population will be faced with water-related problems by the 2030s.

A less visible water problem involves international trade, especially in agricultural and industrial products. For example, when Japan buys crops (which are water-intensive to produce) from the United States, pressure is put on American water supplies. People throughout the world are using water from elsewhere on the globe. This is called "virtual water" because almost all the water has been used in production of some commodity (Vos and Hinojosa 2016). If people do not realize they are using or abusing water, how can they do anything about it?

Climate Change and Global Warming

The major form of climate change is global warming. The year 2016 was the hottest on record globally, and it was the third consecutive year of record-breaking heat (Patel 2017). All 10 of the hottest days since 1880 have occurred since 1998 (Gillis 2015). As the planet heats up even more, some parts of the world will become wetter, but other parts will grow drier. As a general rule, already wet areas will grow wetter and already dry areas drier; both floods and droughts will intensify. It is in the latter that we are likely to see increasingly desperate and expensive efforts to find water by, for example, drilling ever deeper for underground water supplies (Struck 2007). Among the areas likely to grow drier are Southern Europe, the Middle East, South Australia, Patagonia, and the southwestern United States. In May 2008, Barcelona became the first major city in the world to begin importing large amounts of water by ship to help deal with a long-term drought and a precipitous drop in water resources. There are predictions of Dust Bowl–like conditions in the American Southwest and the resulting possibility of mass migrations. In Mexico, similar conditions may lead to mass migrations to Mexican cities and to the United States. Such increases threaten to create even greater problems and animosities than those that already exist in the United States as a result of both legal and, especially, undocumented immigration from Mexico. In more general terms, we are increasingly likely to see the emergence of an entirely new group of people in the world—climate refugees (Wennersten and Robbins 2017). The United States is planning to resettle its first climate refugees from a waterlogged area, Isle de Jean Charles, in Louisiana. Estimates are that worldwide between 50 and 200 million people will be displaced by rising water (Davenport and Robertson 2016).

Another problem traceable to global warming is the melting of mountaintop glaciers that are important sources of drinking water for many people in the world (Filkins 2016). As those glaciers melt and fail to reform fully, they will produce less and less water for those who need the water to survive. The affected populations, too, are likely to become climate refugees, and they are apt to come into conflict with residents of the still water-rich areas to which they are likely to move.

Humans have produced greenhouse gases that have damaged the atmosphere and, in the view of most experts, are leading to a dramatic rise in the temperature of Earth. During the twentieth century, Earth's temperature rose by about 0.74 degrees centigrade; projections for the twenty-first century are for a rise between 2 and 8 degrees centigrade. Because of the accumulation of greenhouse gases, heat generated by the sun that would ordinarily be reflected back into the atmosphere is trapped and "radiated back to the Earth at a greater rate than before" (Beer 2012). Great concern these days is focused on the burning of fossil fuels (coal, gas, oil), the resulting emission of carbon dioxide, and the role that this plays in the accumulation of greenhouse gases and global warming. Rates of carbon dioxide emissions, mainly from industrialized countries, increased by 80 percent between 1970 and 2004 and have grown by 3 percent per year since 2000. Figure 14.7 shows the relationship between global temperature and carbon dioxide concentration.

There is little or no doubt, at least among scientists, that global warming and more generally climate change are real phenomena with human-made causes (Cook et al. 2013). Furthermore, the predominant view is that global warming is already well advanced and is progressing rapidly. Global warming is expected to affect humans adversely in a number of different ways. It will bring with it more, and more intense, heat waves, and excessive heat can be deadly. A heat wave in Europe in 2003, the worst in almost 500 years, caused about 30,000 deaths from heat-related illnesses. A recent study concludes that heat waves such as the one in 2003 will be "commonplace" in Europe by 2040 (Jolly 2014). The aging of the population makes more people vulnerable to being made ill and dying due to excessive heat. Urbanization also increases the likelihood of death, because cities can become heat islands. There are things that can be done to mitigate the dangers of heat stress, such as greater use of air-conditioning, but many people in the world have no access to air-conditioning or cannot afford it. Further, the use of air-conditioning causes other problems, such as a huge demand on energy resources.

Sea levels are projected to rise dramatically, especially as the glaciers melt. A conservative estimate is that sea levels will rise about 1 meter during the twenty-first century. Approximately 100 million people in the world, mostly in Asia and in island nations, live within 1 meter of sea level, and their homes would be washed away by such a rise.

FIGURE 14.7 • Global Temperature and Carbon Dioxide Concentration, 1880–2012

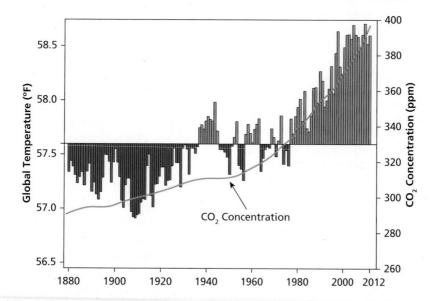

SOURCE: Global Climate Change Indicators, National Oceanic and Atmospheric Administration.

However, this estimate does not take into account the melting of the Greenland and West Antarctic ice sheets, which could add 10 or more meters to the rising seas. In such a case, much larger areas of both the less developed and developed worlds would be inundated.

Global warming and climate change more generally will lead to a wide range of problems, some of which are already upon us:

Wind turbines like these in Honduras hold the promise of supplying cleaner and more affordable energy, but this technology is not without problems. What intergenerational concerns arise in the process of attempting to reduce human reliance on fossil fuels?

- A 2008 typhoon caused the death of almost 140,000 people in Myanmar.

- In the United States, the residents of coastal areas (e.g., the east coast of Florida, the Gulf Coast, southern Louisiana) are in particular danger due to storm surges. In late 2017, Hurricane Harvey caused massive flooding in Houston and other areas of Texas that devastated homes and businesses.

- Carlisle, a small city in northwest England, was hit by a crippling flood in 2005. Flooding of that magnitude was supposed to happen every 200 years, but the city was flooded again in 2009 and then again in 2015 (Schlossberg 2016).

- The Pacific islands and coral atolls of the nation of Kiribati are in the process of being swamped (Ives 2016).

- Coral reefs around the world are being threatened by mass bleaching caused by heat stress (Innis 2016).

- Lake Poopo, the second largest lake in Bolivia, went dry in December 2015, killing all the fish inside it. This destroyed the way of life of those who lived around the lake. It also created a group of climate refugees (Haner 2016).

Figure 14.8 shows all the natural catastrophes around the world in 2015, including extreme weather events.

The incidence of diseases caused by animals and insects may increase due to global warming. For example, it is expected that diseases such as malaria, dengue, and Zika will become more widespread. Exposure to malaria is expected to increase by 25 percent in Africa by 2100. However, actions can be taken to mitigate the spread of the disease, such as controlling the mosquito population with pesticides, instituting a greater use of bed nets (especially by pregnant women and children), and providing better medical care.

GLOBAL RESPONSES

Many global environmental problems, including climate change, are traceable to capitalist economic development (Klein 2014). That is, as economies grow and generate greater wealth, they are likely to do increasing damage to the environment. As concerned as nation-states are becoming about damage to the environment, they are not about to give up the fruits of economic development or cease seeking to become more developed.

As a result, a variety of efforts have arisen to at least reduce the magnitude of environmental problems. We have seen the emergence of a number of environmental movements and organizations, such as Greenpeace, oriented toward this goal (Caniglia 2012). In addition to these movements and organizations, though more general in nature, there has been an increase in environmental activism (Fisher 2012). Environmental activists are generally

FIGURE 14.8 • Natural Catastrophes Worldwide, 2015

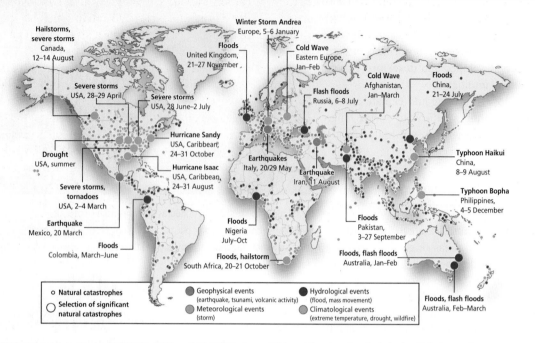

SOURCE: Natural Catastrophes, 2015 World Map. © 2016 Münchener Rückversicherungs-Gesellschaft, Geo Risks Research, NatCatService.

interested either in protecting some aspect of the environment, such as a coral reef or a virgin forest, or in protesting environmental hazards, such as toxic waste or the use of a particular site as a garbage dump. In terms of globalization, activists might oppose the global exportation of environmental problems or support international efforts and treaties to mitigate these problems. While some environmental movements and activists may want to slow or stop economic development, many favor sustainable development.

Sustainable Development

Sustainable development involves economic and environmental changes that meet the needs of the present, especially of the world's poor, without jeopardizing the ability to meet the needs of the future (Blewitt 2014). While the focus of sustainable development is primarily physical sustainability, it is also concerned with promoting equity within the current generation and for future generations.

Globalization can be seen as either a threat or a boon to sustainability. Globalization can threaten sustainable development by reducing the regulatory capacities of governments over environmental threats. On the other hand, globalization can aid sustainable development through the spread of modern, less environmentally destructive technologies and the creation of standards for more efficient resource utilization. Globalization can also lead to a greater demand for cleaner environments.

There are a number of dimensions to the relationship between globalization and sustainability. First, there is the *economic* dimension and the issue of whether economic development irretrievably destroys the environment or whether it gives countries the desire and the ability to better control factors that are adversely affecting the environment. Second, *technology* can be seen as both producing environmental degradation and creating the possibility of limiting the damage. Third, there is the dimension of *awareness* and whether the global media create greater awareness of environmental problems and their causes or whether consumerism, also pushed by the global media, increases people's blindness to these issues. Finally, there is the *politics* of environmentalism, with some global organizations, such as the World Trade Organization (WTO), pushing for more economic growth, while many others, such as Greenpeace, are seeking to reduce it or to limit its negative impact on the environment. Overall, many aspects of globalization adversely affect efforts at sustainable development.

Technological Fixes

There is growing interest in finding technological fixes for at least some global environmental problems, especially those related to climate change There is a longstanding attraction to finding technological solutions to all social problems. To many, creating new technologies seems far easier and less painful than the much harder task of getting large numbers of people to change their behavior. That is, people tend to be reluctant to change their consumption patterns and thus prefer the hope of technological fixes for any resultant ecological problems. Furthermore, many industries have a vested interest in the continuation of high levels of consumption. Thus, even though the burning of fossil fuels is a major cause of global warming, innumerable industries and people are wedded to it. Automobile culture, which exists in both the developed and developing worlds, is one consequential example.

Enter "geoengineering" and a series of relatively new and controversial proposals for dealing with global ecological problems, especially global warming, while leaving untouched and unaddressed the underlying and growing causes of climate change (Asayama 2015). Among the ideas that have been discussed are cooling the Earth's poles by injecting chemicals into the upper atmosphere and putting mirrors in space (Dean 2007). More recently, the focus has been on capturing and storing harmful carbon dioxide emissions, which would permit the Earth's atmosphere to retain less heat, or on reflecting sunlight and its heat away from the Earth (Fountain 2015).

Undertaking such projects would require truly global efforts and a massively funded global governance structure. The hope is that already functioning global governance, such as air traffic control, will be a model for what is needed to deal with global climate problems (Dean 2007). However, it seems unlikely that geoengineering, or any other technological fix, will solve a set of problems that are at their base caused by human actions (Huesemann and Huesemann 2011). While technology can help, the only real solution lies in dramatically changing those behaviors.

The Paris Agreement

Efforts to deal with climate change climaxed, at least for the time being, with the Paris Agreement of the United Nations Climate Change Conference. Negotiated at the end of 2015, the agreement was signed by 174 countries on Earth Day, April 22, 2016. Most notably, the countries involved agreed to limit carbon emissions—largely from the burning of fossil fuels and forest destruction—as soon as possible. Each country will need to set a target to reduce or limit its emissions, but the "nationally determined contribution" will be voluntary. There are no enforcement mechanisms or penalties for failure to meet the targets. Each country also agreed to do its best to keep the temperature increase globally to well below 2 degrees Celsius (3.6 degrees Fahrenheit). Even though it is a weak agreement, President Trump stated in June 2017 that the United States would withdraw from the accord. Although this decision has the potential to further weaken the agreement, or even undermine it completely, it remains to be seen what effect it will actually have, especially in light of strong outcries from the American public and other world leaders about the importance of continuing to uphold the agreement's principles.

DIGITAL LIVING

Smart Cities

Smart cities use digital technology in their attempts to achieve environmental sustainability, quality public services, and an efficient infrastructure for their residents. In addition to bridging the digital divide and ensuring that everyone has access to digital data through wireless networks and web-enabled devices, smart cities are focusing on three key sectors to help residents improve their quality of life: energy, transportation, and security. For example, a smart city might use high-tech sensors to measure how full waste containers are, to count how many seats are available on the next bus or subway, or to turn streetlights on and off (Etezadazdeh 2016, 37, 43). Daily air pollution reports and one-time emergency alerts can be delivered to residents via smartphones. Police and fire departments in smart cities can use digital networks and real-time information to help them respond to emergencies faster. Interactive digital kiosks in these cities can help tourists reserve a table at a popular restaurant or buy a dress at a local shop that can be delivered to their hotel room.

Given that more than 60 percent of the world's population will be living in cities by 2050 and that cities currently consume 75 percent of the world's energy, the growth of smart cities is imperative (MIT Technology Review Custom 2016; United Nations Human Settlements Programme 2016). Digital technologies can help meet future population demands for energy and transportation in an environmentally sustainable and efficient manner. For example, Kansas City, Missouri, has developed smart streetlights that reduce energy consumption. Adelaide, Australia, is using an environment-monitoring system to collect and share data on carbon dioxide, air quality, and temperature (MIT Technology Review Custom 2016). The top five smart cities in the world are Barcelona (Spain), New York City, London (England), Nice (France), and Singapore (High 2015). In order to increase the number of smart cities around the world, partnerships between private technology firms and municipal governments need to be encouraged.

Engaging the Digital World

How "smart" is your college campus? What do you think could be done to make it smarter? Do you see any downsides to living in a smart community? If yes, what are they?

SUMMARY

While overall fertility rates are dropping globally, the world's population continues to increase, although at a declining rate. Demographers focus on three main processes of population change: fertility, or people's reproductive behavior; mortality, or death and death rates; and migration, or the movements of people. Demographic transition theory posits that over time both fertility and mortality rates will decrease, resulting in stabilizing population growth.

Urbanization is the process by which an increasing percentage of a society's population comes to be located in relatively densely populated urban areas. Suburbs are communities adjacent to but outside the political boundaries of central cities. Looking for cheaper land and housing, people have pushed even farther out into areas between the suburbs and rural areas, known as exurbia.

Global cities are the most important of the world's cities and are key locations for leading industries in innovation and financial services. Some global cities are megacities that have populations greater than 10 million. Global cities are cosmopolitan in regard to cultural influences and often attract large numbers of immigrants. Their world appeal and large populations make them potential targets of terrorist attacks and global health problems.

Increasing environmental problems have led sociologists to examine the environment more closely. Most environmental problems are global in nature and scope. The relationship between globalization and sustainability has a number of dimensions, including economic, technological, and political, as well as media awareness. Cooperation between nations is crucial for achieving sustainability, particularly in terms of reducing carbon emissions from burning fossil fuels.

KEY TERMS

asylum seekers, 385
birthrate, 377
cities, 386
cosmopolitan, 389
death rate, 379
demographers, 376
demographic transition, 381
demography, 376

desertification, 397
exurbia, 387
fantasy city, 391
fertility, 378
gated communities, 387
gentrification, 388
global cities, 389
labor migrants, 385
life expectancy, 380

local, 389
megacities, 390
megalopolis, 387
metropolis, 386
migration, 378
mortality, 378
refugees, 384
suburbanization, 387
suburbs, 386

sustainable development, 400
undocumented immigrants, 385
urban, 386
urbanism, 386
urbanization, 386

REVIEW QUESTIONS

1. How does the "demographic dividend" differ from the "financial time bomb"? Overall, is the United States in a period of a demographic dividend or a financial time bomb? Why?

2. According to demographic transition theory, what role do technological advances play in changing demographics? Why is "development the best contraceptive"?

3. How does the nature of today's migrants differ from the nature of migrants in the past? In contrast, how are the barriers to migration consistent with those of the past? How have the "push" and "pull" factors associated with migration changed in the global age?

4. Distinguish among refugees, asylum seekers, labor migrants, and undocumented immigrants.

5. What are the arguments in favor of international migration? How do these fit into today's popular

and political dialogue regarding immigration in the United States?

6. Discuss the contradiction between the two roles played by the world's cities—as the sites of some of the world's worst problems and as the sites of some of its greatest achievements.

7. What makes cities cultural and consumption centers? How is a "fantasy city" different from a traditional urban area? In what ways are fantasy cities related to processes of Americanization?

8. This chapter cites environmental problems arising in cities, yet points to the possibility of new forms of urban development that could be less ecologically destructive. How can sustainable development create a more ecologically friendly city? How would this development differ from that of the last 200 years?

9. What are the world's major environmental problems? Are there technological fixes that can deal with our environmental problems? If so, what are they?

10. Do you think that globalization is ultimately a threat or a boon to sustainability? What current evidence would you cite to support your position?

SOCIAL CHANGE, SOCIAL MOVEMENTS, AND COLLECTIVE ACTION

15

Workers' Rights, Consumer Activism, and Social Change

The fruits and vegetables you purchase in the grocery store were most likely harvested by undocumented workers from Mexico or Central America. These workers pay smugglers thousands of dollars to help them cross the border illegally into the United States. The lucky ones find work on farms for meager pay and substandard working conditions. Hundreds die each year from dehydration, heat stroke, or direct violence as they attempt to cross the border; others are caught by Border Patrol agents and deported (Holmes 2013). Some become trapped in a debt bondage system referred to as modern slavery; they are forced to work off the payment of their border crossing to farm camp operators. Typically, these undocumented farmworkers are not paid in wages, but by the weight of the produce they harvest. Being paid by weight compels many of them to work 10 hours or more per day with few breaks. Those in debt bondage rarely earn enough to pay off their debt and remained enslaved (Tammelleo and Lombardi 2014, 105). This was the scenario for undocumented workers

LEARNING OBJECTIVES

 15.1 Discuss the significance of social movements in the United States.

 15.2 Explain how social movements emerge.

 15.3 Identify different types of collective action.

15.4 Describe contemporary examples of global social change.

---

edge.sagepub.com/ritzeressentials3e

- Take the chapter quiz
- Review key terms with eFlashcards
- Explore multimedia links and SAGE readings

$SAGE edge™

who picked tomatoes in Immokalee, Florida, until the Coalition of Immokalee Workers (CIW) launched a boycott against Taco Bell in 2001.

CIW issued three demands to Taco Bell: (1) that it establish a program to stop human rights violations in its supply chain; (2) that it pay 1 penny more per pound of tomatoes, which would go to the workers; and (3) that it encourage other major retailers to follow its lead (Tammelleo and Lombardi 2014, 105). With pressure from consumer activists, particularly college students and members of religious organizations, Taco Bell agreed to these demands in 2005. More recently, McDonald's, Burger King, Trader Joe's, and Whole Foods have also agreed to these demands. Currently, CIW is boycotting Wendy's and Publix, two large purchasers of tomatoes who refuse to consent to its demands. In March 2017, CIW coordinated the Return to Human Rights Tour in Columbus, Ohio, near Wendy's headquarters to exert more public pressure on this fast-food chain to treat its workers better.

CIW boycotts could not succeed without consumers' using their purchasing power as a tactic to persuade corporations to change their unjust business practices. Boycotts, or the threat of withholding consumer spending from unethical companies, have a long history in the United States. In the nineteenth century, abolitionists refused to purchase sugar and other commodities that were produced with slave labor. In the early twentieth century, the National Consumers' League organized consumer boycotts of various products in order to force corporations to improve working conditions for women and to eliminate child labor. During the same time, the American Federation of Labor issued boycotts against businesses that refused to sell union-made products and companies that would not hire union workers (Forno 2013; Glickman 2009; Wiedenhoft Murphy 2017a). In 2017, a national "Day Without Immigrants" encouraged immigrant workers to stay home from their jobs to highlight their significant contributions to the U.S.

economy. Consumer activism can also take the form of buycotts—using purchasing power to support ethical business practices. For example, the Fair Trade movement encourages consumers to buy products that have been produced by workers who receive living wages. As corporations come to hold increasing amounts of wealth and power around the world and social media allows for widespread and rapid communication and organization, consumer activism can be a critical and effective way to hold corporations accountable for their actions. ●

S ocial change involves variations over time in every aspect of the social world, ranging from changes affecting individuals to transformations having global impacts (G. Massey 2016; Weinstein 2010). Sociologists are concerned with social change itself, as well as with the ways in which social changes affect the self-concepts of individuals, the structures of society, global economic and political systems, and much more.

A good recent example of social change is the ongoing dramatic transformation of much of the Arab world that began in late 2010 (Worth 2016). Aspects of this change, referred to as Arab Spring, have not always been successful. "Springtime" does not seem to have arrived in many of the countries involved. Among other things, we have seen a return to authoritarianism in Egypt, anarchy in Libya, and continuing civil war in Syria and Iraq, both of which seem to be in the process of being permanently dismembered. This has led Roger Cohen (2016), and others, to describe Arab Spring as an "epic failure."

The most important change wrought, at least initially, by the Arab Spring was the 2011 overthrow of longtime Egyptian dictator Hosni Mubarak and the coming to power of a former leader of the Islamic Brotherhood, Mohamed Morsi. However, Morsi's rule was uneasy and marked by much protest and disorder. In fact, Morsi was overthrown in a military coup in July 2013, and the general—Abdel Fattah el-Sisi—who led the coup became the new Egyptian president with dictatorial powers. As of this writing, in late 2017, an extremely bloody rebellion in Syria has been ongoing for more than six years, with

Protestors rally to support Turkey's president, Recep Tayyip Erdoğan, after a failed attempt to overthrow him. What happens to a society when a revolution fails?

President Bashar al-Assad clinging to control over an ever-smaller part of the country (Lynch, Freelon, and Aday 2014; Ma'oz 2014). The rest of Syria is in disarray with various groups, especially the Sunni-based terrorist organization the Islamic State, vying for control. The social movements associated with, and set in motion by, the Arab Spring continue to reverberate throughout the world, especially the Middle East (Lynch 2013; Moss 2013).

What is most important for our purposes is that even though it now seems misnamed, the Arab Spring is an excellent illustration of the major sociological ideas to be discussed in this chapter. It brought about *social change,* and it exemplifies both *collective action* and *social movements.* We begin this discussion with the latter idea.

SOCIAL MOVEMENTS

A **social movement** is a sustained and intentional collective effort, usually operating outside established institutional channels, either to bring about or to retard social change (Della Porta and Diani 2015; Snow et al. 2013). The social movements associated with the Arab Spring sought to bring about social change, while the Tea Party seeks to retard, or even reverse, changes in the United States associated with liberalism, such as former president Obama's Patient Protection and Affordable Care Act (ACA; Skocpol and Williamson 2016). Having already touched on the Arab Spring movements, we discuss other examples of social movements later in this chapter. Beyond the Tea Party, the chapter addresses the feminist movement, the LGBTQ movement, and the civil rights movement. Following brief overviews of those movements, various sociological concepts and ideas that help us better understand these social movements will be discussed.

THE TEA PARTY

The Tea Party is a national movement named for the Boston Tea Party of 1773. In the contemporary context, the word *tea* in the name serves as an

Strangers in Their Own Land: Anger and Mourning on the American Right (The New Press, 2016)

Arlie Russell Hochschild (Professor of Sociology at the University of California, Berkeley; PhD, University of California, Berkeley, 1969)

A sign placed by St. Amant, Louisiana, resident Doug Ford welcomes Republican presidential candidate Donald Trump, who toured flood-ravaged Louisiana on the campaign trail.

The election of Donald Trump to the presidency in 2016 caught many liberals by surprise. They questioned why so many poor and working-class Americans would vote for a Republican who vowed to dismantle government programs such as the Affordable Care Act, which were enacted to help them. Arlie Russell Hochschild spent five years in Louisiana, a strongly conservative "red" state, to learn about what she calls the Great Paradox: People who need federal assistance the most are turning away from it and toward marketplace solutions to their economic problems (2016, 9). Hochschild found that one of the main reasons for this is the emotion that shapes opinions and actions relating to such matters. Political feelings are dividing Americans, many of whom retreat into segregated "emotionally toned enclaves" and surround themselves with like-minded friends and acquaintances (2016, 6). Examples of emotionally toned enclaves may be found on social media, where friends and followers are likely to share similar beliefs. Most troublesome is the fact that invisible "empathy walls" are being constructed that "can make us feel indifferent or even hostile to those who hold different beliefs" (2016, 5). These empathy walls are particularly pronounced in the case of controversial issues, such as immigration and same-sex marriage. Hochschild explains that conservatives believe that liberals are trying to force them to feel "happy for the gay newlywed, [and] sad at the plight of the Syrian refugee," while liberals reduce conservatives' lack of requisite feelings in such cases to prejudice or ignorance (2016, 15).

In order to better understand the empathy walls dividing liberals and conservatives, Hochschild interviewed a core group of 40 highly conservative Tea Party advocates. From this group, she selected six people to profile. She engaged in participant observations of their lives, which included attending political rallies, community meetings, and church services with them. Hochschild focused her research on one specific example of the Great Paradox: resistance to government regulation of environmental hazards caused by private companies. Louisiana is a state that suffers from some of the worst environmental hazards, such as air and water pollution, created by petrochemical corporations, but has some of the most lenient environmental regulations. Hochschild finds that conservatives want a clean environment, but many do not believe that government regulation is the best way to achieve it. Some of them view environmental risk as natural or inevitable, while others think it is a gamble one has to take in order to increase job opportunities. Even people in her study who were forced to relocate because their homes had been swallowed by an enormous sinkhole caused by a drilling company refused to turn to the government for help. Some even blamed government agencies for their lack of oversight instead of the negligent practices of the company. While it is easy to blame the victims of the Great Paradox for contributing to—if not creating—their own hardships, Hochschild warns that this reasoning is too simplistic and reinforces empathy walls. It dismisses structural and cultural reasons why some individuals might oppose "big government" and support companies that promise them jobs. Climbing empathy walls by deliberating interacting with individuals who espouse different beliefs from our own is admittedly difficult at time when political polarization is high. However, it might help us acknowledge the intense emotions supporting these walls and encourage those on both sides to be more inclusive and trusting.

Supplementary Resources
- Watch Hochschild discuss her book *Strangers in Their Own Land* on *Democracy Now!* at https://www.democracynow.org/2016/9/28/what_drives_trump_supporters_sociologist_arlie.

- Learn more about Hochschild's findings and the individuals she interviewed in this article that appeared in the *New Yorker:* http://www.newyorker.com/news/benjamin-wallace-wells/arlie-russell-hochschilds-view-of-small-town-decay-and-support-for-trump.

acronym for "taxed enough already." The Tea Party is *not* a political party, but it wields great power over and within the Republican Party. It emerged in the United States in 2009 as a protest against high taxes and other government actions (Pullum 2013; van Dyke and Meyer 2014). It especially targeted the Obama administration's efforts to address the Great Recession and the associated housing crisis, as well as efforts to stimulate the economy through the American Recovery and Reinvestment Act of 2009. The Tea Party also opposed passage of the Affordable Care Act (ACA), or "Obamacare," which was signed into law in 2010 (see Chapter 13). Similarly, it was later enraged by President Obama's 2014 executive order—blocked by the Supreme Court in 2016—shielding as many as 5 million undocumented immigrants from deportation (Peters 2014). Since the 2016 election, the Tea Party is in an even stronger position to see its agenda enacted now that sympathetic conservative Republicans control two branches of the federal government. In fact, it could be argued that Republicans actually control all three branches, now that President Trump's nominee for the Supreme Court, Neil Gorsuch, has been approved by the Senate and installed on the bench.

The initial impetus for the Tea Party movement was a February 19, 2009, on-air rant by commentator Rick Santelli on the conservative and pro-business cable TV network CNBC. Among other things, Santelli said, "The government is promoting bad behavior. . . . How many of you people want to pay your neighbor's mortgage, that has an extra bathroom, and can't pay their bills? Raise their hand! . . . We're thinking of having a Chicago Tea Party in July. . . . I'm going to start organizing" (quoted in Williamson, Skocpol, and Coggin 2011, 37). Senators Rand Paul (Kentucky), Ted Cruz (Texas), and Marco Rubio (Florida) and Governor Scott Walker (Wisconsin) are Tea Party favorites who have also been failed Republican presidential candidates.

Interest in the Tea Party boomed in 2009 and beyond. However, it remains a loosely organized group of local and national conservative organizations. According to one estimate, there are only a few hundred active Tea Party groups in the United States, and only a fraction of them have more than 500 members (Williamson et al. 2011). The organization's impact has been greatly magnified by the media, especially the "advocacy journalism" of cable television news networks, particularly the conservative and pro–Tea Party Fox News and the liberal and anti–Tea Party MSNBC (Boykoff and Laschever 2011). Media coverage brought a degree of attention and influence to the Tea Party far out of proportion to the number of active participants in the movement.

The Tea Party is unlikely to become a new political party, in part because the United States has long been dominated by a two-party system. However, if the Tea Party were to become a full-fledged political party and became institutionalized, it would no longer be a social movement. It would also no longer be a social movement if it were to peter out and die. It is possible that the Tea Party will remain what it is, a social movement, for some time to come.

Mark Wilson/Getty Images

Is the Tea Party a social movement, a political party in the making, or a flash in the pan?

Like the other examples to be discussed later, the Tea Party has *the basic characteristics of a social movement:*

- It is a *collective effort* because it includes *a significant number of people* from throughout the United States.

- It has been *sustained* for a number of years.

- It was certainly brought into being *intentionally.*

- It has been *outside established institutional channels,* because it was not, and still is not, formally affiliated with either political party.

- It has been an *effort to retard some political changes,* such as former president Obama's tax increases and health care reform act.

- It has been an *attempt to bring about substantial political change* in the Republican Party and the government as a whole. The Tea Party sought to change the Republican Party by moving it further to the right and to change the American government by forcing it to reduce taxes, better control government spending and debt, and shrink its size and power. With the election of Donald Trump, many of those goals are likely to be achieved.

Since the election of Donald Trump, the Democratic Party has started to copy some of the tactics of the Tea Party by mobilizing activists at the grassroots level. Democratic activists are attending the hometown meetings of their Republican representatives, making phone calls, and sending e-mails to protest their support of Donald Trump. They are also organizing marches and rallies across the country to express their discontent with Trump's policies and misogynist remarks (Martin 2017; Nguyen 2017). Almost half a million people attended the Women's March in Washington in January 2017 to demonstrate their outrage with the Trump administration, with millions more attending sister marches across the country (the total number of marchers across the United States was estimated to be between 3 and 5 million) and even in cities around the world.

FEMINIST MOVEMENTS

The movements of concern here are based on **feminism**, or the belief that women are equal to men, especially socially, politically, and economically (see Chapter 9). These movements have all of the characteristics of a social movement outlined previously (Crossley and Hurwitz 2013). The people involved certainly intended to bring the movements into being and to maintain them. Feminist movements—often called women's movements—have, at least until recently, had to work outside established institutional channels. Historically, women were likely to be denied access to these channels by the men in control of the institutions. For example, U.S. women did not gain the right to vote until 1920. The movements have certainly demonstrated durability, as you will soon learn, both in the United States and around the world (Basu 2010). And they are oriented toward dramatically improving the position of women throughout the world.

The Women's Movement in the United States

The women's movement can be traced back to England and Mary Wollstonecroft's 1792 book *A Vindication of the Rights of Women,* which made the case for women's equality (Reid 2014; Tetrault 2014). The first wave of the women's movement in the United States is traditionally traced to the 1840s (Reger 2007). It was focused largely on the issue of suffrage, or gaining the right to vote for women. It had its roots in the early involvement of women in the anti-alcohol (temperance) movement and especially the antislavery movement. However, women were largely subordinated and ignored in these movements. Anger about such treatment led to the 1848 Seneca Falls Convention, which focused on such issues as restrictions on women's roles within the family, women's rights in terms of education and property, and, especially, women's suffrage (Wellman 2004). Decades of meetings, protests, marches, and social activism followed, including the arrest of prominent suffrage leaders (for attempting to vote). Several national organizations were formed to push forward women's right to vote. The movement included battles between black and white women, with prominent white suffragist Susan B. Anthony saying, "I will cut off this right arm of

FIGURE 15.1 • When Women Won the Right to Vote in Selected Countries, Twentieth Century

SOURCE: Data from "Women's Suffrage: When Did Women Vote?" Interactive Map. Scholastic.com.

mine before I will ever work or demand the ballot for the Negro and not the [white] woman" (quoted in Wilson and Russell 1996, 30). Black suffragists, including Ida B. Wells and Anna Julia Cooper, were routinely excluded from the white women's marches and protests. Although the Nineteenth Amendment gave women voting rights as early as 1848, it did not become law until August 26, 1920. (Figure 15.1 shows when women won the right to vote in select countries in the twentieth century.) By the 1930s, black women's voting rights had become severely circumscribed; their political disenfranchisement lasted until the civil rights movement of the 1960s.

The second wave of the women's movement began in the 1960s. It drew from the first wave but went beyond it in various ways. Several key books, including Simone de Beauvoir's *The Second Sex* ([1952] 1973) and Betty Friedan's *The Feminine Mystique* (1963), had a strong effect on the movement and articulated a number of its key ideas. More practically, the second wave, like the first, grew out of the dissatisfaction of activists with their involvement in other social movements, especially the New Left and civil rights movements (Houck and Dixon 2011), and their failure to deal with gender issues. Activists were also angered by the fact that these movements themselves were patriarchal. An important event in the midst of the second wave was the founding of the National Organization for Women (NOW) on October 29, 1966. The founders were women in government dissatisfied with its failure to deal with sex discrimination against women in the workplace. NOW eventually came to focus on a much wider range of issues, such as discrimination against women in education, the rights of women within the family, and the problems of poor women.

The second wave reached its peak between 1972 and 1982. A number of developments occurred during this period, including the founding of *Ms.* magazine; the appearance of women's studies programs on college campuses; the passage of Title IX of the U.S. Education Amendments, ending discrimination on the basis of sex in publicly funded education; and the 1973 Supreme Court decision in the case of *Roe v. Wade,* legalizing abortion. However, the second wave was soon wracked by internal conflicts. Some women—women of color, lesbians, and working-class women—protested that their interests were not being adequately reflected in or addressed by the more publicly visible women's movement (Boris 2012; Roth 2004). These internal conflicts resulted in a polarization of feminism. More conservative feminists, the reformists, were primarily concerned about gender equality in the workplace. Revolutionary feminists criticized the limited goals of the reformists, who focused primarily on the concerns of white middle-class women (hooks 2000). They also emphasized the ways in which conservative feminists often acted in a patriarchal and sexist manner toward other women.

By the early 1990s, a third wave of the women's movement emerged. This wave, which is ongoing, has been marked by a reaction against the problems confronted by the movement in the 1980s. The defining characteristics of the third wave are greater racial and ethnic inclusivity and more focus on problems such as racism, classism, transphobia, and homophobia. The movement also addresses the place of women in the larger culture and a variety of specific issues, such as the wage gap between men and women, sexual harassment, violence against women, and sexual assault and rape.

Cyberfeminism and activism on the internet can be seen as part of the third wave (Carty 2013; Haraway 1991; Wajcman 2010), although there are those who see these developments as marking the dawning of a fourth wave (Baumgardner 2011; Munro 2013). Feminists discuss, debate, and mobilize on a variety of websites, including the Crunk Feminist Collective (www.crunkfeministcollective.com), The F-Word (www.thefword.org.uk), and Feministing (http://feministing.com). They use social media and write blogs to raise awareness about the right to bodily autonomy and share knitting patterns for pink pussyhats. The emerging fourth wave of feminism is centered on the idea that gender and sexuality are fluid and aims to "queer" the binary bias of these identities (Sollee 2015). Reproductive justice is a key issue in fourth-wave feminism, as is the struggle for women to achieve full human rights. These rights include not just gender equality in social institutions, such as the workplace and school, but also the physical and emotional well-being of women and girls.

The Global Women's Movement

Organizing women on a transnational basis began between the 1830s and the 1860s (Berkovitch 1999,

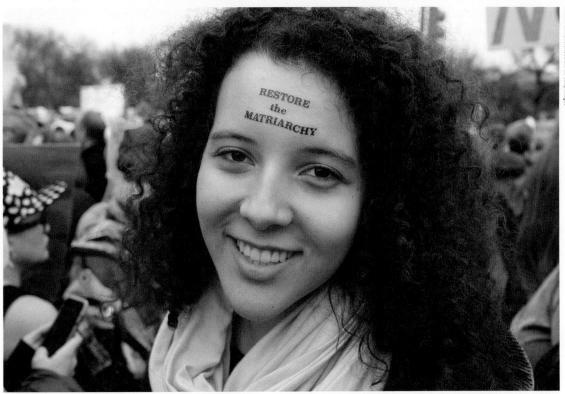

The vertical text reads: Andrew Lichtenstein/Corbis via Getty Images

The Women's March in January 2017, held in cities around the world, drew an estimated 5 million participants in total. What is the role for a women's movement today, and what should be its goals?

2012). At first, this was highly informal, but formal organizations did emerge, such as the World Women's Christian Temperance Union (WWCTU), founded in 1874. While the WWCTU focused on the problem of alcohol, it was concerned about other issues as well, such as political equality for women. By the time of its first international convention in 1891, the WWCTU had branches in 26 countries. Members adopted the view that "universal sisterhood" existed and that women throughout the world experienced a common fate. Suffrage became an increasingly important issue globally, and that led to the founding of the International Woman Suffrage Alliance (IWSA) in 1904 (Rupp and Taylor 1999).

One of the most striking events in the early twentieth century was the gathering of more than 1,000 women in the Netherlands in 1915 at the International Congress of Women. This meeting took place in spite of the fact that World War I raged around the attendees, which made it very difficult to pass through national borders. The main goal of the meeting was to find ways to resolve conflicts and prevent future wars. After World War I, the founding of the League of Nations and the International Labour Organization (ILO) created new opportunities for global action by women (and others). However, women's activities in and through these organizations achieved few tangible results, in part because leaders within the organizations tended to be "elite, White, Christian women from Northern and Western Europe" (Freedman 2009, 48). Many women within these groups supported colonialism, despite the presence of fellow members who suffered under colonial rule. Moreover, the reproduction of colonial relationships within the movement was yet another facet of the contentious beginnings of an international women's movement. In reaction to this, black women from Africa and the United States formed the International Council of Women of the Darker Races in 1920. They called for support in their struggle not only for personal independence but also national independence from colonial domination (Alexander and Mohanty 2013; Freedman 2009).

Much greater strides were made as a result of the founding of the United Nations after World

War II. Instrumental in this progress was the UN Commission on the Status of Women. Its initiative led to a world conference on women in 1975 and to the declaration of that year as the UN International Women's Year. Yet men dominated the speeches and leadership positions at the 1975 conference; they tended to represent the interests of their respective governments rather than those of women's organizations. Women continued to press for equality, however, and were eventually granted more leadership roles to foster discussions about the gaps between male and female opportunities. This was followed by the UN Decade for Women (1976–1985), conferences during that decade, and follow-up conferences held in 1995 (30,000 people attended the UN Fourth World Conference on Women in Beijing) and 2005. Because of such meetings, women from all over the world were able to interact on a face-to-face basis and to develop various transnational interpersonal ties (Davis [1991] 1999). As a result of these associations, many local and transnational women's organizations emerged (Fernandes 2013).

In addition to these formal organizations, many transnational feminist networks have developed in recent years (Ferree and Tripp 2006). These are more fluid organizational forms, lacking formal membership and bureaucratic structures. They have been aided in their formation and interaction by new communication technologies, especially the internet. However, rather than these developments leading to a single global sisterhood, fractures and divisions have grown stronger in the global women's movement. For example, women of the Global South often resist initiatives supported by women of the Global North. This resistance is due in part to Southern women's need to prevent the imposition of Northern notions of superiority and to recognize that injustice and emancipation can take various forms (Freedman 2009). In spite of these divisions, the women's movement today is far more global than ever. It is not only having an impact on the position of women throughout the world but also shaping, and being shaped by, globalization (Basu 2010; Crossley and Hurwitz 2013). This can be seen, for example, in the millions of women around the world who participated in the Women's March on January 21, 2017.

ASK YOURSELF

Does it surprise you to learn that the women's movement and its global arm are characterized by fractures? What might heal these divisions? Do men need to play a role in women's movements? Why or why not?

LGBTQ MOVEMENTS[1]

The origins of U.S.-based LGBTQ movement can be traced back to the 1890s (Shroedel and Fiber 2000). There were earlier LGBTQ movements in other places, such as Germany (Newton 2009), and there are, of course, LGBTQ movements throughout the world today (Tremblay, Paternotte, and Johnson 2013). These movements still have much work to do. For example, same-sex acts remain illegal in at least 72 countries (Carroll 2016; Hildebrandt 2014).

The focus here is mainly on LGBTQ movements in the United States (Ghaziani, Taylor, and Stone 2016). The LGBTQ movement will be discussed as the successor to such previous movements as gay liberation, lesbian feminism, and queer activism. It encompasses those earlier movements, but goes beyond them to "embrace bisexuality and transgender issues" (Ghaziani, Taylor, and Stone 2016, 171).

World War II and the Lavender Scare

Some problems for gays and lesbians (such as mobilization against them in the military) developed during the World War II era (Bérubé 2010). However, in general, that period was something of a golden age for gays and lesbians in the United States. Men and women engaged in new experiences as they left home, settled in new living situations, and found themselves in same-sex milieus in the military or in civilian workplaces. This period has been described as "somewhat of a nationwide coming out experience" (Allan Bérubé, quoted in Johnson 2004: 51). The war years allowed for increased possibilities and opportunities for sexual encounters, as well as an "anything goes" mentality. However, beginning in 1948, the United States entered a period of

---

[1] This section is printed with the permission of Tracy Royce and Danielle Antoinette Hidalgo.

mounting public criticism of the "moral decay" of homosexuality, as well as of communism.

What came to be known as the "Lavender Scare" signaled a turning point for the history of LGBTQ movements in the United States. Starting in 1950, the Lavender Scare was a government-sponsored attack on sexual minorities—those who engaged in, or were suspected of, same-sex sexual behaviors (Johnson 2004). As in the better-known Red Scare (a response to fears of communism), government agents attempted to ferret out employees who were considered security risks. In this case, those suspected of engaging in "sexual perversions" or homosexuality were vulnerable because it was feared that they might reveal government secrets to foreign agents under pressure to prevent their sexual activities from being made public. Thousands were discharged from the government; some committed suicide. This institutionalized attack on homosexuality also sparked political organization among gays and lesbians. The Mattachine Society (see the following section), founded by a government worker, marked the start of 25 years of efforts to dismantle federal job discrimination laws. In 1975, it became illegal to discriminate against gays and lesbian in hiring and firing decisions. Thus, the "crackdown" on gays and lesbians, "perverts," and those engaged in "immoral" sexual relations fostered a long-lasting collective movement to fight for LGBTQ rights.

The U.S.-Based Homophile Movement

Early efforts to organize "homophile" (i.e., gay rights) movements crystallized in 1950–1951 in the formation of the Mattachine Society, originally based in Los Angeles. Other cities started chapters, and by 1966, there were 15 gay and lesbian rights organizations in the United States; by 1969, there were 50 (D'Emilio 1983; Hay 2012). The Daughters of Bilitis (DOB), an offshoot of the Mattachine Society focusing on the rights of gay women, was founded in 1955 (Rutledge 1992; Valocchi 2007). These organizations emphasized education and largely embraced assimilationist strategies in order to gain mainstream acceptance. Although gay and lesbian activists worked alongside each other, gender privilege (particularly male) remained and was a source of dissatisfaction for lesbians active in the homophile movement. As one

lesbian activist stated, "There wasn't a Women's Movement yet. . . . We knew our place—we were always the coffee makers. . . . There was a clear set of chores for women" (Shroedel and Fiber 2000, 99).

Stonewall

The 1969 uprisings at Greenwich Village's Mafia-owned gay bar the Stonewall Inn are regarded by many as pivotal in the twentieth-century struggle for LGBTQ rights and as denoting the beginning of the modern gay rights movement (Armstrong and Crage 2006, 2013; Duberman 1994). On June 27, 1969, the patrons of the Stonewall Inn—"Puerto Rican drag queens, lesbians, effeminate men, and young street people" (Nardi, Sanders, and Marmor 1994, 14)—reacted violently to a police raid. Law enforcement officials and members of the gay community alike credited this event with inspiring gays and lesbians to more aggressively demand equality and freedom from abuse. Within a few years, there were more than 800 gay and lesbian groups all over the United States. Today, gay pride days and marches continue to commemorate the assertion of collective queer identity and entitlement to rights that emerged as a result of Stonewall. However, some question LGBTQ history's emphasis on the Stonewall uprisings. They remind us that new forms of the LGBTQ movement owe much to the foundational work of homophile groups, as well as to twentieth-century civil rights, antiwar, and feminist organizations (Jay 1999).

Lesbian Herstory

Given the underlying male privilege that was embodied in groups such as the Mattachine Society, many lesbians were dissatisfied with their organizing experiences alongside gay men. And although lesbians found a respite from sexism in the mainstream second-wave women's movement, the heterosexism and sometimes overt hostility encountered by lesbians in feminist groups made these organizing spaces less than hospitable. Consequently, many lesbians split off from the mainstream gay and feminist movements. Numerous lesbian separatist groups emerged, such as the Furies, who framed lesbianism as a political choice in opposition to male supremacy.

Not all lesbians politicized their sexual identities in this way. For women who desired other

NY Daily News Archive via Getty Images

Patrons of the Stonewall Inn in Greenwich Village fought back when police raided the gay enclave in 1969, in what proved to be a watershed moment. Do you agree with those who feel that the civil rights, antiwar, and feminist movements had an impact on the struggle for LGBTQ rights? If so, what was that impact?

women in butch/femme (traditionally male/traditionally female) space, a masculine–feminine relationship continued. But lesbian separatists argued that in order to truly be feminists, women had to remove themselves completely from the male sphere. In practice, this resulted in the formation of women-only communities or "womyn's lands" and lesbian-driven, woman-centered activism. These women "wanted to create entirely new institutions and to shape a women's culture that would embody all of the best values that were not male" (Faderman 1991, 216).

ASK YOURSELF

Why do all LGBTQ individuals not have the same goals or try to achieve equality by the same means? Do their philosophical and practical divisions help or hinder their efforts? Why?

HIV/AIDS, ACT UP, and Queer Nation

The recognition of HIV/AIDS in 1981 by the Centers for Disease Control and Prevention had a tremendous impact on LGBTQ politics and communities. The activism that emerged from this period was embodied in the early efforts of the AIDS Coalition to Unleash Power (ACT UP; Stockdill

2013). In 1989, ACT UP pressured pharmaceutical company Burroughs Wellcome to make its new antiretroviral drug, AZT, more affordable for HIV-positive patients. ACT UP embodied a new kind of activism that included civil disobedience, activist art, and other forms of creative activities and representations. ACT UP chapters opened throughout the nation. In 1990, some ACT UP activists formed a new group, Queer Nation, which, although short-lived, served as the beginning of a public and direct representation of LGBTQ issues. Out of HIV/AIDS activism and via the efforts of Queer Nation, the gay and lesbian movement shifted into a politics of queer spaces and identities.

The Ongoing Fight for Marriage Equality

Almost from the inception of the LGBTQ movement, marriage equality was a part of its national agenda. That effort really took off when the movement legally challenged the 1996 Defense of Marriage Act (Ghaziani, Taylor, and Stone 2016). That act restricted marriage to "one man and one woman" and barred federal recognition of same-sex marriages. The efforts of the LGBTQ movement—and others—met with considerable success, and in 2011 President Obama determined that the act was unconstitutional and directed the Justice Department to stop defending the law in court. In 2013, the U.S. Supreme Court struck down the section of the act that defined marriage as involving one man and one woman. It also declared unconstitutional the barring of federal recognition of same-sex marriages. As a result of the 2013 Supreme Court decision, gays and lesbians gained many federal and state benefits that were formerly denied to them and that are automatically conferred on heterosexual couples. By mid-2015, the Supreme Court legalized same-sex marriage for the nation as a whole. Globally, same-sex couples enjoy the legal right to marry in a number of other countries.

In spite of these successes, resistance to same-sex marriage continues to come from both outside and within the LGBTQ rights movement. Religious conservatives oppose same-sex marriage, arguing that it threatens the sanctity of marriage and the traditional family. But queer-identified groups have also offered criticisms of same-sex marriage. For example, emphasizing the central importance of securing legal marriage is criticized for failing to address the inequalities inherent in the institution of marriage itself (BeyondMarriage.org 2006).

Perhaps no one symbolizes the civil rights movement so well as Martin Luther King Jr. Here King waves to supporters from the steps of the Lincoln Memorial during the 1963 March on Washington.

THE CIVIL RIGHTS MOVEMENT

Arguably, the most notable social movement in the United States was, and may still be, the civil rights movement (Fleming and Morris 2015; Morris 1984; Santoro 2015). Perhaps the key event in the history of the civil rights movement was the successful 1955 boycott of segregated city buses in Montgomery, Alabama. At the time, blacks had to ride in the back of public buses. While the movement was organized locally, it was led by the Reverend Martin Luther King Jr. His success there catapulted him into the position of leader of the national civil rights movement. The Montgomery boycott served as a model for future civil rights action and all other subsequent social movements. It emphasized nonviolent action, made it clear that the black community could overcome internal divisions to become an effective force for change, showed the central role that the black church could play in such a social movement, and demonstrated that the black community was able to finance these actions with little or no outside help.

The success of the Montgomery bus boycott led black organizations to become more involved in civil rights activities. These included the National Association for the Advancement of Colored People (NAACP), formed in 1910, and the Congress of Racial Equality (CORE), organized in 1942. It also led to the formation of new organizations, especially the Southern Christian Leadership Conference (SCLC), and to the creation and active involvement of innumerable local groups. The actions spurred on by these groups and organizations encountered significant opposition from whites, sometimes leading to violence. A key development in 1960 was the large-scale involvement of black college students in sit-ins at segregated lunch counters throughout the South. These students were crucial to the formation of another new organization, the Student Nonviolent Coordinating Committee (SNCC), in 1960. The SNCC, in turn, drew many white students into the movement.

In the 1960s, the civil rights movement became a significant force through boycotts, sit-ins, freedom rides, mass marches, and mass arrests. Both blacks and their white allies participated. In some cases, media coverage of vicious attacks against black activists gave the movement great visibility and elicited much sympathy from those not initially inclined to support it.

Many of the "invisible leaders" of the civil rights movement were black women, such as Fannie Lou Hamer, Septima Poinsette Clark, and Ella Baker. Their invisibility in leadership positions was an unfortunate byproduct of the gender hierarchy as it existed in the 1950s. When women spearheaded successful civil rights campaigns, more "visible" men in the movement took the credit and usurped women's leadership positions (Olson 2002). The many women who participated in the movement served as volunteers, and their numbers far surpassed those of their male counterparts.

ASK YOURSELF

Why are the black women who served as "invisible leaders" of the civil rights movement not more widely known today? Do you think women who are fighting racism today, whatever their color, are sufficiently recognized by the public? Why or why not?

The movement had great success, manifest especially in the Civil Rights Act of 1964, which banned discrimination on the basis not only of race but also of sex, religion, and national identity. Of course, the larger goal of eliminating racism in America eluded the civil rights movement and continues to elude it to this day (Coates 2015; Kiuchi 2016).

The global nature of the civil rights movement is especially clear in the antiapartheid movement led by Nelson Mandela in South Africa. Apartheid was a system of racial separation that had been made legal in 1948. Soon thereafter, a social movement against it emerged, led by the African National Congress. It garnered great international support and succeeded in achieving its goals in less than a half-century (Waldmeir [1997] 2001). By 1994, apartheid in South Africa legally had ended, and victims were offered reparations for their suffering. However, many of the victims of apartheid continue to experience distress from memories of human rights violations under the system (Kesselring 2017).

EMERGENCE, MOBILIZATION, AND IMPACT OF SOCIAL MOVEMENTS

A variety of conditions determine whether or not a social movement will emerge. To start with, there must be grievances, or matters that large numbers of people find troublesome (Snow 2013). However, grievances alone are not sufficient for a social movement to arise. Individuals and organizations must be mobilized in order to do something about them. All of the movements discussed previously were successful in mobilizing people to act.

FACTORS IN THE EMERGENCE OF A SOCIAL MOVEMENT

Assuming a set of grievances and efforts at mobilization, certain other conditions must exist for a social movement to emerge. First, there must be openings or opportunities within the political system. For example, a deep and stubborn recession, high unemployment rates, a massive bailout of banks and large corporations, and a dramatic escalation in the national debt provided an opening for the rise of the Tea Party (Macdonald 2010; Pace 2010). That opening was widened as these and related problems, as well as public concern about them, increased (Crutsinger 2010).

A second factor involves various spatial arrangements, such as the physical proximity of those involved. Clearly, social movements develop more easily when those who at least have the potential to become involved come into contact with one another fairly easily or on a regular basis. Another spatial factor is whether or not there are "free spaces" where those involved can meet. It is in such spaces that a movement can develop, out of the limelight and free of external surveillance and control. Women on college campuses existed in close proximity to one another, and this helped in the formation of the women's movement, while free spaces such as churches were especially important to the development of the civil rights movement.

A third factor is the availability of resources. This is the concern of **resource mobilization theory**, one of the most popular approaches to understanding social movements today (Edwards and Gillham 2013; Jenkins 1983; Tarrow 1994). The focus is on what groups of people need to do in order to mobilize effectively to bring about social change. This theory assumes that there is some strain within the larger society and that there are groups of people who have grievances that result from those strains. One of the most important works in this tradition is that of Jack Goldstone (1991; Rojas and Goodwin 2013) on *revolutions*. These are social movements in which the strains produced by state breakdown (e.g., failure of the government to function properly, fiscal distress) play a key role in the development of revolutionary movements. Major examples include the French, American, and Russian revolutions. Once a strain exists, the issue, then, is what resources are needed for these groups to become social movements, perhaps even successful social movements.

RESOURCES AND MOBILIZATION OF SOCIAL MOVEMENTS

Five types of resources have been identified as important to the mobilization of social movements:

- First are *material resources,* such as money, property, and equipment. It is costly to mount a successful social movement, and money and other material resources are mandatory (Snow, Soule, and Cress 2005).

- Second are *social-organizational resources,* which include infrastructure (internet access is especially important today), social networks (insiders with access to important groups and organizations), and the organizations that are formed by the social movement (Stepan-Norris and Southworth 2007).

- Third are *human resources,* such as the leadership, expertise, skills, and day-to-day labor of those in the organization (Stevenson 2016; Tsutsui and Wotipka 2004).

- Fourth are *moral resources,* such as the degree to which the larger public regards the movement as legitimate (Lowe 2002).

- Finally, *cultural resources* are important—such as bodies of knowledge or skills that are tacitly shared by at least some members of the movement.

Another important issue is the source of such resources. One source is simply having members who themselves are able to produce the resources by, for example, raising money, developing networks, or socializing their children to become part of the movement as adults. Another is aggregating external resources, such as soliciting donations from a wide range of donors. Also of importance is the need to locate patrons who can be relied on to support the group monetarily and in many other ways (e.g., by providing staff members). Finally, a social movement can coopt the resources of other organizations. For example, social movements in the United States have often coopted the resources of churches by, for example, using their buildings, their staff, and their moral authority.

Participation

Once a social movement is underway, methods must be found to ensure member participation. First, people need to be asked to participate. For that to occur, they need to be embedded in social networks involving other movement members. Second, a variety of social psychological factors are involved. These include personally identifying with the movement and its causes, being aroused emotionally by the issues involved and becoming committed to dealing with them, and being at a point in life—retired, unemployed, in college—where one is available to participate in the movement. Third, incentives need to be offered so that the gains to members for their involvement outweigh the risks and costs. For example, for participants in the civil rights movement, the achievement of greater rights for blacks outweighed the risk of being beaten or murdered and the cost of lost time and income. While material incentives are important, of far greater significance are the social incentives associated with joining with others as part of the movement, as well as the moral incentive of being involved in something one believes in strongly (Quadagno and Rohlinger 2009).

Goals, Strategy, and Tactics

Once formed, a social movement needs to have goals, a strategy, and a variety of tactics in order to succeed. *Goals* relate to what the movement seeks to do, such as cut taxes or make society more equal. *Strategy* involves the movement's long-term plan for achieving its goals. Once a strategy is in place, tactics become important. *Tactics* are more short-term in nature. They need to be quite fluid and able to adapt quickly in light of changes taking place in the immediate or larger environment. In the case of the civil rights movement, the strategy was to create situations that brought the plight of black Americans, especially those who lived in the South,

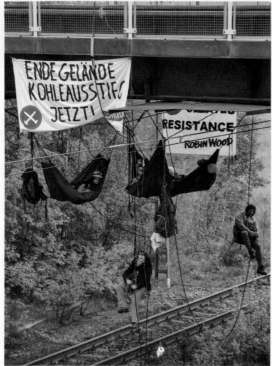

Members of an environmental organization called Robin Wood protested the use of fossil fuels from hammocks hung above railroad tracks leading to a coal-fired power plant in Germany. What other strategies and tactics relating to climate change are you aware of? Which do you think will be successful?

to the attention of the media, the public, and political leaders. Tactics, in this case, involved engaging in *civil disobedience,* or nonviolent public acts that are against the law and aimed at changing the law or government policies (Tescione 2013). For example, blacks attempted to order food at segregated lunch counters. The acts of civil disobedience produced reactions (e.g., white protests, police action) that attracted media and public attention and eventually public outrage. Of particular importance are the actions of countermovements and government officials. For example, the civil rights movement had to adapt to the hostile actions of both white supremacists and many local government officials.

Factors in Success

A variety of factors help determine whether or not a social movement will succeed (Cross and Snow 2012; Rochon 1990). One is its sheer *size.* All social movements start small, but those that succeed are likely to have recruited large numbers of activists and supporters. Another is *novelty,* or the uniqueness of the movement and its goals. Uniqueness and size are important because they lead to a great deal of media attention, which, in turn, is likely to generate additional supporters and funds. The latter are two of the many *resources* social movements need to succeed (see the previous discussion). *Violence* can be useful in achieving results. However, it also can be counterproductive by turning off potential supporters and members. Perhaps more important, it can lead to violent reactions that can end in the suppression of the movement. *Militancy* can also be double-edged, because a highly militant social movement might be able to achieve its goals quickly, but militancy, like violence, can lead to counterreactions and suppression. *Nonviolence* has been a successful method for social movements because it avoids the powerful counterreactions engendered by violent and militant social movements. The nonviolent approach is traceable largely to Mahatma Gandhi and his use of such means as noncooperation with the British-controlled government to gain Indian independence in 1947. Today, a large number of social movements, including the Tea Party and the women's and LGBTQ movements, have adopted a nonviolent approach. More generally, the ability of social movements to network—with individuals involved, as well as with other movements nationally and internationally—is increasingly a key to success (Castells 2015). Part of that, and important in itself, is the ability of the movement and its members to utilize social media (see the discussion that follows) to ramp up and maintain broad support (Molaei 2015)

Although various aspects of social movements themselves strongly affect whether or not they will be successful, many other factors are in play. Of great importance is the ability of individuals, groups, or the state (especially the police, the military, and the state more generally) to suppress a social movement (Davenport 2015; Earl 2007). Efforts at suppressing social movements can be covert, such as the FBI's wiretapping of the phones of members of dissident groups. They can also be overt, a major example being the violent suppression in 1989 of antigovernment protests in Tiananmen Square by the Chinese government and the military.

THE IMPACT OF SOCIAL MOVEMENTS

Whether or not they are successful, social movements often leave their mark, which is sometimes a quite powerful imprint. A government may be able to suppress a social movement, but it is likely that aspects of the government and the way it operates will be affected by the movement as well as by the efforts to suppress it. For example, in the 1940s and 1950s, the U.S. government was able to suppress efforts to increase the influence of communism throughout the country. However, while it was successful in those efforts, it engaged in a variety of highly questionable actions. Major examples include the activities of the House Un-American Activities Committee (HUAC) and especially those of the infamous Senator Joseph McCarthy. McCarthy and his associates often made wild public accusations without presenting any supporting evidence. Long-lasting changes were brought about in the government as a result of the public's revulsion over the reprehensible tactics used by McCarthy and his supporters.

Nevertheless, the government retains the ability to suppress social movements, and in many ways that ability and its extent have increased. This is a result, in part, of the fact that distinctions among activism, terrorism, and extremism are being eroded by government agencies, especially those concerned with law enforcement (Monaghan and Walby 2012). The danger here is that many activist social movements with positive goals and legal methods may end up being suppressed along with terroristic and extremist movements that pose a genuine threat to the United States.

Social movements, especially those that achieve some success, often leave strong legacies for, and have powerful impacts on, later movements. For example, the civil rights movement was an inspiration and a model for many later movements in the United States, such as the student, antiwar, environmental, LGBTQ, and disability movements. Social movements outside the United States—for example, South Africa's antiapartheid movement, the Solidarity movement in Poland, and the democracy movement in China—have also been strongly affected by the civil rights movement.

THE INTERNET, GLOBALIZATION, AND SOCIAL MOVEMENTS

Two of the most important recent developments as far as social movements are concerned relate to globalization and the internet, as well as other new media technologies such as smartphones (Carty 2015; Castells 2015; Molaei 2015).

The internet has proven to be an important means of involving and organizing large numbers of people, perhaps millions of them, who are widely separated from one another, perhaps even in different parts of the world. In other words, people no longer need to be in close physical proximity to be involved in social movements. People can also now communicate more easily through the use of smartphones, even from the sites of events. This communication offers new possibilities for mobilizing those engaged in social movements. It is possible for participants in a movement not only to communicate verbally with others in the movement but also to snap pictures or shoot videos with their smartphones and send them instantaneously via YouTube or Facebook to large numbers of interested parties. This allows people to see for themselves what is transpiring in the social movement. As noted previously, the Islamic State (IS) has been effective in using the internet to recruit supporters, many of whom have trekked to Syria to participate in conflict there and in the region. IS has been particularly successful at using Facebook to attract female adherents from the West (Erlanger 2014). There are also now online activists (e-activists) who are creating electronic social movements (e-movements; Dolata and Schrape 2016). At least some e-movements have the possibility of becoming social movements in the nonvirtual world.

The internet and other technologies enable social movements to cover wide geographic areas and even to become global. Like much else in the world today, social movements are less constrained than ever before by national borders. It seems likely that the future will bring an increasing number of global social movements. We will discuss the internet and globalization further later in this chapter.

COLLECTIVE ACTION

Collective action is generated, or engaged in, by a group of people to encourage or retard social change

A rash of widely publicized violence by white police officers against black males in several states led to many instances of collective action, including this rally in Charlotte, North Carolina, to protest the deaths of Michael Brown, Eric Garner, and others. Have you ever taken part in collective action? If not, what would it take to motivate you to do so?

(Oliver 2013, 210). Social movements are one kind of collective action; others include crowds, riots, and disasters. Like all other forms of collective action, social movements usually occur outside established institutional channels. However, social movements are different from all other forms of collective action in at least two ways. First, most forms of collective action are short-lived compared to social movements. Thus, a crowd, for example, can come together and disperse within hours, but a social movement can be sustained for years or decades. Second, a social movement is intentional; other forms of collective action are not. For instance, a community that comes together immediately after a disaster such as an earthquake or a flood does not do so intentionally. It has been brought together and springs into action because of some unanticipated external event. For example, the 2016 wildfire that destroyed many properties in Gatlinburg and Pigeon Forge, Tennessee, saw collective efforts to raise funds to help those communities recover, including a telethon organized by country music singer Dolly Parton.

While social movements have been theorized separately and somewhat differently, the dominant approach to thinking about other forms of collective action is **emergent norm theory** (Arthur and Lemonik 2013; Turner and Killian 1987). This theory is based on the idea that new norms emerge in light of some precipitating event. These norms guide the often nontraditional actions that characterize collective behavior. Implicit in this theory is the idea that in collective behavior, conventional norms cease to be as effective or as important, at least to some degree. Contrary to popular opinion, however, collective behavior is not irrational, random, or out of control. It is rational and guided by the new norms that develop in the situation.

CROWDS

The clearest application of emergent norm theory to collective action involves the case of a **crowd**, a temporary gathering of a relatively large number of people in a common geographic location at a given time (Borch 2013; McPhail 1991). We are all familiar with all sorts of crowds, such as those that gather at the sites of celebrations or catastrophes, but a relatively new type is the flash crowd (or flash mob). Flash crowds have become

DIGITAL LIVING

Crisis Mapping

The proliferation of information and communication technologies such as mobile phones, social media, and wireless internet access has provided new tools that allow individuals to participate in humanitarian action and disaster response efforts. One of the most popular forms of "digital humanitarianism" is crisis mapping. This involves collecting data from "live" events, such as a natural disaster or political uprising (Givoni 2016; Ziemke 2012). These data may consist of text messages, tweets, or photos posted on Facebook by victims in need of assistance. All of this—and much more—is mapped by volunteers around the world on platforms such as MicroMappers. MicroMappers provides an app called "Clickers" that volunteers— referred to as "digital jedis"—can easily use to organize tweets and photos into designated categories, such as "population displacement" or "infrastructure damage." Other data that might be mapped to help victims and first responders include emergency locations of refugee camps and triage centers.

Crisis mapping also involves creating maps of "unmapped" areas before disasters occur. The Missing Map Project asks "remote volunteers to trace satellite imagery into OpenStreetMap," a collaborative, openly licensed map of the world. Local volunteers on the ground digitally add more detailed data to the map, such as street names. The map is used by humanitarian agencies, principally Doctors without Borders and the American and British Red Cross (http://www.missingmaps.org; Givoni 2016). Crisis mapping proved to be a critical tool in the humanitarian efforts to aid victims of the 2010 Haiti and the 2015 Nepal earthquakes.

Crisis mapping depends not only on digital technologies but also on the social practices of crowdsourcing and crowdlearning (Ziemke 2012, 105). In fact, crisis mappers understand the crowd to be the main actor that makes digital humanitarianism possible. Crowdsourcing is the foundation of crisis mappers. Data are freely shared over the internet by a large number of volunteers as a collaborative form of social action. Thus, the crowd is free from the control of any one organization that might attempt to standardize its behavior, set an agenda on what disasters deserve the most attention, or dictate how to respond to the disaster. During a disaster, the crowd learns "from watching others" (Ziemke 2012, 105–106). One of the most significant lessons that it learns is that the crowd has the power to create maps and empower victims to coordinate response efforts at the local level through the use of social media. However, Givoni (2016, 1039) cautions that because the crowd is "open-ended," it is too "fragile" to challenge the dominance of the global humanitarian organizations that are trying to manage it.

Engaging the Digital World

Visit Google's Crisis Map of weather hazards and emergencies (https://www.google.org/crisismap/weather_and_events), MicroMappers (https://micromappers.wordpress.com), or the Missing Map Project (http://www.missingmaps.org) and write a short report on your findings. How helpful do you think the maps and information provided are to residents, first responders, and agencies trying to collect donations to help victims in a disaster? How likely would you be to volunteer your time and to provide information that could help map a crisis?

---

easier to generate as a result of the internet, e-mail, and social networking sites. A flash crowd might gather, for example, to engage in a pillow fight. In fact, in 2008 a kind of global pillow fight took place, involving participants in two dozen cities around the world. In recent years, largely teenage flash crowds have come together in Philadelphia; they have been disorderly, gotten into fights, and attacked bystanders, and police have cracked down on them in unnecessarily aggressive ways (Massarro and Mullaney 2011).

In the modern age, virtual crowds are becoming the new norm, such as through **crowdfunding** sites (Kickstarter, GoFundMe). People come together online from all across the country, or even the world, to fight for a common cause by offering financial support. Examples of crowdfunding include efforts to fund medical bills or travel fees, to raise money that will buy land to protect the environment, or even to support an author in publishing independent stories. Through crowdfunding, people can choose to support charities, businesses, education, and other endeavors. Together, all kinds of people achieve the same goal and represent the interconnectedness of the world through the internet.

One concern in the literature on crowds is the degree to which individuals behave differently in crowds than they do in other social contexts. Emergent norm theory suggests that they do behave differently, but that is because they are conforming to a different set of norms than what exists elsewhere in the social world. That is more comforting than the alternative view, which sees people in crowds as losing control of their cognitive processes, complying blindly with the suggestions of crowd leaders, copying mindlessly what is done by those around them in the crowd, and acting selfishly. A large body of research has failed to find any support for the latter view (Postmes and Spears 1998; von Sivers et al. 2014).

ASK YOURSELF

Do you behave differently when in a crowd than you do when alone? How, and why? Have you ever participating in crowdfunding? What prompted you to do so?

RIOTS

A **riot** is temporary unruly collective action that causes damage to persons or property. There have been a number of major riots in the last half-century in the United States, including race riots in the 1960s in Los Angeles, Detroit, and Washington, D.C. One notable race riot occurred in Los Angeles in 1992 following the acquittal of four police officers charged with the beating of motorist Rodney King. A more recent, if less violent, riot occurred after the 2014 shooting death of an unarmed black man, Michael Brown, by a white police officer in Ferguson, Missouri. Riots, of course, have happened elsewhere in the world; they are a global phenomenon. For example, significant rioting and extensive looting and arson took place in London and in other cities in England in August 2011. Five people died in the riots (Winlow et al. 2015).

We are likely to have negative views of riots and rioters. However, riots may not be irrational outbursts (Waddington 2015). Rather, they may be motivated by frustrations over various kinds of abuses and the inability to do much about them under normal circumstances (Auyero and Moran 2007). Riots have at times led to various programs designed to deal with the conditions that were seen to be at their source, such as poverty and unemployment. It is hard to generalize about rioters, but there is little support in the research for the idea that rioters are more likely to be criminals, unemployed, or uneducated. A few things seem clear about those who participate in riots. They are more likely to be men, to be young, to have been physically close to where the riots occur, and to feel that their actions can make a difference.

It is worth noting that the mass media can contribute to rioting through the ways in which they treat riots. For one thing, live coverage of riots can inflame them by drawing in additional participants. Live, immediate media reports on rioting are also more likely to be inaccurate and to involve inflammatory reporting. For another thing, media reports of riots can suggest that this is a form of action to be emulated at other places and times. Social media can also quickly draw large numbers of people to riot sites.

DISASTERS

Disasters are events that suddenly, unexpectedly, and severely disrupt and harm the environment, the social structure, people, and their property (Silver 2007). They are distinguished from accidents (e.g., automobile and airplane crashes) by their far greater impact. Many U.S. disasters have resulted in billions of dollars' worth of damage, and the numbers of such huge disasters have increased in recent years (see Figure 15.2). One disaster much in the news in 2010 was the earthquake in Haiti that decimated a significant portion of that Caribbean nation, which shares an island (Hispaniola) with the Dominican Republic. No one knows the exact numbers, but it is estimated

FIGURE 15.2 • Billion-Dollar Weather and Climate Disasters in the United States, 1980–2016

SOURCE: National Oceanic and Atmospheric Administration, National Centers for Environmental Information, "Billion-Dollar Weather and Climate Disasters: Time Series," 1980–2016.

that more than 200,000 people were killed and another 300,000 were injured. Innumerable poorly constructed homes, schools, and other buildings were destroyed. The government virtually ceased functioning as its offices collapsed, literally and figuratively, and many officials were killed or injured (Bhatty 2010). By as late as 2014, little progress had been made in rebuilding homes and the infrastructure in Haiti ("Haiti, Unfinished" 2014; Sontag 2012). While it is a stark example, the earthquake in Haiti represents just one of many natural disasters that have occurred in recent years. Most notable in 2017 were a devastating earthquake in Mexico that killed more than 200 people and Hurricane Maria, which destroyed the electrical grid in Puerto Rico, leaving some residents without power for months.

Human Involvement in Disasters

Disasters such as earthquakes are natural phenomena, but humans often play a role in bringing disasters about and in exacerbating the consequences of natural disasters. People frequently build in areas—for example, on geological fault lines or on floodplains—where there should be no significant

building. Furthermore, what they build is often quite flimsy and likely to be destroyed in a natural disaster. Building stronger structures can be very costly, and impoverished nations such as Haiti simply cannot afford it (Interlandi 2010).

There are, of course, disasters that are the result of human error or corruption. On April 20, 2010, a huge explosion on the BP *Deepwater Horizon* oil rig in the Gulf of Mexico killed 11 workers and left oil gushing into the gulf for three months ("Louisiana Oil Rig" 2010). During that period, 206 million U.S. gallons of oil flowed into the water, affecting nearly 1,000 miles of coastline (Morris et al. 2013). There had been warnings for decades about the dangers associated with deep-sea drilling and oil wells. However, such drilling was pushed forward by the desire for ever-escalating profits on the part of corporations like BP and the voracious need for oil in the United States and other developed nations. Once the *Deepwater Horizon* oil gusher occurred, it became clear that no one quite knew how to go about stopping it; the well was not finally capped until July 15. The spilled oil caused great damage to the gulf's marine life, its beaches, and the businesses that depend on tourists drawn to the area.

Recall from Chapter 5 that the space shuttle *Challenger* disintegrated a little over a minute into its flight on January 28, 1986, killing all seven crew members. To get needed funds and to launch space shuttles in a timely manner, NASA had ignored warnings, taken risks, and tolerated mistakes and deception. Charles Perrow (1999) sees such accidents as "normal." That is, highly complex systems such as those associated with NASA and the space shuttle will inevitably have such disasters, although they happen only rarely.

Human-made disasters also can be political in nature, and they are associated with revolutions, riots, and acts of terrorism. For example, the 9/11 disaster was caused by hijackers crashing planes into the World Trade Center towers and the Pentagon, as well as the downing of one plane before it reached its target. These terrorist attacks resulted in the deaths of nearly 3,000 people.

The Effects of Disasters

Disasters have enormous negative long-term consequences for the people and areas involved. Individuals and collectivities are traumatized for long periods after disasters (Erikson 1976; Fothergill and Peek 2015; see also the Trending box in Chapter 14). People's lives are disrupted for years, if not decades, as are the social networks in which they are enmeshed. Disasters also worsen existing inequalities. For example, females in Haiti suffered disproportionately from the effects of the 2010 earthquake. Furthermore, they were less likely than males to receive humanitarian aid in the aftermath of the quake. Haitian women were more likely than their male counterparts to live in tents, which, among other things, provided them little protection and security. They were especially vulnerable to "unwanted sexual advances and assault" (Jean-Charles 2010). Negative effects on social life persisted for years. Among other things, family life was disrupted. More specifically, there was an increase in the proclivity to commit physical and sexual violence against intimate partners for a year or two beyond the quake (Weitzman and Behrman 2016).

However, some people and groups are in a better position than others to handle disasters. Disasters can also bring people and communities together in unprecedented ways to deal with the aftereffects. The heroism of many of those involved in helping after the 9/11 disaster—firefighters, police officers, and citizens—is one example of this. Within Haiti, a number of aid agencies are working to continue to provide aid to women and girls, including the UN Population Fund, the World Food Programme, and World Vision. Moreover, in response to the increased vulnerability of women and girls, Femmes Citoyennes Haiti Solidaire, or Women Citizens Haiti United, formed an alliance of activists to continue addressing gender inequality and injustices within Haiti.

However, efforts to help sometimes cause great problems. In the case of Haiti, some of the UN peacekeepers who were brought in to help introduced cholera from Nepal. A UN-commissioned contractor dumped the contents of the peacekeepers' septic tanks, teeming with the bacteria that cause cholera, into a river. As a result, by 2016 10,000 Haitians had died from the disease, and thousands more are being infected every month. At first, the UN denied that its peacekeepers were responsible for the outbreak, despite early evidence to the contrary. The UN's denial and failure to act to deal with the crisis led to many more people contracting cholera and to many more deaths from the disease (Piarroux 2016).

SOCIAL CHANGE: GLOBALIZATION, CONSUMPTION, AND THE INTERNET

Social change is intimately connected to the topics discussed in the first part of this chapter. Social movements, especially those that are successful, often lead to major social changes. For example, the women's, LGBTQ, and civil rights movements have all led, and continue to lead, to such social changes. Collective action is less likely to lead to social change, but there have certainly been many examples of crowd behavior, riots, and disasters that have led to change. For example, the Los Angeles race riots of 1992 and the more recent demonstrations in Ferguson, Missouri, led to changes not only in police behavior but also in efforts to deal with the underlying causes of the riots.

Although social change occurs throughout the social world, it is particularly characteristic of the

Graffiti outside the World Social Forum (WSF) in Mumbai seems to reflect the group's stance against the lack of democracy in world economic and political decisions. Although inspired by the conviction that concrete alternatives to free market capitalism must be developed, the group has yet to offer any such options. What alternatives should the WSF offer?

three areas that are the signature concerns of this book—globalization, consumption, and the internet. Globalization is, of course, a social process of relatively recent origin; it is changing the world in which we live and is likely to lead to a variety of even more dramatic changes in the future. For example, the changing nature of the global economy, especially the shift of its center away from the United States and in the direction of China and Asia more generally, means that the job prospects of Americans are changing and apt to change even more in the future. Some economic prospects have declined, especially those that relate to the production of goods and the jobs associated with it. However, others have improved. New jobs have arisen—especially those that involve computers and the internet. Clearly, the internet is important not only in this sense but also because it is an arena in which great and extremely rapid change has taken place in recent years. It is an arena that will certainly continue to change and to affect our lives in innumerable ways.

The changes discussed here—globalization, the economy, and the internet—are related to the changing nature of our other core concern—consumption. Consumption has itself become increasingly global as, for example, more of the things we buy come from outside the United States. The American economy has shifted away from one dominated by production to one dominated by consumption. It is clear that more consumption is taking place through the internet, and that trend can only accelerate in the future.

GLOBALIZATION AS THE ULTIMATE SOCIAL CHANGE

Prior to the current epoch of globalization, one of the things that characterized people, things, information, places, and much else was their greater solidity. That is, all of them tended to (figuratively) harden over time, and therefore, among other things, to remain largely in place. As a result, people did not venture very far from where they were born and raised. Their social relationships were limited to those who were nearby. Much the same could be said of most objects (tools, food), which tended to be used where they were produced. The solidity of most material manifestations of information (stone tablets, books) also made them at least somewhat difficult to move very far. Furthermore, because people didn't move very far, neither did information. Places, too, not only were quite solid and immovable but tended to be surrounded by solid barriers (mountains, oceans, walls, borders) that made it difficult for people and things to exit or to enter.

Global "Liquids"

At an increasing rate over the last few centuries, and especially in the last several decades, that which once seemed so solid has tended to "melt." Instead of thinking of people, objects, information, and places as being like solid blocks of ice, we need to see them as tending to melt and as becoming increasingly liquid (Beilharz 2012). Needless to say, it is far more difficult to move blocks of ice than it is to move the water that is produced when those blocks melt. Of course, to extend the metaphor, there continue to exist blocks of ice, even glaciers, in the contemporary world that have not melted, at least not completely. Solid material realities, such as people, cargo, and newspapers, continue to exist, but because of a wide range of technological developments in transportation, communication, and the internet, they can move across the globe far more readily.

Thus, following the work of Zygmunt Bauman (1925–2017), the perspective on globalization presented here involves increasing liquidity (Bauman 2000, 2003, 2005, 2006; Ritzer and Dean 2015). However, there is a constant interplay between liquidity and solidity, with increases in what is liquid (e.g., terrorist attacks launched against Israel from the West Bank) leading to counterreactions and the erection of new solid forms (e.g., a fence between Israel and the West Bank). However, at the moment and for the foreseeable future, the momentum lies with increasing and proliferating global liquidity.

AP Photo/Heribert Proepper

Zygmunt Bauman first studied sociology while he served in the Polish military and went on to teach at universities in Europe and Israel. Among his notable contributions to the field are his work on the problems associated with the rationalized modern world and the increasing liquidity associated with late modernity and globalization.

Global "Flows"

Closely related to the idea of liquidity, and integral to it, is another key concept in thinking about globalization: the idea of "flows" (Appadurai 1996; Inda 2012). After all, liquids flow easily, far more easily than solids. Because so much of the world has "melted," or is in the process of "melting," globalization is increasingly characterized by great flows of increasingly liquid phenomena of all types, including people, objects, information, decisions, and places. In many cases, the flows have become raging floods that are increasingly less likely to be impeded by place-based barriers of any kind, including the oceans, mountains, and especially the borders of nation-states. This was demonstrated once again in late 2008 in the spread of the American credit and financial crisis to Europe and elsewhere: "In a global financial system, national borders are porous" (Landler 2008, C1).

Looking at a very different kind of flow, as we saw in Chapter 14, many people in many parts of the world believe that they are being swamped by migrants, especially poor undocumented migrants (Moses 2006). This is especially true of concerns in the United States about migrants from Latin America and in Europe about Muslim immigrants (Ahmed 2013). Whether or not these are actually floods, they have come to be seen as such by many people, often aided by politicians and media personalities who have established their reputations by portraying migrants in that way. Places, too, can be said to be flowing around the world, as immigrants re-create the places (and cultures) from which they come in new locales (Logan, Alba, and Zhang 2002; Sarwal 2012).

Ideas, images, and information, both legal (blogs) and illegal (child pornography), flow everywhere, undoubtedly because of their immateriality. They do so through interpersonal contact and the media, especially now via the internet. Much of what would have been considered the height of global liquidity only a few years ago now seems increasingly sludgelike. This is especially the case when we focus on the impact of the computer and the internet on the global flow of all sorts of things. For example, instead of scouring an import VHS catalog and waiting weeks for an anime movie to ship from Japan, a person can simply open the Netflix app on her console and stream any number of anime movies instantly.

GLOBALIZATION AND THE INTERNET

Since its birth in the 1990s, the internet has profoundly affected almost every aspect of life, especially in the developed world. The internet has expedited the globalization of many different things and is itself a profound form and aspect of globalization. The internet is global in several senses, but the most important is that while its users are not equally divided between North and South, rich and poor, and so on, they *do* exist virtually everywhere in the world (Drori 2006; Pick and Sarkar 2015). It is also global in the sense that it was produced and is maintained by a number of global and transnational corporations and organizations, including multinational corporations (e.g., Intel), intergovernmental organizations, and international nongovernmental organizations. For instance, the World Intellectual Property Organization regulates intellectual property rights, the Internet Corporation for Assigned Names and Numbers coordinates domain names, and the UN Educational, Scientific, and Cultural Organization promotes computer and internet use in schools throughout the world.

Computer Viruses

The first global computer virus was likely created in Pakistan in 1986. Since then, of course, many different viruses—some benign, some malicious (malware)—have been created, have circled the globe, and in some cases have caused great damage to computer systems. For example, some of these viruses "infect" personal computers and access users' information, such as credit card numbers, which the cyberthieves then use to purchase all sorts of goods and services illegally. In May 2017, hackers used "ransomware" stolen from the National Security Agency to engage in a global cyberattack. Transmitted via e-mail, the virus froze victims' computers. Victims were forced to pay the hackers a ransom in order to get their computers unfrozen (Perlroth and Sanger 2017). Global organizations, including law enforcement agencies, have emerged to try to warn people about new viruses and malware—so-called *Trojans* and *worms*—and to develop countermeasures to protect against them (Chanda 2007). To the degree that they are successful, the latter are barriers to the largely free flow of computer viruses around the globe.

Cyberactivism

For those who do have internet access, the opportunity to connect with like-minded individuals across the country and around the world has contributed to the rise of **cyberactivism**, or using social media and other internet-based communication methods to create, promote, or manage activism. Recent examples of cyberactivism include the ALS (Amyotropic Lateral Sclerosis) Ice Bucket Challenge, which raised several million dollars to increase awareness about that disease; Greenpeace's Greenwire, which digitally connects volunteers with environmental campaigns; and the Women's March on Washington, which was organized online and generated global demonstrations involving millions of women and men.

While cyberactivism has taken some dramatic new directions, it came of age with the creation of the World Social Forum (WSF), formed in 2001. A key concern of the WSF is the lack of democracy in global economic and political affairs. The WSF is a huge social network, and it is based on the "cultural logic of networking." Such networking includes the creation of diverse connections, free and open communication, decentralized coordination, and democratic decision making (Juris 2005). The internet has given the WSF a powerful series of tools with which to mount its opposition on a regional and even a global basis. Those tools include social media such as Facebook, Twitter, and You Tube, as well as the smartphones that link activists to those sites anytime and virtually anywhere.

WikiLeaks is one of the most notable and controversial examples of cyberactivism. A global audience for its release of private documents has developed. The release of such documents often exposes behavior and planning hidden from the public. While WikiLeaks' home was at least originally in Sweden, it is now hosted by a number of servers around the world. In 2010, WikiLeaks began releasing classified diplomatic cables between Washington and many of its consulates around the world. Later that year, documents were released—some classified as confidential or secret—relating to the Afghan and Iraq wars. The documents implicated numerous officials around the world in questionable, if not illegal, acts. Many lost their positions or suffered other adverse consequences as a result of the documents' release.

CONSUMPTION AND GLOBALIZATION

There has been a tendency to associate consumption with America and, as far as the globe is concerned, with Americanization. This is largely traceable to the affluence of the United States after the close of World War II and the economic difficulties encountered by most other societies in the world during that period. Thus, the United States developed an unprecedented and unmatched consumer society for several decades after the end of the war. At the same time, it began exporting consumer society—and its various elements—to much of the rest of the world. Much of American consumer society came to be adopted elsewhere in the world.

Stillerman (2015) argues that the major areas for the expansion of consumer society are not in the Global North, but in the less developed Global South. While much about consumption there is the same or similar, there are also distinctive patterns of consuming an array of unique products and services. Beyond its sources in the United States and the Global North, consumption has roots in many other places in the world. Consumption as a central life interest is now a truly global phenomenon; we have increasingly become "a world of consumers" (Trentmann 2016)

The latter point brings us to the issue of globalization and consumption (Brandle and Ryan 2012; Chen and Ritzer 2015). The emphasis in the global economy is on greatly increasing flows of everything related to consumption and greatly decreasing any barriers to those flows. Especially important is expediting global flows of consumer goods and services of all types and of the financial processes and instruments that facilitate those flows. Thus, for example, the relatively small number of credit (and debit) card brands with origins in the United States, especially Visa and MasterCard, are increasingly accepted and used at ATMs and at checkout counters at various businesses throughout the world (Ritzer 1995). Especially notable in this regard are online consumption sites, some of them global in reach, that allow people to consume many of the same products using their credit cards. Credit cards serve to expedite not only global consumption but also the flow of global consumers, including tourists.

Local and Regional Differences

There was, and continues to be, a significant American component to the globalization of consumption. However, it is important to recognize that the heyday of the United States in this area is long past. In any case, there has always been much more to the globalization of consumption than Americanization (Brewer and Trentmann 2006). That is, local areas have certainly not always, or perhaps ever, been overwhelmed by American imports, but have integrated them into local cultural and economic realities. Furthermore, other nations and regions have been significant exporters of important aspects of consumer society, such as Mercedes-Benz and BMW automobiles from Germany. Finally, much of consumption remains largely, if not totally, local in character. One example is the growing consumption of a mild stimulant, khat, or *qat,* in Kenya, where it is defined in a highly positive way locally. In addition, there is active resistance to external definitions of it, especially the U.S. definition of khat as a dangerous drug (Anderson and Carrier 2006).

Consumption also plays itself out differently in different parts of the world. For example, both the United States and Japan can be seen as consumer societies, but Japanese consumers differ from their U.S. counterparts in many ways. The Japanese have never fully embraced the idea of a consumer society. More specifically, unlike Americans, the Japanese continue to manage to save significant amounts of money (Garon 2006).

While many consumer objects and services remain highly local (e.g., the khat mentioned previously, the services of street-based letter writers for illiterate Indians), an increasing number have been globalized. On the one hand are the global objects, such as automobiles from the United States, Germany, and Japan. On the other hand are global services, such as those offered by accounting firms like KPMG International, as well as package delivery services like DHL.

Global Brands

A **brand** is a symbol that serves to identify and differentiate one product or service from the others. A brand can be contrasted with, and seeks to contrast itself to, generic commodities such as flour and soap (Holt 2004; Schroeder 2015). The process of branding a product or service is undertaken because, if successful, not only is the brand distinguished from the basic commodity; more of it can also be sold and at a higher price. We are all familiar with the most successful brands in the world (Apple, Coca-Cola, McDonald's, Walmart, Mercedes, and so on), and much consumption is oriented toward the purchase of brand-name products and services. Furthermore, even people come to be brand names (Michael Jordan, Angelina Jolie) and as such are "consumed"

globally to a large degree. As brands themselves, they come to be closely associated with various brand-name products, the best-known example being the association of Michael Jordan with Nike and Hanes (Andrews and Mower 2012).

Nike is one of those brands that has made itself so important that it can be said to have created a culture, and, to some degree, we live in Nike culture (Goldman and Papson 1998; Hollister 2008). However, that culture is but a part of the larger *brand culture* in which we live. That is, brands are a key part of the larger culture: They infuse it with meaning, and contemporary society as a whole is profoundly affected by brands.

Brands are of great importance not only within the United States and many other nations but also globally. Indeed, much money and effort is invested in creating brand names that are recognized and trusted throughout the world. Klein ([2000] 2010) details the importance of brands in the contemporary world and the degree to which they are globalized—corporate logos are virtually an international language—and have global impacts.

SUMMARY

Social change creates variations over time in every aspect of the social world. Social movements are sustained and intentional collective efforts, usually operating outside established institutional channels, either to bring about social change or to prevent it. Prominent social movements include the Tea Party, feminist movements, the LGBTQ movement, and the civil rights movement.

The emergence of a social movement requires a set of grievances, efforts at mobilization, opportunities within the political system, the proximity of people, the availability of free space to meet, and the availability of resources. Factors that affect the success of a social movement include its size and uniqueness as well as other groups' ability to suppress the movement. When successful, a social movement can leave a lasting legacy.

Unlike social movements, some collective action is short-lived and spontaneous. For example, crowds are temporary gatherings of a large number of people in a common geographic location. Riots, responses to disasters, and cyberactivism are other types of collective action that lack the organizational structure, resources, and leadership of social movements.

Globalization is arguably the most important change in human history and is characterized by great flows of liquid phenomena across the globe. The internet is both a form and an aspect of globalization and has expedited globalization. The global economy focuses on increasing the flows of everything related to consumption and reducing the barriers to these flows.

brand, 433

collective action, 423

crowd, 424

crowdfunding, 426

cyberactivism, 431

disasters, 426

emergent norm
  theory, 424

feminism, 412

resource mobilization
  theory, 420

riot, 426

social change, 408

social movement, 409

REVIEW QUESTIONS

1. What about the Tea Party makes it a social movement? What were the conditions that brought about the emergence of the Tea Party movement?

2. What have been the three different waves of the women's movement? How did the goals and strategies of the women's movement change during each of these three waves?

3. How have new communication technologies such as the internet and social networking sites (e.g., Facebook and Twitter) aided global social movements? What types of resources move more easily because of these new technologies?

4. According to resource mobilization theory, what do groups of people need in order to mobilize effectively? How can we apply this theory to the discussion of the civil rights movement in this chapter?

5. What mechanisms do social movements use to ensure member participation? How are these mechanisms related to the LGBTQ movements discussed in this chapter?

6. What factors are used to determine whether a social movement is successful? How has the Tea Party movement been successful to date? Has there been any resistance to the movement? What has given it renewed impetus? How might these things affect the movement's future success?

7. According to emergent norm theory, why are individuals likely to behave differently when they are in crowds? How can we explain some deviant behavior in bars (such as fighting or public displays of affection) using emergent norm theory?

8. The 2011 earthquake and tsunami in Japan and the 2015 earthquake in Nepal are examples of disasters. In what ways did humans exacerbate the consequences of these natural disasters? What sorts of negative long-term consequences can be expected from disasters like these?

9. In what ways is globalization the "ultimate social change"? How has the world become more liquid because of globalization? What role have new communication technologies played in making the world more liquid?

10. Why is branding an important process to transnational corporations? In what ways is branding reflective of the process of Americanization?

$SAGE edge™ **Want a better grade?**

Get the tools you need to sharpen your study skills. Access practice quizzes, eFlashcards, video, and multimedia at **edge.sagepub.com/ritzeressentials3e**.

GLOSSARY

absolute poverty: An absolute measure—such as the U.S. poverty line—that makes it clear what level of income people need in order to survive.

achieved status: A position acquired by people on the basis of what they accomplish or the nature of their capacities.

achievement: The accomplishments, or the merit, of the individual.

agency: The potential to disrupt or destroy the structures in which one finds oneself.

agents of socialization: Those who socialize others.

alienation: In a capitalist system, being unconnected to one's work, products, fellow workers, and human nature.

Americanization: The importation by other countries of products, images, technologies, practices, norms, values, and behaviors that are closely associated with the United States.

anomie: The feeling of not knowing what is expected of oneself in society or of being adrift in society without any clear, secure moorings.

anti-Americanism: An aversion to the United States in general, as well as to the influence of its culture abroad.

anticipatory socialization: The teaching (and learning) of what will be expected of one in the future.

ascribed status: A position in which individuals are placed, or to which they move, that has nothing to do with what they have done or their capacities or accomplishments.

ascription: Being born with or inheriting certain characteristics (wealth, high status, and so on).

assimilation: The integration of minorities into the dominant culture.

asylum seekers: People who flee their home country, usually in an effort to escape political oppression or religious persecution.

authority: A particular type of domination: legitimate domination.

back stage: The part of the social world where people feel free to express themselves in ways that are suppressed in the front stage.

beliefs: Ideas that explain the world and identify what should be sacred or held in awe—that is, a religion's ultimate concerns.

birthrate: The number of births per 1,000 people per year.

blended family: A family that includes some combination of children from the partners' previous marriages or relationships, along with one or more children of the currently married or cohabiting couple.

bounded rationality: Rationality limited by, among other things, instabilities and conflicts within most, if not all, organizations, as well as by the limited human capacity to think and act in a rational manner.

brand: A symbol that serves to identify and differentiate one product or service from others.

bureaucracy: A highly rational organization, especially one that is highly efficient.

bureaucratic personality: A type of bureaucrat who slavishly follows the rules of the organization, to such an extent that the ability to achieve organizational goals is subverted.

butterfly effect: The far-ranging or even global impact of a small change in a specific location, over both time and distance.

capitalism: In Marx's view, an economic system based on one group of people (the capitalists, or owners) owning what is needed for production and a second group (the proletariat, or workers) owning little but their capacity for work.

capitalists: Those who own what is needed for production—factories, machines, tools—in a capitalist system.

cathedrals of consumption: Large and lavish consumption sites, created mostly in the United States in the last half of the twentieth century and into the early twenty-first century.

cenogamy: Group marriage.

charismatic authority: Authority based on the devotion of the followers to what they define as the exceptional characteristics, such as heroism, of the leaders.

church: A large group of religiously oriented people into which members are usually born (rather than joining consciously and voluntarily).

cities: Large, permanent, and spatially concentrated human settlements.

citizens: The people represented by a given state, most often born within its territories.

citizenship: The idea that people of a given state can vote for their representatives within the state, but also that they have access to rights and responsibilities as citizens.

civil religion: The beliefs, practices, and symbols that a nation holds sacred.

class consciousness: According to Marx, a mental state in which the workers (proletariat) come to truly understand capitalism, their collective role in it, and their relationship to one another, as well as to the capitalists.

cohabitation: An arrangement in which a couple share a home and a bed without being legally married.

collective action: Action generated, or engaged in, by a group of people to encourage or retard social change.

collective conscience: The set of beliefs shared by people throughout society.

communism: A historical stage following socialism involving the effort by society to plan and organize production consciously and rationally, so that all members of society benefit from it.

companionate love: A kind of love typified by gradual onset and not necessarily tied to sexual passion, but based on more rational assessments of the one who is loved.

companionate marriage: A marriage emphasizing a clear division of labor between a breadwinner and a homemaker and held together by sentiment, friendship, and sexuality; the predominant model of marriage in the mid-twentieth century. *See also* companionate love.

competitive capitalism: A form of capitalism where there are a large number of relatively small firms, with the result that no one or small subset of them can completely dominate and control a given area of the economy.

conflict theory: A theory that sees society as held together by coercion and focuses on its negative aspects.

conformists: People who accept both cultural goals and the traditional means of achieving those goals.

consensual sexual activities: Sexual activities agreed upon by the participants, any of whom have the right to decide to stop at any point and for any reason.

conspicuous consumption: The public demonstration of wealth through consumption.

constructionist theories: Theories of deviance that seek a greater understanding of the process by which people define and classify some behaviors as normal and others as deviant.

consumer crimes: Crimes related to consumption, including shoplifting and using stolen credit cards or credit card numbers.

consumer culture: A culture in which the core ideas and material objects relate to consumption and in which consumption is a primary source of meaning in life.

consumerism: An obsession with consumption.

consumption: The process by which people obtain and utilize goods and services.

content analysis: Systematic and objective analysis of the content of cultural artifacts in print, visual, audio, and digital media, using both qualitative and quantitative analysis.

convenience samples: Readily available groups of people who fit the criteria for participating in a research project.

conversation analysis: The analysis of how people accomplish conversations.

corporate crime: Violation of the law by legal organizations, including antitrust violations and stock market violations.

cosmopolitan: Open to a variety of external and global influences.

counterculture: A group whose culture not only differs in certain ways from the dominant culture but also adheres to norms and values that may be incompatible with those of the dominant culture.

crime: Deviance that is a violation of the criminal law.

criminalization: The process by which the legal system negatively sanctions some form of deviant behavior.

criminology: The study of all aspects of crime.

critical theories of race and racism: A set of ideas arguing that race continues to matter and that racism continues to exist and adversely affect blacks.

critical theory: A set of critical ideas derived from Marxian theory but focusing on culture rather than the economy.

crowd: A temporary gathering of a relatively large number of people in a common geographic location at a given time.

crowdfunding: Collective action in which people come together online from all across the country, or even the world, to financially support a common cause.

cult: A new, innovative, small, voluntary, and exclusive religious tradition that was never associated with any religious organization.

cultural imperialism: The imposition of one culture, more or less consciously, on other cultures.

cultural relativism: The idea that aspects of culture such as norms and values need to be understood within the context of a person's own culture and that there are no universally accepted norms and values.

culture: A collection of ideas, values, practices, and material objects that mean a great deal to a group of people, even an entire society, and that allow them to carry out their collective lives in relative order and harmony.

culture industry: The rationalized and bureaucratized structures that control modern culture.

culture jamming: The radical transformation of an intended message in popular culture, especially one associated with the mass media, to protest underlying realities of which consumers may be unaware.

culture war: A conflict that pits subcultures and countercultures against the dominant culture or that pits dominant groups within society against each other.

cumulative advantage: The process by which the most advantaged individuals are awarded the best opportunities, which increases inequality over time.

cyberactivism: Using social media and other internet-based communication methods to create, promote, or manage activism.

cybercrime: Crime that targets computers, uses computers to commit traditional crimes, or uses computers to transmit illegal information and images.

cyberculture: An emerging online culture that has the characteristics of all culture, including distinctive values and norms.

dangerous giants: Agents who threaten social structures.

death rate: The number of deaths per 1,000 people.

deindustrialization: The decline of manufacturing as well as a corresponding increase in various types of services.

deinstitutionalization: Weakened social norms, especially with regard to the institution of marriage.

democracy: A political system in which people within a given state vote to choose their leaders and in some cases vote on legislation.

demographers: Those who study population dynamics.

demographic transition: Population changes that are related to the shift from an agricultural society to a more industrialized and urbanized society.

demography: The scientific study of population, especially its growth and decline, as well as the movement of people.

denomination: A religious group not linked to the state that exhibits a general spirit of tolerance and acceptance of other religious bodies.

dependent variable: A characteristic or measurement that is the result of manipulating an independent variable.

deprofessionalization: The process whereby a profession's power and autonomy, as well as high status and great wealth, have declined, at least relative to the exalted position the profession once held.

descriptive statistics: Numerical data that allow researchers to see trends over time or compare differences between groups in order to describe some findings based on a phenomenon in the real world.

descriptive survey: A questionnaire or interview used to gather accurate information about those in a group, people in a given geographic area, or members of organizations.

desertification: A decline in the water supply as a result of the degradation and deterioration of soil and vegetation.

deviance: Any action, belief, or human characteristic that a large number of people who are members of a society or a social group consider to be a violation of group norms and for which the violator is likely to be censured or punished.

diaspora: The dispersal, typically involuntary, of a racial or ethnic population from its traditional homeland and over a wide geographic area.

dictatorships: States that are usually totalitarian and are ruled either by a single individual or by a small group of people.

differential association: A theory that focuses on the fact that people learn criminal behavior; therefore, what is crucial is whom a person associates with.

disasters: Events that suddenly, unexpectedly, and severely disrupt and harm the environment, the social structure, people, and their property.

discouraged workers: Those who have sought work within the last year or since their last job ended, if that was less than a year ago, and have not sought work in the last four weeks (and are therefore not in the labor force).

discreditable stigma: A stigma that the affected individual assumes is neither known about nor immediately perceivable.

discredited stigma: A stigma that the affected individual assumes is already known about or readily apparent.

discrimination: The unfavorable treatment of black Americans and other minorities, either formally or informally, simply because of their race or some other such characteristic.

distinction: The need to distinguish oneself from others.

domestic violence: The exertion of power over a partner in an intimate relationship through behavior that is intimidating, threatening, harassing, or harmful.

domination: The probability or likelihood that commands will be obeyed by subordinates.

double consciousness: Among black Americans, the sense of "two-ness," that is, of being both black and American.

dramaturgy: The view that social life is a series of dramatic performances akin to those that take place in a theater and on a stage.

dyad: A two-person group.

dysfunctions: Observable consequences that negatively affect the ability of a given system to survive, adapt, or adjust.

economy: The social system involved in the production and distribution of a wide range of goods and services.

elite pluralism: The formation by political elites of similar interest groups and organizations that vie for power.

emergent norm theory: A theory arguing that, in light of some precipitating event, new norms emerge that guide the often nontraditional actions that characterize collective behavior.

emphasized femininity: A set of socially constructed ideas about "model womanhood" organized around accommodating the interests of men and patriarchy.

empiricism: The gathering of information and evidence using one's senses, especially one's eyes and ears, to experience the social world.

endogamy: Marriage to someone with similar characteristics in terms of race, ethnicity, religion, education level, social class, and so on.

ethics: A set of beliefs concerning right and wrong in the choices that people make and the ways in which those choices are justified.

ethnic cleansing: The establishment by the dominant group of policies that allow or require the forcible removal of people of another ethnic group.

ethnic group: A group typically defined on the basis of some cultural characteristic such as language, religion, traditions, and cultural practices.

ethnicity: A sense, shared by members of the group, of belonging to and identifying with a given ethnic group.

ethnocentrism: The belief that one's own group or culture—including its norms, values, customs, and so on—is superior to, or better than, others.

ethnography: Observational (sometimes participatory) research, usually intensive and conducted over lengthy periods, that leads to an account of what people do and how they live.

ethnomethodology: An inter/actionist theory focusing on what people do rather than on what they think.

ethnoscapes: Landscapes that allow the movement, or fantasies about movement, of various individuals and groups.

exchange relationships: Stable and persistent bonds between individuals who interact, generally formed because their interactions are rewarding.

exchange theory: A set of ideas related to the rewards and costs associated with human behavior.

exogamy: Marriage to someone with characteristics that are dissimilar in terms of race, ethnicity, religion, education level, social class, and so on.

experiment: The manipulation of a characteristic under study (an independent variable) to examine its effect on another characteristic (the dependent variable).

explanatory survey: A questionnaire or interview used to uncover potential causes for some observation.

explanatory theories: Theories of deviance (or some other social phenomenon) that try to explain why it occurs.

exploitation: A feature of capitalism in which the workers (proletariat) produce virtually everything but get few rewards, while the capitalists, who do little, reap the vast majority of the rewards.

expulsion: Removal of a minority group from a territory, either by forcible ejection through military and other government action or by "voluntary" emigration due to the majority's harassment, discrimination, and persecution.

extended family: Two or more generations of a family living in the same household or in close proximity to one another.

exurbia: Outlying areas between the suburbs and rural areas.

false consciousness: In capitalism, the proletariat's lack of understanding of capitalism's nature and the erroneous belief that capitalism operates to workers' benefit.

family: A group of people related by descent, marriage, or adoption.

fantasy city: A city in which great emphasis is placed on creating a spectacle, especially in the areas of consumption, leisure, tourism, and impressive buildings and other real estate developments.

felonies: Serious crimes punishable by a year or more in prison.

female proletarianization: The channeling of an increasing number of women into low-status, poorly paid manual work.

feminism: The belief that women are equal to men, especially socially, politically, and economically.

feminist theory: A set of ideas critical of the social situation confronting women and offering solutions for improving, if not revolutionizing, their situation.

feminization of labor: The rise of female labor participation in all sectors and the movement of women into jobs traditionally held by men.

feminization of poverty: The rise in the number of women falling below the poverty line.

fertility: People's reproductive behavior, especially the number of births.

field experiments: Research that occurs in natural situations but allows researchers to exert at least some control over who participates and what happens during the experiment.

financescapes: Landscapes that use various financial instruments to allow huge sums of money and other things of economic value to move into and across nations and around the world at great speed, almost instantaneously.

folkways: Norms that are relatively unimportant and, if violated, carry few if any sanctions.

food insecurity: Lack of sufficient access to safe and nutritious food.

Fordism: The ideas, principles, and systems created by Henry Ford (who is credited with the development of the modern mass production system) and his associates at the beginning of the twentieth century.

foreign aid: Economic assistance given by countries or global institutions to a foreign country in order to promote its development and social welfare.

front stage: The part of the social world where the social performance is idealized and designed to define the situation for those who observe it.

functions: Observable, positive consequences that help a system survive, adapt, or adjust.

fundamentalism: A strongly held belief in the fundamental or foundational precepts of any religion, or a rejection of the modern secular world.

game stage: Mead's second stage in the socialization process, in which a child develops a self in the full sense of the term, because it is then that the child begins to take on the role of a group of people simultaneously rather than the roles of discrete individuals.

gated communities: Communities in which gates, surveillance cameras, and guards provide the residents with a feeling of security from the problems (e.g., crime, panhandling) that they think they left behind in the city.

gemeinschaft societies: Traditional societies characterized by face-to-face relations.

gender: The physical, behavioral, and personality characteristics that are socially defined as appropriate for one's sex.

gender identity: A person's internal sense of gender.

genderqueer: A term used to refer to gender identities that are not exclusively male or female.

gender roles: The social presentation of gender that includes clothing, hairstyle, and attitudinal and behavioral traits.

gender-swapping: An individual's representation of himself or herself online as a gender that is different from his or her offline gender; also called gender-switching.

general deterrence: The deterrence of the population as a whole from committing crimes, for fear that they will be punished or imprisoned for their actions.

generalized other: The attitude of the entire group or community taken by individuals in the process of developing their own behaviors and attitudes.

genocide: An active, systematic attempt to eliminate an entire group of people.

gentrification: The reinvestment of real estate capital in blighted inner-city areas in order to rebuild residences and create a new infrastructure for the well-to-do.

geopolitics: Political relationships that involve large geographic areas or the globe as a whole.

gesellschaft societies: Modern societies characterized by impersonal, distant, and limited social relationships.

gestures: Movements of one animal or human that elicit a mindless, automatic, and appropriate response from another animal or human.

global care chains: Series of personal relationships between people across the globe based on the paid or unpaid work of caring.

global cities: The cities, especially New York City, London, and Tokyo, with the world's leading industries and marketplaces.

global ethnography: A type of ethnography that is "grounded" in various parts of the world and that seeks to understand globalization as it exists in people's social lives.

globalization: The increasing fluidity of global flows and the structures that expedite and impede those flows.

group: A relatively small number of people who over time develop a patterned relationship based on interaction with one another.

group pluralism: The competition of society's various interest groups and organizations for access to political power in an attempt to further their interests.

habitus: An internalized set of preferences and dispositions that are learned through experience and social interactions in specific social contexts.

hate crimes: Crimes that stem from the fact that the victims are in various ways different from, and disesteemed by, the perpetrators.

hegemonic masculinity: The dominant form or most idealized vision of masculinity; taken for granted as natural and linked to patriarchy.

hegemony: The subordination of one race (or other group) by another, more on the basis of dominant ideas, especially about cultural differences, than through material constraints.

heterosexism: The belief that heterosexuality is superior to other sexual orientations; individual and institutional discrimination against those with other orientations.

heterosexual double standard: A cultural belief system in which men are expected to desire and seek sex from whomever, whenever, while women are expected to be sexual only within committed, romantic relationships.

hidden curriculum: A school's unofficial norms, routines, and structures that transmit dominant cultural norms and values.

high-income economies: Economies in countries with the highest wealth and income in the world, defined by the World Bank in 2014 as having a gross national income per capita of at least $12,746.

historical-comparative research: A research methodology that contrasts how different historical events and conditions in various societies (or components of societies) lead to different societal outcomes.

homophobia: The fear of being, appearing, or seeming gay; fear of anyone or "anything" gay.

horizontal mobility: Movement within one's social class.

hyperconsumption: Consumption of more than one needs, really wants, and can afford.

hyperdebt: Borrowing more than one should, thereby owing more than one will be able to pay back.

hypodescent rule: A law or judicial ruling that classified persons with even one nonwhite ancestor, or a nonwhite ancestor within a certain number of generations, as black or colored.

"I": The immediate response of an individual to others; the part of the self that is incalculable, unpredictable, and creative.

ideal culture: Norms and values indicating what members of a society should believe in and do.

ideal type: An exaggeratedly rational model that is used to study real-world phenomena.

identity politics: The use of a minority group's power to strengthen the position of the cultural group with which it identifies.

ideology: A set of shared beliefs that explains the social world and guides people's actions.

ideoscapes: Landscapes that include images, largely political images, often in line with the ideologies of nation-states.

imagined communities: Communities that are socially constructed by those who see themselves as part of them.

impression management: People's use of a variety of techniques to control the images of themselves that they want to project during their social performances.

income: The amount of money a person earns in a given year from a job, a business, or various types of assets and investments.

independent variable: In an experiment, a condition that can be independently manipulated by the researcher with the goal of producing a change in some other variable.

individualized marriage: A model of marriage emphasizing the satisfaction of the individuals involved.

inequality: The condition whereby some positions in society yield a great deal of money, status, and power, while others yield little, if any, of these.

inferential statistics: Numerical data that allow researchers to use data from a small group to speculate with some level of certainty about a larger group.

informal organization: How an organization actually works, as opposed to the way it is supposed to work.

informationalism: The processing of knowledge.

informed (effective) sexual consent: Participants' understanding of and free consent to specific sexual activities in a mutually understandable way.

in-group: A group to which people belong and with which they identify, perhaps strongly.

innovators: Individuals who accept cultural goals but reject conventional means of achieving success.

institutional marriage: The predominant model of marriage in the early twentieth century, which emphasizes maintenance of the institution of marriage itself.

institutional racism: Race-based discrimination that results from the day-to-day operation of social institutions and social structures and their rules, policies, and practices.

interaction: A social engagement that involves two or more individuals who perceive, and orient their actions to, one another.

interaction order: An area of interaction that is organized and orderly, but in which the order is created informally by those involved in the interaction rather than by some formal structure.

intergenerational mobility: The difference between the parents' social class position and the position achieved by their child(ren).

intersectionality: The confluence, or intersection, of various social statuses and the inequality and oppression associated with each in combination with others; the idea that members of any given minority group are affected by the nature of their position in other systems or other forms of social inequality.

intersex: A general term used for a variety of (medical) conditions in which a person is born with reproductive or sexual anatomy that does not seem to fit the typical definitions of male or female.

interviews: A research method in which information is sought from participants (respondents) who are asked a series of questions that have been spelled out, at least to some degree, before the research is conducted.

intimate relationship: A close, personal, and domestic relationship between partners.

intragenerational mobility: Movement up or down the stratification system in one's lifetime.

labeling theory: Theory contending that a deviant is someone to whom a deviant label has been successfully applied.

laboratory experiments: Research that occurs in a laboratory, giving the researcher great control over both the selection of the participants to be studied and the conditions to which they are exposed.

labor migrants: Those who migrate because they are driven by either "push" factors (e.g., a lack of work, low pay) in their homeland or "pull" factors (e.g., jobs and higher pay available elsewhere).

landscapes (scapes): Fluid, irregular, and variable global flows that produce different results throughout the world.

language: A set of meaningful symbols that makes possible the communication of culture as well as communication more generally within a given culture, and that calls out the same meaning in the person to whom an utterance is aimed as it does to the person making the utterance.

latent functions: Unintended positive consequences.

laws: Norms that have been codified, or written down, and are formally enforced through institutions such as the state.

leisure: A means of escape from the obligations associated with work and family, involving social activities that are uncoerced, relaxing, and perhaps informative and that are set apart in time and often in space.

life expectancy: The number of years an individual can be expected to live.

liminal period: A special time set apart from ordinary reality.

living wage: An income that is high enough to meet the most basic family expenses.

local: Inward looking rather than outward looking.

looking-glass self: The self-image that reflects how others respond to a person, particularly as a child.

low-income economies: Economies in countries with the lowest levels of income in the world, defined by the World Bank as a gross national income per capita below $1,046.

macro: Macroscopic; used to describe large-scale social phenomena, such as groups, organizations, cultures, society, and the globe.

macrofinance: The globalization of money and finance.

majority group: A group in a dominant position along the dimensions of wealth, power, and prestige.

majority-minority population: A population in which more than 50 percent of the members are part of a minority group.

manifest functions: Positive consequences that are brought about consciously and purposely.

marriage: The socially acknowledged and approved and often legal union of two people, allowing them to live together and to have children by birth or adoption.

mass culture: Cultural elements that are administered by large organizations, lack spontaneity, and are phony.

mass production: Production characterized by large numbers of standardized products, highly specialized workers, interchangeable machine parts, precision tools, a high-volume mechanized production process, and

the synchronization of the flow of materials used in production, with the entire process made as continuous as possible.

master status: A position that is more important than any others, both for the person in the position and for all others involved.

material culture: All the material objects that are reflections or manifestations of a culture.

McDonaldization: The process by which the rational principles of the fast-food restaurant are coming to dominate more and more sectors of society and more societies throughout the world.

"me": The organized set of others' attitudes assumed by the individual; involves the adoption by the individual of the generalized other.

mechanical solidarity: Cohesion among a group of people based on the fact that they all do essentially the same things.

mediascapes: Landscapes that include the electronic capability to produce and transmit information and images around the world.

mediated interaction: Social interaction in which technological devices come between the participants, unlike in face-to-face interaction.

medicalization: The process of labeling and defining as medical problems aspects of life that were not previously so labeled and defined.

medical sociology: A field concerned with the social causes and consequences of health and illness.

megacities: Cities with populations greater than 10 million.

megalopolis: A cluster of highly populated cities that can stretch over great distances.

meritocracy: A system based on a dominant ideology involving the widely shared belief that all people have an equal chance of succeeding economically based on their hard work and skills.

metropolis: A large, powerful, and culturally influential urban area that contains a central city and surrounding communities that are economically and socially linked to the center.

micro: Microscopic; used to describe small-scale social phenomena, such as individuals and their thoughts and actions.

micro-macro continuum: The range of social entities from the individual, even the mind and self, to the interaction among individuals, the groups often formed by that interaction, formally structured organizations, societies, and increasingly the global domain.

middle-income economies: Economies in countries with income that is average for the world, defined by the World Bank in 2014 as having a gross national income per capita of between $1,046 and $12,745.

migration: The movements of people and their impact on the sending and receiving locales.

mind: An internal conversation that arises in relation to, and is continuous with, interactions, especially conversations that one has with others in the social world.

minority group: A group in a subordinate position in terms of wealth, power, and prestige.

misdemeanors: Minor offenses punishable by imprisonment of less than a year.

modernization theory: A structural-functionalist theory that explains unequal economic distributions based on the structural (especially technological) and cultural differences between countries.

monogamy: Marriage between two individuals, whether one wife and one husband, two wives, or two husbands.

monopoly capitalism: A form of capitalism in which huge corporations monopolize the market.

moral entrepreneurs: Individuals or groups who come to define an act as a moral outrage, and who lead a campaign to have it defined as deviant and to have it made illegal and therefore subject to legal enforcement.

moral panic: A widespread and disproportionate reaction to a form of deviance.

mores: Important norms whose violation is likely to be met with severe sanctions.

mortality: Deaths and death rates within a population.

multiculturalism: The encouragement of cultural differences within a given environment, both by the state and by the majority group.

nation: A group of people who share similar cultural, religious, ethnic, linguistic, and territorial characteristics.

nation-state: The combination of a nation with a geographic and political structure; encompasses both the populations that define themselves as a nation with various shared characteristics and the organizational structure of the state.

natural experiments: Experiments that occur when researchers take advantage of a naturally occurring event to study its effect on one or more dependent variables.

neomodernization: A structural-functional theory that explains differences in the economic and social development of countries based on technological and cultural differences.

netnography: An ethnographic method in which the internet becomes the research site and what transpires there is the sociologist's research interest.

network organization: A new organizational form that is flat and horizontal, is intertwined with other organizations, is run and managed in very different ways from traditional organizations, uses more flexible production methods, and is composed of a series of interconnected nodes.

networks: "Interconnected nodes" that are open, capable of unlimited expansion, dynamic, and able to innovate without disrupting the system in which they exist.

new religious movements: Movements that attract zealous religious converts, follow charismatic leaders, appeal to an atypical portion of the population, have a tendency to differentiate between "us" and "them," are characterized by distrust of others, and are prone to rapid fundamental changes.

nonfamily household: A household consisting of a person who lives either alone or with nonrelatives.

nonparticipant observation: A research method in which the sociologist plays little or no role in what is being observed.

nonresident parents: Fathers and mothers who live apart from their children.

norms: Informal rules that guide what members of a culture do in given situations and how they live.

nuclear family: A family with two married adults and one or more children.

observation: A research method that involves systematically watching, listening to, and recording what takes place in a natural social setting over some (extended) period of time.

offshore outsourcing: The transfer of work to organizations in other countries.

oligarchy: An organization with a small group of people at the top obtaining, and exercising, far more power than they are supposed to have.

organic solidarity: Cohesion among a group of people based on their differences.

organization: A collective purposely constructed to achieve particular ends.

organized crime: Crime that may involve various types of organizations but is most often associated with syndicated organized crime that uses violence (or its threat) and the corruption of public officials to profit from illegal activities.

Orientalism: A set of ideas and texts produced in the West that served as the basis for dominating, controlling, and exploiting the Orient (the East) and its many minority groups.

out-group: A group to which outsiders (at least from the perspective of the in-group) belong.

outsourcing: The transfer of activities once performed by one organization to another organization in exchange for money.

pangender: A gender identity encompassing all genders.

parole: The supervised early release of a prisoner for such things as good behavior while in prison.

participant observation: A research method in which the researcher actually plays a role, even a minor one, in the group or setting being observed.

passionate love: A kind of love typified by sudden onset, strong sexual feelings, and idealization of the one who is loved.

play stage: Mead's first stage in the socialization process, in which children learn to take on the attitudes of specific others toward themselves.

pluralism: The coexistence of many groups without any of them losing their individual qualities.

political crimes: Crimes involving either illegal offenses against the state to affect its policies or offenses by the state, whether domestically or internationally.

politics: Societal competition through established governmental channels to determine which group's members get what, as well as when and how they get it.

polyandry: Marriage (of a wife) to multiple husbands.

polygamy: Marriage to multiple spouses.

polygyny: Marriage (of a husband) to multiple wives.

post-Fordism: A production environment associated with smaller production runs of more specialized products, especially those high in style and quality; more flexible machinery made possible by advances in technology largely traceable to the computer; more skilled workers with greater flexibility and autonomy; less reliance on economies of scale; and more differentiated markets for those more specialized products.

postindustrial society: A society that was at one time industrial, but where the focus on the manufacture of goods has been replaced by an increase, at least initially, in service work—that is, work in which people are involved in providing services for one another rather than producing goods.

postmodern theory: A set of ideas oriented in opposition to modern theory by, for example, rejecting or deconstructing the grand narratives of modern social theory.

poverty line: The threshold, in terms of income, below which a household is considered poor.

power: The ability to get others to do what you want them to do, even if it is against their will.

power elite theory: A theory holding that power is not dispersed throughout a stable society but is concentrated in a small number of people who control the major institutions of the state, the corporate economy, and the military.

prejudice: Negative attitudes, beliefs, and feelings toward minorities.

primary deviance: Early, non-patterned acts of deviance, or an act here or there that is considered to be strange or out of the ordinary.

primary groups: Groups that are small, are close-knit, and have intimate face-to-face interaction.

primary socialization: The acquisition of language, identities, gender roles, cultural routines, norms, and values from parents and other family members at the earliest stages of an individual's life.

probation: A system by which those who are convicted of less serious crimes may be released into the community, but under supervision and under certain conditions, such as being involved in and completing a substance abuse program.

profane: To Durkheim, what has not been defined as sacred, or what is ordinary and mundane.

profession: An occupation distinguished from other occupations mainly by its power and considerable autonomy.

proletariat: Workers as a group, or those in the capitalist system who own little or nothing except for their capacity for work (labor), which they must sell to the capitalists in order to survive.

property crimes: Crimes that do not involve injury or force, but rather the theft or destruction of property.

prosumer: One who combines the acts of consumption and production.

Protestant ethic: A belief in hard work, frugality, and good work as means to achieve both economic success and heavenly salvation.

pure relationship: A relationship that is entered into for what each partner can get from it, and in which those involved remain only as long as each derives enough satisfaction from it.

qualitative research: Research methods employed in natural settings that produce in-depth, descriptive information (e.g., in respondents' own words) about the social world.

quantitative research: Research methods that involve the analysis of numerical data, usually derived from surveys and experiments.

queer theory: A theory based on the idea that there are no fixed and stable identities (such as "heterosexual" or "homosexual") that determine who we are; a diverse group of ideas about how cultures develop gender and sexuality norms, notions of conformity, and power relations.

questionnaires: Self-administered, written sets of questions.

race: A social definition based on some real or presumed physical, biological characteristic of a person, such as skin color or hair texture, as well as a shared lineage.

racism: The act of defining a group as a race and attributing negative characteristics to that group.

random sample: A subset of a population in which every member of the group has an equal chance of being included.

rape: Penetration, no matter how slight, of the vagina or anus with any body part or object, or oral penetration by a sex organ of another person, without the consent of the victim.

rational choice theory: A set of ideas that sees people as rational and as acting purposively to achieve their goals.

rationalization: The process by which social structures are increasingly characterized by the most direct and efficient means to their ends.

rational-legal authority: Authority that is legitimated on the basis of legally enacted rules and the right of those with authority under those rules to issue commands.

real culture: What people actually think and do in their everyday lives.

rebels: Individuals who reject both traditional means and goals and instead substitute nontraditional goals and means to achieving those goals.

recidivism: The repetition of a criminal act by one who has been convicted of a prior offense.

reciprocity: The expectation that those involved in an interaction will give and receive rewards of roughly equal value.

reference groups: Groups that people take into consideration when evaluating themselves.

refugees: Migrants who are forced to leave their homeland, or who leave involuntarily because they fear for their safety.

relative poverty: The state of being or feeling poor relative to others, irrespective of income.

reliability: The degree to which a given question (or another kind of measure) produces the same results time after time.

religion: A social phenomenon that consists of beliefs about the sacred; the experiences, practices, and rituals that reinforce those beliefs; and the communities that share similar beliefs and practices.

resocialization: The unlearning of old behaviors, norms, and values and the learning of new ones.

resource mobilization theory: An approach to understanding social movements that focuses on what groups of people need to do to mobilize to bring about social change.

retreatists: Individuals who reject both cultural goals and the traditional routes to their attainment; they have completely given up on attaining success within the system.

reverse socialization: The socialization of those who normally do the socializing—for example, children socializing their parents.

riot: Temporary unruly collective behavior that causes damage to persons or property.

risk society: A society in which central issues involve risks and ways to protect oneself from them.

rites of passage: Events, usually rituals, that surround major transitions in life, such as birth, puberty, marriage, and death.

ritual: A set of regularly repeated, prescribed, and traditional behaviors that serve to symbolize some value or belief.

ritualists: Individuals who realize that they will not be able to achieve cultural goals, but who nonetheless continue to engage in the conventional behavior associated with such success.

role: What is generally expected of a person who occupies a given status.

role conflict: Conflicting expectations associated with a given position or multiple positions.

role making: The ability of people to modify their roles, at least to some degree.

role overload: Confrontation with more expectations than a person can possibly handle.

rule creators: Individuals who devise society's rules, norms, and laws.

rule enforcers: Individuals who threaten to or actually enforce the rules.

sacred: To Durkheim, what is extraordinary, set aside, and of ultimate concern and leads to awe and reverence.

sample: A representative portion of the overall population.

sanctions: The application of rewards (positive sanctions) or punishments (negative sanctions) when norms are accepted or violated.

scapes: *See* landscapes (scapes).

scientific method: A structured way to find answers to questions about the world.

secondary data analysis: Reanalysis of data, often survey data, collected by others, including other sociologists.

secondary deviance: Deviant acts that persist, become more common, and eventually cause people to organize their lives and personal identities around their deviant status.

secondary groups: Generally large, impersonal groups in which ties are relatively weak and members do not know one another very well, and whose impact on members is typically not very powerful.

sect: A small group of people who have joined the group consciously and voluntarily to have a personal religious experience.

secularization: The declining significance of religion.

segregation: The physical and social separation of majority and minority groups.

self: The sense of oneself as an object.

sex: A biological term, expressed as *female* or *male*; typically reflected in chromosomes, gonads, genitalia, and hormones.

sex tourism: Activity that occurs when individuals travel to other countries for the purpose of buying sex from men, women, and sometimes children there; sex is the primary or sole purpose of these trips.

sex trafficking: A commercial sex act that includes force, fraud, or coercion and transporting and obtaining a person for sex acts.

sexual assault: Sexual acts of domination, usually enacted by men against women, other men, and children.

sexual harassment: Unwanted sexual attention that takes place in the workplace or other settings.

sexual identity: An internal sense of one's sexual self.

sexuality: The ways in which people think about, and behave toward, themselves and others as sexual beings.

sexual orientation: Involves whom one desires (fantasies), with whom one wants to have sexual relations (behavior), and with whom one has a sense of connectedness (feelings).

significant symbol: A gesture that arouses in the individual the same kind of response, although it need not be identical, as it is supposed to elicit from those to whom the gesture is addressed.

simulation: An inauthentic or fake version of something.

social change: Variations over time in every aspect of the social world, ranging from changes affecting individuals to transformations having an impact on the globe as a whole.

social class: One's economic position in the stratification system, especially one's occupation, which strongly determines and reflects one's income and wealth.

social construction of reality: The continuous process of individual creation of structural realities and the constraint and coercion exercised by those structures.

social control: The process by which a group or society enforces conformity to its demands and expectations.

social control agents: Those who label a person as deviant.

social control theory: A theory that focuses on the reasons why people do not commit deviant acts and the stake people have in engaging in conformist behavior.

social facts: Macro-level phenomena—social structures and cultural norms and values—that stand apart from and impose themselves on people.

socialism: An economic system oriented to the collective, rather than the private, ownership of the means of production.

socialization: The process through which a person learns and generally comes to accept the ways of a group or of society as a whole.

social mobility: The ability or inability to change one's position in the social hierarchy.

social movement: A sustained and intentional collective effort, usually operating outside established institutional channels, either to bring about or to retard social change.

social networks: Networks that involve two or more individuals, groups, organizations, or societies.

social processes: The dynamic and ever-changing aspects of the social world.

social stratification: Hierarchical differences and inequalities in economic positions, as well as in other important areas, especially political power and status or social honor.

social structures: Enduring and regular social arrangements, such as the family and the state.

society: A complex pattern of social relationships that is bounded in space and persists over time.

sociological imagination: A unique perspective that gives sociologists a distinctive way of looking at data and reflecting on the world around them.

sociology: The systematic study of the ways in which people are affected by and affect the social structures and social processes that are associated with the groups, organizations, cultures, societies, and world in which they exist.

specific deterrence: Deterrence from criminal behavior based on the concept that the experience of punishment in general, and incarceration in particular, makes it less likely that an individual will commit crimes in the future.

state: A political body organized for government and civil rule.

statistics: The mathematical method used to analyze numerical data.

status: A dimension of the social stratification system that relates to the prestige attached to people's positions within society.

stepfamily: A family in which two adults are married or cohabiting and at least one of them has a child or children from a previous marriage or cohabitation living with him or her.

stereotype: An exaggerated generalization about an entire category of people that is thought to apply to everyone in that category.

stigma: A person's characteristic that others find, define, and often label as unusual, unpleasant, or deviant.

strain theory: A theory based on the idea that the discrepancy between the larger structure of society and the means available to people to achieve what the society considers to be of value produces strain that may cause an individual to undertake deviant acts.

stratified sample: A sample created when a larger group is divided into a series of subgroups and then random samples are taken within each of these groups.

structural-functionalism: A set of ideas focused on social structures as well as the functions and dysfunctions that such structures perform.

structuralism: A social theory interested in the social impact of hidden or underlying structures.

structural mobility: The effect of changes in the larger society on the position of individuals in the stratification system, especially the occupational structure.

subculture: A group of people who accept much of the dominant culture but are set apart from it by one or more culturally significant characteristics.

suburbanization: The process whereby large numbers of people move out of the city and into nearby, less densely populated, environs.

suburbs: Communities that are adjacent to, but outside the political boundaries of, large central cities.

survey research: A research methodology that involves the collection of information from a population, or more usually a representative portion of a population, through the use of interviews and, more important, questionnaires.

sustainable development: Economic and environmental changes that meet the needs of the present, especially of the world's poor, without jeopardizing the ability to meet the needs of the future.

symbol: A word, gesture, or object that stands in for something or someone (a "label").

symbolic culture: Aspects of culture that exist in nonmaterial forms.

symbolic interaction: Interaction on the basis of not only gestures but also significant symbols.

symbolic interactionism: A sociological perspective focusing on the role of symbols and how their meanings are shared and understood by those involved in human interaction.

technology: The interplay of machines, tools, skills, and procedures for the accomplishment of tasks.

technoscapes: Landscapes that use mechanical and informational technologies as well as the material that moves quickly and freely through them.

telemedicine: Using technology to consult with doctors, such as an online video call, rather than going to a physical office.

terrorism: Acts of violence by nongovernmental actors that target noncombatants, property, or military personnel to influence politics.

theories: Sets of interrelated ideas that have a wide range of application, deal with centrally important issues, and have stood the test of time.

total institution: A closed, all-encompassing place of residence and work set off from the rest of society that meets all of the needs of those enclosed within it.

tracking: Grouping students by ability, which is typically measured by standardized test scores and/or grades.

traditional authority: Authority based on a belief in long-running traditions.

transgender: An umbrella term for people whose gender identity and/or gender presentation differs from the gender assigned at birth or in infancy.

transnational capitalism: An economic system in which transnational economic practices predominate.

triad: A three-person group.

unanticipated consequences: Unexpected social effects, especially negative effects.

underemployment: Employment in jobs that are not consonant with one's training and ability, as a part-time worker when one is capable and desirous of full-time work, or in jobs that are not fully occupying.

undernutrition: A form of malnutrition involving an inadequate intake of nutrients, including calories, vitamins, and minerals.

undocumented immigrants: Immigrants residing in a receiving country without valid authorization.

unemployment: The state of being economically active and in the labor force, being able and willing to work, and seeking employment, but being unable to find a job.

urban: City dwelling; in the United States, to be considered urban, an area must have more than 50,000 inhabitants.

urbanism: The distinctive way of life (lifestyles, attitudes, social relationships) that emerges in, and is closely associated with, urban areas.

urbanization: The process by which an increasing percentage of a society's population comes to be located in relatively densely populated urban areas.

validity: The degree to which a question (or another kind of measure) gets an accurate response, or measures what it is supposed to measure.

values: General and abstract standards defining what a group or society as a whole considers good, desirable, right, or important—in short, its ideals.

vertical mobility: Both upward and downward mobility.

violent crime: Crime that involves the threat of injury or the threat or actual use of force, including murder, rape, robbery, and aggravated assault, as well as terrorism and, globally, war crimes.

vouchers: Government-issued certificates that allow students to use public tax dollars to pay tuition at private schools.

war: An armed conflict in which a nation uses its military to attempt to impose its will on others.

wealth: The total amount of a person's assets less the total of various kinds of debts.

welfare states: States that seek both to run their economic markets efficiently, as capitalism does, and to do so equitably, which capitalism does not do.

white-collar crimes: Crimes committed by responsible and (usually) high-social-status people in the course of their work.

white racial frame: An array of racist ideas, racial stereotypes, racialized stories and tales, racist images, powerful racial emotions, and various inclinations to discriminate against blacks.

world-systems theory: A system of thought that focuses on the stratification of nation-states on a global scale.

worldview: A culture's most comprehensive image of the ways in which life—nature, self, and society—is ordered.

xenophobia: Prejudices that cause people to reject, exclude, and vilify groups who are outsiders or foreigners to the dominant social group.

REFERENCES
Chapter-Opening Vignettes

CHAPTER 1

Fahim, Kareem. 2016. "Freed from Jail, Dissident Flees Bahrain." *New York Times,* June 12.

Ryan, Yasmine. 2011. "How Tunisia's Revolution Began." *Al Jazeera English,* January 26. Accessed May 5, 2011. http://english.aljazeera.net/indepth/features/2011/01/201112612181598 5483.html.

"Tunisia Protests against Ben Ali Left 200 Dead, Says UN." 2011. *BBC News,* February 1. Accessed May 5, 2011. http://www.bbc.co.uk/news/world-africa-12335692.

Worth, Robert F. 2016. *A Rage for Order: The Middle East in Turmoil, from Tahir Square to ISIS.* New York: Farrar, Straus and Giroux.

CHAPTER 2

Freedman, Andrew. 2011. "Public Remains Confused about Global Warming, but Less So." *Washington Post,* June 14. Accessed June 15, 2011. http://www.washingtonpost.com/blogs/capital-weather-gang/post/public-remains-confused-about-global-warming-but-less-so/2011/06/13/AG04TaUH_blog.html.

Oreskes, Naomi. 2004. "Beyond the Ivory Tower: The Scientific Consensus on Climate Change." *Science* 306(5702): 1686. Accessed June 15, 2011. http://www.sciencemag.org/content/306/5702/1686.full.

CHAPTER 3

Carr, Ian. 1998. *Miles Davis: The Definitive Biography.* New York: Thunder Mouth Press.

Smith, Jeff, and Jean Wylie. 2004. "China's Youth Define 'Cool.'" *China Business Review,* July/August. Accessed June 17, 2011. http://www.chinabusinessreview.com/public/0407/smith.html.

Thompson, Robert Farris. 1973. "An Aesthetic of the Cool." *African Arts* 7(1). Accessed June 16, 2011. http://www.jstor.org/pss/3334749.

CHAPTER 4

Associated Press. 2017. "Transgender Boy Wins Texas Girls' Wrestling Title." *New York Times,* February 25. Accessed March 1, 2017. https://www.nytimes.com/2017/02/25/sports/transgender-boys-matches-with-girls-leave-all-unsatisfied.html.

Domonoske, Camila. 2017. "17-Year Old Transgender Boy Wins Texas Girls' Wrestling Championship." *NPR,* February 27. Accessed March 1, 2017. http://www.npr.org/sections/thetwo-way/2017/02/27/517491492/17-year-old-transgender-boy-wins-texas-girls-wrestling-championship.

James, S. E., J. L. Herman, S. Rankin, M. Keisling, L. Mottet, and M. Anafi. 2016. *The Report of the 2015 U.S. Transgender Survey.* Washington, DC: National Center for Transgender Equality.

CHAPTER 5

Castle, Stephen. 2013. "Report of U.S. Spying Angers European Allies." *New York Times,* June 30. Accessed November 3, 2013. http://www.nytimes.com/2013/07/01/world/europe/europeans-angered-by-report-of-us-spying.html?pagewanted=all.

Neuman, William, and Randal C. Archibold. 2013. "U.S. Is Pressuring Latin Americans to Reject Snowden." *New York Times,* July 12. Accessed November 3, 2013. http://www.nytimes.com/2013/07/12/world/americas/us-is-pressing-latin-americans-to-reject-snowden.html?pagewanted=1&ref=todayspaper.

Sanger, David E. 2014. "New N.S.A. Chief Calls Damage from Snowden Leaks Manageable." *New York Times,* June 29.

Savage, Charlie, and Jonathan Weisman. 2015. "N.S.A. Collection of Bulk Call Data Is Ruled Illegal." *New York Times,* May 11.

CHAPTER 6

Ewing, Walter A., Daniel E. Martinez, and Ruben G. Rumbaut. 2015. *The Criminalization of Immigration in the United States.* Washington, DC: Washington Immigration Council. Accessed January 31, 2017. https://www.americanimmigrationcouncil.org/research/criminalization-immigration-united-states.

Fox, Vicente. 2017. Tweet, January 26. Accessed March 8, 2017. https://twitter.com/VicenteFoxQue/status/824619429728288770.

Mandell, Andrea. 2016. "Cheryl Burke Dumps Trump Too." *USA Today,* June 30.

Perez-Pena, Richard. 2017. "Migrants Less Likely to Commit Crime." *New York Times,* January 27.

Sampson, Robert J. 2008. "Rethinking Crime and Immigration." *Contexts* 7: 28–33.

CHAPTER 7

Brams, Rachel, and Jessica Silver-Greenberg. 2014. "Companies That Offer Help with Student Loans Are Often Predatory, Officials Say." *New York Times,* July 13.

Carey, Kevin. 2016. "Donald Trump Isn't Alone in Exploiting the Word 'University.'" *New York Times,* March 21.

Douglas-Gabriel, Danielle. 2016. "The Surprising Growth of Graduate Enrollment at For-Profit Colleges." *Washington Post,* December 1.

"For-Profit Education Scams." 2012. *New York Times,* March 23.

Lewin, Tamar. 2010. "Report Finds Low Graduation Rates at For-Profit Colleges." *New York Times,* November 23.

Olson, Elizabeth. 2014. "Student Loan Debt Burdens More than Just the Young." *New York Times,* September 12.

Shen, Lucinda. 2016. "For-Profit Colleges Account for a Third of all Federal Student Loan Defaults." *Fortune,* September 29.

CHAPTER 8

"Profile: Bolivia's President Evo Morales." 2011. *BBC News,* January 12. Accessed October 21, 2011. http://www.bbc.co.uk/news/world-latin-america-12166905.

Romero, Simon. 2009. "In Bolivia, a Force for Change Endures." *New York Times,* December 5. Accessed October 21, 2011. http://www.nytimes.com/2009/12/06/world/americas/06bolivia.html?ref=evomorales.

Webber, Jeffery R. 2011. *From Rebellion to Reform in Bolivia: Class Struggle, Indigenous Liberation, and the Politics of Evo Morales.* Chicago: Haymarket Books.

CHAPTER 9

Promundo Global. n.d. *MenCare Brazil* (video). Accessed April 22, 2015. http://promundoglobal.org/resources/mencare-brazil-film.

CHAPTER 10

"Lance Loud! A Death in an American Family." 2011. *PBS.* Accessed November 18, 2011. http://www.pbs.org/lanceloud/american.

Winer, Laurie. 2011. "Reality Replay." *New Yorker,* April 25. Accessed November 18, 2011. http://www.newyorker.com/talk/2011/04/25/110425ta_talk_winer.

CHAPTER 11

Associated Press. 2005. "Judge Rules against 'Intelligent Design.'" *MSNBC,* December 20. Retrieved December 1, 2011. http://www.msnbc.msn.com/id/10545387/ns/technology_and_science-science/t/judge-rules-against-intelligent-design.

Kenny, Charles. 2014. "Does More Education Lead to Less Religion?" *Bloomberg Businessweek,* October 27. Retrieved September 4, 2015. http://www.bloomberg.com/bw/articles/2014-10-27/does-more-education-lead-to-less-religion.

"Muslim Medical Students Boycotting Lectures on Evolution . . . Because It 'Clashes with the Koran.'" 2011. *Daily Mail,* November 28. Retrieved December 1, 2011. http://www.dailymail.co.uk/news/article-2066795/Muslim-students-walking-lectures-Darwinism-clashes-Koran.html.

Timpane, John. 2011. "The Politics of Science: Evolution and Climate Change Are Shortcuts Conveying Broader Messages." *Philadelphia Enquirer,* August 23. Retrieved December 1, 2011. http://articles.philly.com/2011-08-23/news/29917822_1_climate-change-evolution-presidential-candidate-jon-huntsman.

Webley, Kayla. 2010. "Brief History: The Textbook Wars." *Time,* March 29. Retrieved December 1, 2011. http://www.time.com/time/magazine/article/0,9171,1973276,00.html.

CHAPTER 12

Brinded, Lianna. 2017. "ING: Bad Brexit Deal for Britain Could Kick Europe Into Recession." *Business Insider,* April 4. Accessed July 20, 2017. www.businessinsider.com/bad-brexit-deal-impact-on-european-and-uk-economy-trade-single-market-2017-4.

Frost, Wilfred. 2016. "Trump and Brexit: How They're Similar—and Different." *CNBC,* June 16. Accessed July 20, 2017. www.cnbc.com/2016/06/15/trump-and-the-brexit-how-theyre-similar—and-different.html.

McGill, Andrew. 2016. "Who Voted for The Brexit?" *The Atlantic,* June 25. Accessed July 20, 2017. www.theatlantic.com/international/archive/2016/06/brexit-vote-statistics-united-kingdom-european-union/488780.

CHAPTER 13

Bostwick, J. Michael. 2012. "Blurred Boundaries: The Therapeutics and Politics of Medical Marijuana." *Mayo Clinic Proceedings* 87: 172–186.

Hoffmann, Diane E., and Ellen Weber. 2010. "Medical Marijuana and the Law." *New England Journal of Medicine* 362: 1453–1457.

Kramer, Joan L. 2015. "Medical Marijuana for Cancer." *CA: A Cancer Journal for Clinicians* 65(2): 109–122.

Saint Louis, Catherine. 2014. "Politicians' Prescriptions for Marijuana Defy Doctors and Data." *New York Times,* June 26.

"A Sensible Bill on Medical Marijuana." 2015. *New York Times,* March 11.

CHAPTER 14

Coleman, Jasmine. 2011. "World's 'Seven Billionth Baby' Is Born." *The Guardian,* October 31. Accessed November 17, 2011. http://www.guardian.co.uk/world/2011/oct/31/seven-billionth-baby-born-philippines.

"Don't Panic: A UN Study Sparks Fears of a Population Explosion. The Alarm Is Misplaced." 2014. *Economist,* September 24. Accessed April 22, 2015. http://www.economist.com/news/international/21619986-un-study-sparks-fears-population-explosion-alarm-misplaced-dont-panic.

McQueeney, Kerry. 2011. "Welcome to a Very Full World, Danica: Was This the World's Seven Billionth Baby?" *Daily Mail,* October 30. Accessed November 17, 2011. http://www.dailymail.co.uk/news/article-2055419/Danica-Camacho-Seven-billionth-baby-born-Philippines.html.

Newcomb, Alyssa. 2011. "7 Billion People: What Number Are You?" *ABC News,* October 30. Accessed November 17, 2011. http://abcnews.go.com/blogs/headlines/2011/10/7-billion-people-what-number-are-you.

World Bank Development Data Group. 2011. "World Development Indicators." Accessed November 17, 2011. http://data.worldbank.org/data-catalog/world-development-indicators?cid=GPD_WDI.

CHAPTER 15

Forno, Francesca. 2013. "Consumer Movements." In *The Wiley-Blackwell Encyclopedia of Social and Political Movements,* 3 vols., edited by D. A. Snow, D. Della Porta, B. Klandermans, and D. McAdam, 253–256. Malden, MA: Wiley-Blackwell.

Glickman, Lawrence B. 2009. *Buying Power: A History of Consumer Activism in America.* Chicago: University of Chicago Press.

Holmes, Seth. 2013. *Fresh Fruit, Broken Bodies: Migrant Farmworkers in the United States.* Berkeley: University of California Press.

Tammelleo, Steve, and Louis Lombardi. 2014. "Consumer Social Responsibility?" *Business & Professional Ethics Journal* 33(1): 99–126.

Wiedenhoft Murphy, Wendy. 2017. "Boycotts, Buycotts, and Legislation: Tactical Lessons from Workers and Consumers during the Progressive Era." In *Shopping for Social Change: Consumer Activism and the Possibilities of Purchasing Power,* edited by Louis Hyman and Joseph Tohill. Ithaca, NY: Cornell University Press.

REFERENCES
Comprehensive List

Aas, Katja Franko. 2013. *Globalization and Crime.* London: Sage.

Abdul, Matin. 2015. "Relevance of Social Exclusion in Castellian Theory of Informationalism for South Asia." *Journal of Exclusion Studies* 5: 103–112.

Abella, Rudolfo. 2006. "An Analysis of the Academic Performance of Voucher Students in the Opportunity Scholarship Program." *Education and Urban Society* 38(40): 406–418.

Abercrombie, Sarah H., and Sarah L. Hastings. 2016. "Feminization of Poverty." In *Wiley-Blackwell Encyclopedia of Gender and Sexuality Studies,* edited by Nancy Naples. Malden, MA: Wiley-Blackwell (published online first).

Abrutyn, Seth. 2012. "Hinduism." In *The Wiley-Blackwell Encyclopedia of Globalization,* edited by George Ritzer, 932–937. Malden, MA: Wiley-Blackwell.

Acemoglu, Daron, and James A. Robinson. 2012. *Why Nations Fail: The Origins of Power, Prosperity, and Poverty.* New York: Crown Business.

Acemoglu, Daron, and Pierre Yared. 2010. "Political Limits to Globalization." Working Paper 15694, National Bureau of Economic Research, Cambridge, MA. Accessed March 28, 2012. http://www.nber.org/papers/w15694.

Acierno, Ron, Melba A. Hernandez, Ananda B. Amstadter, Heidi S. Resnick, Kenneth Steve, Wendy Muzzy, and Dean G. Kilpatrick. 2010. "Prevalence and Correlates of Emotional, Physical, Sexual, and Financial Abuse and Potential Neglect in the United States: The National Elder Mistreatment Study." *American Journal of Public Health* 100: 292–297.

Acker, Joan. 1990. "Hierarchies, Jobs, and Bodies: A Theory of Gendered Organizations." *Gender & Society* 4(2): 139–158.

Acker, Joan. 1992. "Gendered Institutions: From Sex Roles to Gendered Institutions." *Contemporary Sociology* 21: 565–569.

Acker, Joan. 2009. "From Glass Ceiling to Inequality Regimes." *Sociologie du Travail* 51(2): 199–217.

Adam, Barry D. 2006. "Relationship Innovation in Male Couples." *Sexualities* 9: 15–26.

Adams, Ann, Christopher D. Buckingham, Antje Lindenmeyer, John B. McKinlay, Carol Link, Lisa Marceau, and Sara Arber. 2008. "The Influence of Patient and Doctor Gender on Diagnosing Coronary Heart Disease." *Sociology of Health and Illness* 30(1): 1–18.

Adams, Josh. 2009. "Bodies of Change: A Comparative Analysis of Media Representations of Body Modification Practices." *Sociological Perspectives* 52: 103–129.

Adams, Margaret E., and Jacquelyn Campbell. 2012. "Being Undocumented and Intimate Partner Violence (IPV): Multiple Vulnerabilities through the Lens of Feminist Intersectionality." *Women's Health and Urban Life* 11(1): 15–34.

Addington, Lynn A., and Callie Marie Rennison. 2015. "Keeping the Barbarians Outside the Gate? Comparing Burglary Victimization in Gated and Non-gated Communities." *Justice Quarterly* 32(1): 168–192.

Adelman, Miriam, and Lennita Ruggi. 2015. "The Sociology of the Body." *Current Sociology* 64: 1–24. https://www.researchgate.net/publication/282835796_The_sociology_of_the_body.

Adler, Patricia A., and Peter Adler. 2011. *The Tender Cut: Inside the Hidden World of Self-Injury.* New York: New York University Press.

Adler, Patricia A., and Peter Adler. 2012. "Tales from the Field: Reflections on Four Decades of Ethnography." *Qualitative Sociology* 8: 10–32.

Adler, Paul S., et al., eds. 2016. *The Oxford Handbook of Sociology, Social Theory and Organization Studies: Contemporary Currents.* Oxford: Oxford University Press.

Ahituv, Avner, and Robert I. Lerman. 2007. "How Do Marital Status, Work Effort, and Wage Rates Interact?" *Demography* 44(3): 623–647.

Ahmed, Ishtiaq. 2013. "Muslim Immigrants in Europe: The Changing Realities." *India Quarterly* 69: 265–282.

Ahuvia, Aaron, and Elif Izberk-Bilgin. 2011. "Limits of the McDonaldization Thesis: EBayization and Ascendant Trends in Post-industrial Consumer Culture." *Consumption, Markets and Culture* 14: 361–364.

Ajrouch, Kristine A. 2007. "Reference Groups." In *The Blackwell Encyclopedia of Sociology,* edited by George Ritzer, 3828–3829. Malden, MA: Blackwell.

Akers, Donald S. 1967. "On Measuring the Marriage Squeeze." *Demography* 4: 907–924.

Albrow, Martin. 1996. *The Global Age.* Cambridge: Polity Press.

Alderman, Liz. 2016. "Smugglers Sense Opportunity as Borders Shut." *New York Times,* March 12.

Aleman, Ana M., and Katherine Link Wartman. 2008. *Online Social Networking on Campus: Understanding What Matters in Student Culture.* New York: Routledge.

Alexander, Karl, Doris Entwisle, and Linda Olson. 2014. *The Long Shadow: Family Background, Disadvantaged Urban Youth, and the Transition to Adulthood.* New York: Russell Sage Foundation.

Alexander, M. Jacqui, and Chandra Talpade Mohanty, eds. 2013. *Feminist Genealogies, Colonial Legacies, Democratic Futures.* New York: Routledge.

Alexander, Michelle. 2012. *The New Jim Crow: Mass Incarceration in the Age of Colorblindness.* New York: New Press.

Ali, S. Harris. 2012. "Diseases, Borderless." In *The Wiley-Blackwell Encyclopedia of Globalization,* edited by George Ritzer, 446–449. Malden, MA: Wiley-Blackwell.

Allegretto, Sylvia, Marc Doussard, Dave Graham-Squire, Ken Jacobs, Dan Thomson, and Jeremy Thompson. 2013. *Fast Food, Poverty Wages: The Public Cost of Low-Wage Jobs in the Fast Food Industry.* Berkeley: University of California, Center for Labor Research and Education.

Allen, Katherine R., and Ana L. Jaramillo-Sierra. 2015. "Feminist Theory and Research on Family Relationships: Pluralism and Complexity." *Sex Roles:* 73: 93–99.

Allison, Rachel, and Barbara J. Risman. 2013. "A Double Standard for 'Hooking Up': How Far Have We Come toward Gender Equality?" *Social Science Research* 42(5): 1191–1206.

Altman, Dennis. 2001. *Global Sex.* Chicago: University of Chicago Press.

Amato, Paul R., Alan Booth, David A. Johnson, and Stacy J. Rogers. 2007. *Alone Together: How Marriage in America Is Changing.* Cambridge, MA: Harvard University Press.

Amato, Paul R., and Spencer James. 2010. "Divorce in Europe and the United States: Commonalities and Differences across Nations." *Family Science* 1: 2–13.

Amin, Ash, ed. 1994. *Post-Fordism.* Oxford: Blackwell.

Anastasia, Désiré. 2010. "Living Marked: Tattooed Women and Perceptions of Beauty and Femininity." *Advances in Gender Research* 14: 11–33.

Anderson, Allan Heaton. 2013. *An Introduction to Pentecostalism: Global Charismatic Christianity.* Cambridge: Cambridge University Press.

Anderson, Benedict. 1991. *Imagined Communities: Reflections on the Origin and Spread of Nationalism.* 2nd ed. London: Verso Books.

Anderson, Chris. 2009. *Free: The Future of a Radical Price.* New York: Hyperion.

Anderson, David M., and Neil Carrier. 2006. "'Flower of Paradise' or 'Polluting the Nation': Contested Narratives of Khat Consumption." In *Consuming Cultures, Global Perspectives: Historical Trajectories, Transnational Exchanges,* edited by J. Brewer and F. Trentmann, 145–166. Oxford: Berg.

Anderson, Elijah. 2011. *The Cosmopolitan Canopy: Race and Civility in Everyday Life.* New York: W. W. Norton & Company.

Anderson, Monica, and Paul Hitlin. 2016. "Social Media Conversations About Race." Pew Research Center, August 15. Accessed January 27, 2017. http://www.pewinternet.org/2016/08/15/social-media-conversations-about-race.

Andreas, Peter. 2015. "International Politics and the Illicit Global Economy." *Perspectives on Politics* 13: 782–788.

Andreas, Peter, and Ethan Nadelmann. 2006. *Policing the Globe: Criminalization and Crime Control in International Relations.* New York: Oxford University Press.

Andrejevic, Mark. 2009. *Spy: Surveillance and Power in the Interactive Era.* Lawrence: University of Kansas Press.

Andrews, David L., and Ron L. Mower. 2012. "Spectres of Jordan." *Ethnic and Racial Studies* 35: 1059–1077.

Antonio, Robert J. 2014. "Piketty's Nightmare Capitalism: The Return of Rentier Society and De-democratization." *Contemporary Sociology* 43: 783–790.

Antrobus, Peggy. 2004. *The Global Women's Movement: Origins, Issues, and Strategies.* London: Zed Books.

Apel, Robert S., and Daniel Nagin. 2011. "General Deterrence: A Review of Recent Literature." In *Crime and Public Policy,* edited by J. Q. Wilson and J. Petersilia, 411–436. Oxford: Oxford University Press.

Apesoa-Varano, Ester Carolina. 2007. "Educated Caring: The Emergence of Professional Identity among Nurses." *Qualitative Sociology* 30: 249–274.

Appadurai, Arjun. 1996. *Modernity at Large: Cultural Dimensions of Globalization.* Minneapolis: University of Minnesota Press.

Appelbaum, Binyamin. 2014. "The Vanishing Male Worker, Waiting It Out." *New York Times,* December 12.

Arbzadah, Nushin. 2011. "Girls Will Be Boys in Afghanistan." *The Guardian,* November 30. Accessed April 18, 2015. http://www.theguardian.com/global/2011/nov/30/afghanistan-girls-dressing-as-boys.

Archibold, Randal C. 2015. "Mexico Officially Declares Missing Students Dead." *New York Times,* January 28.

Armstrong, Elizabeth A., and Suzanna M. Crage. 2006. "Movements and Memory: The Making of the Stonewall Myth." *American Sociological Review* 71(5): 724–751.

Armstrong, Elizabeth A., and Suzanna M. Crage. 2013. "Stonewall Riots." In *The Wiley-Blackwell Encyclopedia of Social and Political Movements,* 3 vols., edited by D. A. Snow, D. Della Porta, B. Klandermans, and D. McAdam, 1251–1253. Malden, MA: Wiley-Blackwell.

Armstrong, Elizabeth A., Paula England, and Alison C. K. Fogarty. 2012. "Accounting for Women's Orgasm and Sexual Enjoyment in College Hookups and Relationships." *American Sociological Review* 77(3): 435–462.

Armstrong, Elizabeth, and Laura Hamilton. 2013. *Paying for the Party: How College Maintains Inequality.* Cambridge, MA: Harvard University Press.

Aronson, Jay D., and Simon A. Cole. 2009. "Science and the Death Penalty: DNA, Innocence, and the Debate over Capital Punishment in the United States." *Law and Social Inquiry* 34: 603–633.

Arthur, Mikaila, and Mariel Lemonik. 2007. "Race." In *The Blackwell Encyclopedia of Sociology,* edited by George Ritzer, 3731–3734. Malden, MA: Blackwell.

Arthur, Mikaila, and Mariel Lemonik. 2013. "Emergent Norm Theory." In *The Wiley-Blackwell Encyclopedia of Social and Political Movements,* 3 vols., edited by D. A. Snow, D. Della Porta, B. Klandermans, and D. McAdam, 397–399. Malden, MA: Wiley-Blackwell.

Asayama, Shinichiro. 2015. "Catastrophism toward "Opening Up' or 'Closing Down'? Going beyond the Apocalyptic Future and Geoengineering." *Current Sociology* 63(1): 89–93.

Asch, Solomon E. 1952. *Social Psychology.* New York: Prentice Hall.

Ashwin, Sarah, and Olga Isupova. 2014. "'Behind Every Great Man . . .': The Male Marriage Wage Premium Examined Qualitatively." *Journal of Marriage and Family* 76(1): 37–55.

Associated Press. 2015. "Thousands Spend Night Outdoors as Death Toll Rises in Nepal." *New York Times,* May 12.

Atkinson, Lucy, Michelle R. Nelson, and Mark A. Rademacher. 2015. "A Humanistic Approach to Understanding Child Consumer Socialization in US Homes." *Journal of Children and Media* 9(1): 95–112.

Atkinson, Michael. 2003. *Tattooed: The Sociogenesis of a Body Art.* Toronto: University of Toronto Press.

Atkinson, Rowland, and Sarah Blandy. 2005. "Introduction: International Perspectives on the New Enclavism and the Rise of Gated Communities." *Housing Studies* 20: 177–186.

Atsushi, Miura. 2014. *The Rise of Sharing: Fourth-Stage Consumer Society in Japan.* Tokyo: International House of Japan.

Aud, Susan, and Gretchen Hannes, eds. 2011. *The Condition of Education 2011 in Brief* (NCES 2011-034). Washington, DC: U.S. Department of Education, National Center for Education Statistics.

Auster, Carol J. 2016. "Gender Neutral" In *The Wiley Blackwell Encyclopedia of Gender and Sexuality Studies,* edited by Nancy Naples. Published online.

Austin, Scott, Chris Canipe, and Sarah Slobin. 2015. "The Billion Dollar Startup Club." *Wall Street Journal,* February 18. http://graphics.wsj.com/billion-dollar-club.

Auyero, Javier, and Timothy Patrick Moran. 2007. "The Dynamics of Collective Violence: Dissecting Food Riots in Contemporary Argentina." *Social Forces* 85(3): 1341–1367.

Avishai, Orit. 2007. "Managing the Lactating Body: The Breast-Feeding Project and the Privileged Mother." *Qualitative Sociology* 30: 135–142.

Ayanian, John Z., and Arnold M. Epstein. 1991. "Differences in the Use of Procedures between Men and Women Hospitalized for Coronary Heart Disease." *New England Journal of Medicine* 325(1): 221–225.

Ayres, Tammy C., and James Treadwell. 2012. "Bars, Drugs and Football Thugs: Alcohol, Cocaine Use and Violence in the Night Time Economy among English Football Firms." *Criminology and Criminal Justice* 12: 83–100.

Baker, David Mc.A. 2015. "Tourism and the Health Effects of Infectious Diseases: Are There Potential Risks for Tourists?" *International Journal of Safety and Security in Tourism and Hospitality* 1.12: 1–17.

Baran, Paul A., and Paul M. Sweezy. 1966. *Monopoly Capital: An Essay on American Economic and Social Order.* New York: Modern Reader.

Barker, Eileen. 2007. "New Religious Movements." In *The Blackwell Encyclopedia of Sociology,* edited by George Ritzer, 3201–3206. Malden, MA: Blackwell.

Barmaki, Reza. 2016. "On the Origin of the Concept of Deviant Subculture in Criminology: W. I. Thomas and the Chicago School of Sociology." *Deviant Behavior* 37: 795–810.

Barr, Rebecca, and Robert Dreeben. 1983. *How Schools Work.* Chicago: University of Chicago Press.

Barrett, Donald C., and Lance M. Pollack. 2011. "Testing a Typology of Adaptations to Same-Sex Sexual Orientation among Men." *Sociological Perspectives* 54: 619–640.

Basu, Amrita, ed. 2010. *Women's Movements in the Global Era: The Power of Local Feminisms.* Boulder, CO: Westview Press.

Baudrillard, Jean. [1970] 1998. *The Consumer Society.* London: Sage.

Bauman, Kurt, and Camille Ryan. 2015. "Women Now at the Head of the Class, Lead Men in College Attainment." *Random Samplings: The Official Blog of the U.S. Census Bureau.* October 7. Accessed February 1, 2017. http://blogs.census.gov/2015/10/07/women-now-at-the-head-of-the-class-lead-men-in-college-attainment/?cid=RS23.

Bauman, Zygmunt. 1989. *Modernity and the Holocaust.* Ithaca, NY: Cornell University Press.

Bauman, Zygmunt. 1999. "The Self in Consumer Society." *Hedgehog Review* 1(1): 35–40.

Bauman, Zygmunt. 2000. *Liquid Modernity.* Cambridge: Polity Press.

Bauman, Zygmunt. 2003. *Liquid Love.* Cambridge: Polity Press.

Bauman, Zygmunt. 2005. *Liquid Life.* Cambridge: Polity Press.

Bauman, Zygmunt. 2006. *Liquid Fear.* Cambridge: Polity Press.

Bauman, Zygmunt, and David Lyon. 2012. *Liquid Surveillance: A Conversation.* London: Polity Press.

Baumgardner, Jennifer. 2011. *F'em: Goo Goo, Gaga, and Some Thoughts on Balls.* Berkeley, CA: Seal Press.

Bazelon, Emily. 2016. "Oppression or Profession?" *New York Times Magazine,* May 8, 34–43, 55–57.

Beccaria, Cesare. [1764] 1986. *On Crimes and Punishments.* Indianapolis: Hackett.

Beck, Colin, and Emily Minor. 2013. "Who Gets Designated a Terrorist and Why?" *Social Forces* 91: 837–872.

Beck, Ulrich. [1986] 1992. *Risk Society: Towards a New Modernity.* London: Sage.

Beck, Ulrich. 2007. "Cosmopolitanism: A Critical Theory for the Twenty-First Century." In *The Blackwell Companion to Globalization,* edited by George Ritzer, 162–176. Malden, MA: Blackwell.

Beck, Ulrich, and Elisabeth Beck-Gernsheim. 2012. "Families." In *The Wiley-Blackwell Encyclopedia of Globalization,* edited by George Ritzer, 637–639. Malden, MA: Wiley-Blackwell.

Becker, Howard S. 1963. *Outsiders: Studies in the Sociology of Deviance.* New York: Free Press.

Becker, Howard S., and Blanche Geer. 1958. "The Fate of Idealism in Medical School." *American Sociological Review* 23: 50–56.

Becker, Penny Edgell, and Phyllis Moen. 1999. "Scaling Back: Dual Earner Couples' Work-Family Strategies." *Journal of Marriage and the Family* 61: 995–1007.

Beer, Todd. 2012. "Global Warming." In *The Wiley-Blackwell Companion to Sociology,* edited by George Ritzer, 841–844. Malden, MA: Wiley-Blackwell.

Behbehanian, Laleh, and Michael Burawoy. 2014. "Appendix: Global Pedagogy in a Digital Age." *Current Sociology* 62(2): 285–291.

Beilharz, Peter. 2012. "Liquidity." In *The Wiley-Blackwell Encyclopedia of Globalization,* edited by George Ritzer, 1299–1230. Malden, MA: Wiley-Blackwell.

Belk, Russell W. 1987. "A Child's Christmas in America: Santa Claus as Deity, Consumption as Religion." *Journal of American Culture* 10(1): 87–100.

Belk, Russell. 2013. "The Sacred in Consumer Culture." In *Consumption and Spirituality,* edited by D. Rinallo, L. Scott, and P. Maclaren, 69–80. New York: Routledge.

Belk, Russell. 2014. "Sharing vs. Pseudo-Sharing in Web 2.0." *Anthropologist* 18: 7–23.

Bell, Daniel. 1973. *The Coming of Post-industrial Society: A Venture in Social Forecasting.* New York: Basic Books.

Bell, David. 2007. "Sexualities, Cities and." In *The Blackwell Encyclopedia of Sociology,* edited by George Ritzer, 4254–4256. Malden, MA: Blackwell.

Bell, Robert R. 1971. *Social Deviance: A Substantive Analysis.* Homewood, IL: Dorsey.

Bell, Sheri. 2011. "Through a Foucauldian Lens: A Genealogy of Child Abuse." *Journal of Family Violence* 26: 101–108.

Bellah, Robert N. 1967. "Civil Religion in America." *Daedalus,* Winter.

Belson, Ken. 2014. "Brain Trauma to Affect One in Three Players, NFL Agrees." *New York Times,* September 12.

Belson, Ken. 2016. "Pop Warner is Facing a Class-Action Lawsuit Over Concussions." *New York Times,* September 1.

Bendix, Reinhard, and Seymour Martin Lipset, eds. 1966. *Class, Status, and Power: Social Stratification in Comparative Perspective.* 2nd rev. ed. New York: Free Press.

Bengali, Shashank. 2016. "For Hindus Far from Home, Online Religious Services Can Be a Valued Connection." *Los Angeles Times,* May 1.

Benjamin, Walter. 1999. *The Arcades Project.* Cambridge, MA: Belknap.

Benns, Whiteny and Blake Strode. 2016. "Debtors' Prisons in 21st Century America." *The Atlantic* February.

Ben-Yehuda, Nachman. 1980. "The European Witch Craze of the 14th to 17th Centuries: A Sociologist's Perspective." *American Journal of Sociology* 86(1): 1–31.

Ben-Yehuda, Nachman. 1985. *Deviance and Moral Boundaries.* Chicago: University of Chicago Press.

Ben-Yehuda, Nachman. 2012. "Deviance: A Sociology of Unconventionalities." In *The Wiley-Blackwell Companion to Sociology,* edited by George Ritzer, 197–211. Malden, MA: Wiley-Blackwell.

Benzaquen, Adriana. 2006. *Encounters with Wild Children: Temptation and Disappointment in the Study of Human Nature.* Montreal: McGill-Queen's University Press.

Berends, Mark. 2015. "Sociology and School Choice: What We Know After Two

Decades of School Choice." *Annual Review of Sociology* 41: 159–180.

Berger, Arthur Asa. 2015. *Ads, Fads & Consumer Culture.* Lanham, MD: Rowman & Littlefield.

Berger, Peter L. 1969. *The Sacred Canopy: Elements of a Sociological Theory of Religion.* New York: Doubleday.

Berger, Peter L., and Thomas Luckmann. 1967. *The Social Construction of Reality: A Treatise in the Sociology of Knowledge.* New York: Anchor Books.

Bergquist, Magnus. 2003. "Open-Source Software Development as Gift Culture: Work and Identity Formation in an Internet Community." In *New Technologies at Work: People, Screens, and Social Virtuality,* edited by C. Garsten and H. Wulff. New York: Berg.

Berkovitch, Nitza. 1999. *From Motherhood to Citizenship: Women's Rights and International Organizations.* Baltimore: Johns Hopkins University Press.

Berkovitch, Nitza. 2012. "Women's Movement(s), Transnational." In *The Wiley-Blackwell Encyclopedia of Globalization,* edited by George Ritzer, 2233–2242. Malden, MA: Wiley-Blackwell.

Bertrand, Marianne, and Sendhil Mullainathan. 2004. "Are Emily and Greg More Employable than Lakisha and Jamal? A Field Experiment on Labor Market Discrimination." *American Economic Review* 94(4): 991–1013.

Bérubé, Allan. 2010. *Coming Out under Fire: The History of Gay Men and Women in World War II.* Chapel Hill: University of North Carolina Press.

Bethmann, Dirk, and Michael Kvasnicka. 2013. "World War II, Missing Men and Out of Wedlock Childbearing." *Economic Journal* 123: 162–194.

Beynon, Huw. 2016. "Beyond Fordism." In *The SAGE Handbook of the Sociology of Work and Employment,* edited by Stephen Edgell, Heidi Gottfried, and Edward Granter, 306–328. London: Sage.

BeyondMarriage.org. 2006. "Beyond Same-Sex Marriage: A New Strategic Vision for All Our Families and Relationships." July 16. Accessed May 23, 2015. http://www.beyondmarriage.org/full_statement.html.

Bhatnagar, Rashmi, Renu Dube, and Reena Dube. 2006. *Female Infanticide in India: A Feminist Cultural History.* Albany: State University of New York Press.

Bhatty, Ayesha. 2010. "Haiti Devastation Exposes Shoddy Construction." *BBC News,* January 15. Accessed March 31, 2012. http://news.bbc.co.uk/2/hi/8460042.stm.

Bianchi, Suzanne M., and Melissa A. Milkie. 2010. "Work and Family Research in the First Decade of the 21st Century." *Journal of Marriage and Family* 72: 705–725.

Bianchi, Suzanne M., and Vanessa Wight. 2012. "Population." In *The Wiley-Blackwell Companion to Sociology,* edited by George Ritzer, 470–487. Malden, MA: Wiley-Blackwell.

Biblarz, Timothy J., and Judith Stacey. 2010. "How Does the Gender of Parents Matter?" *Journal of Marriage and Family* 72(1): 3–22.

Bielby, Rob, Julie Renee Posselt, Ozan Jaquette, and Michael N. Bastedo. 2014. "Why Are Women Underrepresented in Elite Colleges and Universities? A Non-linear Decomposition Analysis." *Research in Higher Education* 55: 735–760.

Binnie, Jon. 2004. *The Globalization of Sexuality.* London: Sage.

Black, Donald. 2013. "On the Almost Inconceivable Misunderstandings Concerning the Subject of Value-Free Social Science." *British Journal of Sociology* 64: 763–780.

Black, Jeremy. 2016. *Geopolitics and the Quest for Dominance.* Bloomington: Indiana University Press

Blair-Loy, Mary. 2003. *Competing Devotions.* Cambridge, MA: Harvard University Press.

Blakely, Edward J., and M. G. Snyder. 1997. *Fortress America: Gated Communities in the United States.* Washington, DC: Brookings Institution Press.

Blaschke, Steffen, Dennis Schoeneborn, and David Seidl. 2012. "Organizations as Networks of Communication Episodes: Turning the Network Perspective Inside Out." *Organization Studies* 33: 879–906.

Blatt, Jessica. 2007. "Scientific Racism." In *The Blackwell Encyclopedia of Sociology,* edited by George Ritzer, 4113–4115. Malden, MA: Blackwell.

Blau, Francine D., Peter Brummund, and Albert Yung-Hsu Liu. 2012. "Trends in Occupational Segregation by Gender 1970–2009: Adjusting for the Impact of Changes in the Occupational Coding System." Discussion Paper 6490, Institute for the Study of Labor (Bonn, Germany). Accessed April 18, 2015. http://ftp.iza.org/dp6490.pdf.

Blau, Peter. 1963. *The Dynamics of Bureaucracy.* Chicago: University of Chicago Press.

Blau, Peter, and Otis Dudley Duncan. 1967. *The American Occupational Structure.* New York: Wiley.

Blee, Kathleen. 2002. *Inside Organized Racism.* Berkeley: University of California Press.

Blewitt, John. 2014. *Understanding Sustainable Development.* New York: Routledge.

Blight, James G., and Janet M. Lang. 2005. *The Fog of War: Lessons from the Life of Robert S. McNamara.* Lanham, MD: Rowman & Littlefield.

Bloom, Barbara, Lindsey I. Jones, and Gulnur Freeman. 2013. "Summary Health Statistics for U.S. Children: National Health Interview Survey, 2012." *Vital Health Statistics* 10(258). Accessed April 22, 2015. http://www.cdc.gov/nchs/data/series/sr_10/sr10_258.pdf.

Bluestein, Adam. 2014. "DDP Yoga Is Everywhere, but Does It Deliver?" *Men's Journal,* June. Accessed April 18, 2015. http://www.mensjournal.com/health-fitness/exer cise/ddp-yoga-is-everywhere-but-does-it-deliver-20140609.

Bluestone, Barry, and Bennett Harrison. 1984. The Deindustrialization of America: Plant Closings, Community Abandonment, and the Dismantling of Basic Industry. New York: Basic Books.

Boas, Morten. 2012. "Failed States." In *The Wiley-Blackwell Encyclopedia of Globalization,* edited by George Ritzer, 633–635. Malden, MA: Wiley-Blackwell.

Bolkan, Joshua. 2013. "Report: Students Taking Online Courses Jumps 96 Percent over 5 Years." *Campus Technology,* June 24. Accessed April 22, 2015. http://campustechnology.com/articles/2013/06/24/report-students-taking-online-courses-jumps-96-per cent-over-5-years.aspx.

Bonanno, Alessandro. 2012. "Fordism post Fordism." In *The Wiley-Blackwell Encyclopedia of Globalization,* edited by George Ritzer, 680–682. Malden, MA: Wiley-Blackwell.

Bond, Matthew. 2012. "The Bases of Elite Social Behaviour: Patterns of Club Affiliation among Members of the House of Lords." *Sociology* 46: 613–632.

Bonilla-Silva, Eduardo. 2009. Racism without Racists: Color-Blind Racism and the Persistence of Racial Inequality in the United States. Lanham, MD: Rowman & Littlefield.

Bonilla-Silva, Eduardo. 2015. "The Structure of Racism in Color-Blind, "Post–Racial" America." *American Behavioral Scientist* 59: 1358–1376.

Borch, Christian. 2013. *The Politics of Crowds.* Cambridge: Cambridge University Press.

Boris, Eileen. 2012. "Feminist Currents." *Frontiers: A Journal of Women Studies* 33: 101–105.

Boswell, A. Ayres, and Joan Z. Spade. 1996. "Fraternities and Collegiate Rape Culture: Why Are Some Fraternities More Dangerous Places for Women?" *Gender & Society* 10(2): 133–147.

Botz-Bornstein, Thorsten. 2013. "From the Stigmatized Tattoo to the Graffitied Body: Femininity in the Tattoo Renaissance." *Gender, Place and Culture* 20(2): 236–252.

Bourdieu, Pierre. 1984. *Distinction: A Social Critique of the Judgment of Taste.* Cambridge, MA: Harvard University Press.

Bourdieu, Pierre. 1992. *The Logic of Practice.* Palo Alto, CA: Stanford University Press.

Bourdieu, Pierre, and Jean-Claude Passeron. 1977. *Reproduction in Education, Society, and Culture.* Beverly Hills, CA: Sage.

Boushey, Heather. 2008. "Motherhood Penalty and Women's Earnings, Opting Out? The Effect of Children on Women's Employment in the United States." *Feminist Economics* 14(1): 1–36.

Bowen, Ted Smalley. 2001. "English Could Snowball on Net." *Technology Research News,* November 21. Accessed January 3, 2012. http://www.trnmag.com/Stories/2001/112101/English_could_snowball_on_Net_112101.html.

Bowler, Kate, and Wen Reagan. 2014. "Bigger, Better, Louder: The Prosperity Gospel's Impact on Contemporary Christian Worship." *Religion & American Culture* 24: 186–230.

Bowling, Ben, and James W. E. Sheptycki. 2012. *Global Policing.* London: Sage.

Bowman, John R., and Alyson Cole. 2009. "Do Working Mothers Oppress Other Women? The Swedish 'Maid Debate' and the Welfare State Politics of Gender Equality." *Signs* 35(1): 157–184.

Bowring, Finn. 2016. "The Individual and Society in Durkheim: Unpicking the Contradictions." *European Journal of Social Theory* 19: 21–38.

boyd, danah. 2014. *It's Complicated: The Social Lives of Networked Teens.* New Haven: Yale University Press.

Boykoff, Jules, and Eulalie Laschever. 2011. "The Tea Party Movement, Framing, and the U.S. Media." *Social Movement Studies* 10: 341–366.

Brady, David, and Denise Kall. 2008. "Nearly Universal, but Somewhat Distinct: The Feminization of Poverty in Affluent Western Democracies, 1969–2000." *Social Science Research* 37(3): 976–1007.

Braga, Anthony A., and David L. Weisburd. 2012. "The Effects of Focused Deterrence Strategies on Crime: A Systematic Review and Meta-analysis of the Empirical Evidence." *Journal of Research in Crime and Delinquency* 49(3): 323–358.

Branch, John. 2013. "The X Games, Driven by Risk, Have First Death." *New York Times,* January 31.

Brandle, Gaspar, and J. Michael Ryan. 2012. "Consumption." In *The Wiley-Blackwell Encyclopedia of Globalization,* edited by George Ritzer, 289–295. Malden, MA: Wiley-Blackwell.

Braun, Virginia. 2010. "Female Genital Cosmetic Surgery: A Critical Review of Current Knowledge and Contemporary Debates." *Journal of Women's Health* 19: 1393–1407.

Braw, Elisabeth. 2014. "The Three Letter Word Driving a Gender Revolution." *Newsweek,* September 29. Accessed April 17, 2015. http://www.newsweek.com/2014/10/03/three-letter-word-driving-gender-revolution-272654.html.

Breetzke, Gregory D., Karina Landman, and Ellen G. Cohn. 2014. "Is It Safer behind the Gates? Crime and Gated Communities in South Africa." *Journal of Housing and the Built Environment* 29: 123–139.

Brennan, Denise. 2002. "Selling Sex for Visas: Sex Tourism as a Stepping-Stone to International Migration." In *Global Woman: Nannies, Maids, and Sex Workers in the New Economy,* edited by B. Ehrenreich and A. R. Hochschild. New York: Henry Holt.

Brennan, Denise. 2004. *What's Love Got to Do with It? Transnational Desires and Sex Tourism in the Dominican Republic.* Durham: NC: Duke University Press.

Brennan, John, Niccolo Durazzi, and Tanguy Séné. 2013. "Things We Know and Don't Know about the Wider Benefits of Higher Education: A Review of the Recent Literature." BIS Research Paper, URN BIS/13/1244. Department for Business, Innovation and Skills, London.

Brewer, John, and Frank Trentmann. 2006. "Introduction: Space, Time and Value in Consuming Cultures." In *Consuming Cultures, Global Perspectives: Historical Trajectories, Transnational Exchanges,* edited by J. Brewer and F. Trentmann, 1–17. Oxford: Berg.

Briggs, Laura. 2012. *Somebody's Children: The Politics of Transracial and Transnational Adoption.* Durham, NC: Duke University Press.

Brim, Orville. 1968. "Adult Socialization." In *Socialization and Society,* edited by J. A. Clausen, 182–226. Boston: Little, Brown.

Brimeyer, T. M., J. Miller, and R. Perrucci. 2006. "Social Class Sentiments in Formation: Influence of Class Socialization, College Socialization, and Class Aspirations." *Sociological Quarterly* 47: 471–495.

Britannica. 2012. "Religion: Year in Review 2010." In *Britannica Book of the Year.* Accessed May 29, 2012. http://www.britannica.com/EBchecked/topic/1731588/religion-Year-In-Review-2010.

Brody, Jane E. 2009. "Buyer Beware of Home DNA Tests." *New York Times,* September 1.

Bromley, David G. 2016. "Categorizing Religious Organizations: In Search of a Theoretically Meaningful Strategy." In *New Religious Social Movements,* Vol. 2, edited by James R. Lewis and Inga B. Tollefson, eds., 17–24. New York: Oxford University Press.

Bronfenbrenner, Kate, ed. 2007. *Global Unions: Challenging Transnational Capital through Cross-Border Campaigns.* Ithaca, NY: Cornell University Press.

Bronner, Ethan. 2011. "Virtual Bridge Allows Strangers in Mideast to Seem Less Strange." *New York Times,* July 10. Accessed March 29, 2012. http://www.nytimes.com/2011/07/10/world/middleeast/10mideast.html.

Brooks, Robert A. 2011. *Cheaper by the Hour: Temporary Lawyers and the Deprofessionalization of the Law.* Philadelphia: Temple University Press.

Brosdahl, Deborah J. C., and Jason M. Carpenter. 2012. "U.S. Male Generational Cohorts: Retail Format Preferences, Desired Retail Attributes, Satisfaction and Loyalty." *Journal of Retailing & Consumer Services* 19(6): 545–552.

Brouwer, Steve, Paul Gifford, and Susan D. Rose. 2013. *Exporting the American Gospel: Global Christian Fundamentalism.* New York: Routledge.

Brown, Anna and Eileen Patten. 2017. "The Narrowing, but Persistent, Gender Gap in Pay." PEW Research Center, April 3.

Brown, Stephen E. 2007. "Ethnocentrism." In *The Blackwell Encyclopedia of Sociology,* edited by George Ritzer, 1478–1479. Malden, MA: Blackwell.

Brown, Susan L., Wendy D. Manning, and Krista K. Payne, 2015. "Family Structure and Children's Economic Well-Being: Incorporating Same-Sex Cohabiting Mother Families." *Population Research and Policy Review* 35(1): 1–21.

Brown, Timothy C., William B. Bankston, and Craig Forsyth. 2013. "'A Service Town': An Examination of the Offshore Oil Industry, Local Entrepreneurs, and the Civic Community Thesis." *Sociological Spectrum* 33: 1–15.

Brownmiller, Susan. 1975. *Against Our Will: Men, Women, and Rape.* New York: Simon & Schuster.

Brubaker, Ralph, Robert W. Lawless, and Charles J. Tabb. 2012. *A Debtor World: Interdisciplinary Perspectives on Debt.* Oxford: Oxford University Press.

Bruce, Steve. 2013. *Secularization: In Defense of an Unfashionable Theory.* New York: Oxford University Press.

Bryman, A. 2004. *The Disneyization of Society.* London: Sage.

Buchmann, Claudia, and Thomas DiPrete. 2006. "The Growing Female Advantage in College Completion: The Role of Family Background and Academic Achievement." *American Sociological Review* 71(4): 515–541.

Buck, Brad. 2014. "Process Converts Human Waste into Rocket Fuel." University of Florida News Center, November 25. Accessed May 22, 2015. http://news.ufl.edu/archive/2014/11/process-converts-human-waste-into-rocket-fuel.html.

Budig, Michelle J., Joya Misra, and Irene Boeckman. 2012. "The Motherhood Penalty in Cross-National Perspective: The Importance of Work–Family Policies and Cultural Attitudes." *Social Politics* 19: 163–193.

Budig, Michelle J., Joya Misra, and Irene Boeckman. 2016. "Work-Family Policy Tradeoffs for Mothers? Unpacking the Cross-National Variations in Motherhood Earnings Penalties." *Work and Occupations* 43: 119–177.

Bukowski, William M., Melisa Castellanos, Frank Vitaro, and Mara Brendgen. 2015. "Socialization and Experiences with Peers." In *Handbook of Socialization: Theory and Research,* 2nd ed., edited by Joan E. Grusec and Paul D. Hastings, 228–250. New York: Guilford Press.

Bulut, Elif. 2016. "Pride and Prejudice: The Context for Reception of Muslims in the United States." *Contemporary Social Science* May 16 (published online).

Burawoy, Michael. 2000. "Introduction: Reaching for the Global." In *Global Ethnography: Forces, Connections, and Imaginations in a Postmodern World,* edited by M. Burawoy, J. A. Blum, S. George, Z. Gille, T. Gowan, L. Haney, M. Klawiter, S. H. Lopez, S. Ó Riain, and M. Thayer, 1–40. Berkeley: University of California Press.

Burgess, Ernest W., and Harvey J. Locke. 1945. *The Family: From Institution to Companionship.* New York: American Book.

Burke, Kelsey. 2016. *Christians Under Covers: Evangelicals and Sexual Pleasure on the Internet.* Berkeley: University of California Press.

Burnett, Victoria. 2016. "Bathroom Debate Complicates A Town's Acceptance of a Third Gender." *New York Times,* June 22.

Burns, Diane, Paula Hyde, and Anne Killett, 2013. "Wicked Problems or Wicked People? Reconceptualizing Institutional Abuse." *Sociology of Health and Illness* 35: 514–528.

Butler, Judith. 1990. *Gender Trouble: Feminism and the Subversion of Identity.* New York: Routledge.

Cable, Sherry, Thomas E. Shriver, and Tamara L. Mix. 2008. "Risk Society and Contested Illness: The Case of Nuclear Weapons Workers." *American Sociological Review* 73: 380–401.

Cagatay, Nilufer, and Sule Ozler. 1995. "Feminization of the Labor Force: The Effect of Long Term Development and Structural Adjustment." *World Development* 23(11): 1827–1836.

Cahill, Spencer E., William Distler, Cynthia Lachowetz, Andrea Meaney, Robyn Tarallo, and Teena Willard. 1985. "Meanwhile Backstage: Public Bathrooms and the Interaction Order." *Journal of Contemporary Ethnography* 14: 33–58.

Caldwell, Christopher. 2009. *Reflections on the Revolution in Europe: Immigration, Islam, and the West.* New York: Doubleday.

Callimachi, Rukimini. 2016. "To Maintain Supply of Sex Slaves, ISIS Pushes Birth Control." *New York Times* March 12.

Camera, Lauren. 2016. "Achievement Gap Between White and Black Students Still Gaping." *U.S. News & World Report,* January 13. www.usnews.com/news/blogs/data-mine/2016/01/13/achievement-gap-between-white-and-black-students-still-gaping.

Campbell, Colin. 1987. *The Romantic Ethic and the Spirit of Modern Consumerism.* Oxford: Blackwell.

Campbell, Colin. 2007. *The Easternization of the West: A Thematic Account of Cultural Change in the Modern Era.* Boulder, CO: Paradigm Press.

Campbell, Nnenia M. 2010. "Coil Conscious: African American Women's Development of Internet-Based Alternative Hair Communities." Paper presented at the annual meeting of the American Sociological Association, Atlanta, GA.

Caniglia, Beth. 2012. "Environmental Protection Movement." In *The Wiley-Blackwell Encyclopedia of Globalization,* edited by George Ritzer, 536–541. Malden, MA: Wiley-Blackwell.

Cannato, Vincent J. 2009. *American Passage: The History of Ellis Island.* New York: Harper.

Carbonaro, William. 2005. "Tracking, Student Effort, and Academic Achievement." *Sociology of Education* 78: 27–49.

Carbonaro, William, and Elizabeth Covay. 2010. "School Sector and Student Achievement in the Era of Standards Based Reforms." *Sociology of Education* 83: 160–182.

Carey, Stephen. 2011. *A Beginner's Guide to Scientific Method.* Boston: Wadsworth.

Carmichael, Stokely, and Charles V. Hamilton. 1967. *Black Power: The Politics of Liberation.* New York: Vintage Books.

Carmody, Dianne Cyr. 2007. "Domestic Violence." In *The Blackwell Encyclopedia of Sociology,* edited by George Ritzer, 1219–1220. Malden, MA: Blackwell.

Carrillo, Héctor, and Jorge Fontdevila. 2014. "Border Crossings and Shifting Sexualities among Mexican Gay Immigrant Men: Beyond Monolithic Conceptions." *Sexualities* 17(8): 919–938.

Carroll, Aengus. 2016. *State-Sponsored Homophobia, A World Survey of Sexual Orientation Laws: Criminalisation, Protection and Recognition.* 11th ed. International Lesbian, Gay, Bisexual, Trans and Intersex Association, October. Accessed February 15, 2017. http://ilga.org/downloads/02_ILGA_State_Sponsored_Homophobia_2016_ENG_WEB_150516. pdf.

Carson, Rachel. 1962. *Silent Spring.* New York: Houghton Mifflin.

Carter, Bob, and Steve Fenton. 2010. "Not Thinking Ethnicity: A Critique of the Ethnicity Paradigm in an Over-ethnicised Sociology." *Journal for the Theory of Social Behaviour* 40: 1–18.

Carty, Victoria. 2013. "Internet and Social Movements." In *The Wiley-Blackwell Encyclopedia of Social and Political Movements,* 3 vols., edited by D. A. Snow, D. Della Porta, B. Klandermans, and D. McAdam, 620–623. Malden, MA: Wiley-Blackwell.

Carty, Victoria. 2015. *Social Movements and New Technology.* Boulder: Westview Press.

Case, Anne, and Angus Deaton. 2015. "Rising Morbidity and Mortality in Midlife among White Non-Hispanic Americans in the 21st Century." *Proceedings of the National Academy of Science of the United States of America.* 112(49):15078-15083.

Casey, Emma. 2015. "Gender and Consumer Culture." In Daniel Thomas Cook and J. Michael Ryan, eds. *The Wiley Blackwell Encyclopedia of Consumption and Consumer Studies.* Malden, MA: Wiley-Blackwell: 316–321.

Castells, Manuel. 1996. *The Information Age: Economy, Society and Culture, Vol. 1, The Rise of the Network Society.* Oxford: Blackwell.

Castells, Manuel. 1997. *The Information Age: Economy, Society and Culture, Vol. 2, The Power of Identity.* Oxford: Blackwell.

Castells, Manuel. 1998. *The Information Age: Economy, Society and Culture, Vol. 3, End of Millennium.* Oxford: Blackwell.

Castells, Manuel. 2010. *The Rise of the Network Society. The Information Age: Economy, Society and Culture, Vol. 1.* Malden, MA: Wiley-Blackwell.

Castells, Manuel. 2015. *Networks of Outrage and Hope: Social Movements in the Internet Age.* 2nd ed. Cambridge: Polity Press.

Castles, Stephen. 2013. "The Forces Driving Global Migration." *Journal of Intercultural Studies* 34: 122–140.

Center for Research on Education Outcomes, Stanford University. 2013. "National Charter School Study 2013." Accessed May 18, 2015. http://credo.stanford.edu/documents/NCSS%202013%20Final%20Draft.pdf.

Centers for Disease Control and Prevention. 2012. "Child Abuse and Neglect Cost the United States $124 Billion." Press release, February 1. Accessed May 13, 2015. www.cdc.gov/media/releases/2012/p0201_child_abuse.html.

Centers for Disease Control and Prevention. 2014. "Summary Health Statistics: National Health Interview Survey, 2014." Accessed May 16, 2017. http://ftp.cdc.gov/pub/Health_Statistics/NCHS/NHIS/SHS/2014_SHS_Table_C-3.pdf.

Centers for Disease Control and Prevention. 2016a. "Changes in Life Expectancy by Race and Hispanic Origin in the United States, 2013–2014." https://www.cdc.gov/nchs/products/databriefs/db244.htm.

Centers for Disease Control and Prevention. 2016b. "Unmarried Childbearing." Accessed March 9, 2017. https://www.cdc.gov/nchs/fastats/unmarried-child-bearing.htm.

Centers for Disease Control and Prevention. 2017. "Births: Final Data for 2015." *National Vital Statistics Report* 66(1). Accessed February 22, 2017. https://www.cdc.gov/nchs/data/nvsr/nvsr66/nvsr66_01.pdf.

Centers for Medicare and Medicaid Services. 2015. "National Health Expenditures 2015: Highlights2015." Accessed February 11, 2017. https://www.cms.gov/Research-Statistics-Data-and-Systems/Statistics-Trends-and-Reports/NationalHealthExpendData/downloads/highlights.pdf.

Central Intelligence Agency. 2015. "Country Comparison: Life Expectancy at Birth." *World Factbook*. Accessed May 20, 2015. https://www.cia.gov/library/publications/the-world-factbook/rankorder/2102rank.html.

Central Intelligence Agency. 2016. *The World Factbook*. Accessed March 9, 2017. https://www.cia.gov/library/publications/the-world-factbook.

Cerkez, Aida. 2010. "UN Official: Bosnia War Rapes Must Be Prosecuted." *Washington Post*, November 26.

Cha, Youngjoo. 2013. "Overwork and the Persistence of Gender Segregation in Occupations." *Gender & Society* 27: 158–184.

Cha, Youngjoo, and Kim A. Weeden. 2014. "Overwork and the Slow Convergence in the Gender Gap in Wages." *American Sociological Review* 79: 457–484.

Chae, Haesook. 2014. "Marx on the Family and Class Consciousness." *Rethinking Marxism* 26: 262–277.

Chae, Jiyoung. 2015. "Am I a Better Mother Than You?" *Communication Research* 42: 503–525.

Chakravarti, Arjun, Tanya Menon, and Christopher Winship. 2014. "Contact and Group Structure: A Natural Experiment of Interracial College Roommate Groups." *Organization Science* 25(4): 1216–1233.

Chambers, Erve. 2010. *Native Tours: The Anthropology of Travel and Tourism*. Prospect Heights, IL: Waveland Press.

Chambliss, William J. 1964. "A Sociological Analysis of the Law of Vagrancy." *Social Problems* 12: 67–77.

Chanda, Nayan. 2007. *Bound Together: How Traders, Preachers, Adventurers, and Warriors Shaped Globalization*. New Haven, CT: Yale University Press.

Charles, Maria, and Karen Bradley. 2009. "Indulging Our Gendered Selves: Sex Segregation by Field of Study in 44 Countries." *American Journal of Sociology* 114: 924–976.

Chen, Chih-Chin, and George Ritzer, 2015. "Globalization and Consumption." In *The Wiley-Blackwell Encyclopedia of Consumption and Consumer Studies*, edited by Daniel Thomas Cook and J. Michael Ryan, 333–338. Malden, MA: Wiley-Blackwell.

Chen, James K. C., and Dulamjav Zorigt. 2013. "Managing Occupational Health and Safety in the Mining Industry." *Journal of Business Research* 66: 2321–2331.

Chen, Katherine. 2009. *Enabling Creative Chaos: The Organization behind the Burning Man Event*. Chicago: University of Chicago Press.

Chen, Zihong, Ying Ge, Huiwen Lai, and Chi Wan. 2013. "Globalization and Gender Wage Inequality in China." *World Development* 44: 256–266.

Cherlin, Andrew J. 2004. "The Deinstitutionalization of American Marriage." *Journal of Marriage and Family* 66: 848–861.

Cherlin, Andrew J. 2010. "The Housewife Anomaly." *New York Times*, January 24.

Chernilo, Daniel. 2012. "Nation." In *The Wiley-Blackwell Encyclopedia of Globalization*, edited by George Ritzer, 1485–1492. Malden, MA: Wiley-Blackwell.

Chetty, Raj, Nathaniel Hendren, Patrick Kline, Emmanuel Saez, and Nicholas Turner. 2014. "Is the United States Still a Land of Opportunity? Recent Trends in Intergenerational Mobility." *American Economic Review* 104: 141–147.

Chokshi, Niraj. 2017. "Boys Scouts Reversing Century-Old Stance, Will Allow Transgender Boys." *New York Times*, January 30.

Chomsky, Noam. 1985. *Turning the Tide: U.S. Intervention in Central America and the Struggle for Peace*. Boston: South End Press.

Clancy, Michael. 2012. "Cruise Tourism." In *The Wiley-Blackwell Encyclopedia of Globalization*, edited by George Ritzer, 360–362. Malden, MA: Wiley-Blackwell.

Clapson, Mark, and Ray Hutchison, eds. 2010. *Suburbanization in Global Society*. Bingley, UK: Emerald.

Clark, Jocalyn. 2014. "Medicalization of Global Health 2: The Medicalization of Global Mental Health." *Global Health Action* 7: 24000. Accessed April 18, 2015. http://dx.doi.org/10.3402/gha.v7.24000.

Clegg, Stewart, and Michael Lounsbury. 2009. "Sintering the Iron Cage: Translation, Domination and Rationalization." In *The Oxford Handbook of Sociology and Organization Studies: Classical Foundations*, edited by P. S. Adler, 118–145. Oxford: Oxford University Press.

Clogher, R. 1981. "Weaving Spiders Come Not Here: Bohemian Grove: Inside the Secret Retreat of the Power Elite." *Mother Jones*, August, 28–35.

Clough, Patricia Ticineto. 2013. "The Digital, Labor, and Measure beyond Biopolitics." In *Digital Labor: The Internet as Playground and Factory*, edited by T. Scholz, 112–126. New York: Routledge.

Coakley, Jay. 2007. "Socialization and Sport." In *The Blackwell Encyclopedia of Sociology*, edited by George Ritzer, 4576–4579. Malden, MA: Blackwell.

Coates, Ta-Nehisi.2015. *Between the World and Me*. New York: Spiegel & Grau.

Cockerham, William C. 2007. "Medical Sociology." In *The Blackwell Encyclopedia of Sociology*, edited by George Ritzer, 2932–2936. Malden, MA: Blackwell.

Cockerham, William. 2012. "Current Directions in Medical Sociology." In *The Wiley-Blackwell Companion to Sociology*, edited by George Ritzer, 385–401. Malden, MA: Wiley-Blackwell.]

Cockerham, William. 2016. "Current Directions in Medical Sociology." In *The Wiley-Blackwell Companion to Sociology*, edited by George Ritzer, 385–401. Malden, MA: Wiley-Blackwell.

Cockerham, William C., and Brian P. Hinote. 2015. "PAs in a Changing Society: A Sociologic Perspective." *Journal of the American Academy of Physicians Assistants* 28: 18–20.

Cohen, Noam. 2011. "Define Gender Gap? Look Up Wikipedia's Contributor List." *New York Times*, January 30. Accessed December 3,

2011. http://www.nytimes.com/2011/01/31/business/media/31link.html.

Cohen, Patricia. 2010. "'Culture of Poverty' Makes a Comeback." *New York Times,* October 17. Accessed March 29, 2012. http://www.nytimes.com/2010/10/18/us/18poverty.html.

Cohen, Philip. 2014. *The Family: Diversity, Inequality and Social Change.* New York: Norton.

Cohen, Rina. 2015. "Transnational Motherhood: Constructing Intergenerational Relations between Filipina Migrant Workers and Their Children." In *Engendering Transnational Voices,* edited by Guina Man and Rina Cohen, 155–171. Waterloo, Canada: Wilfred Laurier Press.

Cohen, Robin. 1997. *Global Diasporas: An Introduction.* London: Routledge.

Cohen, Roger. 2016. "The Arab Withering." *New York Times,* May 12.

Cohen-Cole, Ethan, Steven Durlauf, Jeffrey Fagan, and Daniel Nagin. 2009. "Model Uncertainty and the Deterrent Effect of Capital Punishment." *American Law and Economics Review* 11: 335–369.

Colby, Sandra L., and Jennifer M. Ortman, 2015. *Projections of the Size and Composition of the U.S. Population: 2014–2060.* Washington, DC: United States Census Bureau.

Coleman, David, and Robert Rowthorn. 2011. "Who's Afraid of Population Decline? A Critical Examination of Its Consequences." *Population and Development Review* 37: 217–248.

Coleman, James. 1966. *Equality of Educational Opportunity.* Washington, DC: U.S. Department of Health, Education, and Welfare.

Coleman, James. 1990. *Foundations of Social Theory.* Cambridge, MA: Belknap Press.

Collins, Patricia Hill. 1990. *Black Feminist Thought: Knowledge, Consciousness, and the Politics of Empowerment.* Boston: Unwin Hyman.

Collins, Patricia Hill. 2000. *Black Feminist Thought: Knowledge, Consciousness, and the Politics of Empowerment.* 2nd ed. New York: Routledge.

Collins, Patricia Hill. 2004. *Black Sexual Politics: African Americans, Gender and the New Racism.* New York: Routledge.

Collins, Patricia Hill, and Sirma Bilge, 2016. *Intersectionality.* Cambridge: Polity.

Collins, Randall. 1975. *Conflict Society: Toward an Explanatory Science.* New York: Academic Press.

Collins, Randall. 2009. "Micro and Macro Causes of Violence." *International Journal of Conflict and Violence* 3: 9–22.

Collins, Randall. 2012. "C-Escalation and D-Escalation: A Theory of the Time-Dynamics of Conflict." *American Sociological Review* 77: 1–20.

Colosi, Rachel. 2010. *Dirty Dancing? An Ethnography of Lap-Dancing.* Abingdon, UK: William.

Common Sense Media. 2013. "Zero to Eight: Children's Media Use in America 2013." Fall. Accessed April 22, 2015. https://www.commonsensemedia.org/research/zero-to-eight-childrens-media-use-in-america-2013.

Common Sense Media. 2015. *The Common Sense Census: Media Use by Teens and Tweens.* San Francisco: Author. https://www.commonsensemedia.org/sites/default/files/uploads/research/census_executivesummary.pdf.

Compton, D'Lane, and Tristan Bridges. 2014. "Power, Pomp, and Plaid: Lumbersexuals and White, Heteromasculine Pageantry." *Society Pages,* December 25. Accessed April 18, 2015. http://thesocietypages.org/feminist/2014/12/25/power-pomp-and-plaid-lumbersexuals-and-white-heteromasculine-pageantry.

Comstock, George, and Erica Scharrer. 2007. *Media and the American Child.* Burlington, MA: Academic Press.

Condron, Dennis J., Daniel Tope, Christina R. Steidl, and Kendralin J. Freeman. 2013. "Racial Segregation and the Black/White Achievement Gap, 1992 to 2009." *Sociological Quarterly* 54(1): 130–157.

Connell, Raewyn. 2009. *Gender.* Cambridge: Polity Press.

Connell, Robert W. 1987. *Gender and Power: Society, the Person and Sexual Politics.* Palo Alto, CA: Stanford University Press.

Connell, Robert W. 1997. "Hegemonic Masculinity and Emphasized Femininity." In *Feminist Frontiers IV,* edited by L. Richardson, V. Taylor, and N. Whittier, 22–25. New York: McGraw-Hill.

Connor, Phillip. 2012. *Faith on the Move: The Religious Affiliation of International Migrants.* Washington, DC: Pew Research Center.

Conrad, Peter. 1986. "Problems in Health Care." In *Social Problems,* 2nd ed., edited by George Ritzer, 415–450. New York: Random House.

Conrad, Peter, Thomas Mackie, and Ateev Mehrota. 2010. "Estimating the Costs of Medicalization." *Social Science & Medicine* 70: 1943–1947.

Conrad, Peter, and Joseph W. Schneider. 1980. *Deviance and Medicalization: From Badness to Sickness.* St. Louis, MO: Mosby.

Contreras, Randol. 2017. *The Stickup Kids: Race, Drugs, Violence, and the American Dream.* Berkeley: University of California Press.

Cook, Alison, and Christy Glass. 2014. "Women and Top Leadership Positions: Towards an Institutional Analysis." *Gender, Work & Organization* 21(1): 91–103.

Cook, Daniel Thomas 2004. *The Commodification of Childhood: The Children's Clothing Industry and the Rise of the Child Consumer.* Durham, NC: Duke University Press.

Cook, Daniel Thomas. 2007. "Consumer Culture, Children's." In *The Blackwell Encyclopedia of Sociology,* edited by George Ritzer, 693–697. Malden, MA: Blackwell.

Cook, Daniel Thomas, and J. Michael Ryan, eds. 2015. *The Wiley-Blackwell Encyclopedia of Consumption and Consumer Studies.* Malden, MA: Wiley-Blackwell.

Cook, John, Dana Nuccitelli, Sarah A. Green, Mark Richardson, Bärbel Winkler, Rob Painting, Robert Way, Peter Jacobs, and Andrew Skuce. 2013. "Quantifying the Consensus on Anthropogenic Global Warming in the Scientific Literature." *Environmental Research Letters* 8(2): 024024. Accessed April 18, 2015. http://iopscience.iop.org/1748-9326/8/2/024024.

Cooksey, Elizabeth. 2007. "Fertility: Adolescent." In *The Blackwell Encyclopedia of Sociology,* edited by George Ritzer, 1725–1729. Malden, MA: Blackwell.

Cooley, Charles Horton. 1909. *Social Organization: A Study of the Larger Mind.* New York: Scribner.

Coontz, Stephanie. 2013. "Why Gender Equality Stalled." *New York Times Sunday Review,* February 17, SR1.

Coontz, Stephanie. 2016. *The Way We Never Were: American Families and the Nostalgia Trap.* New York: Basic Books.

Cooper, Cary L., Alankrita Pandey, and James Quick Campbell, eds. 2012. *Downsizing: Is Less Still More?* Cambridge: Cambridge University Press.

Cooper, Helene. 2016. "U.S. Drops Snark in Favor of Emotion to Undercut Extremists." *New York Times,* July 28.

Copes, Heith, and Crystal Null. 2007. "Property Crime." In *The Blackwell Encyclopedia of Sociology,* edited by George Ritzer, 3675–3676. Malden, MA: Blackwell.

Corak, Miles. 2013. "Income Inequality, Equality of Opportunity, and Intergenerational Mobility." *Journal of Economic Perspectives* 27: 79–102.

Corak, Miles, Matthew J. Lindquist, and Bhashkar Mazumder. 2014. "A Comparison of Upward and Downward Intergenerational Mobility in Canada, Sweden and the United States." *Labour Economics* 30: 185–200.

Corbett, Steven. 2014. "Challenging the Commodification of Public Spheres: The Hacker Work Ethic in a Free Media Lab." *First Monday* 19(12). Accessed

April 18, 2015. http://firstmonday.org/ojs/index.php/fm/article/view/3555.

Corprew, Charles S., III, and Avery D. Mitchell. 2014. "Keeping It Frat: Exploring the Interaction among Fraternity Membership, Disinhibition, and Hypermasculinity on Sexually Aggressive Attitudes in College-Aged Males." *Journal of College Student Development* 55(6): 548–562.

Correll, Shelley J. 2001. "Gender and the Career Choice Process: The Role of Biased Self-Assessments." *American Journal of Sociology* 106(6): 1691–1730.

Correll, Shelley J. 2004. "Constraints into Preferences: Gender, Status, and Emerging Career Aspirations." *American Sociological Review* 69(1): 93–113.

Costalli, Stefano. 2016. "Expulsion." In *The Wiley-Blackwell Encyclopedia of Race, Ethnicity and Nationalism,* edited by John Stone, Rutledge M. Dennis, Polly Rizova, Anthony D. Smith, and Xiaoshuo Hou. Malden, MA: Wiley-Blackwell.

Coventry, Martha. 2006. "Tyranny of the Esthetic: Surgery's Most Intimate Violation." In *Reconstructing Gender: A Multicultural Anthology,* edited by E. Disch, 203–211. New York: McGraw-Hill.

Covey, Herbert C. 2015. *Crips and Bloods: A Guide to An American Subculture.* Santa Barbara, CA: Greenwood.

Cox, Lloyd. 2007. "Socialism." In *The Blackwell Encyclopedia of Sociology,* edited by George Ritzer, 4549–4554. Malden, MA: Blackwell.

Creswell, John. 2008. *Research Design: Qualitative, Quantitative, and Mixed Methods Approaches.* Thousand Oaks, CA: Sage.

Croll, Paul R. 2013. "Explanations for Racial Disadvantage: Beliefs about Both Sides of Inequality in America." *Ethnic and Racial Studies* 36(1): 47–74.

Cross, Remy, and David Snow. 2012. "Social Movements." In *The Wiley-Blackwell Companion to Sociology,* edited by George Ritzer, 522–544. Malden, MA: Wiley-Blackwell.

Crossley, Alison Dahl, and Heather McKee Hurwitz. 2013. "Women's Movements." In *The Wiley-Blackwell Encyclopedia of Social and Political Movements,* 3 vols., edited by D. A. Snow, D. Della Porta, B. Klandermans, and D. McAdam, 1402–1408. Malden, MA: Wiley-Blackwell.

Crothers, Charles. 2011. "Robert K. Merton." In *Wiley-Blackwell Companion to Major Social Theorists,* Vol. 2, *Contemporary Social Theorists,* edited by George Ritzer and Jeffrey Stepnisky, 65–88. West Sussex, UK: Wiley-Blackwell.

Crothers, Lane. 2010. *Globalization and American Popular Culture.* 2nd ed. Lanham, MD: Rowman & Littlefield.

Croucher, Sheila. 2009. *The Other Side of the Fence: American Migrants in Mexico.* Austin: University of Texas Press.

Crowder, Kyle, and Liam Downey. 2010. "Interneighborhood Migration, Race, and Environmental Hazards: Modeling Microlevel Processes of Environmental Inequality." *American Journal of Sociology* 115(4): 1110–1149.

Crutsinger, Martin. 2010. "G20 Leaders Facing Worries about Rising Deficits." *Bloomberg Businessweek,* June 24. Accessed March 29, 2012. http://www.businessweek.com/ap/financialnews/D9GHNNI81.htm.

Cuaresma, Jesus Crespo, Wolfgang Lutz, and Warren Sanderson. 2014. "Is the Demographic Dividend an Education Dividend?" *Demography* 51: 299–315.

Cullen, Francis T., Cheryl Lero Jonson, and Daniel S. Nagin. 2011. "Prisons Do Not Reduce Recidivism: The High Cost of Ignoring Science." *Prison Journal* 91: 48S–65S.

Culver, Leigh. 2007. "Criminal Justice System." In *The Blackwell Encyclopedia of Sociology,* edited by George Ritzer, 851–856. Malden, MA: Blackwell.

Cunningham, Carolyn, ed. 2013. Social Networking and Impression Management: Self-Presentation in the Digital Age. Lanham, MD: Lexington Books.

CursedByTheDiceGods. 2017. "Wal-Mart." *Imgflip.* Accessed February 27, 2017. https://i.img flip.com/4vm17.jpg.

Curtiss, Susan. 1977. *Genie: A Psycholinguistic Study of a Modern-Day "Wild Child."* New York: Academic Press.

Dahlberg, Lincoln. 2010. "Cyber-Libertarianism 2.0: A Discourse Theory/Critical Political Economy Examination." *Cultural Politics* 6: 331–356.

Dahrendorf, Ralf. 1959. *Class and Class Conflict in Industrial Society.* Stanford, CA: Stanford University Press.

Daipha, Phaedra. 2012. "Weathering Risk: Uncertainty, Weather Forecasting, and Expertise." *Sociological Compass* 6: 15–25.

Damer, Sean. 1974. "Wine Alley: The Sociology of a Dreadful Enclosure." *Sociological Review* 22: 221–248.

Dargent, Fanny. 2014. "Scarifications Rituelles = Ritual Scarifications." *Revue Adolescence* 32: 47–56.

Da Silva, Julia. 2015. "Children and Electronic Media: How Much is Too Much?" *In the Public Interest Newsletter,* June. Washington, DC: American Psychological Association. www.apa.org/pi/about/newsletter/2015/06/electronic-media.aspx.

Davenport, Christian. 2015. *How Social Movements Die: Repression and Demobilization of the Republic of New Africa.* Cambridge: Cambridge University Press.

Davenport, Coral, and Campbell Robertson. 2016. "Resettling the First American 'Climate Refugees.'" *New York Times,* May 2.

David, Matthew, and Peter Millwood. 2012. "Football's Coming Home? Digital Reterritorialization, Contradictions in the Transnational Coverage of Sport and the Sociology of Alternative Football Broadcasts." *British Journal of Sociology* 63: 349–369.

David, Richard J., and James W. Collins. 2014. "Layers of Inequality: Power, Policy, and Health." *American Journal of Public Health,* suppl. 104(S1): S8–S10.

Davis, Deborah, and Sara Friedman, eds. 2014. *Wives, Husbands and Lovers: Marriage and Sexuality in Hong Kong, Taiwan and Urban China.* Redwood, CA: Stanford University Press.

Davis, F. James. 1991. *Who Is Black? One Nation's Definition.* Philadelphia: Penn State University Press. Accessed January 27, 2012. http://www.pbs.org/wgbh/pages/frontline/shows/jefferson/mixed/onedrop.html.

Davis, Flora. [1991] 1999. *Moving the Mountain: The Women's Movement in America since 1960.* New York: Simon & Schuster.

Davis, Kingsley. 1940. "Extreme Social Isolation of a Child." *American Journal of Sociology* 45(4): 554–565.

Davis, Kingsley. 1945. "The World Demographic Transition." *Annals of the American Academy of Political and Social Science* 237: 1–110.

Davis, Kingsley. 1947. "Final Note on a Case of Extreme Isolation." *American Journal of Sociology* 50: 432–437.

Davis, Kingsley, and Wilbert E. Moore. 1945. "Some Principles of Stratification." *American Sociological Review* 10(2): 242–249.

Davis, Mike. 2007. *Planet of Slums.* London: Verso Books.

Dean, Cornelia. 2007. "Experts Discuss Engineering Feats, Like Space Mirror, to Slow Climate Change." *New York Times,* November 10.

Death Penalty Information Center. 2016. "Executions and Death Sentences Around the World." http://www.deathpenaltyinfo.org/death-penalty-international-perspective# interexec.

Debas, Haile T. 2010. "Global Health: Priority Agenda for the 21st Century." *UN Chronicle* 47(2). Accessed March 29, 2012. http://www.un.org/wcm/content/site/chronicle/cache/bypass/home/archive/issues2010/achieving_global_health/globalhealth_priorityagendaforthe21stcentury?ctnscroll_articleContainerList=1_0&ctnlistpagination_articleContainerList=true.

de Beauvoir, Simone. [1952] 1973. *The Second Sex,* translated by H. M. Parshley. New York: Vintage Books.

Decker, Scott H., and G. David Curry. 2000. "Addressing Key Features of Gang Membership: Measuring the Involvement of Young Members." *Journal of Criminal Justice* 28: 473–482.

de Kerckhove, Derrick Tupper, Charles Kenneth Minns, and Chu, Cindy. 2015. "Estimating Fish Exploitation and Aquatic Habitat Loss across Diffuse Inland Recreational Fisheries." *PLoS ONE* 10(4).

De Laat, Kim, and Shyon Baumann, 2016. "Caring Consumption as Marketing Schema: Representations of Motherhood in an Era of Hyperconsumption." *Journal of Gender Studies* 25: 183–199.

DeLamater, John. 2012. "Sexual Expression in Later Life: A Review and Synthesis." *Journal of Sex Research* 49(2–3): 125–141.

Delaney, Tim. 2012. "Georg Simmel's Flirting and Secrecy and Its Application to the Facebook Relationship Status—'It's Complicated." *Journalism and Mass Communication* 2: 637–647.

De Lissovoy, Noah, and José García. 2013. "Doing School Time: The Hidden Curriculum Goes to Prison." *Journal of Critical Education Policy Studies* 11(4): 49–68.

Della Porta, Donatella, and Mario Diani, eds. 2015. *The Oxford Handbook of Social Movements.* Oxford: Oxford University Press.

DeLuzio Chasin, C. J. 2011. "Theoretical Issues in the Study of Asexuality." *Archives of Sexual Behavior* 40(4): 713–723.

D'Emilio, John. 1983. *Sexual Politics, Sexual Communities.* Chicago: University of Chicago Press.

DeNavas-Walt, Carmen, and Bernadette Proctor. 2015. *Income and Poverty in the United States: 2014.* Washington, DC: U.S. Census Bureau. https://www.census.gov/content/dam/Census/library/publications/2015/demo/p60-252.pdf.

DeNavas-Walt, Carmen, Bernadette D. Proctor, and Jessica C. Smith. 2012. *Income, Poverty, and Health Insurance Coverage in the United States: 2011.* Current Population Reports P60-243. Washington, DC: U.S. Census Bureau, September. Accessed March 29, 2012. https://www.census.gov/prod/2012pubs/p60-243.pdf.

Denegri-Knott, Janice, and Detlev Zwick. 2012. "Tracking Prosumption Work on eBay: Reproduction of Desire and the Challenge of Slow Re-McDonaldization." *American Behavioral Scientist* 56: 439–458.

Dentler, Robert A., and Kai T. Erikson. 1959. "The Function of Deviance in Small Groups." *Social Problems* 7: 98–107.

Denyer, Simon. 2016. "China's Scary Lesson to the World: Censoring the Internet Works." *The Washington Post,* March 23.

Denzin, Norman K., and Yvonna S. Lincoln. 2011. "Introduction: The Discipline and Practice of Qualitative Research." In *The SAGE Handbook of Qualitative Research,* 4th ed., edited by Norman K. Denzin and Yvonna S. Lincoln, 1–20. Thousand Oaks, CA: Sage.

DeParle, Jason, Robert Gebeloff, and Sabrina Tavernise. 2011. "Older, Suburban and Struggling." *New York Times,* November 19.

de Regt, Marina. 2009. "Preferences and Prejudices: Employers' Views on Domestic Workers in the Republic of Yemen." *Signs* 34(3): 559–581.

Desai, Sonalde. 2010. "The Other Half of the Demographic Dividend." *Economic and Political Weekly* 45(40): 12–14.

De Silva, Dakshina G., Robert P. McComb, Young-Kyu Moh, Anita R. Schiller, and Andres J. Vargas. 2010. "The Effect of Migration on Wages: Evidence from a Natural Experiment." *American Economic Review: Papers and Proceedings* 100(May): 321–326.

Desmond, Matthew. 2016. *Evicted: Poverty and Profit in the American City.* New York: Crown.

Desmond, Matthew. 2017. "House Rules." *New York Times Magazine* May 14.

Deutsch, Kevin. 2014. *The Triangle: A Year on the Ground with New York's Bloods and Crips.* Guilford, CT: Lyons Press.

Deutsch, Nancy L., and Eleni Theodorou. 2010. "Aspiring, Consuming, Becoming: Youth Identity in a Culture of Consumption." *Youth & Society* 42(2): 229–254.

DeVault, Marjorie. 1991. *Feeding the Family: The Social Organization of Caring as Gendered Work.* Chicago: University of Chicago Press.

Dewey, Susan. 2015. "Sex Work." In *Handbook of the Sociology of Sexualities,* edited by J. DeLamater and R. F. Plante. Dordrecht, Netherlands: Springer.

Dey, Eric L. 1997. "Undergraduate Political Attitudes: Peer Influence in Changing Social Contexts." *Journal of Higher Education* 68: 398–416.

Diamond, Jared. 2006. *Collapse: How Societies Choose to Fail or Succeed.* New York: Penguin.

Dicke, Thomas S. 1992. *Franchising in America: The Development of a Business Method, 1840–1980.* Chapel Hill: University of North Carolina Press.

Dickson, Lynda, Richard Dukes, Hilary Smith, and Noel Strapko. 2014. "Stigma of Ink: Tattoo Attitudes among College Students." *Social Science Journal* 51(2): 268–276.

Dikötter, Frank. 2008. "The Racialization of the Globe: An Interactive Interpretation." *Ethnic and Racial Studies* 31(8): 1478–1496.

Dill, Janette S., Kim Price-Glynn, and Carter Rakovski. 2016. "Does the 'Glass Escalator' Compensate for the Devaluation of Care Work Occupations?: The Careers of Men in Low and Middle-Skill Health Care Jobs," *Gender & Society* 0(2): 334–360.

DiMaggio, Paul J., and Walter W. Powell. 1983. "The Iron Cage Revisited: Institutional Isomorphism and Collective Rationality in Organizational Fields." *American Sociological Review* 48: 147–160.

DiPrete, Thomas A., Gregory M. Eirich, Karen S. Cook, and Douglas S. Massey. 2006. "Cumulative Advantage as a Mechanism for Inequality: A Review of Theoretical and Empirical Developments." *Annual Review of Sociology* 32: 271–297.

Directorate-General for Employment, Industrial Relations and Social Affairs. 1998. "Sexual Harassment at the Workplace in the European Union." Brussels, European Commission.

Dodd, Nigel. 2012. "Money." In *The Wiley-Blackwell Encyclopedia of Globalization,* edited by George Ritzer, 1444–1448. Malden, MA: Wiley-Blackwell.

Doherty, Carroll. 2013. "For African Americans, Discrimination Is Not Dead." Pew Research Center, *Fact Tank,* June 28. Accessed May 7, 2015. http://www.pewresearch.org/fact-tank/2013/06/28/for-african-americans-discrimination-is-not-dead.

Dolata, Ulrich, and Jan-Felix Schrape, 2016. "Masses, Crowds, Communities, Movement: Collective Action in the Internet Age." *Social Movement Studies* 15: 1–18.

Dombrowski, Stefan C., Karen L. Gischlar, and Martin Mrazik. 2011. "Feral Children." In *Assessing and Treating Low Incidence/High Severity Psychological Disorders of Childhood,* 81–93. New York: Springer.

Domhoff, G. William. 1974. *The Bohemian Grove and Other Retreats: A Study in Ruling-Class Cohesiveness.* New York: Harper & Row.

Domhoff, G. William. 2013. *Who Rules America? The Triumph of Corporate Rich.* New York: McGraw-Hill.

Dooley, David, and JoAnn Prause. 2009. *The Social Costs of Underemployment: Inadequate Employment as Disguised Unemployment.* Cambridge: Cambridge University Press.

Dorius, Shawn, and Glenn Firebaugh. 2010. "Trends in Global Gender Inequality." *Social Forces* 88(5): 1941–1968.

Dow, Dawn Marie. 2016. "The Deadly Challenges of Raising African American Boys. *Gender & Society* 30: 161–188.

Downey, Douglas B., and Dennis J. Condron. 2016. "Fifty Years Since the Coleman Report: Rethinking the Relationship between Schools and Inequality." *Sociology of Education* 89: 207–220.

Drache, D. (with M. D. Froese). 2008. *Defiant Publics: The Unprecedented Reach of the Global Citizen.* Cambridge: Polity Press.

Drane, John. 2008. *After McDonaldization: Mission, Ministry, and Christian Discipleship in an Age of Uncertainty.* Grand Rapids, MI: Baker.

Drane, John. 2012. *The McDonaldization of the Church: Consumer Culture and the Church's Future.* Macon, GA: Smith and Helwys.

Drori, Gili. 2006. *Global E-litism: Digital Technology, Social Inequality and Transnationality.* New York: Worth.

Drori, Gili S. 2012. "Digital Divide." In *The Wiley-Blackwell Encyclopedia of Globalization,* edited by George Ritzer, 435–438. Malden, MA: Wiley-Blackwell.

Duany, Andrés, Elizabeth Plater-Zyberk, and Jeff Speck. 2010. *Suburban Nation: The Rise of Sprawl and the Decline of the American Dream.* 10th anniversary ed. New York: North Point Press.

Duberman, Martin B. 1994. *Stonewall.* New York: Plume.

Du Bois, W. E. B. [1899] 1996. *The Philadelphia Negro: A Social Study.* Philadelphia: University of Pennsylvania Press.

Du Bois, W. E. B. [1903] 1966. *The Souls of Black Folk.* New York: Modern Library.

Duckworth, Angela L., and Stephanie M. Carlson. 2013. "Self-Regulation and School Success." In *Self-Regulation and Autonomy: Social and Developmental Dimensions of Human Conduct,* edited by B. W. Sokol, F. M. E. Grouzet, and U. Müller, 208–230. New York: Cambridge University Press.

Duckworth, Angela L., and Martin E. P. Seligman. 2005. "Self-Discipline Outdoes IQ in Predicting Academic Performance of Adolescents." *Psychological Science* 16: 939–944.

Duhigg, Charles. 2017. "Business Government." *New York Times,* January 19.

Duhigg, Charles, and Keith Bradsher. 2012. "How the U.S. Lost Out on iPhone Work." *New York Times,* January 22.

Dujarier, Marie-Anne. 2014. "The Three Sociological Types of Consumer Work." *Journal of Consumer Culture,* April 9 (published online). doi: 10.1177/1469540514528198.

Dukes, Richard L., and Judith A. Stein. 2011. "Ink and Holes: Correlates and Predictive Associations of Body Modification

among Adolescents." *Youth & Society* 43: 1547–1569.

Duncan, Greg J., Kathleen M. Ziol-Guest, and Ariel Kalil. 2010. "Early-Childhood Poverty and Adult Attainment, Behavior, and Health." *Child Development* 81: 306–325.

Duncan, Simon. 2014. "Women's Agency in Living Apart Together: Constraint, Strategy, and Vulnerability." *Sociological Review,* September 5 (published online). doi: 10.1111/1467-954X.12184.

Duneier, Mitchell. 1999. *Sidewalk.* New York: Farrar, Straus and Giroux.

Dunham, Lena. 2014. *Not That Kind of Girl: A Young Woman Tells You What She's Learned.* New York: Random House.

Dunlap, Riley E., and William R. Catton Jr. 2002. "Which Functions of the Environment Do We Study? A Comparison of Environmental and Natural Resource Sociology." *Society and Natural Resources* 15: 239–249.

Dunlap, Riley E., and Andrew K. Jorgenson. 2012. "Environmental Problems." In *The Wiley-Blackwell Companion to Sociology,* edited by George Ritzer, 529–536. Malden, MA: Wiley-Blackwell.

Dunn, Gregory. 2013. "Water Wars." *Harvard International Review* 35: 46–49.

Dunn, Jennifer L. 2005. "'Victims' and 'Survivors': Emerging Vocabularies of Motive for 'Battered Women Who Stay.'" *Sociological Inquiry* 75: 1–30.

Dunning, Eric, Patrick Murphy, and John Williams. 1988. *The Roots of Football Hooliganism.* London: Routledge & Kegan Paul.

Durkheim, Émile. [1893] 1964. *The Division of Labor in Society.* New York: Free Press.

Durkheim, Émile. [1897] 1951. *Suicide.* New York: Free Press.

Durkheim, Émile. [1912] 1965. *The Elementary Forms of the Religious Life.* New York: Free Press.

Duster, Troy. 2003. *Backdoor to Eugenics.* New York: Routledge.

Dustin, Donna. 2007. *The McDonaldization of Social Work.* Burlington, VT: Ashgate.

Dutton, Donald G., and Katherine R. White. 2013. "Male Victims of Domestic Violence." *New Male Studies* 2: 5–17.

Earl, Jennifer. 2007. "Social Movements, Repression of." In *The Blackwell Encyclopedia of Sociology,* edited by George Ritzer, 4475–4479. Malden, MA: Blackwell.

Eckenwiler, Lisa. 2014. "Care Worker Migration, Global Health Equity, and Ethical Place-Making." *Women's Studies International Forum* 47: 213–222.

Eckert, Penelope, and Sally McConnell-Ginet. 2013. *Language and Gender.* 2nd ed. New York: Cambridge University Press.

Edin, Kathryn, and Maria Kefalas. 2011. *Promises I Can Keep: Why Poor Women Put Motherhood Before Marriage.* Berkeley: University of California Press.

Edin, Kathryn, and Laura Lein. 1997. *Making Ends Meet: How Single Mothers Survive Welfare and Low-Wage Work.* New York: Russell Sage Foundation.

Edin, Kathryn J., and H. Luke Schaefer, 2015. *$2 a Day: Living on Almost Nothing in America.* New York: Houghton, Mifflin, Harcourt.

Edmonds, Alex. 2010. *Pretty Modern: Beauty, Sex, and Plastic Surgery in Brazil.* Durham, NC: Duke University Press.

Edwards, Bob, and Patrick F. Gillham. 2013. "Resource Mobilization Theory." In *The Wiley-Blackwell Encyclopedia of Social and Political Movements,* 3 vols., edited by D. A. Snow, D. Della Porta, B. Klandermans, and D. McAdam, 1096–1101. Malden, MA: Wiley-Blackwell.

Ehrenreich, Barbara. 2002. "Maid to Order." In *Global Woman: Nannies, Maids, and Sex Workers in the New Economy,* edited by B. Ehrenreich and A. R. Hochschild. New York: Henry Holt.

Ehrenreich, Barbara, and Arlie Russell Hochschild. 2002. "Introduction." In *Global Woman: Nannies, Maids, and Sex Workers in the New Economy,* edited by B. Ehrenreich and A. R. Hochschild, 1–14. New York: Henry Holt.

Ehrlich, Paul. 1968. *The Population Bomb.* New York: Ballantine.

Elborgh-Woytek, Katrina, Monique Newiak, Kalpana Kochhar, Stefania Fabrizo, Kangi Kpodar, Philippe Wingender, Benedict Clements, and Gerd Schwartz. 2016. *Women, Work, and the Economy: Macroeconomic Gains from Gender Equity.* Washington, DC: International Monetary Fund.

Elder, Todd, and Christopher Jepsen. 2014. "Are Catholic Primary Schools More Effective than Public Primary Schools?" *Journal of Urban Economics* 80: 28–38.

Elgin, Duane. 2010. *Voluntary Simplicity: Toward a Way of Life That Is Outwardly Simple, Inwardly Rich.* 2nd ed. New York: Quill.

Elias, Sean, and Joe R. Feagin. 2016. *Racial Theories in Social Science: A Systemic Racism Critique.* New York: Routledge.

Elias, Vicky L., Andrew S. Fullerton, and Joseph M. Simpson. 2015. "Long-Term Changes in Attitudes toward Premarital Sex in the United States: Reexamining the Role of Cohort Replacement." *Journal of Sex Research* 52(2): 129–139.

Ellin, Abby. 2016. "With Coercive Control, the Abuse Is Psychological." *New York Times,* July 11.

Elliott, David L. 2012. "Urbanism." In *The Wiley-Blackwell Encyclopedia of Globalization,* edited by George Ritzer, 2134–2136. Malden, MA: Wiley-Blackwell.

Elliot, Stuart. 2014. "Go Where the Money Is, AARP Tells Marketers." *New York Times*. July 13.

Ellis, Allison M., Talya N. Bauer, and Berrin Erdogan. 2015. "New-Employee Organizational Socialization: Adjusting to New Roles, Colleagues, and Organizations." In *Handbook of Socialization: Theory and Research,* 2nd ed., edited by Joan E. Grusec and Paul D. Hastings, 301–324. New York: Guilford Press.

Ellison, Katherine. 2015. "A.D.H.D. Rates Rise Around the Globe, but Sympathy Often Lags." *New York Times,* November 9.

Elo, Irma T. 2007. "Mortality: Transitions and Measures." In *The Blackwell Encyclopedia of Sociology,* edited by George Ritzer, 3096–3102. Malden, MA: Blackwell.

Elo, Irma T. 2009. "Social Class Differentials in Health and Mortality: Patterns and Explanations in Comparative Perspective." *Annual Review of Sociology* 35: 553–572.

Ember, Sydney. 2014. "On To-Do List: Deposit Cash in Bitcoin ATM." *New York Times,* August 25.

Ender, Morton. 2002. *Military Brats and Other Global Nomads: Growing Up in Organization Families.* Westport, CT: Praeger.

Engels, Friedrich. [1884] 1970. *The Origins of the Family, Private Property and the State.* New York: International Publishers.

England, Paula. 2010. "The Gender Revolution: Uneven and Stalled." *Gender & Society* 24(2): 149–166.

England, Paula, and Kathryn Edin. 2009. "Briefing Paper: Unmarried Couples with Children: Why Don't They Marry? How Can Policy-Makers Promote More Stable Relationships?" In *Families as They Really Are,* edited by B. J. Risman, 307–312. New York: Norton.

EnglishEnglish.com. n.d. "The English Language: Facts and Figures." Accessed January 3, 2012. http://www.englishenglish.com/english_facts_8.htm.

Entwhistle, Joanne. 2015. *The Aesthetic Economy of Fashion: Markets and Value in Clothing and Modelling.* New York: Berg.

Epstein, Richard A. 2014. "Big Law and Big Med: The Deprofessionalization of Legal and Medical Services." *International Review of Law and Economics* 38: 64–76.

Epstein, Steve. 2009. *Inclusion: The Politics of Difference in Medical Research.* Chicago: University of Chicago Press.

Erikson, Kai T. 1964. "Notes on the Sociology of Deviance." In *The Other Side: Perspectives on Deviance,* edited by H. S. Becker. New York: Free Press.

Erikson, Kai T. 1976. *Everything in Its Path: Destruction of Community in the Buffalo Creek Flood.* New York: Simon & Schuster.

Erlanger, Steven. 2014. "In West ISIS Finds Women Eager to Enlist." *New York Times,* October 23.

Esping-Anderson, Gosta. 1990. *The Three Worlds of Welfare Capitalism.* Princeton, NJ: Princeton University Press.

Etezadazdeh, Chirine. 2016. Smart City—Future City? Smart City 2.0 as a Livable City and Future Market. Neu-Isenburg: Springer.

Etzioni, Amitai, ed. 1969. *The Semi-professions and Their Organization: Teachers, Nurses, and Social Workers.* New York: Free Press.

Faderman, Lillian. 1991. *Odd Girls and Twilight Lovers: A History of Lesbian Life in Twentieth-Century America.* New York: Penguin.

Fadiman, Anne. 2012. *The Spirit Catches You and You Fall Down: A Hmong Child, Her American Doctors, and the Collision of Two Cultures.* Rev. ed. New York: Farrar, Straus and Giroux.

Fahim, Kareem. 2010. "Away from Home, Fleeing Domestic Life: Immigrant Maids Suffer Abuse in Kuwait." *New York Times,* August 2.

Faist, Thomas, Margit Fauser, and Eveline Reisenauer. 2013. *Transnational Migration.* Cambridge: Polity Press.

Farber, Henry. 2011. "Job Loss in the Great Recession: Historical Perspective from Displaced Workers Survey, 1984–2010." Paper presented at a Federal Reserve Conference, San Francisco, May.

Farber, Henry S. 2015. *Job loss in the Great Recession and Its Aftermath: U.S. Evidence from the Displaced Workers Survey.* Cambridge, MA: National Bureau of Economic Research.

Farley, John E. 2011. *Majority–Minority Relations.* 6th ed., Census Update. Upper Saddle River, NJ: Prentice Hall.

Farrell, Betty, Alicia VandeVusse, and Abigail Ocobock. 2012. "Family Change and the State of Family Sociology." *Current Sociology* 60(3): 283–301.

Farrell, Caitlin, Priscilla Wohlstetter, and Joanna Smith. 2012. "Charter Management Organizations: An Emerging Approach to Scaling Up What Works." *Educational Policy* 26(4): 499–532.

Farrell, Dan, and James C. Peterson. 2010. "The Growth of Internet Research Methods and the Reluctant Sociologist." *Sociological Inquiry* 80: 114–125.

Fassmann, Heinz, and Rainer Munz. 1992. "Patterns and Trends of International Migration in Western Europe." *Population and Development Review* 18: 457–480.

Fausto-Sterling, A. 1999. "The Five Sexes: Why Female and Male Are Not Enough." *The Sciences,* March/April, 20–24.

Feagin, Joe R. 2006. *Systemic Racism: A Theory of Oppression.* New York: Routledge.

Feagin, Joe R. 2012. White Party, White Government: Race, Class, and U.S. Politics. New York: Routledge.

Feagin, Joe R. 2013. *The White Racial Frame: Centuries of Racial Framing and Counter-framing.* 2nd ed. New York: Routledge.

Feagin, Joe R., and Jose A. Cobas. 2014. *Latinos Facing Racism: Discrimination, Resistance, and Endurance.* New York: Paradigm Publishers.

Federal Bureau of Investigation. 2014. "Frequently Asked Questions about the Change in the UCR Definition of Rape." December 11. Accessed April 19, 2015. http://www.fbi.gov/about-us/cjis/ucr/recent-program-updates/new-rape-definition-frequently-asked-questions.

Ferguson, Ann Arnett. 2001. *Bad Boys: Public Schools in the Making of Black Masculinity.* Ann Arbor: University of Michigan Press.

Fernandes, Leela. 2013. *Transnational Feminism in the United States: Knowledge, Ethics, Power.* New York: New York University Press.

Fernandez, Bina. 2010. "Cheap and Disposable? The Impact of the Global Economic Crisis on the Migration of Ethiopian Women Domestic Workers to the Gulf." *Gender and Development* 8(2): 249–262.

Fernyhough, Charles. 2014. "Do Deaf People Hear an Inner Voice?" *Psychology Today,* Voices Within blog, January 24. Accessed April 27, 2015. https//:www.psychologytoday.com/blog/the-voices-within/201401/do-deaf-people-hear-inner-voice.

Ferrarini, Tommy, and Kenneth Nelson. 2016. "Social Transfers and Poverty in Middle-and High-Income Countries—A Global Perspective." *Global Social Policy* 16: 22–46.

Ferree, Myra Marx, and Aili Mari Tripp. 2006. "Preface." In *Global Feminism: Transnational Women's Activism, Organizing, and Human Rights,* edited by M. M. Ferree and A. M. Tripp, vii–ix. New York: New York University Press.

Ferreira, Vitor Sérgio. 2014. "Becoming a Heavily Tattooed Young Body: From a Bodily Experience to a Body Project." *Youth & Society* 46(3): 303–337.

Fetscherin, Marc, and Renee-Marie Stephano, 2016. "The Medical Tourism Index: Scale Development and Validation." *Tourism Management* 52: 539–556.

Few-Demo, April L., and David H. Demo. 2016. "Family Diversity." In *The Wiley-Blackwell Encyclopedia of Race, Ethnicity and Nationalism,* edited by John Stone, Rutledge M. Dennis, Polly Rizova, Anthony D. Smith, and Xiaoshuo Hou. Malden, MA: Wiley-Blackwell.

Fiddian-Qasmiyeh, Elena. 2012. "Diaspora." In *The Wiley-Blackwell Encyclopedia of Globalization,* edited by George Ritzer, 430–433. Malden, MA: Wiley-Blackwell.

Fielding, A. J. 1989. "Migration and Urbanization in Western Europe since 1950." *Geographical Journal* 155: 60–69.

Fields, Jessica, Martha Copp, and Sherryl Kleinman. 2007. "Symbolic Interactionism, Inequality, and Emotions." In *Handbook of the Sociology of Emotions,* edited by J. E. Stets and J. H. Turner, 155–178. New York: Springer.

Figlio, David, and Cassandra M. Hart. 2014. "Competitive Effects of Means-Tested of School Vouchers." *American Economic Journal: Applied Economics* 6: 133–156.

Filkins, Dexter. 2016. "The End of Ice: Exploring a Himalayan Glacier." *New Yorker,* April 4.

Fillipi, Veronique, Carine Ronsman, Oona M. R. Campbell, Wendy J. Graham, Anne Mills, Jo Borghi, Marjorie Koblinsky, and David Osrin. 2006. "Maternal Health in Poor Countries: The Broader Context and a Call for Action." *The Lancet* 368: 1525–1541.

Fine, Gary Alan. 1987. *With the Boys: Little League Baseball and Preadolescent Culture.* Chicago: University of Chicago.

Fine, Gary Alan. 2008. *Kitchens: The Culture of Restaurant Work.* Berkeley: University of California Press.

Fine, Gary Alan. 2010. *Authors of the Storm: Meteorologists and the Culture of Prediction.* Chicago: University of Chicago Press.

Fine, Gary Alan. 2012. "Group Culture and the Interaction Order: Local Sociology on the Meso-Level." *Annual Review of Sociology* 38: 159–179.

Fine, Gary Alan. 2015. *Players and Pawns: How Chess Builds Community and Culture.* Chicago: University of Chicago Press.

Finke, Roger, and Rodney Stark. 2005. *The Churching of America, 1776–2005: Winners and Losers in Our Religious Economy.* New Brunswick, NJ: Rutgers University Press.

Fischer, Claude S., Michael Hout, Martin Sanchez Jankowski, and Samuel R. Lucas, eds. 1996. *Inequality by Design: Cracking the Bell Curve Myth.* Princeton, NJ: Princeton University Press.

Fisher, Dana. 2012. "Environmental Activism." In *The Wiley-Blackwell Encyclopedia of Globalization,* edited by George Ritzer, 517–519. Malden, MA: Wiley-Blackwell.

Fisher, Max. 2016. "Attack in Nice, France, Represents Terrorism's New Reality." *New York Times,* July 15.

Fitzsimmons, Emma G. 2016. "Subways in Northeast Showing Their Age. That Isn't the Only Problem." *New York Times,* May 27.

Flack, William F., Jr., Kimberly A. Daubman, Marcia L. Caron, Jenica A. Asadorian, Nicole R. D'Aureli, Shannon N. Gigliotti, et al. 2007. "Risk Factors and Consequences of Unwanted Sex among University Students: Hooking Up, Alcohol, and Stress Response." *Journal of Interpersonal Violence* 22(2): 139–157.

Fleming, Crystal M., and Aldon Morris. 2015. "Theorizing Ethnic and Racial Movements in the Global Age: Lessons from the Civil Rights Movement." *Sociology of Race and Ethnicity* 1: 105–126.

Flodgren, Gerd, Antoine Rachas, Andrew Farmer, Marco Inzitiari, and Sasha Shepperd. 2015. "Interactive Telemedicine: Effects on Professional Practice and Healthcare Outcomes." *Cochrane Database of Systemic Reviews,* Issue 9.

Fontana, Andrea. 2007. "Interviewing, Structured, Unstructured, and Postmodern." In *The Blackwell Encyclopedia of Sociology,* edited by George Ritzer, 2407–2411. Malden, MA: Blackwell.

Ford, Martin. 2015. *Rise of the Robots: Technology and the Threat of a Jobless Future.* New York: Basic Books.

Forno, Francesca. 2013. "Consumer Movements." In *The Wiley-Blackwell Encyclopedia of Social and Political Movements,* 3 vols., edited by D. A. Snow, D. Della Porta, B. Klandermans, and D. McAdam, 253–256. Malden, MA: Wiley-Blackwell.

Fothergill, Alice, and Lori Peek. 2015. *Children of Katrina.* Austin: University of Texas Press.

Foucault, Michel. 1975. *The Birth of the Clinic: An Archaeology of Medical Perception.* New York: Vintage Books.

Foucault, Michel. [1975] 1979. *Discipline and Punish: The Birth of the Prison.* New York: Vintage Books.

Foucault, Michel. 1978. *The History of Sexuality,* Vol. 1, *An Introduction.* New York: Vintage Books.

Fountain, Henry. 2015. "Panel Urges Research on Geoengineering as a Tool against Climate Change." *New York Times,* February 10.

Fournier, Marcel. 2013. *Émile Durkheim: A Biography.* Cambridge: Polity Press.

Frakt, Austin. 2016. You Mean I Don't Have to Show Up? The Promise of Telemedicine. *The New York Times,* May 16.

Francis, Mark. 2011. "Herbert Spencer." In *The Wiley-Blackwell Companion to Major Social Theorists,* Vol. 1, *Classical Theorists,* edited by George Ritzer and Jeffrey Stepnisky, 165–184. Malden, MA: Wiley-Blackwell.

Frank, David John. 2012. "Global Sex." In *The Wiley-Blackwell Encyclopedia of Globalization,* edited by George Ritzer. Malden, MA: Wiley-Blackwell.

Frank, Robert H. 2013. *Falling Behind: How Rising Inequality Harms the Middle Class.* Berkeley: University of California Press.

Frank, Robert H. 2016. *Success and Luck: Good Fortune and the Myth of Meritocracy.* Princeton, NJ: Princeton University Press.

Freedman, Russell. 2009. *Freedom Walkers: The Story of the Montgomery Bus Boycott.* New York: Holiday House.

Freedman, Samuel G. 2016. "North Dakota Mosque a Symbol of Muslims' Long Ties in America." *New York Times,* May 27.

Friedan, Betty. 1963. *The Feminine Mystique.* New York: Dell.

Friedkin, N. E. 2001. "Norm Formation in Social Influence Networks." *Social Networks* 23(3): 167–189.

Friedman, Debra, and Michael Hechter. 1988. "The Contribution of Rational Choice Theory to Macrosociological Research." *Sociological Theory* 6: 201–218.

Friedmann, Naama, and Dana Rusou, 2015. "Critical Period for First Language: The Crucial Role of Language Input During the First Year of Life." *Current Opinion in Neurobiology* 35: 27–34.

Fulbrook, Julian. 2007. "Tobacco." In *Encyclopedia of Globalization,* edited by J. A. Scholte and R. Robertson 1146–1149. New York: MTM.

Fung, Archon. 2004. *Empowered Participation: Reinventing Urban Democracy.* Princeton, NJ: Princeton University Press.

Funk, Laura M., and Karen M. Kobayashi. 2016. "From Motivations to Accounts: An Interpretive Analysis of 'Living Apart Together' Relations in Mid- to Later-Life Couples." *Journal of Family Issues* 37: 1101–1122.

Gabaccia, Donna R. Forthcoming. "The Feminization of Migration." In *The Wiley-Blackwell Encyclopedia of Gender and Sexuality Studies,* edited by Nancy Naples.

Gabriel, Yiannis, Marek Korczynski, and Kirsten Rieder, 2015. "Organizations and Their Consumers: Bridging Work and Consumers." *Organization* 22: 629–643.

Galston, William A., Steven Kull, and Clay Ramsay. 2009. *Battleground or Common*

Ground? *American Public Opinion on Health Care Reform.* Washington, DC: Brookings Institution.

Gambino, Matthew. 2013. "Erving Goffman's Asylums and Institutional Culture in the Mid-Twentieth-Century United States." *Harvard Review of Psychiatry* 21: 52–57.

Gamoran, Adam, and Daniel A. Long. 2006. "Equality of Educational Opportunity: A 40-Year Retrospective." WCER Working Paper 2006-9, Wisconsin Center for Education Research, Madison. Accessed July 13, 2013. http://www.wcer.wisc.edu.

Gamoran, Adam, and Robert D. Mare. 1989. "Secondary School Tracking and Educational Inequality: Compensation, Reinforcement, or Neutrality?" *American Journal of Sociology* 94: 1146–1183.

Gamoran, Adam, Martin Nystrand, Mark Berends, and Paul C. LePore. 1995. "An Organizational Analysis of the Effects of Ability Grouping." *American Educational Research Journal* 32: 687–715.

Ganong, Lawrence, and Marilyn Coleman, eds. 2017. *Stepfamily Relationships: Development, Dynamics and Intervention.* 2nd ed. New York: Springer.

Gans, Herbert J. 1979. *Deciding What's News.* New York: Pantheon.

Gans, Herbert J. 2009. "First Generation Decline: Downward Mobility among Refugees and Immigrants." *Ethnic and Racial Studies* 32: 1658–1670.

Gansky, Lisa. 2010. *The Mesh: Why the Future of Business Is Sharing.* New York: Penguin.

Garcia, David. 2008. "The Impact of School Choice on Racial Segregation in Charter Schools." *Educational Policy* 22(6): 805–829.

Garcia, Lorena. 2012. *Respect Yourself, Protect Yourself: Latina Girls and Sexual Identity.* New York: New York University Press.

Garfield, Bob. 1991. "How I Spent (and Spent and Spent) My Disney Vacation." *Washington Post,* July 7.

Garfinkel, Harold. 1967. *Studies in Ethnomethodology.* Malden, MA: Blackwell.

Garlick, Steve. 2014. "The Biopolitics of Masturbation: Masculinity, Complexity, and Security." *Body & Society* 20: 44–67.

Garon, Sheldon. 2006. "Japan's Post-war 'Consumer Revolution,' or Striking a 'Balance' between Consumption and Saving." In *Consuming Cultures, Global Perspectives: Historical Trajectories, Transnational Exchanges,* edited by J. Brewer and F. Trentmann. Oxford: Berg.

Garrett, William R. 2007. "Christianity." In *Encyclopedia of Globalization,* edited by J. A. Scholte and R. Robertson, 139–144. New York: MTM.

Gartner, Rosemary. 2007. "Violent Crime." In *The Blackwell Encyclopedia of Sociology,* edited by George Ritzer, 5206–5208. Malden, MA: Blackwell.

Gauchat, Gordon, Maura Kelly, and Michael Wallace. 2012. "Occupational Gender Segregation, Globalization, and Gender Earnings Inequality in U.S. Metropolitan Areas." *Gender & Society* 26: 718–747.

Gee, Laura K., Jason Jones, and Moira Burke. Forthcoming. "Social Networks and Labor Markets: How Strong Ties Relate to Job Finding on Facebook's Social Network." *Journal of Labor Economics.*

Geertz, Clifford. 1973. *The Interpretation of Cultures.* New York: Basic Books.

Geis, Gilbert. 2007a. "Crime, Corporate." In *The Blackwell Encyclopedia of Sociology,* edited by George Ritzer, 826–828. Malden, MA: Blackwell.

Geis, Gilbert. 2007b. "Crime, White-Collar." In *The Blackwell Encyclopedia of Sociology,* edited by George Ritzer, 850–851. Malden, MA: Blackwell.

Gentina, Elodie, and Isabelle Muratore. 2012. "Environmentalism at Home: The Process of Ecological Resocialization by Teenagers." *Journal of Consumer Behaviour* 11: 162–169.

Gentry, Caron, and Laura Sjoberg. 2015. "Terrorism and Political Violence." In *Gender Matters in Global Politics: A Feminist Introduction to International Relations,* 2nd ed., edited by L. J. Shepherd, 120–130. New York: Routledge.

Gerhardt, H. Carl, and Franz Huber. 2002. *Acoustic Communication in Insects and Anurans: Common Problems and Diverse Solutions.* Chicago: University of Chicago Press.

Gerland, Patrick, Adrian E. Raftery, Hana Ševčíková, Nan Li, Danan Gu, Thomas Spoorenberg, Leontine Alkema, Bailey K. Fosdick, Jennifer Chunn, Nevena Lalic, Guiomar Bay, Thomas Buettner, Gerhard K. Heilig, and John Wilmoth. 2014. "World Population Stabilization Unlikely This Century." *Science* 346(6206): 234–237.

Gerson, Kathleen. 2011. *The Unfinished Revolution: Coming of Age in a New Era of Gender, Work, and Family.* Oxford: Oxford University Press.

Gervais, Sarah J., Arianne M. Holland, and Michael D. Dodd. 2013. "My Eyes Are Up Here: The Nature of the Objectifying Gaze toward Women." *Sex Roles* 69: 557–570.

Gesselamn, Amanda N., Gregory D. Webster, and Justin R. Garcia, 2016. "Has Virginity Lost Its Virtue? Relationship Stigma Associated With Being a Sexually Inexperienced Adult." *Journal of Sex Research,* March 2016 (published online).

Ghaziani, Amin, Verta Taylor, and Amy Stone. 2016. "Cycles of Sameness and Difference in LGBT Social Movements." *Annual Review of Sociology* 42: 165–183.

Ghumman, Sonia, and Ann Maries Ryan. 2013. "Not Welcome Here: Discrimination towards Women Who Wear the Muslim Headscarf." *Human Relations* 66: 671–698.

Giddens, Anthony 1984. *The Constitution of Society: Outline of the Theory of Structuration.* Berkeley: University of California Press.

Giddens, Anthony. 1992. *The Transformation of Intimacy: Sexuality, Love and Eroticism in Modern Societies.* Stanford, CA: Stanford University Press.

Gilbert, Dennis L. 2015. *The American Class Structure in an Age of Growing Inequality.* 9th ed. Thousand Oaks, CA: Sage.

Gilbert, Dennis L., and Joseph A. Kahl. 1993. *The American Class Structure: A New Synthesis.* Belmont, CA: Wadsworth.

Gillis, Justin. 2015. "Climate Accord is a Healing Step, if Not a Cure." *New York Times,* December 12.

Gillis, Justin. 2016. "Flooding of Coast, Caused by Global Warming, Has Already Begun." *New York Times,* September 3.

Gilman, Nils, Jesse Goldhammer, and Steven Weber, eds. 2011. *Deviant Globalization: Black Market Economy in the 21st Century.* London: Continuum.

Gilroy, Paul. 1993. *The Black Atlantic: Modernity and Double Consciousness.* London: Verso Books.

Gimlin, Debra. 2007. "Accounting for Cosmetic Surgery in the USA and Great Britain: A Cross-Cultural Analysis of Women's Narratives." *Body and Society* 13: 41–60.

Giroux, Henry A., and David E. Purpel, eds. 1983. *The Hidden Curriculum and Moral Education.* Berkeley, CA: McCutchan.

Gitlin, Todd. 1993. *The Sixties: Years of Hope, Days of Rage.* New York: Bantam.

Givoni, Michal. 2016. "Between Micro Mappers and Missing Maps: Digital Humanitarianism and the Politics of Material Participation in Disaster Response." *Environment and Planning D: Society and Space* 34(6): 1025–1043.

Gladstone, Rick. 2015. "Report Details New Atrocities in Darfur by Sudanese Forces." *New York Times,* September 9.

Glantz, Michael H., ed. 1977. *Desertification: Environmental Degradation in and around Arid Lands.* Boulder, CO: Westview Press.

Glenny, Misha. 2008. *McMafia: A Journey through the Global Criminal Underworld.* New York: Knopf.

Glenny, Misha. 2015. "The Refugee Crisis Has Produced One Winner: Organized Crime." *New York Times,* September 20.

Global Nonviolent Action Database, Swarthmore College. 2011. "East Los Angeles Students Walkout for Educational Reform (East L.A. Blowouts), 1968." Accessed May 8, 2015. http://nvdatabase.swarthmore.edu/content/east-los-angeles-students-walkout-educational-reform-east-la-blowouts-1968.

Global Nutrition Report. 2016. *From Promise to Impact: Ending Malnutrition by 2030.* Washington, DC: International Food Policy Research Institute.

Gloor, Peter, and Scott Cooper. 2007. *Coolhunting: Chasing Down the Next Big Thing.* New York: AMACOM.

Gmelch, Sharon Bohn, ed. 2010. *Tourists and Tourism: A Reader.* Prospect Heights, IL: Waveland Press.

Godlee, Fiona, Neil Pakenham-Walsh, Dan Ncayiyana, Barbara Cohen, and Abel Packer. 2004. "Can We Achieve Health Information for All by 2015?" *The Lancet* 364: 295–300.

Godwyn, Mary, and Jody Hoffer Gittell, eds. 2011. *Sociology of Organizations: Structures and Relationships.* Thousand Oaks, CA: Pine Forge Press.

Goffman, Alice. 2014. *On the Run: Fugitive Life in an American City.* Chicago: University of Chicago Press.

Goffman, Erving. 1959. *The Presentation of Self in Everyday Life.* Garden City, NY: Anchor Books.

Goffman, Erving. 1961a. *Asylums: Essays on the Social Situation of Mental Patients and Other Inmates.* Garden City, NY: Anchor Books.

Goffman, Erving. 1961b. *Encounters.* Indianapolis: Bobbs-Merrill.

Goffman, Erving. 1963. *Stigma: Notes on the Management of Spoiled Identity.* Englewood Cliffs, NJ: Prentice Hall/Spectrum.

Goffman, Erving. 2000. *Exploring the Interaction Order.* Cambridge: Polity Press.

Goldberg, David Theo. 2009. "Racial Comparisons, Relational Racisms: Some Thoughts on Method." *Ethnic and Racial Studies* 32: 1271–1282.

Goldberg, Gertrude Schaffner, ed. 2010. *Poor Women in Rich Countries: The Feminization of Poverty over the Life Course.* New York: Oxford University Press.

Goldberg, Harvey E. 2007. "Judaism." In *Encyclopedia of Globalization,* edited by J. A. Scholte and R. Robertson, 690–693. New York: MTM.

Goldfield, Michael, and Amy Bromsen. 2013. "The Changing Landscape of U.S. Unions in Historical and Theoretical Perspective." *Annual Review of Political Science* 16: 231–257.

Goldin, Claudia, Lawrence F. Katz, and Ilyana Kuziemko. 2006. "The Homecoming of American College Women: The Reversal of the College Gender Gap." *Journal of Economic Perspectives* 20: 133–156.

Goldman, Liran, Howard Giles, and Michael A. Hogg. 2014. "Going to Extremes: Social Identity and Communication Processes Associated with Gang Membership." *Group Processes & Intergroup Relations* 17: 813–832.

Goldman, Robert, and Stephen Papson. 1998. *Nike Culture.* London: Sage.

Goldscheider, Calvin. 2012. "Judaism." In *The Wiley-Blackwell Encyclopedia of Globalization,* edited by George Ritzer, 1225–1234. Malden, MA: Wiley-Blackwell.

Goldschmied, Nadav, and Jason Kowalczyk. 2016. "Gender Performance in the NCAA Rifle Championship: Where Is the Gap?" *Sex Roles* 74: 310–322.

Goldstein, Amy. 2017. *Janesville: An American Story.* New York: Simon and Schuster.

Goldstone, Jack. 1991. *Revolution and Rebellion in the Early Modern World.* Berkeley: University of California Press.

Goli, Srinivas, Riddhi Doshi, and Arokiasamy Perianayagam. 2013. "Pathways of Economic Inequalities in Maternal and Child Health in Urban India: A Decomposition Analysis." *PloS ONE* 8(3): e58573. Accessed April 19, 2015. http://www.plosone.org/article/info%3Adoi%2F10.1371%2Fjournal.pone.0058573#pone-0058573-g001.

Goode, Erich. 2002. "Sexual Involvement and Social Research in a Fat Civil Rights Organization." *Qualitative Sociology* 25(4): 501–534.

Goode, Erich. 2014. "Labeling Theory." In *Encyclopedia of Criminology and Criminal Justice,* edited by G. Bruinsma and D. Weisburd, 2807–2814. New York: Springer.

Goode, Erich, and Nachman Ben-Yehuda. 2009. *Moral Panics: The Social Constuction of Deviance.* 2nd edition. Malden, MA: Blackwell.

Goodlin, Wendi E., and Christopher S. Dunn. 2011. "Three Patterns of Domestic Violence in Households: Single Victimization, Repeat Victimization, and Co-occurring Victimization." *Journal of Family Violence* 26: 101–108.

Goodman, David M. 2016. "The McDonaldization of Psychotherapy: Processed foods, Processed Therapies, and Economic Class." *Theory and Psychology* 26: 77–95.

Goodwin, Jennifer. 2011. "U.S. Rates of Autism, ADHD Continue to Rise: Report." *U.S. News & World Report,* May 23. Accessed May 25, 2011. http://health.usnews.com/health-news/family-health/brain-and-behavior/articles/2011/05/23/us-rates-of-autism-adhd-continue-to-rise-report.

Gopal, Prashant. 2014. "Brooklyn Worst in U.S. for Home Affordability." *Bloomberg Business,* December 3. Accessed April 19, 2015. http://www.bloomberg.com/news/articles/2014-12-04/brooklyn-worst-in-u-s-for-home-affordability.

Gorman, Elizabeth H., and Julie A. Kmec. 2009. "Hierarchical Rank and Women's Organizational Mobility: Glass Ceilings in Corporate Law Firms." *American Journal of Sociology* 114: 1428–1474.

Gorski, Philip S. 2011. "Barack Obama and Civil Religion." In *Rethinking Obama,* edited by J. Go. Bingley, 179–214. Bingley, UK: Emerald.

Gottman, Jean. 1961. *Megalopolis: The Urbanized Northeastern Seaboard of the United States.* New York: Twentieth Century Fund.

Gottschalk, Simon. 2010. "The Presentation of Avatars in Second Life: Self and Interaction in Social Virtual Spaces." *Symbolic Interaction* 33(4): 501–525.

Gough, Brendan. Forthcoming. "Hegemonic Masculinities." In *The Wiley Blackwell Encyclopedia of Gender and Sexuality Studies,* edited by Nancy Naples.

Gould, Kenneth, David N. Pellow, and Allan Schnaiberg. 2008. *The Treadmill of Production: Injustice and Unsustainability in the Global Economy.* Boulder, CO: Paradigm.

Gouldner, Alvin W. 1960. "The Norm of Reciprocity: A Preliminary Statement." *American Sociological Review* 25(2): 161–178.

Gove, Walter R., and Michael Hughes. 1979. "Possible Causes of the Apparent Sex Differences in Physical Health: An Empirical Investigation." *American Sociological Review* 44: 126–146.

Gozdecka, Dorota A., Slen A. Ercan, and Magdalena Kmak. 2014. "From Multiculturalism to Post-multiculturalism: Trends and Paradoxes." *Journal of Sociology* 50: 51–64.

Grady, Denise. 2015. "Measles: Perilous but Preventable." *New York Times,* February 2.

Grandin, Temple. 2000. "My Experiences with Visual Thinking Sensory Problems and Communication Difficulties." Autism Research Institute. Accessed April 27, 2015. http://www.autism.com/advocacy_grandin_visual%20thinking.

Granfield, Robert. 1992. *Making Elite Lawyers: Visions of Law at Harvard and Beyond.* New York: Routledge, Chapman and Hall.

Granovetter, Mark. 1973. "The Strength of Weak Ties." *American Journal of Sociology* 78(6): 1360–1380.

Granville, Kevin. 2016. "The Trans-Pacific Partnership Trade Accord Explained." *New York Times,* July 26.

Greenhouse, Steven. 2011. "Union Membership in U.S. Fell to a 70-Year Low Last Year." *New York Times,* January 21.

Greenhouse, Steven. 2015. "The Mystery of the Vanishing Pay Raise." *New York Times,* October 31.

Grice, Elizabeth. 2006. "Cry of an Enfant Sauvage." *Daily Telegraph,* July 17.

Griffin, Christine, Isabelle Szmigin, Andrew Bengry-Howell, Chris Hackley, and Willm Mistral. 2012. "Inhabiting the Contradictions: Hypersexual Femininity and the Culture of Intoxication among Young Women in the UK." *Feminism & Psychology* 23(2): 184–206.

Griffin, Sean Patrick. 2007. "Crime, Organized." In *The Blackwell Encyclopedia of Sociology,* edited by George Ritzer, 833–834. Malden, MA: Blackwell.

Griswold, Alison. 2014. "Are Smartphones Ruining the Restaurant Experience?" *Slate,* July 16. Accessed April 22, 2015. http://www.slate.com/articles/business/moneybox/2014/07/viral_craigslist_post_on_smartphones_in_restaurants_is_tech_ruining_the.html.

Gu, Dongfeng, Tanika N. Kelly, Xigui Wu, Jing Chen, Jonathan M. Samet, Jianfeng Huang, Manlu Zhu, Ji-chun Chen, Chung-shiuan Chen, Xiufang Duan, Michael J. Klag, and Jiang He. 2009. "Mortality Attributable to Smoking in China." *New England Journal of Medicine* 360: 150–159.

Gubrium, Jaber F., James A. Holstein, Amir B. Marvasti, and Karyn D. McKinney, eds. 2012. *The SAGE Handbook of Interview Research: The Complexity of the Craft.* 2nd ed. Thousand Oaks, CA: Sage.

Guetterman, Tomothy C., Michael D. Fetters, and John W. Creswell, 2015. "Integrating Quantitative and Qualitative Results in Health Science Mixed Methods Research Through Joint Displays." *Annals of Family Medicine* 13: 554–561.

Gulati, Ranjay, and Phanish Puranam. 2009. "Renewal through Reorganization: The Value of Inconsistencies between Formal and Informal Organization." *Organization Science* 20: 422–440.

Gündüz, Zuhal Yesilyurt. 2013. "The Feminization of Migration: Care and the New Emotional Imperialism." *Monthly Review* 65(7): 32–43.

Guo, Guang, Yilan Fu, Hedwig Lee, Tianji Cai, Kathleen Mullan Harris, and Yi Li. 2014. "Genetic Bio-Ancestry and Social Construction of Racial Classification in Social Surveys in the Contemporary United States." *Demography* 51: 141–172.

Guo, Shibao. 2013. "Economic Integration of Recent Chinese Immigrants in Canada's Second-Tier Cities: The Triple Glass Effect and Immigrants' Downward Social Mobility." *Canadian Ethnic Studies* 45: 95–115.

Gylling, Michael, et al. 2015. "Making Decisions on Offshore Outsourcing and Backsourcing: A Case Study in the Bicycle Industry." *International Journal of Production Economics* 162: 925100

Hacker, Jacob S., and Paul Pierson. 2010. *Winner-Take-All Politics: How Washington Made the Rich Richer—and Turned Its Back on the Middle Class.* New York: Simon & Schuster.

Haddad, Nick M., Lars A. Brudvig, Jean Clobert, Kendi F. Davies, Andrew Gonzalez, Robert D. Holt, Thomas E. Lovejoy, Joseph O. Sexton, Mike P. Austin, Cathy D. Collins, William M. Cook, Ellen I. Damschen, Robert M. Ewers, Bryan L. Foster, Clinton N. Jenkins, Andrew J. King, William F. Laurance, Douglas J. Levey, Chris R. Margules, Brett A. Melbourne, A. O. Nicholls, John L. Orrock, Dan-Xia Song, and John R. Townshend. 2015. "Habitat Fragmentation and Its Lasting Impact on Earth's Ecosystems." *Science Advances* 1: 1–9.

Hadid, Diaa, and Majd al Waheidi, 2016. "As Hamas Tunnels Back Into Israel; Palestinians are, Afraid, Too." *New York Times,* May 20.

Hafferty, Frederic W. 2009. "Professionalism and the Socialization of Medical Students." In *Teaching Medical Professionalism,* edited by R. L. Cruess, S. R. Cruess, and Y. Steinert, 53–69. New York: Cambridge University Press.

Hafferty, Frederic W., and Brian Castellani. 2011. "Two Cultures: Two Ships: The Rise of a Professionalism Movement within Modern Medicine and Medical Sociology's Disappearance from the Professionalism Debate." In *Handbook of the Sociology of Health, Illness, and Healing: A Blueprint for the 21st Century,* edited by B. A. Pescosolido, J. K. Martin, J. D. McLeod, and A. Rogers, 201–220. Dordrecht, Netherlands: Springer.

"Haiti, Unfinished and Forsaken." 2014. *New York Times,* January 10.

Hakim, Catherine. 2011. *Erotic Capital: The Power of Attraction in the Boardroom and the Bedroom.* New York: Basic Books.

Hall, Peter, and David Soskice, eds. 2001. *Varieties of Capitalism: The Institutional Foundations of Comparative Advantage.* New York: Oxford University Press.

Hamermesh, Daniel S. 2011. *Beauty Pays: Why Attractive People Are More Successful.* Princeton, NJ: Princeton University Press.

Hamilton, Laura, and Elizabeth A. Armstrong. 2009. "Gendered Sexuality in Young Adulthood: Double Binds and Flawed Options." *Gender & Society* 23(5): 589–616.

Hammersley, Martyn. 2007. "Ethnography." In *The Blackwell Encyclopedia of Sociology,* edited by George Ritzer, 1479–1483. Malden, MA: Blackwell.

Hamouda, Manel, and Abderrazak Gharbi. 2013. "The Postmodern Consumer: An Identity Constructor?" *International Journal of Marketing Studies* 5(2): 41–49.

Handelman, Jay M., and Robert V. Kozinets. 2007. "Culture Jamming." In *The Blackwell Encyclopedia of Sociology,* edited by George Ritzer, 945–946. Malden, MA: Blackwell.

Haner, Josh. 2016. "Climate Refuges: Bolivia." *New York Times,* July 7.

Hankin, Janet R., and Eric R. Wright. 2010. "Reflections on Fifty Years of Medical Sociology." *Journal of Health and Social Behavior* 51: S10–S14.

Hannigan, John. 2007. "Fantasy City." In *The Blackwell Encyclopedia of Sociology,* edited by George Ritzer, 1641–1644. Malden, MA: Blackwell.

Haraway, Donna. 1991. "A Cyborg Manifesto: Science, Technology, and Socialist-Feminism in the Late Twentieth Century." In *Simians, Cyborgs and Women: The Reinvention of Nature,* 149–181. New York: Routledge.

Hardoon, Deborah. 2015. "Wealth: Having It All and Wanting More." Oxfam International, January. Accessed April 17, 2015. https://www.oxfam.org/sites/www.oxfam.org/files/file_attachments/ib-wealth-having-all-wanting-more-190115-en.pdf.

Harmon, Corinne, Glenda Carne, Kristina Lizardy-Hajbi, and Eugene Wilkerson. 2010. "Access to Higher Education for Undocumented Students: 'Outlaws' of Social Justice, Equity, and Equality." *Journal of Praxis in Multicultural Education* 5(1): 67–82.

Harrigan, Meredith Marko, Sarah Dieter, Jenna Leinwohl, and Laura Marrin. 2015. ""It's Just Who I Am . . . I Have Brown Hair. I Have a Mysterious Father:" An Explanation of Donor-Conceived Offspring's Identity Construction." *Journal of Family Communication* 15:75-93.

Harris, Alexes. 2016. A Pound of Flesh: Monetary Sanctions as Punishment for the Poor. New York: Russell Sage Foundation.

Harris, Douglas N., Carolyn D. Herrington, and Amy Albee. 2007. "The Future of Vouchers: Lessons from the Adoption, Design, and Court Challenges of Florida's Three Voucher Programs." *Educational Policy* 21(1): 215–244.

Harris Interactive. 2016. "Doctor Tops List of Prestigious Occupations." Press release, March 29. Accessed January 23, 2016. http://media.theharrispoll.com/documents/Prestigious+Occupations_Data+Tables.pdf.

Harrison, Bennett. 1994. *Lean and Mean: The Changing Landscape of Corporate Power in the Age of Flexibility.* New York: Basic Books.

Hart, Betty, and Todd Risley. 1995. *Meaningful Differences in the Everyday Experience of Young American Children.* Baltimore: Paul H. Brookes.

Hart, Jeni. 2016. "Dissecting a Gendered Organization: Implications for Career Trajectories for Mid-Career Faculty Women in STEM." *Journal of Higher Education* 87(5):605–634.

Hartigan, John. 2014. "Whiteness, Class and the Legacies of Empire: On Home Ground." *Ethnic and Racial Studies* 37(10): 1941–1944.

Hartmann, Heidi. 1979. "Capitalism, Patriarchy and Job Segregation by Sex." In *Capitalist Patriarchy and the Case for Socialist Feminism,* edited by Z. Eisenstein, 206–247. New York: Monthly Review Press.

Harvey, David. 2005. *A Brief History of Neoliberalism.* Oxford: Oxford University Press.

Harvey, David. 2007. "Poverty and Disrepute." In *The Blackwell Encyclopedia of Sociology,* edited by George Ritzer, 3589–3594. Malden, MA: Blackwell.

Hashemian, Farnoosh, and Derek Yach. 2007. "Public Health in a Globalizing World: Challenges and Opportunities." In *The Blackwell Companion to Globalization,* edited by George Ritzer, 516–538. Malden, MA: Blackwell.

Hatch, Anthony. 2009. *The Politics of Metabolism: The Metabolic Syndrome and the Reproduction of Race and Racism in the United States.* PhD dissertation, University of Maryland.

Hatch, Anthony. 2016. *Blood Sugar: Racial Pharmacology and Food Justice in Black America.* Minneapolis: University of Minnesota Press.

Hatfield, Elaine, Lisamarie Bensman, and Richard L. Rapson. 2012. "A Brief History of Social Scientists' Attempts to Measure Passionate Love." *Journal of Social and Personal Relationships* 29: 143–164.

Hatton, Erin, and Mary Nell Trautner. 2011. "Equal Opportunity Objectification? The Sexualization of Men and Women on the Cover of *Rolling Stone.*" *Sexuality & Culture* 15: 256–278.

Haub, Carl. 2013. "Rising Trend of Births Outside Marriage." Population Reference Bureau, April. Accessed April 20, 2015. http://www.prb.org/Publications/Articles/2013/nonmarital-births.aspx.

Hausmann, Ricardo, Ina Ganguli, and Martina Viarengo. 2009. "The Dynamics of the Gender Gap: How Do Countries Rank in Terms of Making Marriage and Motherhood Compatible with Work?" In *Global Gender Gap Report,* edited by R. Hausmann, L. D. Tyson, and S. Zahidi, 27–29 Geneva: World Economic Forum.

Hawkesworth, Mary. 2006. *Globalization and Feminist Activism.* Lanham, MD: Rowman & Littlefield.

Hay, Harry. 2012. "Birth of a Consciousness." *Gay & Lesbian Review Worldwide* 19: 15–18.

Hayes, Dennis, and Robin Wynyard, eds. 2002. *The McDonaldization of Higher Education.* Westport, CT: Bergin and Garvey.

Hays, Sharon. 1998. *The Cultural Contradictions of Motherhood.* New Haven, CT: Yale University Press.

Heaphy, Brian. 2007. "Same-Sex Marriage/Civil Unions." In *The Blackwell Encyclopedia of Sociology,* edited by George Ritzer, 3995–3998. Malden, MA: Blackwell.

Heckman, James. 2006. "Skill Formation and the Economics of Investing in Disadvantaged Children." *Science* 312: 1900–1902.

Heckman, James J., Seong Hyeok Moon, Rodrigo Pinto, Peter A. Savelyev, and Adam Yavitz. 2010. "The Rate of Return to the HighScope Perry Preschool Program." *Journal of Public Economics* 94: 114–128.

Hedgecoe, Adam. 2016. "Reputational Risk, Academic Freedom and Research Ethics Review." *Sociology* 50: 486–501.

Heintz, James. 2006. "Globalization, Economic Policy and Employment: Poverty and Gender Implications." Employment Strategy Unit, International Labour Organization. Accessed November 4, 2013. http://www.ilo.org/wcmsp5/groups/public/@ed_emp/@emp_elm/documents/publication/wcms_114024.pdf.

Heller, Nathan. 2013. "Laptop U." *New Yorker,* May 20, 80ff.

Helliwell, Christine. 2000. "'It's Only a Penis': Rape, Feminism, and Difference." *Signs* 25(3): 789–816.

Hendershott, Anne. 2002. *The Politics of Deviance.* San Francisco: Encounter Books.

Henningsen, David Dryden. 2004. "Flirting with Meaning: An Examination of Miscommunication in Flirting Interactions." *Sex Roles* 50: 481–489.

Hepburn, Stephanie, and Rita J. Simon. 2013. *Human Trafficking around the World: Hidden in Plain Sight.* New York: Columbia University Press.

Heritage, John, and Tanya Stivers. 2012. "Conversation Analysis and Sociology." In *The Handbook of Conversation Analysis,* edited by J. Sidnell and T. Stivers, 659–673. Malden, MA: Wiley Blackwell.

Herod, Andrew. 2009. *Geographies of Globalization: A Critical Introduction.* Malden, MA: Wiley-Blackwell.

Herrnstein, Richard J., and Charles Murray. 1994. *The Bell Curve: Intelligence and Class Structure in American Life.* New York: Free Press.

Hershkovitz, Shay. 2012. "Nation-State." In *The Wiley-Blackwell Encyclopedia of Globalization,* edited by George Ritzer, 1492–1496. Malden, MA: Wiley-Blackwell.

Herzog, Lawrence A. 2015. *Global Suburbs: Urban Sprawl from the Rio Grande to Rio de Janeiro.* New York: Routledge.

Heslin, Peter A., Myrtle P. Bell, and Pinar O. Fletcher. 2012. "The Devil Without and Within: A Conceptual Model of Social Cognitive Processes Whereby Discrimination Leads Stigmatized Minorities to Become Discouraged Workers." *Journal of Organizational Behavior* 33: 840–862.

Hesse-Biber, Sharlene. 1996. *Am I Thin Enough Yet? The Cult of Thinness and Commercialization of Identity.* London: Oxford University Press.

Heywood, Andrew. 2014. *Global Politics.* 2nd ed. New York: Palgrave Macmillian.

Hier, Sean. 2011. "Tightening the Focus: Moral Panic, Moral Regulation, and Liberal Government." *British Journal of Sociology* 62: 523–541.

High, Peter. 2015. "The Top Five Smart Cities in the World." *Forbes,* March 9.

Higley, John, and Michael Burton. 2006. *Elite Foundations of Liberal Democracy.* Lanham, MD: Rowman & Littlefield.

Hildebrandt, Achim. 2014. "Routes to Decriminalization: A Comparative Analysis of the Legalization of Same-Sex Sexual Acts." *Sexualities* 17: 230–253.

Hill, Jessica, and Pranee Liamputtong. 2011. "Being the Mother of a Child with Asperger's Syndrome: Women's Experiences of Stigma." *Health Care for Women International* 32: 708–722.

Hill, Nancy E., and Joshua B. Marion. 2016. *Introduction to Cybercrime.* Santa Barbara, CA: Praeger.

Himanen, Pekka. 2001. *The Hacker Ethic, and the Spirit of the Information Age.* New York: Random House.

Hirschi, Travis. 1969. *The Causes of Delinquency.* Berkeley: University of California Press.

Hoang, Kimberly Kay. 2015. *Dealing in Desire: Asian Ascendancy, Western Decline, and* the Hidden Currencies of Global Sex Work. Berkeley: University of California Press.

Hobsbawm, E. J., and Chris Wrigley. 1999. *Industry and Empire: The Birth of the Industrial Revolution*. New York: New Press.

Hochschild, Arlie Russell (with Anne Machung). 1989. *The Second Shift*. New York: Viking.

Hochschild, Arlie Russell. 2000. "Global Care Chains and Emotional Surplus Value." In *On the Edge: Living with Global Capitalism*, edited by W. Hutton and A. Giddens. London: Jonathan Cape.

Hochschild, Arlie Russell (with Anne Machung). 2012. *The Second Shift*. Updated ed. New York: Penguin.

Hochschild, Arlie Russell. 2016. *Strangers in Their Own Land: Anger and Mourning on the American Right*. New York: The New Press.

Hodkinson, Paul. 2015. "Bedrooms and Beyond: Youth, Identity and Privacy on Social Network Sites." *New Media and Society* 10.

Hoecker-Drysdale, Susan. 2011. "Harriet Martineau." In *The Wiley-Blackwell Companion to Major Social Theorists*, Vol. 1, *Classical Theorists*, edited by George Ritzer and Jeffrey Stepnisky, 61–95. Malden, MA: Wiley-Blackwell.

Hoekstra, Arjen J. 2012. "Water." In *The Wiley-Blackwell Companion to Sociology*, edited by George Ritzer, 2202–2210. Malden, MA: Wiley-Blackwell.

Hoffman, Jan. 2016. "Estimate of the U.S. Transgender Population Doubles." *New York Times*, July 1.

Hoffman, Lily M., Susan S. Fainstein, and Dennis R. Judd, eds. 2003. *Cities and Visitors: Regulating People, Markets, and City Space*. New York: Blackwell.

Hokayem, Charles, and Misty L. Heggeness. 2014. *Living in Near Poverty in the United States: 1966–2012*. Current Population Reports P60-248. Washington, DC: U.S. Census Bureau, May. Accessed April 19, 2015. https://www.census.gov/prod/2014pubs/p60-248.pdf.

Holdstock, Nick. 2014. "What We Talk about When We Talk about 'the Uyghurs.'" *Dissent* 61: 65–69.

Holland, Samantha. 2013. "Three Generations of Women's Leisure: Changes, Challenges, and Continuities." *Journal of Gender Studies* 22: 309–319.

Hollifield, James E., and David Jacobson. 2012. "Migration and the State." In *The Wiley-Blackwell Encyclopedia of Globalization*, edited by George Ritzer, 1390–1400. Malden, MA: Wiley-Blackwell.

Hollister, Geoff. 2008. *Out of Nowhere: The Inside Story of How Nike Marketed the Culture of Running*. Maidenhead, UK: Meyer and Meyer Sport.

Holmes, Seth. 2013. *Fresh Fruit, Broken Bodies: Migrant Farmworkers in the United States*. Berkeley: University of California Press.

Holt, Douglas B. 2004. *How Brands Become Icons: Principles of Cultural Branding*. Cambridge, MA: Harvard Business School Press.

Holton, Robert J. 2011. *Globalization and the Nation State*. 2nd ed. New York: Palgrave Macmillan.

Homans, George. 1961. *Social Behavior: Its Elementary Forms*. New York: Harcourt, Brace, and World.

Hondagneu-Sotelo, Pierette. 2000. *Doméstica: Immigrant Workers Cleaning and Caring in the Shadows of Affluence*. Berkeley: University of California Press.

Hondagneu-Sotelo, Pierette, and Ernestine Avila. 2005. "'I'm Here, but I'm There': The Meanings of Latina Transnational Motherhood." In *Gender through a Prism of Difference*, edited by M. B. Zinn, P. Hondagneu-Sotelo, and M. Messner. New York: Oxford University Press.

Hood, Roger, and Carolyn Hoyle. 2015. *The Death Penalty: A Worldwide Perspective*. 5th ed. Oxford: Oxford University Press.

hooks, bell. 2000. *Feminist Thought: From Margin to Center*. Cambridge, MA: South End Press.

Horrigan, John. 2008. "Online Shopping." *Pew Internet and American Life Project*, February 13. Accessed April 19, 2015. http://www.pewinternet.org/2008/02/13/online-shopping.

Horton, Richard. 2000. "North and South: Bridging the Information Gap." *The Lancet* 355: 2231–2236.

Houck, Davis W., and David E. Dixon, eds. 2011. *Women and the Civil Rights Movement, 1954–1965*. Jackson: University of Mississippi Press.

Hout, Michael. 2015. "A Summary of What We Know About Social Mobility." *The Annals* 657: 27–36.

Howard, Vicki. 2015. *From Main Street to Mall: The Rise and Fall of the American Department Store*. Philadelphia: University of Pennsylvania Press.

Howe, Peter, Matto Mildenberger, Jennifer Marlon, and Anthony Leiserowitz. 2016. Yale Climate Opinion Maps—U.S. 2016. http://climatecommunication.yale.edu/visualizations-data/ycom-us-2016/

Hu, Winnie. 2017. "An Endangered Call of the New York Wild: Taxi!" *New York Times*, January 16.

Huaco, George. 1966. "The Functionalist Theory of Stratification: Two Decades of Controversy." *Inquiry* 9: 215–240.

Huang, Penelope M., Pamela J. Smock, Wendy D. Manning, and Cara A. Bergstrom-Lynch.

2011. "He Says, She Says: Gender and Cohabitation." *Journal of Family Issues* 32: 876–905.

Hubbard, Phil, Andrew Gormley-Murray, and Catherine J. Nash. 2015. "Cities and Sexualities." In *Handbook of the Sociology of Sexualities*, edited by John DeLamater and Rebecca F. Plante, 287–303. New York: Springer.

Huddleston, Gabriel S., Julie C. Garlen, and Jennifer A. Sandlin. 2016. "The New Dimension of Disney Magic." In *Disney, Culture and Curriculum*, edited by Jennifer A. Sandlin and Julie C. Garlen, 220–232. New York: Routledge.

Huesemann, Michael, and Joyce Huesemann. 2011. *Techno-fix: Why Technology Won't Save Us or the Environment*. Gabriola Island, BC: New Society.

Hughey, Mathew W., and W. Carson Byrd. 2015. "Beautiful Melodies Telling Me Terrible Things: The Future of Race and Genetics for Scholars and Policy-Makers." *The Annals* 661: 238-258.

Human Rights Watch. 2015. "UN: Sexual Violence as a 'Tactic of War.'" Accessed March 8, 2017. https://www.hrw.org/news/2015/04/14/un-sexual-violence-tactic-war.

Humphreys, Laud. 1970. *Tearoom Trade: A Study of Homosexual Encounters in Public Places*. Chicago: Aldine.

Hunter, James Davison. 1992. *Culture Wars: The Struggle to Control the Family, Art, Education, Law, and Politics in America*. New York: Basic Books.

Huntington, Samuel P. 1996. *The Clash of Civilizations and the Remaking of the World Order*. New York: Simon & Schuster.

Hussain, Zaheer, and Mark Griffiths. 2008. "Gender Swapping and Socializing in Cyberspace: An Exploratory Study." *CyberPsychology & Behavior* 11(1): 47–53.

Hutson, David J. 2016. "Training Bodies, Building Status: Negotiating Age and Gender Differences in the U.S. Fitness Industry." *Qualitative Sociology* 39: 49–70.

Hwang, Jinyoung, and Jong Ha Lee. 2014. "Women's Education and the Timing and Level of Fertility." *International Journal of Social Economics* 41: 862–874.

Iceland, John. 2013. *Poverty in America: A Handbook*. Updated ed. Berkeley: University of California Press.

The Illusionists. 2015. Directed by Elena Rossini.

Inda, Jonathan Xavier. 2012. "Flows." In *The Wiley-Blackwell Encyclopedia of Globalization*, edited by George Ritzer, 668–670. Malden, MA: Wiley-Blackwell.

Inda, Jonathan Xavier, and Renato Rosaldo, eds. 2008. *The Anthropology of Globalization: A Reader*. 2nd ed. Malden, MA: Blackwell.

Inglis, David. 2016. "Globalization and Food." In *The Routledge International Handbook of Global Studies,* 2nd ed., edited by Bryan S. Turner and Robert S. Holton, 469–489. New York: Routledge.

Innis, Michelle. 2016. "Climate-Related Death of Coral Around the World Alarms Scientists." *New York Times,* April 9.

Insch, Gary S., Nancy McIntyre, and Nancy C. Napier. 2008. "The Expatriate Glass Ceiling: The Second Layer of Glass." *Journal of Business Ethics* 83: 19–28.

Interlandi, Jeneen. 2010. "Why the Palace Fell: Lessons Learned from the Destruction of Haiti's Presidential Home." *Newsweek,* January 20. Accessed March 31, 2012. http://www.thedailybeast.com/newsweek/2010/01/20/why-the-palace-fell.html.

International Centre for Prison Studies. 2011. "World Prison Brief." Accessed April 27, 2015. http://www.prisonstudies.org/world-prison-brief.

International Labour Organization. 2017. "Forced Labour, Modern Slavery and Human Trafficking." http://www.ilo.org/global/topics/forced-labour/lang—en/index.htm.

Intersex Society of North America. 2008. "FAQ: What Is Intersex?" Accessed May 15, 2015. http://www.isna.org/faq/what_is_intersex.

Ives, Mike. 2016. "A Remote Pacific Nation, Threatened by Rising Seas." *New York Times,* July 2.

Jackson, Michelle and D. R. Cox. 2013. "Principles of Experimental Design and their Application to Sociology." *Annual Review of Sociology* 39: 27–49.

Jackson, Tim. 2014. "Sustainable Consumption." In *Handbook of Sustainable Development,* 2nd ed., edited by Giles Atkinson et al., 279–290. Northampton, MA: Edward Elgar.

Jacobs, Andrew. 2013. "Uighurs in China Say Bias is Growing." *New York Times,* October 8.

Jacobs, Harrison. 2014. "We Ranked YouTube's Biggest Stars by How Much Money They Make." *Business Insider,* March 10. Accessed April 22, 2015. http://www.businessinsider.com/richest-youtube-stars-2014-3?op=1.

Jacobs, Jerry. 1996. "Gender Inequality and Higher Education." *Annual Review of Sociology* 22: 153–185.

Jacobs, Mark D. 2007. "Interaction Order." In *The Blackwell Encyclopedia of Sociology,* edited by George Ritzer, 2365–2366. Malden, MA: Blackwell.

Jacobsen, Joannes. 2015. "Revisiting the Modernization Hypothesis: Longevity and Democracy." *World Development* 67: 174–185.

Jacobsen, Michael Hviid, and Soren Kristiansen. 2015. *The Social Thought of Erving Goffman.* Thousand Oaks, CA: Sage.

Jakobi, Anja P. 2012. "Human Trafficking." In *The Wiley-Blackwell Encyclopedia of Globalization,* edited by George Ritzer, 953–956. Malden, MA: Wiley-Blackwell.

James, Nalita. 2016. "Using Email Interviews in Qualitative Research: Creating Space to Think and Time to Talk." *International Journal of Qualitative Studies in Education* 29: 150–163.

Jamieson, Lynn. 2007. "Intimacy." In *The Blackwell Encyclopedia of Sociology,* edited by George Ritzer, 2411–2414. Malden, MA: Blackwell.

Janoski, Thomas. 2015. "The New Division of Labor as Lean Production." *International Journal of Sociology* 45: 85–94.

Janoski, Thomas, and Darina Lepadatu. 2013. *Dominant Divisions of Labor: Models of Production That Have Transformed the World of Work.* New York: Palgrave Pivot.

Jansen, Jim. 2010. "Online Product Research." Pew Research Center, September 29. Accessed May 27, 2011. http://www.pewinternet.org/~/media//Files/Reports/2010/PIP%20Online%20Product%20Research%20final.pdf.

Jay, Karla. 1999. *Tales of the Lavender Menace: A Memoir of Liberation.* New York: Basic Books.

Jean-Charles, Régine Michelle. 2010. "Cracks of Gender Inequality: Haitian Women after the Earthquake." Social Science Research Council. Accessed March 30, 2012. http://www.ssrc.org/features/pages/haiti-now-and-next/1338/1428.

Jefferson, Gail. 1979. "A Technique for Inviting Laughter and Its Subsequent Acceptance Declination." In *Everyday Language: Studies in Ethnomethodology,* edited by G. Psathas, 79–96. New York: Irvington.

Jemielniak, Dariusz. 2016. "Breaking the Glass Ceiling on Wikipedia." *Feminist Review* 1: 103–108.

Jenkins, J. C. 1983. "Resource Mobilization Theory and the Study of Social Movements." *Annual Review of Sociology* 9: 248–267.

Jensen, Gary F. 1988. "Functional Perspectives on Deviance: A Critical Assessment and Guide for the Future." *Deviant Behavior* 9: 1–17.

Jerolmack, Colin. 2009. "Humans, Animals, and Play: Theorizing Interaction When Intersubjectivity Is Problematic." *Sociological Theory* 27(4): 371–389.

Jerolmack, Colin. 2013. *The Global Pigeon.* Chicago: University of Chicago Press.

Johns, Nicole, Krycia Cowling, and Emmanuela Gakidou. 2013. "The Wealth (and Health) of Nations: A Cross-Country Analysis of the Relation between Wealth and Inequality in Disease Burden Estimation." *The Lancet* 381: S66.

Johnson, Allan. 2005. *The Gender Knot: Unraveling Our Patriarchal Legacy.* Philadelphia: Temple University Press.

Johnson, Cathryn, Rebecca Ford, and Joanne Kaufman. 2000. "Emotional Reactions to Conflict: Do Dependence and Legitimacy Matter?" *Social Forces* 79(1): 107–137.

Johnson, David K. 2004. *The Lavender Scare: The Cold War Persecution of Gays and Lesbians in the Federal Government.* Chicago: University of Chicago Press.

Jolly, David. 2014. "Heat Waves in Europe Will Increase Study Finds. *New York Times,* December 9.

Jones, Adele. 2008. "A Silent but Mighty River: The Costs of Women's Economic Migration." *Signs* 33(4): 761–769.

Jones, Nicholas, and Jungmiwha Bullock. 2013. "Understanding Who Reported Multiple Races in the U.S. Decennial Census: From Census 2000 and the 2010 Census." *Family Relations* 62: 5–16.

Jones, Richard G. 2015. "Queering the Body Politic: Intersectional Reflexivity in the Body Narratives of Queer Men." *Qualitative Inquiry* 21: 766–775.

Jones, Steven T. 2011. *The Tribes of Burning Man: How an Experiment in the Desert Is Shaping the New American Counterculture.* San Francisco: Consortium of Collective Consciousness.

Jorgenson, Andrew, and Jennifer Givens. 2012. "Pollution, Water." In *The Wiley-Blackwell Companion to Sociology,* edited by George Ritzer, 1674. Malden, MA: Wiley-Blackwell.

Joyner, Chris. 2010. "Miss. Prom Canceled after Lesbian's Date Request." *USA Today,* March 11. Accessed March 30, 2012. http://www.usatoday.com/news/nation/2010-03-10-noprom_N.htm.

Jula, Megan, and Julia Preston. 2016. "Delayed Care Faulted in Immigrants' Deaths at Detention Centers." *The New York Times,* July 7.

Juris, Jeffrey S. 2005. "The New Digital Media and Activist Networking within Anti-corporate Globalization Movements." *Annals of the American Academy of Political and Social Science* 597(January): 189–208.

Kaarbo, Juliet, and James Ray. 2010. *Global Politics.* Boston: Cengage.

Kabeer, Naila, Ratna Sudarshan, and Kristi Milward. 2013. Organizing Women Workers in the Informal Economy: Beyond the Weapons of the Weak. London: Zed Books.

Kaeble, Danielle, Laura M. Maruschak, and Thomas P. Bonczar. 2015. "Probation and Parole in the United States U.S. Department of Justice, Bureau of Justice Statistics. Accessed January 25, 2017. https://www.bjs.gov/content/pub/pdf/ppus14.pdf.

Kahlenberg, Richard D., ed. 2010. *Affirmative Action for the Rich: Legacy Preferences in College Admissions.* Washington, DC: Brookings Institution Press.

Kahlenberg, Susan G., and Michelle M. Hein. 2010. "Progression on Nickelodeon? Gender-Role Stereotypes in Toy Commercials." *Sex Roles* 62(11–12): 830–847.

Kaiser Family Foundation. 2015a. "Population Distribution by Gender." Accessed January 25, 2017. http://kff.org/other/state-indicator/distribution-by-gender/?currentTimeframe=0&sort Model=%7B%22colId%22:%22Location%22,%22sort%22:%22asc%22%7D.

Kaiser Family Foundation. 2015b. "Poverty Rate by Race/Ethnicity." Accessed January 26, 2017. http://kff.org/other/state-indicator/poverty-rate-by-race ethnicity/?currentTimeframe=0&sort Model=%7B%22colId%22:%22Location%22,%22sort%22:%22asc%22%7D.

Kalberg, Stephen. 1980. "Max Weber's Types of Rationality: Cornerstones for the Analysis of Rationalization Processes in History." *American Journal of Sociology* 85(5): 1145–1179.

Kalberg, Stephen. 2011. "Max Weber." In *The Wiley-Blackwell Companion to Major Social Theorists,* Vol. 1, *Classical Theorists,* edited by George Ritzer and Jeffrey Stepnisky, 305–372. Malden, MA: Wiley-Blackwell.

Kalberg, Stephen. 2017. *The Social Thought of Max Weber.* Thousand Oaks, CA: Sage.

Kalev, Alexandra. 2009. "Cracking the Glass Cages? Restructuring and Ascriptive Inequality at Work." *American Journal of Sociology* 114: 1591–1643.

Kane, Emily W. 2006. "'No Way My Boys Are Going to Be Like That!' Parents' Responses to Children's Gender Nonconformity." *Gender & Society* 20(2): 149–176.

Kane, Emily W. 2012. *The Gender Trap: Parents and the Pitfalls of Raising Boys and Girls.* New York: New York University Press.

Kang, Cecilia. 2016. "Court Backs Ruling Treating Internet as a Utility, Not Luxury." *New York Times,* June 14.

Kang, Jerry. 2000. "Cyber-race." *Harvard Law Review* 113: 1130–1208.

Kangas, Olli E. 2007. "Welfare State, Retrenchment of." In *The Blackwell Encyclopedia of Sociology,* edited by George Ritzer, 5247–5249. Malden, MA: Blackwell.

Kanter, James, and Sewell Chan. 2016. "Europe, Reeling from Strain, Tells Economic Migrants: Don't Bother." *New York Times,* March 3.

Kaoma, Kapya. 2014. "The Paradox and Tension of Moral Claims: Evangelical Christianity, the Politicization and Globalization of Sexual Politics in Sub-Saharan Africa." *Critical Research on Religion* 2(3): 227–245.

Karlson, Kristian Berndt. 2015. "Expectations on Track? High School Tracking and Adolescent Educational Expectations." *Social Forces* 94: 115–141.

Karraker, Meg Wilkes. 2013. *Global Families.* 2nd Edition. Boston: Pearson.

Karstedt, Susanne. 2007. "Genocide." In *The Blackwell Encyclopedia of Sociology,* edited by George Ritzer, 1909–1913. Malden, MA: Blackwell.

Karstedt, Suzanne. 2016. "Genocide." In *The Wiley-Blackwell Encyclopedia of Race, Ethnicity and Nationalism,* edited by John Stone, Rutledge M. Dennis, Polly Rizova, Anthony D. Smith, and Xiaoshuo Hou. Malden, MA: Wiley-Blackwell.

Kasarda, John D. 2016. "Welcome to Aerotropolis, The City of The Future." *The World Post,* May 1. Accessed March 13, 2017. http://www.huffingtonpost.com/john-d-kasarda/aerotropolis-city-fu ture_b_7269152.html.

Kasarda, John D., and Greg Lindsay. 2011. *Aerotropolis: The Way We'll Live Next.* New York: Farrar, Straus and Giroux.

Katsulis, Yasmina. 2010. "'Living Like a King': Conspicuous Consumption, Virtual Communities, and the Social Construction of Paid Sexual Encounters by U.S. Sex Tourists." *Men and Masculinities* 27: 1–18.

Katz, Jonathan Ned. 2004. "'Homosexual' and 'Heterosexual': Questioning the Terms." In *Sexualities: Identities, Behaviors, and Society,* edited by M. S. Kimmel and R. F. Plante, 44–46. New York: Oxford University Press.

Katz-Gerro, Tally, and Mads Meier Jaeger. 2013. "Top of the Pops, Ascend of the Omnivores, Defeat of the Couch Potatoes: Cultural Consumption Profiles in Denmark 1975–2004." *European Sociological Review* 29(2): 243–260.

Kaufman, Dan. 2016. "Which Side Are You On, Hillary?" *New York Times,* March 12.

Kauppinen, Ilkka. 2013. "Academic Capitalism and the Informational Fraction of the Transnational Capitalist Class." *Globalisation, Societies and Education* 11: 1–22.

Keane, John. 2003. *Global Civil Society.* Cambridge: Cambridge University Press.

Kellerhals, Jean, and Eric D. Widmer. Forthcoming. In George Ritzer, ed.

Encyclopedia of Sociology, 2nd ed. Malden, MA: Wiley-Blackwell.

Kellner, Douglas. 2008. *Guys and Guns Amok.* NY: Routledge.

Kellner, Douglas and Tyson E. Lewis. 2007. "Cultural Critique." In *The Blackwell Encyclopedia of Sociology,* edited by George Ritzer, 896–898. Malden, MA: Blackwell.

Kelly, Sean. 2004. "Are Teachers Tracked? On What Basis and with What Consequences?" *Social Psychology of Education* 7: 55–72.

Kennedy, M. Alexis, Carolin Klein, Jessica T. K. Bristowe, Barry S. Cooper, and John C. Yuille. 2007. "Routes of Recruitment: Pimps' Techniques and Other Circumstances That Lead to Street Prostitution." *Journal of Aggression, Maltreatment and Trauma* 15(2):1–19.

Kennedy, Peter G. 2013. "Clinical Features, Diagnosis, and Treatment of Human African Trypanosomiasis (Sleeping Sickness)." *The Lancet Neurology* 12(2): 186–194.

Kerber, Linda K. 1988. "Separate Spheres, Female Worlds, Woman's Place: The Rhetoric of Women's History." *Journal of American History* 75(1): 9–39.

Kern, Soeren. 2014. "The Islamization of Belgium and the Netherlands in 2013." Gatestone Institute, International Policy Council, January 13. Accessed April 27, 2015. http://www.gatestonein stitute.org/4129/islamization-bel gium-netherlands.

Kershaw, Sarah. 2008. "Starving Themselves, Cocktail in Hand." *New York Times,* March 2. Accessed January 1, 2012. http://www.nytimes.com/2008/03/02/fashion/02drunk.html.

Kershner, Isabel. 2015. "Netanyahu Urges 'Mass Immigration' of Jews from Europe." *New York Times,* April 15.

Kesselring, Rita. 2017. *Bodies of Truth: Law, Memory, and Emancipation in Post-Apartheid South Africa.* Stanford, CA: Stanford University Press.

Kestnbaum, Meyer. 2012. "Organized Coercion and Political Authority: Armed Conflict in a World of States." In *The Wiley-Blackwell Companion to Sociology,* edited by George Ritzer, 588–608. Malden, MA: Wiley-Blackwell.

Khan, Shamus Rahman. 2011. *Privilege: The Making of an Adolescent Elite at St. Paul's School.* Princeton, NJ: Princeton University Press.

Khanna, Nikki, and Cherise A. Harris. 2015. "Discovering Race in a 'Post-racial' World: Teaching Race through Primetime Television." *Teaching Sociology* 43: 39–45.

Kharif, Olga. 2014. "Not Just for Libertarians and Anarchists Anymore." *Bloomberg,* October 9.

Khatchadourian, Raffi. 2007. "Neptune's Navy." *New Yorker,* November 5.

Khrais, Reema. 2013. "Showing Off Shopping Sprees, Fashion 'Haulers' Cash In Online." *NPR,* March 14. Accessed April 19, 2015. http://www.npr.org/2013/03/14/174305909/showing-off-shopping-sprees-fashion-haulers-cash-in-online.

Kiaye, Risper Enid, and Anesh Maniraj Singh. 2013. "The Glass Ceiling: A Perspective of Women Working in Durban." *Gender in Management* 28: 28–42.

Kidder, Jeffrey L. 2012. "Parkour, the Affective Appropriation of Urban Space, and the Real/Virtual Dialectic." *City and Community* 11: 229–253.

Kimmel, Michael S. 2012. *The Gendered Society.* 5th ed. New York: Oxford University Press.

Kimmel, Michael, ed. 2014. *Sexualities, Identities and Behaviors.* 2nd ed. New York: Oxford University Press.

Kimmelman, Michael. 2016. "The Vertical Frontier." *New York Times Magazine,* June 5.

King, Anthony. 2004. *The Structure of Social Theory.* London: Routledge.

Kinney, William J. 2007. "Asch Experiments." In *The Blackwell Encyclopedia of Sociology,* edited by George Ritzer, 189–191. Malden, MA: Blackwell.

Kirk, Roger E. 2007. "Experimental Design." In *The Blackwell Encyclopedia of Sociology,* edited by George Ritzer, 1533–1537. Malden, MA: Blackwell.

Kiuchi, Yuya (Ed.) 2016. *Race Still Matters.* Albany: State University of New York Press.

Kivisto, Peter. 2012. "Fundamentalism." In *The Wiley-Blackwell Encyclopedia of Globalization,* edited by George Ritzer, 709–713. Malden, MA: Wiley-Blackwell.

Kivisto, Peter, and Paul R. Croll. 2012. *Race and Ethnicity: The Basics.* New York: Routledge.

Kivisto, Peter, and Thomas Faist. 2007. *Citizenship: Discourse, Theory, and Transnational Prospects.* Malden, MA: Blackwell.

Kivisto, Peter, and Thomas Faist. 2010. *Beyond a Border: The Causes and Consequences of Contemporary Immigration.* Thousand Oaks, CA: Pine Forge Press.

Klaasen, Marleen J. E., and Jochen Peter. 2015. "Gender (In)equality in Internet Pornography: A Content Analysis of Popular Pornographic Internet Videos." *The Journal of Sex Research* 52: 721–735.

Klein, Alan. 1993. *Little Big Men: Bodybuilding Subculture and Gender Construction.* Albany: State University of New York Press.

Klein, Naomi. [2000] 2010. *No Logo: Taking Aim at the Brand Bullies.* Toronto: Vintage.

Klein, Naomi. 2014. *This Changes Everything: Capitalism vs. the Climate.* New York: Simon and Scuster.

Klinenberg, Eric. 2012. *Going Solo: The Extraordinary Rise and Surprising Appeal of Living Alone.* New York: Penguin.

Knoblauch, Hubert, and Rene Wilke, 2016. "The Common Denominator: The Reception and Impact of Berger and Luckman's *The Social Construction of Reality.*" *Human Studies* 39: 51–69.

Knorr Cetina, Karin. 2012. "Financial Markets." In *The Encyclopedia of Globalization,* edited by George Ritzer, 653–664. Malden, MA: Wiley-Blackwell.

Koblin, John, Emily Steel, and Jim Rutenberg, 2016. "Roger Ailes Leaves Fox News, and Rupert Murdoch Steps In." *New York Times,* July 21.

Kohrmann, M. 2008. "Smoking among Doctors: Governmentality, Embodiment, and the Diversion of Blame in Contemporary China." *Medical Anthropology* 27(1): 9–42.

Koistinen, David. 2013. *Confronting Decline: The Political Economy of Deindustrialization in Twentieth-Century New England.* Gainesville: University Press of Florida.

Koivusalo, Meri and Eeva Ollila. 2014. "Global Health Policies." In *Understanding Global Social Policy,* edited by N. Yeates, 159–186. Cambridge: Polity Press.

Kolata, Gina. 1999. *The Flu: The Story of the Great Influenza Pandemic of 1918 and the Search for the Virus That Caused It.* New York: Touchstone.

Kolbert, Elizabeth. 2015. *The Sixth Extinction: An Unnatural History.* New York: Picador.

Köllen, Thomas. 2013. "Bisexuality and Diversity Management: Addressing the B in LGBT as a Relevant 'Sexual Orientation' in the Workplace." *Journal of Bisexuality* 13(1): 122–137.

Kollmeyer, Christopher. 2009. "Explaining Deindustrialization: How Affluence, Productivity Growth, and Globalization Diminish Manufacturing Employment." *American Journal of Sociology* 114: 1644–1674.

Kollmeyer, Christopher, and Florian Pichler. 2013. "Is Deindustrialization Causing High Unemployment in Affluent Countries? Evidence from 16 OECD Countries, 1970–2003." *Social Forces* 91: 785–812.

Kolodny, Andrew, David T. Courtwright, Catherine S. Hwang, Peter Kreiner, John L. Eadie, Thomas W. Clark, and G. Caleb Alexander. 2015. "The Prescription Opioid and Heroin Crisis: A Public Health Approach to an Epidemic of Addiction." *Annual Review of Public Health* 36: 449–574.

Konrad, Waleca. 2009. "Seeking the Best Medical Care Prices." *New York Times,* November 28.

Koopmans, Ruud. 2015. "Religious Fundamentalism and Hostility against Out-Groups: A Comparison of Muslims and Christians in Western Europe." *Journal of Ethnic and Migration Studies* 41: 33–57.

Korkki, Phyllis. 2012. "When the H.R. Office Leaves the Building." *New York Times,* December 12.

Kosic, Ankica, Arie W. Kruglanski, Antonio Pierro, and Lucia Mannetti. 2004. "The Social Cognition of Immigrants' Acculturation: Effects of the Need for Closure and the Reference Group at Entry." *Journal of Personality and Social Psychology* 86: 796–813.

Kotarba, Joseph A., Andrea Salvini, and Bryce Merrill, eds. 2012. The Present and Future of Symbolic Interactionism: Proceedings of the International Symposium, Pisa 2010. Pisa: Franco Angeli.

Kozinets, Robert. 2015. *Netnography Redefined.* London: Sage.

Krass, Frauke, ed. 2012. *Megacities: Our Global Urban Future.* New York: Springer.

Kraus, Michael W., Shai Davidai, and A. David Nussbaum. 2015. "American Dream? Or Mirage?" *New York Times,* May 3.

Krauss, Clifford. 2004. "Internet Drug Exporters Feel Pressure in Canada." *New York Times,* December 11. Accessed March 30, 2012. http://query.nytimes.com/gst/fullpage.html?res=9F04EED-81131F932A25751C1A9629C8B63&&scp=4&sq=pharmaceutical%20purchase%200ver%20internet&st=cse.

Kreager, Derek. 2007. "Unnecessary Roughness? School Sports, Peer Networks, and Male Adolescent Violence." *American Sociological Review* 72(5): 705–724.

Krinsky, Charles, ed. 2013. *The Ashgate Research Companion to Moral Panics.* Burlington, VT: Ashgate.

Krogstad, Jens Manuel. 2015. "Social Media Preferences Vary by Race and Ethnicity." Pew Research Center, February. 3. Accessed January 27, 2017. http://www.pewresearch.org/fact-tank/2015/02/03/social-media-preferences-vary-by-race-and-ethnicity.

Krogstad, Jens Manual, Jeffrey S. Passel, and D'Vera Cohn. 2016. "5 Facts about Illegal Immigration in the U.S." Pew Research Center, November 3.

Kroneberg, Clemens, and Frank Kalter. 2012. "Rational Choice Theory and Empirical Research: Methodological and Theoretical Contributions in Europe." *Annual Review of Sociology* 38: 73–92.

Kuehn, Kathleen. 2015. "Culture Jamming." In Daniel Thomas Cook and Michael Ryan, eds. *Encyclopedia of Consumption and Consumer Studies* Malden, MA: Wiley-Blackwell, 2015: 236–238.

Kulish, Nicholas. 2007. "Europe Fears That Meth Foothold is Expanding." *New York Times,* November 23.

Kunzman, Robert, and Milton Gaither. 2013. "Homeschooling: A Comprehensive Survey of the Research." *Other Education* 2: 4–59.

Kuo, Janet Chen-Lan, and R. Kelly Raley, 2016. "Diverging Patterns of Union Transition Among Cohabitors by Race/Ethnicity and Education: Trends and Marital Intentions in the United States." *Demography* June 15 (published online first).

Kuperberg, Arielle, and Jospeh E. Padgett, 2015. "The Role of Culture in Explaining College Students' Selection into Hookups, Dates and Long-term Romantic Relationships." *Journal of Social and Personal Relationships:* 1–27.

Kupfer, Antonia. 2012. "A Theoretical Concept of Educational Upward Mobility." *International Studies in Sociology of Education* 22: 57–72.

Kurtz, Annalyn. 2014. "Americans Still Hesitant to Spend More." *CNN Money,* June 26. Accessed April 22, 2015. http://money.cnn.com/2014/06/26/news/economy/americans-not-spend.

Kurtz, Lester R. 2016. *Gods in the Global Village.* 4th ed. Thousand Oaks, CA: Sage.

Kushkush, Isma'il. 2015. "President of Sudan Is Re-elected with 94 Percent of Vote." *New York Times,* April 27.

Kwan, Samantha, and Mary Nell Trautner. 2011. "Judging Books by Their Covers: Teaching about Physical Attractiveness Biases." *Teaching Sociology* 39: 16–26.

Lacey, Marc. 2011. "Rift in Arizona as Latino Class Is Found Illegal." *New York Times,* January 7. Accessed March 30, 2012. http://www.nytimes.com/2011/01/08/us/08ethnic.html.

Lacy, Karyn. 2016. "The Sociology of Suburbs: A Research Agenda for Analysis of Emerging Trends." *Annual Review of Sociology* 42: 369–384.

Lahelma, Eero. Forthcoming. "Health and Social Class." In *The Wiley-Blackwell Encyclopedia of Sociology,* 2nd ed., edited by George Ritzer. Malden, MA: Wiley-Blackwell.

Laible, Deborah, Ross A. Thompson, and Jill Froimson. 2015. "Early Socialization: The Influence of Close Relationships." In *Handbook of Socialization: Theory and Research,* 2nd ed., edited by Joan E. Grusec and Paul D. Hastings, 35–59. New York: Guilford Press.

Landler, Mark. 2008. "Credit Cards Tighten Grip Outside US." *New York Times,* August 30.

Lane, Harlan. 1975. *The Wild Boy of Aveyron.* Cambridge, MA: Harvard University Press.

Lara-Millán, Armando. 2014. "Public Emergency Room Overcrowding in the Era of Mass Imprisonment." *American Sociological Review* 79: 866–887.

Lareau, Annette. 2015. "Cultural Knowledge and Social Inequality." *American Sociological Review* 80: 1–27.

Larsen, Gretchen, Maurice Patterson, and Lucy Markham. 2014. "A Deviant Art: Tattoo-Related Stigma in an Era of Commodification." *Psychology & Marketing* 31: 670–681.

Lash, Scott, and Celia Lury. 2007. *Global Culture Industry.* Cambridge: Polity Press.

Lasn, Kalle. 2000. *Culture Jam: How to Reverse America's Suicidal Consumer Binge—and Why We Must.* New York: Quill.

Lasn, Kalle. 2012. *Meme Wars.* New York: Seven Stories Press.

Lasswell, Harold D. 2012. *Politics: Who Gets What, When, How.* Whitefish, MT: Literary Licensing.

Lauer, Sean, and Carrie Yodanis. 2011. "Individualized Marriage and the Integration of Resources." *Journal of Marriage and Family* 73: 669–683.

Laurie, Nina, Claire Dwyer, Sarah Holloway, and Fiona Smith. 1999. *Geographies of New Femininities.* London: Longman.

LaViollete, Alyce D., and Ola W. Barnett. 2014. *Why Battered Women Stay: It Could Happen to Anyone.* Thousand Oaks, CA: Sage.

Lavorgna, Anita. 2015. "The Online Trade in Counterfeit Pharmaceuticals: New Criminal Opportunities, Trends and Challenges." *European Journal of Criminology* 12(2): 226–241.

Law, Ian. 2012. "Racism." In *The Wiley-Blackwell Encyclopedia of Globalization,* edited by George Ritzer, 1743–1746. Malden, MA: Wiley-Blackwell.

Layte, Richard, and Christopher T. Whelan. 2009. "Explaining Social Class Inequalities in Smoking: The Role of Education, Self-Efficacy, and Deprivation." *European Sociological Review* 25: 399–410.

Lazer, David. Forthcoming. "General Introduction to Big Data." *Annual Review of Sociology.*

Leaper, Campbell, and Timeas Farkas. 2015. "The Socialization of Gender During Childhood and Adolescence." In *Handbook of Socialization: Theory and Research,* 2nd ed., edited by Joan E. Grusec and Paul D. Hastings, 541–565. New York: Guilford Press.

Lechner, Frank J. 1993. "Global Fundamentalism." In *A Future for Religion?,* edited by W. H. Swatos. Thousand Oaks, CA: Sage.

Lechner, Frank J., and John Boli. 2005. *World Culture: Origins and Consequences.* Oxford: Blackwell.

Lee, Jacqueline G. C., Ray Paternoster, and Zachary Rowan. 2016. "Death Penalty and Race." In *The Wiley Encyclopedia of Race, Ethnicity and Nationalism,* edited by John Stone, Rutledge M. Dennis, Polly Rizova, Anthony D. Smith, and Xiaoshuo Hou. Malden, MA Wiley Blackwell.

Lee, Jaekyung. 2012. "Educational Equity and Adequacy for Disadvantaged Minority Students: School and Teacher Resource Gaps toward National Mathematics Proficiency Standard." *Journal of Educational Research* 105: 64–75.

Lee, Ronald D. 2007. *Global Population Aging and Its Economic Consequences.* Washington, DC: American Enterprise Institute Press.

Lee, Teresa Y. 2013. "Top 10 Trends of the Next Generation of Travel: The Millennials." *HVS Global Hospitality Services,* April. Accessed April 22, 2015. http://www.hospitalitynet.org/file/152005087.pdf.

Lees, Loretta, Tom Slater, and Elvin Wyly, eds. 2010. *The Gentrification Reader.* New York: Routledge.

Legerski, Elizabeth Miklya. 2012. "The Cost of Instability: The Effects of Family, Work, and Welfare Change on Low-Income Women's Health Insurance Status." *Sociological Forum* 27: 641–657.

Leicht, Kevin, and Scott Fitzgerald. 2006. *Postindustrial Peasants: The Illusion of Middle-Class Prosperity.* New York: Worth.

Leidner, Robin. 1993. *Fast Food, Fast Talk.* Berkeley: University of California Press.

Lemert, Charles, and Anthony Elliott. 2006. *Deadly Worlds: The Emotional Costs of Globalization.* Lanham, MD: Rowman & Littlefield.

Lemert, Edwin. [1951] 2012. *Social Pathology: A Systematic Approach to the Theory of Sociopathic Behavior.* Whitefish, MT: Literary Licensing.

Lengermann, Patricia Madoo, and Gillian Niebrugge-Brantley. 2014. "Feminist Theory." In *Sociological Theory,* 9th ed., edited by George Ritzer and Jeffrey Stepnisky, 440–485. New York: McGraw-Hill.

Lerum, Kari, and Barbara G. Brents, 2016. "Sociological Perspectives on Sex Work and Human Trafficking." *Sociological Perspectives* 59: 17–26.

Lessenich, Stephan. Forthcoming. "Welfare Regimes." In *The Wiley-Blackwell*

Encyclopedia of Sociology, 2nd ed., edited by George Ritzer. Malden, MA: Wiley-Blackwell.

Lesthaeghe, Ron J. 2010. "The Unfolding Story of the Second Demographic Transition." *Population and Development Review* 36: 211–251.

Leventog̃lu, Bahar. 2014. "Social Mobility, Middle Class, and Political Transitions." *Journal of Conflict Resolution* 58: 825–864.

Levin, Jack. 2007. "Hate Crimes." In *The Blackwell Encyclopedia of Sociology,* edited by George Ritzer, 2048–2050. Malden, MA: Blackwell.

Levy, Steven. 2010. *Hackers: Heroes of the Computer Revolution.* 25th anniversary ed. Sebastopol, CA: O'Reilly Media.

Lewin, Tamar. 2012. "College of Future Could Be Come One, Come All." *New York Times,* November 19.

Lewis, James R., and Inga B. Tollefson, eds. 2016. *New Religious Social Movements,* Vol. 2. New York: Oxford University Press, 2016.

Lewis, Melissa A., Hollie Granato, Jessica A. Blayney, Ty W. Lostutter, and Jason R. Kilmer. 2012. "Predictors of Hooking Up Sexual Behaviors and Emotional Reactions among U.S. College Students." *Archives of Sexual Behavior* 41(5): 1219–1229.

Lewis, Nathaniel. 2014. "Moving 'Out,' Moving On: Gay Men's Migrations through the Life Course." *Annals of the Association of American Geographers* 104(2): 225–233.

Lewis-Kraus, Gideon. 2016. "The Trials of Alice Goffman." *New York Times Magazine,* January 12. www.nytimes .com/2016/01/17/magazine/the-trials-of-alice-goffman.html?_r=0.

Liaw, Karen Ron-Li, and Aron Janssen. 2014. "Not by Convention: Working with People on the Sexual and Gender Continuum." In *Massachusetts General Hospital Textbook on Diversity and Cultural Sensitivity in Mental Health,* edited by R. Parekh, 89–117. New York: Springer.

Liberman, Akiva M., David S. Kirk, and Kideuk Kim. 2014. "Labeling Effects of First Juvenile Arrest: Secondary Deviance and Secondary Sanctioning." *Criminology* 52: 345–370.

Lidskog, Rolf, Arthur P. J. Mol, and Peter Oosterveeer. 2015. "Towards Global Environmental Sociology? Legacies, Trends and Future Directions." *Current Sociology* 63: 339–368.

Liebow, Elliot. 1967. *Tally's Corner: A Study of Negro Streetcorner Men.* New York: Little, Brown.

Limoncelli, Stephanie A. Forthcoming. "Informal Economy." In Nancy Naples,

ed. *The Wiley Blackwell Encyclopedia of Gender and Sexuality Studies.*

Lind, Amy. 2007. "Femininities/Masculinities." In *The Blackwell Encyclopedia of Sociology,* edited by George Ritzer, 1662–1666. Malden, MA: Blackwell.

Linn, James G., and Debra Rose Wilson. 2012. "Health." In *The Wiley-Blackwell Encyclopedia of Globalization,* edited by George Ritzer, 910–923. Malden, MA: Wiley-Blackwell.

Lipovetsky, Gilles. [1987] 2002. *The Empire of Fashion: Dressing Modern Democracy.* Princeton, NJ: Princeton University Press.

Lipovetsky, Gilles. 2005. *Hypermodern Times.* Cambridge: Polity Press.

Lipset, Seymour M. 1981. *Political Man.* Expanded ed. Baltimore: Johns Hopkins University Press.

Lipton, Eric, David E. Sanger, and Scott Shane, 2016. "The Perfect Weapon: How Russian Cyberpower Invaded the U.S." *New York Times,* December 13.

Lipton, Eric, and Scott Shane. 2016. "Democratic House Candidates Were Also Targets of Russian Hacking." *New York Times,* December 13.

Liss, Miriam. 2014. "Inequality in the Division of Household Labor and Childcare." In *Women, Work, and Family: How Companies Thrive with a 21st-Century Multicultural Workforce,* edited by M. A. Paludi, 23–40. Santa Barbara, CA: ABC-CLIO.

Liu, Yu Cheng. 2012. "Ethnomethodology Reconsidered: The Practical Logic of Social Systems Theory." *Current Sociology* 60: 581–598.

Livermore, Michelle, Rebecca S. Powers, Belinda Creel Davis, and Younghee Lim. 2011. "Failing to Make Ends Meet: Dubious Financial Success among Employed Former Welfare to Work Program Participants." *Journal of Family Economic Issues* 32: 73–83.

Lloréns, Hilda. 2013. "Latina Bodies in the Era of Elective Aesthetic Surgery." *Latino Studies* 11(4): 547–569.

Logan, John, Richard Alba, and Wenquan Zhang. 2002. "Immigrant Enclaves and Ethnic Communities in New York and Los Angeles." *American Sociological Review* 67(2): 299–322.

Logan, John R., Elisabeta Minca, and Sinem Adar. 2012. "The Geography of Inequality: Why Separate Means Unequal in American Public Schools." *Sociology of Education* 85(3): 287–301.

Lois, Jennifer. 2013. *Home Is Where the School Is: The Logic of Homeschooling and the Emotional Labor of Mothering.* New York: New York University Press.

Looney, Adam, and Kevin B. Moore, 2016. "Changes in the Distribution of After-Tax

Wealth in the U.S.: Has Income Policy Increased Wealth Inequality?" *Fiscal Studies* 37: 77–104.

Lorber, Judith. 1967. "Deviance as Performance: The Case of Illness." *Social Problems* 14: 302–310.

Lorber, Judith. 2000. "Using Gender to Undo Gender: A Feminist Degendering Movement." *Feminist Theory* 1(1): 79–95.

Lorber, Judith, and Lisa Jean Moore. 2002. *Gender and the Social Construction of Illness.* 2nd ed. Walnut Creek, CA: AltaMira Press.

Lorenz, Edward. 1995. *The Essence of Chaos.* Seattle: University of Washington Press.

"Louisiana Oil Rig Explosion: Underwater Machines Attempt to Plug Leak." 2010. *Telegraph,* April 26. Accessed March 31, 2012. http://www.telegraph.co.uk/finance/news-bysector/energy/oilandgas/7633286/Louisiana-oil-rig-explosion-Underwater-machines-attempt-to-plug-leak.html.

Love, Brad, Charee M. Thompson, and Jessica Knapp. 2014. "The Need to Be Superman: The Psychosocial Support Challenges of Young Men Affected by Cancer." *Oncology Nursing Forum* 41(1): E21–E27.

Lowe, Brian. 2002. "Hearts and Minds and Morality: Analyzing Moral Vocabularies in Qualitative Studies." *Qualitative Sociology* 25(1): 105–112.

Lowrey, Annie. 2014. "Even among the Richest of the Rich, Fortunes Diverge." *New York Times,* February 10.

Lubbers, Marcel, Eva Jaspers, and Wout Ultee. 2009. "Primary and Secondary Socialization Impacts on Support for Same-Sex Marriage after Legalization in the Netherlands." *Journal of Family Issues* 30: 1714–1745.

Lubienski, Christopher. 2006. "School Sector and Academic Achievement: A Multilevel Analysis of NAEP Mathematics Data." *American Educational Research Journal* 43: 651–698.

Lucas, Jeffrey W., Corina Graif, and Michael J. Lovaglia. 2008. "Prosecutorial Misconduct in Serious Cases: Theory and Design of a Laboratory Experiment: Can You Study a Legal System in a Laboratory?" In *Experiments in Criminology and Law: A Research Revolution,* edited by C. Horne and M. J. Lovaglia, 119–136. Lanham, MD: Rowman & Littlefield.

Lui, Li. 2014. "A Comparative Study of Intergenerational Mobility." *Russian Social Science Review* 55(4): 4–15.

Luker, Kristin. 1984. *Abortion and the Politics of Motherhood.* Berkeley: University of California Press.

Lunneborg, Clifford E. 2007. "Convenience Sample." In *The Blackwell Encyclopedia of Sociology,* edited by George Ritzer, 788–790. Malden, MA: Blackwell.

Luo, Wei. 2013. "Aching for the Altered Body: Beauty Economy and Chinese Women's Consumption of Cosmetic Surgery." *Women's Studies International Forum* 38: 1–10.

Lupton, Deborah. 2007. "Health Risk Behavior." In *The Blackwell Encyclopedia of Sociology,* edited by George Ritzer, 2083–2085. Malden, MA: Blackwell.

Lutfey, K., and J. Mortimer. 2006. "Development and Socialization through the Adult Life Course." In *Handbook of Social Psychology,* edited by J. DeLamater. New York: Kluwer Academic/Plenum.

Lutz, Helma, and Ewa Palenga-Mollenbeck. 2016. "Global Care Chains." In *Routledge Handbook of Immigration and Refugee Studies,* edited by Anna Triandafillidou. New York: Routledge:

Lyman, Rick. 2015a. "Bulgaria Puts Up a New Wall, but This One Keeps People Out." *New York Times,* April 5.

Lyman, Rick. 2015b. "Hungary Seals Border With Croatia in Migrant Crackdown." *New York Times,* October 16.

Lynch, Marc. 2013. The Arab Uprising: The Unfinished Revolutions of the New Middle East. New York: PublicAffairs.

Lynch, Marc, Deen Freelon, and Sean Aday. 2014. "Syria in the Arab Spring: The Integration of Syria's Conflict with the Arab Uprisings, 2011–2013." *Research & Politics* 1(3), published online. doi: 10.1177/2053168014549091.

Lynch, Michael Patrick. 2016. *The Internet of Us: Knowing More and Understanding Less in the Age of Big Data.* New York: Liveright.

Macdonald, Neil. 2010. "The Tea Party's Freak Show." *CBC News,* September 27. Accessed March 31, 2012. http://www.cbc.ca/news/world/story/2010/09/24/f-rfa-macdonald.html.

Machida, Satoshi. 2012. "Does Globalization Render People More Ethnocentric? Globalization and People's Views on Cultures." *American Journal of Economics and Sociology* 71: 436–469.

Mackay, Richard. 2014. *The Atlas of Endangered Species.* New York: Routledge.

Maclean, Mairi, Charles Harvey, and Robert Chia. 2010. "Dominant Corporate Agents and the Power Elite in France and Britain." *Organization Studies* 31: 327–348.

Madan, T. N. 2007. "Hinduism." In *Encyclopedia of Globalization,* edited by J. A. Scholte and R. Robertson, 571–573. New York: MTM.

Madhok, Diksha. 2014. "For All Those Jibes about Shopping, Indian Men Buy More Clothes than Women." Quartz, September 4. Accessed April 20, 2015. http://qz.com/259305/for-all-those-jibes-about-shopping-indian-men-buy-more-clothes-than-women.

Maginn, Paul J., and Christine Steinmetz. 2015. "Spatial and Regulatory Contours of the (Sub)Urban Sexscape." In *(Sub)Urban Sexscapes: Geographies and Regulation of the Sex Industry,* edited by P. J. Maginn and C. Steinmetz, 1–17. London: Routledge.

Mahoney, James, and Dietrich Rueschemeyer. 2003. *Comparative Historical Analysis in the Social Sciences.* Cambridge: Cambridge University Press.

Mahoney, James, and Kathleen Thelen, eds., 2015. *Advances in Comparative-Historical Analysis.* Cambridge: Cambridge University Press.

Mak, Athena H. N., Margaret Lumbers, and Anita Eves. 2012. "Globalisation and Food Consumption in Tourism." *Annals of Tourism Research* 39: 171–196.

Malesevic, Sinisa. 2010. *The Sociology of War and Violence.* Cambridge: Cambridge University Press.

Maliepaard, Mieke, and Richard Alba, 2016. "Cultural Integration in the Muslim Second Generation in the Netherlands: The Case of Gender Ideology." *International Migration Review* 50: 70–94.

Mandery, Evan. 2014. "End College Legacy Preferences." *New York Times,* April 24.

Mannheim, Karl. [1931] 1936. *Ideology and Utopia.* New York: Harcourt, Brace, and World.

Manning, Jimmie. 2015. "Communicating Sexual Identities: A Typology of Coming Out." *Sexuality & Culture* 19(1): 122–138.

Manning, Robert D. 2001. *Credit Card Nation: The Consequences of America's Addiction to Debt.* New York: Basic Books.

Manning, Wendy D. 2013. "Trends in Cohabitation: Over Twenty Years of Change, 1987–2010." In *National Family Profiles.* Bowling Green, OH: National Center for Family and Marriage Research.

Manning, Wendy D., and Jessica A. Cohen. 2015. "Teenage Cohabitation, Marriage and Childbearing." *Population Research and Policy Review* 34: 161–177.

Ma'oz, Moshe. 2014. "The Arab Spring in Syria: Domestic and Regional Developments." *Dynamics of Asymmetric Conflict* 7(1): 49–57.

Marginson, Simon. 2016. "The Worldwide Trend to High Participation Higher Education: Dynamics of Social Stratification in Inclusive Systems." *Higher Education* (published online first).

Margono, Belinda Arunarwati, Peter V. Potapov, Svetlana Turubanova, Fred Stolle, and Matthew C. Hansen. 2014. "Primary Forest Cover Loss in Indonesia over 2000–2012." *Nature Climate Change* 4: 730–735.

Marre, Diana, and Laura Briggs. 2009. *International Adoption: Global Inequalities and the Circulation of Children.* New York: New York University Press.

Marron, Donncha. 2009. *Consumer Credit in the United States: A Sociological Perspective from the 19th Century to the Present.* New York: Palgrave Macmillan.

Marsden, Peter V., and Elizabeth H. Gorman. 2001. "Social Networks, Job Changes, and Recruitment." In *Sourcebook on Labor Markets: Evolving Structures and Processes,* edited by I. Berg and A. L. Kalleberg, 467–502. New York: Kluwer Academic/Plenum.

Marshall, Catherine, and Gretchen Rossman. 2010. *Designing Qualitative Research.* Thousand Oaks, CA: Sage.

Martey, Rosa Mikeal, Jennifer Stromer-Galley, Jaime Banks, Jingsi Wu, and Mia Consalvo. 2014. "The Strategic Female: Gender-Switching and Player Behavior in Online Games." *Information, Communication & Society* 17(3): 286–300.

Martin, Jonathan. 2017. "Angry Democrats Study the Tea Party's Playbook." *New York Times* January 23.

Martin, Karin A. 2005. "William Wants a Doll. Can He Have One? Feminists, Child Care Advisors, and Gender-Neutral Child Rearing." *Gender & Society* 19: 456–479.

Martin-Uzzi, Michelle, and Denise Duval-Tsioles. 2013. "The Experience of Remarried Couples in Blended Families." *Journal of Divorce and Remarriage* 54: 43–57.

Marx, Karl. [1857–1858] 1964. *Pre-capitalist Economic Formations.* New York: International Publishers.

Marx, Karl, and Friedrich Engels. 1848. *The Communist Manifesto.* London: Communist League.

Mashal, Mujib. 2016. "Clash of Values Emerges After Afghan Child Bride Burns to Death." *New York Times,* July 18.

Massaro, Vanessa A., and Emma Gaalaas Mullaney. 2011. "Philly's 'Flash Mob Riots' and the Banality of Post-9/11 Securitization." *City* 15: 591–604.

Massey, Douglas. 2003. *Beyond Smoke and Mirrors: Mexican Immigration in an Era of Economic Integration.* New York: Russell Sage Foundation.

Massey, Douglas. 2016. "Residential Segregation is the Linchpin of Racial Stratification." *City and Community* 15: 4–7.

Massey, Garth. 2016. *Ways of Social Change: Making Sense of Modern Times,* 2nd ed. Thousand Oaks, CA: Sage.

Mather, Mark. 2009. *Reports on America: Children in Immigrant Families Chart New Path.* Washington, DC: Population Reference Bureau.

Mathews, Russell A., Doan E. Winkel, and Julie Holiday Wayne. 2014. "A Longitudinal Examination of Role Overload and Work-Family Conflict: The Mediating Role of Interdomain Transfers." *Journal of Organizational Behavior* 35: 72–91.

Matza, David. 1966. "The Disreputable Poor." In *Class, Status, and Power: Social Stratification in Comparative Perspective,* 2nd rev. ed., edited by R. Bendix and S. M. Lipset, 289–302. New York: Free Press.

Mazelis, Joan Maya, 2015. "'I Got to Try to Give Back': How Reciprocity Norms in a Poor Peoples' Organization Influence Members' Social Capital." *Journal of Poverty* 19: 109–131.

McAdams, Dan P., Michelle Albaugh, Emily Farber, Jennifer Daniels, Regina L. Logan, and Brad Olson. 2008. "Family Metaphors and Moral Intuitions: How Conservatives and Liberals Narrate Their Lives." *Journal of Personality and Social Psychology* 95: 978–990.

McCaghy, Charles H., Timothy A. Capron, J. D. Jamieson, and Sandra Harley H. Carey. 2016. *Deviant Behavior: Crime, Conflict and Interest Groups.* 8th ed. New York: Routledge.

McCann, Eugene, and Kevin Ward, eds. 2011. *Mobile Urbanism: Cities and Policymaking in the Global Age.* Minneapolis: University of Minnesota Press.

McCann, Hannah. 2016. "Epistemology of the Subject: Queer Theory's Challenge to Feminist Sociology." *Women's Studies Quarterly* Fall/Winter: 224-243.

McClelland, Robert, Shannon Mok, and Kevin Pierce. 2014. "Labor Force Participation Elasticities of Women and Secondary Earners within Married Couples." Working Paper 2014-06, Congressional Budget Office, September. Accessed April 20, 2015. https://www.cbo .gov/sites/default/files/cbofiles/attach ments/49433-LaborForce.pdf.

McCombs, Brady. 2013. "LDS Church Membership Hits 15 Million as Mormon Women Question Gender Inequality." *Huffington Post,* October 5. Accessed April 20, 2015. http://www.huffing tonpost.com/2013/10/05/lds-member ship-numbers_n_4051539.html.

McEvily, Bill, Giuseppe Soda, and Marco Tortoriello, 2014. "More Formally: Rediscovering the Missing Link between Formal Organization and Informal Social Structure." *The Academy of Management Annals* 8: 299–345.

McGuffey, Shawn. 2008. "'Saving Masculinity': Gender Reaffirmation, Sexuality, Race, and Parental Responses to Male Child Sexual Abuse." *Social Problems* 55(2): 216–237.

McHugh, Maureen C., and Joan C. Chrisler, eds. 2015. *The Wrong Prescription for Women.* Santa Barbara, CA: ABC-CLIO.

McIntosh, Peggy. 2010. "White Privilege: Unpacking the Invisible Knapsack." In *Race, Class and Gender in the United States,* 8th ed., edited by P. S. Rothenberg, 172–177. New York: Worth.

McLanahan, Sara S. 1999. "Father Absence and the Welfare of Children." In *Coping with Divorce, Single Parenting, and Remarriage: A Risk and Resiliency Perspective,* edited by E. M. Hetherington. Mahwah, NJ: Lawrence Erlbaum.

McLanahan, Sara S., and Erin L. Kelly. 1999. "The Feminization of Poverty: Past and Future." In *Handbook of the Sociology of Gender,* edited by J. S. Chafetz, 127–145. New York: Kluwer Academic/Plenum.

McLaughlin, Caitlin, and Jessica Vitak. 2011. "Norm Evolution and Violation on Facebook." *New Media & Society* 14(2) 299–315.

McMichael, Anthony J. 2013. "Globalization, Climate Change, and Human Health." *New England Journal of Medicine* 368: 1335–1343.

McNair, Brian. 2002. *Striptease Culture: Sex, Media and the Democratization of Desire.* London: Routledge.

McNeil, Donald G., Jr. 2016. "Malnutrition and Obesity Coexist in Many Countries, Report Finds." *New York Times,* June 13.

McPhail, Clark. 2007. "Crowd Behavior." In *The Blackwell Encyclopedia of Sociology,* edited by George Ritzer, 880–883. Malden, MA: Blackwell.

McPhate, Mike. 2016. "Ashley Madison Faces F.T.C. Inquiry Amid Rebranding." *New York Times,* July 6.

McShane, Marilyn D., and Frank P. Williams. 2007. "Beccaria, Cesare (1738–94)." In *The Blackwell Encyclopedia of Sociology,* Vol. 1, edited by George Ritzer, 255–256. Malden, MA: Blackwell.

Mead, George Herbert. [1934] 1962. *Mind, Self, and Society: From the Standpoint of a Social Behaviorist.* Chicago: University of Chicago Press.

Meier, Robert F. 2015. "Explanatory Paradigms in the Study of Deviance." In *The Handbook of Deviance,* edited by Erich Goode, 225–235. Malden, MA: Wiley-Blackwell.

Meister, Sandra. 2012. *Brand Communities for Fast-Moving Consumer Goods.* Wiesbaden, Germany: Gabler.

Melde, Chris, Terrance J. Taylor, and Finn Aage Esbensen. 2009. "'I Got Your Back': An Examination of the Protective Function of Gang Membership in Adolescence." *Criminology* 47(2): 565–594.

Melnick, Merrill L., and Daniel L. Wann. 2011. "An Examination of Sport Fandom in Australia: Socialization, Team Identification, and Fan Behavior." *International Review for the Sociology of Sport* 46: 456–470.

Meloni, Maurizio. 2014. "Biology without Biologism: Social Theory in a Postgenomic Age." *Sociology* 48: 731–746.

Merluzzi, Thomas V., Errol J. Philip, Zhiyong Zhang, and Courtney Sullivan. 2014. "Perceived Discrimination, Coping, and Quality of Life for African-American and Caucasian Persons with Cancer." *Cultural Diversity and Ethnic Minority Psychology,* August 4 (published online). doi: 10.1037/a0037543.

Merton, Robert K. [1949] 1968. *Social Theory and Social Structure.* 3rd ed. New York: Free Press.

Merton, Robert K. 1957. *Social Theory and Social Structure.* Rev. ed. Glencoe, IL: Free Press.

Merton, Robert, and Alice S. Kitt. 1950. "Contributions to the Theory of Reference Group Behavior." In *Continuities in Social Research,* edited by R. K. Merton and P. F. Lazarsfeld. Glencoe, IL: Free Press.

Messinger, Adam M. 2014. "Marking 35 Years of Research on Same-Sex Intimate Partner Violence: Lessons and New Directions." In *Handbook of LGBT Communities, Crime, and Justice,* edited by D. Peterson and V. R. Panfil, 65–85. New York: Springer.

Mészáros, István. 2006. *Marx's Theory of Alienation.* 5th ed. London: Merlin Press.

Meuleman, Roza, and Marcel Lubbers. 2016. "Parental Socialization and the Consumption of Domestic Films, Books and Music. *Journal of Consumer Culture.* May 16 (published online).

Meyer, Hans-Dieter, and Aaron Benavot, eds. 2013. *PISA, Power and Policy: The Emergence of Global Educational Governance.* Oxford: Symposium Books.

Meyer, John, J. Boli, and F. Ramirez. 1997. "World Society and the Nation State." *American Journal of Sociology* 103: 144–181.

Michels, Robert. [1915] 1962. *Political Parties.* New York: Collier Books.

Miles, Andrew, Mike Savage, and Felix Bühlmann. 2011. "Telling a Modest Story: Accounts of Men's Upward Mobility from the National Child Development Study." *British Journal of Sociology* 62: 418–441.

Milgram, Stanley. 1974. *Obedience to Authority: An Experimental View.* New York: Harper & Row.

Milibrandt, Tara, and Frank Pearce. 2011. "Émile Durkheim." In *The Wiley-Blackwell*

Companion to Major Social Theorists, Vol. 1., Classical Theorists, edited by George Ritzer and Jeffrey Stepnisky, 236–282. Malden, MA: Wiley-Blackwell.

Miller, Claire Cain. 2016. "Why Women Still Get the Short End of the Dollar." New York Times, March 3: 1, 5.

Miller, Daniel. 1998. A Theory of Shopping. Ithaca, NY: Cornell University Press.

Miller, Daniel, and Donald Slater. 2000. The Internet: An Ethnographic Approach. London: Berg.

Miller, Robert. 2001. "The Industrial Context of Occupational Mobility: Change in Structure." Research in Social Stratification and Mobility 18: 313–353.

Mills, Maura. 2015. Gender and the Work-Family Experience: An Intersection of Two Domains. Cham: Springer.

Mills, C. Wright. 1951. White Collar. New York: Oxford University Press.

Mills, C. Wright. 1956. The Power Elite. New York: Oxford University Press.

Mills, C. Wright. 1959. The Sociological Imagination. New York: Oxford University Press.

Mintel. 2015. "Online Shopping—US—June 2015." http://store.mintel.com/online-shopping-us-june-2015.

Misra, Joya, and Eiko Strader. 2013. "Gender Pay Equity in Advanced Countries: The Role of Parenthood and Policies." Journal of International Affairs 67(1): 27–41.

MIT Technology Review Custom. 2016. "Smart City Living Transforms the Urban Landscape." July 19. Accessed March 9, 2017. https://www.technologyreview.com/s/601928/smart-city-living-transforms-the-urban-landscape.

Moghadam, Valentine M. 1999. "Gender and Globalization: Female Labor and Women's Mobilization." Journal of World-Systems Research 5: 301–314.

Molaei. Hamideh. 2015. "Discursive Opportunity Structure and the Contribution of Social Media to the Success of Social Movements in Indonesia." Information, Communication and Society 18: 94–108.

Molla, Rani, and Shira Ovide. 2016. "The Wars on the Internet." BloombergGadfly, March 23. Accessed January 26, 2017. http://www.bloomberg.com/gadfly/articles/2016-03-23/google-and-media-titans-clash-in-a-war-on-internet-piracy.

Mollard, Elizabeth K. 2014. "A Qualitative Meta-synthesis and Theory of Postpartum Depression." Issues in Mental Health Nursing 35(9): 656–663.

Molm, Linda D. 2010. "The Structure of Reciprocity." Social Psychology Quarterly 73: 119–131.

Molm, Linda D., Monica M. Whithama, and David Melameda. 2012. "Forms of Exchange and Integrative Bonds:

Effects of History and Embeddedness." American Sociological Review 77: 141–165.

Monaghan, Jeffrey, and Kevin Walby. 2012. "Making Up 'Terror Identities': Security Intelligence, Canada's Integrated Threat Assessment Centre and Social Movement Suppression." Policing & Society 22: 133–151.

Monte, Andrew A., Richard D. Zane, and Kennon J. Heard. 2015. "The Implications of Marijuana legalization in Colorado." Journal of the American Medical Association 313: 241–242.

Montoya, I. D. 2005. "Effect of Peers on Employment and Implications for Drug Treatment." American Journal of Drug and Alcohol Abuse 31: 657–668.

Montt, Guillermo. 2011. "Cross-National Differences in Educational Inequality." Sociology of Education 84: 49–68.

Moore, Dahlia. 1995. "Role Conflict: Not Only for Women? A Comparative Analysis of 5 Nations." International Journal of Comparative Sociology 36(1–2): 17–35.

Moore, R. Laurence. 1997. Selling God: American Religion in the Marketplace of Culture. Oxford: Oxford University Press.

Moraga, Cherrie, and Gloria Anzaldua, eds. 2015. This Bridge Called My Back: Writings by Radical Women of Color. 4th ed. Albany: SUNY Press.

Moran, Mary, Javier Guzman, Anne-Laure Ropars, Alina McDonald, Nicole Jameson, Brenda Omune, Sam Ryan, and Lindsey Wu. 2009. "Neglected Disease Research and Development: How Much Are We Really Spending?" PLoS Med 6(2): e1000030.

Morgan, George, and Scott Poynting, eds. 2012. Global Islamaphobia: Muslims and the Moral Panic in the West. New York: Routledge.

Morgan, Stephen G. 2007. "Direct-to-Consumer Advertising and Expenditures on Prescription Drugs: A Comparison of Experiences in the United States and Canada." Open Medicine 1(1): e37–e45.

Morris, Aldon. 1984. The Origins of the Civil Rights Movement: Black Communities Organizing for Change. New York: Free Press.

Morris, Aldon. 2007. "Civil Rights Movement." In The Blackwell Encyclopedia of Sociology, edited by George Ritzer, 507–512. Malden, MA: Blackwell.

Morris, Betsy. 2013. "More Consumers Prefer Online Shopping." Wall Street Journal, June 3.

Morris, J. Glenn, Lynn M. Grattan, Brian M. Mayer, and Jason K. Blackburn. 2013. "Psychological Responses and Resilience of People and Communities

Impacted by the Deepwater Horizon Oil Spill." Transactions of the American Clinical and Climatological Association 124: 191–201.

Moses, Jonathon W. 2006. International Migration: Globalization's Last Frontier. London: Zed Books.

Mosley, Philip E. 2009. "Bigorexia: Body-building and Muscle Dysmorphia." European Eating Disorders Review 17: 191–198.

Moss, Dana M. 2013. "Arab Spring." In The Wiley-Blackwell Encyclopedia of Social and Political Movements, 3 vols., edited by D. A. Snow, D. Della Porta, B. Klandermans, and D. McAdam, 118–125. Malden, MA: Wiley-Blackwell.

Mucherah, Winnie, and Andrea Dawn Frazier. 2013. "How Deep Is Skin-Deep? The Relationship between Skin Color Satisfaction, Estimation of Body Image, and Self-Esteem among Women of African Descent." Journal of Applied Social Psychology 43: 1177–1184.

Mundy, Liza. 2012. The Richer Sex: How the New Majority of Female Breadwinners Is Transforming Our Culture. New York: Free Press.

Munro, Ealasaid. 2013. "Feminism: A Fourth Wave?" Political Insight 4: 22–25.

Murphy, Susan, and Patrick Paul Walsh. 2014. "Social Protection beyond the Bottom Billion." Economic and Social Review 45(2): 261–284.

Murray, Charles. 2013. Coming Apart: The State of White America, 1960–2010. New York: Crown Forum.

Musick, Kelly. 2007. "Fertility: Nonmarital." In The Blackwell Encyclopedia of Sociology, edited by George Ritzer, 1734–1737. Malden, MA: Blackwell.

Nagourney, Adam. 2013. "Unfinished Luxury Tower Is Stark Reminder of Las Vegas's Economic Reversal." New York Times, January 22.

Nagourney, Adam. 2015. "The Debate over California's Drought Crisis." New York Times, April 15.

Naples, Nancy A., and Manisha Desai. 2002. "Women's Local and Transnational Responses: An Introduction to the Volume." In Women's Activism and Globalization: Linking Local Struggles and Transnational Politics, edited by N. A. Naples and M. Desai. New York: Routledge.

Napoli, Lisa. 1999. "Dispensing of Drugs on Internet Stirs Debate." New York Times, April 6. Accessed March 31, 2012. http://query.nytimes.com/gst/fullpage.html?res=9B02E1D61139F935A-35757C0A96F958260&scp=8&sq=pharmaceutical%20purchase%20over%20internet&st=cse.

Naquin, Charles E., Terri R. Kurtzberg, and Liuba Y. Belkin. 2008. "E-mail communication and Group Cooperation in Mixed Motive Contexts." *Social Justice Research* 21: 470–489.

Nardi, Peter M., David Sanders, and Judd Marmor. 1994. *Growing Up before Stonewall: Life Stories of Some Gay Men.* London: Routledge.

Nash, Catherine J., and Andrew Gorman-Murray. 2014. "LGBT Neighbourhoods and 'New Mobilities': Towards Understanding Transformations in Sexual and Gendered Urban Landscapes." *International Journal of Urban & Regional Research* 38(3): 756–772.

National Coalition of Anti-Violence Programs. 2014. "National Report on Hate Violence against Lesbian, Gay, Bisexual, Transgender, Queer and HIV-Affected Communities Released Today." Press release, May 29. Accessed April 17, 2015. http://www.avp.org/storage/documents/2013_mr_ncavp_hvreport.pdf.

Nederveen Pieterse, Jan. 2015. *Globalization and Culture: Global Melange.* 2nd ed. Lanham, MD: Rowman & Littlefield.

Negri, Stefania. 2016. "Transplant Ethics and the International Crime of Organ Trafficking." *International Criminal Law Review* 16: 287–303.

Negrusa, Sebastian, and Brighita Negrusa. 2014. "Home Front: Post-deployment Mental Health and Divorces." *Demography* 51: 895–916.

Negrusa, Sebastian, Brighita Negrusa, and James Hosek. 2014. "Gone to War: Have Deployments Increased Divorces?" *Journal of Population Economics* 27: 473–496.

Neuendorf, Kimberly A., Thomas D. Gore, Amy Dalessandro, Patricie Janstova, and Sharon Snyder-Suh. 2009. "Shaken and Stirred: A Content Analysis of Women's Portrayals in James Bond Films." *Sex Roles* 62: 747–776.

Neuman, William. 2015. "Americans May See Appeal of Medical Tourism in Cuba." *New York Times,* February 17.

Newton, David E. 2009. *Gay and Lesbian Rights: A Reference Handbook.* Santa Barbara, CA: ABC-CLIO.

Newton, David. 2016. *The Global Water Crisis.* Santa Barbara, CA: ABC-CLIO.

Newton, Michael. 2002. *Savage Girls and Wild Boys: A History of Feral Children.* London: Faber and Faber.

New York Times Editorial Board. 2016. "Rethinking the Global War on Drugs." April 25.

Nguyen, Tina. 2017. "Are Democrats Having Their Tea Party Moment?" *Vanity Fair* February 10.

Nichols, Brian J. 2012. "Buddhism." In *The Wiley-Blackwell Encyclopedia of Globalization,* edited by George Ritzer, 142–145. Malden, MA: Wiley-Blackwell.

Nicholson, Linda. 2008. *Identity before Identity Politics.* Cambridge: Cambridge University Press.

Niebuhr, Gustav. 1995. "Where Shopping-Mall Culture Gets a Big Dose of Religion." *New York Times,* April 16.

Nixon, Elizabeth, Sheila Greene, and Diane Hogan. 2015. "'Its's What's Normal for Me:' Children's Experiences of Growing Up in a Continuously Single-Parent Household." *Journal of Family Issues* 36(8):1043–1061.

Noble, David F. 2011. *Forces of Production: A Social History of Industrial Automation.* New Brunswick, NJ: Transaction.

Nobles, Jenna. 2011. "Parenting from Abroad: Migration, Nonresident Father Involvement, and Children's Education in Mexico." *Journal of Marriage and Family* 73: 729–746.

Noller, Patricia, and Gery C. Karantzas. 2012. "Conflict in Family Relationships." In *The Wiley-Blackwell Handbook of Couples and Family Relationships,* edited by P. Noller and G. C. Karantzas, 129–143. Malden, MA: Wiley-Blackwell.

Noppers, Ernst H., Kees Keizer, Jan Willem Bolderdijk, and Linda Steg. 2014. "The Adoption of Sustainable Innovations: Driven by Symbolic and Environmental Motives." *Global Environmental Change:* 1–11.

Nordberg, Jenny. 2014. *The Underground Girls of Kabul: In Search of a Hidden Resistance in Afghanistan.* New York: Crown Group.

Nordenmark, Mikael. 2007. "Unemployment." In *The Blackwell Encyclopedia of Sociology,* edited by George Ritzer, 5090–5091. Malden, MA: Blackwell.

"North Korea Country Profile—Overview." 2015. *BBC News,* April 30. Accessed May 18, 2015. http://www.bbc.com/news/world-asia-pacific-15256929.

Nuru-Jeter, Amani, Tyan Parker Dominguez, Wizdom Powell Hammond, Janxin Leu, Marilyn Skaff, Susan Egerter, Camara P. Jones, and Paula Braveman. 2009. "'It's the Skin You're In': African-American Women Talk about Their Experiences of Racism. An Exploratory Study to Develop Measures of Racism for Birth Outcome Studies." *Maternal Child Health Journal* 13(1): 29–39.

Nwachukwu, Saviour L., and Rajiv P. Dant. 2014. "Consumer Culture in Developing Economies: Is It Really So Different?" *Proceedings of the Academy of Marketing Science 2015,* November 25, 35–40.

Obara-Minnitt, Mika. 2014. "Alternative Globalizations: An Integrative Approach to Studying Dissident Knowledge in the Global Justice Movement." *Journal of Contemporary European Studies* 22: 222–223.

Oberschall, Anthony. 2012. "Ethnic Cleansing." In *The Wiley-Blackwell Encyclopedia of Globalization,* edited by George Ritzer, 547–551. Malden, MA: Wiley-Blackwell.

O'Brien, Jodi. 2016. "Seeing Agnes: Notes on a Transgender Biocultural Ethnomethodology." *Symbolic Interaction* 39: 306-329.

Ochiai, Emiko. 2014. "The Meaning of the Second Demographic Transition and the Establishment of a Mature Society." *European Societies* 16: 343–346.

Ocloo, Josephine Enyonam. 2010. "Harmed Patients Gaining Voice: Challenging Dominant Perspectives in the Construction of Medical Harm and Patient Safety Reforms." *Social Science & Medicine* 71: 510–516.

O'Connor, Brendan, and Martin Griffiths. 2005. *The Rise of Anti-Americanism.* London: Routledge.

Ogas, Ogi, and Sai Gaddam. 2012. *A Billion Wicked Thoughts: What the Internet Tells Us about Sexual Relationships.* New York: Plume.

Oliver, Pamela. 2013. "Collective Action (Collective Behavior)." In *The Wiley-Blackwell Encyclopedia of Social and Political Movements,* 3 vols., edited by D. A. Snow, D. Della Porta, B. Klandermans, and D. McAdam, 210–215. Malden, MA: Wiley-Blackwell.

Olivier, Jos G. J., Greet Janssens-Maenhout, and Jeroen A. H. W. Peters. 2012. *Trends in Global CO_2 Emissions: 2012 Report.* The Hague: PBL Netherlands Environmental Assessment Agency. Accessed April 17, 2015. http://www.pbl.nl/en/publications/2012/trends-in-global-c02-emissions-2012-report.

O'Loughlin, Deirdre M., Isabelle Szmigin, Morven G McEachern, Belem Barbosa, Kalipso Karantinou, and María Eugenia Fernández-Moya. 2016. "Man Thous Art Dust: Rites of Passage in Austere Times." *Sociology* March 15 (published online).

Olson, Lynn. 2002. *Freedom's Daughters: The Unsung Heroines of the Civil Rights Movements from 1830 to 1970.* New York: Scribner.

Opsal, Tara D. 2011. "Women Disrupting a Marginalized Identity: Subverting the Parolee Identity through Narrative." *Journal of Contemporary Ethnography* 40(2): 135–167.

Orfield, Gary. 2001. *Schools More Separate: Consequences of a Decade of Resegregation.* Cambridge, MA: Harvard University, Civil Rights Project. Accessed July

8, 2013. http://www.civilrightsproject.harvard.edu/research/deseg/Schools_More_Separate.pdf.

Organisation for Economic Co-operation and Development. 2016. "Development Aid Rises Again in 2015, Spending on Refugees Doubles." www.oecd.org/dac/development-aid-rises-again-in-2015-spending-on-refu gees-doubles.htm.

Orlikowski, Wanda J. 2010. "Technology and Organization: Contingency All the Way Down." In *Technology and Organization: Essays in Honour of Joan Woodward,* edited by N. Phillips, G. Sewell, and D. Griffiths, 239–246. Bingley, UK: Emerald.

Orr, Martin. 2012. "Great Recession." In *The Encyclopedia of Globalization,* edited by George Ritzer, 890–891. Malden, MA: Wiley-Blackwell.

Ortmeyer, David L., and Michael A. Quinn. 2012. "Coyotes, Migration Duration, and Remittances." *Journal of Developing Areas* 46: 185–203.

Orwell, George. 1949. *Nineteen Eighty-Four.* London: Secker and Warburg.

Osborne, Danny and Chris Sibley. 2015. "Within the Limits of Civic Training: Education Moderates the Relationship between Openness and Political Attitudes." *Political Psychology* 36(3):295–313.

Osman, Suleiman. 2011. *The Invention of Brownstone Brooklyn: Gentrification and the Search for Authenticity in Postwar New York.* New York: Oxford University Press.

Ostergaard, Per, James Fitchett, and Christian Jantzen. 2013. "A Critique of the Ontology of Consumer Enchantment." *Journal of Consumer Behaviour* 12: 337–344.

Otnes, Cele C., and Linda Tuncay Zayre, eds. 2012. *Gender, Culture, and Consumer Behavior.* New York: Routledge.

Oyogoa, Francisca. 2016. "Cruise Ships: Continuity and Change in the World System." *Journal of World-Systems Research* 22: 32–37.

Pace, Julie. 2010. "Obama Takes on Election-Year Fears over Big Debt." *CBS News,* September 19. Accessed March 31, 2012. http://www.cbsnews.com/stories/2010/09/19/national/main6881308.shtml.

Pager, Devah. 2009. *Marked: Race, Crime, and Finding Work in an Era of Mass Incarceration.* Chicago: University of Chicago.

Pager, Devah, and Bruce Western. 2012. "Identifying Discrimination at Work: The Use of Field Experiments." *Journal of Social Issues* 68: 221–237.

Pakulski, Jan. 2014. "Confusions about Multiculturalism." *Journal of Sociology* 50: 23–36.

Palfrey, John, and Urs Gasser. 2008. *Born Digital: Understanding the First Generation of Digital Natives.* New York: Basic Books.

Panitch, Leo. 2009. "Thoroughly Modern Marx." *Foreign Policy,* April 15.

Pantzar, Mike, and Elizabeth Shove. 2010. "Understanding Innovation in Practice: A Discussion of the Production and Re-production of Nordic Walking." *Technology Analysis and Strategic Management* 22: 447–461.

Park, Haeyoun, and Iaryna Mykhyalyshyn, 2016. "Hate Crimes Now Directed at L.G.B.T. People the Most." *New York Times,* June 18.

Park, Julie, and Dowell Myers. 2010. "Intergenerational Mobility in the Post-1965 Immigration Era: Estimates by an Immigrant Generation Cohort Method." *Demography* 47: 369–392.

Parker, Pamela. 2012. "Study: Mobile and Video Are Key Drivers of Apparel Purchases." *Marketing Land,* August 14. Accessed April 20, 2015. http://marketingland.com/study-mobile-and-video-are-key-drivers-of-apparel-purchases-18927.

Parker, Richard, Jonathan Garcia, and Robert M. Buffington. 2014. "Sexuality and the Contemporary World: Globalization and Sexual Rights." In *A Global History of Sexuality: The Modern Era,* edited by R. M. Buffington, E. Luibhéid, and D. J. Guy, 221–260. Chichester, UK: Wiley.

Parkinson, Cyril Northcote. 1955. "Parkinson's Law." *Economist,* November 19.

Parlapiano, Alicia, Robert Gebeloff, and Shan Carter. 2015. "The Shrinking American Middle Class." *New York Times,* January 26.

Pascoe, C. J. 2012. *Dude, You're a Fag: Masculinity and Sexuality in High School.* Berkeley: University of California Press.

Pascoe, John M., David L. Wood, James H. Duffee, and Alice Kuo. 2016. "Mediators and Adverse Effects of Child Poverty in the United States." *Pediatrics* 37: e1–e17.

Passel, Jeffrey. 2010. "Race and the Census: The 'Negro' Controversy." Pew Research Center, January 21. Accessed January 16, 2012. http://www.pew-socialtrends.org/2010/01/21/race-and-the-census-the-%E2%80%9Cnegro%E2%80%9D-controversy.

Patch, Jason, and Neil Brenner. 2007. "Gentrification." In *The Blackwell Encyclopedia of Sociology,* edited by George Ritzer, 1917–1920. Malden, MA: Blackwell.

Patchin, Justin W., and Sameer Hinduja. 2010. "Trends in Online Social Networking: Adolescent Use of MySpace over Time." *New Media and Society* 12: 197–216.

Patel, Jugal K. 2017. "How 2016 Became Earth's Hottest Year on Record." *New York Times,* January 18.

Paternoster, Ray. 2007. "Capital Punishment." In *The Blackwell Encyclopedia of Sociology,* edited by George Ritzer, 385–388. Malden, MA: Blackwell.

Paternoster, Raymond, Robert Brame, and Sarah Bacon. 2007. *The Death Penalty: America's Experience with Capital Punishment.* Oxford: Oxford University Press.

Patterson, Charlotte J., Rachel H. Farr, and Paul D. Hastings. 2015. "Socialization in the Context of Family Diversity." In *Handbook of Socialization: Theory and Research,* 2nd ed., edited by Joan E. Grusec and Paul D. Hastings, 202–227. New York: Guilford Press.

Patterson, Maurice, and Jonathan Schroeder. 2010. "Borderlines: Skin, Tattoos and Consumer Culture Theory." *Marketing Theory* 10: 253–267.

Patterson, Orlando, and Ethan Fosse, eds. 2015. *The Cultural Matrix: Understanding Black Youth.* Cambridge, MA: Harvard University Press.

Patton, Elizabeth, and Mimi Choi, eds. 2014. *Home Sweat Home: Perspectives on Housework and Modern Relationships.* Lanham, MD: Rowman & Littlefield.

Payne, Elizabeth, and Melissa Smith. 2014. "The Big Freak Out: Educator Fear in Response to the Presence of Transgender Elementary School Students." *Journal of Homosexuality* 61(3): 399–418.

Payton, Andrew, and Peggy A. Thoits. 2011. "Medicalization, Direct-to-Consumer Advertising, and Mental Illness Stigma." *Society and Mental Health* 1: 55–70.

Pearce, Diane. 1978. "The Feminization of Poverty: Women, Work, and Welfare." *Urban and Social Change Review* 11: 28–36.

Pearlin, Leonard I. 1989. "The Sociological Study of Stress." *Journal of Health and Social Behavior* 30: 241–256.

Penn, Roger. Forthcoming. "Marital Endogamy, Friendship Homogamy, and Ethnic/Nationality Group." *Journal of Marriage and Family.*

Pennington, Bill. 2015a. "Brady Receives a 4-Game Ban." *New York Times,* May 12.

Pennington, Bill. 2015b. "In a Man's Game: Mark Herzlich is Standing Up for Women." *New York Times,* October 24.

Pennington, Jon C. 2003. "It's Not a Revolution but It Sure Looks Like One: A Statistical Accounting of the Post-sixties Sexual Revolution." *Radical Statistics* 83: 104–116.

Perelli-Harris, Brienna, and Nora Sanchez Gassen. 2012. "How Similar Are Cohabitation and Marriage? Legal Approaches to Cohabitation across Western Europe." *Population and Development Review* 38: 435–467.

Perloff, Richard M., Bette Bonder, George B. Ray, Eileen Berlin Ray, and Laura A Siminoff. 2006. "Doctor–Patient Communication, Cultural Competence, and Minority Health: Theoretical and Empirical Perspectives." *American Behavioral Scientist* 49(6): 835–852.

Perlroth, Nicole, and David Sanger. 2017. "Hackers Hit Dozens of Countries Exploiting Stolen N.S.A. Tool." *New York Times* May 12.

Perrow, Charles. 1999. *Normal Accidents.* Princeton, NJ: Princeton University Press.

Peters, Jeremy W. 2014. "After Immigration Action, a Blast of Energy for the Tea Party." *New York Times,* November 25.

Peterson, Helen. 2016. "Is Managing Academics 'Women's Work'? Exploring the Glass Cliff in Higher Education Management." *Educational Management Administration and Leadership* 44: 112–127.

Peterson, Richard A., and Roger M. Kern. 1996. "Changing Highbrow Taste: From Snob to Omnivore." *American Sociological Review* 61: 900–907.

Pettijohn, Terry F., Erik Frazier, Elizabeth Rieser, Nicholas Vaughn, and Bobbi Hupp-Wilds.2015. "Classroom Texting in College Students." *College Student Journal* 49: 513–516.

Pew Research Center. 2013. "A Survey of LGBT Americans: Attitudes, Experiences and Values in Changing Times." June 13. Accessed April 17, 2015. http://www.pewsocialtrends.org/2013/06/13/a-survey-of-lgbt-americans.

Pfeffer, Max J., and Pilar A. Parra. 2009. "Strong Ties, Weak Ties, and Human Capital: Latino Immigrant Employment outside the Enclave." *Rural Sociology* 74(2): 241–269.

Phelan, Jo C., Bruce G. Link, Ana Diez-Roux, Ichiro Kawachi, and Bruce Levin. 2004. "'Fundamental Causes' of Social Inequalities in Mortality: A Test of the Theory." *Journal of Health and Social Behavior* 45: 265–285.

Phelan, Jo C., Bruce G. Link, and Parisa Tehranifar. 2010. "Social Conditions as Fundamental Causes of Health Inequalities: Theory, Evidence, and Policy Implications." *Journal of Health and Social Behavior* 51: S28–S40.

Phelps, Michelle S. 2011. "Rehabilitation in the Punitive Era: The Gap between Rhetoric and Reality in U.S. Prison Programs." *Law and Society Review* 45: 33–68.

Phelps, Nicholas, and Fulong Wu, eds. 2011. *International Perspectives on Suburbanization: A Post-Suburban World?* New York: Palgrave-Macmilllan.

Philips, Bernard, ed. 2016. *Understanding Terrorism.* New York: Routledge.

Piarroux, Renaud. 2016. "The U.N.'s Responsibility in Haiti's Cholera Crisis." *New York Times,* September 7.

Pick, James B., and Aviit Sarkar. 2015. *The Global Digital Divides: Explaining Change.* Berlin: Springer.

Pickering, Mary. 2011. "Auguste Comte." In *The Wiley-Blackwell Companion to Major Social Theorists,* Vol. 1, *Classical Theorists,* edited by George Ritzer and Jeffrey Stepnisky, 30–60. Malden, MA: Wiley-Blackwell.

Piketty, Thomas. 2014. *Capital in the Twenty-First Century.* Cambridge, MA: Belknap Press.

Pilcher, Jane. 2013. "'Small but Very Determined': A Novel Theorization of Children's Consumption of Culture." *Cultural Sociology* 7: 86–100.

Piquero, Alex R., Raymond Paternoster, Greg Pogarsky, and Thomas Loughran. 2011. "Elaborating the Individual Difference Component in Deterrence Theory." *Annual Review of Law and Social Science* 7: 335–360.

Piquero, Nicole Leeper. 2010. "Causes and Prevention of Intellectual Property Crime." In *Cybercrime: An Introduction to an Emerging Phenomenon,* edited by George Higgins, 88–109. Boston: McGraw Hill.

Pitts, Victoria. 2003. *In the Flesh: The Cultural Politics of Body Modification.* New York: Palgrave Macmillan.

Plante, Rebecca F. 2014. "Sexuality." In *Investigating Social Problems,* edited by A. J. Treviño, 108–133. Thousand Oaks, CA: Sage.

Plante, Rebecca F. 2015. *Sexualities in Context: A Social Perspective.* 2nd ed. New York: Routledge.

Plante, Rebecca F., and Andrew P. Smiler. 2014. "Time for a Sexual-Climate Change." *Chronicle of Higher Education,* November 26. Accessed April 17, 2015. http://chronicle.com/blogs/conversation/2014/11/26/time-for-a-sexual-climate-change.

Pleyers, Geoffrey. 2010. *Alter-Globalization: Becoming Actors in the Global Age.* Cambridge: Polity Press.

Plummer, Ken. 1975. *Sexual Stigma: An Interactionist Account.* London: Routledge.

Plummer, Ken. 2007a. "Sexual Identities." In *The Blackwell Encyclopedia of Sociology,* edited by George Ritzer, 4238–4242. Malden, MA: Blackwell.

Plummer, Ken. 2007b. "Sexual Markets, Commodification, and Consumption." In *The Blackwell Encyclopedia of Sociology,* edited by George Ritzer, 4242–4244. Malden, MA: Blackwell.

Plummer, Ken. 2012. "Critical Sexuality Studies." In *The Wiley-Blackwell Companion to Sociology,* edited by George Ritzer, 243–268. Malden, MA: Wiley-Blackwell.

Pogue, David. 2014. "Smart Sharing." *Scientific American,* June.

"Police Discover Five Children 'Hidden from Society in Squalid Home and Raised without Schooling or Healthcare.'" 2010. *Daily Mail,* November 30. Accessed May 25, 2015. http://www.dailymail.co.uk/news/article-1334132/Police-discover-5-children-hidden-society-squalid-home.html.

Polonko, Karen. 2007. "Child Abuse." In *The Blackwell Encyclopedia of Sociology,* edited by George Ritzer, 448–451. Malden, MA: Blackwell.

Popenoe, David. 2009. "Cohabitation, Marriage, and Child Wellbeing: A Cross-National Perspective." *Society* 46: 429–436.

Popham, James, and Sirotnik, Kenneth. 1973. *Educational Statistics: Use and Interpretation.* New York: Harper & Row.

Popper, Nathaniel. 2015. *Digital Gold.* New York: Harper.

Population Reference Bureau. 2010. "World Population Data Sheet." Accessed October 28, 2010. http://www.prb.org/Publications/Datasheets/2010/2010wpds.aspx.

Porter, Eduardo. 2016a. "The Crumbling Case for a Mexican Border Wall." *New York Times,* September 6.

Porter, Eduardo. 2016b. "Moving on From Farm and Factory." *New York Times,* April 27.

Poster, Winnifred. 2007. "Who's on the Line? Indian Call Center Agents Pose as Americans for U.S.-Outsourced Firms." *Industrial Relations* 46(2): 271–304.

Postmes, Tom, and Russell Spears. 1998. "Deindividuation and Antinormative Behavior: A Meta-analysis." *Psychological Bulletin* 123(3): 238–259.

Potter, Emma, and Katherine Allen. 2016. "Agency and Access: How Gay Fathers Secure Health Insurance for Their Families." *Journal of GLBT Family Studies* 12(3);300-317.

Powell, Brian, Catherine Bolzendahl, Claudia Geist, and Lala Carr Steelman. 2010. *Counted Out: Same-Sex Relations and Americans' Definitions of Family.* New York: Russell Sage Foundation.

Pramuk, Jacob. 2015. "There Are Now More Uber Cars Than Yellow Taxis in NYC." *CNBC,* March 18.

Presser, Harriet B. 2005. *Working in a 24/7 Economy.* New York: Russell Sage Foundation.

Prior, Nick. 2011. "Critique and Renewal in the Sociology of Music: Bourdieu and Beyond." *Cultural Sociology* 5: 121–138.

Pritchard, Mary, and Brooke Cramblitt. 2014. "Media Influence on Drive for Thinness and Drive for Muscularity." *Sex Roles* 71: 208–218.

Proctor, Bernadette D., Jessica L. Semega, and Melissa A. Kollar. 2016. "Income and Poverty in the United States: 2015." Current Population Reports, P60-256(RV). September. Accessed January 26, 2017. http://www.census.gov/content/dam/Census/library/publications/2016/demo/p60-256.pdf.

Prot, Sara, Craig A. Anderson, Douglas A. Gentile, Wayne Warburton, Muniba Saleem, Christopher L. Groves, and Stephanie C. Brown. 2015. "Media as Agents of Socialization." In *Handbook of Socialization: Theory and Research,* 2nd ed., edited by Joan E. Grusec and Paul D. Hastings, 276–300. New York: Guilford Press.

Pugh, Allison. 2015. *The Tumbleweed Society: Working and Caring in an Age of Insecurity.* New York: Oxford University Press.

Pugh, Allison. 2016. *Beyond the Cubicle: Job Insecurity, Intimacy, and the Flexible Self.* New York: Oxford University Press.

Pugh, Derek S., David Hickson, C. R. Hinings, and C. Turner. 1968. "The Context of Organizational Structures." *Administrative Science Quarterly* 14: 91–114.

Pullum, Amanda. 2013. "Tea Party Movement (United States)." In *The Wiley-Blackwell Encyclopedia of Social and Political Movements,* 3 vols., edited by D. A. Snow, D. Della Porta, B. Klandermans, and D. McAdam, 1327–1328. Malden, MA: Wiley-Blackwell.

Pushpa, Ramnath and Sandeep Singh. 2017. "Peer Pressure Among Adolescents in Relation to Family Climate." *Indian Journal of Health and Well-Being* 8(3):196–199.

Purdam, Kingsley, Elisabeth A. Garratt, and Aneez Esmail, 2015. "Hungry? Food Insecurity, Social Stigma, and Embarrassment in the UK." *Sociology* (published online first).

Qian, Zhenchao, and Daniel T. Lichter. 2011. "Changing Patterns of Interracial Marriage in a Multiracial Society." *Journal of Marriage and Family* 73: 1065–1084.

Quach, Thu, Amani Nuru-Jeter, Pagan Morris, Laura Allen, Sarah J. Shema, June K. Winters, Gem M. Le, and Scarlett Lin Gomez. 2012. "Experiences and Perceptions of Medical Discrimination among a Multiethnic Sample of Breast Cancer Patients in the Greater San Francisco Bay Area, California." *American Journal of Public Health* 102: 1027–1034.

Quadagno, Jill, and Deana Rohlinger. 2009. "Religious Conservatives in U.S. Welfare State Politics." In *The Western Welfare State and Its Religious Roots,* edited by K. van Kersbergen and P. Manow, 236–266. New York: Cambridge University Press.

Quealy, Kevin, and Margaret Sanger-Katz. 2016. "The U.S. Is a World Apart at Gun Death Rates." *New York Times,* June 14.

Ragin, Charles. 2014. *The Comparative Method: Moving beyond Qualitative and Quantitative Strategies.* Rev. ed. Berkeley: University of California Press.

Ram, Uri. 2007. *The Globalization of Israel: McWorld in Tel Aviv, Jihad in Jerusalem.* London: Routledge.

Rank, Mark R. 2014. "Challenging the Conventional Understanding of American Poverty." In *Race and Social Problems,* edited by Ralph Bangs and Larry E. Davis, 93–104. New York: Springer.

Rao, Leena. 2016. "Amazon Debuts as a New Grocery Store without Checkout Lines." *Fortune,* December 5. http://fortune.com/2016/12/05/amazon-go-store.

Rape, Abuse, and Incest National Network (RAINN). n.d. "Victims of Sexual Violence: Statistics." Accessed March 8, 2017. https://www.rainn.org/statistics/victims-sexual-violence.

Rappeport, Alan, and Maggie Haberman, 2016. "How Donald Trump Keeps Changing His Mind on Abortion, Torture and Banning Muslims." *New York Times,* June 29.

Ratha, Dilip, and Sanket Mohapatra. 2012. "Remittances and Development." In *The Wiley-Blackwell Encyclopedia of Globalization,* edited by George Ritzer, 1782–1792. Malden, MA: Wiley-Blackwell.

Rauer, Amy J., Gregory S. Pettit, Jennifer E. Lansford, John E. Bates, and Kenneth A. Dodge. 2013. "Romantic Relationship Patterns in Young Adulthood and Their Developmental Antecedents." *Developmental Psychology* 49: 2159–2171.

Ravitch, Diane. 2012. "Schools We Can Envy." *New York Review of Books,* March 8, 19–20.

Rawls, Ann. 2015. "Interaction Order: The Making of Social Facts." In *Order on the Edge of Chaos,* edited by Edward J. Lawler, Shane R. Thye, and Jeongkoo Yoon, 227–247. New York: Cambridge University Press.

Ray, Victor Erik, Antonia Randolph, Megan Underhill, and David Luke. 2017. "Critical Race Theory, Afro-Pessimism, and Racial Progress Narratives." *Sociology of Race and Ethnicity.* 3(2): 147-158.

Reay, Barry. 2014. "Promiscuous Intimacies: Rethinking the History of American Casual Sex." *Journal of Historical Sociology* 27: 1–24.

Recording Industry Association of America. 2015. "IFPI Digital Music Report: Charting the Path to Sustainable Growth." Accessed January 26, 2017. http://www.riaa.com/wp-content/uploads/2015/09/Digital-Music-Report-2015.pdf.

Reed, Mark S., and Lindsay C. Stringer. 2016. *Land Degradation, Desertification and Climate Change: Anticipating, Assessing and Adapting to Future Change.* New York: Routledge.

Reed College. 2015. "Sexual Assault Prevention and Response at Reed." Accessed March 28, 2015. http://www.reed.edu/sexual_assault/definitions/consent.html.

Rees, Karen L. 2013. "The Role of Reflective Practices in Enabling Final Year Nursing Students to Respond to the Distressing Emotional Challenges of Nursing Work." *Nurse Education in Practice* 13: 48–52.

Reger, Jo. 2007. "Feminism, First, Second, and Third Waves." In *The Blackwell Encyclopedia of Sociology,* edited by George Ritzer, 1672–1681. Malden, MA: Blackwell.

Regnerus, Mark, and Jeremy Uecker. 2011. *Premarital Sex in America: How Young Americans Meet, Mate, and Think about Marrying.* Oxford: Oxford University Press.

Reich, Robert. 2016. *Saving Capitalism.* New York: Vintage.

Reid, Charles J. 2014. "The Journey to Seneca Falls: Mary Wollstonecraft, Elizabeth Cady Stanton and the Legal Emancipation of Women." *University of St. Thomas Law Journal* 10(4), art. 9.

Reid, Julie A., Sinikka Elliott, and Gretchen R. Webber. 2011. "Casual Hookups to Formal Dates: Refining the Boundaries of the Sexual Double Standard." *Gender & Society* 25(5): 545–568.

Reilly, Katie. 2017. "Colleges Could Lose $700 Million a Year because of Trump's Immigration Ban." *Fortune* January 31.

Ren, Ping. 2007. "Church or Sect? Exploring a Chuirch of New Chinese Immigrants in Southern California." *Marburg Journal of Religion* 12: 1–25.

Restivo, Emily, and Mark M. Lanier. 2015. "Measuring the Contextual Effects and Mitigating Factors of Labeling Theory." *Justice Quarterly* 32(1): 116–141.

Reuters. 2016a. "Child Hunger Here to Stay Unless World 'Dramatically Changes Course': Charity." *New York Times,* August 5.

Reuters. 2016b. "Indonesia Wages War on Drugs But Cuts Funding for Rehabilitation." *New York Times* August 1.

Reuters. 2017. "Cyber Attack Hits 200,000 in at least 150 Countries: Europol." *New York Times,* May 14.

Reverby, Susan. 2009. *Examining Tuskegee: The Infamous Syphilis Study and Its Legacy.*

Chapel Hill: University of North Carolina Press.

Rich, Motoko. 2015. "Homeschooling: More Pupils, Less Regulation." *New York Times,* January 4.

Richtel, Matt. 2016. "Texting and Driving? Watch out for Textalyzer." *New York Times* April 27.

Rideout, Victoria J., Ulla G. Foehr, and Donald F. Roberts. 2010. *Generation M2: Media in the Lives of 8- to 18-Year-Olds.* Menlo Park, CA: Kaiser Family Foundation.

Ridgeway, Cecilia L., and Shelley L. Correll. 2004. "Unpacking the Gender System: A Theoretical Perspective on Gender Beliefs and Social Relations." *Gender & Society* 18(4): 510–553.

Rieger, Jon H. 2007. "Key Informant." In *The Blackwell Encyclopedia of Sociology,* edited by George Ritzer, 2457–2458. Malden, MA: Blackwell.

Rieker, Patricia R., and Chloe E. Bird. 2000. "Sociological Explanations of Gender Differences in Mental and Physical Health." In *Handbook of Medical Sociology,* edited by C. E. Bird, P. Conrad, and A. Freemont. New York: Prentice Hall.

Riera-Crichton, Daniel. 2012. "Euro Crisis." In *The Encyclopedia of Globalization,* edited by George Ritzer, 566–570. Malden, MA: Wiley-Blackwell.

Riffkin, Rebecca. 2014. "New Record Highs in Moral Acceptability." Gallup, May 30. Accessed April 17, 2015. http://www.gallup.com/poll/170789/new-record-highs-moral-acceptability.aspx.

Rifkin, Jeremy. 1995. *The End of Work.* New York: Putnam.

Riis, Ole. 2012. "Combining Quantitative and Qualitative Methods in the Sociology of Religion." In *Annual Review of the Sociology of Religion: New Methods in Sociology of Religion,* edited by L. Berzano and O. Riis, 91–116. Leiden, Netherlands: Brill.

Rinaldo, Lindsay, and Kenneth Ferraro. 2012. "Inequality, Health." In *The Wiley-Blackwell Encyclopedia of Globalization,* edited by George Ritzer, 1034–1037. Malden, MA: Wiley-Blackwell.

Rindermann, Heiner, and Antonia E. E. Baumeister. 2015. "Parents' SES vs. Parental Educational Behavior and Children's Development: A Reanalysis of the Hart and Risley Study." *Learning and Individual Differences* 37: 133–138.

Ringrose, Jessica, and Laurie Harvey. 2015. "Boobs, Back-Off, Six Packs, and Bits: Mediated Body Parts, Gendered Reward and Sexual Shame in Teens' Sexting Images." *Continuum* 29: 207–215.

Rippeyoug, Phyllis L. F., and Mary C. Noonan. 2012. "Is Breastfeeding Truly Cost Free? Income Consequences of Breastfeeding for Women." *American Sociological Review* 77: 244–267.

Ritzer, George. 1995. *Expressing America: A Critique of the Global Credit Card Society.* Thousand Oaks, CA: Pine Forge Press.

Ritzer, George. 2001. *Explorations in the Sociology of Consumption: Fast Food, Credit Cards, and Casinos.* London: Sage.

Ritzer, George, ed. 2007. *The Blackwell Encyclopedia of Sociology.* Malden, MA: Blackwell.

Ritzer, George. 2010a. "Cathedrals of Consumption: Rationalization, Enchantment, and Disenchantment." In *McDonaldization: The Reader,* 3rd ed., edited by George Ritzer, 234–239. Thousands Oaks, CA: Pine Forge Press.

Ritzer, George. 2010b. *Enchanting a Disenchanted World: Continuity and Change in the Cathedrals of Consumption.* Thousand Oaks, CA: Sage.

Ritzer, George, ed. 2010c. *The McDonaldization of Society: The Reader.* 3rd ed. Thousand Oaks, CA: Pine Forge Press.

Ritzer, George. 2012a. "'Hyperconsumption' and 'Hyperdebt': A 'Hypercritical' Analysis." In *A Debtor World: Interdisciplinary Perspective on Debt,* edited by Ralph Brubaker, Robert W. Lawless, and Charles J. Tabb, 60–80. New York: Oxford University Press.

Ritzer, George, ed. 2012b. *The Wiley-Blackwell Encyclopedia of Globalization.* Malden, MA: Wiley-Blackwell.

Ritzer, George. 2013. "The 'New' Prosumer: Collaboration on the Digital and Material 'New Means of Prosumption.'" Paper presented at the annual meeting of the Eastern Sociological Society, Boston, March.

Ritzer, George. 2015a. *The McDonaldization of Society.* 8th ed. Thousand Oaks, CA: Sage.

Ritzer, George. 2015b. "Prosumer Capitalism." *Sociological Quarterly* 56: 413–445.

Ritzer, George. 2016. "Deglobalization? Not a Chance." November 24. Accessed March 13, 2017. https://georgeritzer.wordpress.com/2016/11/24/deglobalization-not-a-chance.

Ritzer, George. 2017. "Woefully Little 'Sharing' in the Neo-Liberal Sharing Economy." January 10. https://georgeritzer.wordpress.com/2017/01/19/woefully-little-sharing-in-the-neo-liberal-ride-hailing-industry.

Ritzer, George. Forthcoming. *The McDonaldization of Society.* 9th ed. Thousand Oaks, CA: Sage.

Ritzer, George, and Paul Dean. 2015. *Globalization: A Basic Text.* 2nd ed. Malden, MA: Wiley-Blackwell.

Ritzer, George, Paul Dean, and Nathan Jurgenson. 2012. "The Coming of Age of the Prosumer." *American Behavioral Scientist* 56(4): 379–398.

Ritzer, George, Douglas Goodman, and Wendy Wiedenhoft. 2001. "Theories of Consumption." In *Handbook of Social Theory,* edited by George Ritzer and B. Smart, 410–427. London: Sage.

Ritzer, George and Nathan Jurgenson. 2010. "Production, Consumption, Prosumption: The Nature of Capitalism in the Age of the Digital 'Prosumer.'" *Journal of Consumer Culture* 10(1): 13–36.

Ritzer, George, and Jeffrey Stepnisky, eds. 2017. *Sociological Theory.* 10th ed. Thousand Oaks, CA: Sage.

Roberts, Sam. 2009. "In 2025, India to Pass China in Population, U.S. Estimates." *New York Times,* December 16.

Robertson, Craig. 2010. *The Passport in America: The History of a Document.* New York: Oxford University Press.

Rochon, T. R. 1990. "The West European Peace Movements and the Theory of Social Movements." In *Challenging the Political Order,* edited by R. Dalton and M. Kuchler. Cambridge: Polity Press.

Roda, Allison, and Amy Stuart Wells. 2013. "School Choice Policies and Racial Segregation: Where White Parents' Good Intentions, Anxiety, and Privilege Collide." *American Journal of Education* 119: 261–293.

Rodriguez-Franco, Diana. 2016. "Internal Wars, Taxation, and State Building." *American Sociological Review* 81(1): 190–213.

Roehling, Patricia, Loma Hernandez Jarvis, and Heather Swope. 2005. "Variations in Negative Work–Family Spillover among White, Black, and Hispanic American Men and Women." *Journal of Family Issues* 26(6): 840–865.

Rogin, Josh. 2016. "Congress Wary of National Security Implications of Chinese Deal for Chicago Stock Exchange," *Chicago Tribune,* February 17. Accessed March 8, 2017. http://www.chicagotribune.com/business/ct-congress-chicago-stock-exchange-sale-20160217-story.html.

Rojas, Rene, and Jeff Goodwin. 2013. "Revolutions." In *The Wiley-Blackwell Encyclopedia of Social and Political Movements,* 3 vols., edited by D. A. Snow, D. Della Porta, B. Klandermans, and D. McAdam, 1102–1110. Malden, MA: Wiley-Blackwell.

Rojek, Chris. 2005. *Leisure Theory: Principles and Practice.* New York: Palgrave Macmillan.

Rojek, Chris. 2007. *The Labour of Leisure: The Culture of Free Time.* London: Sage.

Roof, Wade Clark. 2001. *Spiritual Marketplace: Baby Boomers and the Remaking of American Religion.* Princeton, NJ: Princeton University Press.

Roscoe, Will. 1998. *Changing Ones: Third and Fourth Genders in Native North America.* New York: Palgrave/St. Martin's Press.

Rose, Arnold. 1967. *The Power Structure.* New York: Oxford University Press.

Rose, Claire. 2010. *Making, Selling, and Wearing Boys' Clothes in Late-Victorian England.* Burlington, VT: Ashgate.

Rosenbaum, James. 2001. *Beyond College for all: Career Paths for the Forgotten Half.* New York: Russell Sage Foundation.

Rosenbaum, James. 2011. "The Complexities of College for All: Beyond Fairy-Tale Dreams." *Sociology of Education* 84: 113–117.

Rosenberg, Matthew. 2016. "Pentagon Removes Barrier for Transgender People." *New York Times,* July 1.

Rosenfeld, Jake. 2014. *What Unions No Longer Do.* Cambridge: Harvard University Press.

Rosenstein, Judith E. 2008. "Individual Threat, Group Threat, and Racial Policy: Exploring the Relationship between Threat and Racial Attitudes." *Social Science Research* 37: 1130–1146.

Rosenthal, Elisabeth. 2007. "W.H.O. Urges Effort to Fight Fast-Spreading Disease." *New York Times,* August 27.

Rosenthal, Lisa, and Marci Lobel, 2016. "Stereotypes of Black American Women Related to Sexuality and Motherhood," *Psychology of Women Quarterly* 40: 414–427.

Rosewarne, Laruen. 2016. *Intimacy on the Internet.* New York: Routledge

Rostow, Walt. 1960. *The Stages of Economic Growth: A Non-Communist Manifesto.* Cambridge: Cambridge University Press.

Rostow, Walt. 1978. *The World Economy: History and Prospect.* Austin: University of Texas Press.

Roszak, Theodore. [1968] 1995. *The Making of a Counter Culture: Reflections on the Technocratic Society and Its Youthful Opposition.* Berkeley: University of California Press.

Roth, Benita. 2004. *Separate Roads to Feminism: Black, Chicana and White Feminist Movements in America's Second Wave.* Cambridge: Cambridge University Press.

Rousseau, Nicole. 2011. *Black Women's Burden: Commodifying Black Reproduction.* New York: Palgrave Macmillan.

Roxburgh, S. 2004. "There Just Aren't Enough Hours in the Day: The Mental Health Consequences of Time Pressures." *Journal of Health and Social Behavior* 45: 115–131.

Rubington, Earl, and Martin Weinberg, eds. 2016. *Deviance: The Interactionist Approach.* 10th ed. New York: Routledge.

Rueschemeyer, Dietrich, Evelyne Stephens, and John Stephens. 1992. *Capitalist Development and Democracy.* Chicago: University of Chicago Press.

Rupp, Leila, and Verta Taylor. 1999. "Forging Feminist Identity in an International Movement: A Collective Identity Approach to Twentieth-Century Feminism." *Signs* 24(2): 363–386.

Rutherford, Paul. 2007. *The World Made Sexy: Freud to Madonna.* Toronto: University of Toronto Press.

Rutledge, Leigh W. 1992. *The Gay Decades: From Stonewall to the Present.* New York: Plume.

Ryan, Michelle K., and S. Alexander Haslam. 2005. "The Glass Cliff: Evidence That Women Are Over-represented in Precarious Leadership Positions." *British Journal of Management* 16: 81–90.

Ryan, William. 1976. *Blaming the Victim.* New York: Pantheon.

Ryave, A. Lincoln, and James N. Schenkein. 1974. "Notes on the Art of Walking." In *Ethnomethodology: Selected Readings,* edited by R. Turner, 265–275. Harmondsworth, UK: Penguin.

Rysst, Mari. 2008. *"I Want to Be Me. I Want to Be Kul": An Anthropological Study of Norwegian Preteen Girls in the Light of a Presumed "Disappearance" of Childhood.* PhD dissertation, University of Oslo.

Sabo, Don. 1998. "Masculinities and Men's Health: Moving Towards Post-Superman Era Prevention." In *Men's Lives,* edited by M. Kimmel and M. Messner. Needham Heights, MA: Allyn & Bacon.

Sadker, Myra, and David Sadker. 1994. *Failing at Fairness: How Our Schools Cheat Girls.* New York: Simon & Schuster.

Saez, Emmanuel, and Gabriel Zucman. 2014. "The Explosion in U.S. Wealth Inequality Has Been Fuelled by Stagnant Wages, Increasing Debt, and a Collapse in Asset Values for the Middle Classes." London School of Economics and Political Science. Accessed April 20, 2015. http://bit.ly/1pXQ30r.

Sahlberg, Pasi. 2011. *Finnish Lessons: What Can the World Learn from Educational Change in Finland?* New York: Teachers College Press.

Said, Edward W. [1979] 1994. *Orientalism.* New York: Knopf.

Salinas, Rebecca. 2014. "Corpus Christi 'Mantique' Store Equips the Man Cave." *San Antonio Express-News, My San Antonio* blog, July 28. Accessed April 21, 2015. http://www.mysanantonio.com/news/local/article/Corpus-Christi-man-opens-mantique-store-5651705.php.

Salkind, Neil. 2004. *Statistics for People Who (Think They) Hate Statistics.* Thousand Oaks, CA: Sage.

Sander, Ake, and Clemen Cavallin. 2015. "Hinduism Meets the Global Order: The 'Easternization of the West'" In *The Changing World Religion Map,* edited by Stanley D. Brunn, 1743–1763. New York: Springer.

Sanders, George. 2014. "Religious Non-places: Corporate Megachurches and Their Contributions to Consumer Capitalism." *Critical Sociology,* July 7 (published online). doi: 10.1177/0896920514531605.

Sanders, Teela. 2013. *Sex Work.* London: Routledge.

Sanford, Victoria, Katerina Stefanos and Cecilia Salvi (Eds). 2016. *Gender Violence in Peace and War: States of Complicity.* New Brunswick: Rutgers University Press.

Sanger, David E., and Nicole Perlroth. 2016. "As Democrats Gather, a Russian Sub-plot Raises Intrigue." *New York Times,* July 24.

Sanger, David, and Scott Shane. 2016. "Russian Hackers Acted to Aid Trump in Election, U.S. Says." *New York Times,* December 9.

Sanger-Katz, Margot. 2016."Obamacare Seems to be Reducing Peoples' Medical Debt." *New York Times,* April 20.

Sanneh, Kelefa. 2015. "Don't Be Like That: Does Black Culture Need to Be Reformed?" *New Yorker,* February 9, 62–69.

Santoro, Wayne A. 2015. "Was the Civil Rights Movement Successful? Tracking and Understanding Black Views." *Sociological Forum* 30: 627–647.

Santos, Fernanda, and Motoko Rich. 2013. "With Vouchers, States Shift Aid for Schools to Families." *New York Times,* March 27.

Santos, Xuan. 2009. "The Chicana Canvas: Doing Class, Gender, Race, and Sexuality through Tattooing in East Los Angeles." *NWSA Journal* 21: 91–120.

Sarwal, Amit. 2012. "A Journey through Places: Politics of Spatial Location in the Stories of South Asian Diaspora in Australia." *South Asian Diaspora* 4: 195–213.

Sassatelli, Roberta. 2007. *Consumer Culture: History, Theory and Politics.* London: Sage.

Sassen, Saskia. 1991. *The Global City: New York, London, Tokyo.* Princeton, NJ: Princeton University Press.

Sassen, Saskia. 2012. "Cities." In *The Wiley-Blackwell Encyclopedia of Globalization,* edited by George Ritzer, 187–202. Malden, MA: Wiley-Blackwell.

Sassler, Sharon, and Amanda J. Miller. 2011. "Class Differences in Cohabitation Processes." *Family Relations* 60: 163–177.

Saussure, Ferdinand de. [1916] 1966. *Course in General Linguistics.* New York: McGraw-Hill.

Sauter, Mike, Thomas C. Frohlich, and Alexander E. M. Hess. 2013. "Fast-Food Chains Costing Taxpayers the Most Money." *Yahoo! Finance,* October 23. Accessed April 21, 2015. http://finance.yahoo.com/news/fast-food-chains-costing-taxpayers-173510741.html.

Savage, Charlie, and Cheryl Gay Stolberg. 2011. "In Shift, U.S. Says Marriage Act Blocks Gay Rights." *New York Times,* February 23. Accessed December 20, 2011. http://www.nytimes.com/2011/02/24/us/24marriage.html.

Sayyid, Salman. 2012. "Political Islam." In *The Wiley-Blackwell Encyclopedia of Globalization,* edited by George Ritzer, 1202–1204. Malden, MA: Wiley-Blackwell.

Scaff, Lawrence A. 2011. "Georg Simmel." In *The Wiley-Blackwell Companion to Major Social Theorists,* Vol. 1, *Classical Theorists,* edited by George Ritzer and Jeffrey Stepnisky, 205–235. Malden, MA: Wiley-Blackwell.

Scambler, Graham, and Frederique Paoli. 2008. "Health Work, Female Sex Workers and HIV/AIDS: Global and Local Dimensions of Stigma and Deviance as Barriers to Effective Interventions." *Social Science & Medicine* 66: 1848–1862.

Scelfo, Julie. 2015. "A University Recognizes a Third Gender: Neutral." *New York Times,* February 3.

Scheffer, David. 2008. "Rape as Genocide in Darfur." *Los Angeles Times,* November 13.

Scheper-Hughes, Nancy. 2001. "Commodity Fetishism in Organs Trafficking." *Body and Society* 7: 31–62.

Schilt, Kristen. 2010. *Just One of the Guys? Transgender Men and the Persistence of Inequality.* Chicago: University of Chicago Press.

Schlossberg, Tatiana. 2016. "Storms in Succession." *New York Times—Science Times,* September 13.

Schlueter, Elmar, and Peer Scheepers. 2010. "The Relationship between Outgroup Size and Anti-outgroup Attitudes: A Theoretical Synthesis and Empirical Test of Group Threat and Intergroup Contact Theory." *Social Science Research* 39(2): 285–295.

Schmidt, John, Kris Warner, and Sarika Gupta. 2010. *The High Budgetary Cost of Incarceration.* Washington, DC: Center for Economic and Policy Research.

Schmidt, Susanne, Ulrike Roesler, Talin Kusserow, and Renate Rau. 2014. "Uncertainty in the Workplace: Examining Role Ambiguity and Role Conflict, and Their Link to Depression—A Meta-analysis." *European Journal of Work and Organizational Psychology* 23(1): 91–106.

Schneider, Barbara, and David Stevenson. 1999. *The Ambitious Generation: America's Teenagers, Motivated but Directionless.* New Haven, CT: Yale University Press.

Schneider, Silke L. 2008. "Anti-immigrant Attitudes in Europe: Outgroup Size and Perceived Ethnic Threat." *European Sociological Review* 24(1): 53–67.

Scholz, Trebor, ed. 2013. *Digital Labor: The Internet as Playground and Factory.* New York: Routledge.

Schor, Juliet. 1993. *The Overworked American: The Unexpected Decline of Leisure.* New York: Basic Books.

Schor, Juliet. 1998. *The Overspent American: Why We Want What We Don't Need.* New York: Basic Books.

Schor, Juliet. 2005. *Born to Buy: The Commercialized Child and the New Consumer Culture.* New York: Scribner.

Schorzman, Cindy M., Melanie A. Gold, Julie S. Downs, and Pamela J. Murray. 2007. "Body Art: Attitudes and Practices regarding Body Piercing among Urban Undergraduates." *Journal of the American Osteopathic Association* 107: 432–438.

Schroeder, Jonathan E. 2015. "Brands and Branding." In Daniel Thomas Cook and J. Michael Ryan, eds. *The Wiley-Blackwell Encyclopedia of Consumption and Consumer Studies.* Malden, MA: Wiley-Blackwell: 59–63.

Schuman, Michael. 2016. "Is China Stealing Jobs? It May be Losing Them, Instead." *New York Times,* July 22.

Schuster, Liza. 2012. "Asylum-Seekers." In *The Wiley-Blackwell Encyclopedia of Globalization,* edited by George Ritzer, 89–92. Malden, MA: Wiley-Blackwell.

Schutt, Russell K. 2007. "Secondary Data Analysis." In *The Blackwell Encyclopedia of Sociology,* edited by George Ritzer, 4127–4129. Malden. MA: Blackwell.

Schwalbe, Michael, Sandra Godwin, Daphne Holden, Douglas Schrock, Shealy Thompson, and Michele Wolkomir. 2000. "Generic Processes in the Reproduction of Inequality: An Interactionist Analysis." *Social Forces* 79: 419–452.

Schwartz, Nelson D. 2016. "Good Jobs, Goodbye." *New York Times—Sunday Business,* March 20.

Schwartz, Nelson. 2017. "Middle Class Contracted in U.S. over 2 Decades, Study Finds." *New York Times* April 25.

Schwartzman, Kathleen C. 2013. *The Chicken Trail: Following Workers, Migrants and Corporations across the Americas.* Ithaca: Cornell University Press.

Schweinhart, Lawrence J. W., Steven Barnett, and Clive R. Belfield. 2005. *Lifetime Effects: The High/Scope Perry Preschool Study through Age 40.* Ypsilanti, MI: High/Scope Press.

Scott, Amy. 2011. "Pumping Up the Pomp: An Exploration of Femininity and Female Bodybuilding." *Explorations in Anthropology* 11: 70–88.

Scott, Barbara Marliene, and Mary Ann A. Schwartz. 2008. *Sociology: Making Sense of the Social World.* New York: Allyn & Bacon.

Scott, John, and Ann Nilsen, eds. 2013. *C. Wright Mills and the Sociological Imagination: Contemporary Perspectives.* Cheltenham: Edward Elgar.

Scott, W. Richard. 2014. *Institutions and Organizations: Ideas and Interests.* 4th ed. Thousand Oaks, CA: Sage.

Searcey, Dionne, and Robert Gebeloff. 2015. "Middle Class Shrinks Further as More Fall Out Instead of Climbing Up." *New York Times,* January 25.

Seidman, Steven. 2003. *The Social Construction of Sexuality.* New York: Norton.

Sekulic, Dusko. 2016. "Ethnic Cleansing and Ethnic Swamping." In *The Wiley-Blackwell Encyclopedia of Race, Ethnicity and Nationalism,* edited by John Stone, Rutledge M. Dennis, Polly Rizova, Anthony D. Smith, and Xiaoshuo Hou. Malden, MA: Wiley-Blackwell.

Seligmann, Linda J. 2013. *Broken Links, Enduring Ties: American Adoption Across Race, Class and Nation.* Stanford, CA: Stanford University Press.

Semple, Kirk. 2016. "Defending Their Nation's Honor on Social Media: #PanamaIsMoreThanPapers." *New York Times,* May 4.

Semple, Kirk, Azam Ahmed, and Eric Lipton. 2016. "Panama Papers Leak Casts Light on a Law Firm Founded on Secrecy." *New York Times,* April 6.

Serra-Majem, Luis and Joy Ngo. 2012. "Undernutrition." In *The Wiley-Blackwell Encyclopedia of Globalization,* edited by George Ritzer, 2055–2058. Malden, MA: Wiley-Blackwell.

Settle, Jaime E., Christopher T. Dawes, Nicholas A. Christakis, and James H. Fowler. 2010. "Friendships Moderate an Association between a Dopamine Gene Variant and Political Ideology." *Journal of Politics* 72: 1189–1198.

Shane, Scott, and Ben Hubbard. 2014. "ISIS Displaying a Deft Command of Varied Media." *New York Times,* August 30.

Sharp, Gwen. 2012. "Gender in the Hidden Curriculum (Update)." *Society Pages,* November 16. Accessed

April 11, 2013. http://www.thesoci-etypages.org/socimages/2012/11/16/gender-in-the-hidden-curriculum.

Shattuck, Roger. 1980. *The Forbidden Experiment: The Story of the Wild Boy.* New York: Kodansha Globe.

Shaw, Susan M., and Janet Lee. 2009. *Women's Voices, Feminist Visions.* New York: McGraw-Hill.

Sheldon, Jane P. 2004. "Gender Stereotypes in Educational Software for Young Children." *Sex Roles* 51(7/8): 433–444.

Shelley, Louise, John Picarelli, and Chris Corpora. 2011. "Global Crime Inc." In *Beyond Sovereignty: Issues for a Global Agenda,* 4th ed., edited by M. C. Love, 141–169. Boston: Wadsworth, Cengage Learning.

Shepherd, Dawn. 2016. *Building Relationships.* Lanham MD,: Lexington Books.

Sherif, Muzafer, O. J. Harvey, William R. Hood, Carolyn W. Sherif, and Jack White. [1954] 1961. *Intergroup Conflict and Cooperation: The Robbers Cave Experiment.* Norman: University of Oklahoma Book Exchange.

Shevchenko, Olga. 2012. "Socialism." In *The Wiley-Blackwell Encyclopedia of Globalization,* edited by George Ritzer, 1882–1886. Malden, MA: Wiley-Blackwell.

Shildrick, Tracy, and Robert MacDonald. 2013. "Poverty Talk: How People Experiencing Poverty Deny Their Poverty and Why They Blame the Poor." *Sociological Review* 61: 285–303.

Shinberg, Diane S. 2007. "Women's Health." In *The Blackwell Encyclopedia of Sociology,* edited by George Ritzer, 5275–5279. Malden, MA: Blackwell.

Shroedel, Jean Reith, and Pamela Fiber. 2000. "Lesbian and Gay Policy Priorities: Commonality and Difference." In *The Politics of Gay Rights,* edited by C. A. Rimmerman, K. D. Wald, and C. Wilcox, 97–118. Chicago: University of Chicago Press.

Shullenberger, Geoff. 2014. "The Rise of the Voluntariat." *Jacobin,* May 15. Accessed April 23, 2015. https://www.jacobinmag.com/2014/05/the-rise-of-the-voluntariat.

Siegel, Larry J., and John L. Worrall. 2014. *Essentials of Criminal Justice.* 9th ed. Stamford, CT: Cengage.

Silva, Jennifer. 2015. *Coming Up Short: Working Class Adulthood in an Age of Uncertainty.* Oxford: Oxford University Press.

Silver, Hilary. 2007. "Disasters." In *The Blackwell Encyclopedia of Sociology,* edited by George Ritzer, 1174–1176. Malden, MA: Blackwell.

Silver, Hilary. 2015. "Editorial: The Urban Sociology of Detroit." *City and Community* 14: 97–101.

Silverman, David, ed. 2016. *Qualitative Research.* 4th ed. London: Sage.

Silvernail, David L., and Amy F. Johnson. 2014. "The Impacts of Public Charter Schools on Students and Traditional Public Schools: What Does the Empirical Evidence Tell Us?" Maine Education Policy Research Institute, University of Southern Maine, January. Accessed April 17, 2015. https://usm.maine.edu/sites/default/files/cepare/PublicCharterSchoolsWeb.pdf.

Simmel, Georg. [1904] 1971. "Fashion." In *Georg Simmel: On Individuality and Social Forms,* edited by D. Levine, 294–323. Chicago: University of Chicago Press.

Simmel, Georg. [1908] 1971. "Domination." In *Georg Simmel: On Individuality and Social Forms,* edited by D. Levine, 96–120. Chicago: University of Chicago Press.

Simmel, Georg. 1950. *The Sociology of Georg Simmel,* edited and translated by K. Wolff. New York: Free Press.

Simon, Bryant. 2009. *Everything but the Coffee: Learning about America from Starbucks.* Berkeley: University of California Press.

Simon, David R. 2012. *Elite Deviance.* 10th ed. Boston: Pearson/Allyn & Bacon.

Simon, Herbert A. [1945] 1976. *Administrative Behavior.* New York: Macmillan.

Simone, Alina. 2015. "How My Mom Got Hacked." *New York Times,* January 2. Accessed April 27, 2015. http://www.nytimes.com/2015/01/04/opinion/sunday/how-my-mom-got-hacked.html?_r=0.

Simooya, Oscar O. 2016. "Editorial: HIV Infection and AIDS in Africa: Issues, Lessons Learnt, and Next Steps." *Open AIDS Journal* 10: 14–15.

Simpson, George Eaton, and J. Milton Yinger. 1985. *Racial and Cultural Minorities: An Analysis of Prejudice and Discrimination.* 5th ed. New York: Plenum Press.

Simpson, Sally S. 2013. "White-Collar Crime: A Review of Recent Developments and Promising Directions for Future Research." *Annual Review of Sociology* 39: 309–331.

Simpson, Sally S., and David Weisburd, eds. 2009. *The Criminology of White-Collar Crime.* New York: Springer.

Singer, Natasha. 2009. "Lawmakers Seek to Curb Drug Commercials." *New York Times,* July 27.

Singer, Natasha. 2010. "The Financial Time Bomb of Longer Lives." *New York Times,* October 16.

Singh, Devendra, and Dorian Singh. 2011. "Shape and Significance of Feminine Beauty: An Evolutionary Perspective." *Sex Roles* 64: 723–731.

Singh, Gopal K., and Mohammad Siahpush. 2014. "Widening Rural–Urban Disparities in Life Expectancy, U.S., 1969–2009." *American Journal of Preventive Medicine* 46: e19–e29.

Sklair, Leslie. 2002. *Globalization: Capitalism and Its Alternatives.* Oxford: Oxford University Press.

Skocpol, Theda, and Vanessa Williamson. 2016. *The Tea Party and the Remaking of Republican Conservatism.* Updated Edition. Oxford: Oxford University Press.

Skoog, Therese, Emma Sobring, and Margareta Bohlin. 2015. "Facebook as a Means to Make New Peers among Early Maturing Girls." *Computers in Human Behavior* 48: 500–505.

Slater, Don. 2015. "Consumer Culture." In *Encyclopedia of Consumption and Consumer Studies,* edited by Daniel Thomas Cook and Michael Ryan, 112–118. Malden, MA: Wiley-Blackwell.

Slatton, Brittany Chevon, and Joe R. Feagin. 2012. "Racial and Ethnic Issues: Critical Race Approaches in the United States." In *The Wiley-Blackwell Companion to Sociology,* edited by George Ritzer, 287–303. Malden, MA: Wiley-Blackwell.

Smangs, Mattias. 2016. "Doing Violence, Making Race: Southern Lynching and White Racial Group Formation." *American Journal of Sociology* 121: 1329–1374.

Smart, Barry, ed. 2011. *Post-industrial Society.* London: Sage.

Smelser, Neil. 1994. *Sociology.* Cambridge, MA: Blackwell.

Smith, Aaron. 2016. "15% of American Adults Have Used Online Dating Site or Mobile Dating Apps." Pew Research Center, February 11. Accessed February 2, 2016. http://www.pewinternet.org/2016/02/11/15-percent-of-american-adults-have-used-online-dating-sites-or-mobile-dating-apps.

Smith, David Norman, Brock Ternes, James P. Ordner, Russell Schloemer, Gabriela Moran, Chris Goode, Joshua Homan, Anna Kern, Lucas Keefer, Nathan Moser, Kevin McCannon, Kaela Byers, Daniel Sullivan, and Rachel Craft. 2011. "Mapping the Great Recession: A Reader's Guide to the First Crisis of 21st Century Capitalism." *New Political Science* 33(4): 577–601.

Smith, Gavin. 2015. *Opening the Black Box: The Work of Watching.* London: Routledge.

Smith, Jessi L., and Meghan Huntoon. 2014. "Women's Bragging Rights: Overcoming Modesty Norms to Facilitate Women's Self-Promotion." *Psychology of Women Quarterly* 38: 447–459.

Smith, Paula. 2007. "Recidivism." In *The Blackwell Encyclopedia of Sociology,* edited by George Ritzer, 3818–3819. Malden, MA: Blackwell.

Smith, William C., Emily Anderson, Daniel Salinas, Renata Horvatek, and David P. Baker. 2015. "A Meta-analysis of Education Effects on Chronic Disease: The Causal Dynamics of the Population Education Transition Curve." *Social Science & Medicine* 127: 29–40.

Smock, Pamela L., and Wendy Manning. 2004. "Living Together Unmarried in the United States: Demographic Perspectives and Implications for Family Policy." *Law and Policy* 26(1): 87–117.

Smyth, Bruce. 2007. "Non-resident Parents." In *The Blackwell Encyclopedia of Sociology*, edited by George Ritzer, 3223–3227. Malden, MA: Blackwell.

Snow, David A. 2013. "Grievances, Individual and Mobilizing." In *The Wiley-Blackwell Encyclopedia of Social and Political Movements*, 3 vols., edited by D. A. Snow, D. Della Porta, B. Klandermans, and D. McAdam, 540–542. Malden, MA: Wiley-Blackwell.

Snow, David A., D. Della Porta, B. Klandermans, and D. McAdam, eds. 2013. *The Wiley-Blackwell Encyclopedia of Social and Political Movements*. 3 vols. Malden, MA: Wiley-Blackwell.

Snow, David A., Sarah A. Soule, and Daniel M. Cress. 2005. "Identifying the Precipitants of Homeless Protest across 17 U.S. Cities, 1980 to 1990." *Social Forces* 83: 1183–1210.

Snyder, Patricia. 2007. "Survey Research." In *The Blackwell Encyclopedia of Sociology*, edited by George Ritzer, 4898–4900. Malden, MA: Blackwell.

Sollee, Kristen. 2015. "6 Things to Know About 4th Wave Feminism." *Bustle*, October 30. Accessed March 9, 2017. https://www.bustle.com/articles/119524-6-things-to-know-about-4th-wave-feminism.

Song, Haeyeop and Jaemin Jung. 2015. "Antecedent and Consequences of Gender Swapping in Online Games." *Journal of Computer-Mediated Communication* 20: 434–449.

Song, Miri. 2007. "Racial Hierarchy." In *The Blackwell Encyclopedia of Sociology*, edited by George Ritzer, 3360–3364. Malden, MA: Blackwell.

Sontag, Deborah. 2012. "Rebuilding in Haiti Lags after Billions in Post-quake Aid." *New York Times*, December 23.

Sontag, Deborah. 2015. "'Every Day I Struggle': Transgender Inmate Cites Attacks and Abuse in Men's Prison." *New York Times*, April 6.

Soysal, Yasemin Nuhoglu. 2012. "Citizenship, Immigration, and the European Social Project: Rights and Obligations of Individuality." *British Journal of Sociology* 63: 1–21.

Spade, Joan Z., and Catherine G. Valentine. 2011. *The Kaleidoscope of Gender: Prisms, Patterns, and Possibilities.* Thousand Oaks, CA: Pine Forge Press.

Sparman, Anna. 2015. "Children' Consumer Culture." In *Encyclopedia of Consumption and Consumer Studies,* edited by Daniel Thomas Cook and Michael Ryan, 75–77. Malden, MA: Wiley-Blackwell, 2015.

Spencer, Herbert. 1851. *Social Statics.* London: Chapman.

Standing, Guy. 1989. "Global Feminization through Flexible Labor: A Theme Revisited." *World Development* 27(3): 583–602.

Staples, Brent. 1986. "Black Men and Public Space." *Harper's Magazine,* December, 19.

Stark, Rodney, and William Sims Bainbridge. 1979. "Of Churches, Sects, and Cults: Preliminary Concepts for a Theory of Religious Movements." *Journal for the Scientific Study of Religion* 18(2): 117–131.

Stearns, Cindy A. 2009. "The Work of Breastfeeding." *Women's Studies Quarterly* 37: 63–80.

Stein, Joel. 2015. "Baby, You Can Drive My Car, and Do My Errands, and Rent My Stuff . . ." *Time,* February 9, 34–40.

Steinmetz, George. 2012. "Geopolitics." In *The Wiley-Blackwell Encyclopedia of Globalization,* edited by George Ritzer, 800–823. Malden, MA: Wiley-Blackwell.

Steinmetz, Katy. 2014. "The Transgender Tipping Point." *Time,* May 29. Accessed April 21, 2015. http://time.com/135480/transgender-tipping-point.

Steinmetz, Suzanne K. 1987. "Family Violence." In *Handbook of Marriage and the Family,* edited by M. B. Sussman and S. K. Steinmetz. New York: Plenum Press.

Stepan-Norris, Judith, and Caleb Southworth. 2007. "Churches as Organizational Resources: A Case Study in the Geography of Religion and Political Voting in Postwar Detroit." *Social Science History* 31(3): 343–380.

Stepfamily Foundation. n.d. "Stepfamily Statistics." www.stepfamily.org/stepfamily-statistics. html.

Sterling, Toby. 2016. "U.S. Blocks Philips' $3.3 Billion Sale of Lumileds to Asian Buyers," *Reuters,* January 22. Accessed March 8, 2017. http://www.reuters.com/article/us-philips-lumileds-sale-idUSKCN0V02D4.

Stevens, Mitchell L. 2001. *Kingdom of Children: Culture and Controversy in the Home Schooling Movement.* Princeton, NJ: Princeton University Press.

Stevens, Mitchell L. 2007. "Schooling, Home." In *The Blackwell Encyclopedia of Sociology,* edited by George Ritzer, 4032–4034. Malden, MA: Blackwell.

Stevenson, Howard. 2016. "Challenging School Reform from Below: Is Leadership the Missing Link in Mobilization Theory?" *Leadership and Policy in Schools* 15: 67–90.

Stewart, Heather. 2013. "Eurozone Bailouts: Which Countries Remain?" *The Guardian,* December 13.

Stewart, Katherine. 2016. "Betsy DeVos and God's Plan for Schools." *New York Times,* December 13.

St. Fleur, Nicholas. 2015. "Deforestation May Threaten Majority of Amazon Tree Species, Study Finds." *New York Times,* November 20.

Stillerman, Joel. 2015. *The Sociology of Consumption: A Global Approach.* London: Polity.

Stockdill, Brett C. 2013. "ACT UP (AIDS Coalition to Unleash Power)." In *The Wiley-Blackwell Encyclopedia of Social and Political Movements,* 3 vols., edited by D. A. Snow, D. Della Porta, B. Klandermans, and D. McAdam, 5–9. Malden, MA: Wiley-Blackwell.

Stockemer, Daniel, and Rodrigo Praino, 2015. "Blinded by Beauty? Physical Attractiveness and Candidate Selection in the U.S. House of Representatives." *Social Science Quarterly* 96: 430–443.

Stokoe, Elizabeth. 2006. "On Ethnomethodology, Feminism, and the Analysis of Categorical Reference to Gender in Talk-in-Interaction." *Sociological Review* 54(3): 467–494.

Stolow, Jeremy. 2004. "Transnationalism and the New Religio-politics: Reflections on a Jewish Orthodox Case." *Theory, Culture and Society* 21(2): 109–137.

Stone, Amy, and Jill Weinberg. 2015. "Sexualities and Social Movements: Three Decades of Sex and Social Change." In *Handbook of the Sociology of Sexualities,* edited by J. DeLamater and R. F. Plante. Dordrecht, Netherlands: Springer.

Stoolmiller, Michael. 1999. "Implications of the Restricted Range of Family Environments for Estimates of Heritability and Nonshared Environments in Behavior-Genetic Adoption Studies." *Psychological Bulletin* 125: 392–409.

Story, Louise, and Stephanie Saul. 2015. "Stream of Foreign Wealth Flows to Elite New York Real Estate." *New York Times,* February 7.

Stouffer, S. A., E. A. Suchman, L. C. DeVinney, S. A. Star, and R. M. Williams. 1949. *The American Soldier: Adjustment during Army Life.* Vol. 1. Princeton, NJ: Princeton University Press.

Stratton, Greg, and Jeremy Northcote. 2014. "When Totems Beget Clans: The Brand

Symbol as the Defining Marker of Brand Communities." *Journal of Consumer Culture,* April 4 (published online). doi: 10.1177/1469540514528194.

Straus, Murray A. 1980. "Victims and Aggressors in Marital Violence." *American Behavioral Scientist* 23: 681–704.

Streitfeld, David. 2014. "Airbnb Listings Mostly Illegal, State Contends." *New York Times,* October 16.

Struck, Doug. 2007. "Warming Will Exacerbate Global Water Conflicts." *Washington Post,* October 22.

Stryker, Sheldon. 1959. "Symbolic Interaction as an Approach to Family Research." *Marriage and Family Living* 21(2): 111–119.

Subramaniam, Mangala, David Whitlock, and Beth Williford. 2012. "Water Crisis." In *The Wiley-Blackwell Encyclopedia of Globalization,* edited by George Ritzer, 2210–2212. Malden, MA: Wiley-Blackwell.

Sullivan, Gail. 2014. "United Kingdom's First 'Poo Bus' Runs on Human Waste." *Washington Post,* November 21. Accessed April 21, 2015. http://www.washingtonpost.com/news/morning-mix/wp/2014/11/21/united-king doms-first-poo-bus-runs-on-human-waste.

Sumner, William Graham. [1906] 1940. Folkways: A Study of the Sociological Implications of Usages, Manners, Customs, Mores and Morals. Boston: Ginn.

Sundarajan, Arun. 2016. *The Sharing Economy: The End of Employment and the Rise of Crowd-Based Capitalism.* Cambridge, MA: MIT Press.

Surk, Barbara. 2015. "Slovenia Builds Border Fence to Stem Flow of Migrants." *New York Times,* November 11.

Surtees, Nicola. 2008. "Teachers Following Children? Heteronormative Responses within a Discourse of Child-Centredness and the Emergent Curriculum." *Australian Journal of Early Childhood* 33(3): 10–17.

Sutherland, Edwin H. 1924. *Criminology.* Chicago: University of Chicago Press.

Swami, Viren, Amy Henry, Nicola Peacock, Ahkin Roberts-Dunn, and Alan Porter. 2013. "'Mirror, Mirror . . . ': A Preliminary Investigation of Skin Tone Dissatisfaction and Its Impact among British Adults." *Cultural Diversity and Ethnic Minority Psychology* 19(4): 468–476.

Sykes, Gresham. [1958] 2007. *The Society of Captives: A Study of a Maximum Security Prison.* Princeton, NJ: Princeton University Press.

Sylvia Rivera Law Project. 2015. "Who Was Sylvia Rivera?" Accessed March 17, 2015. http://srlp.org/about/who-was-sylvia-rivera.

Tabuchi, Hiroko. 2010. "Beef Bowl Economics: In Japan, a Price War in Popular Restaurants Is the Face of Deflation." *New York Times,* January 30, B1, B6.

Tammelleo, Steve, and Louis Lombardi. 2014. "Consumer Social Responsibility?" *Business & Professional Ethics Journal* 33(1): 99–126.

Tan, Celine. 2007. "Liberalization." In *Encyclopedia of Globalization,* edited by J. A. Scholte and R. Robertson, 735–739. New York: MTM.

Tan, Yu, Ping Shaw, Hong Cheng and Kwangmi Ko Kim. 2013. "The Construction of Masculinity: A Cross-Cultural Analysis of Men's Lifestyle Magazine Advertisements." *Sex Roles* 69:237–249.

Taplin, Jonathan. 2016. "Do You Love Music? Silicon Valley Doesn't." *New York Times,* May 26.

Tarrow, Sidney. 1994. *Power in Movement.* Cambridge: Cambridge University Press.

Tatangelo, Gemma L., and Lina A. Ricciardelli. 2013. "A Qualitative Study of Preadolescent Boys' and Girls' Body Image: Gendered Ideals and Sociocultural Influences." *Body Image* 10: 591–598.

Taub, Amanda. 2016. "A Lesson from Brexit: On Immigration, Feelings Trump Facts." *New York Times,* June 26.

Tavernise, Sabrina. 2016. "Life Spans of the Rich Leave the Poor Behind." *New York Times,* February 13.

Tavernise, Sabrina, and Robert Gabeloff. 2016. "Immigrants and Minorities Gain Insurance." *New York Times,* April 18.

Tavernise, Sabrina, and Denise Grady, 2016. "An Infection Raises the Specter of Superbugs Resistant to All Antibiotics." *New York Times,* A12, A15.

Taylor, J. L. 2007. "Buddhism." In *Encyclopedia of Globalization,* edited by J. A. Scholte and R. Robertson, 108–113. New York: MTM.

Taylor, Laura E., and Patrick T. Hurley, eds. 2016. *Exurbia, Planning Environmental Management, and Landscape Change.* Springer.

Taylor, Paul C. 2011. "William Edward Burghardt Du Bois." In *The Wiley-Blackwell Companion to Major Social Theorists,* Vol. 1, *Classical Theorists,* edited by George Ritzer and Jeffrey Stepnisky, 426–447. Malden, MA: Wiley-Blackwell.

Taylor, Yvette. 2007. "Sexualities and Consumption." In *The Blackwell Encyclopedia of Sociology,* edited by George Ritzer, 4256–4260. Malden, MA: Blackwell.

Terranova, Tiziana. 2013. "Free Labor." In *Digital Labor: The Internet as Playground and Factory,* edited by T. Scholz, 33–57. New York: Routledge.

Terrill, Robert E. 2015. *Double-Consciousess and the Rhetoric of Barack Obama; The Price and Promise of Citizenship.* Columbia: University of South Carolina Press.

Tescione, Sara. 2013. "Civil Disobedience." In *The Wiley-Blackwell Encyclopedia of Social and Political Movements,* 3 vols., edited by D. A. Snow, D. Della Porta, B. Klandermans, and D. McAdam, 191–193. Malden, MA: Wiley-Blackwell.

Tetrault, Lisa. 2014. *The Myth of Seneca Falls: Memory and the Women's Suffrage Movement, 1848–1898.* Chapel Hill: University of North Carolina Press.

Thai, Hung Cam. 2014. *Insufficient Funds: The Culture of Money in Low-Wage Transnational Families.* Stanford, CA: Stanford University Press.

Thébaud, Sarah. 2016. "Passing Up the Job: The Role of Gendered Organizations and Families in the Entrepreneurial Career Process." *Entrepreneurship: Theory and Practice* 40(2): 269–287.

Thébaud, Sarah, and David S. Pedulla, 2016. "Masculinity and the Stalled Revolution: How Gender Ideologies and Norms Shape Young Men's Responses to Work-Family Policies." *Gender & Society* 30: 590–617.

Thoits, Peggy A. 1985. "Self-Labeling Processes in Mental Illness: The Role of Emotional Deviance." *American Journal of Sociology* 91(2): 221–249.

Thoits, Peggy A. 2011. "Perceived Social Support and the Voluntary, Mixed, or Pressured Use of Mental Health Services." *Society and Mental Health* 1: 4–19.

Thomas, Jeremy N., Lauren Crosby, and Jessica Milford, 2015. "Gender Differences among Self-Reported Genital Piercing Stories." *Deviant Behavior* 36: 441–462.

Thompson, Beverly Yuen. 2015. *Covered in Ink: Tattoos, Women, and the Politics of the Body.* New York: New York University Press.

Thorne, Barrie. 1993. *Gender Play: Girls and Boys in School.* New Brunswick, NJ: Rutgers University Press.

Thorpe, Holly, and Nida Ahmad, 2015. "Youth Action Sports and Political Agency in the Middle East: Lessons from a Grassroots Parkour Group in Gaza." *International Review for the Sociology of Sport* 50: 678–704.

Timasheff, Nicholas S. 1965. *War and Revolution.* New York: Sheed and Ward.

Timmermans, Stefan, and Hyeyoung Oh. 2010. "The Continued Social Transformation of the Medical Profession." *Journal of Health and Social Behavior* 51: S94–S106.

Tiryakian, Edward. 1991. "Modernization: Exhumateur in Pace (Rethinking Macrosociology in the 1990s)." *International Sociology* 6(2): 165–180.

Tocqueville, Alexis de. [1835–1840] 1969. *Democracy in America*. Garden City, NY: Doubleday.

Toennies, Ferdinand. [1887] 1957. *Community and Society*. New York: Harper Torchbooks.

Tomlinson, John. 2000. "Globalization and Cultural Identity." In *The Global Transformations Reader*, edited by D. Held and A. McGrew, 269–277. Cambridge: Polity Press.

Tomlinson, John. 2012. "Cultural Imperialism." In *The Wiley-Blackwell Encyclopedia of Globalization*, edited by George Ritzer, 371–374. Malden, MA: Wiley-Blackwell.

Tong, Rosemarie. 2009. *Feminist Thought: A More Comprehensive Introduction*. 3rd ed. Boulder, CO: Westview Press.

Torpey, John C. 2000. *The Invention of the Passport: Citizenship, Surveillance, and the State*. New York: Cambridge University Press.

Torpey, John C. 2012. "Passports." In *The Wiley-Blackwell Encyclopedia of Globalization*, edited by George Ritzer, 1644–1647. Malden, MA: Wiley-Blackwell.

Trans Murder Monitoring Project. 2016. Accessed January 30, 2016. http://transrespect.org/en/research/trans-murder-monitoring.

Tranter, Bruce, and Dallas Hanson. 2015. "The Social Bases of Cosmetic Surgery in Australia." *Journal of Sociology* 51: 189–206.

Treas, Judith, Jonathan Lui, and Zoya Gubernskaya. 2014. "Attitudes on Marriage and New Relationships: Cross-National Evidence on the Deinstitutionalization of Marriage." *Demographic Research* 30: 1495–1526.

Treitler, Vilna Bashi. 2016. "Racialization and Its Paradigms: From Ireland to North America." *Current Sociology* 64: 213–227.

Tremblay, Manon, David Paternotte, and Carol Johnson, eds. 2013. *The Lesbian and Gay Movement and the State: Comparative Insights into a Transformed Relationship*. Farnham, UK: Ashgate.

Trentmann, Frank. 2016. *Empire of Things: How We Became a World of Consumers, from the Fifteenth Century to the Twenty-First*. New York: Harper.

Trepagnier, Barbara. 2010. *Silent Racism: How Well-Meaning People Perpetuate the Racial Divide*. Boulder, CO: Paradigm.

Tsuda, Takeyuki, Maria Tapias, and Xavier Escandell. 2014. "Locating the Global in Transnational Ethnography." *Journal of Contemporary Ethnography* 43: 123–147.

Tsutsui, Kiyoteru, and Christine Min Wotipka. 2004. "Global Civil Society and the International Human Rights Movement: Citizen Participation in Human Rights International Nongovernmental Organizations." *Social Forces* 83(2): 587–620.

Tumin, Melvin E. 1953. "Some Principles of Stratification: A Critical Analysis." *American Sociological Review* 18: 387–394.

Tunnell, Kenneth D. 2007. "Crime, Political." In *The Blackwell Encyclopedia of Sociology*, edited by George Ritzer, 835–836. Malden, MA: Blackwell.

Turkle, Sherry. 2011. *Alone Together: Why We Expect More from Technology and Less from Each Other*. New York: Basic Books.

Turner, Bryan S. 2007a. "Body and Cultural Sociology." In *The Blackwell Encyclopedia of Sociology*, edited by George Ritzer, 324–328. Malden, MA: Blackwell.

Turner, Bryan S. 2007b. "Body and Society." In *The Blackwell Encyclopedia of Sociology*, edited by George Ritzer, 335–38. Malden, MA: Blackwell.

Turner, Bryan S. 2008. *The Body and Society: Explorations in Social Theory*. 3rd ed. London: Sage.

Turner, Bryan S. 2011. *Religion and Modern Society: Citizenship, Secularisation and the State*. Cambridge: Cambridge University Press.

Turner, Bryan, ed. 2012. *Routledge Handbook of Body Studies*. New York: Routledge.

Turner, Bryan S. 2014. "Religion and Contemporary Sociological Theories." *Current Sociology* 62: 771–788.

Turner, Fred. 2008. *From Counterculture to Cyberculture: Stewart Brand, the Whole Earth Network, and the Rise of Digital Utopianism*. Chicago: University of Chicago Press.

Turner, Jonathan. 2005. "A New Approach for Theoretically Integrating Micro and Macro Analysis." In *The Sage Handbook of Sociology*, edited by C. Calhoun, C. Rojek, and B. Turner, 403–422. London: Sage.

Turner, Leigh. 2007. "'First World Health Care at Third World Prices': Globalization, Bioethics and Medical Tourism." *BioSocieties* 2: 303–325.

Turner, Ralph H. 1978. "The Role and the Person." *American Journal of Sociology* 84: 1–23.

Turner, Ralph H., and Lewis M. Killian. 1987. *Collective Behavior*. 3rd ed. Englewood Cliffs, NJ: Prentice Hall.

Turner, Victor. 1967. *The Forest of Symbols: Aspects of Ndembu Ritual*. Ithaca, NY: Cornell University Press.

Tweedy, Damon. 2015. "The Case for Black Doctors." *New York Times*, May 15.

Tyler, Meagan, and Kaye Quek, 2016. "Conceptualizing Pornographication: A Lack of Clarity and Problems for Feminist Analysis." *Sexualization, Media & Society* 2(2).

Tynes, Brendesha, Joshua Schuschke, and Safiya Umoja Noble. 2016. "Digital Intersectionality Theory and the #BlackLivesMatter Movment." In *The Intersectional Internet*, edited by Safiya Umoja Noble and Brendesah Tynes, 21–40.

Ultee, Wout. 2007. "Mobility, Horizontal and Vertical." In *The Blackwell Encyclopedia of Sociology*, edited by George Ritzer, 3060–3061. Malden, MA: Blackwell.

United Nations. 2006. "Ending Violence against Women: From Words to Action Study of the Secretary-General, Fact Sheet." Accessed March 31, 2012. http://www.un.org/womenwatch/daw/vaw/launch/english/v.a.w-exeE-use.pdf.

United Nations. 2014. "World Urbanization Prospects." Revised Edition. Accessed February 22, 2017. https://esa.un.org/unpd/wup/publications/files/wup2014-highlights.Pdf.

United Nations. 2016. "The World's Cities in 2016." http://www.un.org/en/development/desa/population/publications/pdf/urbanization/the_worlds_cities_in_2016_data_booklet.pdf.

United Nations Department of Economic and Social Affairs. 2015a. "International Migrant Stock, Total." Accessed March 19, 2015. http://esa.un.org/unmigration/TIMSA2013/migrant stocks2013.htm.

United Nations Department of Economic and Social Affairs. 2015b. "Probabilistic Population Projections Based on the World Population Prospects: The 2012 Revision." Accessed March 19, 2015. http://esa.un.org/unpd/ppp/Data-Output/UN_PPP2012_output-data.htm.

United Nations General Assembly. 2006. *In-Depth Study on All Forms of Violence against Women: Report of the Secretary-General*. A/61/122/Add.1. New York: Author.

United Nations Human Settlements Programme. 2016. "World's Cities Report 2016." Accessed March 9, 2017. http://wcr.unhabitat.org.

United States Elections Project. 2016. *November General Election Turnout Rates*. www.elect project.org/2016g.

UN Women. 2014. "Facts and Figures: Ending Violence against Women." October. Accessed April 18, 2015. http://www.unwomen.org/en/what-we-do/ending-violence-against-women/facts-and-figures# sthash.5L0ZPGBH.dpuf.

Urry, John. 2000. *Sociology beyond Societies: Mobilities for the Twenty-first Century*. London: Routledge.

U.S. Census Bureau. 2011. "2010 Census Shows America's Diversity." Press release, March 24. Accessed May 7, 2015. http://www.census.gov/newsroom/releases/archives/2010_census/cb11-cn125.html.

U.S. Census Bureau. 2012. "Population." 2011 Statistical Abstract. Accessed March 31, 2012. http://www.census.gov/compendia/statab/cats/population.html.

U.S. Census Bureau. 2013. "Trade in Goods with China." Accessed February 14, 2013. http://www.census.gov/foreign-trade/balance/c5700.html.

U.S. Census Bureau. 2014. "Income, Poverty and Health Insurance Coverage in the United States, 2013." Press release CB14-169, September 16. Accessed April 29, 2015. http://www.census.gov/newsroom/press-releases/2014/cb14-169.html.

U.S. Census Bureau. 2015. "Income: Frequently Asked Questions." Accessed February 19, 2015. https://www.census.gov/hhes/www/income/about/faqs.html.

U.S. Department of Commerce, Economics and Statistics Administration; Executive Office of the President, Office of Management and Budget; and White House Council on Women and Girls. 2011. "Women in America: Indicators of Economic and Social Well-Being." Accessed May 25, 2011. http://www.whitehouse.gov/sites/default/files/rss_viewer/Women_in_America.pdf.

U.S. Department of Education, National Center for Education Statistics. 2014. "Fast Facts: Homeschooling." Accessed May 14, 2015. http://nces.ed.gov/fastfacts/display.asp?id=91.

U.S. Department of Health and Human Services. 2014. "HHS Disparities Action Plan." Accessed April 21, 2015. http://minorityhealth.hhs.gov/omh/browse.aspx?lvl= 2&rlvlid=10.

U.S. Department of Health and Human Services, Assistant Secretary for Planning and Evaluation. 2017. "2017 Poverty Guidelines." Accessed February 13, 2017. https://aspe.hhs.gov/poverty-guidelines.

U.S. Department of State. 2016. Trafficking in Persons Report 2016. Accessed January 31, 2017. https://www.state.gov/j/tip/rls/tiprpt/2016.

Useem, Elizabeth L. 1992. "Middle Schools and Math Groups: Parents' Involvement in Children's Placement." Sociology of Education 65: 263–279.

U.S. Equal Employment Opportunity Commission. 2015. "Charges Alleging Sexual Harassment, FY 2010–FY 2015." Accessed March 8, 2016. https://www.eeoc.gov/eeoc/statistics/enforcement/sexual_harassment_new.cfm.

Vaidhyanathan, Siva. 2011. The Googlization of Everything (and Why We Should Worry). Berkeley: University of California Press.

Vail, D. Angus. 2007. "Body Modification." In The Blackwell Encyclopedia of Sociology, edited by George Ritzer, 328–330. Malden. MA: Blackwell.

Valocchi, Stephen. 2007. "Gay and Lesbian Movement." In The Blackwell Encyclopedia of Sociology, edited by George Ritzer, 1833–1838. Malden, MA: Blackwell.

Van de Poel, Ellen, Ahmad Reza Hosseinpoor, Niko Speybroeck, Tom Van Ourti, and Jeanette Vega. 2008. "Socioeconomic Inequality in Malnutrition in Developing Countries." Bulletin of the World Health Organization 86(4): 241–320.

van der Lippe, Tanja, Vincent Frey, and Milena Tsvetkova. 2012. "Outsourcing of Domestic Tasks: A Matter of Preferences?" Journal of Family Issues 34(12): 1574–1597.

Van de Werfhorst, Herman G., and Jonathan J. B. Mij. 2010. "Achievement Inequality and the Institutional Structure of Educational Systems: A Comparative Perspective." Annual Review of Sociology 36: 407–428.

Van Dijk, Jan A. G. M. 2012. The Network Society. 3rd ed. Thousand Oaks, CA: Sage.

van Dyke, Nella, and David S. Meyer, eds. 2014. Understanding the Tea Party Movement. Farnham, UK: Ashgate.

Vanek, Joann, Martha Chen, Ralf Hussmanns, and Francoise Carre. 2014. Women and Men in the Informal Economy: A Statistical Picture. 2nd ed. Geneva: International Labour Organization.

van Gennep, Arnold. 1961. The Rites of Passage. Chicago: University of Chicago Press.

van Leeuwen, Marco H. D., and Ineke Maas. 2010. "Historical Studies of Social Mobility and Stratification." Annual Review of Sociology 36: 429–451.

Van Slyke, Shanna R., Michael L. Benson, and Francis T. Cullen, eds. 2016. The Oxford Handbook of White-Collar Crime. New York: Oxford University Press.

Varcoe, Ian. 2007. "Historical and Comparative Methods." In The Blackwell Encyclopedia of Sociology, edited by George Ritzer, 2133–2136. Malden, MA: Blackwell.

Vaughan, Diane. 1996. The Challenger Launch Decision: Risky Technology, Culture, and Deviance at NASA. Chicago: University of Chicago Press.

Veblen, Thorstein. [1899] 1994. The Theory of the Leisure Class. New York: Penguin.

Veldkamp, Ted I. E., Yoshihide Wada, Hans de Moel, Matti Kummu, Jeroen C. J. H. Aerts, and Philip J. War. 2014. "Impact of Socio-economic Trends and Climate Variability on the Occurrence and Severity of Blue Water Shortage and Stress Events at the Global Scale." EGU General Assembly Conference Abstracts 16. Accessed April 21, 2015. http://meetingorganizer.copernicus.org/EGU2014/EGU2014-2146.pdf.

Venkatesh, Alladi. 2015. "Consumption, Postmodern." In The Wiley-Blackwell Encyclopedia of Consumption and Consumer Studies, edited by Daniel Thomas Cook and J. Michael Ryan, 183–187. Malden, MA: Wiley-Blackwell.

Venkatesh, Sudhir. 2008. Gang Leader for a Day: A Rogue Sociologist Takes to the Streets. New York: Penguin.

Venkatesh, Sudhir. 2014. Floating City: A Rogue Sociologist Lost and Found in New York's Underground Economy. New York: Penguin.

Vertigans, Stephen. 2011. The Sociology of Terrorism: People, Place and Processes. New York: Routledge.

Vidal, Matt. 2016. "Fordism and the Golden Age of Capitalism." In The Sage Handbook of the Sociology of Work and Employment, edited by Stephen Edgell, Heidi Gottfried, and Edward Granter, 283–305. London: Sage.

Viladrich, Anahi, and Rita Baron-Faust. 2014. "Medical Tourism in Tango Paradise: The Internet Branding of Cosmetic Surgery in Argentina." Annals of Tourism Research 45: 116–131.

Villareal, Andres, and Wei-hsin Yu. 2007. "Economic Globalization and Women's Employment: The Case of Manufacturing in Mexico." American Sociological Review 72(3): 365–389.

Voas, David, and Fenella Fleischmann. 2012. "Islam Moves West: Religious Change in the First and Second Generations." Annual Review of Sociology 38: 525–545.

Vogel, Ezra F. 2011. Deng Xiaoping and the Transformation of China. Cambridge, MA: Belknap Press.

Vogli, Roberto De, Anne Kouvonen, Marko Elovainio, and Michael Marmot. 2014. "Economic Globalization, Inequality and Body Mass Index: A Cross-National Analysis of 127 Countries." Critical Public Health 24(1): 7–21.

Vogt, Kristoffer Chelsom. 2016. "The Post-Industrial Society: From Utopia to Ideology." Work, Employment and Society 30: 366–376.

Vohs, Kathleen D., Jaideep Sengupta, and Darren W. Dahl. 2014. "The Price Had Better Be Right: Women's Reactions to Sexual Stimuli Vary with Market Factors." Psychological Science 25(1): 278–283.

vom Lehn, Dirk. 2007. "Interaction." In The Blackwell Encyclopedia of Sociology, edited by George Ritzer, 2361–2365. Malden, MA: Blackwell.

von Sivers, Isabella, Anne Templeton, Gerta Köster, John Drury, and Andrew

Philippides. 2014. "Humans Do Not Always Act Selfishly: Social Identity and Helping in Emergency Evacuation Simulation." *Transportation Research Procedia* 2: 585–593.

Vos, Jeroen, and Leonith Hinojosa, 2016. "Virtual Water Trade and the Contestation of Hydrosocial Territories." *Water International* 41: 37–53.

Waddington, David. 2015. "Riots." In *The Oxford Handbook of Social Movements,* edited by Donatella Della Porta and Mario Diani, 423–439. Oxford: Oxford University Press.

Wade, Lisa. 2017. *American Hookup: The New Culture of Sex on Campus.* New York: Norton.

Wajcman, Judy. 2010. "Feminist Theories of Technology." *Cambridge Journal of Economics* 34: 143–152.

Wakefield, Kelly. 2013. "Global Digital Divide: Inequality and Internet Access." *Geography Review* 26: 10–13.

Waldmeir, Patti. [1997] 2001. *Anatomy of a Miracle: The End of Apartheid and the Birth of a New South Africa.* New Brunswick, NJ: Rutgers University Press.

Walker, Henry A., and David Willer. 2007. "Experimental Methods." In *The Blackwell Encyclopedia of Sociology,* edited by George Ritzer, 1537–1541. Malden. MA: Blackwell.

Wallerstein, Immanuel. 1974. *The Modern World-System.* New York: Academic Press.

Wallerstein, James S., and Clement J. Wyle. 1947. "Our Law-Abiding Law-Breakers." *Federal Probation* 25: 107–112.

Walsh, Declan. 2017. "Trump Targets Muslim Areas in Refugee Ban." *New York Times,* January 28.

Walters, G. D. 2003. "Changes in Criminal Thinking and Identity in Novice and Experienced Inmates: Prisonization Revisited." *Criminal Justice and Behavior* 30(4): 399–421.

Wang, Wendy, Kim Parker, and Paul Taylor. 2013. "Breadwinner Moms." Pew Research Center, Pew Social and Demographic Trends, May 29. Accessed February 27, 2017. http://www.pewsocialtrends.org/files/2013/05/Breadwinner_moms_final.pdf.

Ward, James D., and Mario A. Rivera. 2014. *Institutional Racism, Organizations & Public Policy.* New York: Peter Lang.

Warren, Cortney S. 2014. "Body Area Dissatisfaction in White, Black and Latina Female College Students in the USA: An Examination of Racially Salient Appearance Areas and Ethnic Identity." *Ethnic and Racial Studies* 37: 537–556.

Warren, John Robert, and Elaine M. Hernandez. 2007. "Did Socioeconomic Inequalities in Morbidity and Mortality Change in the United States over the Course of the Twentieth Century?" *Journal of Health and Social Behavior* 48: 335–351.

Waskul, Dennis. 2015. "Sex and the Internet." In Patricia Whelehan and Anne Bolin, eds. *The International Encyclopedia of Human Sexuality.* Malden, MA: Wiley-Blackwell.

Wasserman, J., M. A. Flannery, and J. M. Clair. 2007. "Raising the Ivory Tower: The Production of Knowledge and Distrust of Medicine among African Americans." *Journal of Medical Ethics* 33(3): 177–180.

Wasserman, Varda, and Michal Frenkel. 2015. "Spatial Work In Between Glass Ceiling and Glass Walls: Gender-Class Intersectionality and Organizational Aesthetics." *Organization Studies* 36: 1485–1505.

Wasson, Leslie. 2007. "Identity Politics/Relational Politics." In *The Blackwell Encyclopedia of Sociology,* edited by George Ritzer, 2214–2215. Malden, MA: Blackwell.

Webb, Haley J., Melanie J. Zimmer-Gembeck, and Caroline L. Donovan. 2014. "The Appearance Culture between Friends and Adolescent Appearance-Based Rejection Sensitivity." *Journal of Adolescence* 37: 347–358.

Weber, Max. [1903–1917] 1949. *The Methodology of the Social Sciences.* New York: Free Press.

Weber, Max. [1904–1905] 1958. *The Protestant Ethic and the Spirit of Capitalism.* New York: Scribner.

Weber, Max. [1921] 1968. *Economy and Society: An Outline of Interpretive Sociology,* edited by G. Roth and C. Wittich. Totowa, NJ: Bedminster Press.

Weeks, John R. 2007. "Demographic Transition Theory." In *The Blackwell Encyclopedia of Sociology,* edited by George Ritzer, 1033–1038. Malden, MA: Blackwell.

Weiler, Bernd. 2007. "Cultural Relativism." In *The Blackwell Encyclopedia of Sociology,* edited by George Ritzer, 908–910. Malden, MA: Blackwell.

Weinstein, Jay. 2010. *Social Change.* 3rd ed. Lanham, MD: Rowman & Littlefield.

Weinstein, Mary. 2013. "How Many People Shop Online?" *Ecommerce,* August 9. Accessed April 27, 2015. http://www.cpcstrategy.com/blog/2013/08/ecommerce-infographic.

Weisenthal, Joe. 2013. "Here's the New Ranking of Top Countries in Reading, Science, and Math." *Business Insider,* December 3. Accessed May 17, 2015. http://www.businessinsider.com/pisa-rankings-2013-12#ix zz3SokWhusf.

Weitz, Rose. 2010. *The Sociology of Health, Illness, and Health Care: A Critical Approach.* 5th ed. Boston: Wadsworth Cengage.

Weitzer, Ronald. 2009. "Sociology of Sex Work." *Annual Review of Sociology* 35: 213–234.

Weitzer, Ronald. 2012. *Legalizing Prostitution: From Illicit Vice to Lawful Business.* New York: New York University Press.

Weitzman, Abigail, and Julia Andrea Behrman. 2016. "Disaster, Disruption to Family Life, and Intimate Partner Violence: The Case of the 2010 Earthquake in Haiti." *Sociological Science* 3: 167–189.

Wellard, Ian. 2012. "Body-Reflexive Pleasures: Exploring Bodily Experiences within the Context of Sport and Physical Activity." *Sport, Education and Society* 17: 21–33.

Wellford, Charles. 2012. "Criminology." In *The Wiley-Blackwell Companion to Sociology,* edited by George Ritzer, 229–242. Malden, MA: Wiley-Blackwell.

Wellman, Elizabeth. 2004. *The Road to Seneca Falls: Elizabeth Cady Stanton and the First Woman's Rights Convention.* Champaign: University of Illinois Press.

Welzel, Christian, and Ronald Inglehart. 2009. "Mass Beliefs and Democratization." In *Democratization,* edited by C. W. Haerpfer, P. Bernhagen, R. F. Inglehart, and C. Welzel. New York: Oxford University Press.

Wennersten, John and Denise Robbins. 2017. *Rising Tides: Climate Refugees in the Twenty-first Century.* Bloomington: Indiana University Press.

Wessel, Anika, and Erich Kasten. 2014. "Body Piercing and Self-Mutilation: A Multifaceted Relationship." *American Journal of Applied Psychology* 3(4): 104–109.

West, Candace, and Don Zimmerman. 1987. "Doing Gender." *Gender & Society* 1: 125–151.

Westergaard, Ryan P., Mary Catherine Beach, Somnath Saha, and Elizabeth A. Jacobs. 2014. "Racial/Ethnic Differences in Trust in Health Care: HIV Conspiracy Beliefs and Vaccine Research Participation." *Journal of General Internal Medicine* 29(1): 140–146.

Western, Bruce, and Jake Rosenfeld. 2012. "Workers of the World Divide: The Decline of Labor and the Future of the Middle Class." *Foreign Affairs,* May/June.

Wharton, Amy S., and Mary Blair-Loy. 2006. "Long Work Hours and Family Life: A Cross-National Study of Employees' Concerns." *Journal of Family Issues* 27(3): 415–436.

Whiteside, Alan. 2008. *A Very Short Introduction to HIV/AIDS.* Oxford: Oxford University Press.

Whiteside, Alan. 2012. "AIDS." In *The Wiley-Blackwell Encyclopedia of Globalization,* edited by George Ritzer, 45–49. Malden, MA: Wiley-Blackwell.

Whittier, Nancy. 2016. "Where Are the Children? Theorizing the Missing Piece in Gendered Sexual Violence." *Gender & Society* 30: 95–108.

Whitton, Sarah W., Scott M. Stanley, Howard J. Markman, and Christine A. Johnson. 2013. "Attitudes Toward Divorce, Commitment and Divorce Proneness in First Marriages and Remarriages." *Journal of Marriage and the Family* 75: 276–287.

Whyte, William Foote. 1943. *Street Corner Society: The Social Structure of an Italian Slum.* Chicago: University of Chicago.

Wiedenhoft Murphy, Wendy. 2017a. "Boycotts, Buycotts, and Legislation: Tactical Lessons from Workers and Consumers during the Progressive Era." In *Shopping for Social Change: Consumer Activism and the Possibilities of Purchasing Power,* edited by Louis Hyman and Joseph Tohill. Ithaca, NY: Cornell University Press.

Wiedenhoft Murphy, Wendy. 2017b. *Consumer Culture and Society.* Thousand Oaks, CA: Sage.

Wiegner, Lilian, Dominique Hange, Cecilia Björkelund, and Gunnar Ahlborg Jr. 2015. "Prevalence of Perceived Stress and Associations to Symptoms of Exhaustion, Depression and Anxiety in a Working Age Population Seeking Primary Care—An Observational Study." *BMC Family Practice* 16.

Wieringa, Saskia and Horacio Sívori. 2013. "Sexual Politics in the Global South: Framing the Discourse." In *The Sexual History of the Global South,* edited by S. Wieringa and H. Sívori, 1–21. New York: Zed Books.

Wiklund, Maria, Carita Bengs, Eva-Britt Malmgren-Olsson, and Ann Öhman. 2010. "Young Women Facing Multiple and Intersecting Stressors of Modernity, Gender Orders and Youth." *Social Science Medicine* 71(9): 1567–1575.

Wilk, Kenneth Aarskaug, Eva Bernhardt, and Turid Noack. 2010. "Love or Money? Marriage Intentions among Young Cohabitors in Norway and Sweden." *Acta Sociologica* 53: 269–287.

Williams, Christine L. 1995. *Still a Man's World.* Berkeley: University of California Press.

Williams, Christine L. 2006. *Inside Toyland: Working, Shopping, and Social Inequality.* Berkeley: University of California Press.

Williams, David R. 1999. "Race, Socioeconomic Status, and Health: The Added Effects of Racism and Discrimination."

Annals of the New York Academy of Sciences 896: 173–188.

Williams, Glyn, Paula Meth, and Katie Willis. 2014. *Geographies of Developing Areas: The Global South in a Changing World.* 2nd ed. New York: Routledge.

Williams, Rosalind. [1982] 1991. *Dream Worlds: Mass Consumption in Late Nineteenth-Century France.* Berkeley: University of California Press.

Williams, Stacy J., Laura Pecenco, and Mary Blair-Loy. 2013. "Medical Professions: The Status of Women and Men." Center for Research on Gender in the Professions, University of California, San Diego. Accessed April 21, 2015. http://crgp.ucsd.edu/documents/Genderin-MedicalProfessionsCaseStudy.pdf.

Williams, Timothy. 2016. "One Robber's 3 Life Sentences: '90s Legacy Fills Prisons Today." *New York Times,* July 4.

Williams, Victoria. 2014. "Foreign Aid." In *Encyclopedia Britannica.* Accessed April 21, 2015. http://www.britannica.com/EBchecked/topic/213344/foreign-aid.

Williamson, Oliver E. 1975. *Markets and Hierarchies: Analysis and Antitrust Implications.* New York: Free Press.

Williamson, Oliver E. 1985. *The Economic Institutions of Capitalism.* New York: Free Press.

Williamson, Vanessa, Theda Skocpol, and John Coggin. 2011. "The Tea Party and the Remaking of Republican Conservatism." *Perspectives on Politics* 9: 25–43.

Willyard, Cassandra. 2014. "Malaria Vaccine, Destined for Africa, Seeks OK from Europe." *Nature Medicine* 20: 968–969.

Wilper, Andrew P., Steffie Woolhandler, Karen E. Lasser, Danny McCormick, David H. Bor, and David U. Himmelstein. 2009. "Health Insurance and Mortality in US Adults." *American Journal of Public Health* 99(12): 2289–2295.

Wilson, Bryan R. 1966. *Religion and Secular Society.* London: Watts.

Wilson, George, Vincent J. Roscigno, and Matt L. Huffman. 2013. "Public Sector Transformation, Racial Inequality, and Downward Occupational Mobility." *Social Forces* 91: 975–1006.

Wilson, Midge, and Kathy Russell. 1996. *Divided Sisters: Bridging the Gap between Black and White Women.* New York: Anchor Books.

Wilson, Stephen R. 1984. "Becoming a Yogi: Resocialization and Deconditioning as Conversion Processes." *Sociological Analysis* 45(4): 301–314.

Wilson, William Julius. 1997. *When Work Disappears: The World of the New Urban Poor.* New York: Vintage.

Winchester, M. S., R. BeLue, T. Oni, U. Wittwer-Backofen, D. Deobagkar, H. Onya,

T. A. Samuels, S. A. Matthews, C. Stone, and C. Airhihenbuwa. 2016. "The Pan-University Network for Global Health: Framework for Collaboration and Review of Global Health Needs." *Globalization and Health* 12. Accessed February 7, 2017. https://globalizationandhealth.biomedcentral.com/articles/10.1186/s12992-016-0151-2.

Wines, Michael. 2011. "Picking Brand Names in China Is a Business Itself." *New York Times,* November 11. Accessed April 1, 2012. http://www.nytimes.com/2011/11/12/world/asia/picking-brand-names-in-china-is-a-business-itself.html.

Wingfield, Nick. 2014a. "In Games Like Minecraft, Tech Giants See More than Fun." *New York Times,* September 11.

Wingfield, Nick. 2014b. "Virtual Games Draw Real Crowds and Big Money." *New York Times,* August 31.

Winlow, Simon, Steve Hall, James Treadwell, and Daniel Brigg. 2015. *Riots and Political Protest.* New York: Routledge.

Wisman, Jon D. 2013. "Wage Stagnation, Rising Inequality, and the Financial Crisis of 2008." *Cambridge Journal of Economics* 37: 921–945.

Wolf, Naomi. [1991] 2002. *The Beauty Myth: How Images of Beauty Are Used against Women.* New York: Harper & Row.

Wolff, Kristina. 2007. "Content Analysis." In *The Blackwell Encyclopedia of Sociology,* edited by George Ritzer, 776–779. Malden, MA: Blackwell.

Wong, William, Eleanor Holroyd, and Amie Bingham. 2011. "Stigma and Sex Work from the Perspective of Female Sex Workers in Hong Kong." *Sociology of Health and Illness* 33: 50–65.

Wood, Wendy, and Alice H. Eagly. 2015. "Two Traditions on Research on Gender Identity." *Sex Roles* 73: 461-473.

World Bank. 2015a. "Country and Lending Groups." Accessed January 31, 2017. https://datahelpdesk.worldbank.org/knowledgebase/articles/906519-world-bank-country-and-lending-groups.

World Bank. 2015b. "Urban Population (% of Total)." Accessed February 12, 2017. http://data.worldbank.org/indicator/SP.URB.TOTL.IN.ZS.

World Bank. 2016. "Health Expenditure, Total (% of GDP), 1995–2014." Accessed February 13, 2017. http://data.worldbank.org/indicator/SH.XPD.TOTL.ZS.

World Bank. n.d. "Fertility Rate, Total (Births per Woman)." data.worldbank.org/indicator/SP.DYN.TFRT.IN.

World Economic Forum. 2016. *The Global Gender Gap Report 2015.* Geneva: Author.

World Health Organization. 2010a. "Tobacco Free Initiative: China Releases Its Global Adult Tobacco Survey Data." Accessed April 1, 2012. http://www.who.int/tobacco/surveillance/gats_china/en/index.html.

World Health Organization. 2010b. "World Health Report: Health Systems Financing: The Path to Universal Coverage." Accessed April 1, 2012. http://whqlibdoc.who.int/whr/2010/9789241564021_eng.pdf.

World Health Organization, 2014. "Adolescent Pregnancy: Fact Sheet," September. Accessed February 14, 2017. http://www.who.int/mediacentre/factsheets/fs364/en.

World Health Organization. 2015a. "Global Health Observatory (GHO) Data: Tuberculosis (TB)." http://www.who.int/gho/tb/epidemic/cases_deaths/en.

World Health Organization. 2015b. "Life Expectancy." Accessed March 9, 2017. http://www.who.int/gho/mortality_burden_disease/life_tables/situation_trends_text/en.

World Health Organization. 2015c. "Water Sanitation and Health." Accessed March 19, 2015. http://www.who.int/water_sanitation_health/mdg1/en.

World Health Organization. 2016. "Life Expectancy Increased by 5 Years Since 2000, but Health Inequalities Persist," May 19. Accessed March 8, 2017. http://www.who.int/mediacentre/news/releases/2016/health-inequalities-persist/en.

World Health Organization. 2017. "Tobacco Fact Sheet." www.who.int/mediacentre/factsheets/fs339/en.

Worldometers. 2015. "Current World Population." Accessed March 19, 2015. http://www.worldometers.info/world-population.

Worth, Robert F. 2016. *A Rage for Order: The Middle East in Turmoil, From Tahrir Square to ISIS*. New York: Farrar, Straus and Giroux.

Wortham, Jenna. 2013. "A Growing App Lets You See It, Then You Don't." *New York Times,* February 9.

Wortmann, Susan L. 2007. "Sex Tourism." In *The Blackwell Encyclopedia of Sociology,* edited by George Ritzer, 4200–4203. Malden, MA: Blackwell.

Wren, Anne. 2013. *The Political Economy of the Service Transition*. New York: Oxford University Press.

Wunder, Delores F. 2007. "Agents, Socialization of." In *The Blackwell Encyclopedia of Sociology,* edited by George Ritzer, 4566–4568. Malden, MA: Blackwell.

Yancy, George. 2008. *Black Bodies, White Gazes: The Continuing Significance of Race*. Lanham, MD: Rowman & Littlefield.

Yardley, Jim. 2010. "Soaring above India's Poverty, a 27-Story Single-Family Home." *New York Times,* October 29.

Yeates, Nicola. 2009. *Globalizing Care Economies and Migrant Workers: Explorations in Global Care Chains*. New York: Palgrave Macmillan.

Yeates, Nicola. 2012. "Global Care Chains: A State-of-the-Art Review and Future Directions in Care Transnational Research." *Global Networks* 12(2): 135–154.

Yeginsu, Ceylan, and Anemona Hartocollis, 2015. "Amid Perilous Mediterranean Crossings, Migrants Find a Relatively Easy Path to Greece." *New York Times,* August 16.

Yetman, Norman R., ed. 1991. *Majority and Minority: The Dynamics of Race and Ethnicity in American Life*. 5th ed. Boston: Allyn & Bacon.

Yodanis, Carrie, and Sean Lauer. 2014. "Is Marriage Individualized? What Couples Actually Do." *Journal of Family Theory and Review* 6: 184–197.

Yoshihara, Susan, and Douglas A. Sylva, eds. 2011. *Population Decline and the Remaking of Great Power Politics*. Washington, DC: Potomac Books.

Young, Michael, and Johan Muller, eds. 2014. *Knowledge Expertise and the Professions*. New York: Routledge.

Zafirovski, Milan. 2013. "Beneath Rational Choice: Elements of 'Irrational Choice Theory.'" *Current Sociology* 61: 3–21.

Zammuel, Elnat, Orna Sasson-Levy, and Guy Ben-Porat. 2014. "Voluntary Simplifiers as Political Consumers: Individuals Practicing Politics through Reduced Consumption." *Journal of Consumer Culture* 14: 199–217.

Zeiler, Kristin, and Annette Wickstrom. 2009. "Why Do 'We' Perform Surgery on Newborn Intersexed Children? The Phenomenology of the Parental Experience of Having a Child with Intersex Anatomies." *Feminist Theory* 10: 359–377.

Zellner, William W. 1995. *Counterculture: A Sociological Analysis*. New York: St. Martin's Press.

Zhang, Yang, and Michael John Hitchcock. 2014. "The Chinese Female Tourist Gaze: A Netnography of Young Women's Blogs on Macao." *Current Issues in Tourism,* June 9 (published online). doi: 10.1080/13683500.2014.904845.

Zhou, Yanqui Rachel, and William D. Coleman. 2016. "Accelerated Contagion and Response: Understanding the Relationship Among Globalization, Time and Disease" *Globalizations* 13: 285–299.

Zhuge, Ying, Joyce Kaufman, Diane M. Simeone, Herbert Chen, and Omaida C. Velazquez. 2011. "Is There Still a Glass Ceiling for Women in Academic Surgery?" *Annals of Surgery* 253: 637–643.

Ziemke, Jen. 2012. "Crisis Mapping: The Construction of a New Interdisciplinary Field?" *Journal of Map and Geography Libraries* 8: 191–117.

Zimbardo, Philip. 1973. "On the Ethics of Intervention in Human Psychological Research: With Special Reference to the Stanford Prison Experiment." *Cognition* 2: 243–256.

Zimmer, Ron, and Richard Buddin. 2009. "Is Charter School Competition in California Improving the Performance of Traditional Public Schools?" *Public Administration Review* 69(5): 831–845.

Zinn, Maxine Baca. 2012. "Patricia Hill Collins: Past and Future Innovations." *Gender & Society* 26: 28–32.

Zuev, Dennis. 2015. "The Internet and Consumption." In *Encyclopedia of Consumption and Consumer Studies,* edited by Daniel Thomas Cook and Michael Ryan, 368–372. Malden, MA: Wiley-Blackwell.

Zukin, Sharon. 1982. *Loft Living: Culture and Capital in Urban Change*. Baltimore: Johns Hopkins University Press.

Zukin, Sharon. 2004. *Point of Purchase: How Shopping Changed American Culture*. New York: Routledge.

INDEX